Gritty, Gallant, Glorious

A History and Complete Record

of the Hearts

1946 - 1997

BY

NORRIE PRICE

Author's Note

This book is dedicated to all those who follow the fortunes of the men in Maroon. I took my inspiration from a work colleague Jim Gordon, who for many, many years has been a real true "Jambo" or should it be a "Jam Tart", for he too is from that bygone era. Having heard all about the famous days of old and those of not so long ago, I decided to delve further until I found myself quite genuinely captivated. There are many other excellent publications about the club but I have attempted to trace the fortunes of Hearts and the development of the club since the Second World War in detail. I hope that Hearts supporters will now gain as much satisfaction from reading the finished article as I had researching and putting it together.

Acknowledgments

I would like to express my gratitude to all who assisted me in producing this publication. I am particularly grateful to Alford-based David Young for his encouragement and technical advice and to *Scotscan* of Aberdeen where master-scanner Mike Cheyne put up with my drip feeding of material over the concluding weeks. Thanks are also due to former Hearts player Gary Mackay for agreeing to write the foreword. Gary of course is a life-long Hearts fan and remains a superb ambassador for the Tynecastle Park club.

I would again like to convey my thanks to D.C. Thomson (Dundee) for allowing me to reproduce so many of their splendid photographs and I would particularly like to thank Photofile Library Supervisor Joyce and her staff - Anne, Susan, Sharon, Gaynor and Gwen for their friendliness, assistance and patience in the face of endless requests. Thanks also to Jimmy Galloway at the Daily Record Photofile Library for the first class service and the excellent material provided. Eric Stevenson of Aberdeen Journals was also of great assistance, helping out with some last minute requests.

Other individuals and bodies who provided information, advice, photos or other memorabilia - often at short notice - were Jim Gordon, Abbey Stuart, Richard Pigeon (Sunday Post), John Ure - particularly for his last-minute assistance, Andrew Hoggan, Alan Pattullo, Ian Walker, Ian Murray (Archway Promotions Football Memorabilia Shop, Edinburgh), Pete Rundo, my long-suffering boss Steve Robson, Charlie Taylor, Chorley and Handford, The Evening Telegraph Sports Desk in Dundee, the Scottish Football Association, the National Library in Edinburgh, the Mitchell Library in Glasgow, the Aberdeen's Central and Woodside Libraries and the Wellgate Library in Dundee.

First published in December 1997

ISBN 0 9521426 3 5

Reprographics by Scotscan, Aberdeen (01224-585808. Printed by Martins The Printers, Seaview Works, Spittal, Berwick Upon Tweed (01289-306006). Cover design, layout, publication, sales and distribution by N. Price (01224-818697)

Contents

We're there - Hearts players and fans go wild with delight after after beating Dundee United in the semi-final of the Scottish Cup at Hampden in April 1986.

Foreword

by Gary Mackay

After spending 17 enjoyable years with Hearts, it gives me great pleasure to write the foreword to Norrie's book "Gritty, Gallant, Glorious". Hearts were my home town team and as a pupil of Tynecastle High School and a life-long supporter, I was delighted when manager Bobby Moncur asked me to sign for Hearts back in July 1980.

Those were difficult times for the club but it was my privilege to come under the wing of top professionals like Alex. MacDonald, Sandy Jardine and various others and their experience was of great benefit in my formative years in the game. My early days at Tynecastle coincided with a renewed emphasis on youth development and along with team-mates Dave Bowman, Ian Westwater and of course, John Robertson, I was fortunate enough to carve out a successful career for myself in the professional game.

Soon the club came under new ownership and after achieving promotion in 1983, Hearts went from strength to strength. The 1985-86 campaign saw us come so close to Premier League and Scottish Cup glory and although bitterly disappointed at not collecting any silverware, that season was a mark of our progress after so many years in the doldrums. Over the next few years, we again came within touching distance of success, twice finishing Premier League runners-up and reaching cup semi-finals on no fewer than six occasions. Jim Jefferies looks to have turned Hearts around again and just last year, there was the thrill of reaching two cup finals within the space of six months - and from a personal point of view the great honour of captaining Hearts in that memorable Coca Cola Cup Final.

I was also fortunate to achieve my ambition of playing for Scotland. I made four full international appearances with the highlight my debut in Bulgaria, where I struck a late winner after coming on as substitute. During my time at Tynecastle, I played alongside many talented players and was lucky enough to make numerous trips abroad through European competition and other tours. There were visits to the West Indies, the U.S.A., Germany, Spain, Eire, Czechoslovakia, France, Austria, Yugoslavia, Russia, Italy and Belgium as well as other games South of the Border.

I therefore have many happy memories of my lengthy career with Hearts and I am delighted that Norrie has produced such a detailed account of these events. I am sure his book will provide all true Hearts supporters - you can certainly count me amongst them - with many hours of interesting reading and I wish every success to the author, the Heart of Midlothian Football Club and all their loyal fans over the coming months.

Best Wishes

Gary Mackay

Prologue

A COLOURFUL PAST

Organised football in Scotland had begun with the formation of the Scottish Football Association in 1873, when a new competition, the Scottish Cup, was initiated. Initially, football was played on an amateur basis and the Scottish Cup apart, games consisted of local competitions in addition to friendlies against other Scottish and English sides.

The Heart of Midlothian Football Club itself was founded in 1874, just a year after the Scottish Football Association but there appear to be two theories as to how the club was named. In the early 1870's, there had existed in Washington-Green Court off the South Back Canongate, a dance hall named after the old Tolbooth jail "Heart of Midlothian", which had been demolished in 1817. One story goes that a policeman, in conversation with some lads who frequented the dance hall, suggested that rather than hang around street corners, they might be better employed kicking a ball around. He directed them to the Meadows and after purchasing a ball, they decided to form a new club and name it after their local dance hall.

According to the other theory, some 30 to 40 youths who were in the habit of playing football outside the old Tolbooth area and who were regarded as a public nuisance, were ordered by the Local Authorities to take their ball to the Meadows. Eventually, they formed a team and named it after the place where they had been forbidden to play, "Heart of Midlothian".

The exact story may not be certain but stalwart defender Tom Purdie became their first captain and in 1875 the fledgling Hearts entered the Scottish Cup for the first time. They met the powerful 3rd Edinburgh Rifle Volunteers and after playing two no-scoring draws, both sides proceeded to the next round (as the rules of the day dictated), only for Hearts to fall 2-0 to Drumpellier of Coatbridge.

In 1875, Hearts joined the Edinburgh Football Association and that December, they met the newly formed Hibernian Football Club at the East Meadows. And despite playing without three men for the first 20 minutes, Hearts went on to win their first derby encounter 1-0. By 1877, Hearts and Hibs had emerged as the capital's top teams and in April of the following year, Hearts beat Hibs 3-2 to win the Edinburgh Football Association Cup Final.

The Meadows was a popular venue for dozens of other public park sides but the area soon became overcrowded with hundreds of spectators as the Hearts support increased. Better facilities were required and in the late 1870's, Hearts, who in 1878 had adopted maroon as the club colours after an earlier flirting with red, white and blue hoops, set up at Powderhall then moved to "Old Tynecastle" before making the short trip up Gorgie Road to the present location in 1886.

In 1890, an 11-club Scottish League comprising Hearts, Rangers, Celtic, Dumbarton, Third Lanark, St Mirren, Cambuslang, Abercorn, Vale of Leven, Cowlairs and Renton was formed and it quickly proved a big success. Hearts, whose first game of the 1890-91 season ended in a 5-2 defeat to Rangers at Old Ibrox, finished sixth but they were to fare better in the Cup.

After disposing of Raith Rovers (h) 7-2, Burntisland Thistle (walkover), Methlan Park (a) 3-0, Ayr (a) 4-3, Morton (h) 5-1, East Stirling (a) 3-1, and Third Lanark (a), the Isaac Begbie-inspired Hearts would meet Dumbarton in the final in February. It was a great day for the Hearts for after going ahead through a Willie Mason goal in 15 minutes, resolute defending ensured the Cup was theirs to the delight of the 5,000 or so Hearts fans amongst the 16,000 Hampden crowd.

Within a few years, most of Hearts cup winning side had gone South but in May 1893 professionalism was finally legalised in Scotland. And in 1894-95, a year after finishing runners-up to Celtic, Hearts bounced back to win the Division One Championship, five points ahead of the Glasgow side. Next year, with virtually the same team, Hearts again won the Scottish Cup, beating the holders St Bernards - who had knocked them out at the same stage in 1895 - 1-0 in the semi-final before going on to beat Hibs 3-1 in the final before a crowd of 17,000 at Edinburgh's Logie Green. A penalty by Davie Baird in three minutes set the pattern and the Maroons went on to win 3-1.

Scottish League Division One
Season 1894-95

	P	W	D	L	F A	PTS
Hearts	18	15	1	2	50-18	31
Celtic	18	11	4	3	50-29	26
Rangers	18	10	2	6	41-26	22
Third Lanark	18	10	1	7	51-39	21
St Mirren	18	9	1	8	34-34	19
St Bernards	18	8	1	9	37-40	17
Clyde	18	8	0	10	38-47	16
Dundee	18	8	0	10	28-33	14
Leith Ath.	18	3	1	14	32-64	7
Dumbarton	18	3	1	14	27-58	7

These were halcyon days for Hearts and with the brilliant young Bobby Walker at inside-right, they went on to win their second Championship two points ahead of Hibernian in 1896-97. Two years later, Hearts were runners-up, albeit 10 points behind champions Rangers and in 1900-01, the Maroons, then second-bottom of the league, sensationally beat Celtic 4-3 in the Scottish Cup Final at Ibrox after an inspirational display by Bobby Walker.

Walker was later described as fast in his mind rather than fast on his feet but his reading of the game and his superb passing was to make him an almost automatic choice for Scotland between 1900 and 1913 as he earned a Hearts record of 29 full international caps.

In 1903, Hearts were Scottish Cup runners-up to Rangers and the following year they finished second in the title race, five points behind Third Lanark. Hearts had started to lose players to the big English clubs but in 1905-06, they became a limited company and with their financial position secured they again came second before going on to their fourth Scottish Cup success, a George Wilson goal giving them a 1-0 victory over Third Lanark in the final at

Ibrox. The following season Hearts again reached the final only to lose 3-0 to Celtic, but after four Scottish Cup triumphs and two league title successes between 1890 and 1906, it was to be nearly five decades before they graced another final or savoured the touch of silverware again.

In 1903, Mr William Waugh had succeeded Peter Fairley after his predecessor's two year spell as manager. However, in 1908, Waugh gave way to James McGhee before Mr John McCartney came from St Mirren to take over in February 1910. However, those were depressing times for the Gorgie faithful and by 1914, the year of completion of the new £12,000 stand - still currently in use, Hearts best placing was third in season 1911-12.

That year, international tensions had escalated and in August, Britain joined France and Russia and went to war against Germany and the Central Powers. The Great War had begun and although Scottish League football continued, it had become secondary to the horrors of the Western Front. With a regular team of Boyd; Crossan, Currie; Briggs, Scott, Nellies; Wilson, Wattie, Gracie, Graham and Speedie, Hearts had begun the 1914-15 campaign with eight successive wins. However, in November the entire first-team volunteered for the army and it was no surprise that the depleted Hearts finished second, four points behind Celtic.

Sadly, few of that team would return to play football at Tynecastle. James Speedie, Duncan Currie, Tom Gracie, and Harry Wattie were amongst those to lose their lives over the next four years and in 1922, a memorial was unveiled at Haymarket in memory of the many players and members of the Heart of Midlothian Football Club who had died in the conflict.

Inspired by the scoring feats of Andy Wilson, Hearts reached the 1919 Victory Cup Final only to lose 3-0 to St Mirren. In November of that year, Willie McCartney assumed the managerial duties from his father, who had resigned to join Portsmouth but despite the imediate post-war crowd boom, the 1920's would prove no more successful than the previous decade.

However, although the best that Hearts could manage was third place in seasons 1920-21, 1925-26 and 1928-29, there were famous names like Scottish international goalkeeper Jack Harkness who arrived from Queen's Park in 1928 and that prolific scorer Barney Battles, son of the famous Hearts defender of the 1890's, who returned from Boston to rattle in 29 league goals in 1928-29 and 44 league goals in 1930-31 - still a Tynecastle record.

In the late 1920's, the old "iron stand" or barrel-roofed enclosure on the distillery side - erected in 1911- was removed. The ash bankings all around the ground were replaced with timbered terracing with new tunnel exits constructed at the Gorgie Road End and Wheatfield Street sides. Those costs would prove a millstone round the club's neck and although the 1930's would see many more famous names at Tynecastle, success again proved elusive.

In February 1932, there was a record Tynecastle crowd Hearts of 53,396 to see a 1-0 Scottish Cup defeat by Rangers, the club that, apart from a few brief flurries by Celtic and one noteable success by Motherwell that very season, had dominated and would continue to dominate the championship in the inter-war years.

Tommy Walker had emerged as a star at inside-right and soon his goalscoring record made him a Scotland regular from 1933 until 1939. In 1936, he cooly replaced the ball three times after it had blown off the spot before scoring a memorable penalty equaliser against England at Wembley, and two years later he was again the hero with the winner against England at the same venue.

In 1935, former Notts County boss David Pratt replaced Willie McCartney but although the 1935-36 season saw five players - Andy Anderson, Alec Massie, Tommy Walker, Dave McCulloch and Andy Herd capped for Scotland, Hearts could only finish fifth and deteriorating finances dictated that Massie (to Aston Villa) and McCulloch (to Brentford) were both transfered for £5,500. Soon Pratt resigned after a mid-season players' strike to be replaced by Arsenal and England keeper Frank Moss in March 1937 and next season, Hearts turned on the style.

It was neck and neck with Celtic for the title but after losing 4-2 to their rivals in January 1938, Hearts finished second, three points behind Celtic. In 1938-39, Hearts finished fourth but by now, the menace of Hitler's Nazi Germany was darkening the Continent of Europe. However, despite the imminent threat of war, the Scottish football season began as usual in August 1939 with Hearts taking six points from their opening five games before war was declared on September 3rd.

All further competition was suspended but in October, after it was realised that football would maintain the morale of the population, new leagues were formed. Players wages were fixed at £2 per week and crowds of no more than 8,000 were allowed for fear of German air raids. In 1939-40, Hearts finished second to Falkirk in the Eastern Division but increasingly players volunteered or were called up for military service and teams were bolstered by guest players and youngsters.

In July 1940 Frank Moss returned South and the team played without a manager until Davie McLean's arrival a year later. Over the next five seasons until 1945, Hearts played in the Southern Division but, with depleted resources, they were never to finish higher than fifth.

Legend in Maroon - Hearts inside-right Tommy Walker just fails to connect with a cross in this match against Partick Thistle at Tynecastle.

Chapter One

IN THE SHADOWS

In season 1945-46 the Scottish League recommenced with Divisions One and Two comprising the same clubs as at the outbreak of hostilities in September 1939. However, there was no promotion or relegation since it was regarded as a transitional period for clubs to get themselves in order as their players gradually returned from the armed forces. In the event, Hearts had to be content with seventh place, well behind the top trio of Rangers, Hibernian and Aberdeen.

The 1946-47 season was regarded as the official restart of the Scottish League Championship and on August 10th, 1946, a crowd of 18,000 saw Hearts field the following side for the opening of the new season at Falkirk - Brown; McAra, McClure; Cox, Baxter (capt), Neilson; Briscoe, T. Walker, Garrett, McCrae and Kelly. Archie Garrett (27) scored twice in an entertaining 3-3 draw but a matter of weeks later, the Hearts centre and another pre-war regular, outside-right Jimmy Briscoe (31), were on their way to Northampton Town for a joint fee of £2,250. In September, there was another surprise departure when the popular ex-Scottish international inside-forward Tommy Walker (31), scorer of 190 goals in 354 appearances during his 14 years at Tynecastle, was transferred to Chelsea for £8,000.

Meanwhile, Hearts had made an indifferent start, taking 13 points from their opening 10 games but on September 7th, great encouragement was taken from a 1-0 win over city rivals Hibs at Easter Road. Inside-left Alex. McCrae netted the only goal and he scored again in the following match, a 2-0 win over Kilmarnock at Tynecastle where centre-forward Archie Kelly collided with a goalpost and was taken off with a broken collarbone.

In the League Cup - a competition started in 1944 - Hearts qualified from a section containing Clyde, Kilmarnock and Partick Thistle. A 2-0 defeat in the penultimate game at Rugby Park put them under great pressure not to lose their last game against Partick Thistle at Tynecastle on October 26th but the Maroons managed a 1-1 draw to progress to the quarter-final stage next spring.

Extrovert goalkeeper Jimmy Brown, full-backs Tom McSpadyen and Tommy McKenzie, half-backs Charlie Cox, Bobby Baxter and Archie Miller and forwards Tommy Sloan, Alex. McCrae and Archie Kelly were the mainstays of the team in the opening months while Willie McFarlane - later capped for Scotland against Luxemburg in May - and Johnny Urquhart established themselves on the wings after the turn of the year.

With the League Cup quarter-finals not due until March, Hearts were free to concentrate on league matters and by the end of 1946, they lay fourth within six points of pace - setters Rangers, Aberdeen and Hibs. Disappointingly, the Maroons went down 3-2 to high flying Hibs in a Ne'erday thriller before 35,000 at Tynecastle before another reverse, 4-1 to Third Lanark at Cathkin, and a 0-0 draw at Kilmarnock over the next few days meant any hopes of success now lay with the two cup competitions.

Davie McLean - the Hearts boss believed in fostering local talent.

On March 1st, Hearts lost 1-0 at home to East Fife in the first leg of the League Cup quarter-final and their hopes looked flimsy when Henry Morris scored within a minute of the Bayview return. However, roared on by a large support amongst the 15,000 crowd, Baxter pulled one back from a penalty in 20 minutes before McFarlane headed home an Urquhart cross to make it 2-2 on aggregate soon afterwards. In a titanic struggle, Urquhart gave Hearts the lead only for Duncan to equalise on the hour but in a storming finish, two goals by Jimmy Walker earned Hearts a 5-3 aggregate win and a place in the last four.

Meanwhile, a 3-0 Scottish Cup triumph over St Johnstone at Tynecastle gave Hearts a home tie against another 'B' Division side, Cowdenbeath, in the second round. On a heavily sanded pitch, the Fifers came within an ace of victory. In the dying minutes, Hearts defender Tom McSpadyen booted the ball off the line with the score locked at 1-1 and only a Jimmy Walker effort in extra-time took the Maroons within sight of their second semi-final.

Normally a winger, Walker had scored three cup goals after successfully switching to centre-forward. However, he failed to turn up for the next tie at Arbroath and although they were strong favourites, a disappointing Hearts went down 2-1 to the Red Lichties.

Although many still predicted an all-Edinburgh League Cup Final, both capital sides were eliminated in the semi-finals. At Hampden, Hibs lost 3-2 to Rangers and although Hearts led 2-1 through Archie Kelly and Johnny Urquhart after 27 minutes of the Easter Road tie against strong-going Aberdeen, a tragic own-goal by young centre-half David Wood proved the turning point. In the second-half, the Maroons were torn apart with the brilliant George Hamilton netting three as the Dons raced to a 6-2 triumph and a place in the League Cup Final.

Jimmy Walker's indiscipline cost him a suspension and although it came as little surprise when he moved on to Partick Thistle in exchange for defender Bobby Parker, many were critical of the close season decision to transfer inside-left Alex. McCrae (27), to Charlton for a new Hearts record fee of £9,000.

A year earlier, Hearts had carried out essential safety work around their ground after the disaster at Bolton's Burnden Park when 33 fans were crushed to death. Now, following government recommendations, work had commenced to concrete the entire terracing at Tynecastle - a task which would take four years and cost nearly £1,700.

Hearts made a great start to their 1947-48 campaign, qualifying from their League Cup section despite the efforts of Hibernian, St Mirren and Airdrie. Pacy left-winger Archie Williams, who had just returned from National Service, was particularly prominent in both 2-1 victories over Hibs, but Hearts soon met their match against the up-and-coming East Fife in the one-off quarter-final tie.

The men from Methil triumphed 3-2 in a Tynecastle thriller which went to extra-time and that signalled the start of a disastrous slump as Hearts won just two of their next 14 league games. The defence, where the gritty Davie Laing had replaced 37-year-old Archie Miller - the long-serving veteran joined Blackburn Rovers soon afterwards - was performing well enough but the attack had struggled to find the net.

To remedy this failure, Tynecastle boss Davie McLean splashed out £15,000 for Clyde's free scoring inside-left Arthur Dixon in October. However, with the goals drought continuing, prolific Airdrie marksman Bobby Flavell was signed for £10,000 a couple of months later before the experienced Aberdeen and Scotland inside-forward George Hamilton (30), arrived in an exchange deal for Hearts top scorer Archie Kelly plus £8,000.

Unfortunately, Hamilton struggled to produce his Pittodrie form and at the start of 1948, Hearts, although turning on some sparkling football, continued to labour in the lower regions of the league. In the Scottish Cup, the Maroons travelled to Dundee and recorded a 4-2 win over the Dens outfit who had made a big impression since returning to 'A' Division. And despite a bitterly disappointing 2-1 defeat at struggling Airdrie in the next round, Davie McLean's boys put their relegation worries behind them with a nine game unbeaten run to eventually finish in mid-table.

The close season brought a number of departures. George Hamilton had been unable to settle at Tynecastle and he rejoined Aberdeen for £12,000, while half-backs Bobby Baxter - who had assisted with the coaching after droping out of the side - Tommy Neilson and Jim Pithie were released. Hibernian had continued to be the dominant force in Edinburgh and after achieving the runners-up slot in 1946-47, the Easter Road side had gone one better by pipping Rangers for last term's League Championship. That had provided an added stimulant for football in the capital and now Hearts were desperately keen to emulate the success of their city rivals.

However the Tynecastle club made a disappointing start to the 1948-49 season as they lost five of their opening six league games and failed to qualify from their League Cup section, which also included East Fife, Partick Thistle and Queen of the South. There was the feeling that things could only get better and manager Davie McLean finally struck gold with his team selection for the remaining two League Cup ties.

Eight changes were made for the visit of East Fife on October 9th. Charlie Cox came in at right-half with Davie Laing moving to left-half. Bobby Dougan - a regular at

Heart of Midlothian F.C. 1946-47 (BACK, left to right) Tom McKenzie, Tommy McSpadyen, Arthur Miller, Jimmy Brown, Bobby Baxter, Charlie Cox. FRONT - Tommy Sloan, Alfie Conn, Archie Kelly, Alex. McCrae and Jimmy Wardhaugh. John Ure

Alfie Conn - one of the "Terrible Trio", he packed a powerful shot.

left-half - went to centre-half and brought added solidity to the middle, while Bobby Parker relinquished the number five jersey and switched to right-back to the exclusion of Dougal Matheson.

Up front, the forwards had again struggled to find the net and, in addition to outside-left Johnny Urquhart, out went the inside forward trio of Ken Currie, Bobby Flavell and Arthur Dixon. In for his debut at centre-forward came 20-year-old Willie Bauld, formerly with Newtongrange Star and Edinburgh City, with inside forwards Alfie Conn and Jimmy Wardhaugh, who had both done little of note in previous first-team outings, recalled along with left winger Archie Williams.

The new inside-forward partnership proved an instant success with Bauld netting a glorious hat-trick in a crushing 6-1 win over the runaway section winners from Methil. And just to prove it was no fluke, the centre grabbed another three the following week in a 4-0 home win over Queen of the South before a 2-0 win over Rangers at Tynecastle confirmed that Hearts were indeed on the way back.

By the start of 1949, Hearts lay nine points behind league leaders Hibs in twelfth place but although their rivals retrieved a two-goal deficit to equalise through Bobby Combe with three minutes remaining, Hearts refused to accept the loss of a point in a Ne'erday thriller at Tynecastle. With the Hibs fans in full voice, Willie Bauld fed Alfie Conn and the inside-forward darted through the centre of the Hibs defence to fire the ball past Jimmy Kerr for a last gasp winner.

That brought a measure of revenge for their earlier derby defeat in August for in recent seasons it had been Hibs who had consistently grabbed the headlines with their acclaimed and highly effective "Famous Five" forward line of Gordon Smith, Bobby Johnstone, Lawrie Reilly, Eddie Turnbull and Willie Ormond. Now, however, Hearts had the perfect answer in the form of their "Terrible Trio" of Alfie Conn, Willie Bauld and Jimmy Wardhaugh.

In December, Tynecastle's prodigal son, Tommy Walker, had returned from Chelsea to take up the post of assistant manager but on January 8th, he turned out at right-half in the 1-0 home defeat by Dundee. However, the former international who, at his peak, had merited 20 full Scotland caps, made little impression and henceforth, he would remain on the sidelines and concentrate on learning the ropes of management from Davie McLean.

In the Scottish Cup, Hearts progressed to the quarter-finals with home victories over Airdrie (4-1), Third Lanark (3-1) and Dumbarton (3-0) before being handed another home tie against title challengers Dundee, who they had defeated in last season's opening round. The Dark Blues had already beaten Hearts twice that term, and on March 5th, 1949, a bumper crowd of 37,356 turned out in the expectation of another closely fought encounter.

The fans were not disappointed. On a rain-soaked Tynecastle, Gunn gave Dundee a first minute lead only for Tommy Sloan and Charlie Cox to hit back for Hearts around the half-hour mark. Goals by Hill and Gerrie either side of half-time put Dundee 3-2 ahead but the tie remained in the balance until Hearts were awarded a penalty near the end. Up stepped Davie Laing but to the consternation of the home support, his weak shot was saved by Reuben Bennett and Pattillo finished the game with a fourth for Dundee soon afterwards.

Following their cup disappointment, Hearts were again destined to finish in mid-table but the clever interlinking play and scoring exploits of Conn, Bauld and Wardhaugh had caught the imagination of the fans. Top scorer Willie Bauld's haul of 24 goals included three hat-tricks and now Hearts problem was to find stability in defence to match their new-found scoring prowess.

Jackie Dewar, Atholl McAra and Davie Wood were amongst those released. Centre-half Jim Rodger joined Stirling Albion some months later while Hearts only new signing for the 1949-50 season was Morton outside-left Colin Liddell (24), for a fee of £10,000.

Hearts began their League Cup challenge in devastating fashion, recording 5-1 wins over Stirling Albion and Raith Rovers before struggling to a 1-1 home draw against newly promoted East Fife. Willie Bauld grabbed his second hat-trick of the season against Stirling Albion at Tynecastle only for the Annfield side - Scotland's newest senior team - to depart with a sensational 5-4 win. And, although two goals by Alfie Conn earned a 2-1 win over Raith Rovers at Kirkcaldy, Hearts required a decisive win over East Fife at Bayview to pip the Fifers for a quarter-final place on goal-average.

For the past two years, Hearts League Cup hopes had foundered against East Fife who, flourishing under the astute management of Scott Symon, had won both the League Cup and 'B' Division Championship last season. Now, once again, that task proved beyond Hearts whose shaky defence was largely responsible for a 4-3 defeat and seven days later the Fifers were again the scourge of Tynecastle when they departed with a 1-0 win in the opening league game before a huge 45,000 crowd.

Bobby Parker - an inspirational figure for Hearts down the years. Daily Record

After a seven match absence, the return of influential right-back Bobby Parker brought a big improvement and, despite losing to Celtic at Parkhead, Hearts got the perfect tonic with a timely 5-2 derby win over Hibernian at Tynecastle on September 24th. That was only a temporary respite and four weeks

One for Bauld - it's Willie Bauld at his best as he leaves Aberdeen goalkeeper Curran floundering before crashing the ball home with Dons left-back McKenna making a desperate attempt to prevent the goal at Pittodrie. ABERDEEN JOURNALS

later, Hearts languished at the bottom of 'A' Division with just three points from their opening six league games.

On October 29th, Jimmy Wardhaugh netted four as the Maroons raced to a 6-2 home win over Clyde, a result which propelled them on a run of 12 straight wins, including an astonishing 9-0 home drubbing of Falkirk in November. Not to be outdone, Willie Bauld also grabbed four goals in the 4-2 win over Stirling Albion and with the "Terrible Trio" continuing to wreak havoc in opposing defences, another two forwards moved on. Tommy Martin joined Stirling Albion for £3,000 with Arthur Dixon transferred to Northampton Town for £8,000.

Colin Liddell had yet to fulfil his potential and with Bobby Flavell on the left-wing, Hearts regular line-up over this period was - Brown; Parker, McKenzie; Cox, Dougan, Laing; Sloan, Conn, Bauld, Wardhaugh and Flavell.

December 31st 1949

	P	F A	Pts
Hibs	**15**	**41-15**	**27**
Hearts	**16**	**47-20**	**23**
Rangers	**14**	**29-15**	**23**
Dundee	**16**	**32-19**	**21**
Celtic	**17**	**30-30**	**20**

On Hogmanay, a thrilling victory over fifth-placed Celtic at Tynecastle put Hearts level with second-placed Rangers and just four points behind leaders Hibs. The ever-alert Willie Bauld had taken advantage of defensive slackness to put Hearts in front, only for Bobby Collins to equalise after half-time. However, Bobby Parker thundered home a free-kick then Bauld made it 3-1. And although the dynamic Collins reduced the leeway, Hearts got a decisive fourth when Milne put through his own goal after pressure from Tommy Sloan.

Hibernian had also strung together an impressive run and on January 2nd, 1950, the most vital derby clash for years saw an incredible 65,840 fans - around one thousand more than at the Celtic v. Rangers match that same day - packed into Easter Road. Hearts took a first-half pounding and went behind when Gordon Smith headed in a Willie Ormond cross. Undaunted, the Maroons surged back to level through Alfie Conn after the interval and with the fans in a welter of excitement, Jimmy Wardhaugh fired home a late winner to give Hearts both points.

Once again, big Tom McKenzie had kept the brilliant Gordon Smith subdued and along with the uncompromising Bobby Parker, he formed a redoubtable full-back partnership. All the forwards were capable of finding the net while the half-back line of Cox, Dougan and Laing was one of the most constructive in Scotland. Hearts lay tantalisingly close to the top of the table but although a 34,000 crowd saw St Mirren crushed 5-0 at Tynecastle the following day, defeats by Dundee (a) 1-3 and Rangers (h) 0-1 signalled an end to their headlong rise.

Now hopes turned to the Scottish Cup, which the Maroons had last won by defeating Third Lanark 1-0 in the 1906 final. In the first round, Hearts entertained Dundee but it took a late counter by Willie Bauld to equalise Syd Gerrie's 60th minute goal for the Dark Blues.

In the replay on the Monday afternoon of February 6th, Dundee struck first, a shot by inside-right Jimmy Toner hitting the bar before bouncing into the net off the unlucky Jimmy Brown. Jimmy Wardhaugh equalised before half-time but, despite Dundee losing left-winger Jimmy Andrews through injury, the score remained 1-1. In extra-time, the home side looked like holding out until Gerrie went off with a pulled muscle but now reduced to nine men, they finally succumbed when Willie Bauld got the winner near the end. The second round draw took Hearts to Aberdeen but with little going their way, the Tynecastle Scottish Cup quest was again doomed to failure as they went down 3-1 before a crowd of 42,000.

The sheer consistency of Rangers - famed at this time for their 'Iron Curtain' defence - saw them take the title by a point from Hibs with third placed Hearts a further six points in arrears. Nevertheless, the Maroons, who were capable of some scintillating soccer, had come on leaps and bounds and a 6-2 win over Dundee in their final match at Tynecastle brought their tally to an impressive 86 goals. The defence had also shown a marked improvement, conceding just 40 goals, 14 fewer than the previous season.

Willie Bauld again finished top scorer, this time with an improved tally of 40 goals - 30 in the league including six hat-tricks and towards the end of the season, his prolific scoring was rewarded with three full caps for Scotland. The centre drew a blank against England before 134,000 at Hampden but scored in a 3-1 win over Switzerland and in the 2-2 draw with Portugal. Although the top two teams from the British Championship had been invited to the World Cup Finals in Rio, Scotland had announced that they would only go as Champions.

After trailing 1-0 to a Bentley goal, only two minutes remained when Bauld was unfortunate to see his ferocious shot rebound from the bar. A draw would have ensured that Scotland and England shared the championship and Bauld and Scotland would have been bound for Rio, but sadly it was not to be.

However, another Tynecastle player was headed for South America. In June, Bobby Flavell dropped a bombshell when he walked out on Hearts and flew off to join Bolivian side Millionairos. Despite his absence, Hearts took seven points from their opening four League Cup games before losing 3-2 in a vital clash at Motherwell, a result which saw the Fir Parkers take what proved a decisive one point lead at the top of the section.

The reintroduction of Archie Williams in place of Colin Liddell after seven games appeared to provide added impetus and by October 28th, Hearts had surged to second top of the league. However, Davie McLean's cavalier side continued to slip up when least expected and heavy defeats by mid-table Partick Thistle - 5-2 at Firhill then 5-4 at Tynecastle a fortnight later - demonstrated that the defensive problems remained. Nevertheless, at the turn of the year, the Tynecastle team lay just four points behind pacesetters, Dundee, in fifth position.

Having earlier triumphed 1-0 at Easter Road, Hearts continued their derby dominance over Hibernian when Sloan and Conn scored in a 2-1 win at Tynecastle on January 1st, 1951. Away victories over 'B' Division Alloa (3-2) and East Stirling (5-1) set up a Scottish Cup third round clash against Celtic at Tynecastle on February 24th. Watched by a noisy 47,672 crowd, Alfie Conn levelled an early goal by John McPhail only for the Celtic centre to almost immediately make it 2-1. Try as they might, the gallant Maroons were unable to breach the "hoops" defence and the Parkhead side went on to lift the Cup itself.

Just 10 days earlier, the Tynecastle club had been stunned by the death of manager Davie McLean. At the home match with Third Lanark on February 17th, the crowd sang two lines of "Abide With Me" before standing for a minute's silence. Soon Tommy Walker took over the reins, but whereas Hearts remained dogged by inconsistency, their Easter Road rivals went on to take the League Championship for the second time in four years.

Hibs completed their programme 10 points ahead of second-placed Rangers, with Dundee and Hearts finishing third and fourth. In a somewhat disappointing season, the team had changed little from the year before, although 20-year-old John Cumming had shown great promise in establishing himself at outside-left.

Mark of respect - Hearts (on right) and Third Lanark players and match officials observe a minute's silence following the death of Tynecastle manager Davie McLean in February 1951. DC Thomson

Chapter Two

A TASTE OF GLORY

After an initial settling-in period, Tommy Walker now began in earnest. Earlier, the transfer-seeking John Prentice had been sold to Rangers for £7,000 after failing to displace Davie Laing at left-half. Jim Henderson was amongst those released while Ken Currie, earlier placed on the open-to-transfer list at £4,000, went to Third Lanark for £1,500 after intervention by the Scottish League.

After a four game close season tour of West Germany, Hearts found themselves in a League Cup section alongside Dundee, St Mirren and Raith Rovers. Following his return from South America last December, Bobby Flavell had received a six month S.F.A. suspension and a fine of £150. However, in April, Hearts decided to accept £6,000 for his transfer to Dundee, where, along with Billy Steel, he would prove a key man for the resurgent Dark Blues.

Amidst tremendous excitement, Hearts had dumped the Dens men 5-2 in their penultimate match at Tynecastle before finishing with a 3-1 home win over section leaders St Mirren. Although that appeared to have ensured their qualification, Dundee had also won 3-1 in their final game against Raith Rovers at Stark's Park. Both clubs had seven points but with a fractionally better goal-average, it was Flavell's new club who proceeded to the last eight, ultimately going on to win the League Cup itself.

Autumn brought a number of changes. With Bobby Parker well established, experienced right-back Dougal Matheson was released and Colin Liddell moved on to Rangers in exchange for Ibrox winger Eddie Rutherford. Until recently, Charlie Cox and Tommy Sloan had been first-team regulars at Tynecastle but with Sloan losing his place to Rutherford and Cox also struggling for a game, both joined Motherwell for a joint fee of £6,500.

Willie Bauld had dropped out of the international reckoning, the Selectors preferring that other prolific scorer, Lawrie Reilly of Hibs. In late September, Bobby Dougan, who along with Bauld had been capped by Scotland against Switzerland in 1950, sustained a bad ankle injury while playing for the Scottish League against the League of Ireland. That ruled him out for the rest of the season and former Arbroath defender Jimmy Milne (21), took over at centre-half with Freddie Glidden (23), coming in at right-half after the departure of Charlie Cox.

After a season on loan to Raith Rovers, Johnny Urquhart re-established himself at outside-left, while John Cumming again made a good impression up front along with the industrious Jimmy Whittle. The influx of new blood coincided with an eight game unbeaten run and by December 29th, Hearts lay third, two points behind East Fife and three behind league leaders Hibs. The famous inside-trio of Conn, Bauld and Wardhaugh remained a major influence and two goals each by Willie Bauld and Jimmy Wardhaugh in the 6-1 home win over Airdrie came as the ideal preparation for the Ne-erday clash with Hibs at Easter Road.

Tommy Walker - the new Hearts manager was destined to lead the success-starved Gorgie side to silverware. DC Thomson

However, although Hearts defeated their arch rivals 3-2 to narrow the gap, Hibernian went on to retain the Championship, their third title success since the war. The Maroons had to be content with fourth place, 10 points behind Hibs but they had come very close to reaching the final of the Scottish Cup.

Following a first round bye, wins over Raith Rovers (h) 1-0 and Queen of the South (a) 3-1 took Hearts into the quarter-finals. There, they travelled to Broomfield to meet Airdrie, who despite struggling in the lower reaches of 'A' Division, led 2-0 at half-time before timely scores by Bauld and Conn provided Hearts with a second chance.

Four days later, the sides replayed at Tynecastle but once again an Ian McMillan double gave the spirited Diamonds a two goal lead. In a pulsating cup-tie, Hearts pulled level before the interval and with Willie Bauld back at his brilliant best with a hat-trick, the Maroons went on to win 6-4 and clinch a hard-earned place in the last four.

Now, the Maroons would meet last season's runners-up Motherwell at Hampden on March 29th with Dundee meeting Third Lanark in the other tie at Easter Road. Although conditions were far from ideal with sleet and a sprinkling of snow on the ground, a huge 98,537 crowd greeted the teams as they ran out. Hearts - Brown; Parker, McSpadyen; Glidden, Milne, Laing; Rutherford, Conn, Bauld, Wardhaugh and Whittle. Motherwell, who included three ex-Tynecastle players in Charlie Cox, Tommy Sloan and Archie Kelly, fielded - Johnstone; Kilmarnock, Shaw; Cox, Paton, Redpath; Sloan, Humphries, Kelly, Watson and Aitkenhead.

Just five minutes had elapsed when Eddie Rutherford drove in a low corner and Alfie Conn fairly thundered the ball in off the bar. After the break, Motherwell were in the ascendancy and they deservedly equalised when Jimmy Watson pounced on an Aitkenhead cross to send the ball in off Tom McSpadyen on the goal-line and into the net.

Going for goal - John Cumming moves in as the visiting keeper grabs the ball in this match at Tynecastle. The dynamic half-back was to the fore as Hearts swept to glory in the 1950's.

With the Scotland v. England international at Hampden the following Saturday, the replay took place at the same venue on Monday, April 7th. This time the attendance was just over 80,000 as Hearts brought in McKenzie and Urquhart for McSpadyen and Wardhaugh. Watson put Motherwell in front with a header in seven minutes but Hearts were soon level, Rutherford finishing off a knock-down by Conn following a Glidden free-kick. There were plenty of thrills but, despite 30 minutes of extra-time, the scores again finished level at one goal apiece.

Just two days later the sides returned to Hampden for their second semi-final replay, for the final itself was scheduled for April 19th. Jimmy Wardhaugh returned at the expense of Jimmy Whittle while Motherwell were again unchanged. The Maroons started well but as time wore on, the more methodical play of the Steelmen began to pay dividends.

In 10 minutes, Archie Shaw got the opener from a free-kick and soon afterwards Wilson Humphries made it two before Alfie Conn pulled one back with a cracking drive 10 minutes from time. Now Hearts piled on the pressure but all was in vain when Motherwell left-half Willie Redpath, recently capped against England, cracked home an 18-yard shot to make it 3-1 just on the final whistle.

Nearly, 238,000 fans had watched the cup-tie marathon with the physically stronger Motherwell dominant at wing-half and more direct up front where only Willie Bauld had consistently been prepared to try his luck for a disappointing Hearts. The Fir Parkers certainly had all the attributes of a successful cup side and they went on to prove it by trouncing Dundee 4-0 in the final.

That July, Hearts participated in the St Mungo's Cup, a competition being held by Glasgow Corporation for 'A' Division clubs to celebrate the Festival of Great Britain. However, their interest proved short-lived as they went down 2-1 at Parkhead to a well-conditioned Celtic before a shirt-sleeved crowd of 51,000. Unlike Hearts, Celtic were match-fit, having just returned from a tour of the U.S.A., and the Glasgow club went on to take the trophy.

After several years as understudy, Jimmy Watters (25), replaced Jimmy Brown in goal for the opening League Cup tie against Rangers at Tynecastle on August 9th. Heavy rain restricted the crowd to 41,000 but when Alfie Conn thundered a magnificent 25-yard shot past Ibrox keeper Bobby Brown after 10 minutes, home fans forgot the miserable conditions and soon the Tynecastle attack was moving like a well-oiled machine. By the end the scoreline was 5-0 in favour of Hearts and when that was followed by an impressive 4-2 midweek win at Aberdeen, the Gorgie side looked a good bet to reach the League Cup quarter finals.

However, a 1-0 Tommy Sloan-inflicted home defeat by cock-a-hoop Motherwell, who had previously returned to Tynecastle to sign Archie Williams for £1,000, then a 2-0 defeat by Rangers in the crucial Ibrox return, saw the Maroons lead disappear. The Light Blues took full advantage and it was they who went on to the next stage, two points ahead of Hearts and Motherwell.

Hearts began their championship campaign with a 3-2 win over Third Lanark at Cathkin but a 2-1 reverse at home to St Mirren and then a 3-1 defeat away to Hibs, where Lawrie Reilly grabbed three, set the scene for an erratic series of results which continued until the end of 1952. Now recovered from injury, Bobby Dougan returned at centre-half in place of Jimmy Milne with Doug Armstrong establishing himself at left-half and Davie Laing moving across to the right-half berth.

For the first time in many years, Hibernian completed a derby double by beating Hearts 2-1 at Tynecastle at New Year. That result appeared to jolt the Maroons into greater consistency and a 10-game unbeaten run saw them high and dry in the Scottish Cup semi-finals.

Once again given the benefit of a first round bye, Willie Bauld snatched the only goal against Raith Rovers before a Stark's Park record crowd of 31,306. Then after coasting to a 3-1 home win over Montrose at the next stage, a Bobby Blackwood double gave Hearts a 2-1 triumph against Queen of the South at Tynecastle to put them into the last four. There they would meet the favourites, Rangers with Aberdeen paired against bottom of the league Third Lanark.

On April 4th, a noisy 116,262 crowd lined the Hampden slopes for the semi-final. Rangers fielded - Niven; Young, Little; McColl, Woodburn, Cox; Waddell, Grierson, Simpson, Prentice and Hubbard. Hearts - Watters; Parker, Adie; Laing, Dougan, Armstrong; Rutherford, Conn, Bauld, Wardhaugh and Cumming.

Right from the start, Hearts surged forward and with Bobby Parker and Dougie Armstrong particularly prominent, Rangers were pushed back. In 11 minutes, Eddie Rutherford made ground up the left and to the joy of the thousands of Hearts fans, Jimmy Wardhaugh hooked home his cross from 12 yards.

Now Conn, Bauld and Wardhaugh turned on the style but with Hearts looking sure to add a second, defensive hesitancy between Jimmy Watters and three of his defenders allowed Derek Grierson to grab the equaliser shortly before half-time. A clash with George Young left John Cumming hirpling and with Ian McColl and Sammy Cox taking charge of midfield, it was Rangers who grabbed the winner, a John Prentice shot spinning off Adie and past a despairing Watters, just 15 minutes from time.

Willie Bauld hit the bar in a late rally but this second successive semi-final failure came as a bitter blow to Hearts. For although their second half of the season revival lifted them to fourth place, Hibernian had finished 13 points better off in runners-up spot, only losing the League Championship to Rangers on goal average.

Nevertheless, Tommy Walker had continued Davie McLean's policy of encouraging local young talent and, already another pair of promising attackers, Bobby Blackwood and Jimmy Souness, had broken through to take their places alongside the youthful John Cumming and Jimmy Whittle. A year earlier, Tom McSpadyen and Bobby Buchan had been freed and now long-serving keeper Jimmy Brown - to Kilmarnock - and Dick Whitehead - to Stirling Albion - were released to allow the club's youngsters to progress.

Unfortunately, the start of the 1953-54 season saw the Gorgie side again placed in the same League Cup section as Rangers who finished runaway winners, five points ahead of Hearts. The Tynecastle men could only manage three wins from their opening eight games but on October 31st, a Johnny Urquhart goal provided a rare triumph over Rangers at Ibrox and gave them renewed appetite for the fray. Hearts had given the Light Blues a lesson in teamwork and with just seven minutes remaining, Alfie Conn accepted a pass by Armstrong and when he stabbed the ball betwen McColl and Young, Urquhart, who had had a field day against big George Young, ran on to crack a beauty into Niven's left hand corner.

The following Saturday brought a disappointing 2-1 home defeat by Clyde but the new-look Hearts were to taste defeat in only two of their next 18 games. After a long spell as a reserve, Jock Adie became first choice at left-back. John Cumming was now a fixture at left-half but a bad knee injury to Bobby Dougan allowed Freddie Glidden to switch to centre-half with Davie Laing and Doug Armstrong in contention for the number four jersey.

Whilst at Hibs, Jimmy Souness had struggled in the shadow of the illustrious Gordon Smith before moving across the Capital for £3,000 in December 1952. He had spent another year in the background at Tynecastle but a long-term knee injury to Eddie Rutherford saw the pacy Souness establish himself at outside-right and he quickly made his mark with the opening goal in a 2-1 win over Hibs on New Year's Day.

On February 6th, a Bauld double and another by Wardhaugh contributed to a thrilling 3-2 win over buoyant Celtic at Tynecastle and within a fortnight, Hearts lay seven points clear of the Parkhead side at the top. The Maroons had also done well in the Scottish Cup, reaching the last eight after a 3-0 win at Highland League Fraserburgh and a 2-1 win over Queen of the South at Palmerston - the third successive year Hearts had met the Dumfries outfit in that competition.

However, Hearts were to progress no further as they fell 3-0 before a bumper 45,000 crowd at Aberdeen on March 13th. A week earlier, a surprise 4-2 league defeat at the hands of Raith Rovers handed Celtic the advantage and another 1-0 reverse in the third last game at Aberdeen finally ended their title hopes. Nevertheless, although five points adrift of Celtic, the much improved Hearts had finished second, their best placing since the war.

Big Jimmy Wardhaugh finished top scorer with 34 League and Cup goals with Willie Bauld contributing 14 goals and Alfie Conn netting 13. John Cochrane was released, full-back Ian Gordon having earlier joined Airdrie and in the close season, Hearts accepted an invitation to undertake a prestigious 10-game tour of South Africa. Sixteen players made the trip and although there were plenty of sight-seeing trips and Caledonian Society functions galore, Hearts lost only one of their 10 games during their month-long stay, a 2-1 defeat at the hands of the South African national team in Durban.

Returning bronzed and fit, the Maroons moved straight into top gear with a 3-1 home win over Dundee - now without the brilliant Billy Steel - before a crushing 6-2 win at Falkirk was followed by a 2-1 triumph over League Champions Celtic before 53,000 at Parkhead.

Meanwhile, Dundee had recovered and in the fourth game Hearts went down 4-1 at Dens Park to set up a nail-biting finale. However, Tommy Walker's men held their nerve to beat Falkirk 4-1 at Tynecastle and now they had to beat Celtic at home in their final game and hope that Dundee, who had the better goal-average, might drop something at Brockville.

Jimmy Wardhaugh - the scoring ace was Hearts top scorer in 1953-54 with 34 League and Cup goals. DC Thomson

It's there - Willie Bauld heads the ball past Hastie Weir to open the scoring in the 1954 League Cup Final against Motherwell. Looking on are Hearts Jimmy Wardhaugh and Alfie Conn and 'Well defenders Cox and Kilmarnock. Below - the match programme. John Ure

The brilliant Charlie Tully gave Celtic an early lead but soon after half-time, Jimmy Wardhaugh accepted a brilliantly executed Willie Bauld head-flick to volley past Bonnar. In 51 minutes, Davie Laing netted from the spot after Bertie Peacock had handled but within a minute, the busy Bobby Collins levelled. It had been a real roller-coaster of a game but with 17 minutes remaining, Willie Bauld crashed home the winner and with Dundee losing 4-0, Hearts were through to the quarter-finals.

Dave Mackay, who had been signed from Newtongrange Star two years earlier, had made four appearances towards the end of last season. Now, however, the hard-tackling half-back wrested the number four jersey from veteran Davie Laing and along with another 19-year-old, goalkeeper Willie Duff, he began the 1954-55 campaign as a first-team regular.

In September, Davie Laing was transferred to Clyde for £6,000 but, although destined to miss out on an imminent piece of Tynecastle glory, the long-serving wing-half went on to collect a winner's medal with the Shawfielders when they beat Celtic in the Scottish Cup Final the following April.

League wins over Partick Thistle (h) 5-4 and Hibernian (a) 3-2 put Hearts in fine fettle for their quarter-final tie against 'B' Division opponents, St Johnstone. And on September 22nd, a 5-0 win at Perth ensured the Tynecastle return was a mere formality as the Maroons cruised into the last four, 7-0 on aggregate.

Once again, the draw favoured Hearts with lower league opposition, this time against 'B' Division pace-setters, Airdrie before 34,127 fans at Easter Road. Straight from kick-off, Billy Price finished off a three-man move to put Airdrie ahead and with giant centre-half Doug Baillie a defensive colossus, Hearts struggled until Jimmy Wardhaugh diverted a powerful shot by Alfie Conn into the net for the equaliser in 23 minutes.

Johnny Urquhart made it 2-1 and just on half-time, Hearts keeper Jimmy Watters jumped with joy when Hughie Baird missed a penalty for Airdrie. Now there would be only one winner and second-half goals by Jimmy Wardhaugh and Willie Bauld put the Maroons through to meet Motherwell, who had beaten East Fife 2-1 in the other semi-final.

The Tynecastle men had lost only twice in 12 games that season and a win at East Fife put them in high spirits for the Hampden final on Saturday, October 23rd. Hearts had been virtually unchanged since the start of the season, apart from Jock Adie or Tam McKenzie at left-back with Jimmy Souness and Bobby Blackwood vying for the number seven jersey. Tommy Walker's choice was - Duff; Parker (capt.), McKenzie; Mackay, Glidden, Cumming; Souness, Conn, Bauld, Wardhaugh and Urquhart.

Motherwell had won the Scottish Cup in 1952 but after their relegation the following year the Steelmen had returned as Second Division Champions in 1954. They had provided the biggest shock of the League Cup by beating Rangers 3-2 on aggregate in the quarter-finals and former Tynecastle men Charlie Cox and Archie Williams remained key men as they fielded - Weir; Kilmarnock, McSeveney; Cox, Paton, Redpath; Hunter, Aitken, Bain, Humphries and Williams.

The game began in a steady drizzle but the crowd of 55,640 had to wait only nine minutes for the opener. Jimmy Souness weaved his way past Andy Paton before crossing and Willie Bauld bulleted a header past a helpless Hastie Weir. Six minutes later, Bauld thumped home a second from 16 yards but as Hearts relaxed, Motherwell hit back. Bain went close, a fierce shot by Willie Hunter was brilliantly saved by Willie Duff then Humphries struck the bar, but Motherwell were not to be denied.

In 28 minutes, the dangerous Wilson Humphries was downed in the box by Conn and Willie Redpath reduced the leeway from the penalty spot. However, just before the interval, Souness sent in another telling cross and Jimmy Wardhaugh made it 3-1 with a flying header.

In the second half, Motherwell did most of the pressing but with Dave Mackay, Freddie Glidden and John Cumming in uncompromising mood, the Tynecastle defence held firm. Now, Hearts were reduced to the occasional breakaway attack but with two minutes remaining, Jimmy Wardhaugh crossed perfectly for Willie Bauld to head his third and Hearts were home and dry.

Motherwell's Alex. Bain netted a late consolation but the Fir Parkers could not emulate the rapier-like Tynecastle attack nor the lethal Willie Bauld - so aptly named "King of Hearts". Willie Duff and the half-back line of Mackay, Glidden and Cumming had also been immense and Hearts had richly deserved their 4-2 win.

It was their first trophy success for 48 years and at the end, hundreds of exhuberant fans had streamed on to the pitch to congratulate their heroes, with thousands more lining the Edinburgh streets to welcome the team home. In the Hampden dressing room, Tommy Walker confined himself to the comment, "I'm a happy man tonight" while a delighted skipper Bobby Parker confessed, "We're delighted but it's just so hard to take it all in."

Expectations of a strong league challenge were heightened when Willie Bauld grabbed doubles in high-scoring wins over Stirling Albion (a) 5-0 and Falkirk (h) 5-3 but a 1-0 reverse to league leaders Aberdeen at Pittodrie came as a severe setback. Then came four straight wins before Hearts again slipped up against Rangers at Tynecastle on December 18th. Despite Grierson netting twice early on, goals by Conn, Bauld and Urquhart had given Hearts a 3-2 lead with 20 minutes remaining. However, Simpson levelled in 82 minutes and the Ibrox centre netted the winner two minutes from the end.

Nevertheless, the Tynecastle faithful had the consolation of some superb attacking play as the "Terrible Trio" of Conn, Bauld and Wardhaugh continued to bang in the goals. Yet another point was dropped in a 4-4 draw with Partick Thistle at Firhill but everyone was in agreement that some team was bound to suffer at the hands of Tommy Walker's attack-minded side.

It came as little great surprise when Hearts began 1955 with a 5-1 triumph over Hibs at Tynecastle, a result which confirmed that Hibs were no longer the team of old. In contrast, Hearts were growing ever stronger and it was now clear that the balance of power in Edinburgh had changed. A month earlier, there had been further recognition of the quality of players at Tynecastle when left-half John Cumming and inside-left Jimmy Wardhaugh made their Scotland debuts in the 4-2 defeat by the magical Magyars of Hungary at Hampden.

Indeed, by the summer, Cumming had taken his tally of international caps to four while the tenacious Dave Mackay and goalkeeper Willie Duff both played in Scotland's first-ever Under-23 international against England at Shawfield, an experience tempered by a 6-0 defeat with the prodigious Manchester United half-back Duncan Edwards netting three.

On February 5th, the Maroons again demonstrated their new-found superiority over the Easter Road side by rattling in five goals without reply in the second round of the Scottish Cup. At the next stage, Hearts coasted to a 6-0 romp over Highland League Buckie Thistle at Victoria Park before meeting current league leaders Aberdeen in the quarter-final. Although Tynecastle's capacity had been 54,359 since completing the concreting of the stand enclosure last year, a restriction of 49,000 had been imposed for safety reasons and soon all tickets were sold for the visit of Aberdeen.

Close call - it's Celtic on the attack and Hearts defenders Fred Glidden, Willie Duff and Jock Adie are relieved to see the ball fly over the bar. Charlie Tully and Willie Fernie are the Celts

In the previous round, the high-flying Dons had defeated Rangers and right-half Jackie Allister shocked the huge home support when he headed the opener after just three minutes. Hearts were to dominate the match but although Willie Bauld knocked in the equaliser on the hour, there was no further score. It was a different story in the midweek replay at Pittodrie where, aided by a big home support, goals by Paddy Buckley and Harry Yorston gave Aberdeen a 2-0 win and Hearts dreams of a cup double were over.

The cup exit came as a big disappoint-

Goalmouth thrills - Hearts outside-right Jimmy Souness gets off his mark as Hibernian keeper Tommy Younger misses this cross in the derby at Tynecastle. The Hibs left-back guards his post while Jimmy Wardhaugh is on the right.

ment and although a measure of revenge was gained with a 2-0 win over Aberdeen a few days later, only 10 points were taken from the remaining 10 games. The Tynecastle side - second only to Celtic in terms of goals scored - finished fourth, 10 points behind the new League Champions Aberdeen, who had done well to hold off a strong challenge by Celtic to take their first-ever title.

The preceeding months had seen something of a clearout. Bobby Dougan joined Kilmarnock for £4,300, Eddie Rutherford moved to Raith Rovers for £500 and Wallace King went to Queen of the South, while Willie Grant and Jock Adie - the latter went to East Fife - were amongst those released in May.

The Tynecastle side made an excellent start to the 1955-56 season, winning five and losing just once to bogy team East Fife as they conceded only two goals to finish two points ahead of Partick Thistle and qualify from their League Cup section. A scintillating display in the 4-0 home win over Dundee in their opening league game set the Maroons up nicely for the League Cup quarter-final clash with Aberdeen. However, the Dons were brimful of confidence and little was to go right for Hearts in the first leg at Pittodrie on Wednesday, September 14th.

Two goals by Paddy Buckley and another by Scottish international winger Graham Leggatt had the Dons three ahead after 35 minutes but a splendid header by 18-year-old Alex. Young, playing only his fourth game in place of the injured Willie Bauld, sparked a revival. Johnny Urquhart pulled back another before half-time and Young made it 3-3 when he nipped in between Jim Clunie and goalkeeper Fred Martin. However, left-back Bobby Kirk was taken off for 20 minutes with concussion and with Jimmy Wardhaugh and Alfie Conn both limping badly, handicapped Hearts conceded another two goals.

However, with Dave Mackay back at right-half, a crowd of 37,000 turned out in the hope of seeing Hearts overturn the deficit at Tynecastle three days later. The fans were treated to another feast of goals but, sadly, it was the Dons who again emerged triumphant by four goals to two as the 9-5 aggregate scoreline took them through to the semi-final.

The League Cup defeat came as a severe setback and four of the next eight matches were lost at the hands of Hibernian (h) 0-1, Queen of the South (a) 3-4, St Mirren (a) 1-3 and Rangers (a) 1-4. Ironically, Hearts had scored first against the Light Blues for whom two goals had been scored by South African forward Don Kitchenbrand, a signing target for Hearts two years previously.

Nevertheless, Hearts recovered and by the end of the year a seven game unbeaten run, including an amazing 7-1 triumph over Motherwell at Tynecastle - where Jimmy Wardhaugh netted four goals for the second time in his career - and 5-1 wins at home to Clyde and away to Dunfermline, saw them draw level with second placed Rangers and just two points behind Celtic over whom they had a game in hand.

Bobby Kirk (28), a £2,500 summer signing from Raith Rovers, had begun the season at left-back in place of Tom McKenzie before switching to the right when Bobby Parker was sidelined by cartilege trouble. In early 1956, Jim Souness retired after deciding to concentrate on his actuarial career but Hearts had more than adequate cover in Johnny Hamilton and former Hibs and Hamilton winger Ian Crawford.

The lightning-paced Hamilton (20), recently signed from Lesmahagow Juniors, had soon burst through to the first team where a series of brilliant touchline displays earned him an Under-23 cap against England along with team-mate Alex. Young. It was not a good night for the Scots who lost 3-1 at Hillsborough but there was consolation for the Hearts winger, who netted their only goal.

By the end of February, Hearts had extended their unbeaten run to 16 games to maintain their championship challenge. Along with Aberdeen, they lay just one point behind the leaders Rangers with Hibs and Celtic a couple of points behind and they had also reached the quarter-finals of the Scottish Cup.

On a foggy February afternoon, Alfie Conn set Hearts on the way to a 3-0 win over Forfar at Tynecastle and a fortnight later the Maroons cruised into the last eight with a 5-0 home win over Stirling Albion. Now, they faced an acid test against high-flying Rangers in yet another home tie on March 3rd and over 47,000 saw Hearts take a pummelling in the opening quarter before wing halves Dave Mackay and John Cumming began to take control.

Before long, the home wingers Alex. Young and Ian Crawford were troubling the Ibrox full backs Bobby Shearer and Johnny Little and it was no surprise when Crawford dived to head home the opener past George Niven from a Young cross. A minute later, Tynecastle went wild when Alfie Conn feinted to shoot and slipped the ball to Willie Bauld who made it 2-0.

Hard as they tried, the Ibrox side could find no way past a resolute Glidden-inspired home defence while big George Young and the Ibrox defence struggled to contain the eager Hearts forwards. In 64 minutes, Alfie Conn confirmed their semi-final place when he lashed in a powerful 18-yarder off the underside of the bar and Willie Bauld completed the rout with a fourth soon afterwards.

Three weeks later, Hearts clashed with Raith Rovers in the semi-finals before 58,448 fans at Easter Road. The Fifers took the first-half honours but although Hearts were the dominant force after the interval, the game ended without a goal. Four days later, there were just 4,000 fewer for the midweek replay which saw Alex. Young at inside-right for the injured Alfie Conn with Johnny Hamilton given the number seven jersey.

The Maroons got off to a great start when Jimmy Wardhaugh crashed home a free kick in the opening minute and the inside-left grabbed a second following a fine move by Willie Bauld and Johnny Hamilton. Now, there was little doubt that Hearts were heading for Hampden and four minutes from time, Ian Crawford headed home another fine Hamilton cross to set up a Scottish Cup Final clash against Celtic, 2-1 conquerors of Clyde in the other semi-final.

Meanwhile, the Tynecastle title challenge continued with a 5-0 home win over Dunfermline and, having gone 22 games without defeat, Hearts fans were well entitled to consider the prospect of a league and cup double. However, their dreams were quickly shattered for, with Willie Bauld out through injury and thoughts turning to the cup final, only one point was taken from the next three games as they lost to Partick Thistle (a) 0-2 and Aberdeen (a) 1-4 before drawing 2-2 with Clyde at Shawfield.

There was disappointment for young Johnny Hamilton who dropped out of the side as Hearts bounced back with a morale-boosting 8-3 romp over Falkirk at Tynecastle just a week before the final. Alfie Conn was back to his best with a hat-trick and Hearts were unchanged for the Hampden clash on April 21st. Celtic, who had lost last season's final to Clyde, would be without Scottish international inside-forward Bobby Collins and centre-half and skipper Jock Stein, who were both out injured.

Hearts - Duff; Kirk, McKenzie; Mackay, Glidden (capt.), Cumming; Young, Conn, Bauld, Wardhaugh and Crawford. Celtic - Beattie; Meechan, Fallon; Smith, Evans, Peacock; Craig, Haughney, Mochan, Fernie and Tully. Referee - Bobby Davidson (Airdrie).

The Hearts revival had caught the imagination of the Edinburgh public and numerous extra trains, buses and trams helped transport around 50,000 fans to Glasgow. There was a massive crowd of 132,842 inside Hampden with thousands more outside seeking the elusive briefs. During the warm up, a young mascot in Hearts colours appeared from the terracing and went round shaking the Tynecastle players' hands before disappearing back into the crowd.

Up for the cup - Celtic keeper Dick Beattie is helpless as Ian Crawford fires home his second goal in the 3-1 triumph over the Parkhead side in the 1955-56 Scottish Cup Final at Hampden. THE SCOTSMAN

Hearts, Glorious Hearts - a caricature of the famous Hearts side which lifted the Scottish Cup in 1956. I. White

After winning the toss, Freddie Glidden chose to play with the stiff breeze but both teams took time to settle. In 17 minutes, only a fine save by Dick Beattie prevented Crawford from giving Hearts the lead but the goal was only delayed. Three minutes later the outside-left accepted a pass from Conn before driving a powerful 20-yard shot high past the despairing Celtic keeper.

Backed by a vociferous support Hearts were now in full cry and Crawford and Wardhaugh missed chances before Conn fired over the bar. As expected it was a fiercely fought contest but with half-time approaching, Hearts suffered a severe setback when John Cumming collided with Willie Fernie and was led off with a badly gashed eyebrow.

After the interval, Cumming resumed with a large plaster over his wound but Billy Craig went close for Celtic before Hearts went 2-0 up three minutes after the break. Willie Bauld made ground down the left and beat Scotland centre-half Bobby Evans before crossing. Alex. Young outjumped Sean Fallon and Ian Crawford was on hand to crash the ball into the net. Soon afterwards, Beattie did well to save from Young but in 53 minutes Willie Duff dropped the ball after a mid-air shoulder charge by Haughney and the Celt netted despite a valiant attempt by Dave Mackay to clear.

Celtic battled to get back to equality and no quarter was asked or given. John Cumming used a sponge to control the blood which continued to seep from his wound and despite yet another bad head knock, he fought on bravely. However, Celtic could make little impression against an equally determined Hearts defence and soon after shooting over from a tight angle, Willie Bauld headed down for Alfie Conn to crash the ball into the roof of the net with 10 minutes remaining.

There was no way back for the Parkhead side and when the final whistle blew the Hearts officials, players and supporters went wild with delight. Inspired by two-goal Ian Crawford and the courageous John Cumming and Dave Mackay, Hearts had more than matched Celtic's fighting spirit, and that added to their undoubted ability, had been a key factor in deciding the destination of the cup.

On their return to the capital, the Tynecastle side received a great welcome from every village they passed through and huge crowds lined the streets of Edinburgh. At the Maybury roundabout the club's officials and players transferred to a special roofless double decker bus suitably adorned with the logo, "Hearts are Trumps".

The bus progressed slowly through the Gorgie Road homeland, up the Lawnmarket at the back of the Castle and across the North Bridge to a tumultous welcome on Princess Street where the traffic was brought to a standstill. Slowly the vehicle made it's way through the throngs before finally reaching Charlotte Street where the party alighted for their well deserved celebration dinner in the Charlotte Rooms.

After so many barren years, Hearts had now won a trophy for a second successive season with their Scottish Cup winning side showing three changes - Kirk, Young and Crawford for Parker, Souness and Urquhart from the League Cup heroes of 1954. However, perhaps suffering from a post-final reaction, Hearts then went down to Motherwell (a) 0-1 and Kilmarnock (h) 0-2 before ending the season with a 7-2 trouncing of Raith Rovers at Tynecastle, a result which saw them finish in third place, seven points behind League Champions, Rangers.

The logo says it all - the streets of Edinburgh are mobbed by crowds as the Hearts players make their triumphant return after the Scottish Cup win in 1956. DC Thomson

Chapter Three

A FAMOUS TITLE SUCCESS

Alfie Conn, who until then had made four appearances for the Scottish League, was rewarded with a Scotland appearance against Austria in May but some of the other "old hands" had moved on. Johnny Urquhart joined Raith Rovers for £300, Jimmy Whittle moved to Ayr United while Jimmy Watters and Doug Armstrong were released, later signing for East Fife and Third Lanark, respectively.

Prior to the start of the 1956-57 season, Hearts announced a profit of £5,445 with a 20% dividend payable to shareholders. Total income had been £63,905 less £58,460 expenditure, of which wages comprised £32,556.

Hearts made one change from their Scottish Cup winning side for the League Cup opener against Hibs at Tynecastle, reserve keeper Wilson Brown replacing Willie Duff who had gone to London for two years National Service. Eddie Turnbull headed Hibs into an early lead but once a piece of Conn and Bauld trickery allowed Wardhaugh to blast the equaliser past Wren, Hearts stormed back to win 6-1. However, their subsequent form proved patchy and despite winning 2-1 at Easter Road, the Maroons failed to qualify from their section as they finished two points behind Partick Thistle who went on to reach the final.

Tommy Walker refused to be ruffled and his decision to field an unchanged team was vindicated as Hearts made a great start to their league campaign. However, in September, they received a setback when Alfie Conn accidentally sustained a broken jaw in the 3-2 win over Hibs at Easter Road. The hard-hitting inside-man would be out for four months but with Alex. Young moving inside to take his place, right-wing speed merchant Johnny Hamilton returned and netted twice in a 4-3 win at Airdrie on October 20th. That result saw Hearts remain top of the table with 13 points from eight games, one point ahead of Motherwell who had a game in hand while Raith Rovers and Rangers trailed a couple of points further behind.

On December 8th, a Crawford double and another by Wardhaugh secured a thrilling 3-2 win over Motherwell before 35,000 at Tynecastle. That set Hearts up nicely for their next game away to Rangers, who had just taken a 5-1 mauling from Raith Rovers at Kirkcaldy. Early on, Jimmy Wardhaugh, recently capped for Scotland against Northern Ireland, netted twice and things looked good for a full-strength Hearts. However, Johnny Hubbard and Harold Davis made it 2-2 by the interval before a Max Murray double and another by Jimmy Simpson put the game beyond Hearts reach although Willie Bauld netted a late consolation goal.

Nevertheless, by the end of the year, Hearts retained pole position three points ahead of Motherwell, who had a game in hand and five above Rangers, who had two extra games. On New Year's Day, Hearts went down 2-0 to Hibs at Tynecastle but recovered to take 15 points from their next nine games. Motherwell, meanwhile, had begun to falter while Rangers had surprisingly lost at Ayr and by March 9th, Hearts held a seven point advantage over the Ibrox men, who now had three games in hand.

Dave Mackay - inspirational right-half and captain for Hearts. Daily Record

Although Willie Duff had moved south, the emergence of promising 17-year-old ex-Dalkeith Thistle goalkeeper Gordon Marshall meant Wilson Brown once again had competition for the keeper's jersey. Previously, Hearts had lost careless points to Ayr United, Falkirk and Partick Thistle and on March 16th, they went down 4-1 to a rapidly improving Kilmarnock at Rugby Park. Still the Maroons stuck to their task and there were victories against Queens Park (a) 1-0, Celtic (h) 3-1 and Motherwell (a) 3-1 before they faced Rangers in what was virtually a title decider at Tynecastle on April 13th .

Two months earlier, the Ibrox side had exacted full revenge for their 1956 humiliation by crushing Hearts 4-0 in the fifth round of the Scottish Cup at Tynecastle. Sadly, the recent run of adverse results against the Light Blues continued when Simpson headed past Marshall for the only goal in 35 minutes. Now, Rangers lay just two points behind with two games in hand and athough Hearts finished the season by beating Queen of the South (a) 2-0 and Aberdeen (h) 3-0, the Ibrox men won all four of their remaining games to take the title by a clear two points.

In recent years, Hearts had been notoriously slow starters and at the start of the 1957-58 campaign the trend continued with a disappointing 2-1 League Cup reverse at Kilmarnock. A hat-trick from veteran inside-left Jimmy Wardhaugh in a runaway 9-2 home win over Queens Park brought grounds for renewed optimism but the Jekyll and Hyde Maroons could only draw their next three games. In their final tie, Dundee were defeated 4-2 at Tynecastle but it was too little, too late with Hearts finishing two points behind section winners, Kilmarnock.

A bad ankle injury meant a lengthy absence for Alfie Conn, but Jimmy Murray (24), who had been at Tynecastle since signing from Merchiston Thistle in 1950, stepped in and Hearts began their league campaign with an stunning 6-0 win over Dundee at Tynecastle.

Throughout September, Hearts fielded an unchanged side of Marshall; Kirk, McKenzie; Mackay, Glidden,

On a high - Alex. Young leaps for a high cross but is beaten by keeper Lawrie Leslie. Jimmy Wardhaugh and Jimmy Murray hover expectantly while John Paterson and Eddie Turnbull are the other Hibs.

Cumming; Young, Murray, Bauld, Wardhaugh and Crawford. The commanding Gordon Marshall was now first-choice goalkeeper but it was Hearts brilliant attacking football which brought a succession of remarkable score-lines. A 7-2 win at Airdrie and a 3-1 derby victory over Hibs at Tynecastle were followed by an astonishing 9-0 home win over East Fife, the clever Jimmy Wardhaugh netting hat-tricks against both the Diamonds and the men from Methil.

There was great enthusiasm amongst the Gorgie faithful who once again rolled up to Tynecastle in their thousands. Somewhat surprisingly, Hearts drew a blank in a 0-0 draw against Third Lanark at Cathkin but they soon got back on the goal trail, a double by Jimmy Murray and singles by Jimmy Wardhaugh and Bobby Blackwood earning a 4-0 home win against Aberdeen on October 19th.

Earlier that month, Hearts had entertained Hibs to hansel their recently erected £14,000 floodlighting system. In 1954, Hibs had been amongst the earliest in Scotland to get their own lights although Hearts, who had played numerous floodlit challenge games in England in the early 1950's, had availed themselves of the Easter Road facility on a number of occasions for midweek friendlies. Now Hearts had their own lights and in the following weeks, their fans would be able to see floodlit friendlies against top English clubs like Manchester City and Newcastle - the latter were regular visitors to Edinburgh in the 1950's - in the comfort of their own ground.

On Wednesday October 23rd, the benfits of an effective floodlighting system were clear when 25,000 fans were at Tynecastle for the Scotland v. Holland Under-23 international. Seven months earlier, Johnny Hamilton, Ian Crawford, Dave Mackay and Alex. Young had all turned out at the same level against England with Crawford netting in a 1-1 draw. Now for the third successive Under-23 match, Hearts players were on the scoresheet, Mackay and Young finding the net in a 4-1 win.

Three days later, Hearts faced their biggest test in a confrontation with Rangers at Ibrox - always a vital staging post for a club with title aspirations. The Light Blues lay seven points behind with three games in hand but, after their late surge last term, no-one at Tynecastle was under-estimating the Ibrox challenge.

The large Hearts following in the 60,000 crowd were stunned when a quick one-two by Billy Simpson left Hearts trailing 2-0 after 22 minutes. However, urged on by Dave Mackay and John Cumming, the Gorgie side fought back and Jimmy Wardhaugh reduced the deficit before half-time. Four minutes after the interval, Willie Bauld levelled the scores and with 23 minutes remaining, Alex. Young - "the blond bombshell" - crashed home the winner to set the seal on a memorable afternoon.

With October drawing to a close, Hearts lay two points above Raith Rovers and Hibs, who had both played a game more, with Rangers now nine points in arrears. Another nine points were taken from their six games in November and despite losing to 2-1 to Clyde at Shawfield, Hearts goalscoring reputation was further enhanced by devastating home wins over Queens Park (8-0) and Falkirk (9-1).

On December 7th, Hearts faced a stern test against Raith Rovers at Stark's Park. The Kirkcaldy side were three points behind but any slip up would allow no fewer than six clubs to come within touching distance. Two goals by Wardhaugh and another by Murray ensured the Tynecastle juggernaught rolled on, and with confidence soaring, wins over Kilmarnock (h) 2-1, St Mirren (h) 5-1 and Celtic (a) 2-0 opened up a seven point gap over Edinburgh rivals Hibernian who had moved into second place.

That set up an intriguing Ne'erday encounter on a slippery bone-hard pitch at Easter Road. With Eddie Turnbull back in form and Joe Baker proving a deadly striker, Hibs were having their best spell for years but Hearts were in no mood to falter. The brilliant Alex. Young, who was now preferred to Willie Bauld at centre-forward was bang in form and it was no surprise when he opened the scoring soon after the interval. Hibs battled on but Dave Mackay made sure of both points when his thundering free-kick left Lawrie Leslie helpless 12 minutes from time.

By then, the experienced trio of Tom McKenzie, Freddie Glidden and John Cumming had dropped out through injury. However, former Edinburgh City defender George Thomson (21), previously impressive at wing-half, came in at left-back with Jimmy Milne and with the tenacious Andy Bowman taking the number five and six jerseys, the team pattern remained unchanged. However, Willie Duff, who had been allowed to play for Charlton Athletic during his National Service down South, was finally transferred to the London club on a permanent basis for a fee of £6,500.

The goals continued to flow like fine wine and by the end

of January, another five wins had been recorded over Airdrie (h) 4-0, Dundee (a) 5-0, Partick Thistle (h) 4-1 and East Fife (a) 3-0. Despite the continued absence of top marksmen like Alfie Conn and Willie Bauld, Hearts had now netted an incredible 113 League and Cup goals since the start of the season with great credit due to Jimmy Murray and the brilliant Alex. Young, who had forged another high scoring partnership alongside veteran inside-left and top scorer, Jimmy Wardhaugh. Hearts were well served on the wings with Ian Crawford continuing to get his share of goals from outside-left and the dashing Bobby Blackwood another man of menace down the right wing.

In February, victories over East Fife (a) 2-1 and Albion Rovers (h) 4-1 saw Hearts progress to the third round of the Scottish Cup where they would meet a rejuvenated Hibernian at Tynecastle on March 1st. Johnny Hamilton opened the scoring after 11 minutes but, almost immediately, new Easter Road sensation Joe Baker levelled before putting Hibs ahead 16 minutes later. Jimmy Wardhaugh equalised soon after the break only for that man Baker to grab another two. On the final whistle, Jimmy Murray pulled one back but the day had belonged to four-goal Joe Baker with Hibs now set to go all the way to the final.

Later that month, Alfie Conn scored Hearts 100th league goal in their 4-0 win at Motherwell to put them a massive 15 points ahead of nearest challengers Rangers who had five games in hand. Last term, a lack of strength in depth had cost Hearts dear but this time, there was strong competition for places. Players like Bobby Parker - who was to retire at the end of the season after a recurring knee injury - Tom McKenzie, Freddie Glidden, Willie Bauld and Alfie Conn, were no longer guaranteed a starting place but along with others like Johnny Hamilton and Wilson Brown, they provided the top class back-up necessary to mount a successful title challenge.

The championship came a couple of steps closer with wins over Queens Park (a) 4-1 and Queen of the South (h) 3-1 before Hearts faced another tricky hurdle. With Hibs at home to Third Lanark in the Scottish Cup next day, the home game against Celtic was brought forward to the evening of Friday, March 14th. Hearts opened with a sparkling brand of football, goals by Crawford and Blackwood putting them 2-0 ahead after seven minutes before an injury to Mackay left him limping on the wing and the Celts pulled one back.

However, Jimmy Wardhaugh did a great job at right-half and with Alex. Young the architect in chief - his aggressive bursts of pace constantly troubled Bobby Evans - Jimmy Murray grabbed a second-half hat-trick to give Hearts a thrilling 5-3 victory. That took them a step closer to the title but although Rangers had slipped a further point behind, fourth-placed Clyde, who along with Motherwell were the only side to match Hearts for skill, managed a point in a 2-2 draw at Tynecastle.

On March 22nd, Hearts bounced back with a 4-0 win at Falkirk only to lose Dave Mackay with a broken bone in his foot, an injury that would rule him out for the last five games of the season. As expected, Rangers had continued to grind out results but Hearts showed no sign of faltering as they outgunned Raith Rovers 4-1 at rain-drenched Tynecastle in a game that marked yet another milestone for the men in Maroon.

Although home league gates had averaged over 20,000, the Tynecastle terracings remained uncovered and, disappointingly, a freak rainstorm limited the crowd to just 9,000. Soon after kick-off, a low shot by Jimmy Murray equalled Motherwell's record of 119 league goals in their 1931-32 Championship winning season and five minutes later Jimmy Wardhaugh set a new record when he headed home a Bobby Blackwood cross.

On April 5th, Hearts travelled to Kilmarnock in the hope of clinching the championship but despite Andy Bowman putting them ahead with a tremendous left-footer in 32 minutes, a George Thomson own-goal left the celebrations on hold. Seven days later, the pride of Gorgie returned to the West to face struggling St Mirren at Love Street and this time Hearts would make no mistake.

On a bright sunny day, Hearts fielded - Marshall; Kirk, Thomson; Cumming, Milne, Bowman; Blackwood, Murray, Young, Wardhaugh and Crawford. The Maroons dominated the early stages and in seven minutes they went ahead when Alex. Young punished slack defending to net from close in. Soon afterwards, they had a let-off when a Lapsley shot hit the bar but 13 minutes after the interval, Ryan scrambled in St Mirren's equaliser from a corner. Within a minute, Hearts regained their lead, Jimmy Wardhaugh heading home a John Cumming free-kick but with 22 minutes remaining, John "Cockles" Wilson crashed the ball home to make it 2-2. Hearts were shaken but they were not to be denied. Within five minutes, a cross from the right was lobbed back in by Ian Crawford, Alex. Young reacting first to flick the ball past Saints keeper Lornie for the winner.

St Mirren had battled hard but Hearts were always the more constructive and after an absence of 61 years, the championship flag would again fly at Tynecastle. At full-time, there were joyful scenes amongst the 8,000 Hearts fans in the 22,000 crowd with hundreds invading the pitch to acclaim their heroes.

Rising star - Hearts keeper Gordon Marshall tips the ball over the bar after some hectic goalmouth action against Celtic.

Later there was jubilation in Love Street's away dressing room and following Tommy Walker's interview at the B.B.C. studios in Glasgow, the Hearts party returned to celebrate their success at the Harp Hotel in Corstorphine. Under trainer Johnny Harvey and his assistant Donald McLeod, Hearts were amongst the fittest teams in Scotland. The popular Harvey, who had briefly played for the club in the 1930's, was overjoyed, "I'm very pleased indeed. This is a great day for me as the boys were terrific and we have worked really well as a team all season."

Hearts had long been admired for their fine play but now, under Tommy Walker's influence, punch had been added to poise and with a better balance of power and skill, success had followed success. After winning the League Cup in 1954, Hearts had lifted the Scottish Cup in 1956 and after a near miss last season, their title success had been achieved with a record-breaking 132 goals. Sixty-two points were accumulated from their 34 games as they suffered just one defeat to finish a massive 13 points clear of their nearest challengers Rangers.

There is little doubt that Hearts were at their peak around this time and their strength in depth was further demonstrated by the capture of the Reserve League title and by reaching the Reserve League Cup Final. Alfie Conn and Willie Bauld - key men in earlier glories - had not played the requisite number of games to qualify for League medals but after Scottish League permission was obtained, replica medals were struck.

Like Davie McLean, the well respected Walker had continued to encourage the development of local talent and despite inheriting outstanding players like Conn, Bauld, Wardhaugh and Cumming from his predecessor, the current Hearts boss had signed and groomed seven of the current side. Walker had built a team in the real sense of the word for although Conn, Bauld, Cumming, Mackay and Wardhaugh had all been capped for Scotland in the past, only Dave Mackay and Jimmy Murray were currently in Scotland's plans.

The spirit of the side was epitomised by men like John Cumming and the forceful Dave Mackay, the latter, who having matured from a raw talent into an inspirational leader, was now Hearts youngest-ever skipper. Up front, Jimmy Murray had burst onto the scene with 29 goals after coming in from the reserves. And after impressing for the Scotland X1 in a World Cup trial against Hearts at Tynecastle, he then did well for Scotland in the 1-1 draw with England at Hampden in April.

Along with Dave Mackay, first capped for Scotland against Spain in Madrid a year earlier, Murray would again feature for Scotland in that summer's World Cup Finals in Sweden. However, neither Scotland Under-23 star Alex. Young nor Hearts top scorer Jimmy Wardhaugh, who had scored 37 League and Cup goals, made the final 22, having been included in the original squad of 40.

That summer, Hearts players and officials crossed the Atlantic on the RMS Carinthia for a three week long, nine-match tour of Canada and USA. They suffered just one defeat, losing 7-1 to Manchester City, who they had beaten 5-2 and 6-0. But with an impressive tally of 64 goals and sights tobe seen, the trip was a marvellous experience and a fitting reward after the success of last season.

Heart of Midlothian F.C. Scottish League Champions 1957-58 (BACK, left to right) Alfie Conn, Bobby Blackwood, John Lough, Jimmy Milne, Wilson Brown, George Robertson, Gordon Marshall, Willie Bauld, Billy Higgins, Jimmy Wardhaugh, Tom McKenzie. MIDDLE - Donald McLeod (assistant-trainer), Andy Bowman, Jim McFadzean, John Cumming, Peter Smith, George Thomson, John McIntosh, Bobby Kirk, Willie Lindores, John Harvey (trainer). FRONT - Hugh Goldie, Johnny Hamilton, Andy Fraser, Dave Mackay, Ian Crawford, Jimmy Murray and Danny Paton. Absent - Alex. Young, Bobby Parker, Freddie Glidden.

DC Thomson

Chapter Four

MORE SILVER POLISH

The draw for the 1958-59 League Cup placed Hearts in the same section as Rangers, Third Lanark and Raith Rovers. The opening tie was at Ibrox but after just five minutes, Davie Wilson put Rangers ahead and the Light Blues went on to win 3-0. With Bauld replacing Young, Hearts recovered to beat Third Lanark 3-0 at Tynecastle before an unchanged team beat Raith Rovers 2-1 at Starks Park to set up a crucial return clash against Rangers at Tynecastle on August 23rd.

Eyes down - Hearts Scottish international inside-forward Jimmy Murray races in on Third Lanark keeper George Ramage in this league match at Tynecastle.

Since defeating Hearts, Rangers had lost 3-1 at Kirkcaldy before dropping another point in a 2-2 draw with Thirds and 42,000 fans turned out at Tynecastle for what proved a cup tie thriller. Soon after the interval, Willie Bauld netted after a Bobby Blackwood effort rebounded from a post only for Johhny Hubbard to equalise within a minute. Ibrox keeper Norrie Martin was carried off hurt and his replacement Bobby Shearer was also later injured. Hearts too had their problems as Jimmy Milne limped on the left wing but all turned out well when the big centre-half prodded home the winner in the dying seconds.

A few days later, Willie Bauld fired in a hat-trick in an enthralling 5-4 win over Third Lanark at Cathkin. That guaranteed Hearts a place in the quarter-finals where they would meet Second Division Ayr United but before then, the Maroons would get their first taste of the European Cup.

In 1955, Scottish League Champions Aberdeen declined to enter the first-ever European Cup but fifth-placed Hibernian accepted an invitation to replace them and went on to reach the semi-finals. Over the next two seasons, Rangers made little impression and now it was the turn of Hearts, who would play Standard Liege of Belgium in the first round with the first leg in Liege on September 3rd.

Hearts settled quickly but although Ian Crawford put them ahead after quarter of an hour, the Belgians drew level soon afterwards and at half-time they led 2-1. Hearts emphasis on attack left them vulnerable and inspired by the brilliant African forward Bonga-Bonga, Standard netted three goals in the final 18 minutes to leave Hearts with a mountain to climb in the return.

However, the Maroons league campaign had started brightly with convincing wins over Dunfermline (h) 6-2 and Hibernian (a) 4-0 and with many keen to sample European football at first hand, 37,500 fans flocked to Tynecastle on Tuesday, September 9th. Hearts showed two changes from the first-leg, Murray and Hamilton coming in for Bowman and Wardhaugh and this time they gave a much better account of themselves.

There was no scoring at half-time but midway through the second half, Willie Bauld, who had been involved in a running battle with the Belgian centre-half, netted twice to earn a 2-1 win. And although Hearts went out 6-3 on aggregate, they had regained a large measure of their self-respect.

The following night, Hearts were compelled to play the first leg of their League Cup quarter-final against Ayr United but with three changes they achived a 5-1 lead at Somerset Park. The Tynecastle return was no more than a formality and a 3-1 victory earned Hearts an 8-2 aggregate win and a place in the last four alongside Celtic, Killie and Partick Thistle. Things were going well for the table-topping Maroons who remained unbeaten in the league and another three points were taken from Airdrie (h) 4-3 and St Mirren (a) 1-1 before Willie Bauld went nap with five goals in an 8-3 slaughter of Third Lanark at Tynecastle.

On October 1st, a crowd of 41,000 turned out for the League Cup semi-final against Kilmarnock at Easter Road and with both teams in top form, play soon roared from end to end. Jimmy Brown performed heroics but midway through the first half, the ex-Hearts keeper was helpless to prevent a George Thomson "special" flying into the top right-hand corner. That broke the deadlock and with Willie Bauld again the master craftsman, Crawford and Bauld

One for "the King" - Willie Bauld is on the spot to put Hearts 3-0 ahead in the League Cup Final against Partick Thistle at Hampden in October 1958. Johnny Hamilton is on the right while Ledgerwood, Wright and Hogan are the Thistle defenders. DC Thomson

himself got the second-half goals which assured Hearts of a place in the League Cup Final.

There they would meet Partick Thistle, who had beaten Celtic in the semi-final having previously been runners-up in 1953 when they lost 3-2 to East Fife and in 1956 when they went down 3-0 to Celtic. Meanwhile, another five points from their next three games kept Hearts three points above Motherwell at the top but there had been criticism with some fans believing that too many changes were being made and that the team were not as "convincing" as last season.

Still the Gorgie side remained favourites for the Hampden confrontation on October 25th and their supporters turned out in large numbers. Injuries meant Thistle would be without the services of two regulars, left-back Doug Baird and centre-forward Andy Kerr. However, there was a shock for the Hearts fans in the 59,960 crowd when the teams were announced for there was no place for Alex. Young, who was regarded as one of Scotland's brightest young forwards. Hearts - Marshall; Kirk, Thomson; Mackay, Glidden, Cumming; Hamilton, Murray, Bauld, Wardhaugh and Crawford. Partick Thistle - Ledgerwood; Hogan, Donlevy; Mathers, Davidson, Wright; McKenzie, Thomson, Smith, McParland, Ewing.

The red and yellow hooped Thistle soon buzzed around Marshall's goal but it was Hearts who went ahead after four minutes. Looking suspiciously offside, Jimmy Murray took a Hamilton pass before racing in on Ledgerwood and although his shot appeared to be going wide, Willie Bauld was there to sweep the ball in from close range. Hearts tails were up and five minutes later, a quickly taken free-kick by Kirk found Murray, who evaded Davidson and coolly slipped the ball past Ledgerwood to make it 2-0.

Now, it was all Hearts with the deep-lying Bauld providing great service for the eager Jimmy Murray who was constantly on the move up front. The Firhill defence were under constant pressure and in 27 minutes Murray flicked the ball on from an Ian Crawford corner and Willie Bauld rammed home the third. Seven minutes from the interval, Murray again went through to crash in number four off a post with Thistle defenders appealing in vain for offside.

After the break, the darting Tommy Ewing switched to inside-left and Thistle stormed forward. George Smith pulled one back with a header from a McKenzie cross then a McParland shot hit the bar with Marshall well beaten. However, urged on by Dave Mackay, Hearts weathered the storm and any faint hopes of a Thistle revival ended when Johnny Hamilton netted a fifth after Jimmy Murray set him up with a brilliantly executed back-heel.

Although Thistle had forced 12 corners - just one less than Hearts - the dazzling Maroons were worthy winners for they had been lethal up front. Willie Bauld and the indomitable John Cumming had been outstanding but all were agreed that this was Jimmy Murray's final. His form had fluctuated since his World Cup sojourn but his recent recall was a masterstroke of judgement by Tommy Walker, the inside-right netting twice and having a hand in the other three goals.

Just over three hours later, around 25,000 fans waved scarves and flags and yelled their appreciation as skipper Dave Mackay held the League Cup aloft in Edinburgh's Charlotte Street as the team arrived for their celebration dinner. "I was really proud of the boys today and now we're going all out to achieve the treble," proclaimed an exultant Mackay during his speech.

In their next match, the Maroons ran up another five goals without reply against Raith Rovers at Kirkcaldy before their 18-game unbeaten domestic record ended with a 2-0 defeat to strong-going Motherwell at Tynecastle. Like Tommy Walker, Fir Park boss Bobby Ancell had opted for youth and the emergence of top class players like John Martis, Bert McCann, Pat Quinn, Ian St John, Willie Hunter and Andy Weir, proved it was a highly productive policy.

Hearts stormed back with a total of 15 goals from games against Queen of the South, Falkirk and Aberdeen and despite dropping three points in their next two games against Clyde and Kilmarnock, the Maroons remained two points clear of Rangers when the sides met at Ibrox on December 13th. Injuries ruled out Gordon Marshall and Dave Mackay and with Jimmy Milne and Freddie Glidden also out with knocks, the inexperienced George Robertson made his debut at centre-half.

In a sensational start, a shot from Alex. Young rebounded from the post and within two minutes, the deadly Ralph Brand had opened the scoring. Robertson was toiling and with the Hearts defence in disarray, rampant Rangers added another four by the half-hour mark, as they went on to win 5-0.

The Ibrox humiliation came as a dreadful blow to morale and with confidence low, just two wins were recorded from eight games as Hearts slipped six points behind Rangers by the end of January. Their Scottish Cup hopes were also short-lived for, after beating Queen of the South 3-1 at Palmerston, the "luck of the draw" meant a return to Ibrox where defensive stalwart Bobby Kirk was unfortunate to put through his own goal as an unimpressive Hearts side went went out by a somewhat flattering three goals to two.

On February 21st, Hearts battled to a 2-1 away win against Raith Rovers, who as well as Johnny Urquhart now included another ex-Heart in 32-year-old Alfie Conn after his £2,500 transfer, four months earlier. In a bold move, the versatile George Thomson was played at inside-left with John Lough at left-back but the gamble paid off with Thomson netting the winner to spark Hearts off on a 10-game unbeaten run which left them within an ace of retaining the Scottish League Championship.

Significantly, Dave Mackay had recently returned after a six game absence through injury but Hearts fans were devastated when their dynamic skipper, who had also captained Scotland in recent internationals against Northern Ireland and Wales, was transferred to Tottenham Hotspur for £32,000 on March 8th.

At that stage, the second-placed Tynecastle club lay six points behind Rangers with a game in hand and perhaps the board - comprising Messrs. Kilgour (chairman), Strachan (vice-chairman), Irvine, Tait and Ford - were pessimistic about overhauling the deficit.

Certainly, a floodlighting system costing £14,000 had been installed in 1957 and in the coming months a 15,000-capacity covered enclosure would be erected on the distillery side for a further £23,000. However, these extraordinary costs appeared to be balanced by last season's post-war record profit of £13,000 plus the £15,000 from the 1958 League Cup run and the £10,000 from the European Cup tie against Standard Liege.

Celebrations - Hearts fans are out in force to cheer their heroes after the 1958 League Cup success against Partick Thistle.

The swashbuckling Mackay - the Football Writers' Player of the Year in 1958 - had been a key man in Hearts success of the 1950's and his inspirational qualities would be sorely missed. In the absence of the injured Andy Bowman, George Thomson, who had scored five goals in four games up front, took over at right-half. Bobby Rankin, a recent £4,000 signing from Queen of the South, came in at inside-left to score twice in the 4-0 home win over St Mirren, leaving Hearts four points behind Rangers with the same number of games played.

On March 14th, a home point was dropped in a 2-2 draw with Clyde but Rangers had also shared the points in an incredible 5-5 divide at Falkirk. Hearts maintained their title challenge with wins over Kilmarnock (h) 3-1 and Aberdeen (a) 4-2 and now the April 11th clash with Rangers, who would be without Eric Caldow who was on Scotland duty against England at Wembley, had all the makings of a championship decider. However, despite it's billing as the battle of the giants, there was precious little football played.

There were constant niggles between Shearer and Hamilton and Davis and Cumming and Telfer and Young as the Light Blues attempted to disrupt Hearts. However, in 32 minutes, Thomson cleverly slipped a free-kick wide of the defensive wall to John Cumming who strode forward to send the ball past goalkeeper George Niven. The Ibrox inside-men McMillan and Millar were unable to shake off Cumming and Thomson and with 15 minutes remaining, Tynecastle erupted when Bobby Rankin ran on to a perfect cross by Alex. Young to thunder in the clincher.

Now Hearts trailed by just two points and everything rested on the final game. Astonishingly both clubs had an identical goal average and, should Hearts beat Celtic at Parkhead and Rangers lose to Aberdeen at Ibrox, the title would remain at Tynecastle. Scottish Cup finalists Aberdeen did the needful, two goals by Norrie Davidson earning a 2-1 win but, disappointingly, Hearts went down by a similar scoreline. In the opening 24 minutes, Gordon Marshall made some great saves to keep Celtic at bay before big Bobby Rankin beat Frank Haffey with a stunning drive from 25 yards.

Thereafter, Hearts bombarded the Celtic goal in search of a second but soon after half-time, Bertie Auld levelled and when Eric Smith made it 2-1 in 64 minutes, Hearts went to pieces. There was too much short passing and the usual switch between wingers Blackwood and Hamilton backfired with Hamilton having little effect on Mochan, who had previously been given a torrid time by Blackwood.

With Bobby Kirk joining Andy Bowman on the injury list and George Thomson required at wing-half, Hearts had been forced to field an inexperienced full-back pairing of John McIntosh - who was released soon afterwards - and John Lough. Few could now deny that the untimely sale of Scottish international Dave Mackay had in all likelihood cost Hearts the title.

Nevertheless, Hearts began the 1959-60 campaign at a cracking pace and emerged as comfortable winners from a League Cup section which also contained Aberdeen, Kilmarnock and Stirling Albion. Towards the end of last term, the long-serving Freddie Glidden had joined Dumbarton on a free transfer while the versatile Danny Ferguson and outside-left Bobby Walker were secured from Hamilton for a joint fee of £10,000.

In an effort to further freshen his pool, Tommy Walker signed former Scottish international outside-right Gordon Smith, who had been released after 14 years at Hibs. A year earlier, the winger had undergone ankle surgery but when the problem persisted, Hibs had refused to pay for a second operation and, that summer, Smith had successfully undergone surgery at his own expense.

Some felt that the 34-year-old now had little to offer, but the Hearts boss, who had just pipped Dundee manager Willie Thornton for his signature, thought differently and such was Smith's reputation that 12,000 fans turned out to see his debut for the Hearts reserves. Sensibly, Smith was allowed time to settle, only being brought in to the first team after four games had been played. The polished veteran did well in a 2-0 League Cup win over Kilmarnock at Tynecastle and from then on, he was a first-team regular.

The League Cup quarter-final draw paired Hearts with high-flying Motherwell, who had twice beaten Rangers to top their section. On Wednesday, September 9th, a near capacity crowd of 32,000 saw an action-packed encounter at Fir Park. 'Well turned on the style only to miss a bundle of chances but in 27 minutes, Bobby Blackwood made no mistake when he put Hearts ahead.

The Motherwell trio of Bert McCann, Andy Weir and Ian St John had played in Scotland's 3-2 win over West Germany in May and, just on half-time, the Motherwell centre showed his class with a well taken equaliser. Now the atmosphere was electric and although there was no further score in an exciting second-half, Hearts were happy enough with a 1-1 draw.

Nearly 44,000 rolled up for the second leg in Edinburgh and within 60 seconds of kick-off, Alex. Young set Tynecastle alight when he fired the opener past Hastie Weir. Another spine-tingler looked on the cards when St John equalised on the half hour but an eye injury to 'Well centre-half John Martis saw him retire for 14 minutes in which time a Bobby Blackwood double had swung the tie Hearts way. There was no way back for Bobby Ancell's men and, after the interval, further goals by Young, Hamilton and Murray made it 6-2 in a night of joy for the Tynecastle faithful.

In the semi-final, Hearts met lowly Cowdenbeath before a 27,500 Easter Road crowd on October 7th. Ian Crawford, now playing at inside-right, netted four as a 9-3 triumph took Hearts through to play Third Lanark in the final, but not before the plucky Fifers had given them a fright by narrowing the score to 4-3 shortly after half-time.

So often under the shadow of the "Old Firm", Thirds had been revitalised in Bob Shankly's two year spell as manager. It had come as a bitter blow when he joined Dundee a few weeks earlier but the 'Hi-Hi' had found a worthy successor in big George Young, the famous ex-Rangers and Scotland defender, and their Ibrox semi-final win over Arbroath now gave them the opportunity to achieve a tangible success.

However, Hearts, who were League Cup holders and current league leaders, were playing with great fluency and with an undefeated run of 17 games, they were strong favourites to retain the trophy on Saturday, October 24th. From the start of the season, energetic performances by Andy Bowman made him the natural successor for the

In where it hurts - Hearts centre-forward Alex. Young slides in but young Hibs keeper Lewis Muirhead is first to the ball in the Easter Road derby. Gordon Smith is the other man in maroon.

Hampden delight - Third Lanark keeper Jocky Robertson, who defied Hearts throughout the 1959 League Cup Final, prepares to go for a cross. Ian Crawford and Alex. Young are the Hearts men looking on.

departed Dave Mackay and George Thomson reverted to left-back. However, Hearts suffered a setback when the experienced Jimmy Milne, recently injured in a friendly at Norwich, was ruled out of the final. John Cumming took over at centre-half and assumed the captaincy from Milne with 19-year-old Billy Higgins retaining the left-half berth in only his fifth first-team appearance.

Hearts - Marshall; Kirk, Thomson; Bowman, Cumming (capt.), Higgins; Smith, Crawford, Young, Blackwood, Hamilton. Third Lanark - Robertson; Lewis, Brown; Reilly (capt.), McCallum, Cunningham; McInnes, Craig, D. Hilley, Gray, I. Hilley.

A colour clash between the maroon of Hearts and Third Lanark's red saw both teams changing, Hearts sporting their white and maroon candy-striped outfit with the Cathkin part-timers wearing Wolves-style gold jerseys and black shorts. On a grey, gusty day, the final attracted a crowd of 57,994 to Hampden and the windy conditions may well have influenced what proved a sensational start.

Just over two minutes had gone when Thirds outside-right Joe McInnes eluded Thomson and floated in a high cross. Gordon Marshall went up unchallenged but unaccountably fumbled and Matt Gray pounced to put Thirds ahead. Later, the keeper denied that the notorious Hampden swirl had affected his handling, saying instead that he had lost sight of the ball in the sun which had appeared from above the North Stand.

As the 'Hi-Hi' celebrated, Hearts looked shaken but they soon recovered to pin Thirds back with their fast attacking play. As time wore on, it appeared that the Tynecastle side would never score for their pacy inside men lacked guile and Third Lanark keeper Jocky Robertson, though short in stature, was in inspiring form.

An acrobatic leap blocked a Young header then the keeper made a magnificent one-handed save to claw away another attempt by the Hearts centre. Blackwood missed from six yards, then Robertson dived full-length to push a powerful drive from Bobby Kirk round the post. Thirds had to rely on the occasional breakaway to raise the seige but after half-time, they came under even more intense pressure. First, Brown headed off the line then a Young header finally beat Robertson only for the ball to rebound from the post into the keeper's hands.

Robertson seemed set to defy Hearts but in 57 minutes, Johnny Hamilton levelled the scores. The wee winger cut inside and as the Thirds defence backed off, he unleashed a low 30-yarder which hit a defender before going in off a post. The Hearts players and fans went wild with delight and, almost straight from kick-off, a long kick by Marshall again had Thirds in trouble. Alex. Young picked up a weak clearing header from McCallum then eluded the centre-half before moving in to beat Robertson for number two.

Poor finishing meant Hearts were unable to add to their tally but they got a tremendous reception from their fans at the end and, once again, there was the spectacle of an open-topped bus being welcomed by the joyous multitudes on the streets of "Auld Reekie".

Hearts had thoroughly deserved their third League Cup success for their defence had seldom been stretched. Stand-in skipper John Cumming had blotted out the dangerous Dave Hilley while another key factor was the composure of Gordon Smith - who had earned his first cup medal after three previous cup final failures with Hibs.

Now Hearts could concentrate on the championship and soon after the recalled Willie Bauld grabbed a hat-trick in a 6-2 win over Third Lanark at Tynecastle, they faced a vital top of the table clash with Rangers at Ibrox. In eight minutes, the 70,000 Ibrox crowd were silenced when Korean War veteran Harold Davis scored an own goal and in a tension-racked finale, Bobby Blackwood clinched matters with a second. Now, with 10 games played, Hearts led the Light Blues by two points with Glasgow pair Clyde and Third Lanark another four points behind.

Billy Higgins was turning in some fine performances and both he and the brilliant Alex. Young had played for the Scottish Under-23's against Wales. The future looked bright for the talented duo but time had caught up with another of the "Terrible Trio". Now 30-years old, Jimmy Wardhaugh had joined Dunfermline for £2,000 after losing his place to Bobby Blackwood. However, he would long be remembered for his 270 League and Cup goals in 418 games, and already his name was indelibly written into the history books at Tynecastle. Later in November, Bobby Rankin was another to move, joining Third Lanark for £4,000 after failing to recapture his early form.

Jimmy Murray replaced the injured Ian Crawford at inside-right as Hearts took seven points from their next four games to stretch their unbeaten run to 24 games as they pulled seven points clear at the top. A shaky spell in December saw successive defeats at home to St Mirren (0-2) then away to Motherwell but with Milne and Bauld coming in for Higgins and Murray, impressive home wins over Raith Rovers (4-1) and Dundee (3-0) soon had Tynecastle cheering again.

By the turn of the year, Hearts held a three point advantage over Rangers with Kilmarnock a further three points behind and on New Year's day, they made a bright and breezy start against a resurgent Hibs at Easter Road. Jimmy Milne kept a tight rein on English international centre-forward Joe Baker and with the Maroons a yard faster to the ball, Alex. Young netted three as they raced to a 5-1 win. The following day, Celtic were defeated 3-1 at Tynecastle but the loss of three points from draws against Dunfermline, Ayr United and Motherwell suggested the strain might be taking it's toll.

In February, the return of Ian Crawford after a two month absence through injury helped strengthen the side but by then, any hopes of a glittering treble were over. After two previous postponements due to wintry weather, the Maroons met in-form Kilmarnock in the second round of the Scottish Cup at Tynecastle on Monday, February 22nd. Nearly 34,000 fans turned out but with the frosty conditions all against good football, Hearts were held to a 1-1 draw.

The injured Willie Bauld would miss the Rugby Park replay while Young had returned south to complete his National Service. Blackwood was dropped with Higgins and Murray, whose recent form had been erratic, coming in and Gordon Smith switching to centre-forward. Play raged from end to end but although Hearts were unlucky when Ian Crawford struck the crossbar, Killie led through a Muir goal at half-time. Jimmy Murray equalised but with just four minutes left, Stewart scored the winner for Killie.

By early next month, Hearts remained seven points clear of Rangers who had two games in hand and on March 5th, the two front runners clashed before a crowd of 45,000 at Tynecastle. The Light Blues started well with Jimmy Millar and Davie Wilson going close but by half-time George Niven was the busier keeper. Throughout the second period of a rugged game, Hearts maintained the pressure and with nine minutes remaining,they got the vital breakthrough. An Alex. Young shot was headed off the line by Billy Stevenson and from the resultant corner John Cumming thundered the ball home. With 30,000 Hearts fans still cheering, Johnny Hamilton intercepted the ball from kick-off, made ground down the wing and when his cross came over, Alex. Young drew the keeper and slipped home number two.

The Ibrox side still retained an active interest in the Scottish and European Cup competitions but with seven

Safe hands - Jimmy Milne watches anxiously as Gordon Marshall gets across to save this header from Andy Aitken of Hibernian at Tynecastle. The big keeper went on to play for the England Under-23 team.

Title clincher - a delighted Willie Bauld turns away after netting a late equaliser in a thrilling 4-4 draw against St Mirren at Love Street. That point gave Hearts the title for the second time in three years.

games remaining, they were effectively out of the title race. Strong-going Kilmarnock were now the main danger for under wily ex-Rangers and Scotland winger Willie Waddell, whose strategy was based on an Ibrox-style "iron-curtain" defence, the Ayrshire side were mounting a strong title challenge.

By March 16th, Hearts had gained another four points from midweek wins over Arbroath (h) 4-1 and Partick Thistle (a) 2-1. Meanwhile, Killie had kept pace with a 4-3 win over Third Lanark at Cathkin and now the Rugby Park clash between the pair a few days later took on great significance. Although both sides hit the bar, Hearts dominated the first half in which George Thomson missed a penalty. Hearts were overdoing the passing and although Crawford scored in 61 minutes, fighting Kilmarnock levelled through McInally and took both points with a last-gasp Muir penalty.

Killie now lay five points behind with two games in hand but three days later, they narrowed the gap to three points with a 1-0 win at Aberdeen. On Saturday, March 26th, they kept the pressure on with a 3-1 win over Ayr United in the Ayrshire derby at Somerset Park while Hearts made heavy weather of beating struggling Aberdeen 3-0 at Tynecastle. In 22 minutes, the versatile Jim McFadzean headed a Bobby Kirk free-kick past goalkeeper Harker but it took a second from Willie Bauld to settle matters near the end, Crawford adding a third before the final whistle.

Killie also had their eyes on the Scottish Cup but, two days after a 2-0 semi-final success over Clyde, a stunning 35-yarder by Ron Mailer at East End Park gave relegation-threatened Dunfermline a 1-0 win to end the Rugby Parkers 21-match unbeaten run and virtually finish their flag hopes. The following night at Tynecastle, Hearts held their nerve to defeat fourth-placed Clyde 5-2 and go five points above Killie who had a game in hand and one point from their final two games - away to St Mirren and Raith Rovers - would give the Maroons the championship.

In three minutes, Hearts got an early shock when when Jim Rodger nodded on for Tommy Bryceland to head past Marshall but almost immediately a goalmouth scramble saw Alex.Young sidestep the home keeper to lay on an easy equaliser for Jim McFadzean. In 16 minutes, Tommy Gemmell restored Saints lead and although Ian Crawford was unlucky to hit the post, Hearts pressure paid off when the outside-left took advantage of a Walker fumble to make it 2-2.

A minute from half-time, Rodger was ordered off after a clash with George Thomson but Saints hit back in the second-half. Gerry Baker left three Hearts defenders trailing before shooting past Marshall but urged on by their noisy-fans in the 17,000 crowd, Alex. Young made it 3-3 after another frantic goalmouth melee. Incredibly, 10-man Saints again took the lead when Gemmell netted from the spot but as Hearts pressed frantically, McFadzean hit the bar and a penalty appeal was turned down before they forced yet another corner. Smith took the kick and when Crawford found Bauld eight yards out, "the King" shot home to make the score 4-4.

At the final whistle, hundreds of excited Hearts fans, many waving banners, scarves and dummy championship cups invaded the pitch to congratulate their heroes. It had been an incredible match, laced with goals and thrilling goalmouth action.

For Hearts and their fans, it was the perfect climax to a fantastic season in which they had accomplished a League and League Cup double. Right from the start the Maroons had got into the winning habit and by October, they had lifted the League Cup at the expense of Third Lanark. Soon afterwards came the crucial game against Rangers at Ibrox but Hearts had risen to the occasion and with confidence on a high, they continued to play with great consistency through the gloomy months of winter.

December and January had brought a fleeting hesitancy and with doubts over their ability to last the distance, some questioned the effects of last summer's month-long, 15-

Heart of Midlothian F.C. Season 1959-60 - Scottish League Champions and League Cup Winners. (BACK - left to right) Andy Bowman, Bobby Kirk, Wilson Brown, Billy Higgins, Willie Bauld. MIDDLE -Donald McLeod (assistant-trainer), George Thomson, Gordon Smith, Gordon Marshall, Andy Fraser, Jim McFadzean, Jimmy Murray, Johnny Harvey. FRONT - Ian Crawford, Alex. Young, Jimmy Milne, Tommy Walker (manager), John Cumming, Bobby Blackwood and Johnny Hamilton. Inset - Jimmy Wardhaugh. DC Thomson

match tour of Australia. However, Hearts got over their bad spell and with the mark of real champions, they once again produced elegant football combined with punchy finishing to return to their winning ways.

Much of Hearts success was down to the "Old Guard" of players who had developed winning habits at Tynecastle and no fewer than seven were each paid their £750 benefit money for completing five years at Tynecastle, with the long-serving John Cumming picking up his second benefit for ten years service.

Hearts boss Tommy Walker had been criticised for making too many changes but with 16 players fighting for first team places, that sort of competition could only be good for the club, who had been fortunate not to sustain any serious injuries. The manager left nothing to chance, even getting reports on future opponents which were carefully studied. He introduced new training methods like weight lifting to build up specific muscle areas and Hearts became one of the physically strongest sides in Scotland.

Hearts were certainly well endowed with the will to win, for fighting spirit and determination were just as necessary as sheer skill in the tough battle for the championship. Much credit was due to the strongly built Gordon Marshall, who commanded his goal area so well, and to the sterling defensive work of Bobby Kirk, George Thomson and Jimmy Milne. The hard working Andy Bowman and John Cumming and the emerging Billy Higgins provided the power in the middle and ensured there was plenty of ammunition for the front men. Yet Hearts were an attractive team with players of real quality in Scottish internationalists John Cumming and Alex. Young - the latter Hearts top scorer with 26 league and cup goals. Both had appeared for Scotland in the 1-1 draw with England at Hampden in April and went on to earn further caps against Austria, Hungary and Turkey in the summer tour of Central Europe with Cumming also playing against Poland.

George Thomson and Billy Higgins were in Scotland's Under-23 side which drew 1-1 with Belgium in Ghent in March while Higgins also faced team-mate Gordon Marshall in the 4-4 draw with England's Under-23's. Although at the veteran stage, Gordon Smith - his speciality was cutting in from the wing and letting fly with long-range shots - had been anything but finished. He had played a big part in Hearts flag success and his composure made him one of the best bargains of the season.

Hearts had been fortunate to have plenty of choice up front and in addition to Smith and Young, Bobby Blackwood, Jimmy Murray, Willie Bauld, Ian Crawford, Johnny Hamilton were all players who might have been first-team regulars had they played elsewhere.

Chapter Five

A NEW DECADE

That summer, Hearts undertook a three week tour of Canada, where they achieved four wins and a draw against local opposition only to lose to current English League Champions Burnley. There were also two defeats at the hands of Matt Busby's Manchester United although there was the consolation of a 4-0 win and a draw against the famous Old Trafford side, who were still recovering from the Munich air disaster two years earlier.

Just a few hours before flying back, the news broke that Tommy Walker had been included in the Queen's Birthday Honours list. After leading Hearts to six trophies in his nine years in charge, the unassuming Tynecastle boss had deservedly been awarded the O.B.E. with the medal to be presented at an investiture at Buckingham Palace in November.

The 1960-61 season began in disappointing fashion. Only one point was taken from League Cup ties against St Mirren and Clyde and despite a timely 3-2 win at Motherwell, a 3-1 reverse at Love Street appeared to leave Hearts out of contention with just three points from four games. However, Willie Bauld, who had been dropped after the Shawfield defeat, returned to net twice in a 6-2 home win over Clyde and, with one game remaining, Hearts, Motherwell and Clyde all remained in the hunt for a quarter-final place.

Two first half goals by Alex. Young earned a 2-1 win over section leaders Motherwell in a Tynecastle thriller as Hearts overtook the Fir Park side to finish level with Clyde on seven points. And with both sides holding an identical goal average, a play-off was arranged for Parkhead on Monday, September 12th. Hearts fielded - Marshall; Kirk, Thomson; Cumming, Milne, Bowman; Crawford, Murray, Bauld, Young and Blackwood. The Maroons were shocked when Scottish international inside-right George Herd put Clyde ahead after 30 seconds but although now at the veteran stage, Willie Bauld again showed his flair for the big occasion when he levelled shortly after the half hour mark.

For a number of years Hearts had found the "Bully Wee" something of a bogy, especially in Glasgow and so it proved again when the ever-menacing John McLaughlin scored a decisive second for the Shawfielders just before half-time. The Maroons had the bulk of the pressure but poor finishing let them down and in the end, they were unable to break down a well-organised Clyde defence.

Hearts had made a bright enough start in the championship, beating newly promoted St Johnstone 3-0 at Tynecastle before racing to a 4-1 triumph over Hibernian at Easter Road. But they could only manage draws against Dunfermline and Airdrie, hardly ideal preparation for their European Cup first round tie against the famous Red Eagles of Benfica.

Nearly 30,000 attended the first leg at Tynecastle on September 29th but although the Portugese were slightly

Parting shot - George Thomson thunders home a penalty for the Edinburgh Select against Chelsea at Tynecastle. A few months later the talented defender was on his way to Everton along with Alex. Young in a £58,000 deal. **DC Thomson**

Danger zone - Hearts keeper Gordon Marshall and centre-half Jimmy Milne combine to thwart the danger from livewire Motherwell centre-forward Ian St John at Tynecastle. Pat Quinn is the other Fir Park player. DC Thomson

Match programme from the Hearts v. Benfica European Cup tie.

ruffled at Hearts early onslaught, they soon gained the initiative. They impressed with their slick passing and movement off the ball and eight minutes before the interval a collision between George Thomson and Jimmy Milne allowed Aguas to head the opener. Hearts possessed neither the class nor the power to upset the clever Portugese for whom Germano was a defensive rock and 15 minutes from time, the speedy Augusta added a second following a head-flick by Aguas. Seven minutes later, Alex. Young pulled one back after good work by Willie Bauld but, despite a grandstand finish, Hearts could not draw level.

Within two minutes of the Lisbon return, Hearts hopes were dashed when Aguas made it 3-1 on aggregate for Benfica and the half-empty 65,000-capacity Stadio du Lutz exploded into a frenzy of noisy, cushion-waving fans. However, with Cumming, Milne and Bowman in outstanding form, Hearts settled to a much improved performance. Crawford and Young also showed up well but Hearts lacked the guile to seriously trouble Benfica who cruised to a 3-0 win and a 5-1 aggregate success. In the event, the Portugese went on to win the European Cup for the next two seasons, also reaching the final in 1963.

By November 19th, Hearts had slipped to fourteenth in the table, just four points above bottom club St Mirren. Since losing the League Cup play-off, it had been downhill all the way for Hearts who remained without a win in 13 games. A scoring drought had drained the side's confidence and, in desperation, Tommy Walker dropped experienced forwards like Gordon Smith, Jimmy Murray and Willie Bauld in favour of younger men like John Docherty - a £4,000 signing from St Johnstone, Jim McFadzean, Tommy Henderson, Alan Finlay and Dave Johnston in a vain attempt to find a scoring blend.

Meanwhile, Alex. Young's Scottish international career had gone from strength to strength. Despite a quiet game against England in April, he gained further caps against Austria, Hungary and Turkey on Scotland's summer tour of Central Europe. One goal in Budapest and another in Ankara ensured he retained his place against Wales at Cardiff and, on November 9th, he scored his third international goal in a 5-2 win over Northern Ireland at Hampden.

Scouts from many of the top English clubs were in attendance for Scotland had become a source of outstanding football talent. As well as Dave Mackay, Alex Parker (Falkirk to Everton), Bill Brown (Dundee to Spurs), Bobby Collins (Celtic to Everton), Jimmy Gabriel (Dundee to Everton), Graham Leggatt (Aberdeen to Fulham) had taken the road south in recent years and with the maximum wage shortly to be abolished, this trickle was soon to become a flood.

On November 23rd - just 15 months after Mackay's departure - Hearts fans were again stunned when the Tynecastle board announced that £42,000-rated Alex. Young and George Thomson had been transferred to big-spending Everton in an £58,000 deal. There was uproar amongst supporters who regarded this as an act of treachery and a few days later, there were loud chants of disapproval at the home game against Raith Rovers.

Nevertheless, Hearts managed a 1-0 win to halt the headlong slide and despite going down 2-1 to Hibernian in the Ne'erday match at Easter Road, a slight improvement saw the Maroons slowly begin to edge their way out of the danger area. However, this was not the Hearts of old and with a transitional period in prospect, Tommy Walker's rebuilding exercise was soon in full swing.

Last year, Hearts had signed Queens Park's Scotland Under-23 internationals - goalkeeper Jim Cruickshank (19), and left-back Davie Holt (24). The quick-tackling Holt, so impressive for Great Britain in the 1960 Rome Olympics, proved an excellent replacement for George Thomson but the task of filling Alex. Young's boots was a different matter altogether. Earlier in the season, Hearts had enquired about Partick Thistle's £10,000-rated centre-forward George Smith then failed in a bid to sign Dave Hilley from Third Lanark. However, in February, the experienced Aberdeen centre-forward Norrie Davidson (27), was signed for £7,000 and a short time later, another £3,000 was spent on Queen of the South outside-right Maurice Elliott (19).

In the opening round of the Scottish Cup, Hearts trounced Tarff Rovers 9-0 before beating Kilmarnock 2-1 in a bruising battle at Rugby Park. The third round tie against Partick Thistle attracted nearly 23,000 to the Firhill slopes and although Hearts played second fiddle in the opening stages, Jimmy Murray netted twice from Willie Bauld crosses in a four minute spell before the interval. A late Wright goal was the Jags only consolation but it was a result which greatly rekindled enthusiasm amongst the Hearts support, who could now relish the prospect of a quarter-final tie against struggling St Mirren at Tynecastle.

However, Hearts then received a footballing lesson in a 5-1 home defeat at the hands of a Willie Hunter-inspired Motherwell before going down 3-0 at Ibrox to Rangers, who themselves had lost 5-2 to the Steelmen in the Scottish Cup.

A crowd of 34,325 turned out for the quarter-final on March 11th but a series of first-half misses was to cost Hearts dear. In 41 minutes, Don Kerrigan was on hand to score after Marshall could only parry a fierce shot from McTavish. And, with former Hearts keeper Jimmy Brown and centre-half Jim Clunie rock steady in defence, there was no way back for the Maroons.

New arrivals - the £22,500 spent on the experienced Willie Polland (left) and Willie Wallace would prove money well spent. DC Thomson

For the first time in over a decade, Hearts were deeply involved in the relegation struggle. However, on March 25th, a 4-2 home win over second-bottom Clyde saw them go seven points clear of the beleaguered Shawfield outfit and with the pressure then off, Hearts completed their last five games unbeaten to finish eighth.

In a traumatic campaign, Tommy Walker had used 30 players, nearly twice as many as last term's League and Cup winning side. And, with a tally of just 51 league goals - half of last season's total - Hearts new but much criticised 4-2-4 formation, which featured John Cumming alongside Jimmy Milne in central defence and Danny Ferguson and Billy Higgins as "link-men", could scarcely be labelled a success.

The influx of new blood had continued with a double swoop for two Raith Rovers players. Experienced defender Willie Polland (27), arrived for £7,500 with outside-right Willie Wallace (20), a man with an eye for goal, costing a new Tynecastle record fee of £15,000. In a major end of season clearout, Jimmy Murray - who had never really attained the heights of two years earlier, Jimmy Milne, Gordon Smith, Wilson Brown, John Lough, Alan Finlay, David Johnston and Boston Glegg were all released, Jim McFadzean having earlier joined St Mirren for £3,000.

Ian Crawford would shortly move on to West Ham for £10,000 with Andy Bowman joining Newport County on a free transfer some months later. Later, it was revealed that West Brom and Fulham had offered £15,000 for Johnny Hamilton but both bids had been turned down.

The arrival of established players like Davidson, Polland, and Wallace plus the emergence of Danny Ferguson would pay dividends in the 1961-62 League Cup campaign. A Willie Wallace goal earned an opening day win over Raith Rovers at Tynecastle and prospects looked bright after a stirring fightback brought a 2-1 triumph at Kilmarnock. Then, despite slip-ups at Paisley and Kirkcaldy, Hearts finished strongly with home victories over Kilmarnock (2-0) and St Mirren (3-1) to finish two points ahead of Willie Waddell's Rugby Park side.

In the quarter-final, a double by Scotland Under-23 international wing-half Billy Higgins gave Hearts a 2-0 home win over Hamilton as they progressed to the last four 4-1 on aggregate. Stirling Albion now stood between Hearts and a place in the final and right from the start of the Easter Road semi-final the Annfield men were content to defend in depth. Hearts attacked in waves but with the tricky Johnny Lawlor giving Bobby Kirk some anxious moments, Albion were always dangerous in breakaways .

Three minutes from half-time, the large Hearts following were stunned when Dyson put Stirling ahead but with 19 minutes remaining, the recently recalled Willie Bauld headed the equaliser past Wren. The Maroons continued to make heavy weather of things as the game went to extra-time but with 104 minutes on the clock, Willie Wallace pounced on a Billy Higgins knock-down to thump home the winner.

Hearts League Cup Final opponents would be Rangers, 3-2 conquerors of St Johnstone after extra-time. Despite taking just five points from their opening six league games, victories at Aberdeen (2-0) and at Tynecastle against Celtic (2-1), raised hopes of a fourth League Cup success but Tommy Walker had a surprise for the Hearts

Just in time - Hearts left-back Davie Holt slides in to rob Alex. Scott of Rangers as the winger prepared to shoot in the League Cup Final at Hampden.

fans in the near 90,000 Hampden crowd on October 28th.

Seventeen-year-old Alan Gordon, who had made his debut against Celtic, was preferred to the more experienced Willie Bauld and Bobby Blackwood as Hearts lined up - Marshall; Kirk, Cumming, Polland, Holt; Higgins, Ferguson; Elliott, Wallace, Gordon and Hamilton. Rangers were favourites and were at full strength - Ritchie; Shearer, Caldow; Davis, Paterson, Baxter; Scott; McMillan, Millar, Brand and Wilson.

At the start, Hearts gave as good as they got and Ritchie had to look lively to push over a Willie Wallace shot. However, Rangers took the lead when Jimmy Millar sent in a low curling cross from the left and as Polland and Cumming hesitated, Marshall was unable to prevent the ball skidding in at the post. The Maroons fought back desperately but were denied a penalty when Wallace's scrambled shot from a Gordon cutback appeared to be handled on the line.

Throughout the second period, the Maroons were mainly reduced to long range shots but with 13 minutes remaining, referee Bobby Davidson awarded a penalty after Alan Gordon went for a Johnny Hamilton cross and was pushed by Harry Davis. Skipper John Cumming made no mistake but despite a hectic finale and half-an-hour's extra-time, there was no further scoring. And, due to European committments and a postponement due to frost, the replay would not take place until Monday, December 18th.

Hearts had been invited to play in the Inter-Cities Fairs Cup and despite returning from Luxembourg with a 3-1 advantage over Union Gilloise, the Gorgie men could only add another two goals through Willie Wallace and Robin Stenhouse for a 5-1 aggregate win. The second round draw paired Hearts with the glamourous Italian club Internazionale of Milan, who, in addition to having top Italian internationals like Fachetti, Guaneri and Picci, also boasted England international centre-forward Gerry Hitchens. However, Inter captain and former Barcelona star Luis Suarez - perpetrator of the infamous Easter Road riot - would miss both ties through injury.

In the first leg at Tynecastle on November 6th, Hearts could make little headway against an Inter team who were content to defend in depth and keeper Bugatti was rarely troubled. The Gorgie side had plenty of the ball but, compared to the Italians, their passing was poor and their forwards showed little imagination against the packed Inter defence.

In contrast, the Italians were clever ball players and lightning quick on the break. In 32 minutes, Willie Polland slipped and Humerto skipped through the Hearts defence to score the only goal of the game. In the end, Inter appeared to be toying with Hearts much-vaunted 4-2-4 system and thousands left for the exits well before the end. Internazionale were indeed different class. Even with eight Italian stars rested for the return, Hearts were torn apart, Gerry Hitchens netting two and laying on another in a seemingly effortless 4-0 win before a crowd of just 12,000 in the 100,000-capacity San Siro Stadium.

In the league, Hearts had recorded successive wins over St Johnstone (a) 2-0, Partick Thistle (h) 2-0 and Raith Rovers (a) 1-0 but just prior to the League Cup Final replay, nine goals were conceded in a 6-2 defeat by Motherwell then a 3-3 draw with Kilmarnock at Tynecastle. The Maroons showed four changes from the first game. Jim Cruickshank replaced Gordon Marshall in goal with Norrie Davidson, Willie Bauld and Bobby Blackwood coming in for Maurice Elliott, Willie Wallace and Alan Gordon, while Rangers only change was Doug Baillie for Bill Paterson at centre-half.

Right from the start, Rangers set a cracking pace and Cruickshank did well to save two attempts by McMillan. In seven minutes, the Light Blues early pressure paid off when the speedy Alex. Scott beat two defenders and his cross was headed into the net by Jimmy Millar from six yards. Within a minute, Hearts were level. John Cumming took a quick free kick and Norrie Davidson rose to head the equaliser. However, the influential Jim Baxter and Ian McMillan were soon carving out more openings and just seven minutes later, Cruickshank failed to cut out a Davie

Wilson cross and Ralph Brand nodded home.

Soon afterwards, Ian McMillan made it 3-1 after his first shot had rebounded from the bar and although Hearts made changes for the second half, they made little impression on the powerful Ibrox team. Unlike the Killie game, the Maroons had played 4-2-4 in the hope of holding Rangers early on before switching to a more attacking formation. However, the plan had failed and only the woodwork - three times - and the heroics of Jim Cruickshank had prevented the loss of further goals.

Although Hearts were much improved from last term, they still lacked the consistency to challenge for the championship. By late January, they were out of the title race which appeared a straight fight between Rangers and a Dundee side inspired by former Hearts and Hibs winger Gordon Smith, and now the Gorgie side looked to the Scottish Cup.

After an opening round bye, Alan Gordon netted a hat-trick in a 5-0 victory at Vale of Leithen before Hearts entertained a much improved Celtic in the third round before 35,000 on February 17th. Up until recently, the eager Willie Wallace had been a constant menace in the penalty box but now he hit a barren spell and with Willie Bauld and Norrie Davidson injured, Danny Paton assumed the number nine jersey with recently signed St Mirren outside-right Jim Rodger (29), also included.

In 13 minutes, Celtic went ahead when a Pat Crerand free-kick set up John Divers. Soon afterwards, Bobby Blackwood headed the equaliser and with Hearts well on top, Johnny Hamilton made it 2-1 after Celtic keeper Frank Haffey dropped the ball. However, with only ten minutes remaining, goals by John Divers and Steve Chalmers - the latter from a suspiciously offside position after the Hearts defence had moved out, gave Celtic the lead only for Danny Paton to make it 3-3 in 84 minutes.

It was a rip-roaring encounter and with just four minutes remaining, Celtic were controversially awarded a penalty when Bobby Davidson adjudged that Danny Ferguson had jostled the powerful John Hughes. Gordon Marshall saved Crerand's first effort but when the referee mysteriously ordered a retake, the Scotland half-back made no mistake.

It was a game Hearts ought to have won and although ten games remained, their season was effectively over. In April, Robin Stenhouse - who had somehow fallen from favour despite scoring four goals in five games - was amongst those released, while another fringe player, Tommy Henderson had earlier joined St Mirren for £2,000.

More significantly, the legendary Willie Bauld had announced his retirement after 275 goals in 16 glorious years with Hearts. He was awarded a testimonial and six months later, around 15,000 fans turned out for the match against Sheffield United at Tynecastle to bid farewell to their goalscoring hero. Regretably, the directors saw fit to deduct some £1,000 in match expenses from Bauld's £2,800 cheque, an action which was to leave the player bitterly resentful for many years to come.

On the deck - Celtic keeper Frank Haffey goes down to save at the feet of Hearts inside-forward Alan Gordon in this match at Tynecastle. Scottish international half-back Pat Crerand is the Celtic player on the right.

Somewhat surprisingly, the experienced Bobby Blackwood was allowed to join new English First Division Champions Ipswich for £10,000 but the Maroons were quick to snap up Middlesborough inside-left Willie Hamilton (25), for just £2,500. Hamilton had spent six years at Sheffield United before joining the Ayresome Park side in 1961 but due to injury, he would miss the opening League Cup ties in a tough section which also included League Champions Dundee, Celtic and Dundee United.

With the versatile Willie Polland in for 35-year-old Bobby Kirk at right-back and Roy Barry (19), at centre-half, Hearts went down 3-1 to Celtic at Parkhead but they recovered to beat Dundee United by the same score at Tynecastle a few days later. The Maroons faced a potentially hazardous trip to Dens Park but a spirited performance saw them survive a first-half onslaught before late goals by Johnny Hamilton and Willie Wallace earned a 2-0 win.

On August 25th, Marshall was the busier keeper as Celtic made all the early running at Tynecastle but Hearts went ahead when Danny Paton beat Billy McNeill and sent a low shot into the far corner of the net after 13 minutes. Shortly afterwards, Willie Wallace made it 2-0 before adding a third from the spot just after the interval. Gordon Marshall then saved a Pat Crerand penalty and although Celtic pulled back two goals, Hearts held on for a 3-2 win.

That gave Hearts six points but a shock 2-0 reverse to Dundee United at Tannadice left them sweating after Celtic went to the top of the section on goal-average after beating Dundee 3-0. Now fit-again, Billy Higgins and Willie Hamilton replaced Danny Ferguson and Jim Rodger for the final game against Dundee at Tynecastle. But although Hearts piled on the pressure for long spells, only 19 minutes remained when Danny Paton finally broke the deadlock. A few minutes later, the skilful Willie Hamilton settled the issue with a second and much to the delight of the 18,000 crowd, the Maroons were through to the last eight after Celtic could only draw 0-0 at Tannadice.

Norrie Davidson had emerged as a key figure and two goals by the bustling centre-forward helped earn a 3-0 win over Morton in the first leg of the quarter-final at Cappielow. And although former Scottish international Doug Cowie scored in the Tynecastle return, it was little more than a consolation as Hearts eased themselves into the last four 6-1 on aggregate.

Hearts, Rangers, Kilmarnock and St Johnstone went into the hat for the semi-final draw with the Maroons having the good fortune to be paired with the Perth side who were now back in the Second Division. Like Hearts, this was Saints second successive League Cup semi-final. However, although Davidson, who had scored 10 goals in 14 games that season, was out with a groin injury, Willie Hamilton was again there to pull the strings and a Willie Wallace hat-trick and another from the maestro himself brought a 4-0 triumph beneath the Easter Road floodlights on Wednesday, October 10th. Once again Hearts could look forward to a final where their opponents would be Willie Waddell's Kilmarnock who had come from behind to net a late winner in a 3-2 win over Rangers.

Meanwhile, Hearts were also making a strong challenge for the championship. In August, Norrie Davidson got them off to a great start with a hat-trick in a 3-1 win over Dundee before Danny Paton netted another three in a 4-0 win over Hibernian at Easter Road. And, by the League Cup Final on Saturday, October 27th, the Maroons lay second, just one point behind Rangers with 14 points from their first eight games.

Last term, the team had struggled but now, with many of the same players, they had rediscovered their form and the crowds were flocking back to Tynecastle. There was now a better balance and understanding throughout the side. The uncompromising Roy Barry had added real toughness to the defence while Willie Hamilton had provided the essential blend in attack, his vision and intricate ball skills bringing out the best in his strong-running colleagues. With Davidson now recovered, Hearts were at full strength - Marshall; Polland, Cumming, Barry, Holt; Higgins, W. Hamilton; Wallace, Paton, Davidson and J. Hamilton.

Kilmarnock were also in fine form, having eliminated Airdrie, Dunfermline, Raith Rovers, Partick Thistle and Rangers. The Ayrshire men were seasoned campaigners with Andy Kerr and Hugh Brown always likely to find the net. However, the wily Davie Sneddon had failed a fitness test and his place was taken by the lanky Jackie McInally. Kilmarnock - McLaughlan; Richmond, Watson; O'Connor, McGrory, Beattie; Brown,

The winner - Hearts centre-forward Norrie Davidson is on the spot to ram home an inch-perfect cutback from Willie Hamilton in the 1962 League Cup Final against Kilmarnock at Hampden.

Another trophy success - delighted fans cheer as Hearts skipper John Cumming waves the League Cup after the team's triumphant return to Edinburgh. (RIGHT) The architect - Willie Hamilton was a key man in Hearts latest League Cup success. Daily Record

Black, Kerr, McInally and McIlroy.

A stiff breeze drove heavy rain across the Hampden pitch but roared on by their fans in the 51,280 crowd, Killie went straight into attack. Bertie Black went close when he drew Marshall only to slip on the greasy turf and John Cumming hooked the ball clear. With Killie in command, the Hearts defence survived a shaky opening although Norrie Davidson broke clear to test Sandy McLaughlan with a powerful shot.

Still Killie held the edge but, in 26 minutes, Willie Wallace hit a long ball forward to Willie Hamilton. The inside-left beat McGrory out on the left and when his cut-back came across, Norrie Davidson came storming in to whip the ball into the net from close range. Now Hearts were buzzing and with Willie Hamilton the mainspring in attack, the Gorgie side began to dictate the play.

Killie's forwards had failed to cash in on their early chances and in stamina-sapping conditions their cause was not helped when McInally limped to the left wing. For most of the second half, it was Hearts who showed the greater cohesion and drive in attack and only valiant defending prevented them from adding to their lead.

Still the rain poured down but with 20 minutes remaining, Killie mounted a gallant fightback only for their attacks to founder on the well-drilled Hearts defence. But, with only thirty seconds remaining, Jim Richmond floated in a long free-kick and Frank Beattie leapt high to head the ball past a despairing Gordon Marshall.

The Hearts players could only watch in disbelief as Killie celebrated but referee Tom Wharton had meanwhile signalled a free-kick to Hearts. He had spotted an infringement - later believed to be a handling offence - and despite consulting his linesman, the goal was disallowed.

Later, TV and press photos indicated that Beattie's hand had been raised but, in the end, they were inconclusive. However, despite the controversy, Hearts had deserved to win, and shortly afterwards, skipper John Cumming led his men up the steps of Hampden's South Stand to lift the League Cup, the fourth time in eight years that the trophy had come to Tynecastle.

Three days later, Roy Barry - a defensive hero at Hampden - was ordered off as Hearts went down 2-0 in a bad-tempered game at Falkirk. However, Hearts soon recovered and a seven game unbeaten run left them third, two points behind Partick Thistle and three behind leaders Rangers by December 15th. Then blizzard conditions swept across the British Isles, causing a near wipeout of the Scottish football programme.This Arctic weather would prevail for almost three months and many clubs would be placed under great financial strain.

In that period, Hearts managed only one competitive game, a Scottish Cup first round tie against Forfar Athletic at snow-covered Station Park on January 12th. Although Hearts protests about the the pitch were overruled by the referee, they went on to a comfortable 3-1 win with former Maroon Jimmy Milne netting a penalty consolation for Forfar.

Hearts next game was at Parkhead on March 6th when they played Celtic in the second round of the Scottish Cup.

Heart of Midlothian F.C. Season 1962-63 - League Cup Winners for the fourth time in nine years (BACK, left to right) Willie Polland, Davie Holt, Gordon Marshall, John Cumming (captain), Roy Barry, Billy Higgins. FRONT - Willie Wallace, Danny Paton, Bobby Ross, Willie Hamilton and Johnny Hamilton. Inset - Norrie Davidson. DC Thomson

Unfortunately, Hearts were without the injured Roy Barry and Willie Hamilton, who had been suspended by Tommy Walker for a breach of club discipline, and with the team's balance fatally upset, the Maroons went down 2-1 before a crowd of 38,000.

Hearts now faced a demanding schedule of up to three games a week until the end of the season. The long lay off had taken the edge from the players but after losing 2-1 at Aberdeen, runaway wins were recorded over Falkirk (h) 5-0 and Clyde (a) 6-0. However, a nine day spell in March saw Hearts lose two vital games at Tynecastle. Kilmarnock departed with a 3-2 win before Hearts hit rock-bottom in a 5-0 defeat by Rangers, results which saw them slip back to sixth, nine points behind the Light Blues.

The early season sparkle had gone although there was some consolation in the emergence of two talented youngsters. An accomplished header of the ball, Alan Gordon burst back on the scene with a bundle of goals while 21-year-old full-back Chris Shevlane was another to make his mark.

Shevlane's debut had coincided with a 7-3 defeat at Paisley, where Willie Wallace had been compelled to don the keeper's jersey after Gordon Marshall was carried off with a head injury in 15 minutes. However, the red-headed defender returned to the team a few weeks later and and retained his place.

A succession of injuries - John Cumming sustained a broken rib in a 5-1 defeat by Rangers at Ibrox - confirmedthat Hearts still remained three or four players short of a championship winning side and in the end, they had to be content with fifth position and a place in next season's Fairs Cup.

Nevertheless, coupled with their earlier League Cup success, it had been a remarkable turnaround in fortunes after a traumatic couple of years. The Maroons had managed a much improved total of 85 league goals, with 25 from top scorer Willie Wallace, a total bettered only by Dundee's Alan Gilzean with 32 goals and Jimmy Millar of Rangers with 39.

Veteran defender Bobby Kirk, Bobby Ross and John Docherty were amongst those released while Gordon Marshall was transferred to Newcastle United for £18,000. The big keeper had given Hearts sterling service in his seven years at Tynecastle but with Jim Cruickshank proving an able deputy, Hearts could afford to let Marshall go.

In May, Davie Holt made his Scotland debut when he replaced recent Wembley leg-break victim Eric Caldow for the Hampden clash against Austria. However, it was a violent match best remembered for the dismissal of two Austrians before English referee Jim Finney abandoned the game 11 minutes from time with Scotland leading 4-1. The Hearts defender did well and that summer he gained further caps against Norway (3-4), Eire (0-1) and Spain (6-2) on Scotland's European tour.

Chapter Six

BY A DECIMAL POINT

With 33-year-old John Cumming now at the veteran stage, Danny Ferguson assumed the capaincy and began the 1963-64 season wearing the number two jersey with Chris Shevlane switching to left-back in place of Davie Holt. The Scottish international had re-signed on the eve of the new season but had not recovered from an injury sustained on Scotland's European tour, while other early absentees were Willie Hamilton, Danny Paton and Maurice Elliott, who had all undergone cartilege operations that summer.

The Maroons began well enough with Norrie Davidson grabbing a hat-trick in a 6-2 League Cup win over Falkirk at Tynecastle but a shock was in store. In recent years, Motherwell had lost key men like Ian St John - to Liverpool - and Pat Quinn - to Blackpool - but despite finishing tenth last term they were to be revitalised by the scoring exploits of newly signed centre-forward Joe McBride. On Wednesday, August 12th, Hearts crashed 3-0 to 'Well at Fir Park and despite the recall of Roy Barry and Jim Rodger, another point was lost to Partick Thistle in a 2-2 home draw.

Falkirk were beaten 3-0 at Brockville but Motherwell had won their fourth successive game and only a win against the Fir Parkers in the penultimate game at Tynecastle would give Hearts any chance of reaching the quarter-finals. However, despite their early pressure, the Maroons were unable to break down the well-organized Motherwell defence who held out for a 0-0 draw and ultimately proceeded to the last eight without losing a single goal.

However, Hearts made a better start in the league. Goals by Tommy Traynor and Johnny Hamilton earned a 2-0 win at Airdrie before Hibernian were defeated in a derby thriller at Tynecastle on September 7th. Last term, the Easter Road side had only avoided relegation on the final day but this season they had made a stirring start and were already bound for the League Cup semi-final.

Hearts - Cruickshank; Shevlane, Polland, Barry, Holt; Ferguson, Higgins; Hamilton J., Davidson, Wallace and Traynor. Hibs - Simpson; Fraser, McLelland; Grant, Easton, Preston; Scott, Martin, G. Baker, Byrne, Stevenson. Right from the start, both teams impressed with a crisp brand of entertaining football. With just over half-an-hour played, Hearts led 2-0 through goals by Danny Ferguson and Willie Wallace before Gerry Baker pulled one back for Hibs. After the interval, the ever-dangerous Wallace made it 3-1 only for Baker to again narrow the deficit, but, with 12 minutes remaining, Norrie Davidson crashed home a fourth to secure the points for Hearts.

Eighteen days later, Hearts returned to European action when they met Lausanne in the first round of the Fairs Cup in Switzerland. It had been a tiring journey with a long delay in the flight from Turnhouse due to fog at London. However, Hearts started brightly and took a two-goal lead through Tommy Traynor and Danny Ferguson. This stung the Swiss into action and as the pressure mounted, Lausanne wingers Hertig and Gottardi made it 2-2 and only the crossbar prevented a third in the dying minutes.

Most expected Hearts to win through in the return with talk even turning to prospective second round opponents, Zaragossa. In the interim, Hearts had won 2-1 at Falkirk and although ace marksman Willie Wallace grabbed a hat-trick in a a 3-3 draw against St Johnstone at Tynecastle, their defensive vulnerability had been all too evident.

With the 29-times capped Swiss international Heinz Schneiter pulling the strings in midfield, Lausanne were certainly no soft touch. Cumming put Hearts in front after 18 minutes only for a Swiss 1-2 to leave them struggling. Johnny Hamilton levelled late on but home fans were far from impressed and the players were booed from the field. Now the toss of the coin meant the play-off going ahead in Lausanne and despite goals by Wallace and Ferguson, a 3-2 defeat ensured the continuance of the Tynecastle side's miserable European record.

Meanwhile, Hearts had performed consistently in the league. Only one game had been lost and a 2-0 win over Third Lanark at Cathkin on October 19th left them fifth behind Rangers, Dunfermline, Kilmarnock and Dundee. Only three points separated the five as Hearts faced a vital clash with Kilmarnock at Rugby Park but, unable to handle the wiles of lanky inside-man Jackie McInally, they crashed 3-1 with Willie Hamilton, now back to full fitness, scoring their sole crumb of comfort.

Off the field, however, the transfer-seeking Hamilton had been guilty of some wayward behaviour. His fourth appearance of the season at Kilmarnock would prove his last for, just a few days later, the ball-playing maestro was the subject of a shock £6,000 transfer to Hibernian.

Willie Wallace - the ace scorer grabbed two in 4-2 win over Hibs.

The Rugby Park reverse indicated to Tommy Walker that a shake-up was overdue and Norrie Davidson was another to leave Tynecastle, joining Dundee United for £6,000 shortly afterwards. However, the supporters were bitterly upset at losing Hamilton, who they regarded as a footballing genius. They were particularly embittered at the decision to sell him to Hibs and only 8,000 - the lowest crowd of the season -

So near - Danny Ferguson beats the Motherwell defence to a high cross only to see the ball go over the bar in this match at Tynecastle. Johnny Hamilton and 'Well defenders George Murray and Pat Delaney watch the action.

turned out for the match against Aberdeen at Tynecastle.

Having received £12,000 in transfer fees, Hearts splashed out £8,000 for St Mirren centre-forward Tommy White (24), £3,000 on Alloa inside-right Jim Murphy (21), and another £1,500 for Scunthorpe United's ex-Falkirk, and Millwall centre-half, Alan Anderson (24). White, whose brother John was the 'Spurs and Scotland inside-forward known as the "Ghost of White Hart Lane", was a more physical type of player. And although he drew a blank in his first two games, his Tynecastle career kickstarted with a glorious double against Rangers at Ibrox.

November had brought just one win from four games until the Maroons travelled to a foggy Ibrox on St Andrews Day. There were three minutes on the clock when a fine Gordon-Wallace move down the right culminated in Tommy White heading the opener and 60 seconds before half-time, an Alan Gordon headflick set up Willie Wallace for a second. Ibrox was stunned and when White added a third right on the interval, there was no way back for the Light Blues.

That result came as a tremendous morale-booster for players and fans alike and by the end of 1963, a five game unbeaten run kept Hearts in touch with the top. Despite the presence of clever forwards like Willie Hamilton and Pat Quinn, Hibernian were again in relegation difficulties but Hearts were unable to overcome their rivals in a 1-1 draw before a crowd of 35,000 in the Ne'erday game at Easter Road. The following day, Alan Anderson made his debut in a 2-1 home win over Dunfermline as Hearts moved into third place, five points behind Rangers who trailed leaders Kilmarnock by a point.

By February 8th, Hearts had narrowed the gap behind Killie and Rangers to four and three points respectively after hitting four goals each in wins over East Stirling (h) 4-0, Falkirk (h) 4-1, St Johnstone (a) 4-1 and Queen of the South (a) 4-1. Up front, Johnny Hamilton and the sprightly Tommy Traynor were full of pace and trickery on the wings while Willie Wallace and the bustling Tommy White had formed a deadly scoring partership, nicknamed the "W-formation", which was ably assisted by the spring-heeled Alan Gordon or Jim Murphy who had netted four goals against East Stirling.

There was a settled rearguard with Jim Cruickshank playing behind a solid back four comprising full-backs Chris Shevlane and Davie Holt with the dependable Willie Polland alongside Roy Barry in the middle. Sterling performances by Cruickshank soon helped the fans forget Gordon Marshall and with Shevlane also turning on the style, both were rewarded with Scotland Under-23 caps against Wales and England.

John Cumming, Billy Higgins, Danny Ferguson were in contetion for the two link-man positions and in January, out-of-favour forwards Jim Rodger and Maurice Elliott were transfered to Queen of the South, who coincidentally Hearts would meet at Palmerston in the first round of the Scottish Cup.

However, there was to be no joy for the "Old Boys" as the evergreen Johnny Hamilton netted two in a comfortable 3-0 win for Hearts and the draw for the next stage paired the Maroons with Motherwell at Fir Park. A crowd of nearly 22,000 saw a cup-tie cracker and although a Joe McBride hat-trick gave 'Well a 3-1 advantage by half-time, Hearts fought back and a low drive by Tommy White then another goal by Willie Wallace earned a 3-3 draw.

This was the stuff to draw the fans and 32,500 rolled up for the replay under the Tynecastle lights on Wednesday, February 19th. Motherwell sat deep but goals by Aitken and McBride put them 2-0 ahead after 15 minutes. Hearts, who missed the drive of tonsilitis victim Johnny Hamilton - their top performer at Fir Park - were struggling and although Tommy White pulled one back soon after half-time, Roy Barry could only limp on the wing after taking a knock, and they were unable to save the tie.

A few days later, Hearts entertained Kilmarnock in a top of the table clash before a disappointing attendance of 14,500. For the seventh successive game, Tommy White found the net but Hearts could only manage a 1-1 draw and Rangers slipped back to the top. Nevertheless, the

Wallace-White combination continued to pay dividends and by March 7th, wins over Aberdeen (a) 2-1, Third Lanark (h) 4-1 and St Mirren (a) 2-0 kept the Maroons in contention three points behind Rangers and one behind second-placed Killie, who both had a game in hand.

Hearts received a bad blow when Tommy White was ruled out for a month due to injuries sustained in a car crash and to bolster the side for the crucial five game run-in, East Stirling inside-right and skipper Frank Sandeman (28), was signed for £3,000. It was hoped that Rangers and Killie, who had both reached the Scottish Cup semi-finals, might be distracted by thoughts of cup glory but, in the event, Hearts themselves were unable to deliver.

On March 14th, torrential rain limited the Tynecastle crowd against Dundee United to just 5,500 but once Jimmy Briggs thundered home the opener from 35 yards, Hearts turned on a sorry display before going down 4-0. Effectively their title hopes were over and, in the end Hearts had to be content with fourth place behind Rangers - winners of the Scottish domestic "treble" - Kilmarnock and Celtic. Following his cartilege operation, Danny Paton, had made only a handful of appearances and with his knee continuing to cause problems, he was amongst those released in April.

In May, Jim Cruickshank and Davie Holt were absentees from the team which drew 2-2 with Hibs at Tynecastle in the new Summer Cup competition. Cruickshank's swift rise to prominence was rewarded by his Scotland debut in a 2-2 draw with West Germany at Hanover with Holt - who had initially lost his place to Dave Provan of Rangers then Celtic's Jim Kennedy - earning his fifth cap after substituting for Dundee's Alex. Hamilton. The Maroons went on to top their Summer Cup section but had to withdraw due to their imminent participation in the New York Tourney. Hibs beat Dunfermline in the play-off for the vacant semi-final place, and the resurgent Easter Road outfit went on to beat Aberdeen in the final.

In New York, Hearts met Bahia (Brazil), Werder Bremern (West Germany), Lanerossi Vicenza (Italy) and Blackburn Rovers (England) only to finish second one point behind the West Germans who qualified for the lucrative final against the other group winners Dukla Prague. The three week trip was a marvellous experience for players and officials alike but, added to the earlier games in the Summer Cup, there remained an all too short close season.

Hearts began the 1964-65 campaign with the same team that had promised so much last term only to finish bottom of their League Cup section behind Celtic, Kilmarnock and Partick Thistle with just three points. In the opening games, Frank Sandeman and Jim Murphy were given their chance up front but they struggled to make any impression and soon dropped out of the reckoning.

On Wednesday, August 19th, Tommy Walker's men burst back with a morale-boosting 8-1 league win over Airdrie at Tynecastle only to fall 1-0 at home to Kilmarnock before collapsing 6-1 to Celtic at Parkhead. In Glasgow, the Hearts defence had been overwhelmed. Roy Barry, whose rash tackling had conceded two penalties, lost the number five jersey to Alan Anderson and the giant ex-Scunthorpe defender's recall coincided with a timely 4-3 home win over Partick Thistle in the final sectional tie.

On September 5th, Hibernian fielded an exciting forward-line of Cormack, Hamilton, Scott, Martin and Stevenson but Hearts proved the masters in an Easter Road derby thriller. An Alan Gordon header from a Traynor cross then a 20-yarder by Willie Wallace which left keeper Willie Wilson helpless put Hearts two up at half-time

Desperate derby action - Alan Gordon rises high above the Hibernian defence to flash a header goalwards in the derby at Tynecastle. Danny Ferguson is at the ready with John Parke, Pat Quinn and John McNamee the men from Easter Road.

before Jim Scott pulled one back. Gordon added another only for Scott to again narrow the leeway. Further goals by Tommy White and Tommy Traynor ensured both points for Hearts with a late goal by Neil Martin leaving the final score 5-3 in favour of the Maroons after a breathtaking afternoon of football.

A week later, Hearts dropped a point in a 1-1 Tynecastle thriller with Dunfermline. However, the fast interchanging of the forwards deservedly brought a 5-1 romp over Third Lanark at Cathkin and after taking a three goal lead, a 4-2 win over Celtic at Tynecastle brought revenge over the Parkhead side for the two League Cup defeats to leave Hearts second, one point behind early pace-setters Kilmarnock by the end of September.

That summer had been a desperately sad time for Tommy White, whose brother John had been killed by lightning while sheltering beneath a tree at a golf course in North London. In November, there was an appreciative 25,500 crowd at White Hart Lane for a John White Testimonial game between Tottenham Hotspur and Scotland. Tommy White played as a guest for 'Spurs while Jim Cruickshank and Willie Wallace were in the Scotland side, which won 6-2, White and Wallace scoring one each for their respective sides.

In fact, the bustling White had begun the season impressively for Hearts and he was selected for the Scottish League against the League of Ireland in Dublin before having to pull out with a heavy cold.

Roy Barry was moved forward to a link-man role alongside former Under-23 international Billy Higgins and on October 3rd, a Willie Wallace double and another from 19-year-old Donald Ford earned a 3-1 win over Partick Thistle at Firhill. The team was now brimful of confidence and the next two months saw Hearts maintain their championship challenge with points from St Mirren (h) 1-1, Rangers (a) 1-1, Dundee (a) 2-1, Morton (h) 4-1, Falkirk (a) 2-2, Motherwell (a) 3-1, Clyde (h) 3-0, St Johnstone (a) 3-0 and Dundee United (h) 3-1.

On December 12th, Alan Gordon netted three in a 6-3 Tynecastle trouncing of Aberdeen to extend Hearts unbeaten run to 16 games as they moved two points clear of Kilmarnock. After recently drawing with Motherwell, Rangers and Aberdeen, the Ayrshire side had gone down 5-1 to Morton at Cappielow, but predictions that Killie's bubble had burst were way off the mark.

By now, Hearts were by no means the only Scottish side playing 4-2-4 but their attacking emphasis was clear as they topped the First Division scoring charts with 53 goals in 15 league games, Alan Gordon scoring 13, Tommy White 12 and Willie Wallace 11 goals. Their scoring compared favourably with Kilmarnock who had netted only 20 goals but although the Hearts rearguard of goalkeeper Cruickshank, Shevlane, Polland, Anderson and Holt had conceded just 11, Killie had done even better, having lost a mere five goals at that stage.

However, form went out the window the following week when the pair clashed at Rugby Park. Once again Alan Gordon found the net but sadly for Hearts, that was their only consolation in a 3-1 reverse although they soon regained lost ground with a hard-fought 2-1 win at Airdrie on Boxing Day.

Meanwhile, there were signs of a Hibs revival across the city. After a highly successful spell at Dunfermline, manager Jock Stein had transformed the struggling Easter Road outfit since his arrival towards the end of last term. Hibs had won the Summer Cup and they were now serious Championship contenders, lying just four points off the pace with a game at hand.

Around 35,000 made their way to Tynecastle for the top

Up for the Cup - Willie Wallace puts Morton keeper Eric Sorensen under pressure as the ball flies across the goalmouth in this Scottish Cup replay with Morton under the Tynecastle floodlights. Morton's Jim Reilly and Alan Gordon of Hearts await developments.

In the book - Hearts centre-forward Tommy White gets his name in the referee's notebook at Fir Park. Daily Record

of the table Ne'erday clash at the start of 1965. Throughout the first-half, the Maroons beieged the Hibs goal but were unable to break through. After the interval, exchanges were more even until former Hearts favourite Willie Hamilton accepted a short free-kick from Pat Quinn and thundered an angled shot into the roof of the net from near the byeline. That proved the winner on a bad afternoon for Hearts which also saw Killie and fourth-placed Dunfermline taking full points.

Next day, Norwegian outside-right Raold Jensen made his debut at Dunfermline before a crowd of 20,000 but there was no glory start for the recently signed S.K. Brann player as the Pars triumphed 3-2 in an East End Park thriller. Killie had lost to Airdrie and with Hibs beating Falkirk 6-0, the top of the table was tight indeed.

On January 9th, a 3-1 home win over Third Lanark lifted the Tynecastle gloom before a Johnny Hamilton double earned a 2-1 win over Celtic at Parkhead. Killie and Hibs had begun to falter and when the pacy Jensen endeared himself to the Gorgie faithful with a cracking 20-yarder in a 1-0 win over Partick Thistle at Tynecastle, Hearts found themselves three points clear of Killie at the top.

Then following a shock 2-1 reverse to St Mirren at Love Street, Hearts drew 1-1 with League Cup winners Rangers at Ibrox. Billy Higgins got the opener after eight minutes only for the prolific Jim Forrest to level soon afterwards. Killie had lost 4-1 to Dundee at home but on February 27th, any encouragement Hearts had taken from that result disappeared when they themselves crashed 7-1 to the rampant Dark Blues at Tynecastle.

The normally dependable home defence had simply been torn apart with Dundee inside-forward Charlie Cooke, recently signed for a new Scottish record £40,000 from Aberdeen to replace Scottish international striker Alan Gilzean, in brilliant form. It was a scoreline that would have great significance in the eventual destination of the title although the Maroons had by then progressed to the last eight of the Scottish Cup.

In the first round, they coasted to a 3-0 win at Falkirk before being paired with Morton at Cappielow. The Greenock side had come on leaps and bounds under the astute managership of Hal Stewart, who had signed an impressive clutch of Danish international stars such as keeper Eric Sorensen, Kai Johansen, Carl Bertelsen and Jorn Sorensen.

In a classic cup-tie encounter in the Cappielow mud, Hearts took the lead three times but had to settle for a 3-3 draw. The Maroons had missed chances galore but they made no mistake in the replay. Just after half-time, a Sorensen blunder allowed Chris Shevlane's lob to sail into the net before Alan Gordon scrambled a second near the end to clinch a place in the quarter-finals before nearly 32,000 at Tynecastle. However, just a week after the disastrous defeat by Dundee, any hopes of a Gorgie league and cup double ended at Fir Park. In a match of bone-crunching tackles, which resulted in a booking for Tommy White, Hearts went behind to an early goal by Walter Carlyle. For the rest of the tie, the Maroons competed well but with no-one like Andy Weir to slow play down, they were unable to retrieve the situation against their cup bogy team, Motherwell.

March 30th 1965

	P	F A	PTS
Hearts	**30**	**82-45**	**45**
Hibernian	**30**	**68-36**	**44**
Killie	**30**	**54-32**	**42**
Dunferm'e	**29**	**70-31**	**42**
Rangers	**28**	**64-27**	**36**

All thoughts now turned to the championship run-in. Successive wins over Morton (a) 3-2, Falkirk (h) 5-2, Motherwell (h) 2-0 and Clyde (a) 5-2 kept them top of the table and with just four games remaining, Hearts were right on track for the title.

On April 7th, two goals each by Willie Wallace and Alan Gordon brought Hearts a comfortable 4-1 win over St Johnstone at Tynecastle. Dunfermline and Killie had also won but Hibs hopes were fading after a 2-1 defeat at "title wreckers" Dundee. The Easter Road side had recently lost manager Jock Stein to Celtic and although the experienced Bob Shankly was secured from Dundee, their challenge ended a few days later with a 4-0 home defeat by Celtic.

Dunfermline and Killie kept up the pressure with wins over Third Lanark and Falkirk but, on Saturday April 10th, when most attention was focused on Scotland's 2-2 draw with England at Wembley, Hearts faltered to a 1-1 draw with Dundee United at Tannadice. After a scrambled early goal by Finn Dossing, only home keeper Don Mackay kept Hearts at bay and although Willie Wallace equalised late on, the centre later had a great chance for the winner only to blaze the ball wildly over the bar. The Fifers then beat Rangers 3-1 in their game in hand and with two games remaining, Hearts held a slender two point lead over Dunfermline and Killie and a grandstand finish was assured.

On April 17th, Hearts made the long trip north to face Aberdeen. After a nervy start they played like prospective champions and a Johnny Hamilton penalty and goals by Roy Barry and Willie Wallace left them on course for the title. At one point in mid-March, Willie Cunningham's Dunfermline had relished the prospect of a Fairs Cup, Scottish League and Cup treble. However, after losing to Bilbao Athletic in a third round play-off, their heavy fix-

So near - with time running out in the title decider at Tynecastle Killie keeper Bobby Ferguson brings off a great save from Alan Gordon. Roy Barry can be seen while the Killie defenders are Eric Murray and Andy King. DC Thomson

ture backlog had taken it's toll and the Pars league hopes finally ended with a 1-1 draw against St Johnstone in their penultimate game at East End Park.

Meanwhile, Killie had beaten Morton 3-0 at Rugby Park and now the Hearts versus Kilmarnock game on April 24th would decide the championship. With a two point lead Hearts only required a draw while the Ayrshire men needed to win by two clear goals to take the title on goal average and 37,275 fans packed the Gorgie ground as the teams lined up: Hearts - Cruickshank; Ferguson, Polland, Anderson, Holt; Barry, Higgins; Jensen, Wallace, Gordon, Hamilton. Kilmarnock - Ferguson; King, McGrory, Beattie, Watson; McLean, Murray; McInally, Black, Sneddon and McIlroy.

Hearts stormed into attack and an early shot by Raold Jensen beat Bobby Ferguson only to come back off a post. Kilmarnock were quick to retaliate and soon play roared from end to end as both sides sought the vital opener. Sadly for Hearts, it was Killie who struck first in 27 minutes when a Jackie McInally-Brian McIlroy move down the right culminated in the unmarked Dave Sneddon heading home at the far post.

Hearts were stunned and within two minutes, they found themselves 2-0 down. McIlroy accepted a pass from Bertie Black on the edge of the box and despite home appeals for offside, he cracked the ball into the far corner of the net-past Jim Cruickshank. Hearts responded by putting Killie under intense pressure but by half-time, the scoreline remained unchanged.

After the interval, Hearts again swept into attack although Killie always looked dangerous on the break. Roy Barry was injured in a aeriel duel with Frank Beattie but soon recovered to head just over in another Hearts attack. Just one goal would give Hearts the title and with the game so finely balanced, there was tremendous tension throughout the ground. Chances were few but with just six minutes remaining, Alan Gordon fired a great shot just inside Ferguson's post only to see the keeper bring off a tremendous save.

That was the nearest Hearts would come and at full time, Kilmarnock players, officials and fans went wild with delight. After finishing runners-up in four of the past five seasons they had finally taken the league flag albeit with a goal average advantage of just 0.042 over Hearts. As the despondent Maroons trooped off, they could only reflect on what might have been. A bitterly disappointed Tommy Walker remained gracious in defeat but top scorer Willie Wallace - soon to be the subject of transfer speculation involving an exchange for Ralph Brand of Rangers - was more forthcoming, "There were certainly one or two games we shouldn't have lost but I suppose it was the same for Killie. We'll be back next season at the top."

Curiously, the teams met again in an experimental no-offside game two few months later. Donald Ford came in to blast home five goals in an 8-2 win for Hearts, although the Maroons were match fit, having just returned from a four-game tour of Norway, in contrast to Killie who had just restarted training. That summer saw the arrival of Aberdeen forward Don Kerrigan (23), scorer of four goals in St Mirren's 7-3 win over Hearts in 1963, in exchange for the out-of favour Tommy White although an injury sustained on tour would rule him out for the first two months of the new season.

In their opening League Cup match against Rangers at Tynecastle, two first-half Johnny Hamilton goals allowed Hearts to overcome an earlier goal by Jim Forrest and Willie Wallace made it 3-1 in 66 minutes. Forrest narrowed the deficit from the penalty spot but with 11 minutes remaining, Wallace brought the house down with a cracking fourth goal.

The next match brought a 1-1 draw at Aberdeen where Hearts lost midfielder Billy Higgins with a serious knee injury which would rule him out for four months before they suffered an unexpected 2-1 home reverse to Clyde. An early goal by Willie Johnston then gave Rangers both points in the crucial return at Ibrox and despite beating Aberdeen and Clyde in their remaining games, Hearts could only finish third albeit just a point behind section winners Rangers.

In February, Chris Shevlane, who had skippered Scotland's Under-23's against Wales, had lost his place to Danny Ferguson after a dip in form. Now he came in at left-back for Davie Holt, who along with Cruickshank, and Shevlane would shortly play for the Scottish League against the League of Ireland - but it increasingly appeared that Tommy Walker was unsure of his strongest team. Willie Polland, Danny Ferguson and Roy Barry were constantly moved between defence and midline as the side was reshuffled and, to the surprise of many, 35 year-old John Cumming re-established himself in the midfield boiler-house.

The Maroons began their league campaign with a 2-0 win over newly promoted Hamilton before a Willie Polland goal earned a 1-1 draw at Dunfermline. However, after a humiliating 4-0 home defeat by Hibs and a 3-2 reverse to St Johnstone at Muirton, the gloom deepened when a no-scoring draw with Dundee at Tynecastle was followed by a 5-2 thrashing by Celtic at Parkhead on October 9th.

Unlike last term, Hearts had struggled to find the net until a 3-3 draw with Partick Thistle at home heralded a six-game unbeaten run. Meanwhile, after getting a first round bye, the Maroons progressed to the third round of the Fairs Cup at the expense of Norwegian outfit, Valerengen.

On October 18th, Don Kerrigan made his long awaited debut in the first leg at Tynecastle. Although it was the deadly Willie Wallace who grabbed the only goal, the fair-haired Kerrigan made his mark in the return, netting twice in a 3-1 win as Hearts went through 4-1 on aggregate. And with the next round not due until January, the Gorgie side could now concentrate on improving their league position.

The deadly Wallace had been a popular figure since his arrival from Raith in 1961 and soon his goalscoring exploits brought the inevitable comparisons with the "King of Hearts", Willie Bauld. For a couple of seasons, Wallace had been the outstanding player at Tynecastle and in November 1964, he had made his Scotland debut at outside-right in the 3-2 win over Northern Ireland at Hampden.

In mid-November, Tommy Walker paid a new Tynecastle record fee of £20,000 for Wolves and former Dunfermline half-back George Miller and his arrival preceded a 16-game unbeaten run as Hearts moved from tenth to fifth place in the league table by early March. Dunfermline and Dundee United, the latter now with a strong Scandinavian influence, were strong challengers until the start of 1966 but it then become clear that the title race would be between Glasgow giants, Rangers and Celtic.

Donald Ford and Frank O'Donnell both got their chance in the number seven jersey after a loss of form by Raold Jensen, while another youngster, Frank Sharp, got a run on the left. But it was not long before the more experienced Johnny Hamilton and Tommy Traynor re-established themselves as first-choice wingers.

On New Year's Day, two goals by Kerrigan and another by Wallace earned a 3-2 triumph over fifth placed Hibs at Easter Road. The next day brought a no-scoring draw with strong-going Dunfermline at Tynecastle but a 3-2 home win over league leaders Celtic at the end of January provided further confirmation of the Tynecastle revival.

That month, a 25,000 crowd witnessed a thriller against highly rated Real Zarragoza in the third round of the Fairs Cup at Tynecastle. The Spaniards, who included four Spanish internationalists and one each from Uruguay and Brazil were formidable opponents, having already won the trophy in 1964.

After trailing 2-0 at the interval, goals by Alan Anderson, Wallace and Kerrigan had the fans on their feet, only for Lapetra to grab the equaliser just three minutes from time. Another exciting match in Spain ended 2-2 with the unlucky Danny Ferguson taken off at half-time with a severe leg injury which would sideline him for seven months. That meant a play-off and the toss of a coin sent Hearts back to Zarragoza on March 2nd. But, despite a gallant performance, the Maroons went down by the only goal of the game.

Nevertheless, morale remained high since Hearts had by then progressed to the last eight of the Scottish Cup. After a 2-1 home win over Clyde, goals by Traynor and Higgins brought a similar scoreline against Hibernian at Tynecastle and now the Maroons entertained cup-holders Celtic. Jock Stein's men were much encouraged by last season's Scottish Cup triumph over Dunfermline and, more recently, their League Cup success against Rangers. However, they had only won once at Tynecastle in the past 10 years and a buoyant Hearts were confident of success.

Tommy Traynor - Hearts left-wing speed merchant.

On March 5th, nearly 46,000 packed the Gorgie ground as the teams lined up: Hearts - Cruickshank; Polland, Anderson, Barry, Shevlane; Higgins, Miller; Hamilton, Wallace, Kerrigan, Traynor. Celtic - Simpson; McNeill, Cushley, Clark, Gemmell; Murdoch, Auld; Johnstone, McBride, Chalmers, Hughes.

Right from the start the action was fast and furious with Hearts having the better of the exchanges. In 23 minutes, Johnny Hamilton was the target for several beercans while taking a corner but when his kick came over, Ronnie Simpson could only parry a powerful header by Alan Anderson and Willie Wallace rammed home the loose ball. Almost immediately, Bertie Auld scored the equaliser and when celebrating fans poured onto the pitch from the overcrowded Celtic end, referee Hugh Phillips quickly ushered the players from the field.

After a few minutes, a small army of policemen restored order and play was restarted. Ten minutes from the interval, Alan Anderson restored Hearts lead only for Joe McBride and Steve Chalmers to put Celtic ahead soon after half-time. The match was played at a furious pace, and as the Maroons increased the pressure, they grabbed a deserved equaliser six minutes from time. Some great play out of defence culminated in a right wing cross from Willie Wallace and in a welter of excitement, Johnny Hamilton crashed the ball past Simpson to make it 3-3.

It had been a breathtaking encounter and a few days later a massive 72,000 crowd turned out for the floodlit replay at Parkhead. Donald Ford was preferred to Alan Gordon as a replacement for Kerrigan, who was out with a groin strain. Jock Stein brought in Jim Craig at right-back with Billy McNeill reverting to centre-half in place of John Cushley, while the directness of Charlie Gallacher saw him selected ahead of the more deliberate Auld. Celtic started at a tremendous pace and within nine minutes, Jimmy Johnstone fired home the opener. Now Tommy Walker's men were under constant siege and before the interval, Murdoch pounced on a slack pass-back to make it 2-0. Celtic's pressure was relentless and in 52 minutes Chalmers netted a third, a late counter by Wallace providing the sole consolation for Hearts.

Hearts had missed the speed and experience of Don Kerrigan and with Willie Wallace closely marked, they made little impression in attack. Despite sharing around £25,000 from the two ties, the result was a major blow and the remainder of the season was to prove bitterly disappointing. Unaccountably, Hearts could only manage two wins from their remaining 11 games to finish seventh and their hopes of landing one of next season's three Fairs Cup places lay in tatters.

However, a quick glance at the "goals-for" column revealed just 56 league goals compared to last term's tally of 90 and that, more than anything, was the reason for such a dramatic turn-

Well stopped - Jim Cruickshank gets down well to block this piledriver from John Grieg of Rangers at Ibrox. **Daily Record**

around. Willie Wallace was again top scorer with 27 goals and his fine form was rewarded with further Scotland appearances against England and Holland.

Nineteen of of his tally had been league goals but, significantly, none of his Tynecastle colleagues had even managed double figures. Without being as effective in the penalty box, Don Kerrigan was probably a better all-round player than Tommy White, but Hearts had missed the powerful centre's scoring contribution.

Dundee United and Morton had obtained great value from their Scandinavian signings. Yet, Raold Jensen apart, Hearts had shown little inclination towards that side of the market far less domestic stars such as Dunfermline's Alex. Ferguson and Alex. Edwards and Andy Penman of Dundee. Consequently, the Tynecastle directors' failure to bolster the attack was to result in further decline.

In May, Hearts proposal to alter the Scottish Leagues to a 16-12-12 setup was rejected at the Scottish League AGM and it would be another nine years before re-organisation was sanctioned. Next month, the World Cup finals in England took centre stage but with no new signings, there was little summer cheer for the Tynecastle faithful. In the League Cup, Hearts were placed alongside Clyde, St Mirren and Celtic, who had pipped Rangers for the league by two points in their first title success since 1954. In the opening day fixture, Joe McBride grabbed a double in a Tynecastle thriller as Celtic departed with a 2-0 win but Hearts recovered to take three points from their next two games.

On August 20th, Willie Wallace distinguished himself with all four goals in the 4-3 home win over Clyde, and with a 12th man now permitted in case of injury, Johnny Hamilton replaced Chris Shevlane to become Hearts first-ever substitute. However, Hearts hopes reaching the quarter-finals were dashed when they again failed to break the Celtic stranglehold in a 3-0 defeat at Parkhead.

Hearts had missed three great chances in a goalless opening half but when the league campaign began with a 3-1 defeat by Hibs at Easter Road and a 1-1 home draw with Airdrie, it was clear that fresh blood was urgently required. However, when the next transfer did transpire, it was a departure from Tynecastle, Roy Barry joining Coventry City for £13,000 on September 28th.

More significantly, however, Tommy Walker had resigned as manager earlier that day. Since the start of the season, an undercurrent of feeling had seen no fewer than eight transfer requests from Jim Cruickshank, Willie Wallace, Alan Gordon, Billy Higgins, George Miller, Roy Barry, Jim Murphy and Frank Sharp.

In view of the dressing room unrest, chairman Bill Lindsay had informed Walker that the board were to consider terminating his contract and, in the club's best interests, the manager had chosen to resign. Now 52 years old, Tommy Walker had led Hearts to seven trophy successes in his near 16 years in charge. Between 1950 and 1960, the Maroons had never been out of the top four but since the 1965 title near-miss, it had been downhill all the way.

Chapter Seven

JOHNNY HARVEY

A **fresh hand** was now required at the helm but instead of going for a younger manager with a proven track record, the board turned to John Harvey. Hearts trainer since 1952, he was a popular figure but like Tommy Walker was now in his fifties. There was no doubting Harvey's committment or his ability to get the players in superb physical shape but it would later emerge that he had not really wanted his new post with all it's associated stress.

On October 1st, the interim boss got off to a fine start with a 3-1 home win over Dundee. Willie Wallace netted two while Alan Gordon soared high to head a magnificent third at the School End, before another three points from the next two games assured Harvey of the post on a long-term basis. But with Kerrigan out for a month through injury, Hearts managed just one point from their next four fixtures to languish in mid-table. George Peden came in at left-back and produced some solid performances before Davie Holt reclaimed the number three jersey, while Jim Murphy burst back on the scene with five goals in three games, including a hat-trick in a 4-0 home win over St Mirren on November 19th.

John Harvey - took over as manager in October 1966.

Over the past year, Willie Wallace, who had signed a two year contract with a two year option, had repeatedly had transfer requests rejected by the Tynecastle board and since mid-October his form had dipped. Celtic boss Jock Stein had always held the Hearts goalscorer in the highest esteem and it was now strongly rumoured that he had targetted Wallace as an addition to the already lethal Parkhead front line.

After missing two games in November, Wallace was back in the team which lost 3-0 to Celtic in Glasgow but his Tynecastle career was drawing to a close. Early next month, Celtic dropped their interest in Leicester City's Scottish international Davie Gibson and moved quickly to sign Wallace for a bargain £29,000. Once again, the Hearts board had shown a clear lack of ambition by selling their top star in mid-season for a fee some £20,000 less than might have been expected for an international forward with a proven scoring pedigreee. After all, Dundee's Alan Gilzean had joined Tottenham Hotspur for £72,500 two years previously, while Neil Martin of Hibs had cost Sunderland £50,000 in 1965.

As a replacement, John Harvey paid £8,000 for St Johnstone winger Bobby Kemp (25), but Wallace's scoring prowess would be sadly missed. On Hogmanay, Hearts went down 2-1 at home to Motherwell before drawing 0-0 in the Ne'erday clash with Hibs at Tynecastle - a match distinguished by Jim Cruickshank's courageous triple save. First the keeper stopped a Joe Davis penalty, then he dived full-length to prevent the full-back netting the rebound before completing the save by blocking a shot from Allan McGraw.

These results were to herald a downward spiral although the board felt that a good Scottish Cup run would help placate the Hearts supporters who felt greatly betrayed by the Willie Wallace transfer. On January 28th, the Maroons met Dundee United in the first round at Tynecastle and fielded: Cruickshank; Ferguson, Anderson, A. Thomson, Holt; Higgins, MacDonald; Traynor, G. Fleming, Gordon, Kemp. Sub. - Aitchison. Dundee United - Davie; Millar, Briggs; Neilson, Smith, Wing; Seeman, Hainey, Dossing, Gillespie, Mitchell. Sub. - Graham

However, all the home deficiencies were exposed in a comprehensive 3-0 defeat with United's Danish centre Finn Dossing twice capitalising on defensive blunders which were further highlighted when Hearts crashed 5-1 away to Rangers, themselves fresh from a humiliating Scottish Cup defeat at Berwick. George Fleming put them back on the winning trail with a 1-0 home victory over St Johnstone but the gloom persisted with Hearts failing to find the net in six successive games. By mid-April, the Tynecastle men had managed just one win in 15 games and as they slipped to sixth bottom, home gates slumped to the 5,000 mark.

Frank Sharp was sold to Carlisle for £4,000 before Dunfermline centre Jim Fleming (25), was secured in exchange for Don Kerrigan but although the newcomer proved a skilful, hard-working player, no goals were forthcoming. In contrast, 18-year-old Andy Milne, who had recently arrived on a free-transfer from Arsenal, netted his first goal in a 2-1 defeat by Falkirk, following that up with another three in a 5-1 win over lowly Stirling Albion. A late flourish brought victories over Kilmarnock and Airdrie but Hearts could only finish eleventh, their worst league position since the war.

Willie Wallace's departure - already he had won League, Scottish Cup and European Cup winners' medals with Celtic - had further exacerbated an already serious lack of firepower with Hearts managing just 39 goals in 34 league games. Jim Cruickshank, Davie Holt, Alan Anderson, George Miller and Tommy Traynor remained as pillars of strength but, having used no fewer than 31 players, Hearts were clearly in a state of disarray and they now faced a major transitional period.

Willie Polland had returned to Raith Rovers on a free transfer while John Cumming - who would remain as trainer - and Chris Shevlane decided to hang up their boots, the latter on medical advice after a recurring ankle injury. And amongst those released were other notables such as Johnny Hamilton, Billy Higgins, Danny Ferguson, Alan Gordon, George Peden and Bobby Aitchison. Hearts had wanted to hold on to Alan Gordon - earlier the subject of a £30,000

Star quality - in the mid-1960's Hearts paid a total of £55,000 for Jimmy Irvine (Middlesbrough), George Miller (Wolves) and Jim Townsend (St Johnstone).

bid from Rangers - but the player had requested a leave of absence to further his accountancy career in South Africa. There he would play for Durban City alongside Billy Higgins with his other former colleague Danny Ferguson joining Durban United. In a depressing time for the Tynecastle faithful, yet another blow came with the news that Shevlane had recovered sufficiently to sign for Celtic less than a month after leaving Tynecastle!

In the close season, three Hearts players were involved in Scotland's nine-game "World Tour" of Israel, Hong Kong, Australia, New Zealand and Canada. Former St Johnstone midfielder Jim Townsend (22), a £20,000 signing at the tail end of last term, and Alan Anderson both made seven appearances with Jim Cruickshank playing five times although these were not regarded as full internationals due to the standard of opposition.

Apart from Townsend, there had been further close-season signings for the fans to discuss. Former Dundee United inside-forward Jimmy Irvine (27), arrived from Middlesbrough for £15,000 with Willie Hamilton (29), returning to Hearts on a free-transfer from Aston Villa, who he had joined for £25,000 after two years with Hibs. The old maestro had lost none of his skill but, like Jim Baxter, his extravagent off-field lifestyle and injuries received in a serious car crash had taken their toll on his physical fitness.

The 1967 League Cup draw placed Hearts alongside Falkirk, St Johnstone and Stirling Albion, all of whom had finished beneath them in the league. On August 12th, Raold Jensen gave the Maroons a perfect start by netting the opener against St Johnstone at Tynecastle in just seven minutes. However, with 20 minutes remaining, a rare Cruickshank blunder allowed Kenny Aird to level and four minutes from time, Gordon Whitelaw headed the winner for the Saints .

Indeed, it was the Perth side, whose previous boss Bobby Brown was now in charge of Scotland and who were now managed by Willie Ormond, who were to prove the stumbling block. For, while the new-look Maroons took eight points from Falkirk and Stirling Albion, they conceded a 2-0 lead before losing 3-2 in a Muirton thriller as St Johnstone took another step in their advance to the semi-final .

Once again, Hearts league campaign began badly, Pat Quinn netting three as Hibs departed with a 4-1 win on September 9th. The Tynecastle side had continued with their recently reintroduced orthodox attacking formation which had brought seven goals from their two previous games but it had all gone wrong against the Easter Road side. A shaky display by Jim Cruickshank cost him his place and Kenny Garland (19), who had earlier made three League Cup appearances took over in goal.

However, the summer signings had brought a much needed freshness to the team and with Jim Townsend driving on play from midfield, a seven game unbeaten run against Raith Rovers (a) 4-2, Aberdeen (h) 2-1, Motherwell (a) 5-2, Falkirk (h) 1-0, Dundee United (h) 1-0, Partick Thistle (a) 3-3 and St Johnstone (h) 1-1, left Hearts fourth by late October.

The newcomers apart, a number of bright young reserves had made their breakthrough. Ian Sneddon (20), established himself at right-back while the strapping Arthur Thomson (19), became a fixture alongside the depaendale Alan Anderson in the centre of defence. In early December, yet another youngster, Arthur Mann (19), got his chance and soon his attacking forays down the left earned him the left-back position ahead of the experienced Davie Holt.

Donald Ford, until recently an amateur until completing his accountancy degree, was now a full-time professional and his lively displays and scoring ability soon earned him a regular spot up front alongside the energetic George Fleming and the pacy wing play of Tommy Traynor.

December 31st, 1967

	P	F A	PTS
Rangers	**16**	**42-12**	**30**
Celtic	**16**	**47-13**	**28**
Hearts	**17**	**38-26**	**23**
Hibernian	**16**	**32-20**	**20**

By the end of 1967, Hearts lay third, five points behind Celtic who had won last year's European Cup and the domestic treble, and seven behind leaders Rangers. At this stage, John Harvey's reshaped side looked a vast improvement on last term's strugglers but on January 1st, a Joe Davis penalty gave Hibs the only goal of the Easter Road derby and soon the Maroons were on the slide. The following day, a 34th minute Jim Irvine goal from a Jim Fleming corner put Hearts 1-0 up against Dunfermline at Tynecastle. However, with 20 minutes remaining, Hugh Robertson levelled from the spot and Alex. Edwards laid on the winner for Willie Callaghan near the end.

The slump continued with a 3-2 home defeat by Rangers before a 6-3 humbling by Clyde at Shawfield saw Gorgie hopes turn to the Scottish Cup. In the first round, Hearts recorded a comfortable 4-1 win over Brechin City at Tynecastle before facing a tricky tie away to last year's conquerors, Dundee United on Saturday, February 17th. On police advice, kick off was brought forward to 2pm since Dundee met Rangers down the road at Dens an hour later in a match which would attract a crowd of 33,000.

Hearts powerfully-built Danish international forward Rene Moller, recently signed from Randers Freja on an amateur form, made a spectacular Scottish Cup debut, laying on an early opener for Donald Ford before adding a second goal in 18 minutes. Former Scotland winger Davie Wilson pulled one back after a slack passback and with Seeman and Wilson causing havoc down the flanks, Andy Rolland equalised from the spot before another two goals by Ian Mitchell put United 4-2 ahead.

However, Eddie Thomson reduced the leeway with a thundering shot then home defender Tommy Millar was stretchered off after a fierce tackle by Arthur Thomson. After half-time, the non-stop drama continued, Garland saving a Seeman penalty before Moller made it 4-4 from close in after 54 minutes. It really was an all-action affair and just six minutes later, Billy Hainey again put the home side ahead with a cracking shot from 20 yards out.

The Maroons stormed back and in 75 minutes, their pressure paid off when a Tommy Traynor shot was handled by Jim Cameron on the line. Up stepped skipper George Miller to net from the spot and with just five minutes remaining and both sets of fans in the 9,000 crowd gasping for breath, former United star Jim Irvine intercepted a Gillespie throw-in before crashing the ball into the roof of the net to give Hearts a sensational 6-5 victory!

Meanwhile, Rangers, who had lost only two domestic games all season, went on to dispose of Dundee after a replay and the quarter-final draw sent Hearts to face the Light Blues at Ibrox on March 9th. The Maroons abysmal league form had continued with seven defeats from eight games but against all the odds, Jim Irvine put them ahead in 33 minutes. Another former Dundee United player Orjan Perrson levelled five minutes after the interval but Hearts held out for a replay before a crowd of nearly 58,000.

Alan Anderson and Donald Ford replaced the injured Arthur Thomson and Rene Moller for the Tynecastle replay. The home side looked the likelier in a scrappy, tension-ridden first-half which was halted for 13 minutes after fans from the 44,000 plus crowd spilled onto the pitch due to overcrowding at the Gorgie Road end.

By midway through the second period, it appeared that Rangers strength might give them the edge but with three minutes left and extra-time fast approaching, the deadlock was broken. Accepting a pass from Ian Sneddon, Donald Ford cleverly slipped the ball past Scottish international centre-half Ron McKinnon then beat Eric Sorensen with a low angular shot into the far corner of the net.

Great was the joy as thousands of excited Hearts fans streamed from the floodlit ground but another three league defeats - all by the odd goal - were hardly ideal preparation for the Hampden semi-final against Morton on Saturday, March 30th. Hearts went ahead through Jensen in 11 minutes only for Rankin to level soon afterward but there was no further scoring in what proved a desperately disappointing match.

The midweek replay, which attracted just 11,500 - half the attendance at the first game - proved a much more open contest. Hearts controlled the early play with some speedy interchanges in attack and both Irvine and Ford hit the woodwork. In 32 minutes Morton took the lead when Willie Allan hammered home a fierce 30-yarder but Hearts hit back and again came close when Irvine's shot crashed off the bar. Midway through the second-half, George Miller picked up a loose ball to sweep home the equaliser but with the teams still deadlocked, the game went to extra-time.

Rene Moller replaced Tommy Traynor while Billy Gray substituted for injured Morton skipper Jim Kennedy but the stalemate continued until two minutes from time. A Morton defender miskicked and Donald Ford raced in on goal only to be downed by goalkeeper Bobby Russell. Raold Jensen stepped forward to take the penalty and cooly blasted the ball high into the net to send the Hearts

What joy - Donald Ford turns away in triumph after scoring a late winner in the Scottish Cup quarter-final replay against Rangers at Tynecastle. Ibrox keeper Eric Sorensen and his defenders look stunned as the Gorgie ground erupts.

fans scattered around the darkened Hampden slopes wild with delight.

Now Hearts could look forward to their first Scottish Cup final since wining the trophy in 1956. Their opponents would be Dunfermline, who had beaten St Johnstone 2-1 after a 1-1 draw and who would be contesting their third final since 1961. The Fifers were the perfect example of a successful provincial club in the 1960's and were reknowned for their exciting forays into Europe. Under manager George Farm, they had knocked out the holders, Celtic, and, since the semi-final, the Pars had shown greater consistency than Hearts who had won just two of their previous five games.

Dunfermline were favourites but Hearts cup form was impressive and on Saturday, April 27th, over 30,000 of the Tynecastle faithful joined the East coast exodus. Disappointingly, the Hampden crowd numbered just 56,365 - the lowest Scottish Cup Final attendance since the war - with the vital Rangers v. Aberdeen league clash across the city at Ibrox significantly affecting the Hampden crowd.

Curiously, Hearts were skippered by former Dunfermline player George Miller while the Fifers were led out by ex-Hearts stalwart Roy Barry. After missing three games through injury, Arthur Mann returned in place of Davie Holt while Jim Townsend was passed fit after a troublesome shoulder injury. 21-year-old Eddie Thomson, who had featured prominently in the cup run, did not make Hearts twelve as the teams lined up: Hearts - Cruickshank; Sneddon, Anderson, A. Thomson, Mann; Jensen, Townsend, Miller (capt); Ford, Irvine, Traynor. Sub. Moller. Dunfermline - Martin; W. Callaghan, McGarty, Barry (capt), Lunn; Edwards, T. Callaghan, Robertson; Lister, Paton, Gardner. Sub. Thomson.

On a bumpy pitch, early play was scrappy with Thomson and Townsend both guilty of heavy challenges as the teams sought to stamp their authority on the game. Nevertheless, it was Hearts who looked more adventurous in a dour first-

Up for the Cup - Hearts squad for the 1968 Scottish Cup Final against Dunfermline. (BACK - left to right) - Alan Anderson, Davie Holt, Arthur Thomson, Jim Cruickshank, Ian Sneddon, George Miller. FRONT - John Harvey (manager), Raold Jensen, Donald Ford, Jim Townsend, Tommy Traynor, Arthur Mann, Jim Irvine, John Cumming (coach). Rene Moller is absent **DC Thomson**

One for Hearts - a strong run by Rene Moller (not in picture) ended with his cutback being deflected into his own net past keeper Bent Martin by grounded Dunfermline defender John Lunn in the Scottish Cup Final at Hampden. Tommy Traynor and Alan Anderson look on.

half, Danish keeper Bent Martin pulling off a fine save from a Donald Ford header while Jim Irvine went close with a couple of good efforts.

After the break, Dunfermline upped the pace and inspired by the intelligent promptings of Tommy Callaghan, Hearts were soon under severe pressure. In 56 minutes, an Ian Lister free-kick from the left saw Jim Cruickshank and Arthur Thomson collide as they went for the ball. The keeper could only half clear and Pat Gardner was on the spot to volley into the net.

Three minutes later, Bert Paton looked set to score when he was pulled down by Cruickshank and from the resultant penalty, Lister sent the ball low to the keeper's right. Raold Jensen had made little impact and manager John Harvey replaced him with Rene Moller. Soon the Dane's powerful play had the Pars defence under pressure and when his fiercely hit near-post cutback spun into the net off John Lunn, Hearts were back in business.

Twenty minutes remained as the Hearts fans roared their encouragement but within three minutes, their hopes lay in ruins. George Miller and Bert Paton challenged for a cross and when the ball broke loose, Pat Gardner shot home to make it 3-1. In the end, the Fifers had been the better all-round side and had deserved to win. Hearts, for whom Jim Townsend and Rene Moller had been booked, matched them for effort with George Miller a defensive standout, but they had lacked the skill to seriously worry their opponents and only Donald Ford had caused any real problems to the Dunfermline rearguard.

Their cup run apart, the Maroons league revival had ground to a halt at the turn of the year and a miserable tally of 13 defeats from their last 17 games saw them finish a lowly twelfth in the table. Although affected by injuries, Bobby Kemp had been a big disappointment and in April he was released along with Andy Milne.

Nevertheless, a clutch of promising youngsters had emerged and the 1968-69 campaign began on an optimistic note. Hearts took five points from their opening three League Cup games against Airdrie, Dundee and Kilmarnock and looked a good bet for a place in the quarter-finals. However, a tousy match against Airdrie at Tynecastle resulted in an unexpected 2-0 reverse with bookings for Townsend, MacDonald, Hamilton and Eddie Thomson as well as three Airdrie men.

Four changes were made for the visit to Dens only for Hearts to perform dismally in a 4-0 defeat, a scoreline which provided Dundee with a springboard through to the semi-finals. John Duncan had netted three for the Dark Blues and as a result his marker George Miller lost his place in central defence. The up-and-coming Eddie Thomson seized the opportunity to establish himself and a couple of months later, Miller moved on to Falkirk for a fee of £5,000.

Hearts league challenge began brightly with 3-1 wins away to Hibs and at home to Dunfermline before goals by Jim Fleming and Willie Hamilton - the latter a cracking drive - brought a 2-1 win at Aberdeen on October 5th. That left them one point behind league leaders Dundee United and Rangers after five games but although Hearts then more than matched Celtic at Tynecastle, a Chalmers header rebounded from the post to go in off Alan MacDonald's leg for the only goal late on.

The bad luck continued at Falkirk when skipper Jim Townsend was stretchered off with a broken ankle and Ian Sneddon sustained a badly damaged knee. In addition, Jim Irvine also had knee trouble and with all three likely to be out for a number of months, a 3-1 defeat at Dens Park completed a disastrous month. Dundee were twice awarded

Safe hands - Hearts keeper Jim Cruickshank cuts out the danger from the inrushing Celtic centre-half Billy McNeill while Arthur Mann and Ian Sneddon stand guard on the goal-line. Alan Gordon and Alan MacDonald are the other Maroons. DC Thomson

penalties and at the second, one frustrated Hearts fan found it all too much as he ran onto the pitch to remonstrate with Glasgow referee Jim Callaghan before being hauled off by the local constabulary.

The city of Dundee was anything but a happy hunting ground for Hearts and in November, Raold Jensen and Dundee United's Alex. Reid were ordered off following a heated clash in a 4-2 reverse at Tannadice. Disappointingly, that was Arthur Mann's last appearance in a Maroon jersey for a few days later he joined Manchester City for £65,000 after lengthy interest from wily Maine Road boss Joe Mercer.

Mann had been a firm favourite and the fans were despondent that another top player had been allowed to leave. However, his departure meant a first-team return for 32-year-old Davie Holt. And with Ian Sneddon facing five months on the sidelines due to injury, Dave Clunie (20), and Billy McAlpine (18), vied for the other full-back slot with Alan Anderson or Arthur Thomson partnering Eddie Thomson in central defence.

Hearts could never be faulted for lack of effort. They were solid enough at the back but despite the presence of the highly competitive Alan MacDonald and the industrious George Fleming, the absence of the injured Townsend left them short of creativity in midfield.

Raold Jensen, Donald Ford, Jim Fleming, Rene Moller, Willie Hamilton and Tommy Traynor were the men competing for the jerseys up front. However, the lack of finishing power continued to be a major headache and in November the return of Alan Gordon from South Africa came as a welcome boost.The tall striker had previously enjoyed a successful partnership with Willie Hamilton and he soon showed his value with six goals in his first nine games.

League form continued to be erratic but in the first round of the Scottish Cup, Hearts improved on their dismal record in Dundee with a 2-1 win at Dens Park. Jocky Scott put the Dark Blues ahead after eight minutes, but within 60 seconds George Fleming levelled the scores with a snapshot from 12-yards. And with 18 minutes remaining, Tommy Traynor was first to a Jensen corner to head the winner past the despairing home keeper Ally Donaldson.

The second round draw sent Hearts to face strong-going Rangers at Ibrox on Monday, February 24th. Due to postponements, the Light Blues had not played for three weeks but although Rangers recent £100,000 Scottish record signing Colin Stein was effectively subdued by Eddie Thomson, the Tynecastle attack were unable to take advantage of the situation. In 32 minutes, Willie Johnston headed in a Stein cross and when Swedish winger Orjan Persson added a second soon after half-time, there was no way back for the Maroons.

A few days later, Hearts crashed 5-1 to Partick Thistle at Firhill where Jags centre Jimmy Bone netted a hat-trick. Out of the team went Arthur Thomson and Jim Fleming and for both it was the beginning of the end of their Tynecastle careers. However, Hearts recovered well and after losing just one of their last nine games, they went on to finish eighth, their only first that year being the opening of the Ace of Hearts Club, at that time the largest licensed club in Scotland.

In mid-March, Alan Gordon was transferred to Dundee

United for £8,000 and, in a further clearout of forwards, Jim Fleming, Willie Hamilton and Bobby Elgin were released. However, the Tynecastle faithful were encouraged by the arrival of two new attackers. Former Aberdeen forward Ernie Winchester (25), cost £10,000 from Kansas City Spurs while the lanky Neil Murray (19), was signed for a similar fee from Ross County. Murray started the 1969-70 season on the wing in place of Tommy Traynor but it was the more robust Winchester who got Hearts off to a great start to their 1969 League Cup campaign, netting twice in a 3-2 win over Dundee United at Tannadice.

Disappointingly, their next three ties brought just a single point, leaving the lacklustre Maroons with only an outside chance of reaching the next stage. However, Winchester again scored in a 1-0 win over Dundee United at Tynecastle to give Hearts five points, one less than St Mirren and two fewer than section leaders Morton, who they faced in the final game on Wednesday, August 27th.

A Cappielow crowd of 9,000 saw Joe Harper and Joe Mason miss some great chances for the home side before Ernie Winchester put Hearts ahead just before half-time. Twelve minutes from the end, Alan MacDonald made it 2-0 but Hearts could not add to their tally and despite leapfrogging St Mirren to finish level on points with Morton, the Greenock side went through to the last eight with a superior goal-average.

Another two goals would have put Hearts through but when the pair met again in the opening league game at Tynecastle three days later, there was further disappointmment as Hal Stewart's side departed with a 1-0 win. In September, Raold Jensen and Donald Ford grabbed two apiece in a 4-1 home win over Kilmarnock but it would be another seven games before Hearts again tasted victory with a 3-2 home win over Raith Rovers on November 1st.

The following week, Hearts fielded an unchanged team for the match against Celtic at Parkhead - Cruickshank; Clunie, Anderson, E. Thomson, Oliver; Brown, MacDonald, Lynch; Jensen, Ford, Moller. Sub. Fleming. Celtic - Fallon; Craig, McNeill, Brogan, Gemmell; Johnstone, Murdoch, Callaghan; Dalglish, Hood, Macari. Sub. Hay

In 36 minutes, the mercurial Raold Jensen, who had been in and out of the side that season, lashed the ball past an astonished John Fallon from an almost impossible angle 15 yards wide of the goal. Celtic were stunned and just before the interval, Donald Ford poked in a second in a goalmouth melee. Hearts went on to take full points and by the 12 game mark, the Gorgie side had 13 points, just four less than joint leaders Hibernian, Dundee United and Dunfermline.

At Parkhead, the young Hearts full-back pairing of Dave Clunie and Peter Oliver had impressed in their jousts with stars like Jimmy Johnstone and Lou Macari. Ian Sneddon and Billy McAlpine had begun the season as first-choice full-backs before injuries and loss of form saw the versatile Clunie, who had started the campaign in midfield, switch to right-back with Oliver handed his chance in the number three jersey.

After a bright start, Ernie Winchester had dropped out of the side and once again it was Donald Ford who carried the main goalscoring threat. On December 20th, the little striker netted another two goals in a runaway 5-0 win over Airdrie at Tynecastle but Hearts were unable to repeat this goalscoring form in the Edinburgh derby against Hibs at Easter Road at the start of 1970. The game which was watched by nearly 37,000 fans ended 0-0, but although the Maroons moved up to fourth place in mid-January, front-runners Celtic, Rangers and Hibs had established what would prove an unbridgeable gap.

Twenty-year-old midfielders, Jim Brown and Tommy Veitch were further examples of the Tynecastle youth policy. Both had made good progress and now provided stiff competition for more experienced men like Jim Townsend, Alan MacDonald and George Fleming. As the youngsters continued to break through, departures were almost inevitable and, in January, two players who regularly found their names in referee's notebooks, moved on. Arthur Thomson joined Oldham for £8,000 with Alan MacDonald moving to Kilmarnock for a similar amount.

After narrowly defeating Montrose in a Scottish Cup first round replay, courtesy of a late George Fleming goal, Hearts were paired with Kilmarnock at Rugby Park. Around 14,000 fans saw Killie kick off with a strong wind at their backs and only three minutes elapsed before the home side went ahead through Cook. Hearts played some good football but showed little threat in front of goal and 13 minutes after the break, Ross Mathie capitalised on a Thomson slip to add a decisive second.

Nevertheless, there was a far greater consistency of performance in the early months of 1970 and by the end of the season, the Maroons had suffered just four defeats in 20 games since late December to finish fourth, their best league position since 1965. Significantly, the defence, which was second only to League Champions Celtic in terms of goals conceded, took much of the credit and Jim Cruickshank was deservedly rewarded with a Scotland recall for the Home Internationals.

Have boots will travel - Hearts defender Arthur Mann prepares to leave Tynecastle after his £65,000 transfer to Manchester City.

The big keeper kept a clean sheet in no-scoring draws against Wales and England and the defensive qualities of Eddie Thomson and Dave Clunie were also recognized with the full-back playing for the Scottish League against the Irish League and both defenders making a number of appearances for Scotland's Under-23's.

Hearts problems lay further forward and the lack of punch up front was again the primary concern. The injury-plagued Jim Irvine was given a free-transfer while seven-goal Rene Moller, a regular for much of the season, decided his future lay back home in Denmark. Worryingly, Donald Ford had finished top scorer with just seven goals and he clearly required the support of another proven goalscorer alongside him.

However, although no new attackers were signed, the experienced former Rangers midfielder Wilson Wood (27), was secured from Dundee United in exchange for the transfer-seeking Tommy Traynor, who was no longer guaranteed his place after the emergence of promising youngsters like Neil Murray and Andy Lynch.

Jim Townsend would miss the opening few weeks of the new season through suspension but Ian Sneddon appeared to have put his injury worries behind him and was back in in Hearts starting line-up for the opening League Cup tie against Celtic at Tynecastle on August 8th. Although Hearts went down 2-1, Wood turned in a forceful performance and further encouragement could be taken from a splendid consolation goal by the slimly built 20-year-old Kevin Hegarty who had substituted for Ernie Winchester.

However, Hearts, by now playing a near 4-4-2 system, were unable to recapture the form shown earlier that year and with only one win to their credit, they finished bottom of their section behind Celtic, Dundee United and Clyde. The league campaign began just as badly with a 3-1 reverse to Willie Ormond's dazzling St Johnstone side at Tynecastle where Peter Oliver was ordered off for taking a kick at Muir. And as the slump continued, the Maroons could muster only two wins from their opening nine league games.

The Gorgie fans were becoming increasingly restless but on September 30th, they were treated to a stirring performance in the first round of the Texaco Cup against Burnley. The Lancashire side, who included former England internationals Tony Waiters, John Angus and Ralph Coates, had come north with a 3-1 lead from the first leg at Turf Moor and a crowd of around 16,000 turned out at Tynecastle in the hope that Hearts could turn things around.

Right from the start, Hearts went on the offensive and roared on by a noisy home support, they went ahead through Jim Brown in 14 minutes. The Maroons were masterminded by the busy Jim Townsend and with Andy Lynch in devastating form on the left wing, it was little surprise when Kevin Hegarty added a second before the interval to tie the aggregate scores at 3-3.

Burnley appeared totally unprepared for such an onslaught and when Waldron put through his own goal and Lynch added another in 54 minutes, it was all over for the English side although Casper managed a consolation goal later on. Hearts had turned the tables with a rousing display of old-fashioned Scottish football and in the end, Burnley had simply been overwhelmed.

In the second round, Hearts met Airdrie with the first leg at Broomfield on October 19th. For much of the season, Hearts had played well without finding the vital finishing touch and they had failed to score in their previous three league games. However, the floodlit cup ties appeared to bring out the best in the Maroons and another scintillating display saw them romp to a 5-0 triumph at Broomfield.

Four-goal Donald Ford had been in devastating form but Drew Young - introduced in place of Kevin Hegarty, whose earlier tally of seven goals from his first 13 games had dried up - had made an immediate impact with a cracking drive from 25 yards. Nine days later, the deadly Ford was again on target with a double against Celtic at Parkhead. His second, a flying header, had given Hearts a deserved 2-0 lead soon after half-time but, inspired by the brilliant Jimmy Johnstone, Celtic quickly pulled one back and scored two late goals to win 3-2.

Two years earlier, former Berwick Rangers player-boss Jock Wallace had been appointed assistant-manager at Tynecastle. He had soon proved a major influence, particulary in organising the defence, and there was little doubt he was being groomed to take over from John Harvey. However, in April, those plans were thrown into disarray when Wallace was appointed chief coach under Willie Waddell at Rangers. John Harvey had soldiered on but in November, lengthy behind the scenes discussions over a management change had finally been concluded.

On the deck - St Johnstone keeper John Donaldson goes down to foil the inrushing Donald Ford and Jim Townsend of Hearts in this league match at muddy Tynecastle.

DC Thomson

Chapter Eight

BOBBY SEITH AT THE HELM

At the start of December, Bobby Seith (38), who had been Preston North End boss for two-and-a-half years until his dismissal seven months earlier, was appointed manager. He also had coached at Rangers and Dundee and his intention was to be a "track-suit boss" at Tynecastle. John Harvey, whose health had suffered under the strain of his managerial responsibilities, welcomed the new appointment and would remain as trainer with special responsibility for coaching the youngsters.

Seith's arrival had coincided with an upsurge in form but although Hearts took 12 points from nine games, they remained 13th in the league by the end of 1970. Meanwhile, the Texaco Cup, which featured six teams each from the Scottish and English Leagues and two each from Northen Ireland and Eire, had caught the imagination of the fans. Despite losing 3-2 to Airdrie in the second leg, Hearts had triumphed 7-3 on aggregate and they then met Motherwell in the semi-final with Wolves and Derry City contesting the other tie.

On December 16th, over 21,000 fans, much encouraged by Hearts 2-1 league win over Motherwell a few days earlier, turned out for the first leg of the Texaco clash against the Steelmen at Tynecastle. The Maroons dominated for long spells but just five minutes from half-time, Donald Ford finished off good leading up work by Brown and Carruthers by cracking a tremendous shot past Keith McCrae. Shortly after the break, Motherwell levelled when a Jumbo Muir shot was deflected past Cruickshank but although Hearts continued to hold the edge in a bruising encounter, there was no further score.

With the return not due until March, Hearts could concentrate on improving their league position. However, when a disappointing Ne'erday game against Hibs at Tynecastle again ended 0-0, the teams were booed from the field by both sets of fans in the 28,000 crowd. In the Scottish Cup, two goals by Ford and another from Lynch earned a 3-0 win over Stranraer and a second round derby clash against Hibs at Tynecastle. In the opening quarter, Hearts looked like ending their derby jinx as they besieged the visitors' goal but it was the Easter Road side who went ahead when John Hazel headed home a free kick.

Halfway through the second period, Kevin Hegarty had the maroon scarves flying again when he rose to head a Dave Clunie free kick past former Hearts keeper Gordon Marshall. But, with a replay looking increasingly likely, Arthur Duncan ended a fine run by firing home the winner from an acute angle. Hearts had failed to capitalise on their many chances and it was now seven league and cup games since they had last beaten their city rivals.

A month earlier, Hearts had suffered another blow when the talented Peter Oliver, who had been capped for Scotland's Under-21's against Wales just days before, was carried off at Airdrie with badly damaged knee ligaments. Sadly it would be nearly a year before the left-back would make his first-team return although his absence allowed another talented youngster, Roy Kay (21), the opportunity to make his first-team breakthrough.

Bobby Seith - a new manager for Hearts in December 1970.

In November, Jim Cruickshank, who had been capped against Wales and England last season, had returned for Scotland's 1-0 home win over Denmark before making his fifth international appearance in the 3-0 defeat in Belgium in February 1971. Donald Ford was also recognized, appearing for the Scottish League in a 1-0 reverse in Glasgow.

Hearts remained in contention for a UEFA Cup place but on Wednesday, March 3rd came the keenly anticipated return leg of the Texaco Cup semi-final at Fir Park. Despite being televised live, there was a near-capacity attendance of 25,259 and although Hearts looked the likelier throughout the first period, Brian Heron put Motherwell ahead 11 minutes after the break. The atmosphere was electric as Hearts battled back with the rugged clashes between Alan Anderson and Dixie Deans just one of the highlights of a real ding-dong cup-tie thriller.

Just seconds remained when Donald Ford fired in a shot which 'Well keeper Billy Ritchie was unable to hold and George Fleming raced in to score at the far post. The pace hardly let up throughout extra-time but with only 10 minutes left, Fleming set up Ford to net the winner and the huge Hearts support went wild with delight.

In the final, Hearts would meet Wolves, who had previously defeated Derry City, Dundee and Morton. A quarter of the league programme remained but with Celtic and Aberdeen fighting it out for the title, Hearts hopes of a UEFA Cup place were fast diminishing. They could only manage six points from seven games, including successive defeats to Aberdeen (a) 1-3, Ayr United (a) 0-1 and Morton (a) 0-3 just prior to the Texaco Cup Final on April 14th.

In a change of routine, Bobby Seith took 15 players away to Peebles to escape the excitement gripping Edinburgh. Both Hearts and Wolves were clubs of great tradition and although prices were more than doubled, there were over 25,000 for the first leg at Tynecastle. Hard hitting winger Andy Lynch, who had missed nine games after being injured at Stranraer, was now out with a virus as Hearts retained the side beaten by Morton four days earlier - Cruickshank; Sneddon, Thomson (capt.), Anderson, Kay; Brown, Townsend, Wood; Carruthers, Ford, Fleming. Subs. Young, Garland. Wolves - Parkes; Taylor, McCalle, Munro, Parkin; Wagstaffe, Bailey, O'Grady; McCalliog,

Curran, Gould. Subs. Dougan, Smith.

Much to the delight of the large home crowd, Hearts got off to a great start when Donald Ford headed home a deflected cross by Townsend in just eight minutes. After the opening quarter, the faster, stronger Wolves, who lay third in the English First Division, took over and a fine run by the pacy Wagstaffe ended with Bailey thundering home the equaliser. Scotland striker Hugh Curran added a second before half-time and with Hearts making little impression, Wolves - who were essentially a counter-attacking side - made it 3-1 through Curran, two minutes from time.

On May 3rd, a large Hearts support made the trip to Molineux where Hearts showed two changes from the first game. Tommy Veitch, now recovered from an early season heel operation, replaced the injured Jim Brown with Brian Laing in for Eric Carruthers who was on the bench. The Maroons opened strongly and with Wood and Townsend tireless workers in midfield, it was no surprise when George Fleming put them ahead after 25 minutes.

That left Hearts just one goal behind on aggregate but although they continued to press, they were unable to further penetrate a well-organised Wolves defence. In the end, the Maroons had to be content with runners-up medals but they had had done Scottish football proud with a rousing display and it was now clear that there was the nucleus of a successful side at Tynecastle.

Raold Jensen, Drew Young, Billy McAlpine and Brian Laing were released before Hearts went on to win six and draw three of a 10-game close season tour of the U.S.A and Canada. There had been little time for sightseeing but the trip had been ideal for building up team spirit. On August 7th, Hearts entertained Tottenham Hotspur in a pre-season friendly and although Spurs included a host of top internationals like Pat Jennings, Alan Mullery, Mike England, Alan Gilzean and Martin Peters, goals by Neil Murray and Roy Kay earned a 2-1 win to leave Hearts fans eager for the start of the new campaign.

Bobby Seith's men made a bright start in the League Cup, defeating last season's beaten finalists St Johnstone 4-1 at Tynecastle before returning from Airdrie with a 3-1 win. The midfield of Brown, Townsend and Wood looked particularly impressive until Wood went off with a knee injury at Broomfield. He would be out for five months and in his immediate absence, Hearts stuttered to a 1-0 defeat at Dunfermline before falling 2-1 at home to Airdrie.

Hearts had been well on top until Cruickshank was deceived by a dipping 35-yarder from Whiteford in 68 minutes. Fleming levelled from close range but as Hearts went all-out for the winner, Eddie Thomson was ordered off for throwing the ball at Drew Jarvie and Menzies netted Airdrie's winner from the spot, four minutes from time.

Now Hearts faced St Johnstone in a crucial tie at Muirton, where victory would restore them to pole position. However, they were unable to recover from the loss of an early Jim Pearson goal and the Saints went on to reach the quarter-final. There was a further dent to morale with yet another derby reverse to Hibs at Tynecastle on September 4th. With just six minutes remaining, another no-scoring draw looked certain until Alex. Cropley cracked home a fierce drive, John Hamilton making it 2-0 near the end.

The steadying influence of Wilson Wood had been missed, leaving Jim Townsend as the only player with the skill and confidence to hold the ball and probe for openings. However, too often Townsend got little response from his younger colleagues and with fresh blood required, former Airdrie forward Tommy Murray (28), was signed from Carlisle United in exchange for the out-of-favour Kevin Hegarty. Murray made an immediate impact with two goals in a 4-1 win at Dunfermline and shortly afterwards, he was involved in the Texaco Cup first round clash with Newcastle United at Tynecastle.

Newcastle, who had won the Fairs Cup in 1969, fielded £180,000 England international centre-forward Malcolm MacDonald only to play a surprisingly defensive game. Hearts could make little headway with only Tommy Murray causing any problems but, nine minutes after half-time, Andy Lynch delighted the 18,000 crowd when he headed the only goal of the game.

On September 28th, a large Edinburgh contingent were at St James' Park for the return. For long spells, Hearts were in control of midfield but they were unable to cap-

On the mark - Hearts striker Donald Ford in typical all-out action against St Johnstone at Tynecastle. Neil Murray is on the left with Saints Alex. Rennie appealing for offside

A dramatic day at Pittodrie - Aberdeen's Davie Robb and Jim Forrest prepare to take a free-kick from the edge of the box as Hearts line up a six-man defensive wall. The Maroons won a sensational 3-2 victory against the league leaders with two goals in the dying minutes.

italise and in the last 20 minutes, they came under intense pressure. Jim Cruickshank made a couple of brilliant saves from MacDonald but with only five minutes remaining, the big striker equalised from close-in. However, his goal had appeared suspiciously offside and as Hearts players appealed, angry Scots fans poured on to the field.

Order was quickly restored only for MacDonald to score again six minutes into extra-time. But, in a sensational finish, Alan Anderson made it 2-2 on aggregate when he headed home a Murray cross just four minutes from the end. Now the tie would be decided on penalties. Townsend hit the post with Hearts first while Cruickshank saved from Hibbett. Murray and Thomson then scored but when Ford's effort was stopped by McFaul, Tudor scored with the final kick to give Newcastle the tie, 4-3 on penalties.

Nevertheless, Hearts bounced back with a 2-1 home win over Rangers and although an eight game unbeaten league run ended with a 5-3 defeat at Motherwell, the Maroons responded with a decisive 6-1 victory over Morton at Tynecastle. Donald Ford was the executioner in chief with a hat-trick but Tommy Murray had shown his worth by netting his seventh goal in 12 games since joining Hearts.

Two weeks later, Ford hit another hat-trick in a sensational win over league leaders Aberdeen at Pittodrie. Derek Renton, signed earlier on a free transfer from Rangers, made his debut in midfield but although Ford opened the scoring just after half-time, the Dons hit back with goals from Joe Harper and Davie Robb. The influential but volatile Townsend was ordered off for protesting too vehemently over the second goal but, against all the odds, Ford netted twice in the last four minutes to give Aberdeen their first league defeat of the season.

That left Hearts third, three points behind the Dons and five behind new leaders Celtic but defeats at Falkirk and Parkhead extended the gap behind Celtic to 10 points by the turn of the year. Astonishingly, the slump continued into 1972, a 5-2 defeat by Dundee at Tynecastle then a 6-0 mauling by Rangers at Ibrox leaving them without a win in eight games.

Jim Cruickshank lost his place to Kenny Garland and, in the absence of car crash victim Donald Ford and Jim Townsend, who had required an operation to remove his swallowed dentures, a 2-0 home win over St Johnstone in the first round of the Scottish Cup came as a much needed boost to morale. In February, Wilson Wood returned to the side while transfer-seeking George Fleming moved on to Dundee United for £7,000. But although Peter Oliver regained the number three jersey, he was not the player of old and soon lost his place to 21-year-old Jim Jefferies.

A 4-0 home win over Clydebank earned a quarter-final tie against Celtic at Parkhead on March 18th. Soon after the start, Hearts lost Townsend with a nasty leg gash after his own reckless foul on Bobby Lennox. Celtic dominated the first-half and took the lead through Deans. However, Hearts battled back and with just 60 seconds remaining, a brilliant run by Jim Brown ended with Donald Ford setting up Derek Renton for the equaliser.

Over 40,000 saw a fast and furious replay at Tynecastle but although there was little between the sides, slack defending towards the end of the first-half allowed little Lou Macari to head the only goal from just three yards out.

At times, the team had shown great promise but injuries to key players had taken their toll as Hearts went on to finish sixth in the league. Once again they had missed out on a European place and it was now six years since their last Continental sojourn, although there was at least the consolation of the Texaco Cup. In the close season, Ernie Winchester, used in midfield in the absence of Wilson Wood, joined Arbroath for £2,500 while Tommy Veitch moved on to Tranmere but disappointingly there were no signings despite the obvious lack of firepower up front.

Hearts got off to a nightmare start to their 1972-73 League Cup section comprising Airdrie, newly-promoted Dumbarton and Berwick Rangers. After losing 1-0 at Dumbarton, Hearts struggled to a 0-0 draw with Airdrie at Tynecastle before being held to a 1-1 draw at lowly Berwick. Then, after losing 2-1 at Airdrie, the nervy Maroons could only manage a 1-1 draw at home to Dumbarton and, even this early in the season, there was widespread booing and slow handclapping from disgruntled fans.

Hearts cause had not been helped by the absence of Jim Cruickshank, who was involved in another contractual dispute while skipper Eddie Thomson would miss the opening month of the season through injury. However, the real problems lay in attack, where only three goals were scored in five games before the 3-0 win over Berwick in a nothing at stake final game. Bobby Seith had little room for manuevre as he tried to perm a winning combine from a basic 15 players and the board's failure to strengthen the squad had meant the loss of valuable revenue from the quarter-final stage and beyond.

In the opening league match on September 2nd, Tommy Murray netted in a 1-0 home victory over 10-man St Johnstone, who had Whitelaw ordered off following an incident with Renton, but almost immediately came a 2-0 reverse to rejuvenated Hibernian at Easter Road. A few days later, things looked bleak during a dour struggle against a defence-minded Crystal Palace in the Texaco Cup at Tynecastle. Towards the end, home fans in the 9,500 crowd started to turn on their team but the jeers soon turned to cheers when Palace keeper John Jackson fisted out a Jim Brown effort and Tommy Murray lofted home the winner.

Jim Townsend had made his first appearance of the season but he was no longer in favour and in October, he was transferred to Morton for £6,000. Reserve striker Harry Kinnear and even centre-half Eddie Thomson were given their chance up front but neither was a success and soon the fair-haired Eric Carruthers, later a transfer target for Rangers, established himself alongside Donald Ford.

On September 26th, Hearts faced a tricky return at Selhurst Park but with Kenny Garland and Alan Anderson inspirational figures in a backs-to-wall display, Andy Lynch snatched another last-gasp goal to ensure Hearts progress to the second round. Now the Gorgie side met Motherwell but, without the drive of the injured Andy Lynch, there was little to cheer in a drab no-scoring first leg at Tynecastle. On November 8th, around 11,000 fans turned out for the Fir Park return with Hearts hopeful that former Inverness Caley winger Donald Park might provide the necessary flair to lift the side to victory.

Beaten to the punch - Eric Carruthers is beaten to a high ball by Aberdeen keeper Bobby Clark. **DC Thomson**

However, it was speedy 'Well winger Billy Campbell who took the eye and in 11 minutes, Ian Sneddon was booked for fouling the Irish international. That sparked terracing trouble which resulted in 30 arrests but, shortly after play restarted, Tommy Murray put Hearts ahead with a deflected shot, Dave Clunie adding a second from the spot after Carruthers was downed by Goodwin, just before half-time.

In the first half, Hearts had held the edge but when a frustrated Sneddon was ordered off for another foul on Campbell, Motherwell took control. In 59 minutes, McCabe lashed home a 25-yarder before Campbell made it 2-2 shortly afterwards. The blitzkrieg continued and although Kenny Garland performed heroics, Wark and McClymont completed a miserable night for the Maroons.

After a shaky start, Hearts, who looked particularly impressive at home, had made steady progress in the league and by mid-December they lay third, five points behind Celtic and one behind Hibs, with only one defeat - 4-2 to Celtic at Parkhead - in their previous nine games. On December 2nd, Hearts had withstood intense pressure for much of the match against Rangers at Ibrox. Only two minutes remained when Tommy Murray cheekily sat on the ball to waste time but, as Rangers players converged, he got up to send over a cross from which Donald Ford headed the winner!

Hearts were spoiled for choice at full-back with Dave Clunie partnered by either Ian Sneddon, Peter Oliver, Jim Jefferies or Roy Kay, who like Clunie could also perform the sweeper role in central defence. Strangely, just like a year earlier, a festive season slump brought defeats to Dundee (h) 1-2 and St Johnstone (a) 2-3 before the Ne'erday match with Hibernian at the start of 1973. Despite not having won an Edinburgh derby since September 1968, Hearts began in great style only to miss an easy chance before poor defending at a long throw allowed Jim O'Rourke to put Hibs ahead.

Blunders by Anderson and Clunie cost another two goals and with Hibs starting to run riot, Hearts trailed by five goals at the interval. After half-time, Eric Carruthers was replaced by the speedy Andy Lynch but although this helped curb the attacking forays of Hibs right-back John Brownlie, the rampant Easter Road side went on to win 7-0 to the utter humiliation of all in maroon amongst the 36,000 Tynecastle crowd.

Hearts could only manage three points from three games throughout the remainder of that black January before they met bottom of the league Airdrie in the Scottish Cup on February 3rd. Hearts had already struggled against the Diamonds in the League Cup and the bogy continued with an undistinguished 0-0 draw at Tynecastle. For the replay, Ian Sneddon and John Gallacher replaced Dave Clunie and Derek Renton with Eddie Thomson moving up front as Hearts fielded - Garland; Sneddon, Gallacher, Anderson, Jefferies; Park, Kay, Brown; Ford, Thomson, T. Murray. Sub - Carruthers. Airdrie were unchanged - McKenzie; Jonquin, Menzies, Whiteford, Caldwell; McCann, Fraser, Walker; Cowan, Busby, Wilson. Sub. Clark.

Unlike the first game, the Broomfield tie was an end-to-end thriller and although Hearts went behind when Busby headed home a free-kick in 20 minutes, Alan Anderson headed down for Ford to equalise shortly afterwards. Soon

Close call - Kenny Garland scrambles desperately across goal but Derek Parlane of Rangers fails to connect much to the relief of the Hearts keeper and the watching Alan Anderson. DC Thomson

after half-time, Hearts were again caught out when Wilson headed home and when Menzies made it 3-1, there was no way back for Hearts, whose misery was complete when Jim Jefferies was ordered off for fouling the speedy McCann - his second bookable offence.

Prior to the Cup replay, Andy Lynch, who had found himself second choice winger behind Donald Park, was transferred to Celtic for £30,000. Neil Murray was another to depart, joining Jim Townsend at Morton for £5,000 with Bobby Seith spending £17,500 on St Johnstone right-winger Kenny Aird (25). In February, Hearts had hit the headlines with an imaginative but ultimately abortive bid to land Manchester United's veteran Scottish international striker Denis Law, who later signed for Manchester City. However, Hearts early Scottish Cup exit came as severe blow to the club's finances and Hearts fans were stunned when club captain Eddie Thomson was transferred to Aberdeen for £60,000 in the middle of March.

Across the city, Hibs went on to finish third - their third top four placing in the past four years as they blossomed under Eddie Turnbull - while Hearts had to be content with a lowly tenth place. Since the turn of the year, the Maroons had managed only seven points from a possible 32 with just 39 goals scored in 34 league games all season.

With Jim Brown now a fixture in midfield and young Billy Menmuir and John Stevenson - the latter a recent free-transfer signing from Coventry City - showing great promise, Wilson Wood and Derek Renton were amongst those released. However, the fans got a welcome boost when Hearts paid a new club record fee of £35,000 for powerful Airdrie striker Drew Busby (26), with the speedy Bobby Prentice also secured on a free-transfer from Celtic.

Two goals by Donald Ford, one from the penalty spot, got the Maroons off to a 2-0 win over Partick Thistle in the opening sectional tie of the 1973 League Cup at Tynecastle. Ford struck again just three minutes into the match against St Johnstone at Muirton but mercurial left-winger Fred Aitken cracked home the equaliser from 20 yards and ten minutes from the end, young sweeper Jim Cant, making just his third first-team appearance, headed an Aitken cross into his own net.

Then came a further reverse at Dundee before Hearts gave themselves an outside hope of qualification with a resounding 4-1 home win over St Johnstone. But with full points required from their remaining two games, the Maroons struggled to successive 0-0 draws and it was Dundee, skippered by former Celtic defender Tommy Gemmell, who qualified and went on to lift the trophy itself.

Nevertheless, this was the prelude to a fine spell for the Tynecastle men. After opening with a 3-2 win over Morton at Cappielow, Hearts avenged that seven-goal Ne-erday debacle and finally ended their astonishing five year, 10-game league and cup derby jinx which had seen them score just a solitary goal, with a decisive 4-1 victory over Hibernian at Tynecastle.

Leading through an early Erich Schaedler own-goal, Kenny Aird capped a storming run with a second in 54 minutes. Cropley pulled one back but almost immediately, Donald Ford made it 3-1 following a lung-bursting run by John Stevenson before Drew Busby completed a wonderful day with a cracking 30-yarder.

That came as a tremendous morale-booster and Busby - who had added much-needed bite up front - was again on the mark when he headed the only goal in a 1-0 win over Everton in the Texaco Cup first round tie at Goodison. The Maroons followed that up with a thrilling 2-2 draw with Dundee at Tynecastle before the following team took on Rangers at Ibrox - Garland; Sneddon, Anderson, Cant, Clunie; Aird, Brown, Stevenson; Ford, Busby, Prentice. Subs. - Murray, Park.

Hearts immediately went into attack. With 25 minutes gone, Kenny Aird beat Mathieson before squaring to Ford.

On the wing - the speedy Rab Prentice proves a hot handful for Sandy Jardine of Rangers in this touchline joust at Tynecastle.

and although the wee striker's shot was blocked by McCloy, Rab Prentice was on the spot to hammer home the rebound. Four minutes later, the darting Ford caught the ball near the byeline before setting up Busby for a second and now Hearts turned on the style. Soon after half-time, Busby pounced on a weak passback to add a third and there was no way back for the Light Blues. Rangers had been outclassed and now Bobby Seith's side were top of the table with eight points from their first five games.

The remarkable turnaround had the fans streaming back to Tynecastle with 25,000 turning out for the return with Everton on Wednesday, October 3rd. Although the Goodison side, who included the highly rated Scots strikers Joe Harper and John Connolly, had recently been overshadowed by their Anfield rivals, they remained one of England's top clubs. However, the game itself proved a major disappointment although the no-scoring stalemate ensured Hearts involvement at the next stage.

The second round draw paired them with old adverseries Burnley with the first leg at Tynecastle on October 24th. By then, Hearts had stretched their unbeaten run to 13 games but their Texaco Cup sojourn was to come to an abrupt end. There was little between the sides but when Garland misjudged a soft header by Noble after the break and conceded another soon afterwards, the writing was on the wall for Hearts.

Near the end, a third goal by Welsh international winger Leighton-James left Hearts with an uphill struggle in the Turf Moor return. And despite their early dogged resistance, Hearts were unable to cope with the strength and skill of Burnley, who went on to win 5-0.

Ten days earlier, Hearts had lost the leadership and their unbeaten league record when they lost 3-1 to Celtic in a top of the table clash before 33,000 at Tynecastle. Sadly, the early momentum had gone and when the experienced Kenny Aird dropped out with a shoulder injury in early November, Hearts began to falter. Eight points were dropped from the next eight games and by the end of 1973, the Tynecastle men had slipped back to third, seven points behind league leaders Celtic.

On New Year's Day, Hearts got off to a great start against hibs at Easter Road when Ford, who recently gained his first Scotland cap after substituting for Denis Law in Czechoslovakia, scored in just five minutes. However, defensive slackness allowed Cropley to shoot low past Garland and before half-time, further goals by Cropley and Duncan proved too big a hurdle to overcome. Over the next month, further defeats by Rangers and St Johnstone effectively ended Hearts title challenge but on January 26th, a Drew Busby header set them on the road to a 3-1 Scottish Cup win over Clyde at Tynecastle.

The fourth round draw sent Partick Thistle to Edinburgh where Willie Gibson, who had come off the bench to score against Clyde, was again on the mark as the sides battled to a 1-1 draw. A crowd of 10,000 saw the young striker net another in the Firhill replay - played on Tuesday afternoon due to the power crisis - and although Joe Craig levelled before the interval, a superb second-half hat-trick by a razor-sharp Donald Ford put Hearts through with a rattled Thistle threatening to lose the place towards the end.

League form remained indifferent but on March 9th, over 18,000 were at Tynecastle for the quarter-final against Ally McLeod's Ayr United and, despite Hearts having the bulk of the play it took a late equaliser by skipper Alan Anderson to level the scores. Hearts carried a large support to Somerset Park which housed a 15,000 crowd for the midweek replay. Inspired by experienced campaigners like George McLean and Alex. Ferguson, Ayr fought tenaciously but although Hearts missed three great chances, neither side was able to break the deadlock in the regulation 90 minutes.

However, the pacy Prentice was a constant menace and, in the 16th minute of extra-time, he crossed for Ford to head the opener. With seven minutes remaining, Hearts were stunned when Rikki Fleming headed the equaliser from a McAnespie free-kick but straight from kick-off, Prentice raced away to send over another perfectly flighted cross and Ford made it 2-1. At the end, manager Bobby Seith jumped for joy for now, along with Celtic, Dundee and Dundee United, Hearts had reached the Scottish Cup semi-finals for the first time since 1968.

The draw paired Hearts with the least fancied side Dundee United, with whom the Maroons had recently drawn 3-3 at Tannadice, the tie going ahead at Hampden on Saturday, April 6th. Hearts fielded - Cruickshank; Sneddon, Clunie, Anderson, Jefferies; Aird, Brown, Stevenson, Prentice; Ford and Busby. Subs. Murray, Gibson. Dundee United, who included former Tynecastle favourites, George Fleming and Tommy Traynor, lined up - Davie; Rolland, Copland, D. Smith, Kopel; Payne, W. Smith, Fleming, Traynor; Knox, Gray. Subs. - Gardner, White.

After a nervy opening spell, Hearts went ahead when Alan Anderson headed home Kenny Aird's corner in 12 minutes. With Prentice a constant danger down the left, the Maroons finished the first-half well on top but to the dismay of their fans in the 23,000 crowd, they sat back to protect their lead. Shrewdly, Tannadice boss Jim McLean countered Prentice by bringing on the experienced Pat Gardner for Andy Rolland and the move paid off when the ex-Dunfermline player sent a perfectly placed 25-yard free-kick past the stranded Cruickshank.

Although there was no further score, United had finished on top and it was little surprise when they retained the players who had finished so strongly with Hearts also unchanged for the midweek replay at Hampden, three days later. Once again, Hearts took the game to United with Drew Busby and Donald Ford causing the Tannadice side all sorts of problems. In 23 minutes, Alan Anderson and Drew Busby drew the United markers and Donald Ford stole in to head Rab Prentice's free-kick past the helpless Sandy Davie.

However, 10 minutes after the interval, Jim Jefferies was harshly adjudged to have to have fouled George Fleming and United skipper Doug Smith levelled from the penalty spot. Two minutes later, Graeme Payne controlled a long lob by Gardner and beat the offside trap to score but, urged on by their fans in the much-reduced 13,000 crowd, Hearts battled back. Willie Gibson had replaced Kenny Aird after 70 minutes, and with 12 minutes remaining, the youngster hooked home an Ian Sneddon pass to make it 2-2. However, just 20 seconds later, 18-year-old Andy Gray restored United's lead and Hearts lost another when Archie Knox made it 4-2, five minutes from time.

The Tannadice side could look forward to a money-spinning final against Celtic and a place in next season's European Cup-Winners' Cup, but for Hearts, there was only despair. In a season which had promised much, they had once again missed out on Europe, finishing sixth, 15 points behind Celtic, who were League Champions for the ninth successive time. Former Under-23 international full-back Peter Oliver had failed to recapture his pre-injury form and was amongst those released, while big Harry Kinnear had earlier joined East Fife for £5,000.

The industrious Donald Ford, who had brought his tally of Scotland caps to three with appearances against West Germany and Wales, was included in Scotland's 22-man squad for the World Cup finals in West Germany that summer. The Hearts striker found himself behind established internationals like Joe Jordan, Kenny Dalglish and Peter Lorimer and did not play, but his inclusion ahead of others like Joe Harper of Hibs and Dundee's Jocky Scott and John Duncan was ample testimony to his ability.

Although Scotland failed to qualify for the next stage, the fans were delighted at their courageous display and with August 1974 marking the Centenary of the Heart of Midlothian Football Club, the start of the 1974-75 season was eagerly awaited. In the League Cup, Hearts found themselves alongside Aberdeen, Morton and Dunfermline. However, the Pars had not fully recovered from their relegation in 1972 and while Aberdeen were expected to pose the biggest threat, they remained a shadow of their successful side of the early 1970's.

John Gallacher began the season at centre-half in place of the injured Alan Anderson and, on August 10th, the Maroons

Heads you win - Hearts striker Donald Ford steals in to head the opener in the Scottish Cup semi-final replay against Dundee United at Hampden. Team-mate Drew Busby and United's Sandy Davie, Doug Smith and Frank Kopel are the others on view. DC Thomson

got off to the ideal start when Donald Ford netted the only goal at Aberdeen. Dunfermline then departed from Tynecastle with a 3-2 win before a crushing 5-0 victory over Morton at Cappielow left Hearts and the Pars neck and neck. Jim Leishman did a successful marking job on Donald Ford until breaking a leg in a tackle with Jim Jefferies but once again Hearts came off second best in the clash at Dunfermline. A Jimmy Cant double earned a 2-0 home win over Morton and, with Dunfermline falling 3-0 at Aberdeen, Hearts regained the section leadership on goal difference.

Aberdeen lay just one point behind and with only Morton out of contention, the final day would be decisive. Kenny Aird delighted the 14,000 Tynecastle crowd with a 10th minute opener and shortly after the interval, Kenny Garland saved a Jim Hermiston penalty. The excitement was intense but with just 18 minutes remaining, Aird struck again to put Hearts into the last eight of the League Cup for the first time since 1962.

However, Hearts were unable to penetrate the Falkirk rear-guard in the first leg of the quarter-final at Tynecastle on Wednesday, September 11th. They found it no easier in the Brockville return and with Gallacher carried off with a broken leg and time running out, Hearts were stunned when Kirkie Lawson grabbed a shock winner for the Second Division outfit.

Hearts had made a poor start to their league campaign with only two points from their opening five games. Two weeks earlier, they had restricted Oldham Athletic to a 1-0 win at Boundary Park in the Texaco Cup and with six changes from the side so comprehensively beaten at Firhill, Hearts were confident of turning the tables in the second leg at Tynecastle. However, Oldham took the lead with an early breakaway goal by Garwood and although Ford netted a penalty after Busby's header was fisted clear, the Maroons were unable to convert their undoubted superiority into goals.

Nothing was going right for the beleaguered Bobby Seith and, although there had already been rumblings of discontent on the terraces, this turned into open revolt when Aberdeen won 4-1 at Tynecastle on October 5th. For many supporters it was the last straw and, after the game, there were noisy demonstrations behind the stand.

Since the early 1960's, attendances in Scotland had fallen steadily. There had been frequent discussions on league reconstruction but these had always been blocked by smaller clubs and clandestine meetings by Scotland's "big six" of Rangers, Celtic, Hearts, Hibs, Aberdeen and Dundee had brought the threat of a breakaway league. Finally it was agreed that a 10-10-14 set-up would start in season 1975-76 and with a place in the new 10-club Premier League at stake, the Tynecastle manager and board were under great pressure. Hearts had now gone 10 games without a win and it was little surprise when Bobby Seith announced his resignation on October 11th.

In the wake of Seith's departure, the Maroons crashed 5-0 to Dundee United at Tannadice. Now they were bottom of the league with only two points from their first seven games and even this early, it appeared Hearts might struggle to get into the Premier League.

Heart of Midlothian F.C. 1974-75 - (BACK, left to right) - Rab Prentice, John Gallacher, Jim Cant, David Graham, Kenny Garland, Jim Cruickshank, Roy Kay, Ian Sneddon, Jim Brown, Dave Clunie. MIDDLE - Donald Park, Ralph Callachan, Eric Carruthers, Alan Anderson, Jim Jefferies, David Dick, Drew Busby, Billy Bennett, Willie Gibson. FRONT - Alan Wilson, John Stevenson, Kenny Aird, Gordon Welsh, Tommy Murray, George Donaldson, Sandy Burrell.

DC Thomson

Chapter Nine

PREMIER LEAGUE BLUES

The Tynecastle board announced their intention to advertise the post and, following an abortive attempt to lure Jim McLean from Dundee United, over 60 applications were received. However, a 2-1 win over Airdrie at Tynecastle and draws against Rangers (h) 1-1 and Ayr United (a) 3-3 tripled Hearts pointage since the Tannadice rout and on November 7th, interim boss John Hagart (36), who had been Hearts coach for the past two years was appointed manager. "Never in my wildest dreams did I think I would get the chance to manage Hearts", said the delighted Hagart, who had played for Berwick Rangers and Luton Town and was an SFA staff coach at Largs.

John Haggart - made a bright start at Tynecastle.

On November 9th, Ralph Callachan netted the winner in a 2-1 home win over Dumbarton as Hearts finally moved off the basement where only four points separated the bottom 13 teams. Hagart quickly realised that experience was vital for the cut-throat battle for a Premier League place and the return of Jim Cruickshank, Dave Clunie and Alan Anderson, who was now recovered from a broken cheekbone, helped steady things and the next 15 league games brought just a single defeat.

Gradually, Hearts edged up the table and by the end of 1974, they lay eighth. The New Year derby with Hibs attracted a crowd of nearly 37,000 and although Donald Ford almost broke the deadlock when he hit the post in the dying minutes, the match ended 0-0. Nevertheless, the steady progress continued and on March 1st, only a last minute Tommy McLean goal for title-chasing Rangers gave Hearts their first defeat in three-and-a-half months. That month, Eric Carruthers, who was no longer in the first team plans, was allowed to join Derby County for £25,000 and by then, Hearts had also reached the last eight of the Scottish Cup after defeating Kilmarnock 2-0 at Tynecastle then Queen of the South by a similar scoreline at Palmerston.

Now Dundee, who lay just two points above them in the table, stood between Hearts and a second successive semi-final place. With both teams doing well, over 27,000 fans turned out at a sun-bathed Tynecastle. Hearts fielded - Cruickshank; Kay, Anderson, D. Murray, Jefferies; Clunie, T. Murray, Callachan; Busby, Ford, Gibson. Subs. Brown, Park. Dundee - Allan; Wilson, Stewart, Ford, Gemmell; Hoggan, Anderson, Robinson; Gordon, Wallace, J. Scott. Subs - Johnston, I. Scott.

After just three minutes, Jim Cruickshank saved a Jocky Scott penalty and soon afterwards Hearts early pressure was rewarded when Tommy Murray cracked home the opener from the edge of the box. Dundee hit back only to find Don Murray a defensive colossus but with just minutes remaining of a fast open game, Gordon Wallace headed a last-gasp equaliser from a free kick. Jim Brown replaced Roy Kay for the Dens Park replay while Dundee brought in Bobby Hutchinson for former Maroon, Alan Gordon, who, remarkably, had now played for all four senior clubs in Edinburgh and Dundee.

In 25 minutes, Hearts came close when a powerful Busby header was swept off the line by Wilson but within six minutes, Hearts trailed 2-0 following goals by Stewart and Hutchinson. Soon afterwards, Ralph Callachan netted from the spot when Donald Ford was stretchered off with an ankle injury after being downed in the box and just seconds from the interval, Busby rose to head the equaliser. After the break, Hearts piled on the pressure but it was Dundee who scored, Gordon Wallace springing Hearts offside trap for Bobby Robinson to net the winner.

It had been a pulsating struggle which neither side had deserved to lose but Hearts took eight points from their eight remaining games to finish eighth and qualify for the Premier League, albeit just four points above 11th placed Airdrie. Just as significantly, there was a new name on the League Championship trophy for Rangers had finally ended nearly a decade of Parkhead domination.

Last term, John Hagart's enthusiasm and tactical knowledge had helped guide Hearts from bottom of the table to a position of respectability. However, a no scoring draw with the unknown F.C. Roda of Holland and a 2-0 defeat by Arsenal in pre-season friendlies at Tynecastle did little to suggest that things might be better this time around.

For the second successive season, Hearts were placed in the same League Cup section as Aberdeen with Celtic and Dumbarton the other clubs involved. However, the Maroons got off to a bad start, unexpectedly losing 2-1 at First Division Dumbarton, whose Boghead ground was something of a footballing backwater where the Edinburgh side rarely did well.

Expectations were that bit lower for the home clash with Celtic a few days later but the unpredictables in Maroon bounced back with a 2-0 victory. In 15 minutes, Steve Hancock raced in to score after Latchford fumbled a Brown shot and, soon afterwards, Jim Cruickshank saved a penalty from McCluskey. Hearts were playing with great spirit and, near the end, Donald Ford clinched matters with a second from the penalty spot after being brought down by McGrain.

Now nearing 32-years-old, Ford was a veteran compared to the youthful Hancock but the pair scored again in a 2-1 win at Aberdeen, a result which set up a crucial clash with Celtic at Parkhead. There, Hearts got an early shock when Glavin netted after just 90 seconds and despite a brave attacking performance, they finally went down 3-1. The

Braveheart - Hearts centre-half John Gallacher is in the thick of the action as he heads clear from Bobby Lennox of Celtic. Others involved are Celtic's Ronnie Glavin, Joe Craig and Roddy MacDonald. Jim Brown, Jim Cruickshank and Roy Kay are the men in maroon. DC Thomson

Tynecastle club went on to win their remaining two games but they were unable to prevent Celtic progressing to the quarter-finals.

Up front, Ford was now struggling to overcome injury but Hancock had made an impressive start with three League Cup goals. Dave Clunie had been in top form at right-back while the commanding Don Murray, who was again partnered by Alan Anderson in central defence, was given the captaincy. After years as back-up to Jim Cruickshank, Kenny Garland had begun the new season in goal. But when the Scottish international keeper regained his place a couple of weeks later, Garland, who now also faced competition from Davie Graham, decided to quit football. The experienced Tommy Murray was another to go, leaving Tynecastle on a free transfer later that month, to join Easter F.C. in Hong Kong .

Now came the start of the long-awaited 10-team Premier League. Each club would play the others four times, but with two sides to be relegated - the original concept had been just one - many felt the penalty for failure to be too harsh. Dundee United boss Jim McLean was amongst those who had favoured a 12-12-14 format, and he predicted that the Premier League would bring an increased emphasis on defensive football.

On August 30th, Hearts made the short trip to Easter Road for their opening Premier League fixture. Under Eddie Turnbull's management, Hibs had never been out of the top four in the past three years and although Hearts again matched their rivals for effort, the Leith outfit had the edge in finesse. Stanton, Edwards and Munro were the masters in midfield and it was little surprise when Joe Harper grabbed the only goal of the game for Hibs.

Hearts fared little better in their next game, losing 2-0 to Rangers at Tynecastle where central defenders Alan Anderson and Don Murray both conceded own goals in the first half-hour of the game. However, a morale-boosting 3-2 win over Dundee at Dens was followed by draws against Aberdeen and Motherwell and home wins over Dundee United and Ayr before another two points from St Johnstone in Perth left Hearts second alongside Hibs, Rangers and Motherwell by the start of November. League leaders Celtic lay just one point ahead but with 10 games played, the competitiveness of the new league setup was evident with ninth-placed Aberdeen just four points behind the Maroons.

After five years, the Texaco Cup was no more after Texaco ended their sponsorship but a new tournament, the Anglo-Scottish Cup had emerged instead. In the opening round, Hearts beat First Division Queen of the South 6-3 on aggregate to earn a match against Fulham, who featured former England international stars Bobby Moore and Alan Mullery. Willie Gibson netted twice as Hearts went down 3-2 in the first leg at Craven Cottage but with only one goal between the sides, a crowd of 14,000 turned out for the Tynecastle return on October 1st.

In 21 minutes, things looked bleak when Slough put Fulham ahead but Jim Jefferies quickly pulled one back with a stunning drive from 25 yards. Shortly afterwards, Willie Gibson nodded in a Prentice cross to make it 3-3 on aggregate but although Hearts - with Prentice in dazzling form - besieged the Londoners, the decisive third goal was not forthcoming. With extra-time looking likely, Scrivens was downed by Jefferies five minutes from time and from the resultant penalty, Alan Mullery blasted home the winner for Fulham.

Nevertheless, Hearts were playing well and, although a last-gasp counter by Pat Stanton denied them a Tynecastle derby win over against Hibs, two first-half goals by Willie Gibson earned a 2-1 win over Rangers at Ibrox on November 8th. In a settled side, Jim Cruickshank's fine form in goal was reflected by a Scotland recall against Rumania while the back four comprised Clunie, Anderson and Murray with Jefferies or Kay on the left. Brown, Busby and Callachan formed the midfield with either Aird or Park, Gibson and Prentice up front.

At the end of the year, Hearts remained fifth, four points behind the leaders Celtic but, with the exception of luckless St Johnstone who remained anchored at the bottom of the table, it was clear that there was little between the teams in the new ultra-tight Premier League.

However, a 3-0 Ne-erday defeat by Hibs at Easter Road prompted Hearts to pay £20,000 for the powerful Dunfermline striker Graham Shaw (25), but although the newcomer was on target in his debut against Dundee, his goal was the only consolation in a 4-1 defeat at Dens.

After a sticky spell in January, the Maroons got back on the rails with a Scottish Cup replay win over Clyde at Shawfield. The Bully Wee had recovered from a two-goal deficit to draw 2-2 at Tynecastle but with only a minute of the replay remaining, the ever-alert Willie Gibson pounced on a half-hit shot by Jim Brown to guide the ball past Cairney. A Busby double and another from Callachan ensured a comfortable 3-0 home win over Stirling Albion in the fourth round to set up a quarter-final tie against First Division Montrose who were currently third top of the First Division, having earlier conquered high-flying Hibs in the League Cup quarter-finals.

However, Hearts had not tasted victory in their seven league games since New Year and, along with Aberdeen, Dundee, Dundee United and Ayr United, they now found themselves deeply involved in the struggle to avoid the drop. By then, John Gallacher had replaced Alan Anderson at centre-half and on February 28th, some vital respite was gained when Willie Gibson netted in a 1-0 win over relegation favourites Ayr United at Tynecastle.

On March 6th, Montrose gave Hearts a shock at Links

Power play - Hearts striker Drew Busby thunders a penalty kick high into the net past St Johnstone keeper Derek Robertson in this Premier League clash at Tynecastle. DC Thomson

***Hampden hoodoo** - Jim Jefferies and keeper Jim Cruickshank were defensive stalwarts but this time they were too late to prevent Derek Johnstone scoring his second goal for Rangers in the 1976 Scottish Cup Final at Hampden.* DC Thomson

Park. Former East Fife and Aberdeen winger Bertie Miller was a constant menace with his darting runs and seven minutes after half-time, Lowe took advantage of a defensive slip to put Montrose ahead. Two minutes later, the sides were level when Dave McNicoll backheaded a long throw past Cruickshank but 19 minutes from time, Montrose regained the lead through Stewart. In desperation, Hearts threw everything forward and with less than 60 seconds remaining, Graham Shaw got on the end of another long throw to head a dramatic last gasp equaliser.

Three days later, over 16,000 saw the Tynecastle replay and once again Montrose took the initiative. With quarter of an hour on the clock, Bertie Miller beat two men on the right before setting up Johnston for the opener and 90 seconds later, the winger was brought down in the box by Gallacher before Les Barr made it 2-0 from the penalty spot. There was no quarter asked or given in a fiercely competitive game and following a clash with burly Montrose defender Dennis D'Arcy, Hearts striker Drew Busby was taken to hospital with a broken nose.

At half-time, Hearts were booed from the field but a tremendous fightback saw Graham Shaw pull one back in 65 minutes. It had been a tension packed thriller and with five minutes remaining, a crude D'Arcy foul on Park proved a flashpoint as a massed brawl broke out in the Montrose penalty box. When order was restored, Ralph Callachan and Jimmy Cant of Montrose were sent off for their part in the melee and Hearts were awarded a penalty.

Home fans despaired when Cammy Fraser's poorly struck kick was saved by Gorman but just on time came relief as Willie Gibson headed a dramatic last gasp equaliser from an Aird corner. The excitement continued throughout extra-time but there was no further scoring. The second replay at Muirton Park before a crowd of 10,000 provided yet another enthralling encounter for the fans. Once again, Hearts came from behind to level through Shaw and they were somewhat fortunate to remain level after 90 minutes. In extra-time, the tie remained finely balanced until a finely judged 20-yard lob by Ralph Callachan left Gorman stranded and that was enough to send Hearts into the last four alongside Rangers, Motherwell and Dumbarton.

March 27th, 1976

	P	Pts
Aberdeen	**29**	**27**
Hearts	**29**	**26**
Dundee	**29**	**25**
Dundee Utd	**27**	**24**
Ayr United	**28**	**24**
St Johnstone	**28**	**6**

Once again, the Maroons were paired with lower league opposition, this time former League Cup foes Dumbarton, and their cup hopes were boosted when a vital relegation match against Dundee at Tynecastle resulted in a 3-0 win to leave them sixth although still within two points of the secondbottom relegation spot.

On April 3rd, a crowd of 16,087 turned out at a chilly, rain-swept Hampden for the Scottish Cup semi-final with

Dumbarton but, surprisingly, it was the Sons who held the edge with Jumbo Muir and Hughie McLean controlling midfield for long spells. In addition, Hearts had found the nippy red-headed Ian Wallace a constant threat up front but although Cruickshank had to pull off a couple of excellent saves, the Maroons survived a no-scoring draw.

Meanwhile, with seven league games remaining and their Premier fate still in the balance, Hearts won 3-0 at struggling Aberdeen before a 2-1 home defeat by Motherwell again left them within three points of second bottom place.

Willie Gibson was recalled for the midweek replay against Dumbarton and with Roy Kay and Ralph Callachan quickly stamping their authority on midfield, Hearts went ahead when Walter Smith spectacularly headed a Kay cross into his own net after eight minutes. This time, Wallace was effectively shackled and further scores by Rab Prentice and Drew Busby ensured Hearts would return to Hampden for the Scottish Cup Final on May 1st.

Three days later, Hearts were brought back to earth when they lost 2-0 to Dundee United in a vital basement clash at Tannadice and with four games remaining, the Gorgie side lay just one point ahead of ninth placed Dundee who had played a game more. However, on Wednesday, April 21st, Donald Park grabbed the winner in a tension-ridden match against fellow strugglers Ayr United at Somerset Park and with nerves again very much in evidence, only a last minute own goal by Bobby Thomson brought another 1-0 win over the long-since doomed St Johnstone a few days later.

That took Hearts to the 32 point mark and, although they went on to take three points from their remaining two games, their superior goal difference had meant they were already safe. Aberdeen, Dundee United and Dundee all finished on 32 points and it was the Dark Blues who took the drop on goal difference.

Now the Tynecastle men, whose cup run had required four replays against First Division sides, could concentrate on the Scottish Cup Final against Rangers. Don Murray and Dave Clunie had been automatic choices in defence until both were injured in March. Their places were taken by Roy Kay and 20-year-old Sandy Burrell but there was no place for another promising youngster, Cammy Fraser, as Hearts lined up - Cruickshank; Brown (capt), Gallacher, Kay, Burrell; Callachan, Shaw, Jefferies; Busby, Gibson, Prentice. Subs. Aird, Park. Rangers - McCloy; Grieg (capt), Forsyth, Jackson, Miller; McLean, Hamilton, MacDonald; Johnstone, Henderson, McKean. Subs.- Jardine, Parlane.

There was a crowd of 85,250 at kick off but Hearts got off to a dreadful start, conceding a goal after just 42 seconds. In the first tackle of the game, Jim Jefferies brought down Derek Johnstone and when Tommy McLean floated over the free-kick, the big striker headed past Cruickshank for his 30th goal of the season. In 15 minutes, neat interpassing between Shaw, Callachan and Brown gave Prentice a chance at the far post but the winger lifted the ball over the bar. However, Hearts were living dangerously and just before half-time, Alex. MacDonald met a headed clearance by Gallacher to volley through a ruck of players and the Maroons were 2-0 down.

After the interval, John Hagart brought on Kenny Aird in place of Sandy Burrell, who had been booked, with Jim Jefferies dropping back into defence. Now Hearts threw caution to the winds but although John Greig was forced to clear off the line, John Gallacher twice did likewise at the other end and both teams struck the bar. In 63 minutes, Park replaced a surprisingly ineffectual Gibson but it was no real surprise when Derek Johnstone converted a Bobby McKean cross to make it 3-0 with nine minutes remaining.

Graham Shaw pulled one back soon afterwards, but that was no more than a consolation. Crucialy, Hearts had got their tactics wrong, for, despite their first-half wind advantage, they had been reluctant to push forward and in the end, they were well beaten by an Ibrox side who had taken their first domestic treble since 1964. However, Jim Brown - watched by Notts County earlier in the season - had been outstanding while Cruickshank, Gallacher, Kay, Callachan, Busby and Aird all performed valiantly.

Now 35-years-old, Alan Anderson announced his retiral while that other grand servant, Donald Ford, who had been plagued by injury, was given a free-transfer along with Steve Hancock and Davie Graham, John Stevenson having been released some months earlier. However, with contract rebel Jim Cruickshank again in dispute over wages and his inability to secure a well-deserved testimonial, Graham accompanied Hearts on their close season World tour.

No chance - Donald Park breaks through the Motherwell defence to leave former Scotland keeper Ally Hunter helpless in this Premier League game at Fir Park. **DC Thomson**

Well done - Hearts boss John Haggart congratulates Willie Gibson after his dramatic winner against Locomotiv Leipzig. Daily Record

Despite the glamour of reaching the Scottish Cup Final, Hearts had had a dangerous flirtation with relegation and surprisingly their only new signing was goalkeeper Brian Wilson on a free transfer from Arbroath, whose first choice was none other than old Tynecastle favourite Gordon Marshall. Nevertheless, the 1976-77 season started brightly as Hearts qualified from a League Cup section comprising Motherwell - fourth in last season's Premier, newly promoted Partick Thistle and relegated Dundee.

Goals by Drew Busby and Willie Gibson within an eight minute spell soon after the break got Hearts off to a 2-0 win over Dundee at Tynecastle. It was a scoreline that might have been greater had it not been for keeper Thomson Allan, who saved a first half penalty by Busby and pulled off a string of brilliant stops.

The Maroons followed that up with 2-0 wins away to Partick Thistle and at home to Motherwell and there was now a new confidence around Tynecastle. There was plenty of spirit about the side with powerful performers like Jim Jefferies and Drew Busby complementing the flair and industry of Ralph Callachan and Donald Park and the scoring ability of Willie Gibson. The crowds were returning to Tynecastle and 12,000 fans witnessed an exciting 3-3 draw with Thistle before a magnificent 4-1 win over Motherwell at Fir Park put Hearts in an unassailable position at the top of the section.

Although much encouraged by their League Cup showing, the Tynecastle side had to be content with three successive league draws which included visits to Pittodrie and Parkhead. Then, an inspired performance by Graham Shaw saw Hearts take a major step towards the League Cup semi-final by defeating Falkirk 4-1 at Tynecastle on Wednesday, September 22nd.

The Brockville return should have been a formality but it was was to prove a costly evening for the Maroons. Sixteen minutes from the end, Ralph Callachan was stretchered off with a bad knee injury and Hearts conceded two late goals to go down 4-3 although they progressed to the last four 7-5 on aggregate.

However, it was the loss of the creative Callachan, who would be out of action until December, which would prove highly significant. In September, the midfield schemer had been a key man in the European Cup Winners' Cup first round win over Lokomotiv Leipzig. After conceding two early goals, the Maroons had survived a late penalty miss by Lok to return from East Germany 2-0 down, but it had proved a different story before 18,000 at Tynecastle on September 29th.

In 12 minutes, Roy Kay pulled one back with a cracking 20-yard shot and Willie Gibson levelled the aggregate score quarter of an hour later. Near half-time, the home fans were silenced when Fritche blasted home a cross and with away goals counting double in the event of a draw, Hearts now required two goals to win the tie.

However, with Callachan prominent, Hearts maintained their pressure and, 16 minutes from time, they got the breakthrough. A finely-judged chip by Jim Brown made it 3-3 on aggregate and 60 seconds later, Drew Busby headed them in front. Now Tynecastle was in a ferment and, five minutes from time, Willie Gibson capped one of the most sensational nights in the club's history with a fifth goal. It had been an unforgettable night of drama and at the end, hundreds of exultant fans poured on to mob the players an action which later cost Hearts 1000 Swiss Francs.

In the second round, the Maroons again conceded an early goal, this time to SV Hamburg in the first leg in West Germany. Drew Busby headed the equaliser in 15 minutes but in the end Hearts, by then without the artistry of Callachan, could have few complaints at their 4-2 defeat. Crucially, the Edinburgh side had lost the fourth goal in the dying minutes but with two away goals they still remained hopeful of overturning the deficit on November 3rd.

Backed by a 25,000 crowd, Hearts went all out for an early goal but their fans were stunned when Eigl scored in 11 minutes, Magath making it 6-2 on aggregate shortly before half-time. The Maroons tried to power their way back but made little headway against the super efficient Germans. Willie Gibson did pull one back but it was a disheartened home side who trudged from the field after going down 4-1 for an 8-3 aggregate defeat.

Nine nights earlier, the Maroons had faced Celtic in the League Cup semi-final at Hampden. They had fielded - Wilson; Brown, Gallacher, Clunie, Kay; Fraser, Shaw, Busby; Park, Gibson, Prentice. Subs. Jefferies, Cant. Celtic - Latchford; McGrain, Edvaldsson, MacDonald, Lynch; Doyle, Aitken, Callaghan; Dalglish, Glavin, Wilson. Subs - McCluskey, Lennox.

Right from kick-off Hearts took the game to Celtic and three minutes from the interval, Willie Gibson accepted a Drew Busby cross with his back to goal to set up the oncoming Jim Brown who shot low past the diving Latchford. Sixty seconds later, a lack of concentration in defence allowed Kenny Dalglish to head the equaliser and although Hearts continued to battle all the way, Celtic were awarded a controversial penalty 18 minutes from the end.

Celtic's Scottish international striker Kenny Dalglish appeared to hold back John Gallacher at the junction of the penalty box and byeline, and Hearts players were stunned when referee Hugh Alexander pointed to the spot.

Dalgish made no mistake with the penalty and almost immediately Rab Prentice was ordered off for a bad tackle on Johnny Doyle. Mayhem then broke out amongst the players and Danny McGrain and Graham Shaw were booked for their part in the ensuing fracas.

Sadly, there was no way back for Hearts, whose early Premier form had been unconvincing with two defeats and six draws from their first eight games but on November 10th, a Jim Jefferies double finally ensured their first league victory with a 2-1 home success over Aberdeen.

Then came three successive defeats including a 4-3 reverse to Celtic at Tynecastle where a Willie Gibson hat-trick had given Hearts a 3-2 lead until the loss of two late goals. In December, Jim Cruickshank regained his place from Brian Wilson while 19-year-old Cammy Fraser established himself in midfield. Every point was now a prisoner in the highly competitive Premier League but narrow wins at Ayr and at home to Motherwell then a draw at Tannadice, left Hearts in sixth position by the end of 1976.

More than a few managers were now voicing their criticism of the Premier set-up where a couple of defeats could plunge a club from near the top of the table straight into the relegation struggle. However, Hearts boss John Hagart had few complaints, "The quality has suffered because there are only ten teams but I'm reasonably satisfied with the way things are."

On January 3rd, Hearts went down 4-1 to Aberdeen on a bone-hard Pittodrie pitch where John Gallacher was given a torrid time by Dons hat-trickster Joe Harper. Hearts and Aberdeen were clubs of similar stature but in recent months, the Dons - managed by the exhuberant Ally McLeod - had ambitiously spent £180,000 on talented performers like Joe Harper, Stuart Kennedy, Jim Shirra, Ian Fleming and Dom Sullivan. They had been transformed from relegation strugglers to genuine title contenders and had won the League Cup Final against Celtic in November. Hearts, on the other hand, had failed dismally to invest in players and, increasingly, had the look of a club going nowhere.

On February 5th, a Willie Gibson hat-trick helped achieve a 4-0 home win over struggling Kilmarnock but it would be another dozen games before Hearts next paid a Premier League winning bonus. For some months, it had been obvious that the team required strengthening but soon afterwards Tynecastle fans were stunned to learn that the talented Ralph Callachan, described by many critics as Hearts most creative youngster since the days of Dave Mackay and Alex. Young, had been transferred to Newcastle United for £90,000.

The move brought a storm of protest but Hearts chairman Bobby Parker explained that Callachan had wanted a transfer and the club felt unable to stand in his way. That was not an angle which *Sunday Mail* journalist and long-time Hearts fan John Fairgrieve could readily accept and he was scathing in his comments, "No doubt the board are good men and true but they are strongly lacking in imagination and are presiding over the decline of a great club."

In the aftermath of Callachan's departure, Hearts struggled to three successive league defeats but, by the end of March, they had reached their second semi-final of the season. In the first round of the Scottish Cup, old cup rivals Dumbarton had scored a late equaliser at Tynecastle and it had taken an extra-time goal by Willie Gibson to eliminate the Sons at Boghead.

At the next stage, a Davie Cooper-inspired Clydebank caused plenty of problems until Drew Busby headed the only goal of the game midway through the second half. The quarter-final draw paired Hearts with yet another First Division side, East Fife, and the Maroons struggled to cope

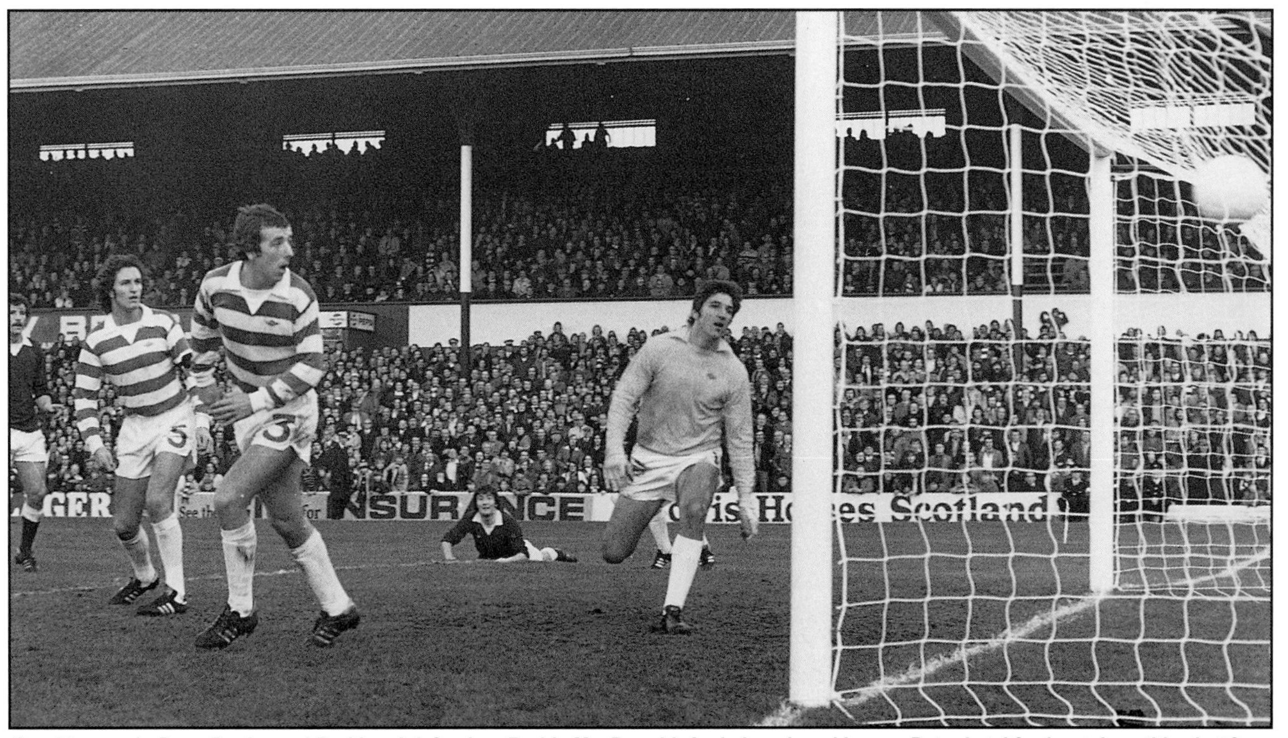

Cracking goal - Drew Busby and Parkhead defenders Roddy MacDonald, Andy Lynch and keeper Peter Latchford watch as this shot from the grounded Rab Prentice sails into the Celtic net. DC Thomson

with former team-mates Harry Kinnear and Kevin Hegarty in a disappointing 0-0 draw at Tynecastle. In the replay at Methil, Hearts survived the loss of an early goal to lead 2-1 at half-time and, although Gillies equalised, John Gallacher put them through to the last four when he headed home a Park cross six minutes from time.

Despite their cup progress, a lack-lustre Hearts had taken just two points from their seven league games since beating Killie and, with their confidence at a low ebb, Ayr United winger Malcolm Robertson was signed for a fee of £25,000 in March just before the transfer deadline.

Rangers, by their own standards, were having a miserable season and the Hampden semi-final was a dour affair. Hearts, who were 5/1 underdogs, looked particularly bereft of ideas and once Jackson broke the deadlock in 67 minutes, there was no way back with Sandy Jardine adding a second from the penalty spot towards the end.

March 26th, 1977

	P	Pts
Partick This.	**28**	**25**
Motherwell	**25**	**23**
Ayr United	**28**	**22**
Hearts	**28**	**20**
Kilmarnock	**29**	**14**

Now, Hearts could fully concentrate on their Premier League predicament for, with just eight matches remaining, they lay second bottom, six points above an almost certainly doomed Kilmarnock. On April 2nd, Donald Park received a second booking for deliberate handball and was ordered off as Hearts crashed to a disastrous 3-0 defeat against Celtic at Tynecastle. Now, the Maroons faced their most vital match of the season at home to Ayr United, who, after recently taking full points at Tannadice and Pittodrie, held a four point advantage.

Amidst an atmosphere of great tension in the 11,500 crowd, Hearts got off to the worst possible start when the unmarked Crammond headed home after four minutes. The Maroons lacked the composure and craft of hard-hitting Ayr but just before half-time, their spirited efforts paid off when Jim Brown thundered a 25 yard shot past Sproat. After the break, Ayr regained the lead through an equally good goal by Walker McCall and although Hearts came close, they were unable to retrieve the situation. It was a miserable evening for the home support, made even worse when Malcolm Robertson was ordered off for retaliation on former team-mate Jim McSherry in the dying seconds.

The writing was on the wall for Hearts and thousands of fans were posted missing as Rangers won 3-1 before a Tynecastle crowd of only 12,500 a few days later. That left Hearts six points behind eighth-placed Motherwell and when the Gorgie men could only manage 2-2 draws at home to Hibs and away to Kilmarnock, they found themselves relegated for the first time in their proud 104 year history.

Those were sad times indeed for Hearts for John Harvey and the legendary Willie Bauld - great servants to the Tynecastle club - had both died in early March. And now, instead of meeting top class opposition like Celtic, Rangers and Hibs, the once mighty Hearts faced trips to footballing backwaters like Alloa, Montrose and Methil.

For too long, Hearts had been no more than honest toilers and, despite John Hagart's continuing faith in his players, there was a distinct lack of class at Tynecastle. Only 49 goals had been scored but, more significantly, the previously reliable defence had too often looked vulnerable in conceding 66 league goals.

On April 19th, John Haggart resigned under pressure from the directors. However, many believed that he was merely the scapegoat for some glaring boardroom blunders - noteably the sale of Ralph Callachan, whose composure would have been invaluable at a crucial stage of the season. But, although clearly upset, Hagart would only comment, "I think too much of the club to say anything."

It had not been a sudden collapse for Hearts had been in decline for some 12 years and the directors had to accept their share of the blame. Repeatedly, top stars had been sold with the board failing to reinvest in quality players to exploit the potentially massive Hearts support.

Towards the end of 1976, Hearts had released Jimmy Cant and Don Murray but now in a massive end of season clearout, a further 14 players including the long-serving Jim Cruickshank, Dave Clunie, Kenny Aird, Roy Kay, Brian Wilson, George Donaldson and Sandy Burrell were given free transfers, as the Tynecastle paying staff was reduced to just 18 full-time players.

Farewell - Jim Cruickshank prepares to leave Tynecastle for the last time after nearly 17 years with Hearts. **DC Thomson**

Chapter Ten

A DOWNWARD SPIRAL

On **May 5th,** Willie Ormond (50), was appointed manager at Tynecastle after resigning as Scottish international team boss, a post which he had held since 1973. Unlike his predecessor, the likeable Ormond had played at the highest level with Hibs and Scotland. He had also been a managerial success with St Johnstone and Scotland, who he had led to the World Cup Finals in 1974 before receiving the O.B.E. for his services to football the following year.

Hearts were installed as promotion favourites along with demoted Kilmarnock and Dundee. Last term, the Dens Park side had failed to gain promotion and it was more than a touch ironic that they and Hearts, who were amongst the originators of the Premier League, both now found themselves in Division One. Following the departure of Jim Cruickshank and Brian Wilson, one of Willie Ormond's first moves was to spend £10,000 on Stenhousemuir keeper Ray Dunlop (27). However, Hearts kicked off their new league campaign with a disappointing 2-2 draw at Dumbarton and, thus early, it was clear that other teams would be all out to beat one of the biggest names in Scottish football.

On August 20th, 12,000 fans turned out for the visit of Dundee and constant home pressure paid off when Graham Shaw beat Ally Donaldson after 32 minutes. Shortly after the interval, Drew Busby thundered in a glorious 30-yarder to make it 2-0 and although the Dark Blues pulled one back late on, Hearts title challenge was back on track.

Over the following weeks, Willie Ormond fielded a virtually unchanged team - Dunlop; Brown, Fraser, Gallacher, Jefferies; Bannon, Shaw, Busby; Park, Gibson, Prentice with Lawrie Tierney and Malcolm Robertson on the fringes. And by October, Hearts lay second, two points behind Morton, after an eight game unbeaten run against Dumbarton (a) 2-2, Dundee (h) 2-1, Kilmarnock (a) 1-1, East Fife (h) 4-1, Queen of the South (a) 3-3, St Johnstone (h) 3-0, Stirling Albion (a) 4-2, Alloa (h) 1-0.

However, the Maroons then lost to Hamilton (h) 0-2, Morton (a) 3-5, Montrose (a) 1-3, Kilmarnock (h) 1-2 and East Fife (a) 0-2 and with just five points from their next eight league games, they slipped seven points behind leaders Morton and four behind Dundee by mid-November. John Gallacher would be out for a number of months with a foot injury, and with the centre of defence looking vulnerable, Willie Ormond moved quickly to sign the experienced Dave McNicoll (27), from Montrose for £10,000.

From an early stage, it had become apparent that Morton and Dundee would be Hearts closest challengers and with little between the trio, matches between them would be vital. Just days after beating Morton 3-0 at Tynecastle in the League Cup, Hearts went down 5-3 to the Greenock side in the league at Cappielow. The Maroons had struggled to control the skilful Andy Ritchie and the pacy Mark McGhee and Morton had extracted their full revenge.

Willie Ormond - Scotland boss took over at Hearts.

There was another setback when skipper Jim Brown suffered a broken leg in the home game with Kilmarnock just days before meeting Premier League Dundee United in the first-leg of the League Cup quarter final. In the second round, the Maroons had disposed of Second Division Stenhousemuir (6-0), before defeating Morton 3-2 on aggregate after second-half goals by McGhee and Ritchie set up a nail-biting finale in the second leg at Greenock. But although Dave McNicoll's experience would prove invaluable to the promotion challenge, he was was unavailable for the League Cup having already been cup-tied with Montrose.

At Tannadice, Hearts trailed to an early Billy Kirkwood goal only for Drew Busby to loop a header past McAlpine from a Jim Jefferies free kick after 22 minutes. However, a quick one-two by United's Wallace and Hegarty left Hearts trailing 3-1 at the interval and with 18 minutes remaining, Cammy Fraser, earlier booked for fouling Kirkwood, was sent off for kicking the ball into the terracing after hotly disputing a decision by referee David Syme

There was no further score but, disappointingly, severe rain and sleet restricted the crowd to just 7,500 at the Tynecastle return in mid-November. However, despite the large puddles on the pitch, it proved a fast entertaining game. United looked the more accomplished side but nine minutes after half-time, 19-year-old Walter Kidd, who had replaced Jim Brown at right-back, pulled one back.

Hearts could not match United's neat football but in the muddy conditions, their own direct style paid dividends. Just 12 minutes from the end, Busby brought the hoose down when he made it 3-3 on aggregate. And with no scoring in extra-time, the mud-spattered Ray Dunlop made a couple of tremendous saves from Narey and McAlpine to pave the way for a 4-3 penalty shoot-out triumph.

That put Hearts into the last four alongside Rangers, Celtic and Forfar and with the semi-finals held over until March, improved league form saw Hearts, with Malcolm Robertson back in place of Rab Prentice, take 11 points from six games to approach the end of 1977 in third place.

Now came three games in a hectic seven day spell over the New Year period. On Hogmanay, Eamonn Bannon emulated Willie Gibson and Drew Busby, who had both notched hat-tricks in the 7-0 demolition of Arbroath the previous week, by grabbing three in an emphatic 3-0 win over Kilmarnock at Tynecastle. On January 2nd, the Maroons followed that up with a battling 2-1 win over East Fife at Methil - a result tinged with sadness following the death of prolific scorer Jimmy Wardhaugh later that day -

and with league leaders Dundee going down 4-3 at home to St Johnstone, the stage was set for a Tynecastle showdown five days later.

That season, the fans had rallied round the side with never less than 8,000 at Tynecastle. Indeed, the last two home games against Morton and Killie had attracted crowds of over 12,000 and with Dundee also flourishing, a bumper crowd of 19,720 - still a record for Division One - passed through the Tynecastle turnstiles. Hearts stormed into attack but although Willie Gibson put them ahead in 10 minutes, Dundee hit back through the prolific Billy Pirie soon after half-time. A good run and cross by Prentice resulted in the ball deflecting off Caldwell to put Hearts 2-1 up but, 18 minutes from time, McDougall levelled for Dundee to keep them alongside Morton at the top with Hearts looking over their shoulders, just two points behind.

The Scottish Cup campaign began with a hard fought 3-2 win at Airdrie before Hearts were paired with Dumbarton for the third successive season. However, just hours before the Boghead tie, the players threatened strike action because they were unhappy about the £125 bonus on offer. The crisis was averted following a lunchtime showdown with the board but Willie Ormond was disgusted, "As professionals, they let the club and the fans down. Had they refused to play, we would have had to concede the tie and, even though it would have cost us promotion, I would have fielded reserves until the end of the season."

Dumbarton took an early lead when Fyfe lofted the ball over Hearts defensive wall for Whiteford to head past Dunlop but in 61 minutes Bannon levelled from the spot after Robertson was downed in the box. The replay, which was played on Monday, February 2nd, was a stop-start affair as the stuffy Sons repeatedly frustrated Hearts. However, they were also capable of hitting fast on the break and, seven minutes from half-time, the speedy Brian

Will o' the Wisp - the popular Willie Gibson was a deadly marksman for Hearts in the 1970's. DC Thomson

Gallacher scored after a shaky-looking Dunlop could only push a cross onto the bar. That brought a hush over Tynecastle and despite dominating the second half, Hearts were unable to equalise and the chance of a money-spinning tie against Hibs in the next round had gone.

Alarmingly, Hearts had looked short of ideas with only the clever Eamonn Bannon showing the necessary composure and, just two days later, they faced Celtic in the League Cup semi-final at Hampden. The Parkhead side were without a win from their previous six games and there were only 18,840 fans scattered around the wide open spaces of Hampden to see Hearts make a shaky start.

It was little surprise when Joe Craig finished off a jinking run by George McCluskey to put Celtic ahead after 17 minutes. And although Hearts then brought out a couple of saves from Latchford, the ever-alert McCluskey pounced on a short passback by Jim Jefferies to net a decisive second goal for Celtic just before half-time.

On that form, there was a considerable gulf between the Premier League and First Division standards and following their second cup exit in three days, the Hearts slump continued with the loss of a home point to bogy side Dumbarton. On Wednesday, March 8th, Hearts faced a real test of their title resolve when they met Morton in a vital league clash at Cappielow, a ground at which they had lost on their previous two visits. In a match littered with untidy tackles, two Morton players were booked along with Kidd, Robertson and Jefferies of Hearts and according to next day's *Daily Record*, "It was a night for brave men."

Nevertheless, the Hearts midfield of Bannon, Busby and Shaw again proved a major influence and in 20 minutes, Busby headed down a Robertson cross for Willie Gibson to beat Connaghan for the only goal of the game. Dundee remained top with 43 points from 30 games with Hearts and Morton just two points behind with respectively, one and two games in hand.

The Cappielow win had come as a tremendous morale booster but after struggling to victories at Alloa and Stirling Albion, successive draws against Montrose seriously threatened to derail Hearts promotion efforts. With six games remaining, the Gorgie men lay second, three points behind Dundee, who had played a game more. Morton were two points behind Hearts but, although they had two games in hand over the Maroons, the Greenock side had two tough games against the Dens Park side.

A planned double header at Perth and Hamilton fell through due to a waterlogged pitch at Muirton on Saturday April 1st but next day Hearts got back on track with a 2-0 win at Hamilton. After twice going behind to Arbroath, a late Busby goal earned another two points in a 3-2 win at Tynecastle to set up a tough midweek test against St Johnstone at Perth.

The Maroons were denied a legitimate penalty claim when Bobby Thomson handled in the box but goals by Bannon and Robertson ensured another 2-0 win. That put them two points clear of Dundee, who, after dropping a home point to Morton, had tumbled 2-1 at Dumbarton and three ahead of the Cappielow side who had two games in hand. Now, promotion was in sight but three days later, Hearts could only manage a 1-1 draw against Queen of the South at Dumfries. Despite dominating proceedings, it was

Magic moment - Eamonn Bannon outjumps the Arbroath defence to head the only goal at Gayfield to put Hearts back in the Premier League. DC Thomson

just after half-time when Donald Park beat three men and shot past Ball. John Brough kept the lead intact when he saved a Hood penalty but there was a late blow when Dickson netted a last-gasp equaliser for the home side.

In their penultimate game, Hearts were strong favourites to beat Alloa at Tynecastle but the Maroons found it hard to break down the well-organised Recreation Park defence. However, six minutes from half-time, Bannon whipped over a delightful free-kick and Busby's header looked net-bound before Malcolm Robertson put the Maroons ahead from close range. Ten minutes after the break, the home support were silenced when Irvine netted the equaliser but shortly afterwards Drew Busby put Hearts back in front and that was enough to keep them on course for the Premier League.

By the last day of the season on April 29th, Morton were assured of promotion with 58 points. However, Hearts who lay two points behind with an inferior goal-difference, had to win their last game at Arbroath - scene of their seven-goal triumph in December - to be certain of going up. Dundee, who lay a point behind Hearts, faced a stiffer task against First Division Champions Morton at Cappielow. However, Hearts had little margin for error for should they drop a point and third-placed Dundee win, the Gorgie side would lose out on goal difference.

Hearts made a nervy start at rain-soaked Gayfield and the home side gave as good as they got in the tense opening exchanges. Albert Kidd came close on a couple of occasions but, much to the relief of the large Hearts following in the 8,389 crowd, Eamonn Bannon rose to head home a Malcolm Robertson corner with 18 minutes on the clock.

Now the Maroons were in full cry but try as they might, a decisive second goal was not forthcoming and that made it an uncomfortable last quarter of an hour before the final whistle signalled wild scenes of jubilation. However, according to Willie Ormond, the dressing room celebrations turned from joy to great relief just seconds after the final whistle.

"When we came off the park, we thought Dundee had lost 3-2 but I almost collapsed when I found they had actually won and only Eamonn Bannon's goal stood between us and failing to go up. That's how close it really was and in the last few weeks of the season the strain on everyone was unbearable with that last day the worst I can ever remember as a club manager."

Operating with a basic squad of just 15 players, Hearts had swept to promotion with a magnificent 23 game unbeaten run stretching back to November. Willie Ormond was optimistic about their Premier League prospects in season 1978-79."Last season our objective was to get out of the First Division in a year and that target was successfully achieved. I look forward to the top ten challenge with confidence and there is no reason why we can't do well. The difference in standards between the two divisions is now very marginal but with such keen competition a good home record is essential."

Heart of Midlothian F.C. August 1978 (BACK) David Park, Willie Gibson, Ronnie McLafferty, John Brough, Ray Dunlop, Brian Stanwick, Grant Tierney, Des O'Sullivan, Cammy Fraser. MIDDLE - Bert Paton (coach), Gordon Smith, Drew Busby, Paul Rodger, Frank Liddell, Gordon Brown, Rab Stewart, Kenny McLeod, Ian Black, Eamonn Bannon, Jim Lennie. FRONT - Andy Stevenson (physio), David Scott, Bobby Prentice, Graham Shaw, Jim Jefferies, Lawrie Tierney, Malcolm Robertson, Walter Kidd, Donald Park, Willie Ormond (manager).

Now, Hearts faced a baptism of fire with an opening day clash against last season's Premier League and Scottish Cup runners-up Aberdeen at Tynecastle. Once again, Drew Busby missed the start of the season through suspension but the Maroons included the hard-tackling Frank Liddell after his £15,000 transfer from Alloa. McNicoll partnered Liddell in central defence with Jim Jefferies at left-back and Cammy Fraser moving to midfield.

In four minutes, Bannon swept the ball past Leighton after an incisive Gibson-Fraser move down the right and Bannon almost added a second when his header came back off the bar. However, Aberdeen took advantage of shaky defending to lead 2-1 at the interval and with Hearts beginning to labour, Steve Archibald added another two to make it 4-1. The Maroons then went down 4-0 to Celtic at Parkhead and a 3-2 aggregate defeat by Partick Thistle in the Anglo-Scottish Cup came as a further blow to morale.

On August 26th, Hearts managed a creditable 1-1 draw against Hibs at sun-bathed Tynecastle but the occasion was marred by mindless terracing violence. In nine minutes, Donald Park put Hearts ahead only to be dismissed on the half-hour after getting involved with McLeod. In 89 minutes, Hearts skipper Jim Jefferies, earlier booked along with Malcolm Robertson and Rab Kilgour and trainer John Lambie of Hibs, became the second player to get his marching orders for a second yellow card before controversial referee Ian Foote of Glasgow was attacked by an irate Hearts supporter.

Still the Maroons looked certain to get their first derby win in 11 games but in the second minute of injury-time, Hibs striker Ally McLeod headed the equaliser to spark a monor pitch invasion before the final whistle was blown two minutes later.

In an afternoon of shame, there had been 53 arrests with dozens more ejected but in recent years, Hearts - in common with all the other city clubs - had been dogged by the disorderly behaviour of some of their fans. The Tynecastle club had intended segregating opposing fans and erecting a £8,000 pitch perimeter fence but now these plans were expedited with Hearts also fined £5,000 by the SFA.

The Tynecastle gloom further deepened when the Maroons crashed out to Morton in the first round of the League Cup. Far from retrieving a 3-1 first leg deficit, the Cappielow return resulted in a 4-1 rout and a 7-2 aggregate defeat as Hearts failed to win any of their opening seven games and even this early, the signs were ominous.

Hearts chairman Bobby Parker expressed his concern over a planned boycott by unhappy fans but emphasised his backing for Willie Ormond. For his part, the manger was blunt, "We will find it hard to survive although we lost some bad goals today." Within a few days, former Aberdeen midfielder John Craig and the tricky Dennis McQuade arrived in exchange for the industrious Donald Park who had hardly missed a game that season. Soon afterwards, Hearts suffered another blow when they lost the experienced Graham Shaw with achilles trouble, an injury that would keep him out until March.

Nevertheless, Hearts recorded their first win in 10 games when Malcolm Robertson netted the only goal at Motherwell on September 23rd. Then, after losing 3-1 to Dundee United at Tannadice, eight points were taken from their next five games against St Mirren (h) 1-1, Rangers (h) 0-0, Aberdeen (a) 2-1, Celtic (h) 2-0 and Hibernian (a) 2-1, a record that might have been even better had Eamonn

Bannon - recently awarded his second Under-21 cap against Norway at Easter Road - not missed a late penalty against Rangers.

St Johnstone's Derek O'Connor was signed for £25,000, and the powerful striker - a lifelong Hearts fan with an impressive scoring tally at Muirton - proved an instant hit. He found the net within 60 seconds of his Pittodrie debut and Dennis McQuade later thundered home a spectacular 30-yarder to secure a 2-1 win.

On October 28th, a fit-again Jim Brown replaced Walter Kidd for the clash with Celtic at Tynecastle. Play was fast and furious with fouls galore before Drew Busby put Hearts ahead with a glorious 25 yarder just after half-time. In 65 minutes, Malky Robertson, himself the victim of some cynical fouls, was ordered off after a clash with former Maroon Andy Lynch but almost immediately Busby clinched both points with another long range effort.

Hearts were bang in form and only one change was made for the Easter Road derby against Hibs the following week. Dennis McQuade replaced the suspended Robertson as Hearts fielded - Dunlop; Brown, McNicoll, Liddell, Jefferies; Fraser, Busby, Bannon; Gibson, O'Connor, McQuade. Subs - Tierney, Craig. Hibs - McDonald; Duncan, Stewart, McNamara, Smith; Callachan, Bremner, Higgins; Rae, McLeod, Hutchinson. Subs. O'Brien, Murray.

With the crowd even more heavily policed than usual, there was little trouble. In 46 minutes, McQuade accepted the ball with his back to goal before wheeling to shoot past the helpless McDonald from 18 yards. Twelve minutes later Derek O'Connor punished a weak McNamara pass-back with a second and although Rae pulled one back late on, a 2-1 win elevated Hearts to sixth, three points behind surprise league leaders Dundee United yet still just one point above second-bottom Morton.

Willie Ormond's men were now unbeaten in five games with successive wins over three of Scotland's top sides but a series of shaky defensive displays - particularly in a 5-3 defeat by Rangers at Ibrox - brought just one win from their next six games. By December 23rd, the Tynecastle club were again second bottom and with the harsh winter weather causing massive disruption to the football programme, Hearts managed just another three league games by the end of February.

Over the past two years, Eamonn Bannon (20), had developed into the outstanding player at Tynecastle, his penetrating runs from wide midfield complementing the strength and industry of Cammy Fraser and Drew Busby in the midfield boilerhouse. His form had already earned him four Scotland Under-21 caps and with excellent prospects of full international honours, there were soon a host of big English clubs making regular visits to the Gorgie ground.

With debts of around £150,000, the club's financial situation had continued to cause concern but Hearts fans were shocked when Bannon - a P.T. student at Jordanhill and a part-timer - was sold to Chelsea for a new Tynecastle record fee of £215,000 towards the end of January. It was a near carbon copy of the Ralph Callachan transfer to Newcastle two years earlier and amidst talk of an organised boycott by despairing fans, a 2-1 home defeat by St Mirren before just 5,800 fans brought vociferous demands for the resignation of Tynecastle chairman Bobby Parker.

In an effort to bolster an increasingly leaky defence, Hearts paid Dundee £15,000 for Thomson Allan and on February 24th, the former Scottish international goalkeeper played his part in a 3-2 Tynecastle win over Rangers, which despite a supposed boycott attracted 16,500 fans - only a couple of thousand less than the corresponding match in October. Early goals by Malcolm Robertson and Derek O'Connor gave Hearts a 2-0 lead only for a stunning one-two by Gordon Smith and Derek Parlane to level things after 24 minutes. However, the fired-up Maroons were not to be denied and, 19 minutes from time, Derek O'Connor brilliantly headed home a Cammy Fraser corner.

That brought O'Connor's haul to an impressive seven goals in 13 games but the other new signings, John Craig and Dennis McQuade, had been disappointing. Although clever enough, Craig lacked the physique to make any real

Spot king - Eamonn Bannon strokes home a penalty against Dumbarton in a Scottish Cup tie at Boghead. However, the classy midfielder was soon on this way to Chelsea due to the deteriorating financial situation at Tynecastle. DC Thomson

The winner - Hearts striker Derek O'Connor leaps high after heading the winning goal in a 3-2 triumph over Rangers at Tynecastle. Malcolm Robertson is on the left with Willie Gibson the other man in Maroon.

Daily Record

impact and while McQuade could be brilliant on occasion, he remained frustratingly inconsistent.

In the first round of the Scottish Cup, Hearts beat Raith Rovers 2-0 at Starks Park before meeting old adversaries Morton at Tynecastle. On March 3rd, Willie Gibson put Hearts ahead with an early penalty but despite dominating a hard physical game, the home side were stunned when Anderson headed an 86th minute equaliser. Then following an inswinging corner by Andy Ritchie, the game exploded when Hearts keeper Ray Dunlop clashed with Morton's Bobby Thomson.

As others joined the goalmouth fracas, fists and boots flew in all directions before Dunlop and Thomson were dismissed along with Morton's Roddy Hutchison and at full-time, Cappielow manager Benny Rooney was also cautioned for his angry comments to referee Brian McGinlay in the players' tunnel. With Ray Dunlop suspended and Thomson Allan already cup-tied after a previous loan-spell with Meadowbank, young John Brough came in and excelled with some splendid saves in a strictly controlled replay at Cappielow. This time Hearts made no mistake, Drew Busby heading the only goal in 53 minutes following a quickly taken free-kick by John Craig.

Hibernian barred Hearts progress to the semi-final and the Leith side were to prove a major obstacle before a crowd of 22,600 at Easter Road. In an all-action cup tie, Hibs had the better of the opening exchanges and they went ahead when George Stewart rose to head home a free kick, seven minutes from the interval. Soon after half-time, Rae made it 2-0 from 12 yards and although O'Connor narrowed the deficit, Hearts were unable to draw level.

Due to the winter backlog, 15 league games remained but, at the turn of April, Hearts took five points from successive matches against Morton (a) 2-2, strong-going Dundee United (h) 2-0 and Motherwell (h) 3-0. And although still ninth, they now lay just two points behind Partick Thistle and six behind Morton with three games in hand over the Greenock side.

On April 11th, the Maroons faced Partick in a crucial clash at Tynecastle but despite controlling the game, poor finishing was to cost Hearts dear. Midway through the first period, Doug Somner put Thistle ahead and although Hearts were unlucky when a Robertson cross hit the bar and McQuade headed narrowly past, the home support were silenced when former favourite Donald Park raced through to thump a decisive second past Thomson Allan with just three minutes remaining.

Within the next seven days, Hearts suffered 3-0 home defeats at the hands of Dundee United and Celtic and those three results were to have a devastating effect on the players' morale. Changes were made but Hearts could manage just two goals in 10 successive defeats as they crashed back to the First Division along with bottom markers Motherwell. Only 2,700 fans bothered to attend the final home game with Morton as the demoralised Maroons finished 11 points adrift of safety.

The Gorgie side's biggest failing was their tally of just 39 goals in 36 league games. Derek O'Connor had finished top scorer with eight goals from 18 league games and, perhaps, significantly, had missed the last nine games after injuring an arm in the crunch game against Partick Thistle.

Hearts had used no fewer than 29 players and, quite clearly, were a club in turmoil. Almost invitably, there was another major clearout with Jim Brown, Drew Busby, Dave McNicoll, Ray Dunlop, John Craig, Dennis McQuade, Pat McShane, Paul Rodger, Kenny McLeod, Gordon Smith and Ian Paterson all given free transfers while Bobby Prentice joined Toronto Blizzard for £8,000.

Chapter Eleven

THE TWILIGHT ZONE

Morale amongst the fans at Tynecastle was at a low ebb and with little money to spend, many wondered just where the club went from here. Chairman Bobby Parker, Alex. Naylor and Tommy Walker continued as directors with Archie Martin and Ian Watt pledging major changes at Tynecastle after being elected to the board in place of John Young and George Davis.

Willie Ormond remained as manager but there were few new faces at Tynecastle for the start of the 1979-80 season. A striker, Pat McShane and right-back Steve Hamilton arrived on free-transfers from Leicester City while former Scottish international midfielder Bobby Robinson (29), was signed for £20,000 from Dundee United, having turned down a move to Hearts from Dundee two years earlier in order to complete a University course on Tayside.

Hearts did little to impress in an Edinburgh-based preseason tourney which also involved Hibs, Manchester City and Coventry. Their best effort was a 1-1 draw with Manchester City but, along with Motherwell, Ayr United and Airdrie, the Tynecastle side remained promotion favourites, their league campaign beginning with wins against Arbroath (a) 2-1 and Ayr United (h) 4-2 before a Derek O'Connor hat-trick brought a 3-1 victory over Berwick Rangers at Shielfield.

The opening round of the League Cup saw Hearts back in action against Ayr United but this time the tables were to be turned. Despite the absence of the injured O'Connor, Hearts managed a 2-2 draw in the first leg at Somerset Park. The big striker was back for the return on September 3rd but the 6,800 Tynecastle crowd were stunned when Brian McLaughlin netted against the run of play in 20 minutes and that goal was enough to put the 'Honest Men' through to the next round.

Willie Ormond spent another £15,000 on Rangers utility player Jim Denny but although the Maroons managed 2-1 wins over St Johnstone and Clydebank, the team continued to struggle. The fans had jeered them from the field after an abysmal display against the Bankies and it was no great surprise when Hearts faltered in their next match at Kirkcaldy on September 11th.

At half-time, Hearts had led 2-1 through two Derek O'Connor headers but a poor second half performance culminated in Bobby Ford grabbing a last gasp winner for Raith. After the game, some frustrated Hearts supporters went on the rampage outside the ground and an embarrassed Willie Ormond commented, "The last thing we need right at this moment are fans like those."

Soon afterwards, Hearts returned to the transfer market to sign Queen of the South defender Crawford Boyd for £25,000 but his debut coincided with another disastrous defeat at Motherwell. Towards the end, Hearts lost two late goals and left-back Ian Black was ordered off for a second bookable offence as the Tynecastle club went down 4-2 to slip a point behind leaders Dumbarton with Airdrie and Ayr three points further in arrears.

A shaky performance by Thomson Allan resulted in John Brough taking over in goal and by the end of 1979, Hearts remained in the vanguard of the title race with 15 points from their last 12 games. There had been a fairly settled line-up of - Brough; Kidd, Liddell, Boyd, Denny or Black; Robinson, Fraser, Jefferies; Gibson, O'Connor and Robertson with Shaw and Tierney stepping in from time to time.

However, that spell had brought only five wins and little in the way of goals and excitement with the result that Hearts core support had dwindled to no more than 5,000. As a former Hibs star, Willie Ormond had always taken stick from a certain section of the fans. But in recent months, the Hearts boss had increasingly come under fire from the rank and file support and on January 5th, the criticism reached a crescendo when Clydebank departed from Tynecastle with a 3-3 draw despite a first-half hat-trick by Derek O'Connor.

John Brough - went on to appear for the Scotland Under-21 team.

Hearts remained joint top with Airdrie but performances had been poor and the writing was on the wall for Willie Ormond. Three days later, the Hearts boss, who owned a pub in Musselburgh, was dismissed due to the lack of progress being made at Tynecastle. A shocked and somewhat gaunt Ormond, who many believed had been on a top salary, declared he had been working for "sweeties" and had earned just £9,000 per annum. He denied rumours that he was unwell and went on to say the board were the worst that he had known in football, but although he pledged to take his case to an industrial tribunal, a settlement was later agreed.

However, the Hearts board were now looking to the future with chairman Bobby Parker describing the ideal profile for the new Hearts manager candidate as " A young tracksuit manager with a proven track record who can lead Hearts into a new era." Morton's Benny Rooney was one of the favourites but Ormond's assistant Alex. Rennie took over as interim boss and the Tynecastle promotion challenge was maintained with six points from their next four league games with the team also progressing to the last eight of the Scottish Cup.

A spectacular Cammy Fraser strike earned a 1-0 third round win at Alloa after the earlier game was abandoned in 51 minutes due to fog with the Second Division side leading 1-0. At the next stage, two Graham Shaw goals brought a 2-0 home win over Stirling Albion and now Hearts would return to the big-time with a quarter-final tie against Rangers at Ibrox on March 8th. In a sensational start, Tom Forsyth put through his own goal before a minute was played but although Hearts had a splendid opening 20 minutes, Rangers led 2-1 at the interval. Soon after half-time, Bobby Russell added a third and as Hearts resistance crumbled, Rangers went on to win 6-1.

Bobby Moncur - new man at the helm in March 1980.

Just seven days earlier, Carlisle manager and former Scotland international centre-half Bobby Moncur had taken over as Hearts boss. According to Moncur, whose entire playing career had been spent south of the border, "The whole atmosphere at Tynecastle suggests the club has gone to seed but I hope to bring a breath of fresh air. Hearts are not the most skilful of sides but the attitude is good and there are more good things than most people would have you believe."

In his spell as caretaker boss, Alex. Rennie had signed two wingers - Jim Docherty (23), and Paul O'Brien (17), on free transfers from Dundee United and now Bobby Moncur paid £5,000 for another wide man, Oxford United's 21-year-old Scot, Archie White.

By early April, Hearts had taken another seven points from their next five games to lie second, four points behind league leaders Airdrie with Ayr United another two points behind. Due to their extended cup run, Hearts had games in hand over their nearest challengers but on April 5th they faced a vital clash against Airdrie at Broomfield. Throughout the first half, Hearts soaked up some heavy home pressure but almost on half-time, Malcolm Robertson jinked past two defenders to set up Willie Gibson for the only goal of the game.

With just seven games remaining, Hearts were right on course for the Premier League but now they dropped three points from their next two games, drawing 2-2 with Raith Rovers at Tynecastle, where young right-back Steve Hamilton suffered a broken ankle, before losing 2-1 to Clyde at Shawfield.

Another priceless Willie Gibson goal at Muirton ensured a 1-0 triumph against St Johnstone but although Hearts might have clinched promotion against Dunfermline at Tynecastle on April 19th, they were unable to break down a stuffy Pars defence in a disappointing 0-0 draw. And with front-runners Airdrie beating Motherwell 3-1, Hearts remained a point behind with a game in hand.

Four days later, Hearts entertained lowly Berwick Rangers and once again the Maroons were badly affected by nerves. In 10 minutes, the Gorgie side went behind when a poor Denny clearance allowed Tait to put Berwick ahead and at half-time, the Hearts players were booed from the field. Graham Shaw replaced Cammy Fraser in midfield and two minutes after the restart, Frank Liddell outjumped the Berwick keeper to head the equaliser from a Malcolm Robertson corner.

In the end, Hearts had to be content with a 1-1 draw but at last the Tynecastle club were assured of promotion and now the aim was to win the First Division title. Malcolm Robertson summed up the players' feelings after the match, "The pressure on us over the past month has been immense. Nobody realised the strain we had been under until promotion was finally achieved."

With the pressure off, Hearts turned on their best performance of the season at Muirton in a 3-0 win over St Johnstone, who had just appointed Alex. Rennie as manager. In three minutes, O'Connor headed on a corner for Willie Gibson to head home. Jim Jefferies added a second before Gibson made it 3-0 from the penalty spot and only the heroics of Saints keeper George Tulloch prevented an even more emphatic scoreline.

Now both Hearts and Airdrie had 51 points although the Broomfield side remained top on goal difference. On Saturday, April 30th, 13,229 fans, Hearts best home attendance of the season, turned out for the First Division Championship decider at Tynecastle with the Gorgie side having to win to take the title. Hearts fielded - Brough; Robinson, Boyd, Liddell, Denny; Kidd; Fraser, Jefferies; Gibson, O'Connor, Robertson. Subs. - Shaw, White. Airdrie - McGarr; Erwin, March, Anderson, Rodger; Walker, Russell, McGuire; McCulloch, Clark, Gordon. Subs. - McKeown, McClymont.

The elusive Willie Gibson was a constant danger, crashing a header off the bar in 24 minutes before another attempt rebounded from a post with McGarr beaten shortly afterwards. It was an ill-tempered match which threatened to boil over and although Gibson came close on several occasions, it was centre-half Frank Liddell who did the needful, heading home the winner three minutes from time, much to the delight of the large home support.

Once the celebrations were over, Bobby Moncur took stock of the situation. In February, the skilful but inconsistent midfielder Lawrie Tierney had joined Hibs on a free-transfer. Now Graham Shaw, Ian Black, Rab Stewart, Gordon Brown, David Scott and Des O'Sullivan were amongst the eleven released and, with the out-of-favour Thomson Allan transferred to Falkirk for £5,000, just 17 full-timers remained at Tynecastle.

Across the city, there was gloom around Leith for just as Hearts were about to make their Premier return as First Division Champions, city rivals Hibernian had been relegated and there would be no Edinburgh derbies in the 1980-81 season. Behind the scenes at Tynecastle, Bobby Moncur appointed Englishman Tony Ford as his assistant with David Johnston - briefly on the Hearts playing staff in the 1960's - named as Hearts first full-time chief scout with the intention of once again concentrating on

Programme from final game shows Liddell's goal against Berwick.

Heart of Midlothian F.C. 1980-81 with last term's First Division Championship trophy. (BACK, left to right) Alfie Conn, Rab Stewart, Colin More, Craig Robertson, Ian Westwater, John Brough, Ronnie McClafferty, Gary Mackay, Frank Liddell, Jim Docherty, Jim Denny. MIDDLE - Bobby Moncur (manager), Walter Kidd, Dave Bowman, Chris Robertson, Stewart Gauld, Pat McShane, John Porter, Bobby Masterton, Scott Maxwell, Steve Hamilton, Andy Stevenson (trainer). FRONT - Archie White, Malcolm Robertson, Gordon Marr, Derek O'Connor, Jim Jefferies, Cammy Fraser, David Scott, Willie Gibson and Paul O'Brien. DC Thomson

the development of local young talent.

Moncur had no illusions over the task facing Hearts and he fully recognized that experience was vital for Premier survival. There was little money to spend for, that summer, 3,000 bench seats had been installed beneath the enclosure at the brewery side to reduce the ground capacity to 27,169. However, the battle-hardened Rangers midfielder Alex. MacDonald (32), was signed for £30,000 while Motherwell stopper Willie McVie (32), Rangers striker Chris Robertson (22), and former Rangers, Spurs, Celtic and Pittsburgh forward Alfie Conn (28), were all obtained on free transfers.

The newcomers would require a settling-in period but the early signs were far from promising with friendlies against Chelsea (h) 0-1, Newcastle (h) 1-1 and Glenavon (a) 3-3 and Anglo-Scottish Cup ties against Airdrie (a) 0-3 and (h) 3-3 draw yielding not a single win. Now, Hearts faced Partick Thistle at Firhill in their opening Premier League fixture. On paper, the opening two fixtures against seventh-placed Partick Thistle and newly promoted Airdrie looked as straightforward as Hearts could expect. But disappointingly, the Maroons lost 3-2 at Firhill before going down 2-0 to the Diamonds at Tynecastle.

On August 23rd, the deadly Derek O'Connor netted twice at Paisley in a 3-1 triumph over a St Mirren side that had finished in third place last season. Hearts had fielded the following side - Brough; Kidd, Boyd, Liddell, Jefferies; Robinson, MacDonald, Bowman; Conn, O'Connor and C. Robertson. Subs.- Gibson, More. But despite following that up with a 1-0 win at Kilmarnock, the next three league games brought just one more point by the end of September.

By then, Chris Robertson had proved his worth with four goals over the two ties as Hearts recorded a 5-2 aggregate win over Montrose in the first round of the Bell's League Cup. However, they were to progress no further. After losing 3-2 at home to First Division Ayr United, the Maroons had Frank Liddell ordered off in the Somerset Park return, where they crashed 4-0 in a humiliating 7-2 aggregate defeat.

Malcolm Robertson and Cammy Fraser had been key men in last season's title success. Fraser had netted an impressive 13 goals from midfield but after starting the new league campaign on the bench, an increasingly strained relationship with Bobby Moncur resulted in his £60,000 transfer to Dundee in early September. Robertson, too, came into conflict with the manager and after dropping out of the team, he moved to Toronto Blizzard on a free transfer in early 1981.

Ipswich left-back Peter Shields arrived for £12,500 but although Jim Jefferies replaced Crawford Boyd and Willie McVie came in for Frank Liddell in the other central defensive position, the onset of October brought further league defeats at the hands of Aberdeen, Rangers, Partick Thistle and Airdrie.

For a spell at the start of the season the forward pairing of Gibson, O'Connor and Chris Robertson had looked promising before a knee injury and subsequent operation ruled out Robertson until April. In October, 19-year-old midfielder Alex. Hamill arrived on a free transfer from Tottenham Hotspur with former Bo'ness midfielder Bobby Masterton also given his chance.

In goal, the fair-haired John Brough had performed heroics and in November, his efforts were rewarded with an Under-21 cap against Denmark at Pittodrie. That month brought draws with St Mirren (1-1) and Rangers (0-0) at home and with Morton at Cappielow where defensive deficiencies saw Hearts squander a 2-0 lead. However, on December 6th, Hearts recorded their first home league success, Alex. MacDonald latching onto a Gibson flick to stick the ball past the outrushing keeper for the first in 57 minutes before Paul O'Brien grabbed a second in a 2-0 win

Mac to the rescue - Alex. MacDonald clears off the line with Mark McGhee and Doug Rougvie of Aberdeen in close attendance. Peter Shields is grounded with Colin More on the right Daily Record

over bottom markers Kilmarnock at Tynecastle.

The following week, Hearts turned in another fine performance against Celtic at Parkhead. A Denny-Conn move culminated in MacDonald giving Hearts a sixth minute lead but once again defensive lapes proved costly in a 3-2 defeat.

Alex. MacDonald had proved the pick of the new signings and after earlier assuming the captaincy from the injured Jim Jefferies, the industrious midfielder was made skipper on a permanent basis.

In December, Hearts were dealt another blow when Derek O'Connor was forced to go part-time due to persistent knee trouble and by the end of 1980, the Tynecastle club remained ninth, four points behind Airdrie and six behind Partick Thistle. On January 1st, goals by Willie Gibson and Paul O'Brien gave Hearts a 2-0 lead in the vital relegation struggle against Airdrie at Tynecastle only to concede three in the final 20 minutes and, two days later, they went down 1-0 to struggling Partick Thistle at Firhill.

Those reverses left Hearts seven points adrift and when their next five games yielded just a single point, the Gorgie club appeared doomed. In January, Bobby Moncur's men had fared no better in the Scottish Cup against Morton at Cappielow where, inspired by the roving play of Alex MacDonald in midfield they had the lions share of the play and hit the bar through O'Brien, only to draw 0-0.

For the replay, Shields came in at right back with Hamill replacing 16-year-old Dave Bowman as Hearts fielded - Brough; Hamilton, F. Liddell, More, Hamill; Kidd, Bowman, Mackay; Gibson, McShane, G. Liddell. Subs. - Masterton, O'Brien. Hearts again started the more dangerous only to lose a kamikaze goal before half-time, a Shields clearance going straight to Ritchie and although Liddell intercepted the Morton player's cross, the centre-half was caught in possession and Tolmie netted the opener.

After the break, Archie White replaced Hamill but although a Liddell knock down was thundered against a post by Shields, Hearts were caught on the break, Jimmy Rooney crashing home from 25 yards before Thomson added a third as Morton departed with a 3-1 win before a diappointingly low 8,000 crowd.

An almost palpable gloom was settling over Tynecastle and with Derek O'Connor and Chris Robertson out through injury, Hearts signed ex-Grimsby striker Gary Liddell (27), on a free-transfer in February. However, the newcomer made no impression. The team was shuffled and reshuffled but to no avail.

In contrast to Alex. MacDonald, Alfie Conn and Willie McVie looked well past their best and, after the turn of the year, both had dropped out of the side. For the third time in five years, the once-proud Tynecastle club were doomed to relegation as they lost seven of their remaining 10 matches, including a 6-0 humiliation by Celtic at Parkhead.

It had been another nightmare season and although Hearts had twice escaped from the First Division, they were clearly not good enough for the Premier League. Hearts home league gates had averaged 7,742, considerably better than the likes of Morton, St Mirren, Partick Thistle and Airdrie, yet these clubs, all with far less potential than Hearts, had retained their Premier status and once again, Tynecastle fans wondered just where the club went from here.

On the positive side, Bobby Moncur had installed a youth scheme which would reap some rich rewards and already promising 16-year-old midfielders Dave Bowman and Gary Mackay had been given a taste of first-team football. Bowman, whose father Andy had been part of Hearts 1958 championship winning squad, had impressed with his competitive style, while the talented Mackay displayed all the skills of an old style inside forward.

In February, transfer-listed Crawford Boyd returned to Queen of the South on a free transfer while Willie Gibson, with only four goals to his credit, was sold to Partick Thistle for £10,000. Earlier, seven players - Alfie Conn, Bobby Robinson, Jim Denny, Derek O'Connor, Steve Hamilton, Pat McShane and Gary Liddell had been put on the open-to-transfer list and at the end of the season, Conn, Robinson, Denny, and Hamilton were released along with Willie McVie and Archie White.

Chapter Twelve

ENTER WALLACE MERCER

Wallace Mercer - rescued Hearts from closure in May 1981.

With debts of some £300,000, Hearts were in deep financial trouble and the implications of another spell in the First Division were dire. The club had large overheads and amidst sugestions that they might struggle to maintain full-time football and, even worse, go out of business, thousands of concerned Hearts fans and others throughout the country watched as events unfolded throughout May.

After an approach by Hearts chairman Archie Martin, city bookmaker Kenny Waugh offered £255,000 for a controlling interest but that was bettered by a £350,000 bid from a consortium involving former Hearts star Donald Ford and headed by local property developer, Wallace Mercer. On June 3rd, Mercer took control and later it was revealed that the club had been within days of closure if funding had not been found.

Soon afterwards, Martin resigned but despite his majority shareholding, Mercer contented himself with the vice-chairmanship. Edinburgh publican Alex. Naylor became chairman with Bobby Parker, Ian Watt and Bob Haig the other directors. However, it was soon clear that the new vice-chairman and Bobby Moncur were not compatible and within weeks, the former international resigned before joining Plymouth Argyle as manager.

Unsuccessful approaches were made for Dundee United's Jim McLean and Leicester City boss Jock Wallace before assistant-manager Tony Ford (36), was given the job with Walter Borthwick as coach. Money was made available for signings and, after failing with a bid for Aberdeen's Willie Gardner, Celtic centre-half Roddy MacDonald (26), was signed for a new Hearts record fee of £55,000. Experienced Dundee skipper Stewart MacLaren (28), who had just led his side to promotion, arrived on freedom of contract for £30,000 while goalkeeper Henry Smith (24), cost £2,000 from Leeds United. Leicester City midfielder Paddy Byrne (24), Rangers forward Derek Strickland (21), and Plymouth full-back Brian McNeill (25), were all signed on free transfers, with striker Gerry McCoy (20), arriving from Queens Park.

The 1981-82 season commenced with the League Cup reverting to the old sectional format. Hearts were placed alongside Aberdeen, Airdrie and Kilmarnock and the new-look Maroons made an impressive start, Chris Robertson netting the only goal at Airdrie and again in a 1-0 win over Aberdeen before 10,400 enthusiastic fans at Tynecastle. Another point was taken in a 1-1 home draw with Killie but Hearts quarter-final hopes were to dissolve with three defeats from their final three games.

Clearly, it would take time to adjust with so many new players but early optimism gave way to despair when the Maroons also failed to win any of their opening three league fixtures. On September 16th, Hearts recorded their first league win with a 2-1 home success over Hamilton Accies but they were struggling to find the net. In a highly ambitious deal, Hearts paid a new Tynecastle record fee of £110,000 for Dundee United's ex-Scottish international striker Willie Pettigrew (27), with another £55,000 spent on Tannadice midfielder Derek Addison (26).

The newcomers made their debut against Clydebank at Tynecastle with the 6,000 attendance some 40% larger than that against Hamilton. At half-time, Addison retired with a head injury but Pettigrew made his mark, beating Fallon before crossing for O'Connor to head the only goal of the game. Although playing well enough, the pacy Pettigrew drew a blank in his first four games before finally netting in the 3-1 win over St Johnstone at Tynecastle on October 7th, a result which kept Hearts third, four points behind front-runners Motherwell and Airdrie.

Roddy MacDonald and Stewart MacLaren had formed an effective partnership in central defence and Hearts contin-

Fresh blood - Stewart MacLaren, Tony Ford (manager) and Derek Strickland. Gerry McCoy, Roddy MacDonald and Paddy Byrne.

Top gun - Willie Pettigrew was signed from Dundee United for a new Tynecastle record fee of £110,000. DC Thomson

ued to do well throughout the Autumn. However, in November, Hearts slipped 1-0 at home to lowly East Stirling before drawing with Kilmarnock and Dunfermline. After failing to sign Celtic's Johnny Doyle or Willie Johnston of Rangers, the Maroons finally secured an experienced winger in the form of Peter Marinello (31), formerly of Hibs, Arsenal, Portsmouth, Motherwell and U.S. outfit Phoenix Inferno.

Marinello had little chance to shine when he came on as substitute in the 3-1 defeat at Dumbarton and now time was rapidly running out for the tactically-cautious Tony Ford. On December 5th, fifth-placed Hearts struggled to a 1-1 draw with lowly Queens Park at Tynecastle and, four days later, the manager was dismissed. Ford, who had been in charge for just five months, pointed out that Hearts were only two points adrift of second placed Ayr United. He believed too much had been expected too soon, but the board were unhappy at performances and the trend of poor results despite an outlay of nearly £300,000 on players.

There was little question that Dundee United's Jim McLean had been first-choice and with Wallace Mercer later stating that he had never seen Ford as the long-term answer, McLean's decision to sign a new long-term contract at Tannadice earlier that week seemed to have sealed Ford's fate. Alex. MacDonald was handed the duties of player-coach with Walter Borthwick continuing as coach and Wallace Mercer taking on the administrative duties.

Hearts already shaky financial position was further exacerbated by the onset of Arctic conditions and it was January 28th before their next competitive game. The resulting loss of revenue meant Hearts were unable to pay the balance due to Dundee United for Pettigrew and Addison, whose purchase they had hoped to offset by the ultimately abortive attempts to sell Peter Shields and Alex. MacDonald in September.

The ensuing furore resulted in the resignation of chairman Alex. Naylor, who claimed the board had wanted to offload the talented Dave Bowman to United - a view hotly disputed by Wallace Mercer. Morale was at a low ebb and, on January 30th, a 3-0 home defeat by runaway league leaders Motherwell left Hearts sixth in the table, 11 points adrift of the Fir Parkers and five behind second-placed Clydebank who were closely followed by Ayr United, Kilmarnock and St Johnstone.

After a 4-1 Scottish Cup win over East Stirling at Firs Park, Hearts entertained Forfar in the second round on February 13th. The Maroons dominated from the start but were unable to break down the stuffy Station Park outfit. Seven minutes after half-time, Ray Farningham sent Steve Hancock clear and the former Tynecastle striker evaded MacLaren and Shields to shoot past Henry Smith.

That proved the only goal of the game and the result came as a stunning blow to a board desperate for the extra income which a decent cup run would have generated. Many felt that it was one of the worst-ever experiences in the history of the Heart of Midlothian Football Club. *Sunday Mail* reporter and Hearts afficionado John Fairgrieve certainly agreed and went so far as to venture that Tynecastle might as well be converted to a car park!

Alex. MacDonald was appointed player-manager and, although only 2,397 fans turned out for the next match against Queen of the South, 17-year-old John Robertson made his debut as a substitute alongside elder brother Chris, and a 4-1 win kept Hearts in the promotion hunt.

On March 13th, Hearts bounced back from a 3-1 defeat at Falkirk with Willie Pettigrew contributing three in a 5-1 win over Queen of the South at Palmerston. Then after falling 2-1 at Clydebank, Alex. MacDonald returned to the side to inpire the Maroons to seven successive wins against Raith Rovers (a) 3-0, St Johnstone (h) 3-0, Hamilton (a) 2-0, Clydebank (a) 5-1, Ayr United (h) 2-1, Dunfermline (a) 2-1 and East Stirling (h) 2-0.

At last, Hearts looked to have found a better balance. In front of the dependable Henry Smith, full-backs Walter Kidd and Peter Shields both liked to move into attack, and in central defence, Roddy MacDonald's aerial power was balanced by the grit and composure of the experienced Stewart MacLaren. The hard-working midfield consisted of Irishman Paddy Byrne, Alex. MacDonald and either Derek Addison or Dave Bowman while, up front, Willie Pettigrew - scorer of four goals at Clydebank - was again to the fore.

Gerry McCoy and Chris Robertson were also getting their share of the goals and with the experienced Peter Marinello and the youthful enthusiasm of Gary Mackay to call on, second-placed Hearts, who held a three point lead over Kilmarnock with three games remaining - Dumbarton (h), Killie (a) and Motherwell (h) - looked a good bet for promotion.

However, Hearts would be without the suspended Roddy MacDonald and Walter Kidd for the crucial run-in and Brian McNeill and Alex Hamill, normally a midfielder, were brought in against struggling Dumbarton. The Sons, who had former Maroon John Gallagher at centre-half, took an early lead but headed goals by Byrne and Pettigrew put Hearts 2-1 ahead by half-time. Now, however, Hearts appeared to be seriously affected by nerves and with the speedy Raymond Blair causing havoc in defence, a second-half collapse resulted in a calamitous 5-2 defeat with the team booed from the field at the end.

That result came as a shattering blow for Killie had won 5-1 and now Hearts would be without the experienced Alex. MacDonald and Derek Addison, who were suspended, for the final two games. In came Dave Bowman and Peter Marinello with Stuart Gauld, Colin More and Gerry McCoy replacing Alex. Hamill, Brian McNeill and Chris Robertson for the vital clash against Killie at Rugby Park.

The 10,000 crowd were treated to a tough, tension-ridden affair with neither defence standing on any ceremony. No quarter was asked or given and with tempers running high, Gerry McCoy and Killie's Keith Robin were ordered off following an off-the-ball incident. In the end, Hearts had to be content with a 0-0 draw which maintained their one point lead but, despite having a goal-difference advantage of four, they faced League Champions Motherwell in their final game at Tynecastle while Killie met the bottom markers, Queen of the South.

On May 15th, the start was delayed by five minutes to allow a crowd of nearly 15,000 into Tynecastle as the teams lined up: Hearts - Smith; Gauld, More, McLaren, Shields; Byrne, Bowman, Hamill; Marinello, C. Robertson, Pettigrew. Subs. Mackay, J. Robertson. Motherwell - Sproat; McLeod, O'Hara, Coyne, McClelland; Conn, McLaughlin, McClair; Clelland, Irvine, Gahagan. Subs. Rafferty, Mackay.

Another nervy performance saw Hearts make little headway against the free-flowing Fir Parkers. It took the Maroons 20 minutes before they had a direct attempt at goal, a powerful Willie Pettigrew header being brilliantly tipped over the bar by Hugh Sproat. Seven minutes later, the huge Tynecastle support were silenced when Irvine headed home a Gahagen cross and Hearts continued to struggle, rarely putting together any concerted attacks.

Soon after half-time, there were several arrests after trouble errupted amongst frustrated home fans. In 61 minutes, Mackay replaced Hamill, who had been booked, but Hearts lacked the composure of Davie Hay's Motherwell, who had players of the calibre of Brian McLaughlin, Brian McClair and Willie Irvine. There was no further score and when it was confirmed that Killie had won 6-0 to clinch promotion by a point, dozens of disgruntled Hearts fans hurled their scarves onto the Tynecastle pitch in disgust.

Although Hearts had faltered at the death, they had shown a big improvement in the final third of the season. In the end, their poor disciplinary record allied to a lack of quality in depth had cost them dear. In a drastic cost-cutting exercise, basic salaries were reduced, physio Andy Stevenson was sacked, the reserve team scrapped and the playing staff cut to the bone with Frank and Gary Liddell, Alex. Hamill, Colin More, Derek Strickland, Brian McNeill, Pat McShane and Scott Maxwell all released, Jim Docherty and Paul O'Brien having earlier rejoined Alex. Rennie at St Johnstone.

Earlier, Hearts had backed league reconstruction proposals for a 16-12-12 set-up but when those were rejected, the Tynecastle club were doomed to another season in the First Division. A bitterly disappointed Wallace Mercer made his views plain, "Leadership must come from somewhere to prevent football clubs strangling each other." A summertime boardroom shuffle saw the arrival of Hamilton coach operator Douglas Park and Edinburgh bookmaker Pilmar Smith to replace Iain Watt and Bob Haig with Wallace Mercer diluting his shareholding to 43%.

Hearts decision to remain full-time allied to their transfer outlay had meant an operating loss of £382,873 which left them some £500,000 in debt. To relieve the pressure, Derek Addison was transferred to St Johnstone for £65,000 with the fee immediately going to the bank as major creditor. In July, the vastly experienced Sandy Jardine, who was from Edinburgh, arrived as player-assistant manager from Rangers after receiving a free-transfer.

This was now the only market available to Hearts, whose

True grit - Stewart MacLaren and Peter Shields are on their toes as keeper Henry Smith fists the ball away from the inrushing Stuart Beedie of St Johnstone at Tynecastle. DC Thomson

Anxious faces - the Hearts directors look apprehensive as they follow the play. Commercial manager Robin Fry is seated second from left at the back. In front of him to the right are Pilmar Smith, Douglas Park, Bobby Parker and Wallace Mercer.

failure to settle their outstanding transfer fees with Dundee United and Celtic had caused the S.F.A. to ban them from purchasing players until repayment was made.

In desperation, Hearts proposed selling starlets Dave Bowman and Gary Mackay as reparation to Dundee United. However, the Tannadice club already had as fine a crop of up-and-coming talent as any other Scottish side bar Aberdeen, and they offered a derisory £30,000 for each player. The offer was refused and the whole affair was to result in a further deterioration of the relationship between the clubs although Hearts were undoubtedly glad of the continued presence of Bowman and Mackay at Tynecastle.

Pre-season friendly successes at Tynecastle against Sheffield United (4-2) and Leeds United (1-0) augered well for the new campaign and, despite suffering an opening day setback at Motherwell, who were now under the management of Jock Wallace, the Maroons went on to qualify from a League Cup section which also included Forfar Athletic and Clyde.

Derek O'Connor, who had returned from loan spells at Berwick and Meadowbank, scored twice as Hearts bounced back with a 2-1 home win over Forfar before ace scorer Willie Pettigrew took advantage of sterling service from midfielder Paddy Byrne to net four in a resounding 7-1 victory over Clyde at Shawfield.

Another win at Forfar set up a section decider against Motherwell at Tynecastle where around 9,000 fans saw Hearts pile on the pressure throughout the first half. A number of chances were missed but just when it appeared that they might never score, Walter Kidd set up Alex. MacDonald who cleverly lobbed Sproat for the winner with just nine minutes remaining. That gave Hearts a two point advantage and a 3-0 home win in the final game against Clyde earned a quarter-final tie against St Mirren.

The Premier League outfit had top quality performers in Billy Thomson, Tony Fitzpatrick, Billy Stark, Frank McAvennie and Frank McDougall but Hearts looked anything but overawed in the first leg at Love Street on September 8th. In the opening stages, play swung from end to end until Willie Pettigrew collected a Byrne pass, beat Copland and thumped a great shot in off the underside of the bar with 25 minutes gone.

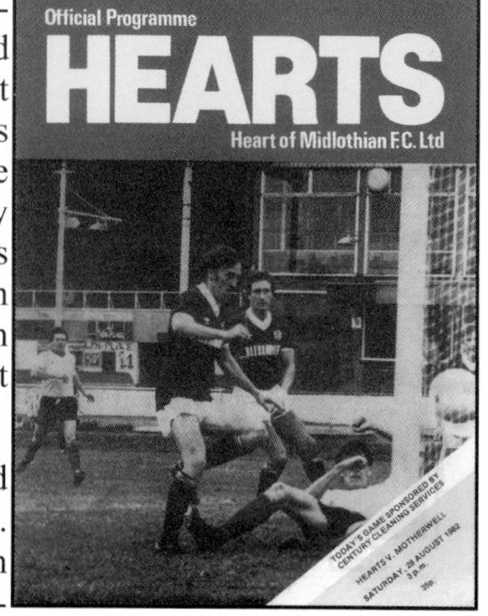

O'Connor netted a second but was adjudged offside and throughout the second half, Hearts soaked up frenzied home attacks only for Henry Smith to let a harmless looking header by Alan Logan spin beneath him for the equaliser, just eight minutes from time.

Nevertheless, it had been a fine performance. Sandy Jardine had soon settled at sweeper alongside the powerful Roddy MacDonald and the pair formed a highly effective defensive barrier. On Wednesday, September 22nd, an already intriguing Tynecastle return was given added spice when former Rangers and Scotland wing star Willie Johnston, signed on a free transfer after a summer with Vancouver Whitecaps, was listed as substitute.

There was a crowd of 12,000 at the start with Hearts, unchanged from the first leg, again recalling Stewart MacLaren, who had been out of favour since Jardine's arrival, to stiffen the vital midfield area. Hearts immediately swept into attack and, midway through the first half, Tynecastle errupted when Alex. MacDonald swerved a low shot past Billy Thomson from the edge of the box. In 66 minutes, Billy Stark nipped in to equalise against the run of play but with just 12 minutes remaining and excitement at fever pitch, the lanky Pettigrew, who had twice earlier struck woodwork, made no mistake from 12 yards.

Despite a tense finish, that was enough to take the rejuvenated Maroons, for whom the tenacious Davie Bowman had been a tower of strength, through to the last four. The draw matched them with Rangers, while Celtic met Dundee United and, by the evening of the first leg at Ibrox on October 27th, Hearts lay second, two points behind St Johnstone with just one defeat in 18 games that season.

Earlier, the meticulous Alex. MacDonald had taken his players to Glasgow to watch their opponents against

Cologne in the UEFA Cup and the value of this exercise was evident as Hearts - fielding the same 4-4-2 formation that had been so successful in the previous round - withstood unremitting Rangers pressure at Ibrox. However, Hearts lost their concentration when Davie Cooper broke the deadlock with six minutes remaining and Jim Bett made it 2-0 shortly afterwards.

Now, Hearts had it all to do in the second leg at Tynecastle. There were three changes, Gary Mackay and John Robertson replacing Alex. MacDonald and Willie Pettigrew, with Willie Johnston coming in for Stewart MacLaren. Incessant rain limited the crowd to 19,000 but although Hearts pushed strongly, they made little impression on John McLelland's well-marshalled defence.

In 20 minutes, a controversial award for handling by Shields allowed Jim Bett to score from the spot but the Willie Johnston-inspired Hearts fought, hustled and harried their way back into the game before Derek O'Connor steered the winger's low cross past Stewart shortly before the interval. However, Hearts never really looked like making further inroads into the deficit and, eight minutes from the end, the unmarked Derek Johnstone rose to head the winner for Rangers.

Nevertheless, the innovative Wallace Mercer had provided the dynamic approach so sadly lacking in previous years. A highlight of the Tynecastle quarter-final had been the half-time draw for a car, supplied by Hearts first-ever jersey sponsors, Alexanders the Ford dealers, while the semi-final featured a similar offer with the lucky programme owner winning a car and a house provided by Miller Homes. The crowds were starting to return and allied to this new commercial awareness, big inroads were being made into the outstanding debts.

Three days after their League Cup exit, a 3-0 win at Clydebank left Hearts one point behind league leaders St Johnstone with Airdrie, Clydebank and Raith Rovers still in hot pursuit and another nine points from their next five games set up a Ne'erday confrontation with the Perth side, who had gone from strength to strength under former Hearts coach, Alex. Rennie.

Nearly 14,500 saw Willie Pettigrew, who had made a scoring return with three goals in his last two games, bundle in the all-important goal in the 16th minute of a Tynecastle thriller. On January 3rd, the big striker again ensured both points in a hard-fought match at Airdrie and, a few days later, he grabbed another in a 2-1 home triumph over Hamilton in Hearts sixth successive win as they remained one point behind the Perth men with a game in hand.

That was Pettigrew's 15th goal of the season - one more than Derek O'Connor, whose power in the air made him the perfect foil for the long-striding runs of his striking partner. Unaccountably, Hearts title challenge then foundered with just one point taken from their next three matches. Those included a 1-0 home defeat by Partick Thistle, whose goal had come from former Maroon, Donald Park in the last minute. And despite a 5-1 victory over Ayr at Tynecastle and a 3-0 win over Queens Park at Hampden, Hearts again slipped up when they lost 2-1 at home to Falkirk on March 5th .

By then, Hearts had reached the quarter-final of the Scottish Cup. In the third round tie against Queen of the South at Palmerston, John Robertson and Jim Wilkie of the Dumfries side were sent off following an unseemly scuffle and only a tremendous angular drive by Peter Shields in the dying minutes earned Hearts a 1-1 draw.

The Tynecastle replay was another ill-tempered affair with Willie Johnston and two Queen of the South players receiving their marching orders. Earlier, however, the veteran Hearts winger had sent over a perfectly flighted cross for Derek O'Connor to head home and that was enough to give Hearts a Sunday tie against Second Division East Fife at Tynecastle on February 20th.

Nearly 10,000 fans saw the Maroons come from behind to level through Alex. MacDonald before a great run and cross by Paddy Byrne allowed Derek O'Connor to head the winner, 15 minutes from time. That earned a clash with Celtic at Parkhead but with only 12 minutes gone, Murdo McLeod put Celtic ahead after a Charlie Nicholas shot was parried by Henry Smith. Nevertheless, for the rest of the first-half it was Hearts who turned on the style with Derek O'Connor scraping the bar and Willie Johnston and Alex. MacDonald both hitting the post.

However, with the first half coming to a close, the underlying nastiness boiled over when Peter Shields - earlier the perpetrator of a bad tackle on Danny McGrain - was himself stretchered off with a broken leg following a crunching challenge by the Scottish international right-back.

Almost immediately, Celtic's Davie Provan fell to the ground following a long throw-in by Willie Johnston. The Hearts winger had just returned from a four-match suspension but referee Brian McGinlay, who had missed the incident, sent him off for an alleged head-butting offence on the advice of his linesman.

Soon after the interval, McGarvey added a second and, taking full advantage of their extra man, Celtic went on to win 4-1. It was the 19th dismissal of Johnston's career but he vehemently denied the charge and with a strong element of doubt, Wallace Mercer's appeal to the S.F.A. for clemency saw the winger receive just a one-game ban.

Willie Johnston - the fiery former Scotland international brought vital experience to the Tynecastle squad for their promotion push in 1982-83.

Eyes down - Sandy Jardine, seen here in a duel with Dundee's Ray Stephen, was a major influence in Hearts promotion success

Now, Hearts could concentrate on securing promotion but despite disposing of strong-going Partick Thistle and Clyde at Tynecastle, their poor disciplinary record continued with player-boss Alex. MacDonald ordered off for dissent in a 4-2 defeat by Raith Rovers at Kirkcaldy. With eight games remaining, Hearts trailed St Johnstone by two points but 2-0 wins, at Airdrie - where Willie Johnston hit the bar with a penalty - and at home to Queens Park, left them top, two points ahead of the Perth men.

That set up a top of the table clash at Muirton on April 9th and backed by a large Hearts support amongst the 7,500 crowd, the game began at a tremendous pace. Early play was punctuated by a series of fouls but two minutes from half-time, Jim Morton headed home a cross by Brannigan. Shortly after the interval, Davie Bowman took advantage of a poor punch-out by keeper Mike McDonald to make it 1-1 only for Saints to regain the lead through Blair with 20 minutes remaining.

And although Alex. MacDonald appeared to have scored a last-gasp equaliser, the whistle had already blown for full-time. Now Hearts and St Johnstone were neck and neck on 47 points and with Clydebank just three points behind with five games remaining, the championship race was again wide open.

At the start of the season, Paddy Byrne, Davie Bowman and Alex. MacDonald had formed the midfield with Gary Mackay gradually introduced to MacDonald's role of midfield general. Following Addison's departure, the red-headed Bowman had gone from strength to strength and by early 1983, Mackay had rejoined his former Salveson Boys Club team-mate as a regular in midfield.

Following his suspension, Robertson (17), who had also been at Salvesons before joining Edina Hibs, made a scoring return and soon he was an established first-team player. His darting, effervescent style of play was a constant menace to opposing defences and there were memorable hat-tricks against Queens Park at Hampden and Partick Thistle at Tynecastle. On April 16th, the wee striker scored twice in a 2-2 draw with Clydebank at Tynecastle, to leave Hearts second, four points ahead of Clydebank and Partick but still a point behind St Johnstone.

At last the Premier League was in sight but a 1-1 draw at Alloa, where Gary Mackay missed a penalty, then a 3-3 draw with relegation-threatened Dunfermline, in which the Maroons squandered a 3-1 lead following yet another treble by the prolific Robertson, left Hearts without a win from their past four games. Alarmingly, Clydebank and Partick Thistle were only two points behind and some, recalling last season's late collapse, wondered whether the players could hold their nerve this time around.

Just two points from their final two games - away to Dumbarton and at home to Hamilton - would guarantee promotion but mere mention of bogy team Dumbarton brought uneasy memories. In particular, there was last season's 5-2 debacle which had cost Hearts so dear for the Sons, especially at Boghead, had often caused problems in the past decade. Alex. MacDonald was more forthcoming, "Our players have been shielded all season but now it's time for them to show their mettle."

It was with a certain degree of apprehension that over 3,000 of the Tynecastle faithful made the trip west but Alex. MacDonald was in a positive frame of mind as he fielded an unchanged team - Smith; Kidd, R. MacDonald, Jardine, Gauld; Mackay, Bowman, A. MacDonald; J. Robertson, O'Connor, Johnston. Subs. - McCoy, Byrne.

This time, calmed by experienced campaigners like Alex. MacDonald, Willie Johnston, Sandy Jardine and Derek O'Connor, Hearts made no mistake. In 13 minutes, the prolific John Robertson - who Sandy Jardine rated as good a striker as Charlie Nicholas - controlled an awkward cross from Kidd before hooking the ball past Tom Carson and just four minutes later he added a second.

Another penetrating run and cross by skipper Walter Kidd provided the ammunition for Derek O'Connor to grab number three with a diving header, Gary Mackay netting a fourth from 20 yards in the final minute for a 4-0 win. To the delight of the noisy Tynecastle support, promotion was assured and, at the end, hundreds of fans ran on to celebrate with the players reappearing in the directors' box at the front of the tiny Boghead stand.

Meanwhile, St Johnstone had drawn at Alloa to leave Hearts just one point behind. The Maroons had a far superior goal average and should they beat Hamilton at Tynecastle and Saints drop a point to Dunfermline at Muirton on the final day, Hearts would go up as champions. A reduced entry fee of £1 ensured a 9,000-plus crowd at Tynecastle where goals by Willie Johnston and Derek O'Connor earned a 2-0 win over the Douglas Park side.

However, St Johnstone had made no mistake with a 1-0 win which condemned the once-proud Fifers to Division Two. Hearts, who had been the fifth best supported club in Scotland, finished with 20 goals more than their Perth rivals, but, in the end, they had to be content with promotion to the Premier League as Division One runners-up.

Chapter Thirteen

FORTUNE FAVOURS THE BRAVE

In keeping with the prevailing spirit at Tynecastle, around 30 volunteers repainted the ground and assisted with terracing repairs during the close season - an exercise much appreciated by their cash-strapped club.

Hearts had used just 17 players during the 1982-83 season although some of those had already moved on. Peter Marinello, who was surplus to requirements after Willie Johnston's arrival, joined Partick Thistle in March while Paddy Byrne was given a free transfer. For a year, the Irishman had commuted from Dublin on a weekly basis after his family failed to settle in Edinburgh and, after losing his place to the pacier Gary Mackay, he was happy to continue his career in Eire.

The Scottish League ban on purchasing players remained and to bolster his squad, Alex. MacDonald signed another three experienced men on free transfers. Donald Park (30), returned to Tynecastle after a five year spell with Partick Thistle. George Cowie (22), a former Scottish Youth international left-back, joined up from West Ham while veteran striker Jimmy Bone (34), formerly with St Mirren, Arbroath, Celtic, Sheffield United, Norwich City and Partick Thistle, arrived from Hong Kong Rangers.

Hearts had a number of promising youngsters like Davie Bowman, Gary Mackay, John Robertson and reserve keeper Ian Westwater, all of whom had recently represented Scotland at youth level. Indeed, Bowman and Mackay had been targets for Newcastle United until the English club were told they were not for sale. However, there were also a good number of players at the veteran stage, giving concern that Hearts might again find it hard going in the Premier League. Current Champions Dundee United, Aberdeen and the Old Firm looked particularly strong and the Tynecastle club's immediate aim was to preserve their hard-earned Premier status and take things from there.

A short pre-season Highland tour brought wins over Nairn, Inverness Caley and Elgin City. Then Hearts made a quite sensational start to the Premier League, five successive victories over St Johnstone (a) 1-0, Hibernian (h) 3-2, Rangers (h) 3-1, Dundee (a) 2-1 and St Mirren (a) 1-0 leaving them alongside Dundee United and Celtic at the top of the league.

Star strikers Willie Pettigrew and Derek O'Connor, who last term had netted 39 goals between them, were dropped for the opening game at Muirton on August 20th as Alex. MacDonald fielded - Smith; Kidd, R. MacDonald, Jardine, Cowie; Park, Bowman, MacLaren, A. MacDonald; Robertson, Bone. Subs. - Johnston, Murray.

It was a big day for St Johnstone who unfurled the First Division Championship flag before kick-off. But although Henry Smith made some vital saves in a hard, physical match, Jimmy Bone fired home an angular shot for the winner midway through the second-half.

Then came the eagerly awaited Tynecastle derby, incredibly the first for over four years, and at half-time, Hibernian fully deserved their 1-0 lead. At the interval, Alex. MacDonald brought himself on for Gary Mackay and soon Hearts were in control. First, John Robertson swerved home a spectacular equaliser but Hibs regained the lead through Irvine before Robertson made it 2-2. And with just 14 minutes remaining, Jimmy Bone was on the spot to head home a Park cross for the winner.

By then, Hearts had reached the third round of the League Cup with a 4-2 win on penalties over Cowdenbeath, after extra-time in the second leg at Tynecastle left the aggregate scores tied at 1-1. The next stage of the new-look competition involved sectional ties against Rangers, St Mirren and Clydebank over the next three months but a 2-2 draw at Paisley and a 3-0 home defeat by Rangers meant an uphill struggle to qualify.

However, on September 10th, the Maroons maintained their early league momentum with a 3-1 revenge win over Rangers at Tynecastle. The fans were returning to Tynecastle in their droves with over 18,000 - an increase of 2,000 on the Rangers game - turning out for the visit of Aberdeen on October 1st.

A Peter Weir double gave the Dons a 2-0 win as Hearts struggled to just two points from four games until beating St Johnstone 2-0 at the end of the month. George Cowie had quickly fitted in to a well-organised defence while up front, the hard-working Jimmy Bone had already proved his worth with five goals in eight games and his strength, control and positional sense made him the ideal foil for the lively John Robertson who had also found the net five times.

Shrewd move - Donald Park's return to Hearts worked out well.

Hearts were certainly getting their share of the breaks but a good start had been vital. This had lessened the pressure on their younger players and, by the end of October, Hearts lay fourth, two points behind joint leaders Aberdeen and Dundee United and eight points clear of the second relegation spot after ten games.

The management team of Alex. MacDonald

and Sandy Jardine had got their tactics right for the players at their disposal and their flexible 4-4-2 system, which involved a quick short-passing style, was proving extremely effective. However, much of Hearts progress was due to the players' willingness to battle for each other and with the calming influence of Sandy Jardine at the back and the solid professionalism of men like Stewart MacLaren - now in midfield - and Jimmy Bone up front, there was solidity right down the middle.

In the League Cup, Hearts had failed to qualify for the next stage as they finished six points behind Rangers and their Premier League form over the final two months of 1983 proved equally disappointing. The goals began to dry up and defensive mistakes proved costly as the Gorgie men managed just six points from eight games although they still remained fourth after Boxing Day.

However, on Hogmanay, Hearts recovered from a goal down, Donald Park cracking home the equaliser before George Cowie grabbed a 61st minute winner in a 2-1 success over the luckless St Johnstone at Muirton. The busy Park was another who typified the new spirit down Gorgie way and on January 2nd, he was again on the mark in a 1-1 draw against Hibs before a crowd of 23,500 at Tynecastle, Hearts highest home gate of the season.

Nineteen-year-old Craig Levein had looked a tremendous prospect against the Maroons in the League Cup and, in November, Hearts were finally able to pay Cowdenbeath £30,000 for the central defender. The youngster would be carefully groomed - initially in midfield - and, in January, former Motherwell and Leicester City defender Gregor Stevens (29), was signed on a short-term loan from Rangers to replace the suspended Roddy MacDonald.

Throughout that month, wintry weather had caused a major disruption to fixtures and the Hearts squad took the opportunity of a five-day break in Marbella. Much refreshed, the Maroons returned to Scottish Cup action on Monday, February 6th, George Cowie and Jimmy Bone netting in a 2-0 win over Partick Thistle at Tynecastle to set up a fourth round tie against Dundee United at Tannadice.

In 26 minutes, Cowie stopped an inswinging corner by Bannon on the line only for Sturrock put United ahead. Since the Pettigrew-Addison transfer, the behind-the-scenes acrimony appeared to have spilled onto the park, with last October's encounter resulting in three bookings apiece. In another tousy game, Bone, McLaren, Mackay, Jardine all received first-half bookings before Jimmy Bone was ordered off three minutes from the interval after yet another clash with Paul Hegarty.

That sparked crowd trouble but Hearts battled on and 20 minutes from time, John Robertson levelled from the spot after Dave Narey had twice handled his netbound shot. However, just six minutes from time, Hegarty headed on a free kick for Davie Dodds to bundle home the winner from a suspiciously offside position and Hearts Scottish Cup hopes were over for another year.

In March, 2-1 home wins over Motherwell and St Mirren assured Hearts of Premier League football and with the new target a place in next season's UEFA Cup, a keen struggle with St Mirren ensued until the third last game on May 5th. Almost fittingly, it was 37-year-old veteran Willie Johnston who came off the bench for the 18th time that season to grab the vital goal in a 1-1 draw with Celtic at Tynecastle. Hearts had clinched their European return and manager, players and even chairman Wallace Mercer celebrated with champage in the bath!

Lifted by the challenge of facing top opposition, the

Dynamic duo - John Robertson and Jimmy Bone pressurise Dundee United defender Derek Stark at Tynecastle. Bone's experience and strength made him the perfect foil for the youthful Robertson as Hearts consolidated in season 1983-84. DC Thomson

youthful trio of Dave Bowman, Gary Mackay and John Robertson had flourished. The prolific Robertson, subject of an abortive £400,000 bid by 'Spurs, finished top scorer with 20 goals in League and Cup and he was deservedly named Scotland's Young player of the Year.

Just over two years earlier, Hearts had been at rock-bottom when Alex. MacDonald took charge. But they had gained promotion and having retained their Premier place, they could now look forward to the return of European football. The manager and his assistant, Sandy Jardine, had fostered a great dressing room spirit and both were rewarded by three year contracts with MacDonald granted a lucrative Tynecastle testimonial against Rangers.

However, Wallace Mercer had been the key to the club's overall progress for it was his initial investment, subsequent organisation and judgement that had rejuvenated the club. He had negotiated one of the first jersey sponsorships in Scotland, first with Alexanders then Renault, and with the club getting tremendous backing from the local business community, a new Executive Business Club Sponsors' Lounge and a restaurant was created at Tynecastle. In addition, the board had given tremendous encouragement to the Supporters' Clubs by providing subsidised coaches for away games and in turn the fans were now solidly behind the club.

Willie Pettigrew had been unable to regain his place and in January he was transferred to Morton for £10,000. Out on free-transfers went Chris Robertson to Meadowbank, John Brough and Peter Shields - the latter who had never recovered his pre-injury form - signing for Partick Thistle while Gerry McCoy went to Falkirk. However, Hearts had been well supported and with average home gates of 12,000, they were able to strengthen the side by paying £25,000 for Celtic left-back Brian Whittaker while former Rangers left-back or midfielder Kenny Black (21), was signed for £30,000 from Motherwell.

Hearts took encouragement from a 3-2 pre-season friendly win over QPR at Tynecastle but they were to find the Premier League harder going, second time around. A 2-0 opening day defeat to Dundee United at Tannadice was followed by a 2-1 home reverse to newly promoted Morton. And when they went behind to a suspiciously offside goal by Paul Kane just before the interval at Easter Road on August 25th, it looked like a third defeat might be on the cards. Kane's goal sparked trouble at the Hearts end while, onfield, the football became secondary as several players got themselves embroiled in personal vendettas.

Shortly after the restart, Craig Levein latched onto a long ball to toe-end the equaliser and in the dying seconds, Bowman laid on a pass for substitute Derek O'Connor to rifle the ball past Alan Rough. However, it had been one of the ugliest Edinburgh derbies in years with play constantly interrupted by no less than 55 fouls. Both sides had three players booked and only the restraint of referee Andrew Waddell prevented the prospect of a full-scale riot. After Hibs goal, several "fans" in maroon went on to the pitch and this hooliganism came as a severe setback to Hearts, who now appealed for those travelling to Paris for the forthcoming UEFA Cup tie to be on their best behaviour. Although Park ensured a 1-0 victory over Dumbarton at Tynecastle, Hearts league performances were giving cause for concern. By the end of September, the Maroons had lost four successive games to St Mirren (h) 1-2, Celtic (a) 0-1, Dundee (h) 0-2 and Aberdeen (a) 0-4 to lie joint-bottom with Morton, after eight games.

Derek O'Connor - grabbed winner at Easter Road .

At Parkhead, Brian Whittaker had come on as a half-time substitute against his former club Celtic. Within minutes he was booked for a scything tackle on John Colquhoun and shortly afterwards, he was ordered off for another wild challenge on the winger. Nevertheless, this proved but a temporary lapse and soon Whittaker's exciting attacking forays saw him take possession of the number three jersey from George Cowie.

Meanwhile, the Tynecastle men had made good progress in the Skol League Cup, defeating East Stirling 4-0 at home before Derek O'Connor made a scoring return with a 36th minute header in a hard-fought 1-0 triumph over Ayr United at Tynecastle. The quarter-final took Hearts to Dens Park to meet Dundee. With half-time approaching, there was little between the sides until Roddy MacDonald headed home a cross by Park to break the deadlock. After the interval, Dundee threw everything forward but with the defence holding firm and Henry Smith producing some splendid saves, Hearts were through to the last four.

On September 19th, Hearts returned to European action for the first time since 1976 against Paris St Germain in the Parc Des Princes Stadium in Paris. The team got a tremendous cheer from their 4,000 fans in the 28,000 crowd and, with Roddy MacDonald out with a two-game European ban from his Celtic days, Hearts lined up - Smith; Kidd, Jardine, Levein, Whittaker; Mackay, Bowman, Black, A. MacDonald; Park, Bone. Subs. Johnston, Cherry.

For most of the first half, Hearts found themselves virtually pinned into their own penalty box as they struggled to cope with the skill and experience of the star-studded PSG side. Safet Susic was the man who mattered and in 22 minutes, the Yugoslav international brilliantly drifted a free-kick around the Hearts defensive wall to put the French side ahead. Near half-time, Rocheteau made it 2-0 and a second-half one-two from Susic and Rocheteau left Hearts with an uphill struggle in Edinburgh.

However, the fans had been on their best behaviour and back on the domestic scene, Hearts faced Dundee United in the the semi-final of the League Cup. In the first leg at Tynecastle, John Robertson sent the home fans wild with delight when he flashed a free-kick past Hamish McAlpine within sixty seconds of the start. However, it proved an ill-tempered game particularly after Henry Smith was carried off following a clash with Paul Hegarty.

Dave Bowman went in goal and although a groggy Smith resumed soon afterwards, the tackles got ever fiercer. Soon after the interval, two headed goals by John Clark put United ahead and almost immediately Dave Bowman and Dave Narey came to blows. Referee Alan Ferguson had little option but to send both off and by the end of yet another stormy clash between the two clubs, eight players had received yellow cards.

The league defeat by Aberdeen was Hearts sixth match without a win but in early October, a 2-2 draw with Paris St Germain at Tynecastle marked the first step on the road to recovery. It had been unrealistic to hope to overturn the four goal deficit but a John Robertson double helped restore some pride and a few days later the striker again netted in an vital 1-0 home win over Rangers at Tynecastle.

The no-nonsense Brian McGinlay was in charge for the second leg against United at Tannadice and, despite another five bookings, there was little chance of things getting out of control. However, Gorgie hopes of overturning the 2-1 deficit virtually disappeared when Eamonn Bannon netted a first-half penalty. United went on to win 3-1 although Hearts gained some revenge with a 2-0 league win over the Tangerines at Tynecastle a few days later.

Worryingly, only John Robertson had been scoring regularly and in October Hearts paid £30,000 for Rangers striker Sandy Clark (28). Clark's arrival coincided with an upturn in fortunes before another disastrous slump brought just one point from the next five games, including a humiliating 5-1 defeat by Celtic at Tynecastle.

In early December, Davie Bowman, capped for Scotland's Under-21's three months earlier, was the subject of a shock transfer to Coventry City and a few days later Hearts crashed 5-2 to Dundee United at Tannadice. The competitive spirit of the red-headed Bowman had somehow epitomised the "new Hearts" yet, according to chairman Wallace Mercer, the £170,000 offer was one which cash-strapped Hearts were in no position to refuse.

The midfield area had been badly affected by injuries. Following his suspension in September, Bowman had missed another seven games through injury while Gary Mackay had only made a couple of appearances due to a persistent foot problem and Stewart MacLaren had been sidelined by back and pelvic muscle injuries. Thus it was no surprise when Hearts signed former Aberdeen playmaker Andy Watson (25), for £70,000 from Leeds United, while Edinburgh-born Neil Berry, (21), was also secured on a free transfer from Bolton.

Red card - Brian Whittaker gets his marching orders at Parkhead as Dave Bowman, Sandy Jardine, Alex. MacDonald and John Robertson appeal in vain to referee Louis Thow.

Watson went straight into the team and over the New Year period, three successive wins over Morton (h) 1-0, Hibs (a) 2-1 and Dumbarton (h) 5-1 looked to have put Hearts back on the rails. The forceful Kenny Black had emerged as an influential performer straight from the Bowman mould. Strong in the tackle with a good left foot, he also got his share of the goals from midfield, netting a hat-trick in the five goal-spree against Dumbarton.The good spell continued and by early March, Hearts remained fifth, well-placed for a UEFA Cup place, having progressed to the quarter-finals of the Scottish Cup.

In January, Hearts had won the prestigious Tennent's Sixes indoor competition before four-goal Gary Mackay led them to a six goal Scottish Cup romp against plucky Inverness Caley beneath the Tynecastle floodlights. At the next stage, Hearts came from behind to draw 1-1 at Brechin and it took a Sandy McNaughton goal in the Tynecastle replay to ensure a place in the last eight.

On March 9th, nearly 24,000 provided a tingling atmosphere for the quarter-final tie against Scottish Cup holders Aberdeen at Tynecastle. Hearts played some of their best football of the season and just after the interval, Clark rammed the ball into the net after Leighton was unable to hold a Whittaker header. Despite a desperate Dons fightback, Hearts looked set for the last four but, with just 12 minutes remaining, a lack of concentration allowed Eric Black to head the equaliser.

The Pittodrie replay attracted a 23,000 capacity crowd with hundreds of unlucky Hearts fans locked out. Early play swung from end to end but, in 15 minutes, Roddy MacDonald was sent off for elbowing Eric Black. Ten minutes later, Billy Stark stole in to head home from a corner and although 10-man Hearts battled hard, the loss of MacDonald was crucial and there was to be no way back.

Sadly, that reverse signalled a Tynecastle collapse with seven defeats from their remaining nine games, a run which cost them a UEFA Cup place as they finished seventh in the table. However, they had again maintained their Premier status while the youngsters had another year's experience under their belts. The ever-improving Craig Levein was named Scotland's "Young Player of the Year" and, along with John Robertson represented Scotland at Under-21 level.

By early 1985, the veteran trio of Jimmy Bone, Willie Johnston and Alex. MacDonald were making only the occasional appearance, their task of bringing on the youngsters and consolidating Hearts Premier League status complete. Bone went to Arbroath as player-manager, the mercurial Johnston joined East Fife with Derek O'Connor moving to Dunfermline on a free transfer. Reserve goalkeeper Ian Westwater joined O'Connor at East End Park for £4,000, Stewart MacLaren retired due to injury while Stuart Gauld was another to depart on a "free".

Chapter Fourteen

THE NEARLY MEN

Effectively, Willie Johnston's departure had left Hearts without a recognized winger and to remedy this, Alex. MacDonald paid £50,000 for the speedy John Colquhoun of Celtic while former Kilmarnock and Partick Thistle midfielder Ian Jardine was secured on a free transfer from the Cypriot club Anorthosis.

July and August saw Hearts undertake a successful pre-season trip to West Germany before opening their 1985-86 Premier League campaign at Tynecastle with a 1-1 draw against last term's runners-up, Celtic. John Colquhoun made a scoring debut against his old club and the winger then grabbed the opening goal against St Mirren only for Hearts to crumble to a 6-2 defeat at Love Street.

Only later would the full significance of that scoreline be realised but the misery continued with a 3-1 defeat by Rangers. In a tousy encounter at Ibrox, three players were ordered off and eight booked. Walter Kidd and Ally McCoist of Rangers were red-carded after an exchange of blows and Sandy Clark was also sent off although he had appeared to be trying to separate the antagonists.

August concluded with a welcome 2-1 win over Hibs at Tynecastle and now Hearts travelled to Aberdeen for the League Cup quarter-final hoping to reach the money-spinning last four for the second successive year. In earlier rounds, the Gorgie men had disposed of Montrose 3-1 at Links Park, but Stirling Albion provided stiffer opposition, only an extra-time header by substitute Paul Cherry separating the sides after a deadlocked opening 90 minutes.

For the Pittodrie clash, manager MacDonald opted for a four man midfield and recalled Gary Mackay in place of the more direct John Colquhoun. However, it was a game that Hearts never looked like winning although the only goal came in bizarre fashion when a Roddy MacDonald clearance rebounded off Eric Black and flew into the net.

Three days later, Hearts returned to Aberdeen, only to go down 3-0 on league business, and, despite a 2-0 success over Dundee United at Tynecastle, defeats at Motherwell (1-2) and Clydebank (0-1) then a 1-1 home draw with Dundee left the Gorgie side two points off the bottom with just six points from their first nine games.

Injuries and suspensions had prevented any semblance of a settled team but there had been a couple of significant changes for the match against Dundee. Out went Andy Watson and Roddy MacDonald with Ian Jardine and Neil Berry coming into midfield and Craig Levein falling back to partner Sandy Jardine in central defence. Hearts had only managed a draw but there now appeared to be a better balance to the side which had played really well.

Ian Jardine had celebrated his first full appearance with a goal and an unchanged side completed October with three straight victories away to Celtic and against St Mirren and Aberdeen at Tynecastle, results which suggested that better times lay ahead for the Gorgie faithful.

It's there - arms aloft, John Colquhoun turns away after netting the opener for Hearts against Hibs at Tynecastle. DC Thomson

At Parkhead, a well-marshalled defence had withstood intense pressure before John Robertson put Hearts ahead in 33 minutes.The striker was later stretchered off with a neck injury, having coincidentally been carried off the same field with concussion, six months earlier

In November, the Maroons had to be content with a point apiece from visits to Tannadice and Easter Road but Alex. MacDonald now had a settled team who were to prove much too strong for Rangers at Tynecastle. The Walter Kidd-inspired Hearts were masters throughout the first-half but a series of missed chances left the game in the balance until Sandy Clark netted the first of two goals, 12 minutes after the restart. Near the end, John Robertson completed the rout and with confidence now sky high, another 3-0 victory over Motherwell then a 4-1 win over Clydebank - both at Tynecastle - left the Edinburgh side within touching distance of the top of the table.

With Aberdeen not playing, victory over Dundee at Dens on December 7th would propel Hearts to pole position. John Brown gave Dundee an early lead but although Kenny Black, who had recently returned from a lengthy spell on the bench in place of Brian Whittaker, missed a penalty before half-time, Ian Jardine fired home the equaliser near the end.

Another three points were taken from the next two games and now the forthcoming festive programme would be a good indicator of Hearts ability to maintain their challenge. Three days after Christmas, the Tynecastle men went to Ibrox, a vital staging post for any title hopefuls, but

Parkhead delight - Ian Jardine acclaims John Robertson's winner against Celtic at Parkhead. Celtic keeper Pat Bonner sprawls helplessly and Paul McStay can only look on as Robertson turns away. DC Thomson

they were to pass the test with flying colours, two early goals by the darting John Colquhoun earning their first Ibrox triumph since November 1975.

The midfield blend of skill and competitiveness provided by Ian Jardine, Neil Berry and Gary Mackay had given their Ibrox counterparts Derek Ferguson, Ian Durrant and Bobby Russell little scope for manouevre and, in the end, Hearts had finished streets ahead of the Light Blues.

By now Hearts were top of the Premier League, two points ahead of Dundee United with Aberdeen and the Old Firm, just behind. And with recent victories in Glasgow over both Celtic and Rangers, the media finally accepted that Hearts had the credentials for success. The fans certainly, thought so and four days later, nearly 26,000 flocked to Tynecastle for the Ne'erday derby against Hibs.

As well as bringing composure to midfield, Ian Jardine also had a good eye for goal and in 25 minutes he cracked home a short free-kick from Gary Mackay for his sixth goal of the season. In a fast end-to-end game, Hearts held the edge before Robertson added a second, 19 minutes from time. Almost immediately, Colin Harris reduced the deficit but Sandy Clark made it 3-1 after a rapier-like move involving Colquhoun and Robertson to send the huge Hearts support into raptures all around the ground.

On January 4th, the Maroons displayed great character to come from behind in a 3-1 win at snow-swept Motherwell. Incredibly, that extended their unbeaten run to 15 games and with their closest rivals all dropping points over the festive period, they had a four point lead although they would now face two of their closest rivals. At a wintry Tynecastle, Gary Mackay made amends for an earlier penalty miss by netting the opener against Dundee United only for old favourite Eamonn Bannon to score a spectacular equaliser in a 1-1 draw.

January 18th was another bitterly cold afternoon as Hearts battled it out with current champions Aberdeen in a tense struggle at Pittodrie but with just eight minutes remaining John Colquhoun did the needful, racing through to beat Leighton for the only goal of the game.

February began with a 1-1 draw at Clydebank, courtesy of a late equaliser by Sandy Clark, before Hearts stretched their unbeaten league run to 19 games with a 3-1 victory over Dundee at Tynecastle. In a report for *The Sunday Post*, former Tynecastle defender Alan Anderson made favourable comparisons with the 1964-65 side that had come so close. "On this display, I reckon they could go one better. There are no great stars in the side but they work hard for each other and never give in."

Since early October, Hearts had used just 12 players and their determined title challenge had made them the talk of Scottish football with Tynecastle league gates now averaging 15,000. On February 22nd, that fighting spirit was again in evidence in the crucial clash with Celtic at Parkhead. A home win would narrow the gap to just one point but with Henry Smith and Craig Levein rock solid at the back, Hearts again recovered from the loss of an early goal to earn a 1-1 draw. That kept them three points clear of Aberdeen at the top, with Dundee United and Celtic a couple of points further behind.

On January 25th, Hearts had eliminated Rangers from the third round of the Scottish Cup in a torrid encounter at Tynecastle. In 30 minutes, a fierce aerial collision resulted in the withdrawal of Sandy Clark and Rangers centre-half Craig Paterson. The Hearts centre was replaced by ex-Ranger Colin McAdam, a recent free transfer signing from Australian outfit Adelaide City. Ally McCoist put Rangers ahead but shortly after half-time, McAdam rammed in the equaliser when a Colquhoun shot rebounded from the post.

Soon afterwards, Gary Mackay made it 2-1 with an angled drive from near the byeline but Ian Durrant equalised in 70 minutes before an incident with Gary Mackay resulted in Derek Ferguson getting his marching orders. A replay looked on the cards but five minutes from time, Tynecastle erupted when John Robertson pounced on a Nicky Walker mistake to fire in the winner.

After four earlier postponements, Hearts progressed to

the last eight by overcoming Hamilton 2-1 at Douglas Park to set up a Tynecastle quarter-final clash with St Mirren on Sunday, March 9th. The Paisley side suffered an early blow when Campbell Money was concussed in a collision with Sandy Clark but although the dazed keeper remained in goal, he retired soon after John Colquhoun capitalised on a slack passback to put Hearts ahead. Before the interval, Robertson added a second as the Maroons progressed to the last four with a comfortable 4-1 win.

Meanwhile, Ian Jardine had dropped out through injury and the forceful Kenny Black moved into midfield with Brian Whittaker returning at left-back. Once recovered, Jardine found himself confined to the bench as victories over Motherwell (h) 2-0, Hibs (a) 2-1 and St Mirren (h) 3-0 left Hearts five points clear of Dundee United and seven above Aberdeen with Celtic, who had three games in hand, nine points in arrears.

Five league games remained against Rangers (h), Dundee United (a), Aberdeen (h), Clydebank (h) and Dundee (a) and with a forthcoming Scottish Cup semi-final against Dundee United, Hearts remained on course for the League and Scottish Cup double - a state of affairs none could have envisaged after such an indifferent start. Rangers, who languished in mid-table, were again no match for Hearts, a John Robertson double and a late goal by the industrious Sandy Clark clinching a 3-1 win to put the Maroons in fine fettle for their Hampden semi-final on April 5th.

There were over 20,000 Hearts fans in the 31,000 crowd and despite United's clutch of international class stars like Narey, Gough, Malpas, Hegarty, Bannon, and Sturrock, it was Hearts who did all the early attacking. In 13 minutes, they were rewarded when John Colquhoun pounced on a slack clearance before hooking a tremendous volley into the roof of the net. Thereafter, United turned up the heat, but the well-organised Tynecastle defence held firm and to the delight of their large support, Hearts were through to the Scottish Cup Final for the first time since 1976.

Now Alex. MacDonald's men faced a perilous trip to Tannadice where United, midweek conquerors of Aberdeen, needed a revenge win to remain in contention for the title. Midway through the first half, John Robertson thundered a spectacular 30-yarder past Billy Thomson and although Henry Smith made a miraculous save from Maurice Malpas, Sandy Clark capped a splendid spell of Hearts ascendency with a second before Robertson made it 3-0 in 66 minutes.

Now, Hearts held a five point advantage over Dundee United and Celtic and four points from their last three games would give them the championship. On Sunday, April 20th, Hearts entertained Aberdeen, whose own title aspirations had foundered with defeats to Celtic and Dundee United, in what proved a tension-wracked occasion.

Alex. Ferguson's men looked the likelier as a jittery Hearts showed little of their usual composure and with 18 minutes remaining, the Dons went ahead with a hotly disputed penalty. Referee Bob Valentine decided that Ian Jardine had handled a cross although Jim Bett had also made contact a split second earlier. Peter Weir scored from the spot but Hearts battled back and, three minutes from time, there was great relief when John Colquhoun fired home the equaliser.

In the end, Hearts were glad of a point but the following week, there was another nervy performance against Clydebank at Tynecastle. The struggling Bankies caused plenty of early problems and although Gary Mackay finally broke the deadlock in 33 minutes, players and fans alike were relieved to hear the final whistle.

Incredibly, Hearts were undefeated in 31 games, 27 of them in the league, although Celtic, who had trailed by nine points a few weeks earlier, remained in hot pursuit. The Parkhead club had won two of their games in hand and, three days before the final league match, their 2-0 win at Motherwell hauled them within two points of Hearts, who still held a goal-difference advantage of four.

However, one point from their final fixture against Dundee at Dens Park would give the Tynecastle men the title for the first time since 1960, while Celtic required a four-goal win over St Mirren at Paisley while hoping for a Hearts defeat. Despite Hearts recent shaky form, the return of skipper Walter Kidd after a three-game suspension would bring added resolve although, behind the scenes, there was growing concern after Tynecastle was struck by a flu virus.

Although affected, Brian Whittaker and John Colquhoun would play but the highly influential Craig Levein was out and Kenny Black could only make the bench. Levein's replacement was the experienced Roddy MacDonald with another victim, Ian Jardine, coming in for Black as Alex. MacDonald fielded - Smith, Kidd, MacDonald, S. Jardine, Whittaker; I. Jardine, Berry, G. Mackay; Colquhoun, Clark, Robertson. Subs. - Black, B. Mackay.

On Saturday, May 3rd, there were some 10,000 Gorgie fans at Dens, singing and waving flags and balloons amidst a pre-match carnival atmosphere which belied the underlying tension. Hearts, who sported their silvery-grey away strip, showed no sign of the nerves of the past two games. They went straight into attack only to be denied an early penalty after a clumsy Colin Hendry tackle sent Sandy

Happy days - a joyous Gary Mackay celebrates his goal against Rangers in the Scottish Cup. DC Thomson

Clark tumbling in the box - with Edinburgh referee Bill Crombie later agreeing he got it wrong. Still Hearts went forward and with Walter Kidd, Gary Mackay and John Colquhoun looking sprightly, the momentum was maintained with four successive corners.

Dundee were pinned back but, despite another couple of corners, Hearts were not creating many real chances and had begun to run out of ideas against Dundee's three-man central defence of Glennie, Duffy and Hendry. Meanwhile, news that Celtic had scored three goals in five minutes began to filter through and by the half-hour mark, the Hearts fans' early exhuberance had given way to tension-ridden anxiety whenever Dundee moved forward.

By half-time, the pressure intensified when it became known that Celtic were four goals ahead and within nine minutes of the restart, Billy McNeill's side had added a fifth. The exhausted Whittaker went off to be replaced by Black but although Dundee appeared to have only Harvey in attack, they were increasingly taking control. To counter this, Hearts withdrew Clark and Robertson to midfield, leaving just Colquhoun up front but although forced back, a couple of lightning breaks almost brought the all-important goal, first Colquhoun then Robertson coming close.

By now, half the Edinburgh team were visibly struggling and, with 15 minutes remaining, Dundee started to exert tremendous pressure in the belief that Rangers, their rivals for a UEFA Cup place, were losing to Motherwell. Hearts hung on grimly but with just seven minutes left, John Brown headed down a Connor corner and the unmarked Albert Kidd shot past Henry Smith from four yards. Tynecastle players and fans slumped in disbelief and although Billy Mackay replaced Ian Jardine, Hearts had nothing left to give and their fate was sealed when Dundee substitute Kidd struck again, three minutes from time.

At the final whistle, the Hearts players and officials were devastated and there were heart-wrending scenes amongst the Gorgie faithful, who were stunned that their dreams of glory had been so cruelly shattered. Ironically, the title had been lost by three goals yet it had been five months since Hearts themselves had last failed to score and few could recall an instance when their well-drilled defence had conceded a goal from a corner kick.

Now the Hearts management had the unenviable task of raising morale for the Scottish Cup Final and seven days later, there was a remarkable turnout of nearly 40,000 Hearts fans amongst the 62,841 crowd at blustery Hampden. Craig Levein and Kenny Black returned but Ian Jardine had not recovered from illness. Hearts - Smith; Kidd, S. Jardine, Levein, Whittaker; G. Mackay, Berry, Black; Colquhoun, Clark, Robertson. Subs. B. Mackay, Cowie. Aberdeen - Leighton; McKimmie, McLeish, W. Miller, McQueen; Bett, Cooper, McMaster, Weir; McDougall, Hewitt. Subs. Stark, J. Miller.

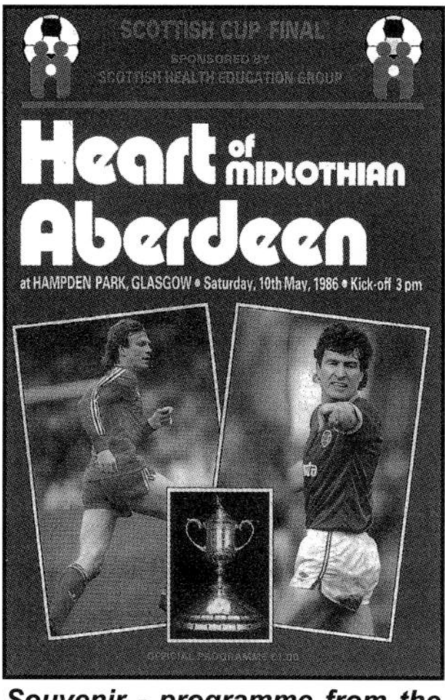

Souvenir - programme from the 1986 Scottish Cup Final.

End of the road - the Hearts bench are disconsolate after Dundee score their second in the crucial game at Dens. DC Thomson

Surprisingly, Aberdeen's ace striker Eric Black had been left out after announcing his departure to Metz but his deputy John Hewitt was to have a major influence on the outcome. Some crisp attacking play earned Hearts two corners in the opening stages but with five minutes gone, Hewitt controlled a long through ball and as the Hearts defence backed off, he advanced to crack a fierce grounder past Smith from the edge of the box.

Desperately, Hearts fought back and with Neil Berry and Gary Mackay getting through a power of work in midfield, they remained in contention. However, Aberdeen's iron curtain defence allowed few opportunities although John Robertson - constantly shadowed by Neale Cooper, managed to beat the offside trap and lob the advancing Jim Leighton only to send the ball just over the bar.

The first-half had been a battle perhaps best epitomised by the fierce clashes between Sandy Clark and Alex. McLeish. At half-time, Hearts trailed 1-0 but just four minutes into the second-half, a cross by the troublesome Peter Weir was brilliantly dummied by Frank McDougall and Hewitt made it 2-0 from close in.

Still Hearts refused to lie down and soon after a Neil Berry shot crashed off the bar in 63 minutes, there were penalty appeals when Walter Kidd was sent crashing by Cooper. By now there were signs of frustration creeping into Hearts play with Robertson and Mackay booked before Dons substitute Billy Stark netted a decisive third with 15 minutes remaining.

Two minutes later, Hearts skipper Walter Kidd, earlier booked for a reckless foul on Hewitt, bounced the ball off Neale Cooper's head before throwing it at Frank McDougall and referee Hugh Alexander had no option but to send him off. Aberdeen's big-occasion experience had been the decisive factor but more significantly, luck had turned it's back on Hearts over the past two weeks.

Nevertheless, the huge Gorgie support remained to applaud for it had been Hearts brightest season in 21 years. Craig Levein was again named Scotland's "Young Player of the Year" while Sandy Jardine, who had been named the Scottish Football Writers' Association "Player of the Year", was rewarded with the post of co-manager. Alex. MacDonald commented, "I didn't feel we deserved to lose by three goals. We played a lot of good football. I really feel sorry for the supporters but I'm certain we can go on from here. It's not the end, just the beginning."

Chapter Fifteen

HEARTBREAK AND MORE

Manager Alex MacDonald had proved himself a shrewd judge of ability and his skill in the transfer market was second to none. Clark, Black, Whittaker, Berry and both Jardines had all been excellent acquisitions but the pace, directness and scoring ability of John Colquhoun and the athleticism and authoritative defensive play of Craig Levein had made them key figures in the recent evolution of Hearts.

Meanwhile, Donald Park and Brian McNaughton had been released with Paul Cherry joining Cowdenbeath but the only newcomers were goalkeeper Andy Bruce from Rangers and former Preston North End striker Wayne Foster (22), who were both obtained on free transfers .

A £300,000 deal to sign Dundee midfielder John Brown, which involved £75,000-rated Andy Watson going to Dens, had collapsed at the last minute when Brown failed a medical on account of a long-term knee problem. The midfield powerhouse had netted 23 goals over the past two seasons and Hearts loss would prove Rangers gain when he later moved to Ibrox to play an integral part in the Souness revolution.

In May, the players had been rewarded for their efforts by a trip to the West Indies, where they played three games in Barbados and Trinidad. Pre-season preparation consisted of matches against Stoke, Wigan and Bohemians of Dublin in the Isle of Man Festival Trophy but although expectations remained high amongst the Tynecastle faithful, things did not go to plan at the start of the 1986-87 campaign. A no-scoring draw at Paisley and 1-0 home wins over promoted pair Hamilton and Falkirk did little to inspire while their League Cup sojourn was sharply curtailed by a shock 2-0 defeat by First Division Montrose at Links Park.

Clearly, the team was not firing on all cylinders, particularly up front and in an effort to remedy the goals drought, John Robertson was relegated to the bench for the match against Dundee United at Tannadice. Wayne Foster, formerly a team-mate of Neil Berry at Bolton was introduced for his debut, but it was to no avail with United scoring the only goal of the game.

Indeed, it took a local derby win against Hibs to kick-start Hearts season. There had been a bad atmosphere from the start of the game at Easter Road and both Kidd and Levein were hit by coins thrown from the home section. However, Hearts concentrated on the game and when Fulton miscued, Gary Mackay crossed smartly for Sandy Clark to head home. Six minutes from half-time, good leading-up work by Colquhoun and Mackay allowed Ian Jardine to crash the ball in off a post and halfway through the second period, a third by Robertson settled the issue.

That was just the boost Hearts required and 10 points from their next six games took them to third, one point behind Celtic and two behind Dundee United with almost a quarter of the marathon 44-game programme - caused by the new 12-club Premier League - already completed.

Up go the heads - defensive stalwart Walter Kidd tangles with Dundee United's Ian Redford and Richard Gough. DC Thomson

By then, the Maroons had no further interest in the UEFA Cup following a first round clash with the Czechoslovakian army side Dukla Prague, who last year had reached the semi-final of the European Cup-Winners' Cup.

On Wednesday, September 17th, Wayne Foster set Tynecastle alight when he put Hearts ahead within 60 seconds of kick-off. However, after the initial home surge, the more experienced Czechs gradually took control and 18 minutes into the second-half, they led 2-1. The Maroons fought back to level through Sandy Clark and backed by tremendous support from the 19,000 crowd, they got the winner when Foster's shot was blocked by the Czech keeper and substitute John Robertson crashed home the rebound just 11 minutes from time.

A fortnight later, the Tynecastle club made the trip behind the Iron Curtain but despite the unreal atmosphere provided by a crowd of just 3,500, which included many from Edinburgh, Hearts held the edge throughout the opening period. In five minutes, they might have gone ahead when Kosternik could only push out a fierce drive by Foster and Colquhoun fired the rebound narrowly past.

After the break, Dukla were transformed and in 53 minutes, Griga swivelled and beat Smith from 10 yards to make the aggregate score 3-3. Hard though Hearts tried, they were unable to get the crucial away goal that would have swung the tie their way and it was the Czechs who went through to the next round on the away goals rule.

On October 8th, Hearts six game unbeaten league run ended when they lost 2-0 in a top of the table clash with Celtic at Parkhead. However, worse was to follow when Craig Levein - on the verge of full international honours - sustained torn knee ligaments in a reserve game at Easter Road and was unlikely to reappear that season.

Roddy MacDonald returned and by the end of the year, 19 points from their next 14 games, including home and away wins over Aberdeen, a 1-0 win against Celtic and a 7-0 Tynecastle romp over struggling Hamilton Accies, left Hearts fourth, hard on the heels of Dundee United and Rangers and within six points of leaders Celtic.

However, the Maroons had been unable to put one over Rangers, who were now under the influence of player-manager and former Scotland international Graeme Souness. Already, he had spent over £2 million on England internationals Chris Woods, Terry Butcher and Graham Roberts as well as Colin West and Jimmy Nicholl and although Hearts had earlier matched them in a 1-1 draw at Tynecastle, a 3-0 defeat in Glasgow indicated that the Ibrox money men were on their way back.

Hearts themselves had spent £80,000 on 21-year-old Dumbarton winger Alan Moore but with John Colquhoun, maintaining his fine scoring partnership with John Robertson, Moore's appearances were largely confined to the bench.

Down and out - Pat Bonner is grounded as Kenny Black celebrates John Robertson's free-kick winner against Celtic in the Scottish Cup at Tynecastle.

On January 23rd, Wallace Mercer unsuccessfully appealed to the Scottish League for the postponement of the match at Dundee for, in a near carbon copy of last May, eight Hearts players were affected by injury or illness. In the event, Smith, Kidd, Watson and Colquhoun left their sick beds to play and a penalty save by Henry Smith helped clinch a 1-0 win.

Hearts had opened their Scottish Cup campaign with a no-scoring draw against First Division Kilmarnock at Tynecastle and four days later the pair were again inseperable after extra-time in a tousy Rugby Park replay. In a sixty-second spell of madness before half-time, Whittaker was ordered off for a waist-high challenge on Harkness then Killie went ahead from the spot after a rash tackle by Kenny Black. In 66 minutes, Foster levelled and, although the second replay sent Hearts back to Ayrshire, they made no mistake third time around, goals from Mackay, Black and Foster clinching a 3-1 victory to ensure a lucrative fourth round clash with Celtic at Tynecastle.

On February 7th, Hearts had entertained Rangers - fresh from a stunning Scottish Cup defeat by Hamilton - in a vital league game. However, the leg weary Maroons were without the injured Gary Mackay and disappointingly they crashed 5-2 in their first home reverse in 32 games since August 1985. That result came as a fatal blow to their already flimsy title hopes and with all hopes now resting on the Scottish Cup, 28,891 fans flocked to Tynecastle for the clash against Celtic on February 21st.

The large crowd were treated to a typically hard-fought cup-tie and although there were few chances, Alan McInally crashed a shot off the crossbar with a Roddy MacDonald header hitting woodwork at the other end. After half-time, a Kenny Black cross was cleared onto his own bar by a Celtic defender but with time running out, Hearts were awarded a free-kick at the edge of the box.

At a recent Scotland international training session, Henry Smith had learned that Pat Bonner tended to position himself too near his far post at free-kicks. This information had been passed to John Robertson and after shaping to chip the ball, the striker instead delivered a deadly lob to the near post which went in for the winner.

In the quarter-finals, Hearts were paired with Tommy McLean's Motherwell at Tynecastle. John Robertson put them in front with a diving header and they looked sure to reach the last four until a careless passback by Roddy MacDonald allowed Andy Walker to equalise. A near-capacity 15,000 crowd saw Hearts dominate the Fir Park replay before the ever-alert John Colquhoun headed home the only goal when Kenny Black's cross rebounded from the post with just five minutes remaining.

With nine league games left, Hearts remained on course for a European place through their league position but the loss of valuable points at Falkirk and Clydebank came as a serious setback. Since early February, the goals had dried up with only the dynamic duo of John Robertson and John

Holding job - Roddy MacDonald clears from St Mirren striker Kenny McDowall in the Scottish Cup semi-final at Hampden in 1987. Looking on are St Mirren's Ian Ferguson and Henry Smith, Sandy Jardine, Kenny Black and Malcolm Murray of Hearts. DC Thomson

Colquhoun scoring regularly.

It was no coincidence that Hearts most creative midfielder Gary Mackay had gone through a sticky spell. After encountering difficulties over a new contract, Mackay's form had dipped and he found himself on the bench for five successive games. Aberdeen took a keen interest but, just when it appeared that his Tynecastle days might be numbered, a new deal was agreed.

Hearts appeared to have a great chance of lifting the Scottish Cup for Aberdeen and both members of the Old Firm were already out of the competition. The semi-final draw had matched them with Alex. Smith's St Mirren while the two Dundee clubs would meet in the other tie at Tynecastle.

However, Hearts would be without six of their top players. John Robertson, recently sent off at Brockville, and Brian Whittaker were suspended, while Craig Levein, Walter Kidd, Neil Berry and Ian Jardine were all out through injury. Nevertheless, around two-thirds of the 31,000 Hampden crowd sported maroon favours for the semi on Saturday, April 11th. Hearts - Smith; Murray, S. Jardine, R. MacDonald, Cowie; Watson, G. Mackay, Black; Colquhoun, Clark, Foster. Subs. - Crabbe, Sandison. St Mirren - Money; Wilson, Winnie, Cooper, D. Hamilton; B. Hamilton, Abercromby, Lambert; Ferguson, McDowell, McGarvey. Subs, Cameron, McWhirter.

In the early stages, Hearts carried the greater threat. but the lively young Saints settled and in 33 minutes, a long ball by Winnie caught Hearts square at the back, allowing Ian Ferguson to go through to score despite a valiant effort by George Cowie on the line. Hearts looked a jaded team but with 16 minutes left, Gary Mackay thumped a glorious 20-yarder past Campbell Money for the equaliser. Now the Maroons went all out for the winner but in the dying minutes, they were caught on the break. Saints substitute Ian Cameron set off on a run before cutting the ball back and although McDowall failed to connect, veteran striker Frank McGarvey was on hand to whip the ball home.

Realising that Hearts had lost a golden opportunity, Alex. MacDonald was furious, "That was a real sickener. My men didn't play to their capabilities and I hope it hurts them as much as it hurts me." However, the loss of so many key players, particularly the prolific Robertson, had proved too big a handicap and although the possibility of a UEFA Cup place remained, the Maroons could muster only six points from their remaining six games to finish fifth, three points behind Aberdeen.

Average home league gates were just 1,500 down on last season and with this level of revenue, there had been a number of ground improvements such as improved toilet facilities and the construction of new turnstiles. However, more importantly, the board could now provide substantial funds for new players.

Towards the end of 1986, Sandy Jardine had been sidelined for a lengthy period by a persistant calf muscle injury. Jimmy Sandison proved a capable deputy but with Craig Levein still recovering and Jardine fast approaching the end of his playing career, Hearts paid a new Tynecastle record fee of £350,000 for Rangers central defender Dave McPherson (23). Ibrox right-back Hugh Burns (21), was included in the estimated £500,000 deal and to recoup some of their outlay, a number of players were moved on.

Last Autumn, Colin McAdam had joined Partick Thistle on a free transfer. Now George Cowie was transferred to Dunfermline for £15,000, Billy Mackay retired due to persistant knee trouble and a few months later, Andy Watson would join Hibs for £30,000 with Roddy MacDonald moving on to Morton for £25,000.

In May, Hearts had undertaken a short four-game tour of sunny California and two months later, the passports were again required for pre-season preparations in West Germany. Apart from Craig Levein, Hearts were free of injuries and suspension, and although Hugh Burns had featured in the pre-season build-up, there was no place for him in the opening league match against Falkirk at Tynecastle on August 8th - Smith; Kidd, S. Jardine,

Top class - Dave McPherson, seen here in a tussle with former team-mate Ian Durrant, cost Hearts a Tynecastle record fee of £350,000 from Rangers. DC Thomson

McPherson, Whittaker; Mackay, Berry, Black; Colquhoun, Clark, Robertson. Subs. - I. Jardine, Foster.

A John Robertson double helped the Gorgie side to a 4-2 win and by early September, Hearts were level with Dundee, just one point behind joint leaders Aberdeen and Celtic. Seven points had been taken from their opening five games and the quality of football produced in the 4-1 hammering of Dundee United at Tynecastle emphasised that Hearts were back to their best.

By then, the Maroons had reached the last eight of the League Cup after home victories over First Division Kilmarnock (6-1) and Clyde (2-0) and with just one defeat in seven games, they were confident of beating Rangers, who would be without the injured Terry Butcher and Graeme Souness, in the quarter-final at Ibrox.

Last term, the rejuvenated Light Blues had taken the Premier title by six points from Celtic but despite their League Cup progress, they had made a disastrous start in the league. However, Hearts appeared to freeze before the 39,303 Ibrox crowd while Rangers returned to form with a vengence. Pre-match flu-doubt Ian Durrant hit a deadly double and a third by Ally McCoist just before the interval finished the match which Hearts eventually lost 4-1.

Although virtually unchanged since the start of the season, Allan Moore and Kenny Black returned at the expense of the injured Sandy Clark and Ian Jardine as Hearts bounced back with a 2-1 win over Morton at Cappielow. A couple of weeks later, Craig Levein made his long-awaited comeback in place of Sandy Jardine and with Wayne Foster replacing Allan Moore, a seven-game unbeaten run took Hearts to the top of the league.

On October 17th, Hearts impressive run temporarily ground to a halt when goals by May and Kane gave Hibs a 2-1 win at Easter Road. That was their first derby defeat in 18 meetings since March 1979 but, orchestrated by the incisive attacking play of Gary Mackay from midfield, Hearts were soon back turning on the style.

There was an abundance of flair and fluency with goals galore from the new bantam strike-force of Colquhoun, Foster and Robertson and there were 3-0 victories against Morton at home - where the unfortunate Ian Jardine broke his ankle - and at Motherwell, before a 4-2 win over Dundee at Tynecastle left Hearts three points clear of second-placed Celtic at the end of October. Seven days later, Colquhoun gave Hearts a first-half lead in the top of the table showdown against Celtic in Edinburgh. Shortly after half-time, Celtic's Mick McCarthy was ordered off for a second bookable offence but despite their numerical advantage, Hearts were unable to subdue the Parkhead side who equalised four minutes from time.

Gary Mackay's sparkling form had resulted in a late call-up to the Scotland squad for the European Championship match against Bulgaria in Sofia. At half-time, he replaced the injured Paul McStay and, near the end, capped a fine display by curling the ball past the Bulgarian keeper for the only goal. Scotland were already out of contention but that result was enough to put Eire through to next summer's finals in West Germany with Mackay - the first Hearts player to score for Scotland since Alex. Young against Northern Ireland in 1960, by now an Irish national hero.

Meanwhile, the writing was on the wall for Sandy Jardine, who had been a defensive lynch-pin in his five years at Tynecastle. He had made well over 1,000 top class appearances throughout his lengthy career, but now Craig Levein's return had prompted him to retire and henceforth he would concentrate on his managerial duties.

By November, Hugh Burns had made his breakthrough as an attacking right-back. But although the squad was further strengthened by the £60,000 signing of the versatile Mike Galloway (23), from English Fourth Division side Halifax, Hearts could only draw seven of their next 10 games as they slipped to third, one point behind Aberdeen and four less than Celtic. Crucially, they had lost a 2-0 lead to Celtic at Parkhead on December 12th, conceding a debatable penalty near the end before McStay cracked home the equaliser in the dying seconds

The New Year began with a bumper 28,992 fans packing Tynecastle for the Ne'erday clash with Hibs. Largely due to the brilliance of Hibs keeper Andy Goram, Hearts drew their third successive blank as the match finished 0-0. But within two weeks, Tynecastle had it's fourth capacity crowd of the season for the visit of a resurgent Rangers, who were now just a few points behind.

Sandy Clark returned to score in a 1-1 draw but the forfeiture of a point paled into insignificance compared to the loss of Craig Levein, who had been stretchered off with a recurrence of his knee ligament injury. Over the past three months, the cultured defender had formed an impressive double act with Dave McPherson but he faced another lengthy spell on the sidelines and now there were fears that his highly promising career might be over.

Either Mike Galloway or Neil Berry could have gone to

central defence but, preferring to utilise their running power in midfield, Alex. MacDonald chose to switch Brian Whittaker and he soon proved a tower of strength alongside the classy Dave McPherson. Earlier, McPherson himself had required a period of adjustment to his new role of ball-winner but such was his progress that he was now on the fringes of full international honours.

A 3-1 win at Falkirk and a 2-0 home success over Morton took Hearts into the last eight of the Scottish Cup and with nearly three quarters of the league programme completed, they remained alongside Rangers, just a couple of points behind leaders Celtic, who had a game in hand. Their quarter-final opponents were again from the Premier League, this time Dunfermline, who, despite struggling in the bread and butter of the league, had provided a fourth round sensation by knocking out Rangers.

On March 12th, there was a vociferous following from Fife amongst the 22,000 Tynecastle crowd. However, once Colquhoun, a hat-trick hero in the recent 6-0 humbling of St Mirren at Paisley, put Hearts ahead in 25 minutes, there was no way back for the disappointing Pars. Foster added a second and midway through the second-half, a thundering shot by Gary Mackay beat on-loan Notts Forest keeper Hans Segars to ease Hearts into the semi-final for the third successive season.

A couple of weeks earlier, Hearts had returned to Brockville on league business only to go down 2-0. A number of good chances had been missed and the loss of another two points in draws with Aberdeen at home and away to Hibs sounded the death-knell of their title hopes as they trailed eight points behind Celtic.

Celtic showed no sign of loosening their vice-like grip at the top of the table but, with the Scottish Cup offering Hearts their only realistic chance of trophy success, they now found themselves paired with the strong-going Parkhead outfit on April 9th, while Aberdeen met Dundee United in the other semi-final tie at Dens. Last summer, Billy McNeill, who was now in his second spell as Celtic boss, had lost Brian McClair to Manchester United and Maurice Johnston to Nantes. However, his gamble of spending big money on Frank McAvennie and Mark McGhee had paid off handsomely with Celtic now aiming to celebrate their Centenary season with a League and Scottish Cup double.

In a change of routine, Hearts spent a few days at Troon preparing for the big game. Walter Kidd, whose 10 years service had been rewarded by a Testimonial match against Everton last October, was out after a recent cartilege operation - the second of his career - as the teams lined up: Hearts - Smith; Murray, McPherson, Whittaker, Black; Galloway, Berry, Mackay; Colquhoun, Foster, Robertson. Subs. - Clark, I. Jardine. Celtic - Bonner; Morris, Aitken, Whyte, Rogan; Stark, McStay, Burns; J. Miller, McAvennie, Walker. Subs. McGhee, Baillie.

The Hampden crowd of almost 66,000 provided a tremendous atmosphere and, in a frantic opening spell, Bonner pushed away a netbound header by Galloway. Initially, play raged from end to end but gradually exchanges degenerated into a dour midfield battle before Hearts went ahead on the hour. Brian Whittaker sent in a high lob but there seemed little danger until Celtic keeper Pat Bonner was distracted by the inrushing Dave McPherson and the ball sailed high into the net.

Celtic surged forward but could make little impression on the Tynecastle rearguard and, with time fast running out, they became increasingly desperate. Throughout the season, the Gorgie defence had played with great discipline but, on three previous occasions that term, the loss of late goals to Celtic had cost them crucial championship points. With only three minutes remaining, Hearts looked certain to reach the final but when Tommy Burns sent over a cor-

On the mark - Wayne Foster slams home the second goal in the 3-0 win over Dunfermline in the Scottish Cup quarter-final. Norrie McCathie, goalkeeper Hans Segars and Graeme Robertson are the helpless Pars defenders. DC Thomson

Braveheart - Dave McPherson and Kenny Black of Hearts and Rangers Scott Nisbet await the outcome of an airborne duel between Mike Galloway and Richard Gough of Rangers.
DC Thomson

ner, Henry Smith dropped the ball and substitute Mark McGhee lashed in the equaliser. Hearts were stunned and, now under intense pressure from the rejuvenated Celts, Smith was again at fault when he fumbled a McGhee header and a grateful Andy Walker stabbed home the winner.

Just seconds had remained and at the final whistle, several Hearts players were on their knees in despair. A great chance of reaching the final had gone and Alex. MacDonald made no excuses, "We blew it. Henry is the one guy we cannot afford to have making mistakes."

However, the Hearts strikers had been equally unimpressive and four days later, John Robertson was not even on the bench for the match against Dunfermline. Sandy Jardine maintained that the striker had not played well for weeks and was not a scapegoat for the Celtic game. Nevertheless, Robertson had played a key role in Hearts return to prominence over the past six years and, already that term, he had netted his best-ever haul of 31 goals.

However, contract talks with Wallace Mercer had broken down amidst suggestions that the prolific striker wanted a signing-on fee of £100,000 and £1,000 per week. The Hearts chairman was adamant that to prevent dressing-room unrest, the wage structure should remain unbroken, particularly as Gary Mackay, Henry Smith and John Colquhoun, who had all made their Scottish international breakthrough, had already agreed new deals.

Strong media speculation over Robertson's future had arisen at a critical stage of the season and in late February, the player was transfer-listed and his agent Bill McMurdo banned from Tynecastle. Now, however, Hearts were out of contention for both league and cup and nine days after the semi-final defeat, John Robertson was transferred to Newcastle United for a Tynecastle record fee of £625,000.

Hearts fans were devastated but with Robertson able to move abroad on Freedom of Contract for a lesser fee - Maurice Johnston had joined Nantes for £375,000 - the board had a dilemma. Wallace Mercer explained, "Directors and management are disappointed to lose John Robertson but it was in the best interests of both parties. That money and more is available to Alex. MacDonald and Sandy Jardine to reinvest in suitable players."

Acting skipper Gary Mackay sustained a depressed jaw fracture in a 2-1 revenge win over Celtic. He thus became the third Hearts captain - after Craig Levein and Walter Kidd - to pick up a serious injury that term and although the Maroons pipped Rangers for the runners-up spot, they finished 10 points behind Celtic in a depressing end to what had begun as a season of great promise.

Chapter Sixteen

EUROPEAN NIGHTS

Over the past three seasons, Hearts had twice been Premier League runners-up and had reached three successive Scottish Cup semi-finals. Financially, they had been in the black for five years - last term had brought a profit of £308,824 - but while appreciating that this was far removed from the dark days of the early 1980's, the fans now hungered for tangible onfield success.

Last season, around £600,000 had been spent on Dave McPherson, Hugh Burns, Mike Galloway and Rochdale left-winger Mark Gavin - the last named a £30,000 acquisition in January. However, Tynecastle fans could only view the sale of the prolific and hugely popular John Robertson as an act of betrayal and almost inevitably, the board - particularly the high-profile figure of Wallace Mercer - had come in for fierce criticism. However, the directors remained genuinely ambitious and new dressing rooms, a club restaurant and a Private Members' Club were created at Tynecastle in the close season.

In addition, Dundee United's out-of-contract midfielder Eamonn Bannon, now 30-years-old, was persuaded to return to his old stamping ground for a fee of £225,000 and just before the start of the new campaign Hearts also signed United striker Iain Ferguson (26), on freedom of contract. The Maroons saw the ex-Dundee and Rangers goalscorer as the ideal replacement for John Robertson but although United demanded £500,000, a fee of £325,000 was agreed just prior to a meeting of the transfer tribunal.

Relations between the clubs had been strained since the Pettigrew-Addison transfer in 1981 and soon afterwards, the pair were again at loggerheads. The Tannadice outfit, upset at losing two quality players to Hearts, went public after making an abortive bid for Gary Mackay, who soon afterwards signed a new three year deal for Hearts.

Once again, Hearts did their pre-season training in West Germany before 12,000 Tynecastle fans took the opportunity to watch the glamour friendly against Brazilian club Cruzeiro. Most departed happy when new signing Iain Ferguson netted in a 2-1 win but, despite their summer spending spree, Hearts went down by the only goal of the game to Celtic in the big league opener at Parkhead.

That was to herald a disastrous start to their 1988-89 title challenge for, by the end of the first quarter of their programme on October 8th, Hearts lay third bottom of the table with just six points. Two years earlier, Rangers, Celtic, Hearts, Hibs, Aberdeen and Motherwell had discussed a possible breakaway after the decision to implement a 12-team Premier League and to counter this threat, further reconstruction saw the league revert to 10 clubs with only one to go down.

Meanwhile, Hearts had made good progress in the Skol Cup. A first-half hat-trick by Iain Ferguson helped endear him to the home support in a 5-0 win over St Johnstone before a 2-0 success over Meadowbank Thistle took them into the last eight. Sandy Clark had looked like forming a useful partnership alongside Ferguson but a serious achilles tendon injury sustained against Meadowbank was to spell the end of his first-team career at Tynecastle.

On Wednesday, August 31st, Hearts met Dunfermline in a thrilling quarter-final at East End Park. In three minutes, Gary Mackay lashed in the opener only for the Fifers to level through John Watson on the half-hour. It was end to end stuff but although John Colquhoun made it 2-1 soon after the interval, the Pars refused to accept defeat and it took two opportunist strikes by Iain Ferguson in the last 10 minutes before the issue was finally settled.

In the semi-final, Hearts would play Rangers with Aberdeen and Dundee United contesting the other tie. Successive 2-1 league defeats by St Mirren and Rangers at Tynecastle offered little encouragement but their Skol Cup progress coupled with the recent 2-0 first-leg UEFA Cup first round win over St Patrick's Athletic in Dublin suggested that Hearts might well be better equipped for the cut and thrust of cup football.

On September 21st, Hampden housed an all-ticket crowd of 53,623 for the semi-final which was also shown live on T.V. Top scorer Iain Ferguson was relegated to the bench as Hearts fielded - Smith; Kidd, McPherson, Whittaker, Berry; Galloway, Mackay, Black, Bannon; Colquhoun, Foster. Subs. Ferguson, Murray. Rangers - Woods; Stevens, Butcher, Gough, Brown; Nisbet, Wilkins, Durrant; Walters, I. Ferguson, Cooper. Subs. - Souness, Gray.

Against the run of play, Hearts went behind after 11 minutes when Henry Smith could only parry a close-in attempt by Terry Butcher and Ibrox winger Mark Walters slammed home the rebound. The Tynecastle men fought back with Berry, Colquhoun and Bannon all coming close to equalising but six minutes after the break, Henry Smith fumbled a harmless looking Walters' cross and Nisbet made it 2-0. That proved the turning point for although Colquhoun again went near and a Gary Mackay shot crashed off the bar, Walters grabbed a third for the Light Blues towards the

"The Boss" - Alex. MacDonald was the manager behind Hearts revival throughout the 1980's. **DC Thomson**

end as luckless Hearts tumbled to their third successive semi-final defeat at Hampden.

Despite their disappointment, Hearts again defeated St Patrick's Athletic 2-0 in the Tynecastle return to reach the next stage of the UEFA Cup. Kenny Black opened the scoring after 23 minutes and although the Irishmen battled gamely, a Mike Galloway strike midway through the second half gave the Maroons a 4-0 aggregate success. The draw for the second round paired Hearts with Austria Vienna, but despite almost totally dominating the first leg at Tynecastle in late October, Hearts were unable to penetrate the well-organised Austrian defence.

Back on the domestic front, Hearts continued to struggle and two days after a 3-0 defeat by Rangers at Ibrox in early November, Sandy Jardine was dismissed from his post of co-manager. Hearts now lay third bottom with just two wins from 13 games and although Wallace Mercer maintained it was time to revert to one man in charge, a bitterly disappointed Jardine claimed that the chairman had not made the cash available for top quality players. Walter Borthwick, a coach at Tynecastle since 1981, was appointed assistant-manager with Sandy Clark now player-coach.

Curiously, Douglas Park, a key figure in Hearts resurgence of the early 1980's, had resigned 24 hours earlier, his place on the board being taken by long-serving secretary Les Porteous. The vice-chairman, fined £1,000 by the SFA for locking referee David Syme in his dressing-room after a home defeat by Rangers in September, was unwilling to elaborate on his departure. Nevertheless, rumours of a power struggle with Wallace Mercer appeared well-founded when he talked of forming a consortium to mount a takeover bid. However, the chairman indicated that the club was not for sale, later purchasing Park's 20% shareholding to take his own stake in the club to 70%.

Big match - programme from game against Bayern Munich.

It had been a most unsettling period and when Hearts flew to Vienna soon afterwards, few expected them to survive their UEFA Cup second round tie. It was a bitterly cold night in the Prater Stadium but Hearts, who had the versatile Jimmy Sandison keeping a tight rein on influential midfielder Herbert Prohaska, were quick to settle. Wayne Foster shot just wide before a crude tackle ended his involvement and as both sides began to create chances, the match developed into a highly intriguing tie.

From the start, Austria Vienna had played a frustrating offside game. However, in 55 minutes the wily Eamonn Bannon released Walter Kidd down the right and when the ball was swept back, Mike Galloway dived to head home at the near post. The home side stepped up the pace but, well marshalled by Dave McPherson, Hearts defended diligently and that single goal was sufficient to ensure a 1-0 win. It had been a well-planned and splendidly disciplined performance and now they would meet the Yougoslavians, Velez Mostar in the third round.

On November 23rd, nearly 17,500 fans turned out for the home clash against Velez. A spectacular overhead kick from Iain Ferguson then two efforts by John Colquhoun went close before Eamonn Bannon broke the deadlock with a cracking drive in 19 minutes. Velez remained dangerous on the break but when Hearts began to exert tremendous presure after half-time, Mike Galloway took advantage of a goalkeeping blunder to make it 2-0. As the visotors became increasingly rattled, Susic was red-carded for a brutal foul on Colquhoun but the wee striker had the final say, Gary Mackay setting him up for a decisive third goal near the end.

Two weeks later, the Tynecastle party flew to Split on the Adriatic coast before undertaking a lengthy coach trip to Mostar, an ancient town deep in the heart of the Bosnian mountains. Amidst a volatile and intimidating atmosphere fireworks exploded and a couple of tumblers were thrown at the Hearts dugout. However, the brave Maroons had no intention of throwing away their three-goal advantage and, apart from a 26th minute Repak header which hit the bar, Velez created few real chances.

Five minutes later, Toce did pull one back but although the Gorgie men faced a torrid finish before the hostile 17,000 crowd, their well-organised defence was rarely in difficulty. Although mostly used in midfield, the powerful Mike Galloway was capable of wreaking havoc in opposing defences, particularly in the air. Shrewdly, the Tynecastle management had played him up front in earlier UEFA ties and this had paid off handsomely with four

Well done - Jimmy Sandison congratulates Mike Galloway after a goal at Tynecastle. Galloway netted five UEFA Cup goals in season 1988-89.

Head start - Dave McPherson and Craig Levein look suitably impressed as Eamonn Bannon heads clear from Terry Butcher and John Brown of Rangers in this match at Ibrox. DC Thomson

goals. Now, with 25 minutes remaining, the red-headed Galloway again demonstrated his aerial ability when he got on the end of a well-worked free-kick to head the equaliser. And although a sloppy passback allowed Gudelj to net the winner in the dying seconds, Hearts were home and dry in the last eight, 4-2 on aggregate.

In his short spell at Newcastle, John Robertson had struggled to make an impact and there was speculation that the dismissal of Sandy Jardine, who it was rumoured had not seen eye to eye with the striker, might pave the way for Robertson's return. With a scoring famine - only 16 goals had been scored in 18 league games - Hearts were indeed keen to have him back and aware of interest from Hibs and Dundee United, they splashed out a new Tynecastle record fee of £750,000 to ensure Robertson's return.

That brought Hearts recent spending to over £1-million for a few days earlier, Dundee's Tosh McKinlay had been signed for £300,000 to fill the left-back spot, a problem position since Brian Whittaker's switch to central defence. On December 10th, Robertson made an emotional homecoming and along with McKinlay his reappearance attracted a 26,500 crowd for the home match with Rangers.

Tynecastle's favourite son was back and a 26th minute goal by Galloway - ordered off soon afterwards - and another by substitute Ferguson near the end, earned a 2-0 win over the league leaders, who also had Mark Walters red-carded in a tough, bruising battle. However, although Robertson returned to the goal trail in the 4-2 Hogmanay defeat by Celtic, a niggling pelvic injury left him struggling for fitness as Hearts erratic league form continued. By the end of February, they remained fourth bottom although by then, much of the attention was focussed on the forthcoming UEFA Cup clash against Bayern Munich.

Under coach Jupp Heynckes, the Germans, with stars like Augenthaler, Thon and Ekstrom, had netted 12 goals in their three away ties including three against Inter Milan at the San Siro Stadium. There was a huge demand for tickets and, despite speculation that the match might be switched to a larger venue like Hampden or Murrayfield, the first leg went ahead at Tynecastle on February 28th with prices increased for all parts of the ground.

Brian Whittaker had recently broken his leg but Craig Levein had made a successful comeback. The injured John Robertson was absent and the transfer-listed Iain Ferguson, who had earlier rejected moves to Dundee and Aberdeen, was drafted in as Hearts fielded - Smith; McLaren, McPherson, Levein, McKinlay; Bannon, Berry, Galloway, Black; Colquhoun, Ferguson. Subs. - Mackay, Foster.

The atmosphere was electric as the game kicked off but although Hearts failed to get an early goal, they were not thrown out of their stride. Exchanges were fairly even with Bayern lightning quick on the break but six minutes from half-time, Ferguson went close with a dipping shot. After the interval, Hearts took control and in 55 minutes, they went ahead when Iain Ferguson accepted a short free-kick from McKinlay before bulleting a tremendous 25-yarder past the German wall and high into the net. Tynecastle erupted and as Hearts pushed for a second, McPherson missed a golden opportunity in the dying minutes. It had been another memorable night down Gorgie way, with young Alan McLaren, Walter Kidd's successor at right-back, outstanding in a fine all-round team performance.

Two weeks later, Hearts, who had Gary Mackay in for Iain Ferguson with Galloway up front from the first-leg, came under heavy pressure in the quarter-full 100,000-capacity Olympic Stadium in Munich. However, just when they looked like weathering the storm, Bayern's West German international defender Augenthaler blasted a 30-yard shot high past Henry Smith in 17 minutes.

Soon afterwards, a rapier-like move allowed John Colquhoun to go right through from the halfway line only to shoot just wide. After the break, Bayern continued to make chances but Hearts were again unfortunate when Colquhoun's header rebounded from a post before Dave McPherson's shot was blocked on the line. Hearts were to regret their missed chances for with 20 minutes remaining, a Stefan Reuter cross left the Tynecastle defence in disarray as Danish defender Erland Johnsen made it 2-0.

In a last-ditch effort, Alex. MacDonald threw on substitutes John Robertson and Iain Ferguson but despite a gallant finish, Hearts were unable to get the vital away goal that would have put them through. Nevertheless, the Gorgie men had done themselves proud and at the end they were given a standing ovation from their 3,000 fans.

Now, just days after their European exit, Hearts, who had earlier disposed of First Division Ayr United (4-1) and Partick Thistle (2-0) at Tynecastle, returned to face Celtic in the Scottish Cup quarter-final at Parkhead. Celtic made all the early running and in 18 minutes Mark McGhee outpaced Craig Levein - still struggling from an earlier knock - and went on to open the scoring.

Nine minutes from the interval, a Roy Aitken penalty made it 2-0 after Dave McPherson was harshly adjudged to have fouled McGhee in the box and furious Hearts protests ended with a red card for Alan McLaren. Soon afterwards, Tosh McKinlay scythed down Billy Stark and following an unseemly melee involving at least a dozen players, McKinlay and Celtic centre-half Mick McCarthy joined McLaren in the dressing room. After the break, nine-man Hearts had the better of exchanges but although Eamonn Bannon pulled one back 17 minutes from time, they were unable to save the tie.

After all the cup excitement, the remaining half dozen league games proved something of an anti-climax and sixth place was insufficient to ensure a European return. League performances had been disappointingly inconsistent and although Hearts had often played well, they had failed to convert their outfield supremacy into goals. Up front, Iain Ferguson had never looked the complete answer while John Robertson's appearances had been severely curtailed by his troublesome pelvic complaint which finally necessitated a hernia operation in the close season.

Nevertheless, Dave McPherson had been a tower of strength and after gaining a couple of Under-21 caps as an over-age player, his outstanding performances in Europe brought him full international honours against Cyprus and England, while Alan McLaren's rise to prominence was recognised with a Scotland Under-21 appearance and a new three year contract at Tynecastle.

Several players had moved on. Andy Bruce joined the police and the veteran Murray McDermott, on the Tynecastle books during the 1985-86 campaign, was signed as a short-term back-up keeper. The arrival of the experienced Eamonn Bannon meant the departure of Mark Gavin to Bristol City for £35,000 after just a handful of games while Hugh Burns had moved on to Dunfermline for £25,000 in December.

The £1-million outlay on Robertson and McKinlay had ensured a trading loss of £1,005,522 and to help balance the books, Malcolm Murray was sold to Hull City for £40,000, Alan Moore joined St Johnstone for £85,000 while Kenny Black joined the out of favour Iain Ferguson and Wayne Foster on the transfer-list after failing to agree a new contract. In May, Black, a good servant in his five years at Tynecastle, was transferred to Portsmouth for £280,000 and the following month Mike Galloway, whose fine work in midfield had been rewarded with a Scotland Under-21 appearance, joined Celtic for £550,000.

In an effort to reinforce his midline, Alex. MacDonald paid £100,000 for Rangers midfielder Davie Kirkwood (22), while £200,000 was spent on Red Star Belgrade striker Husref Musemic (28), a regular at Under-21 international level with one full international appearance for Yugoslavia. The 6'2" Musemic got off to a good start with the only goal in a pre-season friendly against Sunderland but there was a disappointing start to the 1989-90 league season with a 3-1 home defeat by Celtic.

Hearts recovered to beat St Mirren 2-1 at Paisley before a Musemic header from a well-flighted Kirkwood free-kick brought a 1-0 derby success against Hibs at Tynecastle. Alex. MacDonald further strengthened the side by bringing in former Manchester United and Newcastle midfielder Dave McCreery (32), on a free-transfer from Swedish club Sudsvall. Operating in a deep-lying role, the 66-times capped Northern Ireland international midfielder soon settled and by the end of the first quarter of the league programme on October 14th, Hearts lay second alongside Motherwell, Hibs, Aberdeen, and just two points behind Celtic.

In his first seven games, the skilful Musemic netted four times but he was soon on the sidelines, Alex. MacDonald preferring a more industrious style of striker who would put opposing defenders under pressure. In addition, the Yugoslav's English was limited, and it was no surprise when he joined Yugoslavian side Sarajevo on a free transfer a few months later.

Perfect balance - Gary Mackay shows his skills against Dundee's Stuart Beedie.

In contrast, Scott Crabbe, who had made just seven appearances over the past three sea-

Heart of Midlothian F.C. 1989-90. BACK - Tosh McKinlay, Eamonn Bannon, Davie Kirkwood, Neil Berry, Ian Jardine, Walter Kidd. MIDDLE - Wayne Foster, Brian Whittaker, Husref Musemic, Henry Smith, Craig Levein, Alan McLaren, Jimmy Sandison. FRONT - Walter Borthwick (coach), Scott Crabbe, Gary Mackay, Dave McPherson, John Robertson, Iain Ferguson, John Colquhoun, and Alex. MacDonald (manager)

sons, had burst back on the scene with a series of energetic performances to net nine goals in 11 games. With John Robertson still recuperating, Crabbe had seized his chance and his impressive form earned him a Scotland Under-21 appearance against Yugoslavia along with team-mates Alan McLaren and Davie Kirkwood.

Hearts had again reached the last eight of the Skol Cup. First they disposed of Montrose 3-0 at Tynecastle before defeating First Division Falkirk 4-1 in a real rough house at Brockville, where Neil Berry and Scott Crabbe were taken off injured and the Bairns reduced to eight men following the dismissal of McWilliams, Beaton and Callaghan. On August 30th, 25,000 fans turned out for the quarter-final against Celtic at Tynecastle. Early Hearts pressure forced Bonner into some good saves before Scott Crabbe put them ahead with a 19th minute free-kick and, as Celtic hit back, it developed into an end-to-end thriller.

Jackie Dziekanowski levelled in 65 minutes but in the dying seconds only a timely save by Bonner kept out a Musemic header. In the ninth minute of extra-time, Andy Walker put Celtic in front but with time running out, John Robertson, on as substitute in his first appearance of the season, picked up a Gary Mackay pass to make it 2-2. Hearts had played well but in the penalty shoot-out, Bonner saved from Colquhoun and McLaren while Robertson hit the post as Celtic went on to win 3-1.

Still short of match fitness, John Robertson was brought back gradually, and with Musemic and Iain Ferguson out of the picture, Wayne Foster was given an extended run alongside Crabbe and Colquhoun. Dave McPherson had attracted interest from Spurs and Borrussia Dortmund but transfer speculation ended when the Scottish international signed a new two year deal with Hearts.

Hearts continued to mount a determined title challenge and a fine 6-3 home win over Dundee on November 11th elevated them to the top of the Premier League ahead of Aberdeen and Rangers on goal-difference. The elusive John Colquhoun - scorer of 16 goals last term - was the star performer with a hat-trick and two assists, the pick of the bunch coming just before half-time when he cut past two defenders before rifling a 18-yard shot past Carson.

However, an inexplicable slump brought just two wins from their next six games before a John Robertson double ensured a 2-0 home victory over Hibs on New Year's Day. Further victories against Dundee (a) 1-0, Motherwell (a) 3-0 and Dundee United (h) 3-2 and a 2-0 Scottish Cup success at Falkirk took the tally to five successive wins and by the end of January, the buzz was back at Tynecastle.

Second-placed Hearts still remained six points behind Rangers and now they faced two crucial away games against their nearest title rivals. On February 3rd, Iain Ferguson came off the bench to snatch the equaliser in a four-goal thriller at Aberdeen but the slender lifeline was all but severed the following week when struggling Dunfermline departed from Tynecastle with a shock 2-0 win. Then came a no-scoring draw against Rangers at Ibrox to leave Hearts eight points behind with nine games left, and all hopes now lay with the Scottish Cup.

Motherwell, who Hearts had already decisively defeated in three tousy league encounters - in which Kidd, Foster and Mackay were dismissed - stood in the way of a place in the last eight. However, the Steelmen again proved no match for a rampant Hearts who ran up a comprehensive 4-0 home win to set up a quarter-final clash with strong-going Aberdeen at Pittodrie on March 17th.

The Dons made a whirlwind start and in seven minutes Bett beat Kidd before firing past Henry Smith. Gradually, Hearts fought back and just before half-time, John Colquhoun made it 1-1 after Scott Crabbe's shot was blocked on the line from a corner. However, prompted by the midfield skills of Jim Bett and Charlie Nicholas, Aberdeen took control and with 15 minutes remaining, Hearts hopes foundered when Gillhaus and Irvine struck twice in two minutes, Nicholas making it 4-1 near the end.

That result came as a major blow, for after such an impressive run, it had been Hearts worst display of the season, and they could only look on in envy as Aberdeen proceeded to lift the Scottish Cup. Hearts went on to finish third behind the Dons on goal-difference with the champions Rangers, seven points better off. However, there was the consolation of a place in next season's UEFA Cup and there was no doubting the quality of players at Tynecastle.

Craig Levein had capped a successful comeback with Scotland appearances against Argentina and East Germany and along with Dave McPherson, he played in that summer's World Cup Finals in Italy. Now Hearts had no fewer than seven players - Levein, McPherson, Mackay, Smith, Colquhoun, Bannon and McCreery with full international experience. In addition, top scorer John Robertson had appeared twice for the Scotland 'B' team while five others had played for Scotland's Under-21's.

Last December, Sandy Clark had become manager of Partick Thistle with Ian Jardine joining him as player-coach for a fee of £25,000. However, with just two wins from 17 games, Clark had been sacked and after spending a short period as a player at Dunfermline, he returned to Tynecastle as coach in April. However, intriguing as Clark's return had been, it was nothing compared to the sensational developments of the close season.

For the record - Hearts signed Derek Ferguson from Rangers for £750,000, equalling the record fee paid for John Robertson.

Just prior to the start of the World Cup in June, Wallace Mercer had mounted an ultimately abortive £6.2 million takeover bid for Edinburgh rivals Hibernian, who were in serious financial difficulties. He envisaged selling both grounds then playing at a new stadium on a greenfield site on the outskirts of Edinburgh. However, the merger was lambasted by both sets of supporters, particularly those of Hibs, who proceeded to mount a successful "Hands off Hibs" campaign. Bricks were thrown through his office windows and after a number of death threats, police guards were stationed at the home of the Tynecastle chairman.

Later that summer, Alex. MacDonald made a bold attempt to add what he hoped might be the final piece to the team jigsaw, equalling Hearts transfer record by paying £750,000 for the talented Rangers Scottish international midfielder Derek Ferguson (23). However, things did not go to plan and the opening two league games of the 1990-91 campaign against St Mirren and Dunfermline yielded just a single point.

Wins over Cowdenbeath and St Mirren - the latter, courtesy of an extra-time strike by Scotland's "Young Player of the Year" Scott Crabbe - took Hearts into the last eight the Skol Cup. But on Wednesday, September 5th, Pittodrie once again proved the graveyard of their hopes as they crashed 3-0 to a rampant Aberdeen.

The writing was on the wall for the Hearts boss, for after the Musemic fiasco, thus far, Derek Ferguson also had done little to justify his massive transfer fee, whereas it had not gone unnoticed that the Dons had got excellent value from their moderately-priced Dutch imports, particularly goalkeeper Theo Snelders and striker Hans Gillhaus. A few days later, the Maroons went down 3-1 to Rangers at Ibrox and with just two wins from their opening six games, Alex. MacDonald was dismissed along with assistant-boss Walter Borthwick. "There is obviously something missing and we need someone who can now take the club forward," explained Wallace Mercer. MacDonald was stunned but his thoughts remained with the supporters, "We have hit the crossbar so often in recent seasons - it would have been nice to give the fans a trophy."

MacDonald had been popular with his players who were openly critical of the board. John Robertson commented, "It's scandalous, a shocking decision, pandering to the whims of a couple of hundred fans. In his eight-and-a-half years at Tynecastle, Alex. MacDonald sweated blood for Hearts, taking us from the First Division back to the higher echelons of Scottish football." The revolt was short-lived but after the furore caused by his abortive takeover, the increasingly unpopular Wallace Mercer wisely absented himself from the potentially explosive derby clash against Hibs at Easter Road.

Under interim manager Sandy Clark, two first-half goals by John Robertson and another by Craig Levein gave Hearts a 3-0 win - their biggest derby winning margin since the start of the Premier League. Sadly, however, it was an afternoon of shame with 30 arrests and John Robertson attacked by a Hibs "fan" who was restrained by home keeper Andy Goram, the referee then taking the players off the field before order was restored.

Chapter Seventeen

JOE JORDAN

On September 21st, Hearts announced that former Scotland striker Joe Jordan (38), one of the biggest names in British football, would be their new manager. Jordan, who had played for Morton, Leeds United, Manchester United, A.C. Milan, Southampton and Bristol City before becoming boss of the Ashton Gate club, would receive £100,000 per annum, a salary second only to Graeme Souness of Rangers in Scotland.

The rugged Jordan, who had come highly recommended by Kenny Dalglish, Alex. Ferguson and Jock Wallace, was a popular choice. However, the new boss was blunt, "I'm here to manage Hearts and I'll do it my way. I want to be successful at Tynecastle and to win things but I'm under no illusions over how difficult that will be. I know how the players felt about Alex. MacDonald and I want to continue his good work."

Despite their initial claim of £175,000 - Hearts had offered £40,000 - Bristol City were later awarded £75,000 compensation by an international tribunal, who cleared Hearts of poaching Jordan since he had a get-out clause in his contract and had applied for the job. A few days before Jordan's arrival, Hearts - minus suspended skipper Dave McPherson - had returned from the sparsely populated Meteor Stadium in Dnepropetrovsk with a creditable 1-1 draw from their UEFA Cup, first round, first leg clash against the Ukranian side Dniepr Dnepropetrovsk.

Joe Jordan's Tynecastle career got off to an inauspicious start with a 3-0 defeat by Celtic at Parkhead but the following week, an Eamonn Bannon goal brought a 1-0 home win over Dundee United prior to the second leg against Dniepr on October 3rd. Scenting further European glory and boosted by Joe Jordan's arrival, nearly 19,000 fans made their way to Tynecastle.

Derek Ferguson, who had not yet shown his true form, was dropped, while Iain Ferguson, who had started just one game last term before going on loan to Charlton Athletic then Joe Jordan's Bristol City, had replaced Scott Crabbe, who was still recovering from food poisoning contracted before the Skol Cup match at Aberdeen. Hearts - Smith; McLaren, McPherson, Levein, McKinlay; Colquhoun, Wright, Kirkwood, Bannon; Robertson, I. Ferguson. Subs. - Mackay, D. Ferguson.

With 19 minutes gone, Dave McPherson dived to head home a Tosh McKinlay free-kick and with the Soviets reeling, John Robertson made it 2-0 with a penalty soon afterwards. Midway through the first period, George Wright, who had recently been drafted into the Scotland Under-21 squad after impressing in the Hearts midfield, was stretchered off with a leg injury and almost on half-time, Shakhov pulled one back from the spot after Bagmut was brought down by McKinlay.

However, within 60 seconds, the fans were back on their feet when Colquhoun nodded on a McLaren cross for Robertson to head Hearts into a 3-1 lead and orchestrated by Euro veteran Eamonn Bannon, a fine disciplined performance in the second period put the Maroons through to meet Bologna in the second round.

Joe Jordan - fans hoped the new boss would lead Hearts to silverware.

The next three Premier League games brought just one point courtesy of a 1-1 draw at Motherwell with disappointing defeats by St Johnstone (h) 2-3 and Aberdeen (a) 0-3 and to the consternation of the fans, prices would be almost doubled for the visit of Bologna on October 24th. Fans who purchased a £1 programme at the St Johnstone game were entitled to a £2 Euro discount but the ploy backfired when only 5,000 of the 15,000 programmes printed were sold and the Bologna game attracted nearly 8,000 fans less than had watched Dniepr.

There were two changes from the side that had beaten the Russians, Wayne Foster and Neil Berry coming in for the injured John Robertson and George Wright. It took only six minutes to breach the Italian defence, Foster working a slick one-two with Ferguson before hitting home a fierce left-footer.

As Hearts maintained the pressure, a Ferguson shot was cleared off the line and when Colquhoun cut the ball back, Foster was on hand to make it 2-0. Shortly before half-time, Ferguson saw his header touched onto the bar by Cusin but revelling in the big-match atmosphere, the fair-haired striker raced in to nod home the rebound.

Hearts had dominated but, in 60 minutes, Bologna were awarded an indirect free-kick in the box when Henry Smith was booked for time-wasting. Bonini rolled the ball to Notaristefano whose shot deflected off the defensive wall and into the net and Tynecastle was momentarily stunned to silence. Three minutes later, West German striker Herbert Wass was ordered off for a wild tackle on McPherson but although the scoreline remained 3-1 for Hearts, the Italians had grabbed a priceless away goal.

Meanwhile, there appeared to be a crisis of confidence as Hearts fell 2-1 to lowly St Mirren at Paisley before the loss of another point at home to Dunfermline left them bottom of the Premier League prior to the return leg at Bologna's Dall'Ora Stadium on November 7th. And to freshen things up, Joe Jordan appointed as his asistant-manager Raith Rovers boss Frank Connor (54), who had extensive managerial experience after spells at Cowdenbeath, Berwick,

Motherwell and Celtic.

The Hearts boss made two changes from the first-leg, Mackay and Robertson replacing McLaren and the flu-stricken Foster. However, after weathering the early pressure, Hearts went behind in 20 minutes when Bologna golden boy, Lajos Detari, a Hungarian who had cost £3million from Olympiakos of Greece, latched onto a long ball which dropped behind Craig Levein, and went on to beat Henry Smith.

Before kick-off, fireworks had exploded amongst the crowd but onfield a disappointing Hearts created few chances. As Bologna turned the screw, only sterling work by Henry Smith and Dave McPherson kept them in the hunt but with just 16 minutes remaining, home skipper Villa got on the end of a Detari cross to make it 3-3 on aggregate. However, Bologna had a vital away goal and with Hearts now compelled to push forward, Mariani finished the tie with a third, six minutes from the end.

Hearts could have few complaints as their UEFA dreams evaporated in the afternoon sun. However, a John Colquhoun goal brought a welcome 1-0 win against Celtic at Tynecastle three days later although Derek Ferguson, who had just regained his place after 12 games on the sidelines, was ordered off for a bad tackle on Mike Galloway.

In December, Hearts parted company with Davie Kirkwood who joined Airdrie for £100,000, a similar fee taking Iain Ferguson to Motherwell where he would win a Scottish Cup Winner's medal just five months later. By the end of the month, home wins over joint-leaders, Aberdeen (1-0) and Motherwell (3-2) and a 1-1 draw at Parkhead left Hearts sixth though still three points off the bottom and on January 2nd, the revival continued against Alex. Miller's struggling Hibernian at Easter Road. In eight minutes, McKinlay thundered a 30-yard shot past the helpless Andy Goram with McPherson adding a second soon afterwards.

Just minutes from the interval, Robertson challenged Goram for a long ball at the edge of the box and Gary Mackay netted despite the desperate efforts of two defenders on the goal-line. After half-time, Pat McGinlay was ordered off for a foul on Crabbe and although Hibs pulled one back through an own-goal by Mackay, Craig Levein made it 4-1 in a match shown live on T.V.

As Hearts moved into mid-table, there was further encouragement when the Tynecastle club earned themselves £16,000 by winning the Tennents Sixes indoor tournament for the second time. However, the third round draw of the Scottish Cup threw up a tricky tie at Broomfield on January 26th against First Division Airdrie who were managed by former Hearts striker Jimmy Bone.

Hearts made a dream start in 10 minutes when a Gary Mackay 20-yarder was fumbled over the line by John Martin. Five minutes later, Scott Crabbe, just recently back after his illness, was taken off with damaged knee ligaments. he was replaced by Wayne Foster and although Airdrie showed plenty of fighting spirit, it was Hearts who made and wasted several good opportunities.

Shortly after the break, Paul Jack equalised and Hearts were stunned when Airdrie went ahead, John Watson heading home from a corner in 58 minutes. With an upset on the cards, the Gorgie men piled on the pressure and with time running out, a Robertson header was cleared off the line by Stewart. However, Hearts battle was in vain and at the end the players were booed off by the fans who threw their scarves onto the track.

The premature cup exit was a financial disaster for the Tynecastle club who were now some £2.5 million in the red. Hearts did not have their troubles to seek and the following week John Robertson required six stitches in a bad head wound with Neil Berry sustaining serious cruciate ligament damage which would sideline him for over a year as the Maroons slumped to a 5-0 defeat at Aberdeen.

However, Wallace Mercer had made it clear that he was not willing to take on further debt to rebuild the side and Joe Jordan commented, "Ideally, we could just add to the squad but without the finance, some players will have to leave before others are brought in." That brought renewed

Beginning of the end - Renate Villa turns away after netting Bologna's second goal to make the aggregate score 3-3 in the Dall'Ora Stadium. Disconsolate Hearts are Iain Ferguson, Henry Smith, Davie Kirkwood and Dave McPherson.

speculation over the future of £1.5-million-rated Dave McPherson, who was now a Scotland regular, with Chelsea, Southampton and Manchester City all reportedly showing interest.

Lethal weapon - Ian Baird looks on as Hearts striker John Robertson finds the net in a 1-1 draw against Hibs in the Edinburgh derby in November 1991. DC Thomson

After a long spell in the wings, Nicky Walker now got his chance in goals but from then until the end of the season, Hearts form was erratic although only the goalkeeping heroics of Andy Goram prevented them bettering their 3-1 winning margin over struggling Hibs at Tynecastle on March 23rd.

By then Jordan was planning for next season and the promising Tommy Harrison was introduced to first-team football as Hearts went on to finish a disappointing fifth. The defence, normally the strongest part of the team, had lost 55 league goals, the worst defensive record since 1984-85 while the forwards had had a frustrating season.

John Robertson had finished top scorer with only 16 goals but he had finally made his full international breakthrough, netting Scotland's winner against Romania after coming off the bench. He went on to earn five caps that season while Dave McPherson, recently named Player of the Year for the third successive season by the 44-strong Federation of Hearts Supporters Clubs, was again a Scotland regular. Craig Levein also made a couple of apearances with Alan McLaren again featuring for the Under-21's.

In addition to Ian Ferguson and Davie Kirkwood, a number of the old guard had moved on. The long-serving Walter Kidd was given a free transfer while Brian Whittaker, who remained on the Tynecastle commercial staff, had earlier joined Falkirk for £30,000. After turning down a move to Airdrie in October, Jimmy Sandison established himself at right-back before accepting a new two-year deal but when he again fell from favour late in the season, he decided to rejoin old boss Alex. MacDonald at Broomfield with Hearts accepting a fee of £100,000.

In July, John Colquhoun was transferred to Millwall for £400,000 while reserve midfielder Max Christie joined Meadowbank for £40,000 in August. After an early season injury, Dave McCreery had also become surplus to requirements and he later moved on to Hartlepool on a free transfer. The sale of Colquhoun and Sandison had generated £500,000 and now Joe Jordan could begin to reshape his side. He spent £350,000 on bustling Middlesbrough striker Ian Baird, who had previously played for Southampton, Leeds United and Portsmouth. In addition, Blackburn midfielder John Millar (25), arrived on a free transfer while former Northern Ireland international winger Steve Penney (27), was another free transfer signing from Brighton.

Although Nicky Walker had finished last season as the number one keeper, a nasty cheekbone injury sustained in a closed-doors match meant Henry Smith starting the 1991-92 season in goal. League reconstruction had brought the Premier League back to 12 teams, as it had been between 1986 and 1988, entailing a marathon 44-game programme. Hearts faced a tricky start away to Dunfermline and Airdrie but despite the dismissal of Tosh McKinlay at East End Park then Craig Levein at Broomfield, full points were taken as their league campaign got off to a flier.

On August 17th, the Maroons faced their first major test with a home game against Rangers who were now under the management of Walter Smith. After just 80 seconds, a rejuvenated Scott Crabbe hammered a dipping volley past Goram. Hard as they tried, Rangers could not penetrate the stubborn home defence, where skipper Dave McPherson made an excellent job of subduing the formidable Mark Hateley, and Hearts 100% record remained intact.

The Maroons continued with a 3-0 win over Clydebank in the Skol Cup before the squad was further strengthened by the £200,000 signing of powerfully built Portsmouth defender Graeme Hogg (27). Joe Jordan denied that this was a prelude to Dave McPherson's departure and the former Manchester United and Scotland Under-21 international looked a sound investment although he was ordered off for jersey-pulling at Hamilton in the third round of the Skol Cup. However, in a game of few chances, Hearts still did enough to reach the quarter-finals, Robertson putting them ahead with a 47th minute penalty and Baird settling the issue near the end after a shot by substitute Tommy Harrison rebounded from the post.

Hearts had also made a splendid start in the Premier League, taking nine points from their opening five games to lie joint top of the table with Aberdeen. Hearts had switched to a 3-4-3 formation and a delighted Joe Jordan was full of praise for Gary Mackay and Tosh McKinlay in their new wing-back roles with Henry Smith getting a special mention for keeping five successive clean sheets.

The Skol Cup quarter-final draw ensured a swift return to Tynecastle for Rangers but it was Hearts who began in full flight. Goram saved from Baird and Robertson but although Rangers were only seen in flashes, they went ahead when Hateley headed down a David Robertson cross for Ally McCoist to squeeze the ball home in 25 minutes. After that, Rangers defended well and although Hearts expended plenty of effort, they were unable to retrieve the situation.

Hearts recovered to take seven points from their next four games before going down 3-1 to Celtic at Parkhead in their first league defeat of the season. Four days later, nearly 16,000 flocked to Tynecastle for the top of the table clash against Aberdeen on Tuesday, October 9th. Once again, Hearts got off to a great start, Scott Crabbe taking a short free-kick from Baird before shooting past Theo Snelders. That proved the only goal of a titanic struggle and now Hearts were one point clear of Rangers at the top of the Premier League after 11 games.

In October, the Tynecastle title challenge was bolstered by the £100,000 signing of Raith Rovers striker Ian Ferguson (22). The lanky newcomer grabbed the only goal on his starting debut at Motherwell but over the next few months his appearances would mainly be confined to the bench.

Joe Jordan had instilled the will to win and from the start of the season a virtually unchanged team of Smith; McLaren, McPherson, Levein; Mackay, D. Ferguson, Millar, McKinlay; Crabbe, Baird, Robertson with Wright, Bannon, Hogg and now Ferguson available to step in, had performed with great consistency. By the end of 1991, only two games away to Celtic (1-3) and to Rangers (0-2) had been lost from 21 league games as Hearts remained top, two points clear of Rangers.

The gritty John Millar had proved a highly effective ball-winner in midfield while alongside him, Derek Ferguson was again carving out the opportunities. Up front, the powerful Ian Baird played the traditional target-man, a role which brought out the best in Robertson and Crabbe, who were both scoring on a regular basis.

In October, Hibernian had beaten Dunfermline to win the Skol Cup but despite having to settle for a 1-1 draw with their old rivals in the Ne'erday clash at Tynecastle, Hearts bounced back to beat Celtic 2-1 at Parkhead a few days later. However, three successive defeats to Aberdeen (h) 0-4, Airdrie (a) 1-2 and league leaders Rangers (h) 0-1 came as a near fatal blow to their title hopes and it was now imperative that Hearts put together a decent Scottish Cup run.

The third round draw sent sent the Gorgie men to Paisley where they found themselves down to ten men after Ian Baird was red-carded for a late challenge on home keeper Campbell Money. The injured Money was taken off and although the match ended 0-0, St Mirren's anger remained for the Tynecastle replay on Wednesday, February 5th.

In a ragged opening period, Kenny McDowall was booked for a foul on Tosh McKinlay before being sent off for sarcastically applauding Edinburgh whistler George Smith. Strangely, it was 10-man Saints who looked the more lively, a Chic Charnley shot striking the bar before Hearts were awarded a controversial 68th minute penalty when Ian Ferguson appeared to be fouled just outside the box. John Robertson made no mistake from the spot, going on to complete his hat-trick, although not before Charnley had been dismissed for stamping on Ian Ferguson.

In the fourth round, a Billy Davies free-kick put Dunfermline ahead after only 85 seconds at East End Park. Graeme Hogg scrambled an equaliser but despite Hearts almost total domination, Pars keeper Andy Rhodes looked almost unbeatable until Scott Crabbe diverted a John

Spot on - John Millar looks on as Scott Crabbe nets from the spot against Motherwell at Tynecastle. The Hearts striker burst back to form with 17 goals in the 1991-92 campaign.
DC Thomson

Millar shot into the net in the dying seconds. Now, the Maroons faced Falkirk in the quarter-final at Tynecastle on Sunday, March 8th. Live TV coverage had cut the attendance to 11,227 but even before a ball had been kicked there was drama when Ian Baird pulled a muscle in the pre-match warm-up.

Joe Jordan requested that Scott Crabbe - not listed as one of the substitutes - be allowed to play. However, Bairns boss and former Tynecastle stalwart Jim Jefferies refused and Baird was replaced by substitute Eamonn Bannon with Steve Penney joining Wayne Foster on the bench.

In two minutes, Ian Ferguson put Hearts ahead with a cracking volley and although Sam McGivern levelled within four minutes, Hearts soon regained their lead, Dave McPherson flicking on a McKinlay free-kick for John Robertson to net at the back post. In 32 minutes, Crawford Baptie was ordered off for a "professional foul" on Ian Ferguson and although Hearts made heavy weather of things, a late Gary Mackay goal put Hearts into the last four.

In the semi-final, Hearts would meet Airdrie, now managed by former Tynecastle manager Alex. MacDonald and who included no fewer than five former Tynecastle men - Walter Kidd, Jimmy Sandison, Kenny Black, Davie Kirkwood and Sandy Stewart. Recently, Hearts had signed left-back Glynn Snodin (32), on a free-transfer from Leeds United and with Baird injured, they fielded - Smith; McLaren, McPherson, Levein, McKinlay; Mackay, Wright, D. Ferguson, Bannon; I. Ferguson, Robertson. Subs. Crabbe, Snodin. Airdrie, who, like Hearts had had nine players red-carded that season, fielded - Martin; Kidd, Sandison, Honor, Stewart; Boyle, Kirkwood, Balfour, Black; Lawrence, Coyle. Subs - Conn, Jack.

Although Alan McLaren and Dave Kirkwood came close to breaking the deadlock, the 27,310 crowd witnessed a Hampden shocker with long spells of scrappy play. Hearts were unable to throw off the shackles of tight marking Airdrie but, with just 15 minutes remaining, Dave McPherson found the net with a header only to have the "goal" controversially disallowed for a push on Evan Balfour. In the dying seconds, Airdrie keeper John Martin clawed back a John Robertson shot that appeared to have crossed the line but despite strong appeals by Hearts, no goal was given as the game finished goalless.

Hearts continued to struggle with a 1-0 win at Motherwell and a no-scoring home draw against St Mirren and it was little surprise when only 11,163 fans took the trouble to attend the semi-final replay, 10 days later. Snodin, Millar, Baird and Crabbe came in for McKinlay, Wright, Ferguson and Mackay - the latter out with a back injury - with Ferguson and Wright on the bench.

Despite the cold windy weather, both sides were much improved although Airdrie - who had no fewer than six players booked - were again quick to close Hearts down. In 28 minutes, Henry Smith was penalised for taking four steps with the ball and Kenny Black thundered the free-kick high into the net. Hearts battled back and were unlucky when a Snodin shot crashed off the bar. But with only 90 seconds remaining, a low skidding cross by Eamonn Bannon eluded the Broomfield defence and Alan McLaren slid the ball home at the far post.

Bounce of the ball - Alan McLaren holds off Airdrie's Alan Lawrence in the Scottish Cup semi-final at Hampden. DC Thomson

In extra time, Hearts pounded the Airdrie goal, Robertson twice hitting woodwork before the game went to a penalty shoot-out to decide who would meet Rangers in the final. As skipper, Dave McPherson elected to take Hearts first kick only for John Martin to save and although Derek Ferguson and John Robertson scored, Scott Crabbe hit the bar with the fourth kick as Airdrie went on to win 4-2.

That result came as a bitter blow and although Hearts went on to finish runners-up, nine points behind Premier League Champions Rangers, home attendances had slumped to below the 7,000 mark. Although Hearts disciplinary record - nine red cards and 68 bookings - left a lot to be desired, Jordan had brought a significant improvement, particularly in defence where just 37 goals were conceded compared to 55 in season 1990-91 when six games less had been played.

Dave McPherson was again a Scotland regular and although Craig Levein dropped out of the reckoning, John Robertson and the recalled Henry Smith both added to their tally of caps with Alan McLaren on the fringes of full international recognition.

Backed by the Federation of Hearts Supporters' Clubs and the Shareholders' Association, the Hearts board which comprised Wallace Mercer, Pilmar Smith, Jim Clydesdale, Colin Wilson, Bobby Parker and Les Porteous had submitted a planning application for a 50 acre site at Millerhill which encompassed a new 20,000 capacity stadium with various other leisure activities. However, this scheme was rejected, as was a re-application for a slimmed-down ver-

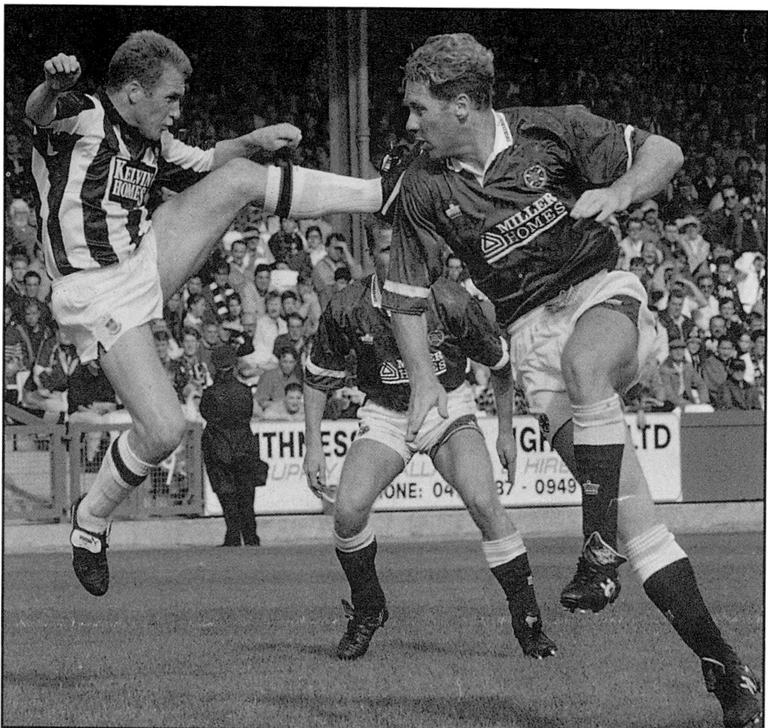

In where it hurts - Chic Charnley of St Mirren and Hearts striker Ian Baird challenge for the ball in this clash at Love Street. DC Thomson

sion before Hearts were also unsuccessful in their request to the Royal Highland Show Authority for suitable land at Ingliston.

The £750,000 fee for Derek Ferguson plus expenses incurred during the abortive takeover of Hibs, compensation paid to the departing managerial team and to Bristol City at the time of Joe Jordan's arrival, increased expenditure on salaries, the loss of revenue from falling gates and, not least, the resultant interest charges, were all contributory factors as Hearts slipped further and further into the red. Last term, average home league gates had slipped to just over 13,000 and with debts estimated as approaching £3 million, it was no great surprise when Hearts skipper and 23-times capped Scottish international Dave McPherson was transferred to Rangers for £1.3 million just before the European Championships in May.

The departure of the popular McPherson came as the latest blow to the fans' ever-decreasing morale, even although £90,000 was spent on Aberdeen's versatile Dutchman Peter Van De Ven as a replacement, the squad being further augmented by former Killie and Motherwell midfielder Ally Mauchlen (32), from Leicester City and ex-St Mirren full-back Tommy Wilson from Dunfermline, on free transfers.

Prior to the new season, John Robertson's Testimonial game against Newcastle, which Hearts won 1-0, attracted over 11,000 fans while the visit of Tottenham Hotspur, who departed with a 2-1 win, was also well attended with 1950's hero Dave Mackay given a rousing reception when he took his place as a guest in the directors' box.

Despite an opening day league reverse to Celtic at Parkhead, Hearts proceeded to take 12 points from their opening eight league games with an assured Peter Van De Ven slotting in well at the back. In the Skol Cup, it took a late header from newly appointed captain Alan McLaren to see off Clydebank (1-0) at Tynecastle with extra-time required to dispose of plucky Brechin City (2-1) at Glebe Park. That set up a lucrative home tie against Celtic in the quarter-finals on Wednesday, August 26th but although Hearts did most of the attacking, it was Celtic who went in front through Andy Payton in 36 minutes.

Six minutes later, Gary Mackay delighted the Tynecastle faithful by cracking in the equaliser from 20 yards. However, eight minutes after the break, Hearts were stunned when Polish left-back Dariusz Wdowczyk scored direct from a corner and despite dominating for long spells, they were unable to retrieve the situation.

By early November, Hearts had also lost interest in the UEFA Cup. On September 16th, they had travelled to the Czech Republic for their UEFA Cup tie against Slavia Prague who had soon impressed with their fast, incisive play. However, with Henry Smith in top form and Neil Berry, now recovered after 18 months out with cruciate trouble, proving a splendid deputy for the suspended Levein, Hearts defended valiantly against the speedy Czechs.

In 54 minutes, Hearts rode their luck when a Novak free-kick hit the post, rolled along the line and rebounded from the other upright. But with just seven minutes remaining, Slavia's Russian midfielder Tatarchuk lashed a free-kick from fully 35-yards out near the touchline, over the defensive wall and high past the poorly positioned Henry Smith for the only goal of the game.

Still, Hearts remained confident of overturning the narrow deficit and a fortnight later, the 16,000 Tynecastle crowd - three times the meagre attendance in Prague - went wild with delight when Gary Mackay shot low past Janos for the opener. Shortly afterwards, Silhavy flicked home the equaliser but in 21 minutes, Bannon played a one-two with Robertson before crossing for Baird to head home.

Three minutes from half-time, Tynecastle went wild when Levein backheaded into the net from a corner to put Hearts 3-2 ahead on aggregate. Snodin and McKinlay were booked along with Slavia's Penicka but the rough stuff continued and after twice ignoring Silhavy's off-the-ball challenges on John Robertson, referee Larsson sent off Penicka for a foul on Baird.

Although Slavia were down to 10-men, there was little between the sides and Kuka sent a hush around the Gorgie ground when he made it 3-3 after 65 minutes. Under the away goals rule, Hearts now trailed by two goals but, roared on by their fans, they pinned back the Czechs, who nevertheless, remained razor-sharp on the break. The atmposphere was electric but with just 11 minutes remaining, Glyn Snodin cracked a powerful 30-yard free-kick through the gap left by Eamonn Bannon at the end of the wall and past the despairing Janos for the winner.

It had been a Tynecastle classic and now Hearts would play Standard Liege of Belgium, who had been their first-ever opponents in European competition in 1958 and were currently joint top of the Belgian League along with Anderlecht. Prior to the first leg at Tynecastle on October 21st, Standard's Dutch coach Arie Haan declared himself unimpressed with Hearts, and after creating a number of early chances, the slick-passing Belgians went ahead through Alain Bettagno in just seven minutes. Mackay and Robertson both went close but although Hearts pinned the Belgians back after the interval they were unable to make any real impression and now it would be an uphill struggle in Liege on November 4th.

With Ian Ferguson replacing the suspended Ian Baird and Derek Ferguson also included after passing a late fitmess test, the Maroons began well. After missing a couple of half-chances, Robertson set up McKinlay whose shot was blocked by keeper Bodart who was injured and later substituted at half-time. Hearts had silenced the home support with their disciplined play but despite starting the second half in similar vein, Wilmots scored the vital goal for Standard in 63 minutes, and in the end the Belgians qualified comfortably for the next round, 2-0 on aggregate.

Back in September, a John Robertson goal had earned a 1-0 win over Aberdeen at Tynecastle to put Hearts alongside Rangers at the top of the Premier League. With Smith in goal and a back three of McLaren, Levein, Van De Ven or Hogg, a midfield of Mackay, Mauchlen, D. Ferguson and McKinlay and a front trio of Crabbe or Foster, Baird and Robertson, Hearts had a fairly settled side. However, the next four games brought just two points for the Maroons had flattered to deceive, too often labouring to low scoring single goal wins with the fans increasingly disgruntled with the fare on offer.

In October, Hearts had transferred Scott Crabbe, scorer of 17 goals last term, to Dundee United in part-exchange for the pacy Allan Preston plus £215,000 before putting together a six-game unbeaten run, which included a 1-0 win over Hibs at Tynecastle. Ian Baird scored the only goal with a back-post header while Gary Mackay bravely continued after suffering a broken cheekbone in an accidental clash with Hibs defender Gordon Hunter. However, the victory was further marred when Ally Mauchlen stamped on Darren Jackson, an unsavoury incident which surprisingly merited just a yellow card. However, it was widely seen on television and was not the sort of behaviour condoned by the vast majority of decent Hearts fans.

On November 28th, Hearts, who until then had the best defensive record in the league, crumbled to a 6-2 defeat at Aberdeen after Baird and Hogg had earlier retrieved a two-goal half-time deficit to make it 2-2 after 58 minutes. After the fifth goal, Tosh McKinlay was red-carded for a second booking and when the next two games brought further reverses at the hands of Falkirk (a) 1-2 and Airdrie (h) 1-3 angry fans demonstrated outside Tynecastle.

Nicky Walker had replaced Henry Smith and, despite losing three to Airdrie, the former Ibrox keeper went on to concede only another four goals in his next 12 games, well deserving his Scotland debut against Germany a few months later. Alongside him were Tynecastle colleagues, Craig Levein who captained the side - the first Hearts player to skipper Scotland in a full international since Dave Mackay against Northern Ireland in 1958, John Robertson and Alan McLaren - who had made his full international breakthrough in America last summer. On December 19th, Ian Ferguson netted in a 1-0 home win over Celtic before just 13,500 but that was to be Hearts sole success in nine games as they slipped to fourth, 11 points behind leaders Rangers.

The third round of the Scottish Cup brought a 6-0 romp against Huntly with former Bristol Rovers defender Adrian Boothroyd, who had arrived on a free-transfer in December, coming off the bench to net twice. In the next round, Hearts defeated Dundee 2-0 at Tynecastle with John Robertson shooting past Mathers from near the byeline for the decisive second with eight minutes remaining.

For the second successive season, the quarter-final draw paired Hearts with Falkirk who had belied their lowly league position by defeating Celtic 2-0 at the previous stage. Just after half-time, Hearts had a let off when Kevin Drinkell headed narrowly wide but almost immediately Preston put them ahead after Mackay's cross was not properly cleared. Falkirk had matched Hearts throughout but with eight minutes remaining, Neil Duffy brought down Baird and John Robertson beat Marshall from the spot to clinch a semi-final clash against a powerful Rangers side, who had also reached the semi-final of that season's European Cup.

With ground reconstruction at Hampden, the semi-final went ahead at Parkhead on Saturday, April 3rd as Hearts fielded - Walker; McLaren, Levein, Van De Ven; Mackay, D. Ferguson, Millar, McKinlay; Robertson, Baird, Preston. Subs. I. Ferguson, Snodin. Rangers - Goram; McCall, Gough, McPherson, Robertson; Steven, I.

Up in attack - John Robertson looks on as Hearts skipper Craig Levein rises high in attempt to reach this corner kick in the UEFA Cup classic against Slavia Prague at Tynecastle. Daily Record

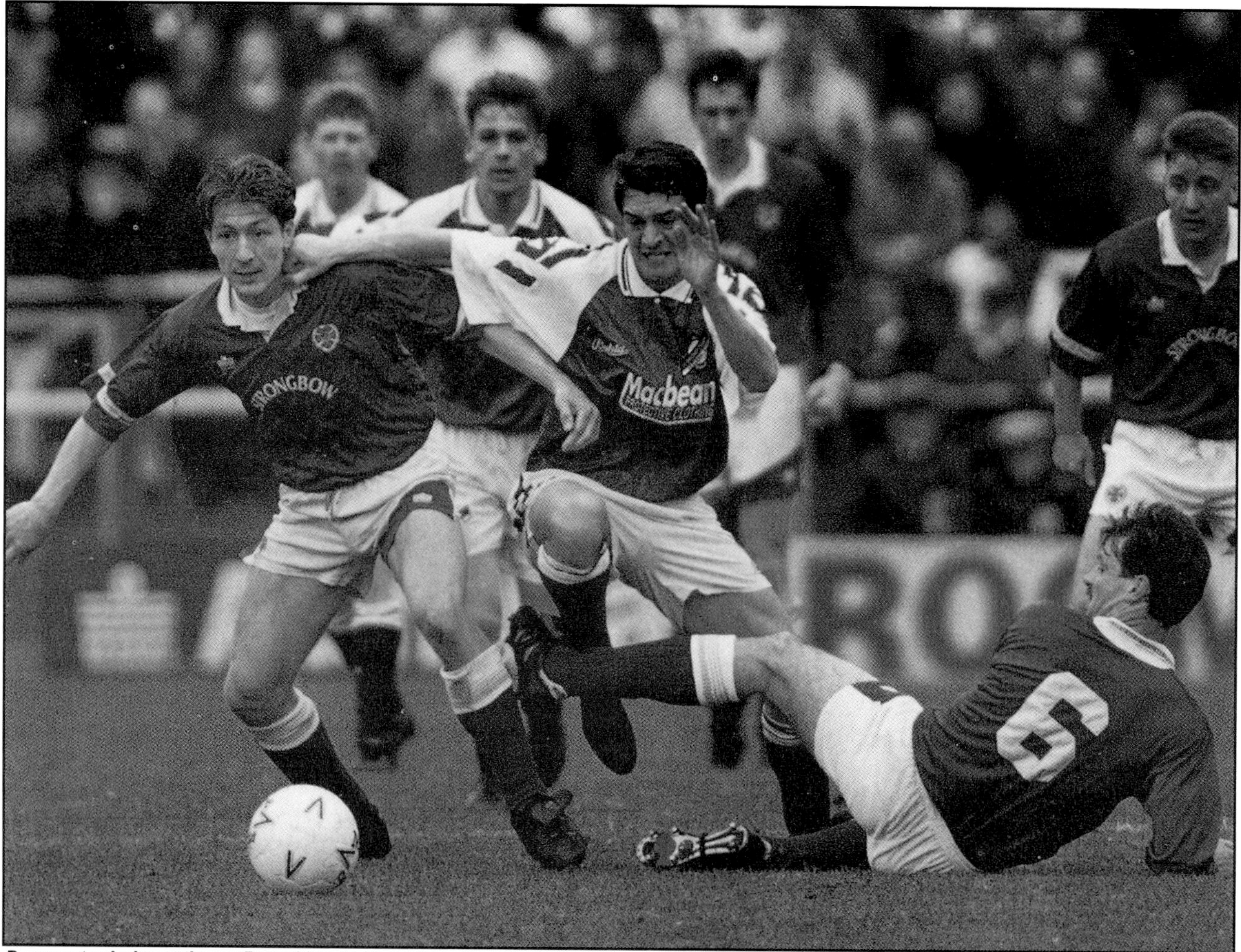

Desperate derby action - Peter Van de Ven slides in with John Millar and John Robertson standing by as Pat McGinlay of Hibs tries to make a breakthrough in this derby match against Hibernian at Tynecastle.
DC Thomson

Ferguson, Brown; McCoist, Hately, Hagen. Subs. Murray, Durrant.

There was little flowing football in a tense and often scrappy tie but with Derek Ferguson pulling the strings in midfield, Hearts held the edge for much of the opening period. Thirteen minutes after the interval, the Gorgie men went ahead when Alan Preston darted between Dave McPherson and Richard Gough to meet John Robertson's cross and send a superb flying header into the net. However, the Ibrox men fought back and from a disputed corner Dave McPherson equalised when a slack John Millar headed clearance fell at his feet. Now Hearts were up against it and with 15 minutes to go, their defence was beaten by a long through ball which prolific Ibrox striker Ally McCoist lofted over Nicky Walker and into the net, a split second before colliding with the keeper.

Hearts had been worth a draw with Derek Ferguson the most polished performer afield, but, unusually, defensive slackness had cost them dear. It was only the latest of a long catalogue of disappointments but the gloom continued with three successive defeats at the hands of Rangers (h) 2-3, Aberdeen (a) 2-3 and Motherwell (a) 1-2 following a goalless home draw with Dundee which ended hopes of a UEFA Cup place.

For weeks, there had been rumours of disharmony between manager and players and clearly time was running out for Joe Jordan. On May 1st, the Maroons crashed 6-0 to relegation-threatened Falkirk after a disgraceful performance at Brockville. The fans had howled for Jordan's head for it was clear that several players had no stomach for the fray as Hearts went down to their biggest defeat since the derby debacle against Hibs in January 1973.

A number of months earlier, a disillusioned Jordan had failed to get certain assurances from the board and had turned down the offer to extend his contract which would expire in September 1993. Two days after the Brockville debacle, Wallace Mercer, who had mysteriously disappeared to the south of France five weeks earlier, reappeared at Tynecastle to announce Joe Jordan's dismissal with Sandy Clark taking over as caretaker-manager.

Jordan's only surprise appeared to be over the timing of the announcement but he maintained that he had been successful with the limited resources available, "My time spent here has been invaluable and my successor will have something to build on with so many good youngsters."

Undoubtedly the manager had been a victim of the deteriorating financial situation at Tynecastle but he had come across as a man of few words and with rumours of internal conflict, it appeared highly significant that he had departed without saying goodbye to his players. And although his teams were certainly well-organised, they had never generated the same excitement as some of the famous teams he had played for and it was significant that average league gates were down by some 4,000 to just below the 10,000 mark.

Chapter Eighteen

TWO MORE IN THE HOT SEAT

Troubled times appeared to lie ahead for Hearts, who now faced a number of major problems. If anything, the financial position appeared to be worsening with a number of players having to appeal to the Scottish Professional Footballers' Association before their bonuses were paid. After failing to secure permission for a new stadium at a suitable location on the outskirts of Edinburgh, it was decided to to comply with the Taylor Report by redeveloping Tynecastle, a project which would require major capital investment of some £5 million.

After recently splitting from his property group, Wallace Mercer had moved to the South of France on medical advice . However, although many long-suffering fans felt a change of ownership was now overdue, the chairman scotched rumours of a takeover by former Rangers boss Graeme Souness, insisting the club was not for sale.

Last term, Sandy Clark had guided the club's youngsters to the BP Youth Cup and the Premier Reserve League title. Now, after an initial spell as caretaker-boss, he was appointed as Joe Jordan's successor. Frank Connor departed and Alloa boss Hugh McCann was named assistant-manager with two former Maroons Walter Kidd and Brian Whittaker joining the coaching staff.

Hearts had failed to win any of their final 10 games last season as they finished fifth, a massive 29 points behind five-in-a row Premier League Champions, Rangers. As Clark settled to his task of restoring Hearts fortunes, Eamonn Bannon and Glynn Snodin were released, while star midfielder Derek Ferguson was transferred to Sunderland for £500,000 with John Colquhoun returning to Tynecastle as part of the deal.

Ian Baird joined Bristol City on freedom of contract with Hearts later awarded £295,000 by the transfer tribunal. To replace him, Hearts brought in another experienced striker, the strapping Justin Fashanu (31), who had played for no fewer than 12 clubs. In his heyday, he had cost Nottingham Forest a massive £1 million and had recently impressed while on a short-term contract at Airdrie.

For the first time since 1988, Hearts did their pre-season work in Germany before going down 2-1 to Rangers in the opening league game at Ibrox. A John Robertson double then gave them a 2-0 League Cup win over Stranraer at Tynecastle to set up a third round clash against First Division Falkirk on Wednesday, August 25th.

Prior to that, Hearts had recorded 1-0 victories over newly promoted Raith Rovers and Hibs at Tynecastle, where 19-year-old Allan Johnston came off the bench to net the winner in a hard-fought Edinburgh derby. With seven minutes remaining, the youngster had cooly pulled down a Locke cross before turning inside Hunter to rifle a stunning shot high past Leighton.

Like any new manager, Sandy Clark had his own ideas of the type of players he wanted and Neil Berry - latterly a fringe player under Joe Jordan - returned to midfield alongside Gary Mackay and the promising George Wright. Hamilton sweeper Jim Weir (23), was signed for £300,000 despite interest by Blackburn and Dundee United. Peter Van De Ven then moved on to Racing Genk of Belgium for £90,000 while Allan Preston was exchanged for the industrious Dunfermline midfielder Scott Leitch.

Weir was already cup-tied and ineligible to face Falkirk but although Hearts had the lion's share of possession they lacked the guile to create many clear-cut chances. And with just seconds remaining, they paid the penalty when Bairns midfielder Eddie May swept a Duffy cross high past Henry Smith from the edge of the box.

The early cup exit was a serious blow to cash-strapped Hearts and by September 11th, indifferent league form left them in mid-table after six games. Justin Fashanu had proved well capable of upsetting opposing defences. However, he had managed just one goal in seven games, netting in a 2-1 win over Partick Thistle at Tynecastle, only to be red-carded after an off-the-ball incident which left Grant Tierney badly concussed.

The UEFA Cup draw had paired Hearts with Atletico Madrid, who although often overshadowed by the more illustrious Real Madrid, had previously reached four European finals and the match attracted nearly 16,000 to Tynecastle on September 14th. Alan McLaren, who had recovered from his early-season cartilege operation was included as Hearts lined up - Smith; Weir, Levein, McLaren; Locke, Mackay, Leitch, McKinlay; Colquhoun, Fashanu, Robertson. Subs. Thomas, Johnston.

Although the Atletico defence had been decimated through suspension and injury, Hearts were unable to break the deadlock in an ill-tempered first-half. Soon after the break, Hearts were denied a certain penalty when Lopez downed John Robertson but with 20 minutes remaining, the little striker raced in to lash the ball into the roof of the net after Atletico keeper Diego could only parry a powerful Fashanu header.

Urged on by the crowd, Hearts surged forward and they got another when John Colquhoun picked up a long diagonal pass by Locke and darted in to beat the outrushing keeper. That should have been the signal to shut up shop but with 13 minutes left, Atletico substitute and Polish international skipper Roman Kesecki burst past Alan McLaren before shooting past Smith.

Sandy Clark - top job after youth team successes.

A couple of weeks later, the 62,000 capacity Vicente Calderon Stadium in Madrid was just over half full as Hearts made one change from the first leg, Graeme Hogg, a standout in

On the spot - John Robertson has scored against Atletico Madrid at Tynecastle after keeper Diego could only parry a powerful header by Justin Fashanu. That broke the deadlock against the Spanish aces and Hearts went on to win the first leg 2-1. Daily Record

the recent 1-0 win over Celtic, retaining his place to the exclusion of Jim Weir. Hearts weathered a torrid opening spell but with just 10 minutes to the interval, a long-range free-kick from Pedro took a deflection, spinning away from Henry Smith to make it 2-2 on aggregate.

However, the slick-passing Atletico now led on away goals and although Fashanu had a shot blocked and Thomas and Ferguson were thrown on after the break to try and get a vital away goal, the roof fell in on Hearts with 18 minutes remaining. First, Gary Mackay was dispossessed in his own box and Manolo steered the ball home, then Henry Smith allowed an harmless-looking header by Luis Garcia to squirm through his hands and the more experienced Spaniards were through, 4-2 on aggregate.

On their return, Smith and Mackay were dropped but the Hearts scoring famine continued. Only one goal was scored in four games as a 1-0 defeat by Raith Rovers at Starks Park on October 16th left them third bottom in a season where three clubs would be relegated as the Premier League reverted to ten teams after the threat of a breakaway Scottish Super League two years earlier.

Hearts were desperate for a proven striker and when Everton cut their losses by releasing Mo Johnston - a flop since his £1.5 million transfer from Rangers - the former Scotland striker was lured to Tynecastle on a lucrative seven month "pay-as-you-play" deal. Johnston's arrival marked the end of the road for the highly paid Justin Fashanu and to further cut costs Ian Ferguson moved on to St Johnstone for £110,000, while Ally Mauchlen and Adrian Boothroyd joined Irish League side Glenavon and Mansfield Town, respectively, on free transfers.

Johnston's debut coincided with a 0-0 draw with Partick Thistle at Firhill but a 2-0 win over Hibs at Easter Road and a 2-2 draw against Rangers at Tynecastle appeared to mark a turning point in Hearts fortunes. However, the next 12 games brought just seven points and by January 12th, Hearts remained just a couple of points above the bottom trio of St Johnstone, Raith Rovers and Dundee.

The Scottish Cup third round draw threw up a tricky tie against Partick Thistle at Firhill. Almost on half-time, Maurice Johnston fired home the only goal of a scrappy game in which the controversial Chic Charnley was never far from the action. Two minutes previously, the Thistle midfielder had appeared to elbow Colquhoun, and although the Hearts winger was ordered-off for retaliation, Charnley himself escaped with a booking.

On February 20th, Hearts faced Hibs at Easter Road in the fourth round in a Sunday televised spectacular. Only two minutes had elapsed when Tosh McKinlay beat Willie Miller and from his low cross, John Robertson put Hearts ahead with his 20th derby goal. It was a tough tense affair which would end with three players from each side booked and, just before half-time, Hibs were level when Keith Wright headed home a Michael O'Neill cross.

The green-and-whites went close when McAllister hit a post but, three minutes from time, substitute Wayne Foster raced onto a splendid through ball by Gary Mackay to clip a low shot past Jim Leighton. That was the winner and there were wild celebrations amongst the Hearts legions who could now celebrate an astonishing unbeaten run of 21 derby games since January 1989.

That paved the way for a quarter-final clash against Rangers at Ibrox on March 12th. In the early stages, Hearts struggled to contain the Light Blues before themselves squandering a clutch of good chances before half-time. However, once John Brown thundered home a 30-yarder soon after the restart, there was no way back, Mark Hateley adding a second midway through the second-half.

Now Hearts could concentrate on escaping the relegation struggle which involved half the clubs in the Premier League. With nine games remaining, Raith Rovers and Dundee were almost certainly down and to bolster the side, Dundee midfielder Stevie Frail was signed for £130,000 before the transfer deadline. But despite taking four points from their next three games, a disastrous 2-0 defeat to Dundee on April 16th, left Hearts locked alongside the struggling Partick Thistle, St Johnstone and Kilmarnock.

Following a 0-0 draw with St Johnstone at McDiarmid Park, the board slashed admission prices for the vital midweek game against Aberdeen. Their initiative was rewarded when 14,000 fans - double the gate for the Dundee match - turned out as Hearts managed a 1-1 draw before another hard-earned point was taken from a 0-0 draw against Hibs at Easter Road. But with two games left, the grisly spectre of relegation remained, just two points separating four teams in the battle to escape relegation.

Hearts faced a tension-wracked finale but Stevie Frail, who had impressed with his attacking forays as a right wing-back, grabbed the vital opener in 29 minutes, and much to the relief of the partisan crowd, Craig Levein clinched matters with a second on the hour to earn a crucial 2-0 home win over Dundee United.

Now Hearts and Partick Thistle, who would meet in the final game at Firhill on May 14th, had 40 points with Killie a point behind and St Johnstone on 38 points. Hearts had a goal-difference advantage of seven over Paul Sturrock's men and only an extraordinary combination of results could put them down although that was exactly what had occurred when they lost the title in May 1986.

However, a grimly determined Hearts played it tight at Firhill and with four minutes remaining Alan McLaren struck the winner. St Johnstone had won 1-0 but although now alongside Partick and Killie - who had drawn 0-0 with Hibs at Easter Road - on the 40 point mark, the Perth side were down since Partick Thistle had a goal-difference advantage of one.

Nevertheless Hearts escape had been too close for comfort and after failing with an earlier offer, Wheatsheaf Catering supremo Chris Robinson and local solicitor Leslie Deans returned to conclude a £2.1 million deal for 51% of Wallace Mercer's shareholding in June. The new majority shareholders believed an experienced manager was crucial for the club's progress and later that month, Sandy Clark and Hugh McCann were sacked.

Tommy McLean, who had recently resigned after leading Motherwell to Scottish Cup glory in 1992 and third place in last term's Premier League, was appointed manager. Eamonn Bannon was brought in as assistant-manager with Tom Forsyth joining Walter Kidd on the coaching staff.

By now the redevelopment of Tynecastle had begun in earnest with the McLeod Street and School End terracings levelled and the pitch shifted towards the main stand after the Dundee United game on May 6th. Onfield, Tommy McLean would need time to assess his new charges but the 1994-95 season got off to a bad start when Craig Levein and Graeme Hogg were ordered off after exchanging blows during a pre-season friendly against Raith Rovers in Kirkcaldy. Hearts imposed the maximum possible fine but both would later receive a hefty S.F.A. ban.

The league campaign opened with a 3-1 defeat at Aberdeen and a 1-1 draw at Motherwell before Hibs finally broke their derby hoodoo with a 1-0 victory at Tynecastle. Meanwhile in the League Cup - now sponsored by Coca Cola - an Allan Johnston double contributed to a 4-0 win at Dumbarton to ensure a third round tie against St Johnstone at Tynecastle on August 31st.

Hearts started well, Gary Locke heading an early goal and setting up John Colquhoun for a second in 31 minutes. before the Maroons were reduced to ten men when Stevie Frail was red-carded for touching over a John O'Neill shot. Hearts had a let off when Nicky Walker saved George O'Boyle's penalty but Saints were right back in the game a minute after the restart, O'Neill getting in at the near post to head past the static Hearts keeper.

Hearts were struggling badly and although Tommy Harrison substituted for Alan Johnston, Colin Miller levelled the scores from a free-kick midway through the second half before George O'Boyle and Davie Irons capitalised on poor defending at corner kicks to make it 4-2 for St Johnstone in the last 11 minutes. It had been a shocker and Tommy McLean demonstrated his anger by substituting Wayne Foster for the ineffectual Tommy Harrison. Along with Nicky Walker and Jim Weir, Harrison was axed for the next game - a 3-0 defeat by Rangers at Ibrox - and none would appear for the first team again.

Undaunted, McLean set about revamping the team which, by October 22nd, lay fifth after winning five of their next six games. Former Rangers and Aberdeen midfield star Jim Bett (35), was signed on a free-transfer from Icelandic club Reykjavik and although now short on pace, his passing ability and positional sense pace soon made him a key figure in central midfield.

According to Chris Robinson, the new owners had inherited debts of around £4.4 million and it was little surprise when Scottish international defender Alan McLaren was transferred to Rangers for £1.25 million with £750,000-rated Dave McPherson returning to Tynecastle. Early next month, the overdraft was further cut when Tosh McKinlay joined Celtic for £350,000, with the out-of-favour Jim Weir moving to St Johnstone in exchange for Canadian international defender Colin Miller plus £80,000.

In November, Hearts hit a bad slump and with Craig Levein and Graeme Hogg both starting their nine-game S.F.A ban, 36-year old coach Walter Kidd was drafted in at Kilmarnock on November 26th. However, the slide continued and soon Tommy McLean was back in the transfer market. Partick Thistle's Under-21 keeper Craig Nelson and veteran centre-half Willie Jamieson would join Hearts in exchange for Nicky Walker and Wayne Foster with Thistle also receiving £160,000, while another £150,000 was spent on Rangers ex-Scotland Under-21 international forward David Hagen (21).

A 3-0 Boxing Day victory over struggling Partick Thistle brought relief for it was Hearts first win in seven games and by the end of 1994, they lay sixth, although still within a couple of points of second-bottom Aberdeen. In January, Graeme Hogg was allowed to join Notts County for £75,000 but Tommy McLean reinforced his squad by signing Brian Hamilton of Hibs on freedom of contract with a £260,000 fee later set by the transfer tribunal.

Tommy McLean - the new Hearts boss proved an astute tactician.

The hard-working midfielder netted a debut goal in 2-1 win at Motherwell and with Craig Levein back, the reshaped team went from strength to

Top-notch - former Scottish international striker Mo Johnston fires in a shot against Partick Thistle at Firhill. DC Thomson

strength. By March 21st, Hearts had reached the semi-final of the Scottish Cup with just two defeats from 14 games. Following a 1-1 draw at Kilbowie, Hearts 2-1 home win over Clydebank set up a fourth round glamour tie against Rangers on Monday, February 20th. By now the Wheatfield Stand was complete but due to the continuing construction work at the School End, Tynecastle's capacity was limited to just over 12,000.

However, with the match live on Sky TV, the fans and viewers alike were to get full value for money. A thundering free-kick by Colin Miller then a McPherson header just before the interval gave Hearts a 2-0 half-time lead only for Laudrup and Durie to level the scores soon after the restart. However, on a rain-swept night, Hearts were not to be denied and when Ally Maxwell could only palm out an angled drive by Jim Bett, John Robertson pounced to make it 3-2. A famous victory was in sight and two minutes from time, substitute Kevin Thomas clinched matters with a fourth to give Hearts their first win over the Ibrox side in 17 games since August 1991.

In the quarter-final, Hearts were again at home in a sunday televised game against cup holders, Dundee United. It had been 10 years since United had last beaten Hearts at Tynecastle but after just four minutes Brazilian forward Sergio wriggled clear of Millar and McPherson to put United ahead. Seventeen minutes later, Hearts were level when John Millar met a perfectly flighted free-kick by Stevie Frail to drift a header past the helpless O'Hanlon and just before the interval the hard-working Millar headed a second after a Gary Mackay corner was headed back by Willie Jamieson and with Hearts flooding the midfield after the break, they held on to win.

Shortly before his own departure, Sandy Clark had given Mo Johnston a two year extension to his lucrative contract. However, after just a handful of games under McLean, Johnston, whose salary was an unwanted burden to the cash-strapped Tynecastle club, had fallen from favour. Over the next few months, there were constant rows between the player, his agent Bill McMurdo and the Hearts manager before Falkirk stepped in to sign Johnston on a free-transfer in March with promising Bairns striker Colin Cramb joining Hearts for £50,000, an amount reputedly used as a settlement for the remainder of Johnston's contract with Hearts.

Meanwhile, guided by the tactically astute McLean, Hearts were entitled to believe that this could be their year particularly when the semi-final draw matched them against First Division Airdrie with Celtic and Hibs contesting the other tie. However, the loss of the increasingly influential Stevie Frail - recently tipped for international honours - with a recurrence of his knee ligament injury soon afterwards, came as a severe blow. Frail would be out for a year and to replace him, Tommy McLean made his eighth signing, snapping up former Motherwell, St Mirren and Falkirk full-back Fraser Wishart (30), on a free-transfer from Rangers.

League defeats by Falkirk and Partick Thistle did little for morale while Wishart was "cup-tied" and ineligible for the Hampden semi-final on April 8th. Hearts - Nelson; Levein, Jamieson, McPherson; Mackay, Hamilton, Bett, Millar, Miller; Hagen, Robertson. Subs. - Colquhoun, Thomas, H. Smith. Airdrie - Martin; Boyle, Stewart, Sandison, Jack; Lawrence, A. Smith, Black, Davies; Cooper, Harvey. Subs. - McCulloch, T. Smith, Hay.

Soon after kick-off, John Robertson went for a bouncing ball only to receive a kick on the head and lengthy treatment was required before he could resume with his head heavily bandaged. Once again, Hearts laboured against Airdrie and just on the half-hour, a Paul Harvey-Andy Smith move down the right ended with the unmarked Steve Cooper heading home at the far post.

Immediately, Tommy McLean replaced Brian Hamilton with John Colquhoun to provide more width and as Hearts stepped up a gear, John Martin was kept busy. After the break, the game degenerated with Jamieson, Hagen, Bett and Airdrie's Black all yellow-carded. And although a McPherson try was headed off the line, Hearts were unable to recover, a frustrated John Robertson geting his marching orders for lashing out at Tony Smith in an off the ball incident.

Hearts had lost their way and now four defeats from their next five league games plunged them into serious relegation trouble. For months, the once mighty Aberdeen had struggled at the bottom but they had battled back and on April 29th, a late Billy Dodds goal giving them a 2-1 win at Tynecastle. That gave the Dons a lifeline, but with two games remaining, only five points covered bottom-placed Aberdeen, Dundee United, Partick Thistle and seventh-placed Hearts in a season where the second-bottom side would play off with the runners-up in Division One.

In their penultimate game, Hearts went ahead through a 34th minute David Hagen header only for Hibs to net three goals in seven minutes in the second-half. It was the doomsday scenario once again for with Aberdeen now within two points after beating Dundee United, the Maroons required to beat Motherwell to avoid the possibility of having to play off.

Right from the start, Hearts piled on the pressure and in 23 minutes, Tynecastle erupted when Brian Hamilton scored with a diving header past Woods from a Colquhoun cross. Although Hearts dominated, it proved a nervy afternoon for the Gorgie fans but with just a minute remaining, John Robertson, who had come off the substitutes bench, clinched matters with a second from the penalty spot.

Chapter Nineteen

A NEW DIRECTION

For a number of months it had been clear that Tommy McLean was unhappy with his lot at Tynecastle. Last Autumn's share issue, which perhaps significantly was for non-voting shares, had raised only £200,000, little more than required to cover the cost of the issue and, frustrated at the same financial restrictions which had led him to part company with Motherwell, McLean had offered to resign in December. That had ensured a strained relationship with chairman Chris Robinson and a parting of the ways appeared inevitable.

There was little doubt that McLean had the credentials to be a top manager although there were suggestions that all was not as it might have been between him and his players. With Hearts debt now approaching £5-million, McLean knew there was little prospect of bringing in quality players and every chance that talented youngsters like Allan Johnston would follow Alan McLaren and Tosh McKinlay out of Tynecastle to ensure the club's short-term survival.

In June, the manager hinted strongly that he would resign only to reject a £50,000 compensation offer by Hearts to do so. However, the club declared themselves unhappy at statements attributed to McLean and on July 21st, the manager was dismissed with the club citing his "unreasonable behaviour". McLean challenged his sacking but after later taking Hearts to court for unfair dismissal, the matter was settled out of court.

However, speculation now turned to McLean's successor with Jimmy Nicholl, who had twice led Raith Rovers to promotion as well as Coca Cola Cup success in 1994, and Jim Jefferies, who had also twice gained promotion with Falkirk, the favourites for the Tynecastle post.

However, there was little doubt that Jefferies, pipped by McLean for the Tynecastle post a year earlier, was the man Hearts wanted. On August 4th, the former Hearts skipper was offered the manager's job and after accepting, he met Falkirk chairman George Fulston to tender his resignation. The persuasive Bairns supremo talked Jefferies into remaining but a few days later, Jefferies sensationally made a second turnaround to join Hearts on a five-year contract along with his assistant Billy Brown, .

Later, Jefferies commented, "Any number of people told me not to take the Hearts job but I had to do it. I had been there so long that it's in the blood but it was a mistake to go to Brockville and walk past all the fans. It was probably the worst week in my life but I knew deep down that I should go to Tynecastle."

"The problems are very deep- rooted but I will do what I have to do and what some will argue should have been done years ago. There will be casualties along the way for that's the nature of the business. Hearts are at just about as low an ebb as I can remember and if I can swing it around, people will remember once again that this is a big club."

It had been a hectic prelude to the new season and when a 3-3 at Derby and a 1-0 home defeat to Newcastle were follwed by an impressive 5-1 victory over Manchester City at Tynecastle, the 1995-96 campaign began in earnest. The Jim Jefferies era began brightly enough, wins over Alloa (3-0) and Dunfermline (2-1) taking Hearts into the last eight of the Coca Cola Cup while the opening two Premier League games against Motherwell and Falkirk, which were also played at Tynecastle, yielded four points.

The new Hearts boss had not been slow to enter the transfer market. The pacy Alan Lawrence was signed from Airdrie for £30,000 with another £50,000 spent on Aberdeen defender David Winnie to replace Fraser Wishart, who had been injured against Motherwell a few days earlier.

A few months earlier, First Division Dunfermline had lost heavily to Aberdeen in the Premier League play-off but Hearts cup clash with the Fifers proved a real thriller for the 12,500 Tynecastle crowd. However, victory had been achieved at a high cost with defensive stalwart Craig Levein stretchered off with a recurrence of the cruciate ligament injury which had so blighted his Tynecastle career.

The Coca Cola Cup quarter-final draw paired Hearts with First Division Dundee at Dens Park on September 20th and with John Robertson back from an early season injury, they fielded - Smith; Locke, Berry, McPherson, Winnie; Colquhoun, Mackay, Hamilton; Lawrence, Hagen, Robertson. Subs. Jamieson, Leitch, Nelson.

Hearts were shocked when the lively George Shaw struck

Jim Jefferies - the ex-Hearts skipper had a good track record at Falkirk and was a popular choice with the fans. DC Thomson

Heart of Midlothian F.C. 1995-96 (BACK) Gary Mackay, Fraser Wishart, Gary Locke, Dave McPherson, Willie Jamieson, Brian Hamilton, Neil Berry. MIDDLE - Scott Leitch, Steve Frail, David Hagen, Craig Nelson, Henry Smith, Allan Johnston, John Millar, Colin Miller. FRONT - John Colquhoun, John Robertson, Jim Jefferies (manager), Craig Levein, Billy Brown (assistant-manager), George Wright, Kevin Thomas.

twice for Dundee shortly before the break but a half-time pep-talk by Jim Jefferies brought a more determined response. Within nine minutes, Dave McPherson headed home a Colquhoun free-kick and as Hearts piled on the pressure, Colquhoun made it 2-2 after Pageaud could only parry a Robertson drive with 17 minutes remaining.

Hearts went all out for the winner but it was Dundee who scored, a crazily miscued clearance by Henry Smith going right across the penalty box for Paul Tosh to shoot into the empty net. The Maroons threw everything into attack and with just two minutes left, Alan Lawrence took a knock-down from substitute Willie Jamieson to shoot high into the net. With the atmosphere now almost electric, the drama continued as play surged from end to end throughout extra-time. Within four minutes, Morten Wieghorst powered home a dipping shot but, early in the second period, John Robertson made it 4-4 from the spot after Alan Lawrence was downed in the box.

There was no further score in a nail-biting finale and now the tie would be decided on penalties. Both sides netted four with Henry Smith missing for Hearts but with the tension-ridden shoot-out going to sudden death, Willie Jamieson hit the post before Wieghorst beat Smith to end Hearts hopes of cup glory and the substantial cash rewards available for reaching the last four.

Five changes were made but a few days later, Hearts went down 4-0 to Celtic at Tynecastle. The slump continued with just one win from their next six games and by the end of October, the Gorgie men lay bottom of the table on goal-difference behind Kilmarnock and Falkirk after 10 Premier League games. Predictably, Jim Jefferies received a hostile reception at Brockville where Hearts had stumbled to a 2-0 defeat by fellow-strugglers Falkirk. David Weir, a player much admired by Jefferies, opened the scoring but it was former Maroon Derek Ferguson who had pulled the strings for the Bairns. It was a defeat compounded by the loss of former Scotland defender Dave McPherson, whose pelvic injury would rule him out for the next couple of months. Once again, it was crisis time at Tynecastle where the worrying financial situation meant there was little money available for players.

There were suggestions that tax-exile Wallace Mercer might want to regain control at Tynecastle but John Borthwick, general secretary of the Hearts Supporters' Federation had his own views, "If there's someone out there who could come in with money, most Hearts fans would welcome him but the majority would not like to see Mr Mercer back in control. I'm sure Mr Robinson and Mr Deans would admit they've made mistakes but they should be given time to get things right."

Whilst at Falkirk, Jim Jefferies had proved a shrewd judge of footballing talent. Now, after giving his players the chance to prove themselves, he realised that drastic surgery was required and by early November, there were six new faces at Tynecastle. In had come the experienced Oldham left-back Neil Pointon for £30,000 with ex-Celtic and Bolton midfielder Steve Fulton (24), secured from Falkirk in exchange for David Hagen.

Veteran keeper Henry Smith had been axed after the Dens Park debacle and although Craig Nelson and young Gary O'Connor were given their chance in goal, the manager decided to look elsewhere before bringing in former French international keeper Gilles Rousset, (32) who had previously played for Sochaux, Rennes, Lyons and Marseilles. Next to arrive was tough Italian sweeper Pasquale Bruno (33), who had previously played with Fiorentina, Juventus and Torino. Versatile Dunfermline midfielder Paul Smith arrived in exchange for Colin Miller with former Swedish international striker Hans Eskilsson obtained on a free-transfer from Vallerund.

The home match against Partick Thistle on Saturday, November 4th was to prove a watershed for Hearts. In 10 minutes, they went ahead when Derek McWilliams put through his own goal, then a clever chip by Johnston allowed John Millar to get a second in 65 minutes before substitute Hans Eskilsson sent the Tynecastle crowd home happy with a third near the end. That lifted Hearts off the bottom and a no-scoring draw at Motherwell then 2-1 home wins over Kilmarnock and Hibernian further restored confidence as Hearts went on to finish 1995 in sixth place, seven points clear of the danger zone.

One of the highlights had been the 2-1 win over Coca Cola Cup Winners Aberdeen at Pittodrie in mid-December. After trailing to an early goal by Dean Windass, Hearts had besieged the Dons with little success. However, only nine minutes had remained when Johnston cut in from the right, played a 1-2 with John Robertson and shot past Michael Watt, John Colquhoun then netting a spectacular winner after a well-placed through ball from the polished left boot of Neil Pointon.

There was a disappointing start to the New Year for although Neil Pointon put Hearts ahead, Hibs went on to win 2-1 at Easter Road. Nevertheless, Jim Jefferies now had Hearts on the right lines and three successive wins over Partick (a) 1-0, Motherwell (h) 4-0, Falkirk (h) 2-1 elevated them to third although still well behind the title-chasing Old Firm. The Maroons then went down 2-1 to Celtic at Tynecastle but on January 20th, they turned on their best performance for years against Rangers at Ibrox.

In six minutes, the quick-thinking Allan Johnston appeared at Andy Goram's near post to flick home a John Colquhoun cross and although the table-topping Light Blues had the lions share of the play, Hearts, who were playing an intelligent counter-attacking game, were never seriously troubled. Sixteen minutes into the second-half, they struck again, the lightning-quick Johnston racing on to a perfectly weighted Pointon pass to lob Andy Goram and it was no surprise when the striker completed his hat-trick by dribbling round the Rangers keeper near the end.

It had been a dazzling performance and only careless finishing had prevented a bigger score. Since early November Hearts had managed nine wins and two draws from 15 games and once again, things were buzzing down Tynecastle way. The arrival of the formidable Bruno and the towering 6'5" Rousset, the latter the subject of an abortive £300,000 bid by Sunderland, had brought stability at the back and Hearts fortunes had been transformed. Neil Pointon had brought an added attacking dimension down the left while the deft prompts and clever passing of a rejuvenated Steve Fulton was another telling factor in the Hearts revival.

The presence of the experienced newcomers had brought out the best in the talented youngsters at Tynecastle. Under Tommy McLean, Scotland Under-21 defender Gary Locke (20), had dropped out of the plans and might have been transferred to Motherwell. Now he was a fixture at right-back and his infectious enthusiam had earned him the captaincy. Paul Ritchie had also been successfully brought into defence with another promising young defender, Alan McManus - who had turned down the offer of a free-transfer by Tommy McLean - also making his breakthrough in early 1996. Up front, Allan Johnston was, like Locke a regular at Under-21 level. Brimful of confidence, he was now realising his full potential wide on the right and his clever footwork had quickly earned him the nickname of "Magic" Johnston.

On January 31st, Hearts dominated the Scottish Cup tie against Partick Thistle before a near-capacity Tynecastle crowd of 13,770. However, they found former keeper Nicky Walker in near unbeatable form until midway through the second-half. Neil Pointon sent over a corner and Paul Ritchie stole in at the near post to score with a powerful downward header for the only goal of the game.

The fourth round draw threw up a tricky tie at Kilmarnock where Hearts would be without the suspended Gary Locke and Pasquale Bruno. A week earlier, the Italian, who had arrived with the reputation of a poor disciplinary record, had been sent off for elbowing Aberdeen's Dean Windass and already Scott Leitch (v. Celtic in October), Gary Mackay (v. Hibs in November), Neil Berry and Gary Locke (both v. Raith Rovers) had all been ordered off.

Due to the Taylor Report recommendations, most Premier League clubs had changed or were changing to all-seater stadia and the revamped Rugby Park was a perfect setting for a thrilling encounter on February 17th. There was no scoring at half-time but 12 minutes after the restart, Paul Ritchie again made the breakthrough, running on to a Mackay pass to shoot low into the net. And although Anderson equalised for Killie in 67 minutes, Neil Berry got the winner when his shot was defected past Killie keeper Lekovic, near the end.

In the the quarter-final, Hearts met the in-form St Johnstone at Perth and although played on Thursday, March 7th for live television, there was a near-capacity 10,000 crowd at McDiarmid Park. In the first-half, Saints

Pasquale Bruno - the Italian central defender brought solidity to the Tynecastle defence. **DC Thomson**

belied their First Division status by putting Hearts under severe pressure but with half-time fast approaching, a Robertson-Mackay move down the left gave Alan Lawrence the opportunity to put Hearts ahead against the run of play. Former Coventry winger Leigh Jenkinson was in top form and two minutes after the restart, George O'Boyle made it 1-1. Within five minutes, Dave McPherson headed home a Steve Fulton free-kick to restore Hearts lead and with the supply to Jenkinson finally cut off, it was Hearts who marched into the last four alongside Rangers, Celtic and Aberdeen.

Star quality - Gary Locke and Alan Johnston soon become regulars for the Scotland Under-21 side. DC Thomson

However, league form had been erratic and a humiliating 5-2 home defeat by Partick Thistle did little for morale prior to the Hampden semi-final against Aberdeen on Saturday April 6th. A shaky performance cost Dave McPherson his place but John Colquhoun had fought his way back into the team and now he was paired with the nippy Alan Lawrence to the exclusion of John Robertson.

Remarkably it was the seventh time Hearts had reached the last four since 1986 and although the Dons had already beaten them three times that season, there was little between the sides. As was often the case, the semi-final was no spectacle for the sun-drenched crowd of 27,785 who were treated to a tough, tense and often scrappy game.

Only 17 minutes remained when McPherson and Robertson replaced Fulton and Lawrence but within seven minutes Hearts were ahead. An inswinging corner by Pointon was headed into the six-yard box by McPherson and Robertson reacted first to nod the ball in at the post. With two minutes left, Hearts looked home and dry but when Gilles Rousset failed to cut out a Stephen Glass free-kick, Dons substitute Duncan Shearer was lying handy to head home the equaliser.

Now a replay looked certain but 30 seconds into injury time, John Robertson swung in a cross from the left and Allan Johnston raced in to head the ball beyond a static Michael Watt. The 18,000 Hearts fans had been stunned by Aberdeen's equaliser, but now they celebrated in style, for there was no way back for the Dons.

It was Hearts first final for 10 years and although they had previously reached that stage in 1976 and 1986, it was forty years since they had last lifted the trophy in 1956. In the final they would face the all-conquering Rangers, who were on their way to an eighth successive title and, by the day of the Hampden clash on May 18th, Hearts were confident of success after a seven game unbeaten run.

"Leading Hearts out to play a cup final at Hampden will be the greatest day of my life", claimed Jim Jefferies. "Our fans will lap it up for too often we've deprived them of a day out." However, apart from an impressive 2-0 league win over Rangers at Tynecastle - where Neil Pointon crashed in a stunning goal - Hearts had not been at their best, particularly up front, where they had struggled to find the net. There was now strong competition for places and although six players remained from the near-miss side of 1985-86, there was no guaranteed place for any of the "Old Guard". All were aware that they had to perform to earn their place and although Rousset, Bruno and Mackay were all rested in the build-up to Hampden, John Robertson was relegated to the bench at Motherwell and, to the surprise of many, was again a substitute for the final.

Jefferies had made just one change from his semi-final team, Dave McPherson coming in to stiffen the midfield to the exclusion of Allan Lawrence with Allan Johnston and John Colquhoun up front.

With both teams favouring a 3-5-2 formation, the line up was: Hearts - Rousset; Ritchie, Bruno, McManus; Locke, McPherson, Mackay, Fulton, Pointon; Colquhoun, Johnston. Subs. Lawrence, Robertson, Hogarth. Rangers - Goram; McLaren, Gough, Brown; Cleland, Ferguson, Gascoigne, McCall, Robertson; Durie, Laudrup. Subs. Petric, Durrant, Anderson.

Before the match, lifelong Hearts fan Gary Locke described the occasion as one of the greatest days of his life. However, within eight minutes of kick-off, the young Hearts skipper had caught his studs in the ground and was stretchered off with damaged knee ligaments. With no other defensive player on the bench, Alan Lawrence came on up front with Allan Johnston dropping back to midfield to assume Locke's role of shadowing the influential Paul Gascoigne.

Rangers were well fired up and quickly asserted control in midfield although both Ian Ferguson and Alex. Cleland were booked for a series of wild tackles. Although the Light Blues had most of the pressure, Hearts had given a good account of themselves and a 25-yard shot by Alan Lawrence was tipped over by Andy Goram. However, with half-time approaching, Brian Laudrup headed the ball to Gordon Durie in the centre-circle then strode through the middle for the return before beating Rousset who had remained on his six-yard line.

The goal had come at a bad time and soon after the restart Gilles Rousset allowed a long-range effort by Laudrup to squirm beneath him for Rangers second. Hearts now had a mountain to climb for they had to take the game to Rangers, who could sit back and hit on the break. In 59 minutes, Jim Jefferies took off Pasquale Bruno and brought on John Robertson to give a three-man strike force but all was to no avail when Durie volleyed in a third soon afterwards.

Fourteen minutes from the end, John Colquhoun gave the Hearts fans something to cheer, first controlling a Lawrence pass before cracking a low 25-yarder past Goram from the edge of the box. Now Hearts poured men forward but with the brilliant Laudrup in particular taking full advantage of the gaping holes at the back, Durie grabbed another two to complete his hat-trick and give Rangers a 5-1 win.

In the latter stages, Hearts had been totally outclassed

and it was a sad end to what had started as a day full of promise. The early loss of Locke had been a severe blow while the towering McPherson had looked exposed in the wide right defensive area but it had been a lack of discipline and inexperience at the back that had cost Hearts dear.

Hearts had no-one to match Ibrox hat-trickster Gordon Durie or the brilliant Brian Laudrup, who himself had scored two and made three goals. However, John Colquhoun had been their most effective player with Bruno, Mackay, Pointon and Ritchie - fortunate to remain on the park after a rash challenge on Gascoigne just before half-time - also battling bravely.

Before the game, the long-serving Gary Mackay had maintained that Hearts would need eight players to be at their very best to win but this had not been the case. Rousset had looked nervous from the start but Jim Jefferies defended his keeper, “Gilles was distraught about his error and you have to feel sorry for him. He has been magnificent all season and his performances have been one of the main reasons we got to Hampden in the first place. We had been playing some of our best stuff up to that point but ended up getting destroyed. I felt a lot of our players failed to perform to their ability on the day but hopefully they will go on and learn from the experience.”

Nevertheless, Hearts had come a long way since October and in the close season, they edged above Aberdeen as Scotland’s third top club in terms of their 9,000-plus season ticket sales. Meanwhile, the Jim Jefferies Tynecastle revolution continued unabated for since last October, there had been a massive clearout. George Wright had departed on a free transfer, while Willie Jamieson joined Ayr United for £10,000 in November with Henry Smith moving to Somerset Park in early 1996.

By Spring, Scott Leitch had joined Swindon for £15,000, Colin Cramb going to Doncaster Rovers for a similar amount, Gary O’Connor (to Notts County), Paul Smith (to Ayr United), Fraser Wishart (to Motherwell) and Hans Eskilsson who was allowed to return to Sweden, all joining the Tynecastle exodus on free-transfers at the end of the season. And before the start of the 1996-97 campaign, Alan Lawrence had returned to Airdrie for £20,000 while David Winnie was soon on his way to Dundee for £30,000.

Contrary to rumours, Pasquale Bruno, who was now something of a cult hero with the fans, would remain at Tynecastle while Jefferies had also been busy bringing in fresh talent. Prior to the transfer deadline in March, the Hearts boss had snapped up Scotland “B’ international midfielder Colin Cameron from Raith Rovers in a £350,000 deal which involved John Millar going to Stark’s Park after Cameron, like his team-mate Stevie Crawford, had previously refused to talk to Aberdeen.

However, although talented youngsters Gary Locke, Paul Ritchie and Allan McManus had all signed new two-and-a-half year contracts in February, Allan Johnston, who last term, had produced several spellbinding performances, had held off. There had been regular rumours that Rangers were interested but in July, the £750,000-rated striker joined French club Rennes on freedom of contract with Hearts not entitled to any compensation after the Bosman ruling 12 months earlier.

His departure came as a big blow to all involved at Tynecastle but, at the end of July, the Hearts boss produced an amazing triple swoop to sign Dundee’s Scotland Under-21 international left-winger Neil McCann (22), Falkirk defender David Weir (25), and former Norwich and Wales midfielder Jeremy Goss (31). McCann, who had been on the point of signing for Sturm Graz of Austria, had cost £200,000 with Weir secured for the same amount with Craig Nelson, Brian Hamilton and Neil Berry joining Falkirk in part-exchange, their departures meaning that no fewer than 14 first-team squad players had left Tynecastle since October 1995.

Walter Kidd left his coaching job to become assistant-manager at Falkirk and his post was taken by Peter Houston. The fans got a further boost with the return to fitness of Kevin Thomas and Stevie Frail after their long-term cruciate ligament injuries. They, along with the newcomers showed up well in pre-season games in Eire against Dundlak (3-1) and Shamrock Rovers (1-1) and although Hearts went down 3-1 at home to Euro aces F.C. Porto, there was the consolation of a 1-0 victory over Graeme Souness’s Southampton at Tynecastle.

However, Hearts faced a difficult start to their competitve season, being plunged straight into a European Cup-

Push and pull - Gary Mackay battles for possession with Rangers England international midfielder Paul Gascoigne. DC Thomson

New brigade - former Scotland'B' international Colin Cameron was one of the exciting new players brought in by Jim Jefferies as he reshaped his side. Here the midfielder turns away to celebrate after netting against his old club Raith Rovers at Stark's Park. **DC Thomson**

Winners Cup Preliminary round tie against Red Star in Belgrade on August 8th. There were concerns that the Scots might not be sufficiently tuned up but in the event, Hearts - who had Cameron and Colquhoun up front - turned in a fine disciplined performance to earn a 0-0 draw against the talented Serbs, whose average age was just twenty-three. Dave McPherson had been an inspiration at the back, the experience of Goss in midfield had been significant, while Rousset had brought off three magnificent saves to defy Red Star.

Two weeks later, just over 15,000 were at Tynecastle for the return with all aware of Hearts vulnerability to an away goal. At the start, Red Star were content to lie deep but Hearts again approached their task in a controlled manner and were unwilling to throw too many men forward for fear of being hit on the break. Just before half-time, their patience paid off when they went ahead, Dave McPherson soaring high to meet a Neil McCann corner and head the ball down and into the net.

However, 13 minutes after the restart, Tynecastle was silenced when a fatal loss of concentration in defence allowed the dangerous Dino Marinovic to level despite a valiant effort by Rousset. Now trailing on the "away-goals" rule, Bruno missed a good chance and although Hearts tried to up the pace in the closing stages, they were unable to make any further headway against the men from Belgrade.

Meanwhile, the domestic campaign had started encouragingly with a 3-2 win over Killie at Tynecastle but although Dundee United were also defeated (1-0) at home, the Maroons away form gave cause for concern with defeats at newly-promoted Dunfermline (1-2), Aberdeen (0-4) and Rangers (0-3).

Over the past year, the Bosman ruling had meant many mainland Europeans coming to Scotland as trialists and by early September, Hearts had further strengthened their squad with the addition of ex-Oldham striker Darren Beckford and former AC Milan, Fiorentina and Atalanta midfielder Stefano Salvatori (29), who as free agents were both signed on short-term contracts.

In the League Cup, again sponsored by Coca Cola, Hearts struggled to overcome lowly Stenhousemuir in the second round at Tynecastle with Weir hitting the bar before several other good chances were squandered. The Maroons were shocked when Adrian Sprott netted a penalty before half-time and although Neil McCann equalised with 17 minutes left and former Maroon Max Christie was ordered off in the final minute, the sides remained locked at 1-1 Stevie Frail missed the first kick but the powerfully-built Beckford, a £1-million signing earlier in his career, netted the decisive fifth goal as the shoot-out moved to sudden death and Hearts were through 5-4 on penalties.

The third round draw sent Hearts back to McDiarmid Park to play Paul Sturrock's much-improved St Johnstone who had earlier caused the Maroons problems in the Scottish Cup and who had narrowly been pipped for the First Division-Premier play-off place by Dundee United.

In 15 minutes, Colin Cameron opened the scoring but Hearts paid the penalty for a succession of missed chances when O'Boyle levelled soon after half-time. It was Saints who finished the stronger but in extra-time, Neil McCann outpaced McCluskey to set up Darren Beckford and John Robertson made it 3-1 soon afterwards. The quarter-final draw paired Hearts with the star-studded Celtic who included top players like Pierre Van Hooijdonk, Jorge Cadete and Paulo Di Canio, but the Maroons would be short of some of their own top men after astonishing scenes against Rangers at Ibrox a few days earlier.

After conceding two goals late in the first-half, Hearts had Pasquale Bruno ordered off for his second bookable offence soon after the restart. Ten minutes later, Hearts felt hard done by when referee Gerry Evans ignored an initial foul by Gordon Durie on David Weir but sent off the Hearts defender after he and Durie had gone head-to-head. At this point the Hearts players lost their discipline and within four minutes both Neil Pointon - previously booked - and Paul Ritchie joined their team-mates for an early bath after using foul and abusive language towards the assistant-referee who had missed the Durie incident.

At this stage, with 25 minutes remaining, the game was in serious danger of being abandoned - as would have happened had Hearts lost another player - with the possibility of disturbances amongst the 47,240 fans. In the end, the game was completed with Hearts going down 3-0 but, whatever the rights and wrongs of the matter, it was not an afternoon to be remembered with pride as Hearts thoughts turned to the quarter-final tie against Celtic.

In came Alan McManus, Gary Naysmith and Kevin Thomas, the latter who was back in the Scotland Under-21 team to play Austria, with a surprise newcomer in the number six jersey, Jim Jefferies having moved quickly to sign the experienced Andy Thorn on loan from Wimbledon as a direct replacement for David Weir.

Thorn was immense in the centre of defence but the youngsters, Naysmith in particular, also did well in a tight, tense match. There was not a lot of good football and chances were few and far between in a poor match. In 61 minutes, Stefano Salvatori committed one foul too many and was red-carded but things were evened up three minutes into extra-time when Celtic's Peter Grant was sent off for fouling Thorn. Rousset made a brilliant save from a Van Hooijdonk free-kick and with 110 minutes on the clock, Neil McCann turned the ball inside and John Robertson beat Marshall with a powerful low shot for the only goal of the game

Once again, "Robbo" was the Gorgie hero for after struggling to get a game at the end of last term and at the start of the current campaign, the striker had patiently awaited his chance. From then, he had scored a string of important goals and manager Jim Jefferies had been unable to keep him out of the side.

In the semi-final, the Gorgie men would face last season's conquerors Dundee, who had remained in the First Division for a third successive season. By the evening of the Easter Road match on Wednesday, October 23rd, Hearts had completed the first quarter of their league campaign to lie in mid-table. At the end of September, Colin Cameron had netted twice in a 3-1 win over derby rivals Hibernian at the same venue and Hearts, with more than 10,000 of the near 16,000 crowd behind them, were in confident mood.

There were doubts whether Beckford, a useful but relatively immobile target man, was the right player to partner John Robertson and earlier that month Hearts had signed Frenchman Stephane Paille, previously suspended for a year in his home country for drugs offences. Paille had soon impressed as an industrious and technically sound striker but the new Paille-Robertson partnership lasted just 15 minutes, before pre-match injury doubt Robertson hobbled off with a hamstring injury.

However, within five minutes, Hearts were ahead. Young Stuart Callaghan - who had turned down the chance of joining Dundee in part-exchange for the currently injured Neil McCann, raced after a long punt by Rousset and when Dundee keeper Billy Thomson could only parry a pass-back with his chest due to the new pass-back rule, Beckford - who had substituted for Robertson - netted after the keeper had saved his first attempt. Ten minutes later, Hearts went 2-0 up when the speedy Callaghan was downed by Adamczuk and Colin Cameron converted with ease.

After the break, the game opened up as Dundee threw everything forward but in 59 minutes, Hearts broke with lightning speed. Pointon lofted the ball forward and when Beckford headed down, Paille, who had run from the halfway line, cracked a beauty into the net. Jim Hamilton netted a late consolation for Dundee but, apart from a brief flurry from the Dens side, Hearts had never really been troubled. In the final - held at Parkhead due to the demolition of the South Stand at Hampden, Hearts would again meet Rangers, 6-1 conquerors of Dunfermline, and many

Spot the ball - Gary Mackay, shortly to leave Tynecastle after a record 547 domestic games for Hearts, and Celtic's Peter Grant appear to have lost the ball. Daily Record

Keep on running - John Robertson has made it 2-2 in the Coca Cola Cup Final thriller against Rangers at Parkhead. Later that season, the prolific striker scored his 207th league goal to beat the previous record held by Jimmy Wardhaugh. Daily Record

wondered if the Maroons could improve on last May's dismal showing.

By the big day on Sunday, November 24th, Hearts lay fourth but skipper Dave McPherson was out after injuring his ankle against Hibs a week earlier. Pasquale Bruno, out of favour since his dismissal at Ibrox, stepped in as Hearts lined up - Rousset; Weir, Ritchie, Bruno; Mackay (capt), Cameron, Fulton, Pointon, McCann; Paille, Robertson. Subs. Goss, Beckford, McManus. Rangers - Goram; Gough (capt), Petric, Bjorklund; Moore, Gascoigne, Miller, Albertz, Cleland; Laudrup, McCoist. Subs. Van Vossen, Robertson, Snelders. Referee - Hugh Dallas.

Right up to an hour before kick-off, driving rain and sleet cast doubts on the game before Hugh Dallas finally gave the go-ahead and by kick-off, conditions were clear. There was plenty of noise from the Gorgie faithful amongst the 48,559 crowd but in 10 minutes they were silenced when Rangers went ahead. Laudrup beat Paul Ritchie then slipped the ball into the box where the unmarked McCoist swivelled to shoot low past Rousset.

Hearts were struggling to make any impact and when an Albertz corner was headed on, first by Petric, then by Moore, the deadly McCoist headed a second from just one yard out. After 27 minutes, it seemed all over for the Tyecastle side but with Hearts pushing forward and Neil McCann in sparking form down the left, they pulled one back just a minute before the break.

A short corner from the Scotland Under-21 international winger broke to Steve Fulton and the midfielder turned to send an angled left footer past Goram. After half-time, Hearts came out with their tails up. Goram saved well from Colin Cameron then Steve Fulton went close with a header before John Robertson threw himself forward to stab

Neil McCann - the left-wing speed merchant gave Rangers a torrid time in the Coca Cola Cup Final at Hampden. Daily Record

home a superb cross by Neil McCann for a 59th minute equaliser. Hearts were in full flow and with Rangers in disarray, the game was there for the taking.

However, five minutes later came the turning point of the game. John Robertson was obstructed by Bjorklund on the

Fabulous Fifties - a programme from the Scottish Cup Final in 1956 when Hearts beat Celtic 3-1 before 132,840 fans at Hampden. John Ure

Glorious Hearts - this pennant celebrates Hearts League Cup win over Kilmarnock in 1962. John Ure

A Hearts line up from 1970 - (BACK, left to right), John Cumming (trainer), Alan MacDonald, Dave Clunie, Rene Moller, Jim Cruickshank, Alan Anderson, Eddie Thomson, Ernie Winchester. FRONT - Raold Jensen, Tommy Traynor, Peter Oliver, Donald Ford, Jim Brown, Andy Lynch, Neil Murray and George Fleming. John Ure

Five of Hearts - Iain Ferguson, Davie Kirkwood, Nicky Walker, Dave McPherson with Derek Ferguson at the front. **DC Thomson**

John Colquhoun - the darting attacker shows his determination in an Edinburgh derby match. **DC Thomson**

Steady heroic and sure - the central defensive partnership of Craig Levein and Dave McPherson proved a rock-solid foundation for Hearts. Between them the pair made nearly 40 appearances for Scotland. **DC Thomson**

Memories are made of this - "Old Tynecastle" in February 1994 before the ground was transformed by the construction of three new stands. Gorgie Road is at the bottom of the picture.

Paul Proctor, Chorley and Handford

Heart of Midlothian F.C. 1997-98 (BACK, left to right), Steve Fulton, Dave McPherson, Roddy McKenzie, Gilles Rousset, Myles Hogarth, David Weir, Paul Ritchie. MIDDLE - Colin Cameron, David Murie, Stuart Callaghan, Thomas Flogel, Neil Pointon, Stefan Adam, Grant Murray, Jim Hamilton, Allan McManus, Jeremy Goss, Gary Naysmith. FRONT - Stefano Salvatori, Neil McCann, Bert Logan, Paul Hegarty, Billy Brown, Gary Locke, Jim Jefferies (manager), Peter Houston, Allan Rae, John Robertson and Steve Frail.

DC Thomson

Doughty defender - the accomplished Alan McLaren was a regular Scotland international while at Tynecastle. DC Thomson

"Ace of Hearts" - the popular John Robertson has been a prolific scorer for Hearts and was a full Scotland international. DC Thomson

Head man - Davie Weir outjumps Sean Dennis of Raith Rovers to head the ball clear. The commanding central defender has come on leaps and bounds in his time at Tynecastle and has already made his Scottish international breakthrough. DC Thomson

touchline but instead of a free-kick to Hearts, assistant-referee Alan Freeland of Aberdeen indicated a Rangers throw which quickly went to Paul Gascoigne, who ran 20 yards before curling a shot past Rousset, much to the anger of the Hearts bench.

Hearts were stunned for that goal was completely against the run of play and within 90 seconds, the mercurial Gascoigne played a 1-2 with Miller to put the Light Blues two goals ahead. With 12 minutes remaining, Beckford replaced the ineffectual Paille and Hearts efforts were rewarded when Davie Weir headed home a McCann free-kick. However, although Rangers had an uncomfortable last sixty seconds, an equaliser was not forthcoming and Hearts could only ponder what might have been.

At the end, an angry Jim Jefferies had to be restrained, "The incident turned it because the players stopped. Otherwise I think we would have gone on to win." Stand-in Hearts skipper Gary Mackay was also distraught at the Robertson affair, "The result is hard to take but the players were magnificent. I was disappointed but I am probably as chuffed as I've ever been of my team-mates during my time at Hearts. We couldn't have given any more than we did."

The fans thought so too and the team were given a tremendous ovation from their fans at the end. The game had hinged on that controversial moment and also on two flashes of brilliance by £4.3 million Paul Gascoigne. At times, Rangers, who had five players booked compared to just Bruno of Hearts, had threatened to lose the place, for the dazzling display by Neil McCann had led Richard Gough and company a merry dance and the winger was deservedly voted Coca Cola's "Man of the Match". At half-time, Cleland had been taken off to be replaced by David Robertson with Moore going to right-back but the Australian was also unable to cope with the pace and directness of McCann.

However, although there were lessons to be learned by Hearts - for a striker of McCoist's calibre should never have been left unmarked in the box, Hearts performance had been a vast improvement on five months earlier. And despite a Parkhead return and a thrilling 2-2 draw with Celtic six days later, the next five games were something of an anti-climax after the heady excitement of the Coca Cola Cup Final. Only two points were taken from a possible 15 and in mid-December, Jim Jefferies paid £200,000 to cash-strapped Dundee for their Scotland Under-21 international striker Jim Hamilton.

The newcomer's arrival saw the formation of a new striking partnership with John Robertson and coincided with wins over Dunfermline (a) 3-2 and Motherwell (h) 4-1. In both games, Hamilton, who was rather like Sandy Clark in style, played cleverly without scoring but on New Year's Day, the fair-haired striker exploded on the scene with a derby double as Hearts raced to a 4-0 win at Easter Road. Hamilton then brought his goals tally to five in his first five starts although a 2-1 home defeat by Celtic again illustrated that Hearts still struggled to defeat the Old Firm, Aberdeen and Dundee United.

At the end of January, two goals by John Robertson contributed towards a 5-0 romp over Cowdenbeath to set up a fourth round clash at Tynecastle against Dundee United on February 16th. The Tannadice side, who were third in the league, five points ahead ahead of Hearts, were riding the crest of a wave and had been named as one of the cup favourites. Just four weeks earlier, Hearts had dominated the corresponding league game only to lose 2-1 after twice being hit on the break by pacy United strikers, Olofsson and Winters.

Now, once again, the Dundee team sat in and it was Hearts who held the edge for long spells. In 13 minutes, David Weir was unlucky to see Dykstra touch his powerful 30-yard shot on to his right-hand post. Referee Hugh

Perfect Balance - Hearts striker Jim Hamilton uses his body to shield the ball from a Dundee United defender in the Scottish Cup tie at Tynecastle.

DC Thomson

Dallas then rejected Hearts penalty claims when Hamilton was bundled to the ground by Malpas while trying to get to a Pointon cross and Hearts were again unfortunate to see a long-range McPherson shot rebound from the crossbar.

However, it was United who went ahead in 67 minutes, Alan McManus diving in front of Rousset to head the ball into his own net when there had been little danger. For much of the game, United had ridden their luck but nine minutes from time, Neil McCann nodded down a long ball by David Weir and Jim Hamilton prodded the ball past Sieb Dykstra with United unsuccessfully claiming for off-side.

In the midweek replay at Tannadice, a crowd of 12,282 were treated to a typically fast and furious cup-tie. In four minutes, Zetterlund thundered a shot against the bar and from the resultant clearance, Hearts fell behind. McLaren's corner fell to Malpas at the edge of the box and when he headed towards the far post, the unmarked Winters nodded home. After that Hearts had most of the ball but although few chances were created, only a desperate save by Dykstra denied Dave McPherson.

Tynecastle boss Jim Jefferies could not hide his disappointment, "We gave a goal away and that's why we are out of the cup - not because we were beaten by a better football side. I warned my players to be alert to Dundee United's threat at set-pieces but we then allowed them to score from a corner we had two chances to clear.

A few days later, Gary Mackay, who had spent most of February on the bench, returned in the 2-0 defeat at Parkhead for what proved his last appearance in a Hearts jersey. The popular midfielder had graced Tynecastle for almost 17 years and he had made a Hearts record of 547 League, League Cup and Scottish Cup appearances. Shortly afterwards, the 33-year-old joined Airdrie on a free-transfer although Jim Jefferies indicated that the club would have liked him to stay until the end of season,"He has been a fantastic servant to Hearts and we hope to see him back here in some capacity."

In many ways, it was the end of an era. Just before the transfer deadline, another of the 1985-86 side, John Colquhoun (33), who had made only a handful of appearances that term, joined First Division St Johnstone on a free-transfer and not long afterwards, defensive stalwart Craig Levein (32) - a player who might have made many more than his 16 Scottish international appearances had it not been for injury - announced his retirement due to his recurring knee problem.

On the right track - Hearts have made good progress under the direction of Chris Robinson and Leslie Deans,

However, for another 32-year-old, the season went on. Since January 18th, John Robertson had been within one goal of equalling Jimmy Wardhaugh's record of 206 league goals for Hearts only for injuries to restrict his appearances and it would be nearer the end of the season before his chance would come.

After their cup exit, eight league games had remained but in essence Hearts season was over although an outside hope of a UEFA Cup place remained should Celtic or Dundee United win the Scottish Cup. However, on March 15th, Neil McCann played a delightful 1-2 with Neil Pointon before beating Jim Leighton with a late goal in a 1-0 win over Hibs at Tynecastle.

On April 19th, John Robertson had returned from injury to play Dunfermline. In recent weeks, Hearts had found goals hard to come by and with the game edging towards injury time, the Pars looked like departing with a 1-0 win. However, a Neil McCann corner then a Jim Hamilton knockdown gave Robertson the chance to bundle the ball over the line and, at last the long-awaited goal that equalled Jimmy Wardhaugh's 46 year-old record for league goals had arrived.

After the game, Robertson, a player who had been worth his weight in goals over the years was delighted, "It's been a long time coming but that goal has taken the pressure off me. I know the fans have been willing me to get there and I'm happy to have done it at Tynecastle. I have unfortunately been unable to win a major trophy during my years at Hearts but joining Jimmy Wardhaugh of "Terrible Trio" fame in the record books is a distinction I will always cherish." Now his aim was to break the record but despite failing to score in a 1-0 reverse at Tannadice, Robertson grabbed the vital goal then added another in the dying minutes of a 3-1 win over against Rangers in the final game of the season at Tynecastle on May 10th.

Those had been moments of great joy for the Hearts supporters in the crowd of 13,097, both in beating Rangers and in watching a player, who had contributed so much to the club over so many years, finally achieve his goal. However, there had also been disgrace, for Frenchman Stephane Paille had failed a drugs test at Kilmarnock in April. The S.F.A. had then suspended the player for four months and in view of his previous offence in his home country, Hearts decided to terminate Paille's contract.

It had been a season of transition for Hearts, who had used thirty players. The waygoing of older players like Mackay, Colquhoun, and Bruno - the latter who was released at the end of the season, left Hearts with a young squad but this was balanced out when Jim Jefferies signed experienced men in Austrian midfielder Thomas Flogel and another French striker Stephane Adam.

Things appear to be moving well for Hearts both on and off the field. Jim Jefferies has substantially reduced the average age of his playing staff while keeping the club on

Derby delight - John Robertson despatches the ball into the net for the opening goal against Hibs in November 1997. (RIGHT) The striker leads Salvatori and Fulton on a victory run. Daily Record

an even keel and achieving the most acceptable record of reaching two cup finals within a six month period.

As earlier demonstrated at Falkirk, the manager insists on an attractive style of football and things have been no different at Tynecastle. Jefferies has taken a three-pronged approach to building his playing squad. The Tynecastle youth system, which was developed back in the days of Sandy Clark has blossomed and has to be the future for all clubs outwith the Old Firm.

Previously, players like Paul Ritchie, Gary Locke, Alan McManus, Kevin Thomas and Stuart Callaghan have come through the ranks and more recently they were joined by goalkeeper Roddy McKenzie, defenders Gary Naysmith, David Murie and Robbie Horn, midfielder Grant Murray and promising strikers Derek Holmes and John-Paul Burns. All were given a taste of first-team football and did not look out of place and some have been also involved in the Scotland Under-21 international set-up.

However, the Premier League is a tough environment and requires players of experience. Here, Jefferies has brought in a clutch of signings from Scottish clubs, having shrewdly secured David Weir, Neil McCann, Colin Cameron, Jim Hamilton - all players of quality for less than £1 million in total. David Weir has been a big success for Hearts and has gone on to win full international honours for Scotland.

Outstanding performances also saw him short listed alongside top stars like Paulo Di Canio and Brian Laudrup for the SPFA Player of the Year Award. Jim Hamilton is a fine leader of the line with an eye for a goal and his ability to hold up the ball makes him a good target for pacy and exciting players like Colin Cameron and Neil McCann - players the fans want to pay to see. The third source of players is the now popular foreign market where experi-

enced players like Adam and Flogel can be obtained without paying transfer fees after Bosman. In short, things are beginning to come together and there is a real air of optimism down Gorgie way.

At this time, in mid-November, Hearts are playing attractive football and are top of the Premier League after twice putting four goals past Aberdeen while another exciting player, the Angolan, Jose Quitongo has been secured.

Off the field, Hearts are also in good hands under co-owners Chris Robinson and Leslie Deans. In the Spring a successful share issue raised £5.5 million, an amount which will at last allow the club to throw off the shackles of debt, while the completion of the Gorgie Road Stand has provided a new ground capacity of 18,500 and the fans now have facilities of which they can be really proud.

Season 1946-47

Date		Opponents		Score	Crowd	Scorers
Aug 10th	L	Falkirk	a	3-3	18,000	Garrett 2; Cox
14th	L	Partick Thistle	h	1-4	27,000	T. Walker
17th	L	Third Lanark	h	4-1	24,000	McCrae 2; T. Walker; Kelly
21st	L	Celtic	a	3-2	15,000	Wardhaugh; Kelly 2
24th	L	Motherwell	a	2-0	9,000	Kelly 2
28th	L	St Mirren	h	2-2	12,000	Sloan; Barrett
31st	L	Queen of the South	h	1-1	22,000	Kelly
Sep 4th	L	Hamilton	a	1-3	10,000	T. Walker
7th	L	Hibernian	a	1-0	39,000	McCrae
14th	L	Kilmarnock	h	2-0	20,000	McCrae; Sloan
21st	LC	Clyde	a	2-1	10,000	McCrae 2
28th	LC	Kilmarnock	h	3-1	30,000	Currie 2; Conn
Oct 5th	LC	Partick Thistle	a	4-4	25,000	Currie; McCrae; Sloan; own-goal
12th	LC	Clyde	h	2-1	30,000	Currie 2
19th	LC	Kilmarnock	a	0-2	20,000	-
26th	LC	Partick Thistle	h	1-1	35,000	J. Walker
Nov 2nd	L	Queens Park	a	2-2	15,000	McCrae; Millar
9th	L	Clyde	h	2-1	15,000	Whitehead; Sloan
16th	L	Morton	a	1-0	10,000	Sloan
23rd	L	Aberdeen	a	1-2	14,000	Conn
30th	L	Rangers	h	0-3	45,000	-
Dec 7th	L	Falkirk	h	1-1	20,000	McCrae
14th	L	Partick Thistle	a	2-1	12,000	McCrae; Sloan
21st	L	Celtic	h	2-1	28,000	J. Walker; McCrae
28th	L	St Mirren	a	0-1	10,000	-
Jan 1st	L	Hibernian	h	2-3	35,000	Whitehead; Kelly
2nd	L	Third Lanark	a	1-4	15,000	Kelly
4th	L	Kilmarnock	a	0-0	10,000	-
11th	L	Motherwell	h	2-1	25,000	Kelly; Urquhart
18th	L	Hamilton	h	4-3	20,000	McCrae; McFarlane; Urquhart; Kelly
25th	SC1	St Johnstone	h	3-0	19,238	Miller (pen); Conn; Kelly
Feb 1st	L	Queen of the South	a	1-0	7,000	McFarlane
8th	L	Clyde	a	2-0	8,000	Wardhaugh; Urquhart
Mar 1st	LCQ	East Fife	h	0-1	19,804	-
5th	LCQ	East Fife	a	5-2 (5-3)	15,000	J. Walker 2; Baxter; McFarlane; Urquhart
8th	SC2	Cowdenbeath	h	2-1*	18,700	Baxter; J. Walker
15th	SCQ	Arbroath	a	1-2	9,000	Currie
22nd	LCS	Aberdeen	Easter Rd	2-6	36,200	Kelly; Urquhart
29th	L	Queens Park	h	1-3	6,000	Dewar
Apr 5th	L	Morton	h	2-0	7,000	Dewar; McKenzie
7th	L	Rangers	a	2-1	12,000	Conn; Dewar
May 17th	L	Aberdeen	h	4-0	16,000	Conn 2; Kelly; McCrae

Cup Cash v. St Johnstone £1,089; Cowdenbeath £1,100: Arbroath £650; v. Aberdeen £4,240

Alfie Conn - the hard-hitting inside-man was one of the legendary "Terrible Trio"

The Record		
League	-	Fourth Place, 'A' Division
League Cup	-	Semi-final
Scottish Cup	-	Quarter-final
Top Scorers	-	Archie Kelly (14 goals)
Av. Home Gate	-	21,500
Players used	-	28
Sent off	-	None

Appearances

	League	L/Cup	S/Cup	Total
Jimmy Brown	30	9	3	42
Bobby Baxter	25	7 (1)	3 (1)	35 (2)
Alex. McCrae	24 (10)	7 (3)	2	33 (13)
Tommy McKenzie	21 (1)	9	2	32 (1)
Tom McSpadyen	20	9	2	31
Charlie Cox	21 (1)	7	2	30 (1)
Archie Miller	20 (1)	8	1 (1)	29 (2)
Alfie Conn	12 (3)	6 (1)	2 (1)	20 (5)
Archie Kelly	22 (12)	2 (1)	1 (1)	25 (14)
Tommy Sloan	18 (5)	6 (1)	1	25 (6)
Willie McFarlane	14 (2)	3 (1)	2	19 (3)
Duncan McClure	16	1	2	19
Ken Currie	8	8 (5)	2 (1)	18 (6)
Jimmy Wardhaugh	11 (2)	6	0	17 (2)
Johnny Urquhart	11 (3)	3 (2)	2	16 (4)
Davie Laing	9	1	2	12
Jimmy Walker	8 (1)	2 (3)	1 (1)	11 (5)
Dick Whitehead	7 (2)	1	1	9 (2)
Tommy Walker	9 (3)	0	0	9 (3)
Jackie Dewar	3 (3)	2	2	7 (3)
Tommy Neilson	6	0	0	6
Jim Pithie	4	1	0	5
Archie Garrett	4 (3)	0	0	4 (3)
Jimmy Briscoe	2	0	0	2
Atholl McAra	2	0	0	2
Tommy Martin	2	0	0	2
Stirton Smith	1	0	0	1
Davie Wood	0	1	0	1

Scottish League 'A' Division

		Home			Away			Goals	
	P	W	D	L	W	D	L	F A	PTS
Rangers	30	12	1	2	9	3	3	76-26	46
Hibernian	30	9	4	2	10	2	3	69-33	44
Aberdeen	30	11	3	1	5	4	6	58-41	39
Hearts	**30**	**8**	**3**	**4**	**8**	**3**	**4**	**52-43**	**38**
Partick Thistle	30	10	0	5	6	3	6	74-58	35
Morton	30	7	4	4	5	6	4	58-45	34
Celtic	30	8	2	5	5	4	6	53-55	32
Motherwell	30	8	3	4	4	2	9	58-54	29
Third Lanark	30	7	3	5	4	3	8	56-64	28
Clyde	30	4	5	6	5	4	6	55-65	27
Falkirk	30	5	4	6	3	6	6	62-61	26
Queen of the South	30	4	4	7	5	4	6	44-69	26
Queens Park	30	3	5	7	5	1	9	47-60	22
St Mirren	30	6	2	7	3	2	10	47-65	22
Kilmarnock	30	4	4	7	2	5	5	44-66	21
Hamilton	30	1	6	8	1	1	13	38-85	11

League Cup Section

	P	W	D	L	F A	PTS
Hearts	**6**	**3**	**2**	**1**	**12-10**	**8**
Clyde	6	3	1	2	12-10	7
Killie	6	3	0	3	12-11	6
Partick Thistle	6	0	3	3	11-16	3

Heart of Midlothian F.C. Line-Ups 1946-47

		1	2	3	4	5	6	7	8	9	10	11
Aug	10th	Brown	McAra	McClure	Cox	Baxter	Neilson	Briscoe	Walker T	Garrett	McCrae	Kelly
	14th	Brown	McAra	McClure	Cox	McKenzie	Neilson	Briscoe	Walker T	Garrett	McCrae	Kelly
	17th	Brown	McClure	Miller	Cox	Baxter	Neilson	Sloan	Walker T	Kelly	Garrett	McCrae
	21st	Brown	McSpadyen	McClure	Cox	Baxter	Miller	Sloan	Walker T	Kelly	McCrae	Wardhaugh
	24th	Brown	McSpadyen	McClure	Cox	Baxter	Miller	Sloan	Walker T	Kelly	McCrae	Walker J
	28th	Brown	McSpadyen	McClure	Cox	Baxter	Miller	Sloan	Walker T	Garrett	McCrae	Walker J
	31st	Brown	McSpadyen	McClure	Cox	Baxter	Miller	Sloan	Walker T	Kelly	McCrae	Wardhaugh
Sep	4th	Brown	McSpadyen	McClure	Cox	Baxter	Miller	Sloan	Conn	Kelly	Walker T	Wardhaugh
	7th	Brown	McSpadyen	McClure	Walker T	Baxter	Miller	Sloan	Conn	Kelly	McCrae	Wardhaugh
	14th	Brown	McSpadyen	McKenzie	Cox	Baxter	Miller	Sloan	Conn	Kelly	McCrae	Wardhaugh
	21st	Brown	McSpadyen	McKenzie	Cox	Baxter	Miller	Sloan	Conn	Currie	McCrae	Wardhaugh
	28th	Brown	McSpadyen	McKenzie	Cox	Baxter	Miller	Sloan	Conn	Currie	McCrae	Wardhaugh
Oct	5th	Brown	McSpadyen	McKenzie	Cox	Baxter	Miller	Sloan	Conn	Currie	McCrae	Wardhaugh
	12th	Brown	McSpadyen	McKenzie	Cox	Baxter	Miller	Sloan	Conn	Currie	McCrae	Wardhaugh
	19th	Brown	McSpadyen	McKenzie	Cox	Pithie	Miller	Sloan	Conn	Currie	McCrae	Wardhaugh
	26th	Brown	McSpadyen	McClure	Whitehead	McKenzie	Miller	Sloan	Conn	Currie	McCrae	Walker J
Nov	2nd	Brown	McSpadyen	McKenzie	Whitehead	Baxter	Miller	Sloan	Conn	Wardhaugh	McCrae	Walker
	9th	Brown	McSpadyen	McKenzie	Whitehead	Baxter	Miller	Sloan	Conn	Currie	McCrae	Urquhart
	16th	Brown	McSpadyen	McKenzie	Whitehead	Baxter	Laing	Sloan	Martin	Conn	McCrae	Walker J
	23rd	Brown	McSpadyen	McKenzie	Whitehead	Baxter	Laing	Sloan	Martin	Conn	McCrae	Walker J
	30th	Brown	McSpadyen	McKenzie	Cox	Baxter	Miller	Sloan	Conn	Kelly	McCrae	Walker J
Dec	7th	Brown	McSpadyen	McKenzie	Cox	Baxter	Miller	Sloan	Conn	Kelly	McCrae	McFarlane
	14th	Brown	McClure	McKenzie	Cox	Baxter	Miller	Sloan	McFarlane	Currie	McCrae	Wardhaugh
	21st	Brown	McSpadyen	McKenzie	Cox	Baxter	Miller	McFarlane	Wardhaugh	Currie	McCrae	Walker J
	28th	Brown	McSpadyen	McKenzie	Cox	Baxter	Miller	Sloan	McFarlane	Kelly	McCrae	Wardhaugh
Jan	1st	Brown	McSpadyen	McKenzie	Cox	Baxter	Miller	McFarlane	Whitehead	Walker J	Currie	Kelly
	2nd	Brown	McClure	McKenzie	Cox	Pithie	Laing	McFarlane	Whitehead	Kelly	Urquhart	Smith
	4th	Brown	McClure	Miller	Whitehead	Baxter	Laing	McFarlane	McCrae	Kelly	Currie	Urquhart
	11th	Brown	McClure	McKenzie	Cox	Baxter	Miller	McFarlane	Currie	Kelly	McCrae	Urquhart
	18th	Brown	McClure	McKenzie	Cox	Baxter	Laing	McFarlane	Currie	Kelly	McCrae	Urquhart
	25th	Brown	McClure	McKenzie	Cox	Baxter	Miller	McFarlane	Conn	Kelly	McCrae	Urquhart
Feb	1st	Brown	McSpadyen	McKenzie	Cox	Baxter	Miller	McFarlane	Wardhaugh	Kelly	McCrae	Urquhart
	8th	Brown	McSpadyen	McKenzie	Cox	Baxter	Miller	McFarlane	Wardhaugh	Sloan	McCrae	Urquhart
Mar	1st	Brown	McSpadyen	McKenzie	Cox	Baxter	Miller	McFarlane	Wardhaugh	Kelly	McCrae	Urquhart
	5th	Brown	McSpadyen	McKenzie	Cox	Baxter	Laing	McFarlane	Currie	Walker J	Urquhart	Dewar
	8th	Brown	McSpadyen	McKenzie	Cox	Baxter	Laing	McFarlane	Currie	Walker J	Urquhart	Dewar
	15th	Brown	McSpadyen	McClure	Whitehead	Baxter	Laing	Sloan	Conn	Currie	McCrae	Dewar
	22nd	Brown	McSpadyen	McKenzie	Wood	Baxter	Laing	McFarlane	Currie	Kelly	Urquhart	Dewar
	29th	Brown	McSpadyen	McKenzie	Laing	Baxter	Neilson	McFarlane	Currie	Kelly	Urquhart	Dewar
Apr	5th	Brown	McClure	McKenzie	Laing	Pithie	Neilson	McFarlane	Conn	Kelly	Urquhart	Dewar
	7th	Brown	McClure	McKenzie	Laing	Pithie	Neilson	McFarlane	Conn	Kelly	Urquhart	Dewar
	17th	Brown	McSpadyen	McKenzie	Cox	Pithie	Laing	Sloan	Conn	Kelly	McCrae	Urquhart

Heart of Midlothian F.C. 1946-47 (BACK, left to right) Tom McKenzie, Tommy McSpadyen, Arthur Miller, Jimmy Brown, Bobby Baxter, Charlie Cox. FRONT - Tommy Sloan, Alfie Conn, Archie Kelly, Alex. McCrae and Jimmy Wardhaugh. J. Ure

Season 1947-48

Date			Opponents		Score	Crowd	Scorers
Aug	9th	LC	Hibernian	a	2-1	43,000	Urquhart; Kelly
	13th	L	St Mirren	h	3-2	20,000	Kelly 2; Urquhart
	16th	LC	Airdrie	a	2-3	15,000	Currie; Kelly
	23rd	LC	Clyde	h	1-0	25,000	Kelly
	27th	L	Motherwell	a	1-3	14,000	Currie
	30th	LC	Hibernian	h	2-1	45,000	Laing; Kelly
Sep	6th	LC	Airdrie	h	1-0	25,000	Kelly
	13th	LC	Clyde	a	2-5	12,000	Sloan 2
	20th	L	Hibernian	h	2-1	42,000	Laing (pen); Urquhart
	27th	LCQ	East Fife	h	3-4*	24,000	Currie 2; Kelly
Oct	4th	L	Third Lanark	h	1-3	15,000	Kelly
	6th	L	Dundee	a	1-2	26,000	Parker
	18th	L	Partick Thistle	h	1-2	28,000	Urquhart
Nov	1st	L	Queens Park	h	1-0	18,000	Currie
	8th	L	Morton	a	1-1	5,000	Dixon
	15th	L	Aberdeen	a	1-1	10,000	Kelly
	22nd	L	QOS	h	1-0	15,000	Kelly
	29th	L	Airdrie	a	1-1	9,000	Sloan
Dec	6th	L	Rangers	h	1-2	40,000	Sloan
	13th	L	Clyde	a	1-2	12,000	Williams
	20th	L	St Mirren	a	0-1	18,000	-
	25th	L	Celtic	a	2-4	30,000	Martin 2
	27th	L	Motherwell	h	0-1	16,000	
Jan	1st	L	Hibernian	a	1-3	45,000	Dixon
	3rd	L	Celtic	h	1-0	37,000	Flavell
	10th	L	Third Lanark	a	1-4	15,000	Flavell
	17th	L	Dundee	h	0-1	25,000	-
	24th	SC1	Dundee	a	4-2	31,500	Urquhart; Flavell; Currie 2
	31st	L	Partick Thistle	a	1-1	30,000	Hamilton
Feb	7th	SC2	Airdrie	a	1-2	20,000	Hamilton
	14th	L	Falkirk	h	3-2	30,000	Hamilton; Flavell; Sloan
	28th	L	Morton	h	3-0	24,000	Hamilton; Currie; Flavell
Mar	6th	L	Aberdeen	h	1-1	30,000	Dixon
	13th	L	QOS	a	1-0	11,200	Flavell
	20th	L	Airdrie	h	2-2	22,000	Hamilton; Flavell
Apr	3rd	L	Clyde	h	1-1	23,000	Hamilton
	17th	L	Falkirk	a	2-0	9,000	McFarlane 2
	24th	L	Queens Park	a	0-0	12,000	-
May	3rd	L	Rangers	a	2-1	15,000	Laing; Hamilton

* After 30 minutes extra-time, 2-2 after 90 mts. Cup cash v, Dundee £2,000; v. Airdrie £1,400

Bobby Flavell - the prolific Airdrie goal-scorer cost Hearts £10,000.

The Record		
League	-	Ninth Place 'A' Division
League Cup	-	Qualifying stages only
Scottish Cup	-	Second round
Top Scorer	-	Archie Kelly (11 goals)
Av. Home Gate	-	25,900
Players used	-	22
Sent off	-	None

Appearances

	League	L/Cup	S/Cup	Total
Davie Laing	29 (2)	7 (1)	2	38 (3)
Jimmy Brown	27	5	2	34
Bobby Parker	25 (1)	6	2	33 (1)
Tommy McKenzie	25	6	1	32
Arthur Dixon	24 (3)	0	2	26 (3)
Dougal Matheson	24	0	2	26
Archie Williams	19 (1)	7	0	26 (1)
Ken Currie	16 (3)	7 (3)	2 (2)	25 (8)
Johnny Urquhart	17 (3)	7 (1)	2 (1)	26 (5)
Willie McFarlane	17 (2)	7	0	24 (2)
Bobby Flavell	17 (6)	0	2 (1)	19 (7)
Archie Kelly	12 (5)	6 (6)	0	18 (11)
Jimmy Rodger	15	1	2	18
Tom McSpadyen	10	6	1	17
Charlie Cox	10	6	0	16
George Hamilton	13 (6)	0	2 (1)	15 (7)
Bobby Dougan	11	1	0	12
Tommy Sloan	10 (3)	1 (2)	0	11 (5)
George Paton	3	2	0	5
Tommy Martin	4 (2)	0	0	4 (2)
Duncan McClure	1	2	0	3
Jimmy Wardhaugh	1	0	0	1

Scottish League 'A' Division

	P	Home W	Home D	Home L	Away W	Away D	Away L	Goals F-A	PTS
Hibernian	30	13	2	0	9	2	4	86-27	48
Rangers	30	10	2	3	11	2	2	64-28	46
Partick Thistle	30	7	3	5	9	1	5	61-42	36
Dundee	30	10	2	3	5	1	9	67-51	33
St Mirren	30	9	2	4	4	3	8	54-58	31
Clyde	30	8	3	4	4	4	7	52-57	31
Falkirk	30	6	5	4	4	5	6	55-48	30
Motherwell	30	7	2	6	6	1	8	45-47	29
Hearts	**30**	**7**	**3**	**5**	**3**	**5**	**7**	**37-42**	**28**
Aberdeen	30	8	4	3	2	4	9	45-45	27
Third Lanark	30	8	1	6	2	5	8	56-73	26
Celtic	30	5	4	6	5	1	9	41-56	25
QOS	30	7	3	5	3	2	10	49-74	25
Morton	30	3	4	8	6	2	7	47-43	24
Airdrie	30	7	1	7	0	6	9	40-78	21
Queens Park	30	5	2	8	4	0	11	45-75	20

League Cup Section

	P	W	D	L	F A	PTS
Hearts	**6**	**4**	**0**	**2**	**10-10**	**8**
Hibernian	6	3	1	2	17- 9	7
Airdrie	6	2	1	3	9-14	5
Clyde	6	2	0	4	14-17	4

Heart of Midlothian F.C. Line-Ups 1947-48

		1	2	3	4	5	6	7	8	9	10	11
Aug	9th	Brown	McSpadyen	McKenzie	Cox	Rodger	Laing	McFarlane	Currie	Kelly	Urquhart	Williams
	13th	Brown	McSpadyen	McKenzie	Cox	Rodger	Laing	McFarlane	Currie	Kelly	Urquhart	Williams
	16th	Brown	McClure	McKenzie	Cox	Parker	Laing	McFarlane	Currie	Kelly	Urquhart	Williams
	23rd	Brown	McSpadyen	McKenzie	Cox	Parker	Laing	McFarlane	Currie	Kelly	Urquhart	Williams
	27th	Brown	McSpadyen	McKenzie	Cox	Parker	Dougan	McFarlane	Currie	Kelly	Urquhart	Williams
	30th	Brown	McSpadyen	McKenzie	Cox	Parker	Laing	McFarlane	Currie	Kelly	Urquhart	Williams
Sep	6th	Brown	McSpadyen	McClure	Cox	Parker	Laing	McFarlane	Currie	Kelly	Urquhart	Williams
	13th	Paton	McSpadyen	McKenzie	Cox	Parker	Laing	McFarlane	Currie	Sloan	Urquhart	Williams
	20th	Paton	McSpadyen	McKenzie	Rodger	Parker	Laing	McFarlane	Currie	Kelly	Urquhart	Williams
	27th	Paton	McSpadyen	McKenzie	Laing	Parker	Dougan	McFarlane	Currie	Kelly	Urquhart	Williams
Oct	4th	Paton	McSpadyen	McKenzie	Laing	Parker	Dougan	McFarlane	Currie	Kelly	Dixon	Urquhart
	6th	Paton	Matheson	McClure	Parker	Rodger	Laing	McFarlane	Currie	Kelly	Dixon	Urquhart
	18th	Brown	Matheson	McKenzie	Parker	Rodger	Laing	McFarlane	Currie	Kelly	Dixon	Urquhart
Nov	1st	Brown	Matheson	McKenzie	Parker	Rodger	Laing	McFarlane	Urquhart	Currie	Dixon	Kelly
	8th	Brown	Matheson	McKenzie	Parker	Rodger	Laing	McFarlane	Urquhart	Currie	Dixon	Kelly
	15th	Brown	Matheson	McKenzie	Cox	Parker	Laing	Sloan	Urquhart	Currie	Dixon	Kelly
	22nd	Brown	Matheson	McKenzie	Cox	Parker	Laing	Sloan	Currie	Kelly	Urquhart	Dixon
	29th	Brown	Matheson	McKenzie	Cox	Parker	Laing	Sloan	Currie	Kelly	Urquhart	Dixon
Dec	6th	Brown	Matheson	McKenzie	Cox	Parker	Laing	Sloan	Urquhart	Kelly	Dixon	Williams
	13th	Brown	Matheson	McKenzie	Parker	Rodger	Laing	Sloan	Urquhart	Currie	Dixon	Williams
	20th	Brown	Matheson	McKenzie	Dougan	Parker	Laing	Sloan	Urquhart	Flavell	Dixon	Williams
	25th	Brown	Matheson	McKenzie	Dougan	Parker	Laing	Sloan	Martin	Flavell	Dixon	Williams
	27th	Brown	Matheson	McKenzie	Cox	Parker	Laing	McFarlane	Martin	Flavell	Currie	Williams
Jan	1st	Brown	Matheson	McKenzie	Dougan	Parker	Laing	McFarlane	Hamilton	Flavell	Martin	Dixon
	3rd	Brown	Matheson	McKenzie	Cox	Parker	Laing	McFarlane	Hamilton	Flavell	Dixon	Williams
	10th	Brown	Matheson	McKenzie	Dougan	Parker	Laing	McFarlane	Hamilton	Flavell	Currie	Williams
	17th	Brown	Matheson	McKenzie	Parker	Rodger	Laing	McFarlane	Hamilton	Flavell	Dixon	Williams
	24th	Brown	Matheson	McKenzie	Parker	Rodger	Laing	Currie	Hamilton	Flavell	Dixon	Urquhart
	31st	Brown	McSpadyen	Matheson	Parker	Rodger	Laing	Currie	Hamilton	Flavell	Dixon	Urquhart
Feb	7th	Brown	McSpadyen	Matheson	Parker	Rodger	Laing	Currie	Hamilton	Flavell	Dixon	Urquhart
	14th	Brown	McSpadyen	Matheson	Parker	Rodger	Laing	Sloan	Hamilton	Flavell	Dixon	Urquhart
	28th	Brown	McSpadyen	McKenzie	Parker	Rodgers	Laing	Currie	Hamilton	Flavell	Dixon	Williams
Mar	6th	Brown	McSpadyen	McKenzie	Laing	Parker	Dougan	Sloan	Hamilton	Flavell	Dixon	Williams
	13th	Brown	McSpadyen	Matheson	Laing	Parker	Dougan	McFarlane	Hamilton	Flavell	Dixon	Williams
	20th	Brown	McSpadyen	Matheson	Laing	Parker	Dougan	McFarlane	Hamilton	Flavell	Dixon	Williams
Apr	3rd	Brown	Matheson	McKenzie	Cox	Rodger	Laing	Flavell	Hamilton	Wardhaugh	Dixon	Williams
	17th	Brown	Matheson	McKenzie	Cox	Rodger	Laing	McFarlane	Hamilton	Flavell	Dixon	Williams
	24th	Brown	Matheson	McKenzie	Laing	Rodger	Dougan	McFarlane	Martin	Flavell	Dixon	Williams
May	3rd	Brown	Matheson	McKenzie	Laing	Rodger	Dougan	Sloan	Hamilton	Flavell	Dixon	Williams

Tynecastle action from the 1940's (LEFT) - Left-back Tom McKenzie leaps high to clear the danger from Motherwell's centre-forward. (RIGHT) - Jimmy Brown watches as McKenzie runs the ball to safety against East Fife.

Season 1948-49

Date			Opponents		Score	Crowd	Scorers
Aug	14th	L	Dundee	a	1-2	30,000	Flavell
	18th	L	Third Lanark	h	3-2	25,000	McFarlane; Flavell 2
	21st	L	Hibernian	a	1-3	40,000	Currie
	28th	L	Celtic	h	1-2	41,000	Flavell
Sep	1st	L	Motherwell	a	0-3	15,000	-
	4th	L	St Mirren	h	1-3	28,000	Conn
	11th	LC	Partick Thistle	h	2-2	23,000	Laing (pen); Dixon
	18th	LC	East Fife	a	0-4	12,000	-
	25th	LC	QOS	a	3-2	11,500	Sloan; Flavell 2
Oct	2nd	LC	Partick Thistle	a	1-3	29,000	Dixon
	9th	LC	East Fife	h	6-1	23,500	Bauld 3; Conn 2; Laing (pen)
	16th	LC	QOS	h	4-0	32,000	Conn; Bauld 3
	23rd	L	Rangers	h	2-0	41,000	Wardhaugh; Conn
	30th	L	Clyde	a	3-3	14,000	Bauld 2; Sloan
Nov	6th	L	Partick Thistle	h	1-3	26,000	Bauld
	13th	L	Falkirk	a	3-5	14,000	Wardhaugh; Bauld; Laing (pen)
	20th	L	QOS	h	1-1	18,000	Bauld
	27th	L	Morton	a	2-0	12,000	Conn 2
Dec	4th	L	Aberdeen	a	2-2	20,000	Wardhaugh; Bauld
	11th	L	East Fife	h	4-0	28,000	Bauld; Sloan; Conn 2 (1 pen)
	18th	L	Albion Rovers	a	5-1	10,000	Wardhaugh 3; Sloan; Bauld
	25th	L	Third Lanark	a	1-1	15,000	Bauld
Jan	1st	L	Hibernian	h	3-2	48,000	Flavell; Conn; Bauld
	3rd	L	Celtic	a	0-2	30,000	-
	8th	L	Dundee	h	0-1	35,000	-
	15th	L	St Mirren	a	2-1	12,000	Bauld; Flavell
	22nd	SC2	Airdrie	h	4-1	29,338	Dixon; Wardhaugh 2; Bauld
	29th	L	Motherwell	h	5-1	30,000	Flavell; Paton o.g.; Bauld; Wardhaugh; Dixon
Feb	5th	SC3	Third Lanark	h	3-1	31,600	Dixon; Wardhaugh; Laing (pen)
	12th	L	Clyde	h	3-0	28,000	Conn 2; McCormack o.g.
	19th	SC4	Dumbarton	h	3-0	30,241	Conn; Dixon; Flavell
	26th	L	Falkirk	h	3-1	23,000	Cox; Laing 2 (1 pen)
Mar	5th	SCQ	Dundee	h	2-4	37,356	Sloan; Cox
	12th	L	Morton	h	2-4	20,000	Conn; Sloan
	19th	L	Aberdeen	h	1-1	20,000	Bauld
Apr	2nd	L	Albion Rovers	h	7-1	15,000	Wardhaugh; Conn; Flavell; Bauld 3; Hunter o.g.
	5th	L	Rangers	a	1-2	45,000	Bauld
	20th	L	Partick Thistle	a	1-1	15,000	Conn
	23rd	L	QOS	a	4-1	8,000	Wardhaugh 2; Conn; Aird o.g.
	29th	L	East Fife	a	1-5	7,000	Wardhaugh (pen)

Cup Cash v.Airdrie £1,858, v. Thirds £2,044, v. Dumbarton £1,933, v. Dundee £3,342

Jimmy Brown - the flamboyant keeper was a firm favourite with the fans.

The Record		
League	-	Eighth Place, 'A' Division
League Cup	-	Qualifying stages only
Scottish Cup	-	Quarter-final
Top Scorer	-	Willie Bauld (24 goals)
Av. Home Gate	-	28,400
Players used	-	24
Sent off	-	None

Appearances

	League	L/Cup	S/Cup	Total
Jimmy Brown	30	6	4	40
Davie Laing	28 (3)	6 (2)	4 (1)	38 (6)
Tommy McKenzie	28	6	4	38
Bobby Dougan	26	6	4	36
Bobby Flavell	26 (8)	4 (2)	4 (1)	34 (11)
Tommy Sloan	23 (4)	5 (1)	4 (1)	32 (6)
Willie Bauld	24 (17)	2 (6)	4 (1)	30 (24)
Alfie Conn	22 (13)	4 (3)	2 (1)	28 (17)
Jimmy Wardhaugh	22 (10)	2	2 (3)	26 (13)
Dougal Matheson	20	2	3	25
Charlie Cox	17 (1)	2	4 (1)	23 (2)
Bobby Parker	15	6	0	21
Arthur Dixon	9 (1)	4 (2)	4 (3)	13 (6)
Archie Williams	8	4	0	12
Ken Currie	6 (1)	3	0	9 (1)
Willie McFarlane	7 (1)	0	0	7
Johnny Urquhart	3	2	0	5
Tommy Darling	2	2	0	4
Jock Adie	4	0	0	4
Jim Henderson	2	0	1	3
Jimmy Rodger	3	0	0	3
Dick Whitehead	2	0	0	2
Bobby Buchan	1	0	0	1
Tommy Martin	1	0	0	1
Tommy Walker	1	0	0	1

Scottish League 'A' Division

		Home			Away			Goals	
	P	W	D	L	W	D	L	F A	PTS
Rangers	30	11	3	1	9	3	3	63-32	46
Dundee	30	13	1	1	7	4	4	71-48	45
Hibernian	30	9	3	3	8	2	5	75-52	39
East Fife	30	9	1	5	7	2	6	64-46	35
Falkirk	30	9	3	3	3	5	7	70-54	32
Celtic	30	7	3	5	5	4	6	48-40	31
Third Lanark	30	9	2	4	4	3	8	56-52	31
Hearts	**30**	**8**	**2**	**5**	**4**	**4**	**7**	**64-54**	**30**
St Mirren	30	9	3	3	4	1	10	51-47	30
Queen of the South	30	8	3	4	3	5	7	47-53	30
Partick Thistle	30	4	8	3	5	1	9	50-63	27
Motherwell	30	7	2	6	3	3	9	44-49	25
Aberdeen	30	5	4	6	2	7	6	39-48	25
Clyde	30	5	4	6	4	2	9	50-67	24
Morton	30	4	6	5	3	2	10	39-51	22
Albion Rovers	30	3	1	11	0	1	14	30-105	8

League Cup Section

	P	W	D	L	F A	PTS
East Fife	6	5	0	1	20- 9	10
Hearts	**6**	**3**	**1**	**2**	**16-12**	**7**
Partick Thistle	6	2	1	3	15-14	5
Queen of the South	6	1	0	5	6-25	2

Heart of Midlothian F.C. Line-Ups 1948-49

		1	2	3	4	5	6	7	8	9	10	11
Aug	14th	Brown	Matheson	McKenzie	Laing	Rodger	Dougan	McFarlane	Currie	Flavell	Dixon	Williams
	18th	Brown	McKenzie	Matheson	Dougan	Rodger	Laing	McFarlane	Martin	Flavell	Dixon	Williams
	21st	Brown	Matheson	McKenzie	Laing	Rodger	Dougan	McFarlane	Currie	Flavell	Dixon	Williams
	28th	Brown	Laing	McKenzie	Cox	Parker	Dougan	Sloan	Conn	Flavell	Urquhart	Williams
Sep	1st	Brown	Laing	Darling	Cox	Parker	Dougan	Sloan	Conn	Flavell	Urquhart	Williams
	4th	Brown	Laing	Darling	Cox	Parker	Dougan	Sloan	Conn	Currie	Urquhart	Williams
	11th	Brown	McKenzie	Darling	Laing	Parker	Dougan	Currie	Conn	Flavell	Dixon	Williams
	18th	Brown	McKenzie	Darling	Laing	Parker	Dougan	Sloan	Conn	Flavell	Dixon	Williams
	25th	Brown	Matheson	McKenzie	Laing	Parker	Dougan	Sloan	Currie	Flavell	Dixon	Urquhart
Oct	2nd	Brown	Matheson	McKenzie	Laing	Parker	Dougan	Sloan	Currie	Flavell	Dixon	Urquhart
	9th	Brown	Parker	McKenzie	Cox	Dougan	Laing	Sloan	Conn	Bauld	Wardhaugh	Williams
	16th	Brown	Parker	McKenzie	Cox	Dougan	Laing	Sloan	Conn	Bauld	Wardhaugh	Williams
	23rd	Brown	Parker	McKenzie	Cox	Dougan	Laing	Sloan	Conn	Bauld	Wardhaugh	Williams
	30th	Brown	Parker	McKenzie	Cox	Dougan	Laing	Sloan	Conn	Bauld	Wardhaugh	Williams
Nov	6th	Brown	Parker	McKenzie	Cox	Dougan	Laing	Sloan	Currie	Bauld	Wardhaugh	Buchan
	13th	Brown	Parker	McKenzie	Whitehead	Dougan	Laing	Sloan	Conn	Bauld	Wardhaugh	Flavell
	20th	Brown	Parker	McKenzie	Cox	Dougan	Laing	Sloan	Conn	Bauld	Wardhaugh	Flavell
	27th	Brown	Matheson	McKenzie	Parker	Dougan	Laing	Sloan	Conn	Bauld	Wardhaugh	Flavell
Dec	4th	Brown	Matheson	McKenzie	Parker	Dougan	Laing	Sloan	Conn	Bauld	Wardhaugh	Flavell
	11th	Brown	Matheson	McKenzie	Parker	Dougan	Laing	Sloan	Conn	Bauld	Wardhaugh	Flavell
	18th	Brown	Matheson	McKenzie	Parker	Dougan	Laing	Sloan	Dixon	Bauld	Wardhaugh	Flavell
	25th	Brown	Matheson	McKenzie	Parker	Dougan	Laing	Sloan	Dixon	Bauld	Wardhaugh	Flavell
Jan	1st	Brown	Matheson	McKenzie	Parker	Dougan	Laing	Sloan	Conn	Bauld	Wardhaugh	Flavell
	3rd	Brown	Matheson	McKenzie	Parker	Dougan	Laing	McFarlane	Conn	Bauld	Wardhaugh	Flavell
	8th	Brown	Matheson	McKenzie	Walker	Dougan	Laing	Sloan	Conn	Bauld	Wardhaugh	Flavell
	15th	Brown	Matheson	McKenzie	Cox	Dougan	Laing	Sloan	Dixon	Bauld	Wardhaugh	Flavell
	22nd	Brown	Matheson	McKenzie	Cox	Dougan	Laing	Sloan	Dixon	Bauld	Wardhaugh	Flavell
	29th	Brown	Matheson	McKenzie	Cox	Adie	Laing	Sloan	Dixon	Bauld	Wardhaugh	Flavell
Feb	5th	Brown	Matheson	McKenzie	Cox	Dougan	Laing	Sloan	Dixon	Bauld	Wardhaugh	Flavell
	12th	Brown	Matheson	McKenzie	Cox	Dougan	Laing	Sloan	Dixon	Bauld	Conn	Flavell
	19th	Brown	Matheson	McKenzie	Cox	Dougan	Laing	Sloan	Dixon	Bauld	Conn	Flavell
	26th	Brown	Henderson	McKenzie	Cox	Dougan	Laing	Sloan	Conn	Bauld	Wardhaugh	Flavell
Mar	5th	Brown	Henderson	McKenzie	Cox	Dougan	Laing	Sloan	Dixon	Bauld	Conn	Flavell
	12th	Brown	Henderson	McKenzie	Cox	Dougan	Laing	Sloan	Dixon	Bauld	Conn	Flavell
	19th	Brown	Matheson	McKenzie	Whitehead	Dougan	Laing	McFarlane	Conn	Bauld	Wardhaugh	Flavell
Apr	2nd	Brown	Matheson	McKenzie	Cox	Dougan	Laing	McFarlane	Conn	Bauld	Wardhaugh	Flavell
	5th	Brown	Matheson	McKenzie	Cox	Dougan	Laing	McFarlane	Conn	Bauld	Wardhaugh	Flavell
	20th	Brown	Matheson	McKenzie	Cox	Adie	Laing	Sloan	Conn	Bauld	Wardhaugh	Flavell
	23rd	Brown	Matheson	McKenzie	Cox	Adie	Currie	Sloan	Conn	Bauld	Wardhaugh	Flavell
	29th	Brown	Matheson	McKenzie	Cox	Adie	Currie	Sloan	Conn	Bauld	Wardhaugh	Flavell

Misty day in Gorgie - Hearts outside-left Bobby Flavell challenges as Dundee keeper Reuben Bennett saves in the Scottish Cup quarter-final at Tynecastle. Gerry Follon and Doug Cowie are the other Dundee defenders. D. Cowie Jnr.

Season 1949-50

Date		Opponents		Score	Crowd	Scorers
Aug 13th	LC	Stirling Albion	a	5-1	20,000	Flavell; Wardhaugh; Bauld 3
17th	LC	Raith Rovers	h	5-1	34,000	Sloan 2; Conn 2; Bauld
20th	LC	East Fife	h	1-1	40,000	Liddell
27th	LC	Stirling Albion	h	4-5	30,000	Bauld 3; Wardhaugh
31st	LC	Raith Rovers	a	2-1	17,000	Conn 2
Sep 3rd	LC	East Fife	a	3-4	20,000	Wardhaugh; McKenzie (pen); Bauld
10th	L	East Fife	h	0-1	32,000	-
17th	L	Celtic	a	2-3	30,000	Wardhaugh 2
24th	L	Hibernian	h	5-2	45,000	Conn 2; Bauld 2; Flavell
Oct 1st	L	St Mirren	a	3-3	25,000	Conn; Bauld 2
15th	L	Third Lanark	a	0-3	16,000	-
22nd	L	Rangers	a	0-1	50,000	-
29th	L	Clyde	h	6-2	25,000	Wardhaugh 4; Sloan; Bauld
Nov 5th	L	Partick Thistle	a	1-0	28,000	Conn
12th	L	Falkirk	h	9-0	20,000	Flavell 2; Laing; Sloan 2; Bauld; Wardhaugh 2; Conn
19th	L	Q.O.S.	a	4-0	10,000	Flavell; Bauld 2; Wardhaugh
26th	L	Motherwell	h	2-0	30,000	Conn; Sloan
Dec 3rd	L	Aberdeen	h	4-1	30,000	Conn 2; Wardhaugh 2
10th	L	Stirling Albion	a	4-2	20,000	Bauld 4
17th	L	Raith Rovers	h	2-0	25,000	Bauld; Conn
24th	L	East Fife	a	1-0	20,000	Flavell
31st	L	Celtic	h	4-2	44,000	Bauld 2; Parker; Milne o.g.
Jan 2nd	L	Hibernian	a	2-1	65,840	Conn; Wardhaugh
3rd	L	St Mirren	h	5-0	34,000	Wardhaugh 2; Conn; Urquhart; Sloan
7th	L	Dundee	a	1-3	33,500	Flavell
14th	L	Third Lanark	h	1-0	25,000	Conn
21st	L	Rangers	h	0-1	46,000	-
28th	SC1	Dundee	h	1-1	39,568	Bauld
Feb 4th	L	Clyde	a	4-3	20,000	Bauld 3; Parker (pen)
6th	SC1R	Dundee	a	2-1*	29,000	Wardhaugh; Bauld
11th	SC2	Aberdeen	a	1-3	42,000	McKenna o.g.
18th	L	Falkirk	a	1-1	14,000	Bauld
25th	L	QOS	h	3-0	18,000	Bauld 2; Liddell
Mar 4th	L	Motherwell	a	3-2	12,000	Flavell; Wardhaugh 2
18th	L	Stirling Albion	h	5-2	12,000	Flavell 2; Bauld 3
25th	L	Raith Rovers	a	0-2	19,000	-
Apr 8th	L	Aberdeen	a	5-0	16,000	Wardhaugh; Bauld 3; Flavell
17th	L	Partick Thistle	h	3-3	12,000	Flavell; McGowan o.g.; Wardhaugh
22nd	L	Dundee	h	6-2	28,000	Bauld 3; Wardhaugh 2; Conn

* Aet, 1-1 after 90 minutes. Cup Cash v. Dundee (h) £2,695; v. Aberdeen £3,700

Bobby Dougan - the Hearts centre-half played for Scotland against Switzerland.

The Record		
League	-	**Third Place, 'A' Division**
League Cup	-	**Qualifying Stages only**
Scottish Cup	-	**Second round**
Top Scorer	-	**Willie Bauld (40 goals)**
Av. Home Gate	-	**27,700**
Players used	-	**21**
Sent off	-	**None**

Appearances

	League	L/Cup	S/Cup	Total
Jimmy Wardhaugh	30 (20)	6 (3)	3 (1)	39 (24)
Willie Bauld	29 (30)	6 (8)	3 (2)	38 (40)
Tommy Sloan	28 (5)	5 (2)	3	36 (7)
Davie Laing	26 (1)	6	3	35 (1)
Tommy McKenzie	26	6 (1)	3	35 (1)
Bobby Dougan	28	4	2	34
Bobby Parker	28 (2)	2	3	33 (2)
Jimmy Brown	24	6	3	33
Charlie Cox	25	6	0	31
Bobby Flavell	26 (11)	1 (1)	3	30 (12)
Alfie Conn	22 (13)	5 (4)	2	29 (15)
Colin Liddell	11 (1)	6 (1)	1	18 (2)
Dougal Matheson	8	6	0	14
Ken Currie	4	0	3	7
Jimmy Watters	6	0	0	6
Jim Henderson	4	0	1	5
John Prentice	2	0	0	2
Arthur Dixon	0	1	0	1
Johnny Urquhart	1 (1)	0	0	1 (1)
Dick Whitehead	1	0	0	1
Archie Williams	1	0	0	1

Scottish League 'A' Division

	P	Home W	Home D	Home L	Away W	Away D	Away L	Goals F-A	PTS
Rangers	30	11	3	1	11	3	1	58-26	50
Hibernian	30	13	0	2	9	5	1	86-34	49
Hearts	**30**	**12**	**1**	**2**	**8**	**2**	**5**	**86-40**	**43**
East Fife	30	8	3	4	7	4	4	58-43	37
Celtic	30	11	4	0	3	3	9	51-50	35
Dundee	30	10	1	4	2	6	7	49-46	31
Partick Thistle	30	8	1	6	3	2	8	55-45	29
Aberdeen	30	7	2	6	4	2	9	48-56	26
Raith Rovers	30	7	4	4	2	4	9	45-54	26
Motherwell	30	6	3	6	4	2	9	53-58	25
St Mirren	30	6	4	5	2	5	8	42-49	25
Third Lanark	30	7	2	6	4	1	10	44-62	25
Clyde	30	6	3	6	4	1	10	56-73	24
Falkirk	30	3	7	5	4	3	8	48-72	24
Queen of the South	30	5	5	5	0	1	14	33-63	16
Stirling Albion	30	4	2	9	2	1	12	38-77	15

League Cup Section

	P	W	D	L	F A	PTS
East Fife	6	5	1	0	17-7	11
Hearts	**6**	**3**	**1**	**2**	**20-13**	**7**
Stirling Albion	6	2	0	4	13-22	4
Raith Rovers	6	1	0	5	11-19	2

Heart of Midlothian F.C. Line-Ups 1949-50

		1	2	3	4	5	6	7	8	9	10	11
Aug	13th	Brown	Matheson	McKenzie	Cox	Dougan	Laing	Flavell	Conn	Bauld	Wardhaugh	Liddell
	17th	Brown	Matheson	McKenzie	Cox	Dougan	Laing	Sloan	Conn	Bauld	Wardhaugh	Liddell
	20th	Brown	Matheson	McKenzie	Cox	Dougan	Laing	Sloan	Conn	Bauld	Wardhaugh	Liddell
	27th	Brown	Matheson	McKenzie	Cox	Dougan	Laing	Sloan	Wardhaugh	Bauld	Dixon	Liddell
	31st	Brown	Matheson	McKenzie	Cox	Parker	Laing	Sloan	Conn	Bauld	Wardhaugh	Liddell
Sep	3rd	Brown	Matheson	McKenzie	Cox	Parker	Laing	Sloan	Conn	Bauld	Wardhaugh	Liddell
	10th	Brown	Matheson	McKenzie	Cox	Parker	Laing	Sloan	Conn	Bauld	Wardhaugh	Liddell
	17th	Brown	Parker	Matheson	Cox	Henderson	Dougan	Sloan	Currie	Bauld	Wardhaugh	Flavell
	24th	Brown	Parker	Matheson	Cox	Henderson	Dougan	Sloan	Conn	Bauld	Wardhaugh	Flavell
Oct	1st	Brown	Parker	Matheson	Currie	Henderson	Dougan	Sloan	Conn	Bauld	Wardhaugh	Flavell
	15th	Brown	Parker	Laing	Cox	McKenzie	Dougan	Sloan	Conn	Bauld	Wardhaugh	Flavell
	22nd	Brown	Parker	McKenzie	Cox	Dougan	Laing	Sloan	Conn	Bauld	Wardhaugh	Flavell
	29th	Brown	Parker	Matheson	Cox	Dougan	Laing	Sloan	Conn	Bauld	Wardhaugh	Flavell
Nov	5th	Brown	Parker	McKenzie	Cox	Dougan	Laing	Sloan	Conn	Bauld	Wardhaugh	Flavell
	12th	Brown	Parker	McKenzie	Cox	Dougan	Laing	Sloan	Conn	Bauld	Wardhaugh	Flavell
	19th	Brown	Parker	McKenzie	Cox	Dougan	Laing	Sloan	Conn	Bauld	Wardhaugh	Flavell
	26th	Brown	Parker	McKenzie	Cox	Dougan	Laing	Sloan	Conn	Bauld	Wardhaugh	Flavell
Dec	3rd	Brown	Parker	McKenzie	Cox	Dougan	Laing	Sloan	Conn	Bauld	Wardhaugh	Flavell
	10th	Brown	Parker	McKenzie	Cox	Dougan	Laing	Sloan	Conn	Bauld	Wardhaugh	Flavell
	17th	Brown	Parker	McKenzie	Cox	Dougan	Laing	Sloan	Conn	Bauld	Wardhaugh	Flavell
	24th	Brown	Parker	McKenzie	Cox	Dougan	Laing	Sloan	Conn	Bauld	Wardhaugh	Flavell
	31st	Brown	Parker	McKenzie	Cox	Dougan	Laing	Sloan	Conn	Bauld	Wardhaugh	Flavell
Jan	2nd	Brown	Parker	McKenzie	Cox	Dougan	Laing	Sloan	Conn	Bauld	Wardhaugh	Flavell
	3rd	Brown	Parker	McKenzie	Cox	Dougan	Laing	Sloan	Conn	Wardhaugh	Urquhart	Liddell
	7th	Brown	Parker	McKenzie	Cox	Dougan	Laing	Sloan	Conn	Bauld	Wardhaugh	Flavell
	14th	Brown	Parker	McKenzie	Whitehead	Dougan	Laing	Sloan	Conn	Bauld	Wardhaugh	Liddell
	21st	Brown	Parker	McKenzie	Cox	Dougan	Laing	Sloan	Conn	Bauld	Wardhaugh	Flavell
	28th	Brown	Parker	McKenzie	Currie	Henderson	Laing	Sloan	Conn	Bauld	Wardhaugh	Flavell
Feb	4th	Brown	Parker	McKenzie	Currie	Henderson	Laing	Sloan	Conn	Bauld	Wardhaugh	Liddell
	6th	Brown	Parker	McKenzie	Currie	Dougan	Laing	Sloan	Flavell	Bauld	Wardhaugh	Liddell
	11th	Brown	Parker	McKenzie	Currie	Dougan	Laing	Sloan	Conn	Bauld	Wardhaugh	Flavell
	18th	Brown	Matheson	McKenzie	Parker	Dougan	Laing	Flavell	Currie	Bauld	Wardhaugh	Liddell
	25th	Brown	Parker	McKenzie	Cox	Dougan	Laing	Sloan	Flavell	Bauld	Wardhaugh	Liddell
Mar	4th	Watters	Parker	McKenzie	Cox	Dougan	Prentice	Sloan	Flavell	Bauld	Wardhaugh	Liddell
	18th	Watters	Matheson	McKenzie	Cox	Dougan	Laing	Sloan	Flavell	Bauld	Wardhaugh	Liddell
	25th	Watters	Matheson	McKenzie	Cox	Dougan	Laing	Sloan	Flavell	Bauld	Wardhaugh	Liddell
Apr	8th	Watters	Parker	McKenzie	Cox	Dougan	Laing	Sloan	Flavell	Bauld	Wardhaugh	Liddell
	17th	Watters	Parker	McKenzie	Prentice	Dougan	Laing	Sloan	Flavell	Bauld	Wardhaugh	Liddell
	22nd	Watters	Parker	McKenzie	Cox	Dougan	Laing	Flavell	Wardhaugh	Bauld	Conn	Williams

Heart of Midlothian F.C. 1949-50 (BACK, left to right) Dougal Matheson, Charlie Cox, Bobby Dougan, Jimmy Brown, Tom McKenzie, Davie Laing. FRONT - Bobby Flavell, Alfie Conn, Willie Bauld, Jimmy Wardhaugh and Colin Liddell.

Season 1950-51

Date			Opponents		Score	Crowd	Scorers
Aug	12th	LC	Partick Thistle	a	1-1	34,000	Wardhaugh
	16th	LC	Motherwell	h	4-1	40,000	Conn 2; Wardhaugh 2
	19th	LC	Airdrie	h	3-2	35,000	Bauld; Wardhaugh 2
	26th	LC	Partick Thistle	h	2-0	30,000	Wardhaugh; Parker (pen)
	30th	LC	Motherwell	a	2-3	24,000	Sloan; Bauld
Sep	3rd	LC	Airdrie	a	3-1	12,500	Parker (pen); Conn; Bauld
	9th	L	Dundee	a	0-1	25,000	-
	16th	L	East Fife	h	5-1	20,000	Bauld 2; Conn 2; Wardhaugh
	23rd	L	Hibernian	a	1-0	50,000	Sloan
	30th	L	St Mirren	h	1-0	30,000	Sloan
Oct	7th	L	East Fife	a	4-1	14,000	Sloan; Laing; Bauld; Conn
	14th	L	Airdrie	h	2-0	25,000	Cox; Bauld
	21st	L	Partick Thistle	a	2-5	22,000	Bauld; Laing (pen)
	28th	L	Clyde	a	2-2	8,000	Urquhart; Bauld
Nov	4th	L	Partick Thistle	h	4-5	25,000	Wardhaugh; Conn 2; Bauld
	11th	L	Third Lanark	a	2-1	10,000	Wardhaugh; Bauld
	18th	L	Motherwell	h	3-3	25,000	Conn 2; Parker (pen)
	25th	L	Morton	a	1-0	11,000	Wardhaugh
Dec	2nd	L	Aberdeen	a	0-2	20,000	-
	9th	L	Falkirk	h	4-2	20,000	Bauld 2; Conn; Wardhaugh
	16th	L	Raith Rovers	a	0-2	12,000	-
	23rd	L	Dundee	h	1-1	18,000	Follon o.g.
	30th	L	Celtic	a	2-2	40,000	Wardhaugh 2
Jan	1st	L	Hibernian	h	2-1	45,000	Sloan; Conn
	2nd	L	St Mirren	a	0-1	15,000	
	20th	L	Rangers	a	1-2	54,000	Wardhaugh
	27th	SC1	Alloa	a	3-2	8,500	Wardhaugh; Conn 2
Feb	3rd	L	Clyde	h	4-0	18,000	Wardhaugh; Mennie o.g.; Conn; Bauld
	10th	SC2	East Stirling	a	5-1	11,000	Wardhaugh; Bauld 2; McKenzie; Sloan
	17th	L	Third Lanark	h	4-0	24,000	Cumming; Laing (pen); Conn; Bauld
	24th	SC3	Celtic	h	1-2	47,672	Conn
Mar	3rd	L	Morton	h	8-0	15,000	Conn 3; Batton o.g.; Mitchell o.g.; Cumming; Whitehead; Wardhaugh
	17th	L	Falkirk	a	4-5	15,000	Wardhaugh 2; Sloan; Conn
	24th	L	Raith Rovers	h	3-1	28,000	Wardhaugh; Urquhart; Cumming
Apr	7th	L	Celtic	h	1-1	16,000	Conn
	14th	L	Airdrie	a	3-2	10,000	Sloan 2; Wardhaugh
	18th	L	Aberdeen	h	4-1	20,000	Bauld; Conn 2; Wardhaugh
	21st	L	Rangers	h	0-1	30,000	-
May	5th	L	Motherwell	a	4-2	7,000	Bauld 2; Cumming; Conn

Cup Cash v. Alloa £353, East Stirling £800: Celtic £3,264-9-8d

Davie Laing - this stalwart half-back was capped twice for the Scottish League.

The Record

League	-	Fourth Place, 'A' Division
League Cup	-	Qualifying stages only
Scottish Cup	-	Third round
Top Scorer	-	Alfie Conn (25 goals)
Av. Home Gate	-	23,900
Players used	-	20
Sent off	-	None

Appearances

	League	L/Cup	S/Cup	Total
Willie Bauld	30 (15)	6 (3)	3 (2)	39 (20)
Bobby Dougan	30	6	3	39
Tommy Sloan	29 (7)	6 (1)	3 (1)	38 (9)
Jimmy Wardhaugh	29 (15)	6 (6)	3 (2)	38 (23)
Alfie Conn	28 (19)	6 (3)	3 (3)	37 (25)
Jimmy Brown	27	6	3	36
Tommy McKenzie	27	6	3 (1)	36 (1)
Davie Laing	27 (3)	5	3	35 (3)
Bobby Parker	27 (1)	6 (2)	2	35 (3)
Charlie Cox	22 (1)	6	3	31 (1)
Archie Williams	15	0	0	15
John Cumming	14 (4)	0	3	17 (4)
Dick Whitehead	8 (1)	0	0	8 (1)
Colin Liddell	1	6	3	7
John Prentice	4	1	0	5
Tom McSpadyen	3	0	1	4
Johnny Urquhart	3 (2)	0	0	3 (2)
Jimmy Watters	3	0	0	3
Jock Adie	2	0	0	2
Jimmy Whittle	1	0	0	1

Scottish League 'A' Division

		Home			Away			Goals	
	P	W	D	L	W	D	L	F A	PTS
Hibernian	30	13	1	1	9	3	3	78-26	48
Rangers	30	10	3	2	7	1	7	64-37	38
Dundee	30	11	3	1	4	5	6	47-30	38
Hearts	**30**	**10**	**3**	**2**	**6**	**2**	**7**	**72-45**	**37**
Aberdeen	30	9	2	4	6	3	6	61-50	35
Partick Thistle	30	9	4	2	4	3	8	57-48	33
Celtic	30	6	3	6	6	2	7	48-46	29
Raith Rovers	30	8	2	5	5	0	10	52-52	28
Motherwell	30	7	3	5	4	3	8	58-65	28
East Fife	30	7	4	4	3	4	8	48-66	28
St Mirren	30	7	3	5	2	4	9	35-51	25
Morton	30	6	0	9	4	4	7	47-59	24
Third Lanark	30	7	1	7	4	1	10	40-51	24
Airdrie	30	6	3	6	4	1	10	52-67	24
Clyde	30	6	4	5	2	3	10	37-57	23
Falkirk	30	6	3	6	1	1	13	35-81	18

League Cup Section

	P	W	D	L	F A	PTS
Motherwell	6	5	0	1	18-12	10
Hearts	**6**	**4**	**1**	**1**	**15- 8**	**9**
Partick Thistle	6	1	1	3	10-11	5
Airdrie	6	0	0	6	9-21	0

Heart of Midlothian F.C. Line-Ups 1950-51

		1	2	3	4	5	6	7	8	9	10	11
Aug	12th	Brown	Parker	McKenzie	Cox	Dougan	Laing	Sloan	Conn	Bauld	Wardhaugh	Liddell
	16th	Brown	Parker	McKenzie	Cox	Dougan	Laing	Sloan	Conn	Bauld	Wardhaugh	Liddell
	19th	Brown	Parker	McKenzie	Cox	Dougan	Laing	Sloan	Conn	Bauld	Wardhaugh	Liddell
	26th	Brown	Parker	McKenzie	Cox	Dougan	Laing	Sloan	Conn	Bauld	Wardhaugh	Liddell
	30th	Brown	Parker	McKenzie	Cox	Dougan	Laing	Sloan	Conn	Bauld	Wardhaugh	Liddell
Sep	4th	Brown	Parker	McKenzie	Cox	Dougan	Prentice	Sloan	Conn	Bauld	Wardhaugh	Liddell
	9th	Brown	Parker	McKenzie	Cox	Dougan	Prentice	Sloan	Conn	Bauld	Wardhaugh	Liddell
	16th	Brown	Parker	McKenzie	Cox	Dougan	Laing	Sloan	Conn	Bauld	Wardhaugh	Williams
	23rd	Brown	Parker	McKenzie	Cox	Dougan	Laing	Sloan	Conn	Bauld	Wardhaugh	Williams
	30th	Brown	Parker	McKenzie	Cox	Dougan	Laing	Sloan	Conn	Bauld	Wardhaugh	Williams
Oct	7th	Brown	Parker	McKenzie	Cox	Dougan	Laing	Sloan	Conn	Bauld	Wardhaugh	Williams
	14th	Brown	Parker	McKenzie	Cox	Dougan	Laing	Sloan	Conn	Bauld	Wardhaugh	Williams
	21st	Watters	Laing	Adie	Cox	Dougan	Prentice	Sloan	Conn	Bauld	Wardhaugh	Williams
	28th	Brown	McSpadyen	Parker	Cox	Dougan	Laing	Sloan	Conn	Bauld	Urquhart	Williams
Nov	4th	Brown	Parker	McKenzie	Cox	Dougan	Laing	Sloan	Conn	Bauld	Wardhaugh	Williams
	11th	Brown	Parker	McKenzie	Cox	Dougan	Prentice	Sloan	Conn	Bauld	Wardhaugh	Williams
	18th	Brown	Parker	McKenzie	Cox	Dougan	Prentice	Sloan	Conn	Bauld	Wardhaugh	Williams
	25th	Brown	Parker	McKenzie	Cox	Dougan	Laing	Sloan	Conn	Bauld	Wardhaugh	Williams
Dec	2nd	Brown	Parker	McKenzie	Cox	Dougan	Laing	Sloan	Conn	Bauld	Wardhaugh	Williams
	9th	Brown	Parker	McKenzie	Cox	Dougan	Laing	Sloan	Conn	Bauld	Wardhaugh	Williams
	16th	Brown	Parker	McKenzie	Cox	Dougan	Laing	Sloan	Whittle	Bauld	Wardhaugh	Williams
	23rd	Brown	Parker	McKenzie	Cox	Dougan	Laing	Sloan	Conn	Bauld	Wardhaugh	Williams
	30th	Brown	Parker	McKenzie	Cox	Dougan	Laing	Sloan	Conn	Bauld	Wardhaugh	Cumming
Jan	1st	Brown	Parker	McKenzie	Cox	Dougan	Laing	Sloan	Conn	Bauld	Wardhaugh	Cumming
	2nd	Watters	Parker	McKenzie	Whitehead	Dougan	Laing	Sloan	Conn	Bauld	Wardhaugh	Cumming
	20th	Watters	Parker	McKenzie	Cox	Dougan	Laing	Sloan	Conn	Bauld	Wardhaugh	Cumming
	27th	Brown	Parker	McKenzie	Cox	Dougan	Laing	Sloan	Conn	Bauld	Wardhaugh	Cumming
Feb	3rd	Brown	McSpadyen	McKenzie	Cox	Dougan	Laing	Sloan	Conn	Bauld	Wardhaugh	Cumming
	10th	Brown	McSpadyen	McKenzie	Cox	Dougan	Laing	Sloan	Conn	Bauld	Wardhaugh	Cumming
	17th	Brown	McSpadyen	McKenzie	Cox	Dougan	Laing	Sloan	Conn	Bauld	Wardhaugh	Cumming
	24th	Brown	Parker	McKenzie	Cox	Dougan	Laing	Sloan	Conn	Bauld	Wardhaugh	Cumming
Mar	3rd	Brown	Parker	McKenzie	Whitehead	Dougan	Laing	Sloan	Conn	Bauld	Wardhaugh	Cumming
	17th	Brown	Parker	McKenzie	Whitehead	Dougan	Laing	Sloan	Conn	Bauld	Wardhaugh	Cumming
	24th	Brown	Parker	McKenzie	Whitehead	Dougan	Laing	Sloan	Urquhart	Bauld	Wardhaugh	Cumming
Apr	7th	Brown	Parker	Adie	Whitehead	Dougan	Laing	Sloan	Conn	Bauld	Wardhaugh	Cumming
	14th	Brown	Parker	McKenzie	Whitehead	Dougan	Laing	Sloan	Conn	Bauld	Wardhaugh	Cumming
	18th	Brown	Parker	McKenzie	Whitehead	Dougan	Laing	Sloan	Conn	Bauld	Wardhaugh	Cumming
	21st	Brown	Parker	McKenzie	Whitehead	Dougan	Laing	Urquhart	Conn	Bauld	Wardhaugh	Cumming
May	5th	Brown	Parker	McKenzie	Cox	Dougan	Laing	Sloan	Conn	Bauld	Wardhaugh	Cumming

Familiar foe - former Tynecastle forward Bobby Flavell gets in amongst his old team-mates to head for goal. Davie Laing and Bobby Dougan are the Hearts defenders while Doug Cowie is also prominent for Dundee. D. Cowie Jnr.

Season 1951-52

Date			Opponents		Score	Crowd	Scorers
Aug	11th	LC	Raith Rovers	h	1-0	26,000	Bauld
	15th	LC	Dundee	a	1-2	22,500	Wardhaugh
	18th	LC	St Mirren	a	5-5	8,000	Bauld 5
	25th	LC	Raith Rovers	a	0-2	14,000	-
	29th	LC	Dundee	h	5-2	30,000	Parker 2 (pens); Bauld 2; Cumming
Sep	1st	LC	St Mirren	h	3-1	37,000	Conn 3
	8th	L	East Fife	h	3-1	23,000	Wardhaugh 2; Bauld
	15th	L	Airdrie	a	0-2	12,000	-
	22nd	L	Hibernian	h	1-1	47,000	Conn
	29th	L	Celtic	a	3-1	48,000	Bauld; Conn; Wardhaugh
Oct	6th	L	Dundee	h	4-2	35,000	Urquhart; Wardhaugh; Bauld; Conn
	13th	L	St Mirren	a	0-1	15,000	-
	20th	L	Rangers	a	0-2	35,000	-
	27th	L	Third Lanark	h	2-2	22,000	Urquhart; Laing
Nov	3rd	L	Partick Thistle	a	0-2	20,000	-
	10th	L	QOS	h	4-3	16,000	Whittle; Cumming; Bauld; Parker (pen)
	17th	L	Motherwell	a	5-0	14,000	Conn; Aitkenhead o.g.; Bauld; Whittle; Parker (pen)
	24th	L	Morton	h	4-1	22,000	Bauld; Rutherford; Conn; Parker (pen)
Dec	1st	L	Aberdeen	h	2-2	28,000	Bauld; Whittle
	8th	L	Stirling Albion	a	4-0	8,000	Rutherford 2; Bauld; Parker (pen)
	15th	L	Raith Rovers	h	4-2	24,000	Whittle; Conn; Bauld; Rutherford
	22nd	L	East Fife	a	4-2	15,000	Rutherford; Wardhaugh; Conn 2
	29th	L	Airdrie	h	6-1	25,000	Parker (pen); Wardhaugh 2; Bauld 2; Whittle
Jan	1st	L	Hibernian	a	3-2	39,000	Bauld 2; Wardhaugh
	2nd	L	Celtic	h	2-1	40,000	Parker (pen); Whittle
	5th	L	Dundee	a	3-3	32,000	Rutherford; Whittle; Wardhaugh
	12th	L	St Mirren	h	2-1	30,000	Wardhaugh; Conn
	19th	L	Rangers	h	2-2	48,000	Rutherford; Wardhaugh
	26th	L	Aberdeen	a	0-3	16,000	-
Feb	9th	SC2	Raith Rovers	h	1-0	47,350	Bauld
	13th	L	Partick Thistle	h	1-2	22,000	Conn
	16th	L	QOS	a	1-1	12,500	Wardhaugh
	23rd	SC3	QOS	a	3-1	24,500	Whittle; Glidden; Conn
Mar	1st	L	Morton	a	1-3	9,500	Bauld
	8th	SCQ	Airdrie	a	2-2	26,000	Bauld; Conn
	12th	SCQR	Airdrie	h	6-4	40,528	Bauld 3; Rutherford 2; Wardhaugh
	15th	L	Stirling Albion	h	5-2	20,000	Murray; Whittle; Rutherford; Conn 2
	22nd	L	Raith Rovers	a	1-2	10,000	Whittle
	29th	SCS	Motherwell	Hamp	1-1	98,547	Conn
Apr	7th	SCSR	Motherwell	Hamp	1-1*	80,209	Rutherford
	9th	SCSR	Motherwell	Hamp	1-3	59,468	Conn
	14th	L	Third Lanark	a	0-4	25,000	-
	30th	L	Motherwell	h	2-2	10,000	Wardhaugh 2

* After extra-time, 1-1 after 90 mts. Cup Cash v. Raith £3,339, QOS £1,718, v. Airdrie (a) £1,950; (h) £2,767, v. Motherwell (1st) £6,600 exc stands; (2nd) £5,730, (3rd) £4,300

Bobby Parker - defensive bulwark for Hearts down the years

Appearances

	League	L/Cup	S/Cup	Total
Willie Bauld	29 (14)	6 (8)	7 (5)	42 (27)
Jimmy Brown	29	6	7	42
Bobby Parker	29 (6)	6 (2)	7	42 (8)
Davie Laing	26 (1)	3	7	36 (1)
Alfie Conn	25 (12)	3 (3)	7 (4)	35 (19)
Tommy McKenzie	23	3	6	32
Jimmy Milne	26	0	7	33
Jimmy Wardhaugh	19 (14)	6 (1)	5 (1)	30 (16)
Fred Glidden	21	0	7 (1)	28 (1)
Eddie Rutherford	20 (8)	0	7 (3)	27 (11)
Johnny Urquhart	18 (2)	5	3	26 (2)
Jimmy Whittle	16 (9)	0	5 (1)	21 (10)
John Cumming	12 (1)	6 (1)	0	18 (2)
Jock Adie	10	0	0	10
Tom McSpadyen	4	5	1	10
Bobby Dougan	3	6	0	9
Charlie Cox	2	4	0	6
Tommy Sloan	2	4	0	6
John Durkin	4	0	0	4
Ian Gordon	3	0	0	3
Archie Williams	2	0	1	3
Doug Armstrong	2	0	0	2
Bobby Buchan	1	0	0	1
Colin Liddell	2	0	0	2
Jimmy Murray	1 (1)	0	0	1 (1)
Jimmy Watters	1	0	0	1

The Record

League	-	**Fourth Place, 'A' Division**
League Cup	-	**Qualifying stages only**
Scottish Cup	-	**Semi-final**
Top Scorer	-	**Willie Bauld (27 goals)**
Av. Home Gate	-	**27,400**
Players used	-	**26**
Sent off	-	**None**

Scottish League 'A' Division

		Home			Away			Goals		
	P	W	D	L	W	D	L	F	A	PTS
Hibernian	30	12	2	1	8	3	4	92-36		45
Rangers	30	10	4	1	6	5	4	61-31		41
East Fife	30	11	2	2	6	1	8	71-49		37
Hearts	**30**	**9**	**5**	**1**	**5**	**2**	**8**	**69-53**		**35**
Raith Rovers	30	9	2	4	5	3	7	43-42		33
Partick Thistle	30	7	3	5	5	4	6	40-51		31
Motherwell	30	8	4	3	4	3	8	51-57		31
Dundee	30	7	3	5	4	3	8	53-52		28
Celtic	30	7	5	3	3	3	9	52-55		28
QOS	30	10	3	2	0	5	10	50-60		28
Aberdeen	30	7	4	4	3	3	9	65-58		27
Third Lanark	30	7	3	5	2	5	8	51-62		26
Airdrie	30	7	3	5	4	1	10	54-69		26
St Mirren	30	9	2	4	1	3	11	43-58		25
Morton	30	7	1	7	2	5	8	49-56		24
Stirling Albion	30	4	4	7	1	1	13	36-99		15

League Cup Section

	P	W	D	L	F A	PTS
Dundee	6	3	1	2	14-10	7
Hearts	**6**	**3**	**1**	**2**	**15-12**	**7**
St Mirren	6	2	2	2	13-13	6
Raith Rovers	6	2	0	4	6-13	4

Heart of Midlothian F.C. Line-Ups 1951-52

		1	2	3	4	5	6	7	8	9	10	11
Aug	11th	Brown	Parker	McSpadyen	Cox	Dougan	Laing	Sloan	Conn	Bauld	Wardhaugh	Cumming
	15th	Brown	Parker	McSpadyen	Whitehead	Dougan	Cox	Sloan	Wardhaugh	Bauld	Cumming	Urquhart
	18th	Brown	Parker	McSpadyen	Whitehead	Dougan	Cox	Sloan	Wardhaugh	Bauld	Cumming	Urquhart
	25th	Brown	Parker	McKenzie	Whitehead	Dougan	Cox	Sloan	Wardhaugh	Bauld	Cumming	Urquhart
	29th	Brown	McSpadyen	McKenzie	Parker	Dougan	Laing	Wardhaugh	Conn	Bauld	Cumming	Urquhart
Sep	1st	Brown	McSpadyen	McKenzie	Parker	Dougan	Laing	Wardhaugh	Conn	Bauld	Cumming	Urquhart
	8th	Brown	McSpadyen	McKenzie	Parker	Dougan	Laing	Wardhaugh	Conn	Bauld	Cumming	Urquhart
	15th	Brown	McSpadyen	McKenzie	Parker	Dougan	Adie	Wardhaugh	Conn	Bauld	Cumming	Urquhart
	22nd	Brown	Parker	McKenzie	Cox	Dougan	Laing	Sloan	Conn	Bauld	Wardhaugh	Cumming
	29th	Brown	Parker	McKenzie	Adie	Milne	Laing	Durkin	Conn	Bauld	Wardhaugh	Urquhart
Oct	6th	Brown	Parker	McKenzie	Adie	Milne	Laing	Durkin	Conn	Bauld	Wardhaugh	Urquhart
	13th	Brown	Parker	McKenzie	Adie	Milne	Laing	Durkin	Conn	Bauld	Urquhart	Liddell
	20th	Brown	Parker	Gordon	Armstrong	Milne	Laing	Liddell	Conn	Bauld	Urquhart	Williams
	27th	Brown	Parker	McKenzie	Gordon	Milne	Laing	Sloan	Conn	Bauld	Urquhart	Cumming
Nov	3rd	Brown	Parker	McKenzie	Laing	Milne	Armstrong	Durkin	Conn	Bauld	Cumming	Urquhart
	10th	Brown	Glidden	McKenzie	Cox	Parker	Laing	Rutherford	Conn	Bauld	Whittle	Cumming
	17th	Brown	Parker	McKenzie	Glidden	Milne	Laing	Rutherford	Conn	Bauld	Whittle	Cumming
	24th	Brown	Parker	McKenzie	Glidden	Milne	Laing	Rutherford	Conn	Bauld	Whittle	Cumming
Dec	1st	Brown	Parker	McKenzie	Glidden	Milne	Laing	Rutherford	Conn	Bauld	Whittle	Cumming
	8th	Brown	Parker	McKenzie	Glidden	Milne	Laing	Rutherford	Conn	Bauld	Whittle	Wardhaugh
	15th	Brown	Parker	McKenzie	Glidden	Milne	Laing	Rutherford	Conn	Bauld	Whittle	Wardhaugh
	22nd	Brown	Parker	McKenzie	Glidden	Milne	Laing	Rutherford	Conn	Bauld	Whittle	Wardhaugh
	29th	Brown	Parker	McKenzie	Glidden	Milne	Laing	Rutherford	Whittle	Bauld	Wardhaugh	Urquhart
Jan	1st	Brown	Parker	Adie	Glidden	Milne	Laing	Rutherford	Conn	Bauld	Wardhaugh	Urquhart
	2nd	Brown	Parker	Adie	Glidden	Milne	Laing	Rutherford	Whittle	Bauld	Wardhaugh	Urquhart
	5th	Brown	Parker	McKenzie	Glidden	Milne	Laing	Rutherford	Whittle	Bauld	Wardhaugh	Urquhart
	12th	Brown	Parker	McKenzie	Glidden	Milne	Laing	Rutherford	Conn	Bauld	Wardhaugh	Urquhart
	19th	Brown	Parker	McKenzie	Glidden	Milne	Laing	Rutherford	Conn	Bauld	Wardhaugh	Urquhart
	26th	Brown	Parker	McKenzie	Glidden	Milne	Laing	Rutherford	Conn	Bauld	Wardhaugh	Urquhart
Feb	9th	Brown	Parker	McKenzie	Glidden	Milne	Laing	Rutherford	Conn	Bauld	Wardhaugh	Urquhart
	13th	Brown	Parker	Gordon	Glidden	Milne	Laing	Wardhaugh	Conn	Bauld	Whittle	Urquhart
	16th	Brown	Parker	Adie	Glidden	Milne	Laing	Rutherford	Whittle	Bauld	Wardhaugh	Williams
	23rd	Brown	Parker	McKenzie	Glidden	Milne	Laing	Rutherford	Conn	Bauld	Whittle	Williams
Mar	1st	Brown	Parker	McKenzie	Glidden	Milne	Adie	Rutherford	Conn	Bauld	Whittle	Cumming
	8th	Brown	Parker	McKenzie	Glidden	Milne	Laing	Rutherford	Conn	Bauld	Whittle	Wardhaugh
	12th	Brown	Parker	McKenzie	Glidden	Milne	Laing	Rutherford	Conn	Bauld	Whittle	Wardhaugh
	15th	Brown	Parker	McSpadyen	Glidden	Milne	Adie	Rutherford	Conn	Murray	Whittle	Cumming
	22nd	Brown	Parker	McSpadyen	Glidden	Milne	Buchan	Rutherford	Conn	Bauld	Wardhaugh	Whittle
	29th	Brown	Parker	McSpadyen	Glidden	Milne	Laing	Rutherford	Conn	Bauld	Wardhaugh	Whittle
Apr	7th	Brown	Parker	McKenzie	Glidden	Milne	Laing	Rutherford	Conn	Bauld	Whittle	Urquhart
	9th	Brown	Parker	McKenzie	Glidden	Milne	Laing	Rutherford	Conn	Bauld	Wardhaugh	Urquhart
	14th	Brown	Adie	McKenzie	Glidden	Milne	Laing	Rutherford	Whittle	Bauld	Cumming	Urquhart
May	1st	Watters	Parker	McKenzie	Glidden	Milne	Laing	Rutherford	Conn	Bauld	Wardhaugh	Urquhart

Heart of Midlothian F.C. 1951-52 (BACK, left to right) Bobby Parker, Tom McSpadyen, Jimmy Brown, Charlie Cox, Bobby Dougan, Davie Laing. FRONT - Tommy Sloan, Alfie Conn, Willie Bauld, Jimmy Wardhaugh and John Cumming.

Season 1952-53

Date			Opponents		Score	Crowd	Scorers
Aug	9th	LC	Rangers	h	5-0	41,000	Conn 2; Bauld 2; Wardhaugh
	13th	LC	Aberdeen	a	4-2	33,000	Bauld 2; Rutherford; Parker (pen)
	16th	LC	Motherwell	h	0-1	29,000	-
	23rd	LC	Rangers	a	0-2	70,000	-
	27th	LC	Aberdeen	h	1-1	22,000	Bauld
	30th	LC	Motherwell	a	2-1	18,000	Whittle; Durkin
Sep	6th	L	Third Lanark	a	3-2	25,000	Glidden; Wardhaugh; Whittle
	13th	L	St Mirren	h	1-2	23,000	Urquhart
	20th	L	Hibernian	a	1-3	50,000	Parker (pen)
	27th	L	Airdrie	h	4-0	22,000	Whittle 2; Urquhart; Wardhaugh
Oct	4th	L	East Fife	a	1-3	12,000	Bauld
	11th	L	Partick Thistle	h	2-1	25,000	Bauld; Urquhart
	18th	L	Dundee	a	1-2	21,000	Urquhart
	25th	L	Celtic	h	1-0	33,000	Urquhart
Nov	1st	L	Falkirk	h	0-1	20,000	-
	8th	L	QOS	a	2-4	9,000	Conn; Urquhart
	15th	L	Aberdeen	a	0-3	15,000	-
	22nd	L	Motherwell	h	3-1	22,000	Bauld; Conn; Urquhart
	29th	L	Raith Rovers	a	1-1	12,000	Urquhart
Dec	6th	L	Clyde	a	2-3	15,000	Wardhaugh 2
	13th	L	Rangers	h	2-2	26,000	Glidden; Conn
	20th	L	Third Lanark	h	3-3	20,000	Conn 3
	27th	L	St Mirren	a	0-1	10,000	-
Jan	1st	L	Hibernian	h	1-2	41,000	Urquhart
	3rd	L	Airdrie	a	2-1	13,000	Urquhart; Wardhaugh
	17th	L	Partick Thistle	a	2-2	18,000	Whittle; Laing
	24th	L	Motherwell	a	3-1	14,000	Parker; Conn; Urquhart
	31st	L	Dundee	h	1-1	16,000	Conn
Feb	7th	SC2	Raith Rovers	a	1-0	31,306	Bauld
	14th	L	Celtic	a	1-1	35,000	Wardhaugh
	21st	SC3	Montrose	h	3-1	21,400	Urquhart; Bauld; Laing (pen)
	28th	L	QOS	h	3-0	25,000	Urquhart; Wardhaugh; Blackwood
Mar	7th	L	Aberdeen	h	3-1	20,000	Wardhaugh 2; Blackwood
	14th	SCQ	QOS	h	2-1	30,477	Blackwood 2
	21st	L	Raith Rovers	h	1-2	30,000	Conn
	28th	L	Clyde	h	7-0	18,000	Wardhaugh; Cumming 2; Rutherford; Bauld 3
Apr	4th	SCS	Rangers	Hamp	1-2	116,262	Wardhaugh
	6th	L	Rangers	a	0-3	40,000	-
	18th	L	Falkirk	a	4-2	12,000	Bauld 3; Conn
	28th	L	East Fife	h	4-2	12,000	Wardhaugh 2; Conn; Bauld

Cup Cash v. Raith £2,430; v. QOS £2,167; Rangers £16,000

Jimmy Watters - the Tynecastle keeper gets his body behind a powerful shot.

The Record		
League	-	Fourth Place, 'A' Division
League Cup	-	Qualifying stages only
Scottish Cup	-	Semi-final
Top Scorer	-	Willie Bauld (17 goals)
Av. Home Gate	-	23,600
Players used	-	22
Sent off	-	None

Appearances

	League	L/Cup	S/Cup	Total
Jimmy Watters	30	6	4	40
Bobby Parker	27 (2)	6 (1)	4	37 (3)
Johnny Urquhart	28 (12)	6	3 (1)	37 (13)
Jimmy Wardhaugh	26 (12)	6 (1)	4 (1)	36 (14)
Davie Laing	23 (1)	6	4 (1)	33 (2)
Tommy McKenzie	24	6	3	33
Willie Bauld	23 (10)	5 (5)	4 (2)	32 (17)
Alfie Conn	25 (11)	3 (2)	4	32 (13)
Doug Armstrong	19	0	4	23
Bobby Dougan	18	1	4	23
Fred Glidden	16 (2)	5	0	21 (2)
Jimmy Milne	14	6	0	20
Bobby Blackwood	14 (2)	0	1 (2)	15 (4)
Jimmy Whittle	12 (4)	2 (1)	0	14 (5)
John Cumming	7 (2)	3	1	11 (2)
Jock Adie	7	1	1	9
Eddie Rutherford	4 (1)	3 (1)	2	9 (2)
John Durkin	5	1 (1)	0	6 (1)
Jim Souness	5	0	1	6
Charlie Ferguson	1	0	0	1
John Kilgannon	1	0	0	1
Dick Whitehead	1	0	0	1

Scottish League 'A' Division

		Home			Away			Goals	
	P	W	D	L	W	D	L	F A	PTS
Rangers	30	12	1	2	6	6	3	80-39	43
Hibernian	30	10	3	2	9	2	4	93-51	43
East Fife	30	11	2	2	5	5	5	72-48	39
Hearts	**30**	**8**	**3**	**4**	**4**	**3**	**8**	**59-50**	**30**
Clyde	30	8	2	5	5	2	8	78-78	30
St Mirren	30	6	6	3	5	2	8	52-58	30
Dundee	30	8	5	2	1	6	9	44-37	29
Celtic	30	7	3	5	4	4	7	51-54	29
Partick Thistle	30	6	4	5	4	5	6	55-63	29
Queen of The South	30	8	3	4	2	5	8	43-61	28
Aberdeen	30	8	5	2	3	0	12	64-68	27
Raith Rovers	30	5	7	3	4	1	10	47-53	26
Falkirk	30	7	1	7	4	3	8	53-63	26
Airdrie	30	6	4	5	4	2	9	53-75	26
Motherwell	30	7	2	6	3	3	9	57-80	25
Third Lanark	30	6	2	7	2	2	11	52-75	20

League Cup Section

	P	W	D	L	F A	PTS
Rangers	6	4	1	1	12-9	9
Hearts	**6**	**3**	**1**	**2**	**12-7**	**7**
Motherwell	6	3	1	2	11-9	7
Aberdeen	6	0	1	5	7-16	1

Heart of Midlothian F.C. Line-Ups 1952-53

		1	2	3	4	5	6	7	8	9	10	11
Aug	9th	Watters	Parker	McKenzie	Glidden	Milne	Laing	Rutherford	Conn	Bauld	Wardhaugh	Urquhart
	13th	Watters	Parker	McKenzie	Glidden	Milne	Laing	Rutherford	Conn	Bauld	Wardhaugh	Urquhart
	16th	Watters	Parker	McKenzie	Glidden	Milne	Laing	Rutherford	Conn	Bauld	Wardhaugh	Urquhart
	23rd	Watters	Parker	McKenzie	Glidden	Milne	Laing	Cumming	Whittle	Bauld	Wardhaugh	Urquhart
	27th	Watters	Parker	McKenzie	Dougan	Milne	Laing	Adie	Cumming	Whittle	Wardhaugh	Urquhart
	30th	Watters	Parker	McKenzie	Glidden	Milne	Laing	Durkin	Cumming	Bauld	Wardhaugh	Urquhart
Sep	6th	Watters	Parker	McKenzie	Glidden	Milne	Laing	Durkin	Cumming	Whittle	Wardhaugh	Urquhart
	13th	Watters	Parker	McKenzie	Glidden	Milne	Laing	Durkin	Cumming	Whittle	Wardhaugh	Urquhart
	20th	Watters	Parker	McKenzie	Glidden	Milne	Laing	Durkin	Urquhart	Wardhaugh	Cumming	Blackwood
	27th	Watters	Parker	McKenzie	Whitehead	Dougan	Laing	Rutherford	Conn	Whittle	Wardhaugh	Urquhart
Oct	4th	Watters	Parker	McKenzie	Glidden	Dougan	Laing	Rutherford	Conn	Bauld	Wardhaugh	Urquhart
	11th	Watters	Parker	McKenzie	Glidden	Milne	Laing	Durkin	Whittle	Bauld	Cumming	Urquhart
	18th	Watters	Ferguson	McKenzie	Glidden	Milne	Laing	Durkin	Conn	Bauld	Wardhaugh	Urquhart
	25th	Watters	Parker	McKenzie	Glidden	Milne	Laing	Whittle	Conn	Bauld	Cumming	Urquhart
Nov	1st	Watters	Parker	McKenzie	Glidden	Milne	Laing	Whittle	Conn	Bauld	Cumming	Urquhart
	8th	Watters	Parker	McKenzie	Milne	Dougan	Laing	Whittle	Conn	Bauld	Cumming	Urquhart
	15th	Watters	Parker	McKenzie	Dougan	Milne	Laing	Kilgannon	Bauld	Whittle	Urquhart	Blackwood
	22nd	Watters	Parker	McKenzie	Glidden	Milne	Armstrong	Blackwood	Conn	Bauld	Wardhaugh	Urquhart
	29th	Watters	Parker	Adie	Glidden	Milne	Armstrong	Blackwood	Conn	Bauld	Wardhaugh	Urquhart
Dec	6th	Watters	Parker	McKenzie	Glidden	Milne	Armstrong	Blackwood	Conn	Bauld	Wardhaugh	Urquhart
	13th	Watters	Parker	Laing	Glidden	Milne	Armstrong	Blackwood	Conn	Bauld	Wardhaugh	Urquhart
	20th	Watters	Parker	Adie	Glidden	Milne	Armstrong	Blackwood	Conn	Bauld	Wardhaugh	Urquhart
	27th	Watters	Parker	McKenzie	Glidden	Dougan	Armstrong	Blackwood	Conn	Bauld	Wardhaugh	Urquhart
Jan	1st	Watters	Parker	McKenzie	Glidden	Dougan	Armstrong	Blackwood	Conn	Bauld	Wardhaugh	Urquhart
	3rd	Watters	Adie	McKenzie	Glidden	Dougan	Armstrong	Whittle	Conn	Bauld	Wardhaugh	Urquhart
	17th	Watters	Parker	Adie	Laing	Dougan	Armstrong	Souness	Conn	Whittle	Wardhaugh	Urquhart
	24th	Watters	Parker	McKenzie	Laing	Dougan	Armstrong	Souness	Conn	Whittle	Cumming	Urquhart
	31st	Watters	Parker	McKenzie	Laing	Dougan	Armstrong	Souness	Conn	Whittle	Cumming	Urquhart
Feb	7th	Watters	Parker	McKenzie	Laing	Dougan	Armstrong	Souness	Conn	Bauld	Wardhaugh	Urquhart
	14th	Watters	Parker	McKenzie	Laing	Dougan	Armstrong	Souness	Conn	Bauld	Wardhaugh	Urquhart
	21st	Watters	Parker	McKenzie	Laing	Dougan	Armstrong	Rutherford	Conn	Bauld	Wardhaugh	Urquhart
	28th	Watters	Parker	McKenzie	Laing	Dougan	Armstrong	Blackwood	Conn	Bauld	Wardhaugh	Urquhart
Mar	7th	Watters	Parker	McKenzie	Laing	Dougan	Armstrong	Blackwood	Conn	Bauld	Wardhaugh	Urquhart
	14th	Watters	Parker	McKenzie	Laing	Dougan	Armstrong	Blackwood	Conn	Bauld	Wardhaugh	Cumming
	21st	Watters	Adie	McKenzie	Laing	Dougan	Armstrong	Blackwood	Conn	Bauld	Wardhaugh	Urquhart
	28th	Watters	Parker	Adie	Laing	Dougan	Armstrong	Rutherford	Conn	Bauld	Wardhaugh	Cumming
Apr	4th	Watters	Parker	Adie	Laing	Dougan	Armstrong	Rutherford	Conn	Bauld	Wardhaugh	Cumming
	6th	Watters	Parker	Adie	Laing	Dougan	Armstrong	Rutherford	Conn	Bauld	Wardhaugh	Urquhart
	18th	Watters	Parker	McKenzie	Laing	Dougan	Armstrong	Souness	Conn	Bauld	Wardhaugh	Blackwood
	28th	Watters	Parker	McKenzie	Laing	Dougan	Armstrong	Blackwood	Conn	Bauld	Wardhaugh	Urquhart

On the alert - Hearts centre-forward Willie Bauld moves in menacingly as the Motherwell keeper collects in this match at Tynecastle.

Season 1953-54

Date		Opponents		Score	Crowd	Scorers
Aug 8th	LC	Hamilton Accies	h	5-0	30,000	Wardhaugh 2; Conn; Bauld 2
12th	LC	Rangers	a	1-4	50,000	Bauld
15th	LC	Raith Rovers	h	2-0	28,000	Wardhaugh; Urquhart
22nd	LC	Hamilton Accies	a	1-1	14,000	Cumming
26th	LC	Rangers	h	1-1	35,000	Bauld
29th	LC	Raith Rovers	a	1-3	9,000	Wardhaugh
Sep 5th	L	East Fife	h	2-2	24,000	Urquhart; Wardhaugh
12th	L	QOS	h	1-4	22,000	Wardhaugh
19th	L	Hibernian	h	4-0	45,000	Bauld; Wardhaugh; Conn; Parker (pen)
26th	L	Airdrie	a	1-2	14,000	Wardhaugh
Oct 3rd	L	Stirling Albion	h	6-1	25,000	Urquhart 2; Rutherford; Wardhaugh 3
10th	L	St Mirren	a	1-1	15,000	Urquhart
17th	L	Dundee	h	2-1	26,000	Wardhaugh; Conn
24th	L	Celtic	a	0-2	20,000	-
31st	L	Rangers	a	1-0	30,000	Urquhart
Nov 7th	L	Clyde	h	1-2	16,000	Wardhaugh
14th	L	Raith Rovers	h	5-1	22,000	Wardhaugh 3; Conn 2
21st	L	Hamilton Accies	a	5-1	10,000	Armstrong; Bauld; Conn; Wardhaugh 2
28th	L	Aberdeen	h	3-2	28,000	Wardhaugh; Conn; Rutherford
Dec 5th	L	QOS	a	2-2	12,000	Wardhaugh 2
12th	L	Falkirk	a	3-1	12,500	Wardhaugh; Conn; Urquhart
19th	L	East Fife	a	2-2	14,000	Urquhart; Parker (pen)
26th	L	Partick Thistle	h	0-2	16,000	-
Jan 1st	L	Hibernian	a	2-1	48,000	Souness; Bauld
2nd	L	Airdrie	h	4-3	24,000	Souness; Bauld; Wardhaugh 2
9th	L	Stirling Albion	a	3-0	16,000	Wardhaugh 2; Souness
16th	L	St Mirren	h	5-1	23,000	Wardhaugh; Souness; Urquhart 2; Bauld
23rd	L	Dundee	a	4-2	25,000	Conn 2; Souness; Bauld
30th	L	Falkirk	h	0-0	25,000	-
Feb 6th	L	Celtic	h	3-2	49,000	Bauld 2; Wardhaugh
13th	SC2	Fraserburgh	a	3-0	5,800	Wardhaugh; Conn; Souness
20th	L	Rangers	h	3-3	49,000	Bauld; Conn; Wardhaugh
27th	SC3	QOS	a	2-1	23,000	Wardhaugh 2
Mar 6th	L	Raith Rovers	a	2-4	17,000	Souness; Conn
13th	SCQ	Aberdeen	a	0-3	45,061	-
17th	L	Hamilton Accies	h	3-0	13,000	Bauld; Urquhart; Cochrane
20th	L	Aberdeen	a	0-1	17,000	-
Apr 17th	L	Clyde	a	1-0	15,000	Wardhaugh
19th	L	Partick Thistle	a	1-2	12,000	Wardhaugh

Cup Cash v. Fraserburgh £640; v. QOS £2,000; v. Aberdeen £3,928

Jock Adie - solid at the back for the Maroons.

The Record		
League	-	**Runners up, 'A' Division**
League Cup	-	**Qualifying stages only**
Scottish Cup	-	**Third round**
Top Scorer	-	**Jimmy Wardhaugh (34 goals)**
Av. Home Gate	-	**27,200**
Players used	-	**20**
Sent off	-	**None**

Appearances

	League	L/Cup	S/Cup	Total
Jimmy Watters	30	6	3	39
Johnny Urquhart	28 (10)	6 (1)	3	37 (11)
Jimmy Wardhaugh	28 (27)	6 (4)	3 (3)	37 (34)
John Cumming	29	4 (1)	3	36 (1)
Alfie Conn	26 (11)	6 (1)	3 (1)	35 (13)
Bobby Parker	26 (2)	6	3	35 (2)
Willie Bauld	21 (10)	6 (4)	3	30 (14)
Jock Adie	26	0	3	29
Davie Laing	23	3	3	29
Fred Glidden	21	0	3	24
Doug Armstrong	16 (1)	6	0	22 (1)
Jimmy Souness	14 (6)	0	3 (1)	17 (7)
Bobby Dougan	9	6	0	15
Eddie Rutherford	14 (2)	0	0	14 (2)
Tommy McKenzie	7	6	0	13
Bobby Blackwood	4	2	0	6
Dave Mackay	4	0	0	4
Wallace King	0	3	0	3
Bobby Campbell	2	0	0	2
John Cochrane	2 (1)	0	0	2 (1)

Scottish League 'A' Division

		Home			Away			Goals	
	P	W	D	L	W	D	L	F A	PTS
Celtic	30	14	1	0	6	2	7	72-29	43
Hearts	**30**	**9**	**3**	**3**	**7**	**3**	**5**	**70-45**	**38**
Partick Thistle	30	9	0	6	8	1	6	76-54	35
Rangers	30	9	4	2	4	4	7	56-35	34
Hibernian	30	9	1	5	6	3	6	72-51	34
East Fife	30	11	3	1	2	5	8	55-45	34
Dundee	30	11	3	1	3	3	9	46-47	34
Clyde	30	8	1	6	7	3	5	64-67	34
Aberdeen	30	10	2	3	5	1	9	66-51	33
Queen of the South	30	10	2	3	4	2	9	72-58	32
St Mirren	30	7	3	5	5	1	9	44-54	28
Raith Rovers	30	7	3	5	3	3	9	56-60	26
Falkirk	30	5	5	5	4	2	9	47-61	25
Stirling Albion	30	8	1	6	2	3	10	39-62	24
Airdrie	30	4	5	6	1	0	14	41-92	15
Hamilton	30	4	1	10	0	2	13	29-94	11

League Cup Section

	P	W	D	L	F A	PTS
Rangers	6	5	1	0	22-4	11
Hearts	**6**	**2**	**2**	**2**	**11-9**	**6**
Raith Rovers	6	3	0	3	8-11	6
Hamilton	6	0	1	5	3-20	1

Heart of Midlothian F.C. Line-Ups 1953-54

		1	2	3	4	5	6	7	8	9	10	11
Aug	8th	Watters	Parker	McKenzie	Laing	Dougan	Armstrong	Blackwood	Conn	Bauld	Wardhaugh	Urquhart
	12th	Watters	Parker	McKenzie	Laing	Dougan	Armstrong	Blackwood	Conn	Bauld	Wardhaugh	Urquhart
	15th	Watters	Parker	McKenzie	Laing	Dougan	Armstrong	Cumming	Conn	Bauld	Wardhaugh	Urquhart
	22nd	Watters	Parker	McKenzie	Armstrong	Dougan	King	Cumming	Conn	Bauld	Wardhaugh	Urquhart
	26th	Watters	Parker	McKenzie	King	Dougan	Armstrong	Conn	Wardhaugh	Bauld	Cumming	Urquhart
	29th	Watters	Parker	McKenzie	King	Dougan	Armstrong	Conn	Wardhaugh	Bauld	Cumming	Urquhart
Sep	5th	Watters	Parker	Campbell	Laing	Dougan	Armstrong	Conn	Wardhaugh	Bauld	Cumming	Urquhart
	12th	Watters	Parker	Campbell	Laing	Dougan	Armstrong	Rutherford	Wardhaugh	Bauld	Cumming	Urquhart
	19th	Watters	Parker	McKenzie	Armstrong	Dougan	Laing	Rutherford	Conn	Bauld	Wardhaugh	Urquhart
	26th	Watters	Parker	McKenzie	Armstrong	Dougan	Laing	Rutherford	Conn	Cumming	Wardhaugh	Urquhart
Oct	3rd	Watters	Parker	Adie	Armstrong	Dougan	Laing	Rutherford	Conn	Wardhaugh	Cumming	Urquhart
	10th	Watters	Parker	Adie	Armstrong	Dougan	Laing	Rutherford	Conn	Wardhaugh	Cumming	Urquhart
	17th	Watters	Parker	Adie	Armstrong	Glidden	Laing	Blackwood	Conn	Wardhaugh	Cumming	Urquhart
	24th	Watters	Parker	Adie	Armstrong	Dougan	Laing	Rutherford	Conn	Wardhaugh	Cumming	Urquhart
	31st	Watters	Adie	McKenzie	Parker	Dougan	Armstrong	Rutherford	Conn	Wardhaugh	Cumming	Urquhart
Nov	7th	Watters	Parker	Adie	Armstrong	Dougan	Mackay	Rutherford	Conn	Wardhaugh	Cumming	Urquhart
	14th	Watters	Parker	Adie	Armstrong	Glidden	Cumming	Rutherford	Conn	Bauld	Wardhaugh	Urquhart
	21st	Watters	Parker	Adie	Armstrong	Glidden	Cumming	Rutherford	Conn	Bauld	Wardhaugh	Urquhart
	28th	Watters	Parker	Adie	Armstrong	Glidden	Cumming	Rutherford	Conn	Bauld	Wardhaugh	Urquhart
Dec	5th	Watters	Parker	Adie	Armstrong	Glidden	Cumming	Rutherford	Laing	Bauld	Wardhaugh	Urquhart
	12th	Watters	Parker	Adie	Laing	Glidden	Cumming	Rutherford	Conn	Bauld	Wardhaugh	Urquhart
	19th	Watters	Parker	Adie	Laing	Glidden	Cumming	Rutherford	Conn	Souness	Wardhaugh	Urquhart
	26th	Watters	Parker	Adie	Armstrong	Glidden	Cumming	Blackwood	Conn	Souness	Wardhaugh	Urquhart
Jan	1st	Watters	Parker	Adie	Laing	Glidden	Cumming	Souness	Conn	Bauld	Wardhaugh	Urquhart
	2nd	Watters	Parker	Adie	Laing	Glidden	Cumming	Souness	Conn	Bauld	Wardhaugh	Urquhart
	9th	Watters	Parker	Adie	Laing	Glidden	Cumming	Souness	Conn	Bauld	Wardhaugh	Urquhart
	16th	Watters	Parker	Adie	Laing	Glidden	Cumming	Souness	Conn	Bauld	Wardhaugh	Urquhart
	23rd	Watters	Parker	Adie	Laing	Glidden	Cumming	Souness	Conn	Bauld	Wardhaugh	Urquhart
	30th	Watters	Parker	Adie	Laing	Glidden	Cumming	Souness	Conn	Bauld	Wardhaugh	Urquhart
Feb	6th	Watters	Parker	Adie	Laing	Glidden	Cumming	Souness	Conn	Bauld	Wardhaugh	Urquhart
	13th	Watters	Parker	Adie	Laing	Glidden	Cumming	Souness	Conn	Bauld	Wardhaugh	Urquhart
	20th	Watters	Parker	Adie	Laing	Glidden	Cumming	Souness	Conn	Bauld	Wardhaugh	Urquhart
	27th	Watters	Parker	Adie	Laing	Glidden	Cumming	Souness	Conn	Bauld	Wardhaugh	Urquhart
Mar	6th	Watters	Parker	Adie	Laing	Glidden	Cumming	Souness	Conn	Bauld	Wardhaugh	Urquhart
	13th	Watters	Parker	Adie	Laing	Glidden	Cumming	Souness	Conn	Bauld	Wardhaugh	Urquhart
	17th	Watters	Adie	McKenzie	Laing	Glidden	Mackay	Souness	Cochrane	Bauld	Cumming	Urquhart
	20th	Watters	Adie	McKenzie	Laing	Glidden	Mackay	Souness	Cochrane	Bauld	Cumming	Urquhart
Apr	17th	Watters	Adie	McKenzie	Mackay	Glidden	Cumming	Souness	Conn	Bauld	Wardhaugh	Blackwood
	19th	Watters	Adie	McKenzie	Laing	Glidden	Armstrong	Blackwood	Conn	Bauld	Wardhaugh	Cumming

Off the line - Aberdeen right-back Jimmy Mitchell blocks a Hearts scoring attempt with goalkeeper Fred Martin off his line. Jimmy Wardhaugh awaits his chance while Dave Caldwell is the other Dons defender.

Season 1954-55

Date		Opponents		Score	Crowd	Scorers
Aug 14th	LC	Dundee	h	3-1	35,000	Blackwood; Urquhart; Conn
18th	LC	Falkirk	a	6-2	17,000	Conn; Mackay; Wardhaugh 2; Bauld 2
21st	LC	Celtic	a	2-1	53,000	Wardhaugh; Peacock o.g.
28th	LC	Dundee	a	1-4	29,500	Bauld
Sep 1st	LC	Falkirk	h	4-1	30,000	Conn; Blackwood; Bauld 2
4th	LC	Celtic	h	3-2	40,000	Wardhaugh; Bauld; Laing (pen)
11th	L	Partick Thistle	h	5-4	30,000	Urquhart 2; Souness; Wardhaugh; Mackay
18th	L	Hibernian	a	3-2	42,000	Conn 2; Wardhaugh
22nd	LCQ	St Johnstone	a	5-0	12,000	Cumming; Conn; Bauld 2; Wardhaugh
25th	LCQ2	St Johnstone	h	2-0 (7-0)	21,000	Parker; Blackwood
Oct 2nd	L	Dundee	a	2-3	20,000	Souness 2
9th	LCS	Airdrie	E.Rd	4-1	34,172	Urquhart; Bauld; Wardhaugh 2
16th	L	East Fife	a	2-0	12,000	Wardhaugh; Souness
23rd	LCF	Motherwell	Hamp	4-2	55,640	Bauld 3; Wardhaugh
30th	L	Stirling Albion	a	5-0	12,000	Parker (pen); Urquhart 2; Bauld 2
Nov 6th	L	Falkirk	h	5-3	30,000	Parker (pen); Bauld 2; Wardhaugh 2
20th	L	Aberdeen	a	0-1	28,000	-
24th	L	Kilmarnock	a	3-1	16,000	Wardhaugh; Conn; Whittle
27th	L	QOS	h	3-1	22,000	Urquhart; Cumming; Bauld
Dec 4th	L	Raith Rovers	a	6-0	12,000	Wardhaugh; Urquhart; Bauld 2; Conn; Souness
11th	L	Clyde	a	3-0	11,000	Bauld 2; Souness
18th	L	Rangers	h	3-4	35,000	Conn; Bauld; Urquhart
25th	L	Partick Thistle	a	4-4	19,000	Wardhaugh; Conn 2; Mackay
Jan 1st	L	Hibernian	h	5-1	49,000	Souness; Wardhaugh; Bauld 2; Conn
3rd	L	St Mirren	a	1-1	15,000	Bauld
8th	L	Dundee	h	2-1	24,000	Wardhaugh; Urquhart
29th	L	Celtic	a	0-2	49,300	-
Feb 5th	SC2	Hibernian	h	5-0	45,770	Conn; Wardhaugh 2; Bauld 2
12th	L	Stirling Albion	h	3-0	10,000	Bauld 2; Wardhaugh
19th	SC3	Buckie Thistle	a	6-0	5,400	Souness; Bauld 3; Wardhaugh 2
26th	L	Falkirk	a	2-2	19,000	Conn 2
Mar 5th	SCQ	Aberdeen	h	1-1	47,500	Bauld
9th	SCQR	Aberdeen	a	0-2	41,000	-
12th	L	Aberdeen	h	2-0	36,000	Bauld
19th	L	QOS	a	1-1	9,500	Urquhart
26th	L	Raith Rovers	h	2-0	20,000	Urquhart; McKenzie
Apr 2nd	L	Clyde	h	3-0	18,000	Souness; Bauld; Wardhaugh
6th	L	Kilmarnock	h	2-2	10,000	Parker; Bauld
9th	L	Rangers	a	1-3	30,000	Parker (pen)
13th	L	East Fife	h	1-3	10,000	Wardhaugh
16th	L	Motherwell	h	1-1	12,000	Wardhaugh
18th	L	Motherwell	a	3-2	12,000	Crawford; Bauld 2
22nd	L	St Mirren	h	1-1	10,000	Wardhaugh
30th	L	Celtic	h	0-3	22,000	-

Willie Duff - was capped for Scotland's Under-23's

The Record

League	-	**Fourth Place, 'A' Division**
League Cup	-	**Winners**
Scottish Cup	-	**Quarter final**
Top Scorer	-	**Willie Bauld (39 goals)**
Av. Home Gate	-	**22,500**
Players used	-	**21**
Sent off	-	**None**

Appearances

	League	L/Cup	S/Cup	Total
Fred Glidden	30	10	4	44
Bobby Parker	30 (4)	10 (1)	4	44 (5)
Jimmy Wardhaugh	30 (15)	10 (8)	4 (4)	44 (27)
John Cumming	29 (1)	10 (1)	4	43 (2)
Johnny Urquhart	29 (10)	10 (2)	4	43 (12)
Willie Duff	26	9	4	39
Willie Bauld	25 (21)	9 (12)	4 (6)	38 (39)
Alfie Conn	22 (10)	10 (4)	4 (1)	36 (15)
Dave Mackay	25 (2)	7 (1)	4	36 (3)
Jim Souness	28 (8)	4	4 (1)	36 (9)
Tommy McKenzie	22 (1)	4	4	30 (1)
Jock Adie	7	6	0	13
Bobby Blackwood	3	7 (3)	0	10 (3)
Doug Armstrong	6	0	0	6
Jimmy Watters	4	1	0	5
Jimmy Whittle	5 (1)	0	0	5 (1)
Jimmy Murray	4	0	0	4
Ian Crawford	3 (1)	0	0	3 (1)
Davie Laing	0	3 (1)	0	3 (1)
Jimmy Milne	1	0	0	1
Willie Grant	1	0	0	1

Scottish League 'A' Division

		Home			Away			Goals	
	P	W	D	L	W	D	L	F A	PTS
Aberdeen	30	14	0	1	10	1	4	73-26	49
Celtic	30	10	4	1	9	4	2	76-37	46
Rangers	30	13	2	0	6	1	8	67-33	41
Hearts	**30**	**10**	**2**	**3**	**6**	**5**	**4**	**74-45**	**39**
Hibernian	30	8	2	5	7	2	6	64-54	34
St Mirren	30	8	3	4	4	5	6	55-54	32
Clyde	30	6	7	2	5	3	7	59-50	31
Dundee	30	9	2	4	4	2	9	48-48	30
Partick Thistle	30	5	5	5	6	2	7	49-61	29
Kilmarnock	30	5	3	7	5	3	7	46-58	26
East Fife	30	6	1	8	3	5	7	51-62	24
Falkirk	30	6	6	3	2	2	11	42-54	24
Queen of the South	30	7	2	6	2	4	9	38-56	24
Raith Rovers	30	9	1	5	1	2	12	49-57	23
Motherwell	30	5	2	8	4	2	9	42-62	22
Stirling Albion	30	2	1	12	0	1	14	29-105	6

League Cup Section

	P	W	D	L	F A	PTS
Hearts	6	5	0	1	19-11	10
Dundee	**6**	**4**	**0**	**2**	**12-10**	**8**
Celtic	6	1	1	4	9-11	3
Falkirk	6	1	1	4	10-18	3

Heart of Midlothian F.C. Line-Ups 1954-55

		1	2	3	4	5	6	7	8	9	10	11
Aug	14th	Duff	Parker	Adie	Mackay	Glidden	Cumming	Blackwood	Conn	Bauld	Wardhaugh	Urquhart
	18th	Duff	Parker	Adie	Mackay	Glidden	Cumming	Blackwood	Conn	Bauld	Wardhaugh	Urquhart
	21st	Duff	Parker	Adie	Mackay	Glidden	Cumming	Blackwood	Conn	Bauld	Wardhaugh	Urquhart
	28th	Duff	Parker	Adie	Laing	Glidden	Cumming	Blackwood	Conn	Bauld	Wardhaugh	Urquhart
Sep	1st	Duff	Parker	Adie	Laing	Glidden	Cumming	Blackwood	Conn	Bauld	Wardhaugh	Urquhart
	4th	Duff	Parker	Adie	Laing	Glidden	Cumming	Blackwood	Conn	Bauld	Wardhaugh	Urquhart
	11th	Duff	Parker	McKenzie	Mackay	Glidden	Cumming	Souness	Conn	Bauld	Wardhaugh	Urquhart
	18th	Duff	Parker	McKenzie	Mackay	Glidden	Cumming	Souness	Conn	Bauld	Wardhaugh	Urquhart
	22nd	Duff	Parker	McKenzie	Mackay	Glidden	Cumming	Souness	Conn	Bauld	Wardhaugh	Urquhart
	25th	Duff	Parker	McKenzie	Mackay	Glidden	Cumming	Blackwood	Conn	Souness	Wardhaugh	Urquhart
Oct	2nd	Duff	Parker	McKenzie	Mackay	Glidden	Cumming	Souness	Conn	Bauld	Wardhaugh	Urquhart
	9th	Watters	Parker	McKenzie	Mackay	Glidden	Cumming	Souness	Conn	Bauld	Wardhaugh	Urquhart
	16th	Duff	Parker	McKenzie	Mackay	Glidden	Cumming	Souness	Whittle	Bauld	Wardhaugh	Urquhart
	23rd	Duff	Parker	McKenzie	Mackay	Glidden	Cumming	Souness	Conn	Bauld	Wardhaugh	Urquhart
	30th	Duff	Parker	Adie	Mackay	Glidden	Cumming	Souness	Conn	Bauld	Wardhaugh	Urquhart
Nov	6th	Duff	Parker	McKenzie	Mackay	Glidden	Cumming	Souness	Conn	Bauld	Wardhaugh	Urquhart
	20th	Duff	Parker	McKenzie	Mackay	Glidden	Cumming	Souness	Conn	Bauld	Wardhaugh	Urquhart
	24th	Duff	Parker	McKenzie	Mackay	Glidden	Cumming	Blackwood	Conn	Whittle	Wardhaugh	Urquhart
	27th	Duff	Parker	Adie	Mackay	Glidden	Cumming	Souness	Conn	Bauld	Wardhaugh	Urquhart
Dec	4th	Duff	Parker	Adie	Mackay	Glidden	Cumming	Souness	Conn	Bauld	Wardhaugh	Urquhart
	11th	Duff	Parker	Adie	Mackay	Glidden	Cumming	Souness	Conn	Bauld	Wardhaugh	Urquhart
	18th	Duff	Parker	Adie	Mackay	Glidden	Cumming	Souness	Conn	Bauld	Wardhaugh	Urquhart
	25th	Duff	Parker	Milne	Mackay	Glidden	Cumming	Souness	Conn	Bauld	Wardhaugh	Urquhart
Jan	1st	Duff	Parker	McKenzie	Mackay	Glidden	Cumming	Souness	Conn	Bauld	Wardhaugh	Urquhart
	3rd	Duff	Parker	McKenzie	Mackay	Glidden	Cumming	Souness	Conn	Bauld	Wardhaugh	Urquhart
	8th	Duff	Parker	McKenzie	Mackay	Glidden	Cumming	Souness	Conn	Bauld	Wardhaugh	Urquhart
	29th	Duff	Parker	McKenzie	Mackay	Glidden	Cumming	Souness	Conn	Bauld	Wardhaugh	Urquhart
Feb	5th	Duff	Parker	McKenzie	Mackay	Glidden	Cumming	Souness	Conn	Bauld	Wardhaugh	Urquhart
	12th	Duff	Parker	McKenzie	Mackay	Glidden	Cumming	Souness	Conn	Bauld	Wardhaugh	Urquhart
	19th	Duff	Parker	McKenzie	Mackay	Glidden	Cumming	Souness	Conn	Bauld	Wardhaugh	Urquhart
	26th	Duff	Parker	McKenzie	Mackay	Glidden	Cumming	Souness	Conn	Bauld	Wardhaugh	Urquhart
Mar	5th	Duff	Parker	McKenzie	Mackay	Glidden	Cumming	Souness	Conn	Bauld	Wardhaugh	Urquhart
	9th	Duff	Parker	McKenzie	Mackay	Glidden	Cumming	Souness	Conn	Bauld	Wardhaugh	Urquhart
	12th	Duff	Parker	McKenzie	Mackay	Glidden	Cumming	Souness	Conn	Bauld	Wardhaugh	Urquhart
	19th	Duff	Parker	McKenzie	Mackay	Glidden	Cumming	Souness	Conn	Bauld	Wardhaugh	Urquhart
	26th	Duff	Parker	McKenzie	Mackay	Glidden	Cumming	Souness	Conn	Bauld	Wardhaugh	Urquhart
Apr	2nd	Duff	Parker	McKenzie	Mackay	Glidden	Armstrong	Souness	Conn	Bauld	Wardhaugh	Urquhart
	6th	Duff	Parker	McKenzie	Mackay	Glidden	Cumming	Souness	Whittle	Bauld	Wardhaugh	Urquhart
	9th	Duff	Parker	Adie	Armstrong	Glidden	Cumming	Souness	Whittle	Wardhaugh	Blackwood	Urquhart
	13th	Duff	Parker	Adie	Mackay	Glidden	Cumming	Blackwood	Whittle	Souness	Wardhaugh	Urquhart
	16th	Watters	Parker	McKenzie	Armstrong	Glidden	Cumming	Souness	Murray	Bauld	Wardhaugh	Urquhart
	18th	Watters	Parker	McKenzie	Armstrong	Glidden	Cumming	Souness	Murray	Bauld	Wardhaugh	Crawford
	22nd	Watters	Parker	McKenzie	Armstrong	Glidden	Cumming	Grant	Murray	Wardhaugh	Urquhart	Crawford
	30th	Watters	Parker	McKenzie	Armstrong	Glidden	Cumming	Souness	Urquhart	Murray	Wardhaugh	Crawford

Going for goal - opposing defenders had to be on their toes when the Hearts forwards were on song. This time the Airdrie keeper grabs the ball before the deadly Jimmy Wardhaugh can apply the finishing touch.

Season 1955-56

Date		Opponents		Score	Crowd	Scorers
Aug 13th	LC	Partick Thistle	a	2-0	25,000	Conn; Wardhaugh
17th	LC	Raith Rovers	h	5-0	25,000	Conn 3; Souness; Urquhart
20th	LC	East Fife	a	0-1	12,000	-
27th	LC	Partick Thistle	h	2-1	30,000	Urquhart; Young
31st	LC	Raith Rovers	a	2-0	9,000	Parker; Young
Sep 3rd	LC	East Fife	h	4-0	24,000	Young 3; Parker (pen)
10th	L	Dundee	h	4-0	20,000	Urquhart 2; Conn; Young
14th	LCQ	Aberdeen	a	3-5	30,000	Young 2; Urquhart
17th	LCQ	Aberdeen	h	2-4 (5-9)	37,000	Urquhart; Conn
24th	L	Hibernian	h	0-1	45,000	-
Oct 1st	L	Airdrie	a	4-1	14,000	Mackay; Urquhart; Wardhaugh 2
8th	L	Celtic	h	2-1	31,000	Urquhart; Boden o.g.
15th	L	QOS	a	3-4	11,000	Cumming; Wardhaugh; Conn
22nd	L	East Fife	h	3-1	21,000	Conn 2; Young
29th	L	St Mirren	a	1-3	12,000	Bauld
Nov 5th	L	Stirling Albion	h	5-0	18,000	Wardhaugh 3; Young 2
12th	L	Rangers	a	1-4	51,000	Young
19th	L	Clyde	h	5-1	16,000	Conn; Wardhaugh 4
26th	L	Dunfermline	a	5-1	14,000	Bauld 2; Young; Wardhaugh
Dec 3rd	L	Aberdeen	h	3-0	27,000	Young 2; Bauld
10th	L	Falkirk	a	1-1	12,000	Young
17th	L	Motherwell	h	7-1	18,000	Bauld 2; Wardhaugh 4; Hamilton
24th	L	Kilmarnock	a	4-2	12,000	Bauld 2; Conn; Wardhaugh
31st	L	Raith Rovers	a	1-1	9,000	Bauld
Jan 2nd	L	Hibernian	a	2-2	60,800	Bauld; Conn
7th	L	Partick Thistle	h	5-0	22,000	Conn 3; Wardhaugh 2
14th	L	Dundee	a	2-0	17,000	Crawford; Conn
21st	L	Airdrie	h	4-1	20,000	Whittle; Crawford; Young; Urquhart
28th	L	Celtic	a	1-1	40,000	Young
Feb 4th	SC5	Forfar Athletic	h	3-0	11,007	Conn 2; Hamilton
11th	L	QOS	h	2-2	20,000	Conn; Wardhaugh
18th	SC6	Stirling Albion	h	5-0	19,465	Bauld; Cumming; Young; Conn; Wardhaugh
25th	L	East Fife	a	4-1	11,000	Adie o.g.; Young; Wardhaugh; Conn
Mar 3rd	SCQ	Rangers	h	4-0	47,258	Bauld 2; Crawford; Conn
7th	L	St Mirren	h	4-1	19,000	Young; Wardhaugh 3
10th	L	Stirling Albion	a	2-0	10,000	Crawford; Bauld
17th	L	Rangers	h	1-1	45,000	Bauld
24th	SCS	Raith Rovers	E. Rd.	0-0	58,448	-
28th	SCSR	Raith Rovers	E. Rd.	3-0	54,233	Wardhaugh 2; Crawford
31st	L	Dunfermline	h	5-0	22,000	Mackay 2; Young; Whittle; Kirk (pen)
Apr 2nd	L	Partick Thistle	a	0-2	25,000	-
7th	L	Aberdeen	a	1-4	20,000	Crawford
11th	L	Clyde	a	2-2	7,000	Conn; Wardhaugh
16th	L	Falkirk	h	8-3	15,000	Conn 3; Wardhaugh 2; Crawford; Young; Bauld
21st	SCF	Celtic	Hamp.	3-1	132,840	Crawford 2; Conn
23rd	L	Motherwell	a	0-1	12,000	-
25th	L	Kilmarnock	h	0-2	10,000	-
28th	L	Raith Rovers	h	7-2	18,000	Bauld 2; Wardhaugh 3 Kirk (pen); Mackay

Freddie Glidden - the stalwart skipper led Hearts to Scottish Cup glory.

The Record		
League	-	Third Place, Division One
League Cup	-	Quarter final
Scottish Cup	-	Winners
Top Scorer	-	Jimmy Wardhaugh (34)
Av. Home Gate	-	22,800
Players used	-	25
Sent off	-	None

Cup Cash v. Forfar £850; Stirling £1,457; Rangers £4,500 v. Raith (1st) £5,615

Appearances

	League	L/Cup	S/Cup	Total
John Cumming	34 (1)	8	6 (1)	48 (2)
Fred Glidden	32	8	6	46
Bobby Kirk	31 (2)	8	6	45 (2)
Jimmy Wardhaugh	32 (30)	7 (1)	6 (3)	45 (34)
Willie Duff	32	4	6	42
Alfie Conn	25 (17)	8 (5)	5 (5)	38 (27)
Alex Young	27 (15)	5 (7)	6 (1)	38 (23)
Dave Mackay	28 (4)	2	6	36 (4)
Willie Bauld	20 (15)	3	5 (3)	28 (18)
Tommy McKenzie	22	0	6	28
Johnny Urquhart	19 (5)	8 (4)	0	27 (9)
Johnny Hamilton	22 (1)	0	2 (1)	24 (2)
Bobby Parker	14	8 (2)	0	22 (2)
Ian Crawford	12 (5)	0	6 (4)	18 (9)
Bobby Blackwood	5	4	0	9
Andy Bowman	2	6	0	8
Jimmy Whittle	6 (2)	0	0	6 (2)
Wilson Brown	1	4	0	5
Jim Souness	1	4 (1)	0	5 (1)
Jimmy Murray	4	0	0	4
Jimmy Milne	2	0	0	2
Bobby Campbell	1	0	0	1
George Campbell	0	1	0	1
John Thomson	1	0	0	1
Jimmy Watters	1	0	0	1

Scottish League Division One

		Home			Away			Goals	
	P	W	D	L	W	D	L	F A	PTS
Rangers	34	12	4	1	10	4	3	88-27	52
Aberdeen	34	11	3	3	7	7	3	87-50	46
Hearts	**34**	**13**	**2**	**2**	**6**	**5**	**6**	**99-47**	**45**
Hibernian	34	11	4	2	8	3	6	86-50	45
Celtic	34	9	4	4	7	5	5	55-39	41
Queen of the South	34	12	2	3	4	3	10	69-73	37
Airdrie	34	8	4	5	6	4	7	85-96	36
Kilmarnock	34	7	6	4	5	4	8	52-45	34
Partick Thistle	34	8	4	5	5	3	9	62-60	33
Motherwell	34	7	6	4	4	5	8	53-59	33
Raith Rovers	34	6	7	4	6	2	9	58-75	33
East Fife	34	11	3	3	2	2	13	60-69	31
Dundee	34	10	2	5	2	4	11	56-65	30
Falkirk	34	9	2	6	2	4	11	58-75	28
St Mirren	34	9	2	6	1	5	11	57-70	27
Dunfermline	34	6	4	7	4	2	11	42-82	26
Clyde	34	2	4	11	6	2	9	50-74	22
Stirling Albion	34	4	3	10	0	2	15	23-82	13

League Cup Section

	P	W	D	L	F A	PTS
Hearts	**6**	**5**	**0**	**1**	**15-2**	**10**
Partick Thistle	6	4	0	2	11-7	8
East Fife	6	2	0	4	5-13	4

Heart of Midlothian F.C. Line-Ups 1955-56

		1	2	3	4	5	6	7	8	9	10	11
Aug	13th	Duff	Parker	Kirk	Bowman	Glidden	Cumming	Souness	Conn	Bauld	Wardhaugh	Urquhart
	17th	Duff	Parker	Kirk	Bowman	Glidden	Cumming	Souness	Conn	Bauld	Wardhaugh	Urquhart
	20th	Duff	Parker	Kirk	Bowman	Glidden	Cumming	Souness	Conn	Bauld	Wardhaugh	Urquhart
	27th	Duff	Parker	Kirk	Bowman	Glidden	Cumming	Souness	Wardhaugh	Young	Conn	Urquhart
	31st	Brown	Parker	Kirk	Bowman	Glidden	Cumming	Blackwood	Conn	Young	Wardhaugh	Urquhart
Sep	3rd	Brown	Parker	Kirk	Mackay	Glidden	Cumming	Blackwood	Conn	Young	Wardhaugh	Urquhart
	10th	Brown	Parker	Kirk	Murray	Glidden	Cumming	Blackwood	Conn	Young	Wardhaugh	Urquhart
	14th	Brown	Parker	Kirk	Bowman	Glidden	Cumming	Blackwood	Conn	Young	Wardhaugh	Urquhart
	17th	Brown	Parker	Kirk	Mackay	Glidden	Cumming	Blackwood	Conn	Young	Campbell	Urquhart
	24th	Watters	Kirk	McKenzie	Conn	Glidden	Cumming	Souness	Blackwood	Young	Wardhaugh	Urquhart
Oct	1st	Duff	Parker	Kirk	Mackay	Glidden	Cumming	Hamilton	Conn	Young	Wardhaugh	Urquhart
	8th	Duff	Parker	Kirk	Mackay	Glidden	Cumming	Hamilton	Conn	Bauld	Wardhaugh	Urquhart
	15th	Duff	Parker	Kirk	Mackay	Glidden	Cumming	Hamilton	Conn	Young	Wardhaugh	Urquhart
	22nd	Duff	Parker	Kirk	Bowman	Glidden	Cumming	Hamilton	Conn	Young	Wardhaugh	Urquhart
	29th	Duff	Parker	McKenzie	Bowman	Glidden	Cumming	Young	Conn	Bauld	Wardhaugh	Hamilton
Nov	5th	Duff	Kirk	McKenzie	Parker	Glidden	Cumming	Hamilton	Conn	Young	Wardhaugh	Urquhart
	12th	Duff	Parker	Kirk	Mackay	Glidden	Cumming	Hamilton	Conn	Whittle	Young	Urquhart
	19th	Duff	Parker	Kirk	Mackay	Glidden	Cumming	Hamilton	Conn	Bauld	Wardhaugh	Urquhart
	26th	Duff	Parker	Kirk	Mackay	Glidden	Cumming	Hamilton	Young	Bauld	Wardhaugh	Urquhart
Dec	3rd	Duff	Parker	Kirk	Mackay	Glidden	Cumming	Hamilton	Young	Bauld	Wardhaugh	Urquhart
	10th	Duff	Parker	Kirk	Mackay	Glidden	Cumming	Hamilton	Young	Bauld	Wardhaugh	Urquhart
	17th	Duff	Kirk	McKenzie	Mackay	Glidden	Cumming	Hamilton	Conn	Bauld	Wardhaugh	Blackwood
	24th	Duff	Kirk	McKenzie	Mackay	Glidden	Cumming	Hamilton	Conn	Bauld	Wardhaugh	Urquhart
	31st	Duff	Kirk	McKenzie	Mackay	Glidden	Cumming	Hamilton	Young	Bauld	Wardhaugh	Blackwood
Jan	2nd	Duff	Parker	McKenzie	Mackay	Glidden	Cumming	Blackwood	Conn	Bauld	Wardhaugh	Urquhart
	7th	Duff	Parker	Kirk	Mackay	Milne	Cumming	Hamilton	Conn	Bauld	Wardhaugh	Urquhart
	14th	Duff	Kirk	McKenzie	Mackay	Milne	Cumming	Hamilton	Conn	Young	Wardhaugh	Crawford
	21st	Duff	Kirk	McKenzie	Mackay	Glidden	Cumming	Crawford	Young	Whittle	Wardhaugh	Urquhart
	28th	Duff	Kirk	McKenzie	Mackay	Glidden	Cumming	Crawford	Conn	Young	Wardhaugh	Urquhart
Feb	4th	Duff	Kirk	McKenzie	Mackay	Glidden	Cumming	Hamilton	Conn	Young	Wardhaugh	Crawford
	11th	Duff	Thomson	McKenzie	Mackay	Glidden	Cumming	Hamilton	Conn	Young	Wardhaugh	Crawford
	18th	Duff	Kirk	McKenzie	Mackay	Glidden	Cumming	Young	Conn	Bauld	Wardhaugh	Crawford
	25th	Duff	Kirk	McKenzie	Mackay	Glidden	Cumming	Young	Conn	Bauld	Wardhaugh	Crawford
Mar	3rd	Duff	Kirk	McKenzie	Mackay	Glidden	Cumming	Young	Conn	Bauld	Wardhaugh	Crawford
	7th	Duff	Kirk	McKenzie	Mackay	Glidden	Cumming	Young	Conn	Bauld	Wardhaugh	Crawford
	10th	Duff	Kirk	McKenzie	Mackay	Glidden	Cumming	Young	Conn	Bauld	Wardhaugh	Crawford
	17th	Duff	Kirk	McKenzie	Mackay	Glidden	Cumming	Young	Urquhart	Bauld	Wardhaugh	Crawford
	24th	Duff	Kirk	McKenzie	Mackay	Glidden	Cumming	Young	Conn	Bauld	Wardhaugh	Crawford
	28th	Duff	Kirk	McKenzie	Mackay	Glidden	Cumming	Hamilton	Young	Bauld	Wardhaugh	Crawford
	31st	Duff	Kirk	McKenzie	Mackay	Glidden	Cumming	Hamilton	Young	Whittle	Wardhaugh	Crawford
Apr	2nd	Duff	Kirk	McKenzie	Mackay	Glidden	Cumming	Hamilton	Young	Whittle	Wardhaugh	Urquhart
	7th	Duff	Kirk	McKenzie	Mackay	Glidden	Cumming	Young	Murray	Whittle	Conn	Crawford
	11th	Duff	Kirk	McKenzie	Mackay	Glidden	Cumming	Young	Conn	Bauld	Wardhaugh	Hamilton
	16th	Duff	Kirk	McKenzie	Mackay	Glidden	Cumming	Young	Conn	Bauld	Wardhaugh	Crawford
	21st	Duff	Kirk	McKenzie	Mackay	Glidden	Cumming	Young	Conn	Bauld	Wardhaugh	Crawford
	23rd	Duff	Kirk	McKenzie	Mackay	Glidden	Cumming	Young	Conn	Bauld	Wardhaugh	Crawford
	25th	Duff	Kirk	Campbell R	Murray	Glidden	Cumming	Young	Whittle	Bauld	Wardhaugh	Hamilton
	28th	Duff	Kirk	McKenzie	Murray	Glidden	Mackay	Hamilton	Conn	Bauld	Wardhaugh	Cumming

Alfie dashes in - Hearts inside-forward Alfie Conn races in on Rangers keeper George Niven as Ibrox right-half Ian McColl looks on.

Season 1956-57

Date		Opponents		Score	Crowd	Scorers
Aug 11th	LC	Hibernian	h	6-1	42,000	Wardhaugh 2; Kirk 2 (pens); Crawford; Conn
15th	LC	Partick Thistle	a	1-3	30,000	Wardhaugh
18th	LC	Falkirk	h	5-0	20,000	Wardhaugh 2; Bauld 2; Crawford
25th	LC	Hibernian	a	2-1	40,000	Young; Wardhaugh
29th	LC	Partick Thistle	h	2-2	35,000	Bauld; Crawford
Sep 1st	LC	Falkirk	a	1-1	15,000	Wardhaugh
8th	L	Dunfermline	a	3-2	15,000	Mackay; Wardhaugh; Conn
15th	L	St Mirren	h	2-2	16,000	Kirk (pen); own-goal
22nd	L	Hibernian	a	3-2	39,000	Wardhaugh 2; McKenzie
29th	L	Dundee	h	2-1	30,000	Wardhaugh; Bauld
Oct 6th	L	Ayr United	a	2-0	14,000	Bauld; Campbell
13th	L	East Fife	h	2-5	25,000	Bauld 2
20th	L	Airdrie	a	4-3	11,000	Hamilton 2; Cumming; Mackay
27th	L	Falkirk	a	2-0	16,000	Bauld; Cumming
Nov 3rd	L	Partick Thistle	h	1-0	20,000	Bauld
10th	L	Raith Rovers	a	3-2	19,000	Wardhaugh 2; Crawford
17th	L	Kilmarnock	h	3-2	14,000	Cumming; Crawford; Wardhaugh
24th	L	Queens Park	h	6-1	24,000	Young; Crawford 2; Murray 2; Wardhaugh
Dec 1st	L	Celtic	a	1-1	30,000	Wardhaugh
8th	L	Motherwell	h	3-2	35,000	Crawford 2; Wardhaugh
15th	L	Rangers	a	3-5	45,000	Wardhaugh 2; Bauld
22nd	L	QOS	h	3-1	11,000	Campbell; Wardhaugh; Hamilton
29th	L	Aberdeen	a	3-2	20,000	Young 2; Murray
Jan 1st	L	Hibernian	h	0-2	35,000	-
2nd	L	St Mirren	a	2-0	12,000	McFadzean; Wardhaugh
5th	L	Dunfermline	h	5-1	19,000	Wardhaugh; Young; Hamilton; Murray; Parker
12th	L	Dundee	a	3-0	20,000	Murray; Kirk (pen); Crawford
19th	L	Ayr United	h	2-2	18,000	Bauld; Wardhaugh
26th	L	East Fife	a	3-1	10,000	Cumming; Mackay; Wardhaugh
Feb 2nd	SC5	Rangers	h	0-4	47,484	-
9th	L	Airdrie	h	2-0	25,000	Young; Murray
23rd	L	Falkirk	h	1-1	18,000	Murray
Mar 2nd	L	Partick Thistle	a	2-2	17,000	Bauld; Crawford
9th	L	Raith Rovers	h	2-1	30,000	Wardhaugh; Bauld
16th	L	Kilmarnock	a	1-4	17,000	Crawford
25th	L	Queens Park	a	1-0	7,700	Wardhaugh
30th	L	Celtic	h	3-1	25,000	Bauld; Young; Crawford
Apr 6th	L	Motherwell	a	3-1	18,000	Mackay; Conn; Crawford
13th	L	Rangers	h	0-1	49,000	-
20th	L	QOS	a	2-0	8,000	Bauld; Wardhaugh
27th	L	Aberdeen	h	3-0	15,000	Wardhaugh 2; Mackay

Cup Cash v. Rangers £5,610

Alex. Young - dazzling performer up front for Hearts.

The Record		
League	-	Runners-up, Division One
League Cup	-	Qualifying stages only
Scottish Cup	-	Fifth round
Top Scorer	-	Jimmy Wardhaugh (29)
Av. Home Gate	-	24,100
Players used	-	23
Sent off	-	None

Appearances

	League	L/Cup	S/Cup	Total
Jimmy Wardhaugh	31 (22)	6 (7)	1	38 (29)
Dave Mackay	31 (5)	6	1	38 (5)
Ian Crawford	30 (11)	6 (3)	1	37 (14)
Bobby Kirk	27 (2)	6 (2)	1	34 (4)
Alex Young	27 (6)	6 (1)	1	34 (7)
John Cumming	25 (4)	6	1	32 (4)
Willie Bauld	24 (12)	6 (3)	1	31 (15)
Tommy McKenzie	21 (1)	6	0	27 (1)
Wilson Brown	19	6	1	26
Fred Glidden	19	6	1	26
Johnny Hamilton	26 (4)	0	0	26 (4)
Bobby Parker	22 (1)	0	1	23 (1)
Alfie Conn	10 (2)	6 (1)	1	17 (3)
Jimmy Milne	15	0	0	15
Jimmy Murray	12 (7)	0	0	12 (7)
Gordon Marshall	11	0	0	11
George Thomson	7	0	0	7
Willie Duff	4	0	0	4
Jim McFadzean	4 (1)	0	0	4 (1)
Andy Bowman	3	0	0	3
George Campbell	3 (2)	0	0	3 (2)
Willie Lindores	2	0	0	2
Jimmy Whittle	1	0	0	1

Scottish League Division One

		Home			Away			Goals	
	P	W	D	L	W	D	L	F A	PTS
Rangers	34	13	2	2	13	1	3	96-48	55
Hearts	**34**	**11**	**3**	**3**	**13**	**2**	**2**	**81-48**	**53**
Kilmarnock	34	9	6	2	7	4	6	57-39	42
Raith Rovers	34	10	2	5	6	5	6	84-58	39
Celtic	34	9	6	2	6	2	9	58-43	38
Aberdeen	34	10	1	6	8	1	8	79-59	38
Motherwell	34	9	2	6	7	3	7	72-66	37
Partick Thistle	34	11	3	3	2	5	10	53-51	34
Hibernian	34	6	8	3	6	1	10	69-56	33
Dundee	34	10	2	5	3	4	10	55-61	32
Airdrie	34	8	2	7	5	2	10	77-89	30
St Mirren	34	8	3	6	4	3	10	58-72	30
Queens Park	34	5	2	10	6	5	6	55-59	29
Falkirk	34	5	2	10	5	6	6	51-70	28
East Fife	34	7	3	7	3	3	11	59-82	26
Queen of the South	34	8	3	6	2	2	13	54-96	25
Dunfermline	34	6	3	8	3	3	11	54-74	24
Ayr United	34	5	2	10	2	3	12	48-89	19

League Cup Section

	P	W	D	L	F A	PTS
Partick Thistle	6	4	2	0	15-6	10
Hearts	**6**	**3**	**2**	**1**	**17-8**	**8**
Falkirk	6	2	1	3	6-10	5
Hibernian	6	0	1	5	5-19	1

Heart of Midlothian F.C. Line-Ups 1956-57

		1	2	3	4	5	6	7	8	9	10	11
Aug	11th	Brown	Kirk	McKenzie	Mackay	Glidden	Cumming	Young	Conn	Bauld	Wardhaugh	Crawford
	15th	Brown	Kirk	McKenzie	Mackay	Glidden	Cumming	Young	Conn	Bauld	Wardhaugh	Crawford
	18th	Brown	Kirk	McKenzie	Mackay	Glidden	Cumming	Young	Conn	Bauld	Wardhaugh	Crawford
	25th	Brown	Kirk	McKenzie	Mackay	Glidden	Cumming	Young	Conn	Bauld	Wardhaugh	Crawford
	29th	Brown	Kirk	McKenzie	Mackay	Glidden	Cumming	Young	Conn	Bauld	Wardhaugh	Crawford
Sep	1st	Brown	Kirk	McKenzie	Mackay	Glidden	Cumming	Young	Conn	Bauld	Wardhaugh	Crawford
	8th	Brown	Kirk	McKenzie	Mackay	Glidden	Cumming	Young	Conn	Bauld	Wardhaugh	Crawford
	15th	Brown	Kirk	McKenzie	Mackay	Milne	Cumming	Young	Conn	Bauld	Wardhaugh	Crawford
	22nd	Duff	Kirk	McKenzie	Mackay	Glidden	Cumming	Hamilton	Young	Wardhaugh	Conn	Crawford
	29th	Duff	Kirk	McKenzie	Mackay	Glidden	Cumming	Young	Campbell	Bauld	Wardhaugh	Hamilton
Oct	6th	Duff	Kirk	McKenzie	Mackay	Glidden	Cumming	Young	Campbell	Bauld	Wardhaugh	Crawford
	13th	Duff	Kirk	McKenzie	Mackay	Glidden	Cumming	Hamilton	Young	Bauld	Wardhaugh	Crawford
	20th	Brown	Kirk	McKenzie	Mackay	Glidden	Cumming	Hamilton	Young	Whittle	Wardhaugh	Crawford
	27th	Brown	Parker	McKenzie	Mackay	Glidden	Cumming	Hamilton	Young	Bauld	Wardhaugh	Crawford
Nov	3rd	Brown	Parker	Lindores	Mackay	Glidden	Cumming	Hamilton	Young	Bauld	Wardhaugh	Crawford
	10th	Brown	Parker	McKenzie	Mackay	Milne	Cumming	Hamilton	McFadzean	Bauld	Wardhaugh	Crawford
	17th	Marshall	Parker	McKenzie	Bowman	Milne	Cumming	Hamilton	McFadzean	Young	Wardhaugh	Crawford
	24th	Marshall	Parker	Lindores	Mackay	Milne	Cumming	Hamilton	Young	Murray	Wardhaugh	Crawford
Dec	1st	Marshall	Kirk	McKenzie	Mackay	Milne	Cumming	Hamilton	Young	Bauld	Wardhaugh	Crawford
	8th	Marshall	Kirk	McKenzie	Mackay	Milne	Cumming	Hamilton	Young	Murray	Wardhaugh	Crawford
	15th	Marshall	Kirk	McKenzie	Mackay	Milne	Cumming	Hamilton	Young	Bauld	Wardhaugh	Crawford
	22nd	Brown	Parker	Kirk	Bowman	Glidden	Cumming	Hamilton	Campbell	Bauld	Wardhaugh	Crawford
	29th	Brown	Parker	Kirk	Mackay	Glidden	Cumming	Hamilton	Murray	Bauld	Young	Crawford
Jan	1st	Brown	Parker	Kirk	Mackay	Glidden	Cumming	Hamilton	Young	Bauld	Wardhaugh	Crawford
	2nd	Brown	Parker	McKenzie	Mackay	Glidden	Cumming	Kirk	Murray	Wardhaugh	McFadzean	Hamilton
	5th	Brown	Parker	Kirk	Mackay	Glidden	Cumming	Hamilton	Murray	Wardhaugh	Young	Crawford
	12th	Brown	Parker	Kirk	Mackay	Glidden	Cumming	Hamilton	Murray	Wardhaugh	Young	Crawford
	19th	Brown	Parker	Kirk	Mackay	Glidden	Cumming	Young	Murray	Bauld	Wardhaugh	Hamilton
	26th	Brown	Parker	Kirk	Mackay	Glidden	Cumming	Hamilton	Conn	Bauld	Wardhaugh	Crawford
Feb	2nd	Brown	Parker	Kirk	Mackay	Glidden	Cumming	Young	Conn	Bauld	Wardhaugh	Crawford
	9th	Brown	Parker	McKenzie	Mackay	Glidden	Cumming	Hamilton	Murray	Wardhaugh	Young	Crawford
	23rd	Brown	Parker	McKenzie	Mackay	Glidden	Thomson	Crawford	Murray	Bauld	Wardhaugh	Cumming
Mar	2nd	Brown	Parker	Kirk	Mackay	Glidden	Thomson	Hamilton	Murray	Bauld	McFadzean	Crawford
	9th	Brown	Parker	Kirk	Mackay	Milne	Thomson	Hamilton	Murray	Bauld	Wardhaugh	Crawford
	16th	Brown	Parker	Kirk	Mackay	Milne	Thomson	Young	Murray	Bauld	Wardhaugh	Crawford
	25th	Marshall	Parker	Kirk	Bowman	Milne	Thomson	Young	Conn	Bauld	Wardhaugh	Hamilton
	30th	Marshall	Kirk	McKenzie	Parker	Milne	Mackay	Hamilton	Conn	Bauld	Young	Crawford
Apr	6th	Marshall	Kirk	McKenzie	Parker	Milne	Mackay	Wardhaugh	Conn	Bauld	Young	Crawford
	13th	Marshall	Kirk	McKenzie	Parker	Milne	Mackay	Wardhaugh	Conn	Bauld	Young	Crawford
	20th	Marshall	Kirk	McKenzie	Mackay	Milne	Thomson	Young	Conn	Bauld	Wardhaugh	Crawford
	27th	Marshall	Kirk	McKenzie	Mackay	Milne	Thomson	Hamilton	Conn	Young	Wardhaugh	Crawford

One for Murray - the grounded Jimmy Murray shoots for goal and although an Airdrie defender slides along the line he cannot stop the ball hitting the back of the net at Tynecastle. Ian Crawford is the other Hearts forward.

Season 1957-58

Date		Opponents		Score	Crowd	Scorers
Aug 10th	LC	Kilmarnock	a	1-2	19,000	Wardhaugh
14th	LC	Queens Park	h	9-2	20,000	Wardhaugh 3; Bauld 2; Crawford 2; Conn; Hamilton
20th	LC	Dundee	a	2-2*	16,200	Wardhaugh; Bauld
24th	LC	Kilmarnock	h	1-1	25,000	Wardhaugh
28th	LC	Queens Park	a	0-0	5,000	-
31st	LC	Dundee	h	4-2	18,000	Bauld 2; Kirk (pen); Wardhaugh
Sep 7th	L	Dundee	h	6-0	19,000	Murray; Bauld; Crawford 2; Kirk (pen); Wardhaugh
14th	L	Airdrie	a	7-2	14,000	Murray; Wardhaugh 3; Crawford 2; Kirk (pen)
21st	L	Hibernian	h	3-1	34,000	Wardhaugh; Crawford; Murray
Oct 5th	L	East Fife	h	9-0	28,000	Bauld 2; Mackay; Wardhaugh 3; Cumming; Young; Murray
12th	L	Third Lanark	a	0-0	19,000	-
19th	L	Aberdeen	h	4-0	30,000	Murray 2; Young; Blackwood
26th	L	Rangers	a	3-2	60,000	Wardhaugh; Bauld; Young
Nov 2nd	L	Motherwell	h	2-2	30,000	Wardhaugh 2
9th	L	Queen of the South	a	4-1	9,500	Murray 2; Cumming; Young
11th	L	Partick Thistle	a	3-1	10,000	Young; Cumming; Wardhaugh
16th	L	Queens Park	h	8-0	20,000	Young 3; Mackay; Wardhaugh; Cumming 2; Paton
23rd	L	Clyde	a	1-2	18,000	Bauld
30th	L	Falkirk	h	9-1	25,000	Mackay 3 (1 pen); Wardhaugh; Young 4; Murray
Dec 7th	L	Raith Rovers	a	3-0	21,000	Wardhaugh 2; Murray
14th	L	Kilmarnock	h	2-1	24,000	Mackay; Wardhaugh
21st	L	St Mirren	h	5-1	18,000	Murray 2; Young; Wardhaugh; Mackay
28th	L	Celtic	a	2-0	25,000	Wardhaugh; Young
Jan 1st	L	Hibernian	a	2-0	49,000	Young; Mackay
2nd	L	Airdrie	h	4-0	19,000	Murray 3; Mackay (pen)
4th	L	Dundee	a	5-0	23,000	Wardhaugh 3; Murray; Mackay (pen)
11th	L	Partick Thistle	h	4-1	22,000	Murray; Mackay; Wardhaugh; Blackwood
18th	L	East Fife	a	3-0	10,000	Young; Hamilton 2
25th	L	Third Lanark	h	7-2	17,000	Young; Blackwood; Murray 2; Hamilton 2; Milne (pen)
Feb 1st	SC5	East Fife	a	2-1	13,500	Murray; Blackwood
15th	SC6	Albion Rovers	h	4-1	23,451	Young 2; Blackwood; Wardhaugh
22nd	L	Motherwell	a	4-0	20,000	Conn 2; Milne (pen); Murray
Mar 1st	SC3	Hibernian	h	3-4	41,668	Hamilton; Wardhaugh; Murray
8th	L	Queens Park	a	4-1	8,200	Conn 2; Young; Mackay
10th	L	Queen of the South	h	3-1	11,000	Murray; Smith o.g.; Milne (pen)
14th	L	Celtic	h	5-3	35,000	Crawford 2; Blackwood; Murray 2
19th	L	Clyde	h	2-2	34,000	Crawford; Young
22nd	L	Falkirk	a	4-0	18,000	Murray 2; Crawford; Young
29th	L	Raith Rovers	h	4-1	9,000	Murray 2; Wardhaugh; Young
Apr 5th	L	Kilmarnock	a	1-1	17,000	Bowman
12th	L	St Mirren	a	3-2	22,000	Young 2; Wardhaugh
16th	L	Aberdeen	a	4-0	12,000	Crawford; Wardhaugh; Young; Bowman
30th	L	Rangers	h	2-1	30,000	Wardhaugh 2

* Earlier match on August 17th abandoned at half-time at 0-0 due to flooding.

Jimmy Murray - scored 27 goals and made Scotland breakthrough.

The Record		
League	-	Division One Champions
League Cup	-	Qualifying stages only
Scottish Cup	-	Quarter final
Top Scorer	-	Jimmy Wardhaugh (37)
Av. Home Gate	-	20,600
Players used	-	22
Sent off	-	None

Cup Cash v. Albion Rovers; £2,114; v. Hibernian £4,166

Appearances

	League	L/Cup	S/Cup	Total
Gordon Marshall	31	6	3	40
Alex Young	34 (24)	3	3 (2)	40 (26)
Bobby Kirk	30 (2)	6 (1)	3	39 (3)
Jimmy Wardhaugh	30 (28)	6 (7)	3 (2)	39 (37)
Dave Mackay	28 (12)	6	3	37 (12)
Jimmy Murray	33 (27)	0	3 (2)	36 (29)
George Thomson	30	2	3	35
Ian Crawford	25 (10)	6 (2)	1	32 (12)
Bobby Blackwood	23 (4)	0	2 (2)	25 (6)
Jimmy Milne	21 (3)	0	3	25 (3)
John Cumming	20 (5)	4	0	24 (5)
Andy Bowman	18 (2)	0	3	21 (2)
Fred Glidden	13	6	0	19
Willie Bauld	9 (5)	6 (5)	0	15 (10)
Tommy McKenzie	8	6	0	14
Johnny Hamilton	4 (4)	4 (1)	3 (1)	11 (6)
Alfie Conn	5 (4)	4 (1)	0	9 (5)
Bobby Parker	4	0	0	4
Wilson Brown	3	0	0	3
Danny Paton	3 (1)	0	0	3 (1)
Billy Higgins	1	0	0	1
Willie Lindores	1	0	0	1
Jim McFadzean	0	1	0	1

Scottish League Division One

		Home			Away			Goals	
	P	W	D	L	W	D	L	F A	PTS
Hearts	**34**	**15**	**2**	**0**	**14**	**2**	**1**	**132-29**	**62**
Rangers	34	10	2	5	12	3	5	89-49	49
Celtic	34	7	6	4	12	2	3	86-47	46
Clyde	34	13	1	3	5	5	7	84-61	42
Kilmarnock	34	8	6	3	6	3	8	60-55	37
Partick Thistle	34	11	1	5	6	2	9	69-71	37
Raith Rovers	34	10	2	5	4	5	8	66-56	35
Motherwell	34	8	3	6	4	5	8	68-67	32
Hibernian	34	6	4	7	7	1	9	59-60	31
Falkirk	34	6	5	6	5	4	8	64-82	31
Dundee	34	10	1	6	3	4	10	49-65	31
Aberdeen	34	8	0	9	6	2	9	68-76	30
St Mirren	34	7	4	6	4	4	9	59-66	30
Third Lanark	34	6	2	9	7	2	8	69-88	30
Queen of the South	34	6	4	7	6	1	10	61-72	29
Airdrie	34	8	2	7	5	0	12	71-92	28
East Fife	34	5	2	10	5	1	11	45-88	23
Queens Park	34	1	0	16	3	1	13	41-114	9

League Cup Section

	P	W	D	L	F A	PTS
Kilmarnock	6	3	3	0	11- 5	9
Hearts	**6**	**2**	**3**	**1**	**17- 9**	**7**
Dundee	6	1	3	2	11-13	5
Queens Park	6	0	3	3	8-20	3

Heart of Midlothian F.C. Line-Ups 1957-58

		1	2	3	4	5	6	7	8	9	10	11
Aug	10th	Marshall	Kirk	McKenzie	Mackay	Glidden	Cumming	Hamilton	Conn	Bauld	Wardhaugh	Crawford
	14th	Marshall	Kirk	McKenzie	Mackay	Glidden	Cumming	Hamilton	Conn	Bauld	Wardhaugh	Crawford
	20th	Marshall	Kirk	McKenzie	Mackay	Glidden	Cumming	Hamilton	Conn	Bauld	Wardhaugh	Crawford
	24th	Marshall	Kirk	McKenzie	Mackay	Glidden	Cumming	Hamilton	Young	Bauld	Wardhaugh	Crawford
	28th	Marshall	Kirk	McKenzie	Mackay	Glidden	Thomson G	Young	Wardhaugh	Bauld	McFadzean	Crawford
	31st	Marshall	Kirk	McKenzie	Mackay	Glidden	Thomson G	Young	Conn	Bauld	Wardhaugh	Crawford
Sep	7th	Marshall	Kirk	McKenzie	Mackay	Glidden	Cumming	Young	Murray	Bauld	Wardhaugh	Crawford
	14th	Marshall	Kirk	McKenzie	Mackay	Glidden	Cumming	Young	Murray	Bauld	Wardhaugh	Crawford
	21st	Marshall	Kirk	McKenzie	Mackay	Glidden	Cumming	Young	Murray	Bauld	Wardhaugh	Crawford
Oct	5th	Marshall	Kirk	McKenzie	Mackay	Glidden	Cumming	Young	Murray	Bauld	Wardhaugh	Crawford
	12th	Marshall	Kirk	Lindores	Mackay	Glidden	Thomson	Young	Murray	Bauld	Wardhaugh	Crawford
	19th	Brown	Kirk	Thomson	Mackay	Glidden	Higgins	Young	Murray	Bauld	Wardhaugh	Blackwood
	26th	Brown	Kirk	Thomson	Mackay	Glidden	Cumming	Young	Murray	Bauld	Wardhaugh	Blackwood
Nov	2nd	Marshall	Kirk	Thomson	Mackay	Glidden	Cumming	Young	Murray	Bauld	Wardhaugh	Crawford
	9th	Marshall	Parker	McKenzie	Mackay	Glidden	Thomson	Blackwood	Murray	Young	Wardhaugh	Cumming
	11th	Marshall	Parker	McKenzie	Mackay	Glidden	Thomson	Paton	Murray	Young	Wardhaugh	Cumming
	16th	Marshall	Parker	McKenzie	Mackay	Glidden	Thomson	Paton	Murray	Young	Wardhaugh	Cumming
	23rd	Marshall	Parker	McKenzie	Mackay	Glidden	Thomson	Young	Murray	Bauld	Wardhaugh	Cumming
	30th	Brown	Kirk	Thomson	Mackay	Glidden	Cumming	Blackwood	Murray	Young	Wardhaugh	Crawford
Dec	7th	Marshall	Kirk	Thomson	Mackay	Milne	Cumming	Blackwood	Murray	Young	Wardhaugh	Crawford
	14th	Marshall	Kirk	Thomson	Mackay	Milne	Cumming	Blackwood	Murray	Young	Wardhaugh	Crawford
	21st	Marshall	Kirk	Thomson	Mackay	Milne	Cumming	Blackwood	Murray	Young	Wardhaugh	Crawford
	28th	Marshall	Kirk	Thomson	Mackay	Milne	Bowman	Blackwood	Murray	Young	Wardhaugh	Crawford
Jan	1st	Marshall	Kirk	Thomson	Mackay	Milne	Bowman	Blackwood	Murray	Young	Wardhaugh	Crawford
	2nd	Marshall	Kirk	Thomson	Mackay	Milne	Bowman	Blackwood	Murray	Young	Wardhaugh	Crawford
	4th	Marshall	Kirk	Thomson	Mackay	Milne	Bowman	Blackwood	Murray	Young	Wardhaugh	Crawford
	11th	Marshall	Kirk	Thomson	Mackay	Milne	Bowman	Blackwood	Murray	Young	Wardhaugh	Crawford
	18th	Marshall	Kirk	Thomson	Mackay	Milne	Bowman	Blackwood	Murray	Young	Wardhaugh	Hamilton
	25th	Marshall	Kirk	Thomson	Mackay	Milne	Bowman	Blackwood	Murray	Young	Conn	Hamilton
Feb	1st	Marshall	Kirk	Thomson	Mackay	Milne	Bowman	Blackwood	Murray	Young	Wardhaugh	Hamilton
	15th	Marshall	Kirk	Thomson	Mackay	Milne	Bowman	Blackwood	Murray	Young	Wardhaugh	Hamilton
	22nd	Marshall	Kirk	Thomson	Mackay	Milne	Bowman	Blackwood	Murray	Young	Conn	Hamilton
Mar	1st	Marshall	Kirk	Thomson	Mackay	Milne	Bowman	Hamilton	Murray	Young	Wardhaugh	Crawford
	8th	Marshall	Kirk	Thomson	Mackay	Milne	Bowman	Hamilton	Murray	Young	Conn	Crawford
	10th	Marshall	Kirk	Thomson	Mackay	Milne	Bowman	Blackwood	Murray	Young	Conn	Crawford
	14th	Marshall	Kirk	Thomson	Mackay	Milne	Bowman	Blackwood	Murray	Young	Wardhaugh	Crawford
	19th	Marshall	Kirk	Thomson	Bowman	Milne	Cumming	Blackwood	Murray	Young	Wardhaugh	Crawford
	22nd	Marshall	Kirk	Thomson	Mackay	Milne	Bowman	Blackwood	Murray	Young	Wardhaugh	Crawford
	29th	Marshall	Kirk	Thomson	Cumming	Milne	Bowman	Blackwood	Murray	Young	Wardhaugh	Crawford
Apr	5th	Marshall	Kirk	Thomson	Cumming	Milne	Bowman	Blackwood	Murray	Young	Wardhaugh	Crawford
	12th	Marshall	Kirk	Thomson	Cumming	Milne	Bowman	Blackwood	Murray	Young	Wardhaugh	Crawford
	16th	Marshall	Kirk	Thomson	Cumming	Milne	Bowman	Blackwood	Conn	Young	Wardhaugh	Crawford
	30th	Marshall	Kirk	Thomson	Cumming	Milne	Bowman	Paton	Murray	Young	Wardhaugh	Crawford

Snap shot - Hearts inside-forward Jimmy Murray tries his luck against Hibernian at Tynecastle but Easter Road keeper Lawrie Leslie makes a good save. Jimmy Wardhaugh is on the alert for any slip-up while Johnny Hamilton is on the left.

Season 1958-59

Date			Opponents		Score	Crowd	Scorers
Aug	9th	LC	Rangers	a	0-3	63,000	-
	13th	LC	Third Lanark	h	3-0	18,000	Hamilton; Bauld; Wardhaugh
	16th	LC	Raith Rovers	a	3-1	18,000	Young 2; Hamilton
	20th	L	Dunfermline	h	6-2	20,000	Crawford 2; Bain o.g.; Wardhaugh 2; Hamilton
	23rd	LC	Rangers	h	2-1	42,000	Bauld; Milne
	27th	LC	Third Lanark	a	5-4	15,000	Wardhaugh; Bauld 3; Crawford
	30th	LC	Raith Rovers	h	3-1	16,000	Crawford; Mackay; Hamilton
Sep	3rd	EC1	Standard Liege	a	1-5	25,000	Crawford
	6th	L	Hibernian	a	4-0	29,500	Mackay; Crawford 2; Murray
	9th	EC1	Standard Liege	h	2-1 (3-6)	39,000	Bauld 2
	10th	LCQ	Ayr United	a	5-1	14,000	Paton; Murray; Thomson o.g. Young; Hamilton
	13th	L	Airdrie	h	4-3	20,000	Wardhaugh; Mackay; Thomson; Bauld
	17th	LCQ	Ayr United	h	3-1 (8-2)	17,000	Cumming; Murray; Bauld
	20th	L	St Mirren	a	1-1	16,000	Crawford
	27th	L	Third Lanark	h	8-3	20,000	Bauld 5; Crawford; Young 2
Oct	1st	LCS	Kilmarnock	E. Rd	3-0	41,000	Thomson; Crawford; Bauld
	4th	L	Stirling Albion	a	2-1	12,000	Bauld 2
	11th	L	Dundee	a	3-3	18,000	Bauld; Murray; Young
	18th	L	Partick Thistle	h	2-0	20,000	Wardhaugh; Thomson (pen)
	25th	LCF	Partick Thistle	Hamp	5-1	59,960	Bauld 2; Murray 2; Hamilton
	29th	L	Raith Rovers	a	5-0	6,000	Murray; Bauld; Wardhaugh; Mackay; Thomson (pen)
Nov	1st	L	Motherwell	h	0-2	30,000	-
	8th	L	QOS	a	5-0	9,000	Wardhaugh 3; Hamilton; Bauld
	15th	L	Clyde	h	2-2	22,000	Wardhaugh; Thomson
	22nd	L	Falkirk	h	5-1	20,000	Blackwood; Young; Wardhaugh 2; Thomson (pen)
	29th	L	Kilmarnock	a	2-3	15,000	Beattie o.g.; Bauld
Dec	6th	L	Aberdeen	h	5-1	22,000	Murray 2; Bauld 3
	13th	L	Rangers	a	0-5	66,000	-
	20th	L	Celtic	h	1-1	30,000	Blackwood
	27th	L	Dunfermline	a	3-3	12,000	Murray 2; Crawford
Jan	1st	L	Hibernian	h	1-3	35,000	Young
	3rd	L	Airdrie	a	3-2	15,000	Murray; Cumming; McFadzean
	24th	L	Stirling Albion	h	1-4	22,000	McFadzean
Feb	4th	SC1	QOS	a	3-1	9,862	Young; Wardhaugh; Murray
	7th	L	Dundee	h	1-0	18,000	Hamilton
	14th	SC2	Rangers	a	2-3	53,000	Murray 2
	18th	L	Partick Thistle	a	1-2	12,000	Crawford
	21st	L	Raith Rovers	h	2-1	12,000	Mackay; Thomson
	25th	L	Third Lanark	a	4-0	3,500	Thomson 3; Hamilton
Mar	4th	L	Motherwell	a	1-0	15,000	Murray
	7th	L	QOS	h	2-1	12,000	Thomson; Murray
	9th	L	St Mirren	h	4-0	12,000	Rankin 2; Murray; Hamilton
	14th	L	Clyde	a	2-2	10,000	Murray; Young
	21st	L	Falkirk	a	2-0	19,000	Rankin 2
	28th	L	Kilmarnock	h	3-1	18,000	Young; Blackwood; Hamilton
Apr	15th	L	Aberdeen	a	4-2	18,000	Rankin 3; Blackwood
	11th	L	Rangers	h	2-0	30,000	Cumming; Rankin
	18th	L	Celtic	a	1-2	20,000	Rankin

Willie Bauld - "King of Hearts" whose scoring exploits made him a firm favourite.

The Record		
League	-	Second Place, Division One
League Cup	-	Winners
Scottish Cup	-	Second round
Top Scorer	-	Willie Bauld (26 goals)
Av. Home Gate	-	21,200
Players used	-	23
Sent off	-	None

Transfixed - Alex. Young and two Hibernian defenders watch as the ball rolls along the line in the derby at Tynecastle.

Heart of Midlothian F.C. Line-Ups 1958-59

		1	2	3	4	5	6	7	8	9	10	11
Aug	9th	Marshall	Kirk	Thomson	Cumming	Milne	Bowman	Hamilton	Murray	Young	Wardhaugh	Crawford
	13th	Marshall	Kirk	Thomson	Cumming	Milne	Bowman	Hamilton	Murray	Bauld	Wardhaugh	Crawford
	16th	Marshall	Kirk	Thomson	Cumming	Milne	Bowman	Hamilton	Young	Bauld	Wardhaugh	Crawford
	20th	Marshall	Kirk	Thomson	Cumming	Milne	Bowman	Hamilton	Murray	Bauld	Wardhaugh	Crawford
	23rd	Marshall	Kirk	Thomson	Murray	Milne	Bowman	Paton	Blackwood	Bauld	Wardhaugh	Crawford
	27th	Marshall	Kirk	Thomson	Murray	Glidden	Bowman	Hamilton	Blackwood	Bauld	Wardhaugh	Crawford
	30th	Marshall	Kirk	Thomson	Mackay	Glidden	Cumming	Hamilton	Murray	Bauld	Blackwood	Crawford
Sep	3rd	Marshall	Kirk	Thomson	Cumming	Glidden	Bowman	Blackwood	Mackay	Bauld	Wardhaugh	Crawford
	6th	Marshall	Kirk	Thomson	Mackay	Glidden	Cumming	Blackwood	Murray	Bauld	Crawford	Hamilton
	9th	Marshall	Kirk	Thomson	Mackay	Glidden	Cumming	Blackwood	Murray	Bauld	Crawford	Hamilton
	10th	Marshall	Kirk	Thomson	Mackay	Glidden	Cumming	Paton	Murray	Young	Wardhaugh	Hamilton
	13th	Marshall	Kirk	Thomson	Mackay	Glidden	Cumming	Hamilton	Young	Bauld	Wardhaugh	Crawford
	17th	Marshall	Kirk	Thomson	Mackay	Glidden	Cumming	Blackwood	Murray	Bauld	Crawford	Hamilton
	20th	Marshall	Kirk	Thomson	Mackay	Glidden	Cumming	Young	Murray	Bauld	Crawford	Hamilton
	27th	Marshall	Kirk	Thomson	Mackay	Glidden	Cumming	Hamilton	Murray	Bauld	Young	Crawford
Oct	1st	Marshall	Kirk	Thomson	Mackay	Glidden	Cumming	Hamilton	Blackwood	Bauld	Young	Crawford
	4th	Marshall	Kirk	Thomson	Mackay	Glidden	Cumming	Hamilton	Bowman	Bauld	Young	Crawford
	11th	Marshall	Kirk	Thomson	Mackay	Glidden	Cumming	Hamilton	Murray	Bauld	Young	Crawford
	18th	Marshall	Kirk	Thomson	Murray	Glidden	Bowman	Hamilton	Wardhaugh	Bauld	Young	Crawford
	25th	Marshall	Kirk	Thomson	Mackay	Glidden	Cumming	Hamilton	Murray	Bauld	Wardhaugh	Crawford
	29th	Marshall	Kirk	Thomson	Mackay	Glidden	Cumming	Hamilton	Murray	Bauld	Wardhaugh	Crawford
Nov	1st	Marshall	Kirk	Thomson	Mackay	Glidden	Cumming	Hamilton	Murray	Bauld	Wardhaugh	Crawford
	8th	Marshall	Kirk	Thomson	Mackay	Glidden	Cumming	Paton	Murray	Bauld	Wardhaugh	Hamilton
	15th	Marshall	Kirk	Thomson	Mackay	Glidden	Cumming	Paton	Murray	Bauld	Wardhaugh	Hamilton
	22nd	Marshall	Kirk	Thomson	Mackay	Glidden	Cumming	Blackwood	Murray	Young	Wardhaugh	Crawford
	29th	Brown	Kirk	Thomson	Mackay	Glidden	Cumming	Blackwood	Young	Bauld	Wardhaugh	Hamilton
Dec	6th	Marshall	Kirk	Thomson	Mackay	Milne	Cumming	Young	Murray	Bauld	Wardhaugh	Crawford
	13th	Brown	Kirk	Thomson	Bowman	Robertson	Cumming	Young	Murray	Bauld	Wardhaugh	Crawford
	20th	Brown	Kirk	Thomson	Bowman	Milne	Cumming	Paton	Murray	Bauld	Blackwood	Hamilton
	27th	Marshall	Kirk	Thomson	Bowman	Milne	Cumming	Paton	Murray	Young	Wardhaugh	Crawford
Jan	1st	Marshall	Kirk	Thomson	Bowman	Milne	Cumming	Paton	Murray	Young	Bauld	Crawford
	3rd	Marshall	Kirk	Thomson	Cumming	Milne	Higgins	Crawford	Murray	Young	McFadzean	Blackwood
	24th	Marshall	Kirk	Thomson	Cumming	Milne	Higgins	Crawford	Murray	Young	McFadzean	Bauld
Feb	4th	Marshall	Kirk	Thomson	Mackay	Milne	Cumming	Young	Murray	Bauld	Wardhaugh	Hamilton
	7th	Marshall	Kirk	Thomson	Mackay	Milne	Cumming	Young	Murray	Bauld	Wardhaugh	Hamilton
	14th	Marshall	Kirk	Thomson	Cumming	Milne	Mackay	Young	Murray	Bauld	Wardhaugh	Hamilton
	18th	Marshall	Kirk	Thomson	Cumming	Milne	Mackay	Young	Crawford	Bauld	McFadzean	Hamilton
	21st	Marshall	Kirk	Lough	Cumming	Milne	Mackay	Hamilton	Murray	Young	Thomson	Blackwood
	25th	Marshall	Kirk	Lough	Cumming	Milne	Mackay	Hamilton	Murray	Young	Thomson	Blackwood
Mar	4th	Marshall	Kirk	Lough	Mackay	Milne	Cumming	Blackwood	Murray	Young	Thomson	Hamilton
	7th	Marshall	Kirk	Lough	Mackay	Milne	Cumming	Blackwood	Murray	Young	Thomson	Hamilton
	9th	Marshall	Kirk	Lough	Thomson	Milne	Cumming	Blackwood	Murray	Young	Rankin	Hamilton
	14th	Marshall	Kirk	Lough	Thomson	Milne	Cumming	Crawford	Murray	Young	Blackwood	Hamilton
	21st	Marshall	Kirk	Lough	Thomson	Milne	Cumming	Blackwood	Murray	Young	Rankin	Hamilton
	28th	Marshall	Kirk	Lough	Thomson	Milne	Cumming	Blackwood	Murray	Young	Wardhaugh	Hamilton
Apr	11th	Marshall	Kirk	Lough	Thomson	Milne	Cumming	Blackwood	Murray	Young	Rankin	Hamilton
	15th	Marshall	Kirk	Lough	Thomson	Milne	Cumming	Blackwood	Murray	Young	Rankin	Hamilton
	18th	Marshall	McIntosh	Lough	Thomson	Milne	Cumming	Blackwood	Murray	Young	Rankin	Hamilton

Appearances

	League	L/Cup	S/Cup	E/Cup	Total
George Thomson	34 (10)	10 (1)	2	2	48 (11)
Bobby Kirk	33	10	2	2	47
Gordon Marshall	31	10	2	2	46
John Cumming	33 (2)	8 (1)	2	2	45 (3)
Jimmy Murray	30 (12)	8 (4)	2 (3)	1	41 (19)
Johnny Hamilton	27 (6)	9 (5)	2	1	39 (11)
Alex Young	27 (7)	4 (3)	2 (1)	0	33 (11)
Willie Bauld	20 (15)	8 (9)	2	2 (2)	32 (26)
Ian Crawford	19 (8)	9 (3)	0	2 (1)	30 (12)
Dave Mackay	19 (4)	5 (1)	2	2	28 (5)
Jimmy Milne	20	4 (1)	2	0	26 (1)
Jimmy Wardhaugh	14 (11)	7 (2)	2 (1)	1	24 (14)
Bobby Blackwood	16 (4)	5	0	2	23 (4)
Fred Glidden	13	6	0	2	21
Andy Bowman	7	5	0	1	13
John Lough	11	0	0	0	11
Danny Paton	5	2 (1)	0	0	7 (1)
Bobby Rankin	5 (9)	0	0	0	5 (9)
Wilson Brown	3	0	0	0	3
Jim McFadzean	3 (2)	0	0	0	3 (2)
Billy Higgins	2	0	0	0	2
John MacIntosh	1	0	0	0	1
George Robertson	1	0	0	0	1

Scottish League Division One

		Home			Away			Goals	
	P	W	D	L	W	D	L	F A	PTS
Rangers	34	13	2	2	8	6	3	92-51	50
Hearts	**34**	**12**	**2**	**3**	**9**	**4**	**4**	**92-51**	**48**
Motherwell	34	11	4	2	7	4	6	83-50	44
Dundee	34	10	5	2	6	4	7	61-51	41
Airdrie	34	8	3	6	7	4	6	64-62	37
Celtic	34	11	4	2	3	4	10	70-53	36
St Mirren	34	8	4	5	6	3	8	71-74	35
Kilmarnock	34	10	3	4	3	5	9	58-51	34
Partick Thistle	34	8	4	5	6	2	9	59-66	34
Hibernian	34	8	3	6	5	3	9	68-70	32
Third Lanark	34	6	5	6	5	5	7	74-83	32
Stirling Albion	34	6	5	6	5	3	9	54-64	30
Aberdeen	34	7	4	6	5	1	11	63-66	29
Raith Rovers	34	9	3	5	1	6	10	60-70	29
Clyde	34	8	2	7	4	2	11	62-66	28
Dunfermline	34	7	3	7	3	5	9	68-87	28
Falkirk	34	6	4	7	4	3	10	58-79	27
Queen of the South	34	4	5	8	2	1	14	38-101	18

League Cup Section

	P	W	D	L	F A	PTS
Hearts	**6**	**5**	**0**	**1**	**16-10**	**10**
Rangers	6	3	1	2	16- 7	7
Raith Rovers	6	2	0	4	10-18	4
Third Lanark	6	1	1	4	11-18	3

Season 1959-60

Date		Comp	Opponents		Score	Crowd	Scorers
Aug	8th	LC	Kilmarnock	a	4-0	16,000	Bauld; Crawford; Wardhaugh 2
	12th	LC	Aberdeen	h	2-2	21,000	Wardhaugh; Crawford
	15th	LC	Stirling Albion	a	2-1	12,000	Crawford 2
	19th	L	Dundee	a	3-1	18,000	Hamilton 2; Cumming
	22nd	LC	Kilmarnock	h	2-0	28,000	McFadzean; Young
	26th	LC	Aberdeen	a	4-1	31,000	Bauld 2; Blackwood; Smith
	29th	LC	Stirling Albion	h	2-2	24,000	Murray 2
Sep	5th	L	Hibernian	h	2-2	40,000	Murray 2
	9th	LCQ	Motherwell	a	1-1	32,000	Blackwood
	12th	L	Celtic	a	4-3	36,000	Murray; Young; Blackwood; Hamilton
	16th	LCQ	Motherwell	h	6-2(7-3)	44,000	Young 2; Blackwood 2; Hamilton; Murray
	19th	L	Dunfermline	h	3-1	18,000	Blackwood; Hamilton; Thomson (pen)
	26th	L	Stirling Albion	a	2-2	12,000	Smith 2
Oct	3rd	L	Ayr United	h	5-3	16,000	Young 2; Murray; Smith; Blackwood
	7th	LCS	Cowdenbeath	E. Rd	9-3	27,500	Crawford 4; Hamilton 2; Blackwood; Smith; Thomson (pen)
	10th	L	Airdrie	a	5-2	12,000	Young 3; Smith; Blackwood
	17th	L	Arbroath	a	4-1	6,866	Smith; Hamilton; Crawford 2
	24th	LCF	Third Lanark	Hamp	2-1	57,994	Hamilton; Young
	28th	L	Third Lanark	h	6-2	20,000	Bauld 3; Blackwood 2; Crawford;
	31st	L	Rangers	a	2-0	70,000	Davis o.g.; Blackwood
Nov	7th	L	Partick Thistle	h	5-3	25,000	Blackwood 2; Young 3
	14th	L	Kilmarnock	h	3-1	18,000	Young; Murray; Higgins
	21st	L	Aberdeen	a	3-1	15,000	Hamilton; Crawford; Young
	28th	L	Clyde	a	2-2	14,000	Blackwood; Murray
Dec	5th	L	St Mirren	h	0-2	25,000	-
	12th	L	Motherwell	a	0-3	22,000	-
	19th	L	Raith Rovers	h	4-1	24,000	Cumming; Young; Smith; Blackwood
	26th	L	Dundee	h	3-0	16,000	Blackwood; Thomson (pen); Smith
Jan	1st	L	Hibernian	a	5-1	54,000	Young 3; Plenderleith o.g.; Smith
	2nd	L	Celtic	h	3-1	26,000	Smith; Bauld; Thomson (pen)
	9th	L	Dunfermline	a	2-2	13,000	Thomson (pen); Young
	16th	L	Stirling Albion	h	4-0	22,000	Bauld 2; Young; Hamilton
	23rd	L	Ayr United	a	1-1	17,000	McLean o.g.
	30th	L	Motherwell	h	1-1	18,000	Bauld
Feb	6th	L	Airdrie	h	3-2	22,000	Cumming 2; Murray
	22nd	SC1	Kilmarnock	h	1-1	33,829	Young
	24th	SC1R	Kilmarnock	a	1-2	23,000	Murray
	27th	L	Third Lanark	a	4-1	14,000	Crawford; Young; Murray; Smith
Mar	5th	L	Rangers	h	2-0	45,000	Cumming; Young
	9th	L	Arbroath	h	4-1	12,000	Crawford; Higgins; Murray 2
	15th	L	Partick Thistle	a	2-1	15,000	Murray; Young
	19th	L	Kilmarnock	a	1-2	22,000	Crawford
	26th	L	Aberdeen	h	3-0	15,000	McFadzean; Bauld; Crawford
Apr	5th	L	Clyde	h	5-2	30,000	Bauld; Crawford 3; Higgins
	16th	L	St Mirren	a	4-4	17,000	Young 2; Crawford; Bauld
	30th	L	Raith Rovers	a	2-2	5,000	Young; Smith

Cup Cash v. Killie (h) £3,883; (a) £2,312

Gordon Smith - classy winger brought poise to the Hearts front line.

The Record

League	-	Division One Champions
League Cup	-	Winners
Scottish Cup	-	First round
Top Scorer	-	Alec Young (28 goals)
Av. Home Gate	-	23,000
Players used	-	18
Sent off	-	None

Appearances

	League	L/Cup	S/Cup	Total
Bobby Kirk	34	10	2	46
George Thomson	34 (4)	10 (1)	2	46 (4)
Gordon Marshall	33	10	2	45
John Cumming	32 (5)	10	2	44 (5)
Johnny Hamilton	27 (7)	10 (4)	2	39 (11)
Bobby Blackwood	28 (12)	9 (5)	1	38 (17)
Gordon Smith	29 (11)	7 (2)	2	38 (13)
Jimmy Milne	25	9	2	36
Alex Young	28 (23)	4 (4)	1 (1)	33 (26)
Andy Bowman	24	6	2	32
Ian Crawford	18 (12)	5 (8)	2	25 (20)
Jimmy Murray	18 (11)	5 (3)	1 (1)	24 (15)
Willie Bauld	17 (10)	6 (3)	0	23 (13)
Billy Higgins	21 (3)	1	1	23 (3)
Jim McFadzean	5 (1)	1 (1)	0	6 (2)
Jimmy Wardhaugh	0	4 (3)	0	4 (3)
Andy Fraser	0	3	0	3
Wilson Brown	1	0	0	1

Scottish League Division One

	P	Home W	Home D	Home L	Away W	Away D	Away L	Goals F-A	PTS
Hearts	**34**	**14**	**2**	**1**	**9**	**6**	**2**	**102-51**	**54**
Kilmarnock	34	13	2	2	11	0	6	67-45	50
Rangers	34	5	6	6	12	2	3	72-38	42
Dundee	34	11	1	5	5	9	3	70-49	42
Motherwell	34	9	4	4	7	4	6	71-61	40
Clyde	34	7	5	5	8	4	5	77-69	39
Hibernian	34	8	4	5	6	3	8	106-85	35
Ayr United	34	9	4	4	5	2	10	65-73	34
Celtic	34	7	5	5	5	4	8	73-59	33
Partick Thistle	34	10	0	7	4	4	9	54-78	32
Raith Rovers	34	7	3	7	7	0	10	64-62	31
Third Lanark	34	7	3	7	6	1	10	75-83	30
Dunfermline	34	7	5	5	3	4	10	72-80	29
St Mirren	34	5	3	9	6	3	8	78-86	28
Aberdeen	34	8	4	5	3	2	12	54-72	28
Airdrie	34	5	1	11	6	5	6	56-80	28
Stirling Albion	34	4	3	10	3	5	9	55-72	22
Arbroath	34	4	5	8	0	2	15	38-106	15

League Cup Section

	P	W	D	L	F-A	PTS
Hearts	**6**	**4**	**2**	**0**	**16-6**	**10**
Aberdeen	6	3	1	2	16-15	7
Kilmarnock	6	2	1	3	13-13	5
Stirling Albion	6	0	2	4	8-19	2

Heart of Midlothian F.C. Line-Ups 1959-60

		1	2	3	4	5	6	7	8	9	10	11
Aug	8th	Marshall	Kirk	Thomson	Fraser	Milne	Cumming	Hamilton	Blackwood	Bauld	Wardhaugh	Crawford
	12th	Marshall	Kirk	Thomson	Fraser	Milne	Cumming	Hamilton	Blackwood	Bauld	Wardhaugh	Crawford
	15th	Marshall	Kirk	Thomson	Fraser	Milne	Cumming	Hamilton	Blackwood	Bauld	Wardhaugh	Crawford
	19th	Marshall	Kirk	Thomson	Murray	Milne	Cumming	Hamilton	Blackwood	Bauld	McFadzean	Crawford
	22nd	Marshall	Kirk	Thomson	Murray	Milne	Cumming	Smith	Young	Bauld	McFadzean	Hamilton
	26th	Marshall	Kirk	Thomson	Bowman	Milne	Cumming	Smith	Murray	Bauld	Blackwood	Hamilton
	29th	Marshall	Kirk	Thomson	Bowman	Milne	Cumming	Smith	Murray	Bauld	Blackwood	Hamilton
Sep	5th	Marshall	Kirk	Thomson	Bowman	Milne	Cumming	Smith	Murray	Bauld	Blackwood	Hamilton
	9th	Marshall	Kirk	Thomson	Bowman	Milne	Cumming	Smith	Murray	Wardhaugh	Blackwood	Hamilton
	12th	Marshall	Kirk	Thomson	Bowman	Milne	Cumming	Smith	Murray	Young	Blackwood	Hamilton
	16th	Marshall	Kirk	Thomson	Bowman	Milne	Cumming	Smith	Murray	Young	Blackwood	Hamilton
	19th	Brown	Kirk	Thomson	Bowman	Milne	Cumming	Smith	Murray	Young	Blackwood	Hamilton
	26th	Marshall	Kirk	Thomson	Bowman	Milne	Cumming	Smith	Murray	Young	Blackwood	Hamilton
Oct	3rd	Marshall	Kirk	Thomson	Bowman	Milne	Higgins	Smith	Murray	Young	Blackwood	Hamilton
	7th	Marshall	Kirk	Thomson	Bowman	Milne	Cumming	Smith	Crawford	Young	Blackwood	Hamilton
	10th	Marshall	Kirk	Thomson	Bowman	Milne	Cumming	Smith	Crawford	Young	Blackwood	Hamilton
	17th	Marshall	Kirk	Thomson	Bowman	Cumming	Higgins	Smith	Crawford	Young	Blackwood	Hamilton
	24th	Marshall	Kirk	Thomson	Bowman	Cumming	Higgins	Smith	Crawford	Young	Blackwood	Hamilton
	28th	Marshall	Kirk	Thomson	Bowman	Cumming	Higgins	Smith	Crawford	Bauld	Blackwood	Hamilton
	31st	Marshall	Kirk	Thomson	Bowman	Cumming	Higgins	Smith	Crawford	Young	Blackwood	Hamilton
Nov	7th	Marshall	Kirk	Thomson	Bowman	Cumming	Higgins	Smith	Crawford	Young	Blackwood	Hamilton
	14th	Marshall	Kirk	Thomson	Bowman	Cumming	Higgins	Smith	Murray	Young	Blackwood	Hamilton
	21st	Marshall	Kirk	Thomson	Bowman	Cumming	Higgins	Crawford	Murray	Young	Blackwood	Hamilton
	28th	Marshall	Kirk	Thomson	Bowman	Cumming	Higgins	Smith	Murray	Young	Blackwood	Hamilton
Dec	5th	Marshall	Kirk	Thomson	Bowman	Cumming	Higgins	Smith	Murray	Young	Blackwood	Hamilton
	12th	Marshall	Kirk	Thomson	Bowman	Cumming	Higgins	Smith	Bauld	Young	Blackwood	Hamilton
	19th	Marshall	Kirk	Thomson	Cumming	Milne	Bowman	Smith	Young	Bauld	Blackwood	Hamilton
	26th	Marshall	Kirk	Thomson	Cumming	Milne	Bowman	Smith	Young	Bauld	Blackwood	Hamilton
Jan	1st	Marshall	Kirk	Thomson	Cumming	Milne	Bowman	Smith	Young	Bauld	Blackwood	Hamilton
	2nd	Marshall	Kirk	Thomson	Cumming	Milne	Bowman	Smith	Young	Bauld	Blackwood	Hamilton
	9th	Marshall	Kirk	Thomson	Cumming	Milne	Bowman	Smith	Young	Bauld	Blackwood	Hamilton
	16th	Marshall	Kirk	Thomson	Bowman	Milne	Higgins	Smith	Young	Bauld	Blackwood	Hamilton
	23rd	Marshall	Kirk	Thomson	Cumming	Milne	Bowman	Smith	Young	Bauld	Blackwood	Hamilton
	30th	Marshall	Kirk	Thomson	Cumming	Milne	Bowman	Hamilton	Young	Bauld	Blackwood	Crawford
Feb	6th	Marshall	Kirk	Thomson	Bowman	Milne	Higgins	Crawford	Murray	Bauld	Cumming	Hamilton
	22nd	Marshall	Kirk	Thomson	Bowman	Milne	Cumming	Smith	Crawford	Young	Blackwood	Hamilton
	24th	Marshall	Kirk	Thomson	Bowman	Milne	Higgins	Crawford	Muray	Smith	Cumming	Hamilton
	27th	Marshall	Kirk	Thomson	Cumming	Milne	Higgins	Smith	Murray	Young	McFadzean	Crawford
Mar	5th	Marshall	Kirk	Thomson	Cumming	Milne	Higgins	Smith	Murray	Young	Crawford	Hamilton
	9th	Marshall	Kirk	Thomson	Cumming	Milne	Higgins	Smith	Murray	Bauld	Blackwood	Crawford
	15th	Marshall	Kirk	Thomson	Cumming	Milne	Higgins	Smith	Murray	Young	Blackwood	Crawford
	19th	Marshall	Kirk	Thomson	Cumming	Milne	Higgins	Hamilton	Murray	Young	Blackwood	Crawford
	26th	Marshall	Kirk	Thomson	Cumming	Milne	Higgins	Smith	Murray	Bauld	McFadzean	Crawford
Apr	5th	Marshall	Kirk	Thomson	Cumming	Milne	Higgins	Smith	Young	Bauld	McFadzean	Crawford
	16th	Marshall	Kirk	Thomson	Cumming	Milne	Higgins	Smith	Young	Bauld	McFadzean	Crawford
	30th	Marshall	Kirk	Thomson	Cumming	Milne	Higgins	Smith	Murray	Young	Blackwood	Crawford

One for Willie - Willie Bauld is on the spot to ram the ball into the Aberdeen net in a League Cup tie at Pittodrie. Dons centre-half Jim Clunie can only look on in anguish.

Season 1960-61

Date		Opponents		Score	Crowd	Scorers
Aug 13th	LC	St Mirren	h	1-1	30,000	Thomson (pen)
17th	LC	Clyde	a	0-2	15,000	-
20th	LC	Motherwell	a	3-2	22,600	Cumming 2; Murray
24th	L	St Johnstone	h	3-1	18,000	Crawford; Smith; Murray
27th	LC	St Mirren	a	1-3	14,500	Murray
31st	LC	Clyde	h	6-2	21,000	Bauld 2; Bowman; Clegg; Young; Murray
Sep 3rd	LC	Motherwell	h	2-1	35,000	Young 2
10th	L	Hibernian	a	4-1	40,000	Bowman; Murray ; Young; Blackwood
12th	LC*	Clyde	Park.	1-2	23,000	Bauld
17th	L	Dunfermline	h	1-1	20,000	Blackwood
24th	L	Airdrie	a	2-2	11,000	Bauld; Blackwood
29th	EC1	Benfica	h	1-2	29,500	Young
Oct 1st	L	Dundee United	h	1-1	15,000	Murray
5th	EC1	Benfica	a	0-3(1-5)	35,000	-
8th	L	Partick Thistle	h	0-1	20,000	-
15th	L	Ayr United	a	0-1	15,000	-
26th	L	Rangers	h	1-3	35,000	Smith
29th	L	Motherwell	a	1-1	17,000	Crawford
Nov 5th	L	Aberdeen	h	3-4	20,000	Cumming; Young; Crawford
12th	L	Kilmarnock	a	1-2	13,000	Finlay
19th	L	Clyde	a	1-1	15,000	Hamilton
26th	L	Raith Rovers	h	1-0	17,000	Blackwood
Dec 3rd	L	Third Lanark	a	3-0	9,000	Crawford (pen); Blackwood; McFadzean
10th	L	St Mirren	a	0-2	12,000	-
17th	L	Celtic	h	2-1	20,000	Crawford 2
24th	L	Dundee	a	2-2	13,000	Crawford; Blackwood
31st	L	St Johnstone	a	3-2	11,000	Blackwood; Murray; Little o.g.
Jan 2nd	L	Hibernian	a	1-2	43,000	Crawford
7th	L	Dunfermline	a	1-2	13,000	Crawford
14th	L	Airdrie	h	3-1	18,000	Bauld; Blackwood; Crawford
21st	L	Dundee United	a	0-3	15,000	-
28th	SC1	Tarff Rovers	h	9-0	13,309	Ferguson 3; Blackwood 2; Finlay; Hamilton (pen); McFadzean 2
Feb 4th	L	Partick Thistle	a	1-4	10,000	Hamilton
11th	SC2	Kilmarnock	a	2-1	18,000	Blackwood; Hamilton
18th	L	Ayr United	h	2-1	15,000	Bauld; Blackwood
25th	SC3	Partick Thistle	a	2-1	22,950	Murray 2
Mar 4th	L	Motherwell	h	1-5	22,000	Crawford
8th	L	Rangers	a	0-3	30,000	-
11th	SCQ	St Mirren	h	0-1	34,325	-
14th	L	Aberdeen	a	2-0	8,000	Cumming (pen); Murray
18th	L	Kilmarnock	h	0-1	17,000	-
25th	L	Clyde	h	4-2	20,000	Docherty; Blackwood 2; Hamilton
Apr 1st	L	Raith Rovers	a	1-1	5,000	Johnston
8th	L	Third Lanark	h	1-0	15,000	Cumming (pen)
15th	L	St Mirren	h	0-0	12,000	_
29th	L	Dundee	h	2-1	14,000	Hamilton; Henderson
May 2nd	L	Celtic	a	3-1	7,000	Wallace; Davidson 2

* Play-off for quarter-final place at Parkhead. Cup Cash v. Tarff £1,347; v. Killie £1,900; v. Partick £2,559: St Mirren £3,873.

Bobby Blackwood - pacy winger with the scoring touch

The Record		
League	-	Eighth Place, Division One
League Cup	-	Qualifying stages only
Scottish Cup	-	Quarter-final
European Cup	-	First round
Top Scorer	-	Bobby Blackwood (14 goals)
Av. Home Gate	-	19,900
Players used	-	30
Sent off	-	None

Appearances

	League	L/Cup	S/Cup	E/Cup	Total
John Cumming	32 (3)	7 (2)	4	2	45 (5)
Gordon Marshall	30	7	3	2	42
Bobby Kirk	30	7	2	2	41
Bobby Blackwood	26 (11)	7	3 (3)	2	38 (14)
Jimmy Milne	19	7	4	2	32
Billy Higgins	26	4	1	0	31
Ian Crawford	20 (11)	5	3	1	29 (11)
Andy Bowman	16 (1)	3 (1)	3	2	24 (2)
Johnny Hamilton	20 (4)	1	3 (2)	0	24 (6)
Davie Holt	21	0	3	0	24
Gordon Smith	13 (2)	4	3	2	22 (2)
Jimmy Murray	13 (5)	5 (3)	1 (2)	2	21 (10)
George Thomson	12	7 (1)	0	2	21 (1)
Willie Bauld	11 (3)	4 (3)	3	1	19 (6)
Alec Young	10 (2)	7 (3)	0	2 (1)	19 (6)
Jim McFadzean	13 (1)	0	1 (2)	0	14 (3)
Danny Ferguson	9	0	3 (3)	0	12 (3)
Alan Finlay	9 (1)	0	1 (1)	0	10 (2)
John Docherty	8 (1)	0	0	0	8 (1)
Norrie Davidson	6 (2)	0	1	0	7 (2)
Tommy Henderson	7 (1)	0	0	0	7 (1)
Jim Cruickshank	4	0	1	0	5
David Johnston	5 (1)	0	0	0	5 (1)
John Lough	3	0	1	0	4
Maurice Elliott	3	0	0	0	3
Bobby Ross	3	0	0	0	3

Scottish League Division One

		Home			Away			Goals	
	P	W	D	L	W	D	L	F A	PTS
Rangers	34	14	1	2	9	4	4	88-46	51
Kilmarnock	34	12	4	1	9	4	4	77-45	50
Third Lanark	34	11	2	4	9	0	8	100-80	42
Celtic	34	9	4	4	6	5	6	64-46	39
Motherwell	34	9	3	5	6	5	6	70-57	38
Aberdeen	34	9	2	6	5	6	6	72-72	36
Hibernian	34	10	3	4	5	1	11	66-69	34
Hearts	**34**	**8**	**3**	**6**	**5**	**5**	**7**	**51-53**	**34**
Dundee United	34	9	3	5	4	4	9	60-58	33
Dundee	34	9	3	5	4	3	10	61-53	32
Partick Thistle	34	8	4	5	5	2	10	59-69	32
Dunfermline	34	8	4	5	4	3	10	65-81	31
Airdrie	34	9	4	4	1	6	10	61-71	30
St Mirren	34	6	5	6	5	2	10	53-50	29
St Johnstone	34	7	5	5	3	4	10	47-63	29
Raith Rovers	34	5	4	8	5	3	9	46-67	27
Clyde	34	5	7	5	1	4	12	55-77	23
Ayr United	34	5	6	6	0	6	11	51-81	22

Appearances (Ctd.)

	League	L/Cup	S/Cup	E/Cup	Total
Willie Polland	2	0	0	0	2
Willie Wallace	2 (1)	0	0	0	2 (1)
Boston Glegg	2	0	0	0	2
Andy Fraser	1	0	0	0	1

Heart of Midlothian F.C. Line-Ups 1960-61

		1	2	3	4	5	6	7	8	9	10	11
Aug	13th	Marshall	Kirk	Thomson	Cumming	Milne	Higgins	Smith	Blackwood	Young	Crawford	Hamilton
	17th	Marshall	Kirk	Thomson	Cumming	Milne	Higgins	Smith	Blackwood	Young	Bauld	Crawford
	20th	Marshall	Kirk	Thomson	Cumming	Milne	Higgins	Smith	Murray	Young	Blackwood	Crawford
	24th	Marshall	Kirk	Thomson	Cumming	Milne	Higgins	Smith	Murray	Young	Blackwood	Crawford
	27th	Marshall	Kirk	Thomson	Cumming	Milne	Higgins	Smith	Murray	Young	Blackwood	Crawford
	31st	Marshall	Kirk	Thomson	Cumming	Milne	Bowman	Glegg	Murray	Bauld	Young	Blackwood
Sep	3rd	Marshall	Kirk	Thomson	Cumming	Milne	Bowman	Glegg	Murray	Bauld	Young	Blackwood
	10th	Marshall	Kirk	Thomson	Cumming	Milne	Bowman	Crawford	Murray	Bauld	Young	Blackwood
	12th	Marshall	Kirk	Thomson	Cumming	Milne	Bowman	Crawford	Murray	Bauld	Young	Blackwood
	17th	Marshall	Kirk	Thomson	Cumming	Milne	Bowman	Crawford	Murray	Bauld	Young	Blackwood
	24th	Marshall	Kirk	Holt	Thomson	Milne	Bowman	Smith	Young	Bauld	Blackwood	Cumming
	29th	Marshall	Kirk	Thomson	Cumming	Milne	Bowman	Young	Murray	Bauld	Blackwood	Smith
Oct	1st	Marshall	Kirk	Holt	Bowman	Milne	Higgins	Blackwood	Murray	Young	Thomson	Crawford
	5th	Marshall	Kirk	Thomson	Cumming	Milne	Bowman	Smith	Murray	Young	Blackwood	Crawford
	8th	Marshall	Kirk	Thomson	Bowman	Milne	Higgins	Henderson	Murray	Young	McFadzean	Smith
	15th	Cruickshank	Lough	Holt	Thomson	Milne	Cumming	Smith	Young	Bauld	Blackwood	Hamilton
	26th	Marshall	Lough	Holt	Thomson	Milne	Cumming	Smith	Murray	Bauld	McFadzean	Crawford
	29th	Marshall	Kirk	Thomson	Cumming	Milne	Higgins	Hamilton	Blackwood	Young	McFadzean	Crawford
Nov	5th	Marshall	Kirk	Thomson	Cumming	Milne	Higgins	Hamilton	Blackwood	Young	McFadzean	Crawford
	12th	Marshall	Kirk	Thomson	Cumming	Milne	Higgins	Hamilton	Young	Blackwood	Finlay	Johnston
	19th	Marshall	Kirk	Thomson	Bowman	Cumming	Higgins	Hamilton	Blackwood	Smith	Finlay	Johnston
	26th	Marshall	Kirk	Holt	Fraser	Cumming	Higgins	Hamilton	Finlay	Blackwood	Crawford	Johnston
Dec	3rd	Marshall	Kirk	Holt	Ferguson	Cumming	Higgins	Hamilton	Finlay	Blackwood	Crawford	McFadzean
	10th	Marshall	Kirk	Holt	Ferguson	Cumming	Higgins	Hamilton	Finlay	Blackwood	Crawford	McFadzean
	17th	Marshall	Kirk	Holt	Ferguson	Cumming	Higgins	Hamilton	Finlay	Blackwood	Crawford	McFadzean
	24th	Marshall	Kirk	Holt	Bowman	Cumming	Higgins	Smith	Finlay	Blackwood	Crawford	McFadzean
	31st	Marshall	Kirk	Holt	Bowman	Cumming	Higgins	Hamilton	Murray	Blackwood	Crawford	McFadzean
Jan	2nd	Marshall	Kirk	Holt	Bowman	Cumming	Higgins	Hamilton	Murray	Blackwood	Crawford	McFadzean
	7th	Marshall	Kirk	Holt	Bowman	Cumming	Higgins	Henderson	Blackwood	Bauld	McFadzean	Crawford
	14th	Cruickshank	Kirk	Holt	Bowman	Cumming	Higgins	Henderson	Blackwood	Bauld	Crawford	McFadzean
	21st	Cruickshank	Kirk	Holt	Bowman	Cumming	Higgins	Henderson	Blackwood	Bauld	Crawford	Hamilton
	28th	Cruickshank	Lough	Holt	Bowman	Milne	Cumming	Blackwood	Finlay	Ferguson	McFadzean	Hamilton
Feb	4th	Cruickshank	Lough	Holt	Bowman	Milne	Cumming	Blackwood	Finlay	Davidson	McFadzean	Hamilton
	11th	Marshall	Kirk	Holt	Bowman	Milne	Cumming	Smith	Hamilton	Bauld	Blackwood	Crawford
	18th	Marshall	Kirk	Holt	Bowman	Cumming	Higgins	Hamilton	Davidson	Bauld	Blackwood	Crawford
	25th	Marshall	Ferguson	Holt	Bowman	Milne	Cumming	Smith	Murray	Bauld	Blackwood	Crawford
Mar	4th	Marshall	Ferguson	Holt	Bowman	Milne	Cumming	Smith	Murray	Bauld	Blackwood	Crawford
	8th	Marshall	Kirk	Holt	Bowman	Milne	Cumming	Smith	Murray	Davidson	Blackwood	Crawford
	11th	Marshall	Kirk	Ferguson	Higgins	Milne	Cumming	Smith	Davidson	Bauld	Crawford	Hamilton
	14th	Marshall	Kirk	Ferguson	Higgins	Milne	Cumming	Smith	Murray	Davidson	Docherty	Hamilton
	18th	Marshall	Kirk	Ferguson	Higgins	Milne	Cumming	Smith	Murray	Elliott	Docherty	Hamilton
	25th	Marshall	Kirk	Holt	Murray	Cumming	Higgins	Smith	Docherty	Blackwood	Elliott	Hamilton
Apr	1st	Marshall	Kirk	Ferguson	Cumming	Milne	Higgins	Ross	Docherty	Bauld	Blackwood	Johnston
	8th	Marshall	Kirk	Holt	Murray	Cumming	Higgins	Ross	Docherty	Smith	Finlay	Johnston
	15th	Marshall	Kirk	Ferguson	Cumming	Milne	Higgins	Henderson	Docherty	Davidson	Ross	Hamilton
	29th	Marshall	Kirk	Holt	Higgins	Polland	Cumming	Henderson	Docherty	Wallace	Elliott	Hamilton
May	2nd	Marshall	Kirk	Ferguson	Higgins	Polland	Cumming	Henderson	Davidson	Wallace	Docherty	Hamilton

League Cup Section

	P	W	D	L	F A	PTS
Clyde	**6**	**2**	**3**	**1**	**13-11**	**7**
Hearts	6	3	2	1	13-11	7
Motherwell	6	2	2	2	17-12	6
St Mirren	6	1	2	3	6-15	4

No chance - George Thomson thunders a penalty past Peter Bonetti of Chelsea at Tynecastle. It was his second of the match between the Edinburgh Select and the English First Division side. **DC Thomson**

Season 1961-62

Date		Opponents		Score	Crowd	Scorers
Aug 12th	LC	Raith Rovers	h	1-0	17,000	Wallace
16th	LC	Kilmarnock	a	2-1	16,000	Higgins; Wallace
19th	LC	St Mirren	a	0-1	20,000	-
23rd	L	St Mirren	h	2-2	16,000	Blackwood; Hamilton
26th	LC	Raith Rovers	a	1-3	6,000	Ross
30th	LC	Kilmarnock	h	2-0	17,000	Hamilton 2
Sep 2nd	LC	St Mirren	h	3-1	22,000	Cumming (pen); Hamilton; Wallace
9th	L	Dunfermline	a	1-2	12,500	Cumming
13th	LCQ	Hamilton	a	2-1	8,000	Cumming (pen); Wallace
16th	L	Hibernian	h	4-2	35,000	Easton o.g.; Hamilton 2; Ross
20th	LCQ	Hamilton	h	2-0 (4-1)	10,000	Higgins 2
23rd	L	Dundee	a	0-2	12,000	-
27th	FC1	Union St Gilloise^	a	3-1 (4-1)	4,000	Blackwood; Davidson 2
30th	L	Airdrie	h	4-1	12,000	Bauld 2; Stenhouse; Cumming (pen)
Oct 4th	FC1	Union St Gilloise	h	2-0	18,000	Wallace; Stenhouse
7th	L	Stirling Albion	a	1-3	9,000	Stenhouse
12th	LCS	Stirling Albion	E. Rd.	2-1*	19,000	Bauld; Wallace
14th	L	Aberdeen	a	2-0	12,000	Stenhouse; Hamilton
21st	L	Celtic	h	2-1	22,000	Wallace; Elliott
28th	LCF	Rangers	Hamp	1-1*	88,635	Cumming (pen)
Nov 4th	L	St Johnstone	a	2-0	10,300	Hamilton; Wallace
6th	FC2	Inter Milan	h	0-1	17,500	-
11th	L	Partick Thistle	h	2-0	10,000	Elliott; Higgins
22nd	FC2	Inter Milan	a	0-4 (0-5)	20,500	-
25th	L	Raith Rovers	a	1-0	6,000	Gordon
Dec 2nd	L	Motherwell	h	2-6	15,000	Gordon; Hamilton
16th	L	Kilmarnock	h	3-3	12,000	Cumming (pen); Bauld; Davidson
18th	LCFR	Rangers	Hamp	1-3	47,552	Davidson
23rd	L	Falkirk	a	2-0	6,000	Wallace; Ross
Jan 6th	L	St Mirren	a	1-0	10,000	Higgins
10th	L	Rangers	a	1-2	25,000	Davidson
13th	L	Dundee	h	0-2	25,000	-
17th	L	Hibernian	a	4-1	16,000	Gordon 2; Wallace; Bauld
20th	L	Airdrie	a	3-2	7,000	Bauld; Wallace; Kirk (pen)
24th	L	Dundee United	h	2-1	7,000	Paton; Wallace
27th	SC2	Vale of Leithen	a	5-0	3,500	Gordon 3; Bauld; Kirk (pen)
31st	L	Dunfermline	h	2-1	12,000	Ferguson; Kirk (pen)
Feb 3rd	L	Stirling Albion	h	0-0	10,000	-
7th	L	Third Lanark	h	2-1	16,000	Rodger; Bauld
10th	L	Aberdeen	h	1-1	14,000	Davidson
17th	SC3	Celtic	h	3-4	35,045	Blackwood; Hamilton; Paton
21st	L	Celtic	a	2-2	23,000	Paton 2
24th	L	Rangers	h	0-1	28,000	-
Mar 3rd	L	St Johnstone	h	1-1	8,000	Ferguson
10th	L	Partick Thistle	a	1-3	8,000	Paton
17th	L	Third Lanark	a	0-1	7,000	-
24th	L	Raith Rovers	h	0-1	8,000	-
Apr 2nd	L	Motherwell	a	2-1	3,000	Blackwood;Gordon
7th	L	Kilmarnock	a	0-2	7,000	-
21st	L	Falkirk	h	2-3	9,000	Hamilton; Higgins
28th	L	Dundee United	a	1-0	4,000	Rodger

* After extra-time, 1-1 at 90 minutes. ^ Luxembourg. Cup Cash v. Vale of Leithen £525; v. Celtic £5,257

John Cumming - Hearts skipper and Scottish international half-back.

The Record		
League	-	Sixth Place, Division One
League Cup	-	Runners-up
Scottish Cup	-	Third round
Top Scorer	-	Willie Wallace (12 goals)
Av. Home Gate	-	15,200
Players used	-	22
Sent off	-	None

Appearances

	League	L/Cup	S/Cup	F/Cup	Total
Davie Holt	34	11	2	4	51
John Cumming	33 (3)	8 (3)	2	4	47 (6)
Billy Higgins	28 (3)	11 (3)	2	4	45 (6)
Gordon Marshall	29	10	1	4	44
Willie Polland	30	10	1	4	45
Johnny Hamilton	27 (7)	11 (3)	1 (1)	4	43 (11)
Bobby Kirk	28 (2)	6	2 (1)	4	40 (3)
Willie Wallace	26 (6)	9 (5)	2	3 (1)	40 (12)
Danny Ferguson	26 (3)	11	1	1	39 (3)
Bobby Blackwood	17 (2)	7	1 (1)	2 (1)	27 (4)
Alan Gordon	22 (5)	1	1 (3)	0	24 (8)
Danny Paton	17 (4)	3	2 (1)	0	22 (5)
Bobby Ross	13 (2)	5 (1)	1	1	20 (3)
Willie Bauld	10 (6)	3 (1)	1 (1)	2	16 (8)
Norrie Davidson	8 (3)	3 (1)	0	1 (2)	12 (6)
John Docherty	1	6	0	3	10
Maurice Elliott	7 (2)	1	0	2	10 (2)
Jim Rodger	7 (2)	0	1	0	8 (2)
Jim Cruickshank	5	1	1	0	7
Robin Stenhouse	3 (3)	1	0	1 (1)	5 (4)
Roy Barry	3	1	0	0	4
Tommy Henderson	0	2	0	0	2

Scottish League Division One

	P	Home W	Home D	Home L	Away W	Away D	Away L	Goals F A	PTS
Dundee	34	13	2	2	12	2	3	80-46	54
Rangers	34	12	2	3	10	5	2	84-31	51
Celtic	34	12	4	1	7	4	6	81-37	46
Dunfermline	34	13	1	3	6	4	7	77-46	43
Kilmarnock	34	10	4	3	6	6	5	74-58	42
Hearts	**34**	**7**	**5**	**5**	**9**	**1**	**7**	**54-49**	**38**
Partick Thistle	34	12	0	5	4	3	10	60-55	35
Hibernian	34	7	5	5	7	0	10	58-72	33
Motherwell	34	7	3	7	6	3	8	66-62	32
Dundee United	34	8	3	6	5	3	9	70-71	32
Third Lanark	34	8	3	6	5	2	10	59-60	31
Aberdeen	34	6	6	5	4	3	10	60-73	29
Raith Rovers	34	5	5	7	5	2	10	51-73	27
Falkirk	34	6	2	9	5	2	10	45-68	26
Airdrie	34	7	2	8	2	5	10	57-78	25
St Mirren	34	7	3	7	3	2	12	52-80	25
St Johnstone	34	4	2	11	5	5	7	35-61	25
Stirling Albion	34	5	3	9	1	3	13	34-76	18

League Cup Section

	P	W	D	L	F A	PTS
Hearts	**6**	**4**	**0**	**2**	**9-6**	**8**
Kilmarnock	6	3	0	3	18-8	6
St Mirren	6	3	0	3	7-11	6
Raith Rovers	6	2	0	4	7-16	4

Heart of Midlothian F.C. Line-Ups 1961-62

		1	2	3	4	5	6	7	8	9	10	11
Aug	12th	Marshall	Ferguson	Holt	Barry	Polland	Higgins	Henderson	Blackwood	Wallace	Docherty	Hamilton
	16th	Marshall	Kirk	Holt	Ferguson	Polland	Higgins	Blackwood	Paton	Wallace	Docherty	Hamilton
	19th	Marshall	Kirk	Holt	Ferguson	Polland	Higgins	Blackwood	Paton	Wallace	Docherty	Hamilton
	23rd	Marshall	Kirk	Holt	Ferguson	Polland	Higgins	Paton	Blackwood	Wallace	Bauld	Hamilton
	26th	Marshall	Ferguson	Holt	Cumming	Polland	Higgins	Ross	Henderson	Wallace	Bauld	Hamilton
	30th	Marshall	Ferguson	Holt	Cumming	Polland	Higgins	Ross	Davidson	Wallace	Docherty	Hamilton
Sep	2nd	Marshall	Ferguson	Holt	Docherty	Cumming	Higgins	Ross	Davidson	Wallace	Blackwood	Hamilton
	9th	Marshall	Ferguson	Holt	Cumming	Polland	Higgins	Ross	Davidson	Wallace	Docherty	Hamilton
	13th	Marshall	Ferguson	Holt	Cumming	Polland	Higgins	Ross	Blackwood	Wallace	Docherty	Hamilton
	16th	Marshall	Kirk	Holt	Ferguson	Polland	Cumming	Ross	Hamilton	Paton	Higgins	Blackwood
	20th	Marshall	Kirk	Holt	Ferguson	Polland	Cumming	Ross	Hamilton	Paton	Higgins	Blackwood
	23rd	Marshall	Kirk	Holt	Ferguson	Polland	Cumming	Wallace	Hamilton	Paton	Higgins	Blackwood
	27th	Marshall	Kirk	Holt	Cumming	Polland	Higgins	Ross	Hamilton	Davidson	Docherty	Blackwood
	30th	Marshall	Kirk	Holt	Cumming	Polland	Higgins	Hamilton	Stenhouse	Bauld	Wallace	Paton
Oct	4th	Marshall	Kirk	Holt	Cumming	Polland	Higgins	Hamilton	Stenhouse	Bauld	Wallace	Docherty
	7th	Marshall	Kirk	Holt	Cumming	Polland	Higgins	Ferguson	Stenhouse	Blackwood	Wallace	Hamilton
	12th	Marshall	Kirk	Holt	Cumming	Polland	Higgins	Ferguson	Stenhouse	Bauld	Wallace	Hamilton
	14th	Marshall	Kirk	Holt	Cumming	Polland	Higgins	Ferguson	Stenhouse	Wallace	Ross	Hamilton
	21st	Marshall	Kirk	Holt	Cumming	Polland	Higgins	Ferguson	Elliott	Wallace	Gordon	Hamilton
	28th	Marshall	Kirk	Holt	Cumming	Polland	Higgins	Ferguson	Elliott	Wallace	Gordon	Hamilton
Nov	4th	Marshall	Kirk	Holt	Ferguson	Polland	Cumming	Blackwood	Elliott	Wallace	Gordon	Hamilton
	6th	Marshall	Kirk	Holt	Cumming	Polland	Higgins	Ferguson	Elliott	Bauld	Wallace	Hamilton
	11th	Marshall	Kirk	Holt	Cumming	Polland	Higgins	Ferguson	Elliott	Bauld	Wallace	Hamilton
	22nd	Marshall	Kirk	Holt	Cumming	Polland	Higgins	Docherty	Blackwood	Wallace	Elliott	Hamilton
	25th	Marshall	Kirk	Holt	Cumming	Polland	Higgins	Ferguson	Hamilton	Blackwood	Gordon	Ross
Dec	2nd	Marshall	Kirk	Holt	Cumming	Polland	Higgins	Ferguson	Hamilton	Blackwood	Gordon	Ross
	16th	Marshall	Kirk	Holt	Ferguson	Polland	Cumming	Blackwood	Davidson	Bauld	Wallace	Hamilton
	18th	Cruickshank	Kirk	Holt	Cumming	Polland	Higgins	Ferguson	Davidson	Bauld	Blackwood	Hamilton
	23rd	Marshall	Kirk	Holt	Cumming	Polland	Higgins	Ferguson	Wallace	Davidson	Gordon	Ross
Jan	6th	Marshall	Kirk	Holt	Cumming	Polland	Higgins	Ferguson	Wallace	Davidson	Gordon	Ross
	10th	Marshall	Kirk	Holt	Cumming	Polland	Higgins	Ross	Hamilton	Davidson	Wallace	Gordon
	13th	Marshall	Kirk	Holt	Ferguson	Polland	Cumming	Paton	Elliott	Wallace	Gordon	Hamilton
	17th	Marshall	Kirk	Holt	Polland	Cumming	Higgins	Paton	Wallace	Bauld	Gordon	Hamilton
	20th	Marshall	Kirk	Holt	Polland	Cumming	Higgins	Paton	Wallace	Bauld	Gordon	Ross
	24th	Cruickshank	Kirk	Holt	Polland	Cumming	Higgins	Paton	Wallace	Bauld	Gordon	Ross
	27th	Cruickshank	Kirk	Holt	Polland	Cumming	Higgins	Paton	Wallace	Bauld	Gordon	Ross
	31st	Cruickshank	Kirk	Holt	Polland	Cumming	Ferguson	Paton	Wallace	Bauld	Gordon	Hamilton
Feb	3rd	Cruickshank	Kirk	Holt	Polland	Cumming	Ferguson	Paton	Wallace	Davidson	Gordon	Hamilton
	7th	Cruickshank	Kirk	Holt	Ferguson	Cumming	Higgins	Rodger	Wallace	Bauld	Gordon	Hamilton
	10th	Cruickshank	Kirk	Holt	Ferguson	Cumming	Higgins	Rodger	Davidson	Bauld	Gordon	Hamilton
	17th	Marshall	Kirk	Holt	Ferguson	Cumming	Higgins	Rodger	Wallace	Paton	Blackwood	Hamilton
	21st	Marshall	Polland	Holt	Ferguson	Cumming	Higgins	Rodger	Blackwood	Paton	Gordon	Hamilton
	24th	Marshall	Kirk	Holt	Polland	Cumming	Higgins	Ferguson	Blackwood	Wallace	Gordon	Hamilton
Mar	3rd	Marshall	Polland	Holt	Ferguson	Cumming	Higgins	Wallace	Blackwood	Bauld	Gordon	Hamilton
	10th	Marshall	Polland	Holt	Barry	Ferguson	Higgins	Rodger	Blackwood	Paton	Davidson	Hamilton
	17th	Marshall	Ferguson	Holt	Barry	Cumming	Higgins	Ross	Elliott	Paton	Gordon	Wallace
	24th	Marshall	Kirk	Holt	Polland	Cumming	Higgins	Blackwood	Ferguson	Rodger	Paton	Hamilton
Apr	2nd	Marshall	Kirk	Holt	Cumming	Polland	Higgins	Hamilton	Paton	Elliott	Blackwood	Gordon
	7th	Marshall	Kirk	Holt	Cumming	Polland	Higgins	Rodger	Paton	Elliott	Blackwood	Wallace
	21st	Marshall	Kirk	Holt	Cumming	Polland	Higgins	Paton	Hamilton	Ross	Blackwood	Wallace
	28th	Marshall	Ferguson	Holt	Cumming	Barry	Higgins	Rodger	Blackwood	Ross	Gordon	Wallace

Goal feast - Hearts were on the wrong end of a seven-goal thriller, losing 4-3 to Celtic in the Scottish Cup at Tynecastle. The Parkhead side were awarded a late penalty and Gordon Marshall is helpless as Pat Crerand made no mistake from the spot.

DC Thomson

Season 1962-63

Date		Opponents		Score	Crowd	Scorers
Aug 11th	LC	Celtic	a	1-3	41,000	Paton
15th	LC	Dundee United	h	3-1	10,000	J. Hamilton; Rodger; Davidson
18th	LC	Dundee	a	2-0	20,000	Wallace; J. Hamilton
22nd	L	Dundee	h	3-1	18,000	Davidson 3
25th	LC	Celtic	h	3-2	33,000	Paton; Wallace 2
29th	LC	Dundee United	a	0-2	12,000	-
Sep 1st	LC	Dundee	h	2-0	18,000	Paton; W. Hamilton
8th	L	Hibernian	a	4-0	32,000	Cumming; Paton 3
12th	LCQ	Morton	a	3-0	16,000	Evans o.g.; Davidson 2
15th	L	Airdrie	h	6-1	15,000	Paton; W. Hamilton; J. Hamilton; Higgins; Wallace (pen); Davidson
19th	LCQ	Morton	h	3-1 (6-1)	16,000	J. Hamilton; W. Hamilton; Paton
22nd	L	Partick Thistle	a	4-3	12,000	Wallace (pen); W. Hamilton; Paton; Davidson
29th	L	QOS	h	3-0	18,000	Davidson 2; W. Hamilton
Oct 6th	L	Dunfermline	a	2-2	19,000	Paton; Wallace (pen)
10th	LCSF	St Johnstone	Ea. Rd	4-0	22,900	W. Hamilton; Wallace 3 (1 pen)
13th	L	Kilmarnock	a	2-2	18,000	Wallace; Higgins
20th	L	Motherwell	h	2-1	22,000	W. Hamilton 2
27th	LCF	Kilmarnock	Hamp	1-0	51,280	Davidson
30th	L	Falkirk	a	0-2	12,000	-
Nov 3rd	L	Aberdeen	h	1-1	20,000	Paton
10th	L	Clyde	h	1-1	10,000	Wallace
17th	L	Third Lanark	a	2-1	5,000	Paton; Gordon
24th	L	St Mirren	h	5-0	14,000	Gordon; Wallace 2; J. Hamilton; Rodger
Dec 1st	L	Raith Rovers	a	3-0	5,000	W. Hamilton; Gordon; Wallace
8th	L	Celtic	a	2-2	30,000	Davidson; J. Hamilton
15th	L	Dundee United	h	2-2	10,000	Rodger; W. Hamilton
Jan 12th	SC1	Forfar Athletic	a	3-1	5,000	Wallace (pen); Higgins; Paton
Mar 6th	SC2	Celtic	a	1-3	38,000	Wallace
9th	L	Aberdeen	a	1-2	11,000	J. Hamilton
13th	L	Falkirk	h	5-0	12,000	Wallace 3 (1 pen); Gordon; Ferguson
16th	L	Clyde	a	6-0	7,000	Gordon 2; Wallace 2; W. Hamilton; J. Hamilton
18th	L	Kilmarnock	h	2-3	15,000	Ross; Gordon
23rd	L	Third Lanark	h	2-0	16,000	Wallace; W. Hamilton
27th	L	Rangers	h	0-5	35,000	-
Apr 2nd	L	St Mirren	a	3-7	8,000	J. Hamilton; Gordon 2
6th	L	Raith Rovers	h	2-1	5,500	Gordon; J. Hamilton
10th	L	Partick Thistle	h	2-4	10,000	Gordon; Wallace
20th	L	Dundee United	a	0-0	7,000	-
24th	L	QOS	a	3-0	6,000	W. Hamilton; Gordon; Wallace (pen)
27th	L	Rangers	a	1-5	40,000	Ferguson
29th	L	Celtic	h	4-3	14,000	Rodger 2; Higgins; J. Hamilton
May 4th	L	Hibernian	h	3-3	18,000	Paton; J. Hamilton; Davidson
6th	L	Dundee	a	2-2	10,000	Rodger; Wallace
11th	L	Motherwell	a	3-1	4,500	Rodger; Barry; J. Hamilton
13th	L	Airdrie	a	2-4	4,000	Paton 2
18th	L	Dunfermline	h	2-0	6,500	Davidson; Ferguson

Cup Cash v. Forfar £500

Norrie Davidson - the Hearts centre grabbed winner in League Cup Final.

The Record		
League	-	Fifth Place, Division One
League Cup	-	Winners
Scottish Cup	-	Secound round
Top Scorer	-	Willie Wallace (25 goals)
Av. Home gate	-	15,200
Players used	-	19
Sent off	-	One

Appearances

	League	L/Cup	S/Cup	Total
Willie Wallace	34 (17)	10 (6)	2 (2)	46 (25)
Johnny Hamilton	33 (10)	10 (3)	1	44 (13)
Davie Holt	32	10	2	44
Gordon Marshall	28	10	2	40
Roy Barry	28 (1)	10	2	40 (1)
Billy Higgins	31 (3)	6	2 (1)	39 (4)
Willie Polland	26	10	2	38
Willie Hamilton	27 (10)	5 (3)	1	33 (13)
John Cumming	20 (1)	10	2	32 (1)
Danny Ferguson	26 (3)	4	2	32 (3)
Danny Paton	19 (11)	10 (4)	2 (1)	31 (16)
Norrie Davidson	13 (10)	9 (4)	1	23 (14)
Jim Rodger	13 (6)	5 (1)	0	18 (7)
Alan Gordon	16 (12)	0	1	17 (12)
Chris Shevlane	10	0	0	10
Bobby Ross	8 (1)	1	0	9 (1)
Jim Cruickshank	6	0	0	6
John Docherty	3	0	0	3
Tommy Traynor	1	0	0	1

Scottish League Division One

		Home			Away			Goals	
	P	W	D	L	W	D	L	F A	PTS
Rangers	34	13	4	0	12	3	2	94-28	57
Kilmarnock	34	12	4	1	8	4	5	92-40	48
Partick Thistle	34	11	1	5	9	5	3	66-44	46
Celtic	34	10	3	4	9	3	5	76-44	44
Hearts	**34**	**10**	**4**	**3**	**7**	**5**	**5**	**85-59**	**43**
Aberdeen	34	10	2	5	7	5	5	70-47	41
Dundee United	34	10	6	1	5	5	7	67-52	41
Dunfermline	34	9	6	2	4	2	11	50-47	34
Dundee	34	9	6	2	3	3	11	60-49	33
Motherwell	34	6	7	4	4	4	9	60-63	31
Airdrie	34	10	0	7	4	2	11	52-76	30
St Mirren	34	6	4	7	4	4	9	52-72	28
Falkirk	34	8	1	8	4	2	11	54-69	27
Third Lanark	34	6	4	7	3	4	10	56-68	26
Queen of the South	34	6	3	8	4	3	10	36-75	26
Hibernian	34	4	5	8	4	4	9	47-67	25
Clyde	34	6	1	10	3	4	10	49-83	23
Raith Rovers	34	0	4	13	2	1	14	35-118	9

League Cup Section

	P	W	D	L	F A	PTS
Hearts	6	4	0	2	11-8	8
Celtic	6	3	1	2	12-5	7
Dundee United	6	2	1	3	7-11	5
Dundee	**6**	**2**	**0**	**4**	**5-11**	**4**

Heart of Midlothian F.C. Line-Ups 1962-63

		1	2	3	4	5	6	7	8	9	10	11
Aug	11th	Marshall	Ferguson	Holt	Polland	Barry	Cumming	Rodger	Hamilton J	Davidson	Wallace	Paton
	15th	Marshall	Polland	Holt	Cumming	Barry	Higgins	Rodger	Paton	Davidson	Wallace	Hamilton J
	18th	Marshall	Polland	Holt	Ferguson	Barry	Cumming	Rodger	Paton	Davidson	Wallace	Hamilton J
	22nd	Marshall	Polland	Holt	Ferguson	Barry	Cumming	Rodger	Paton	Davidson	Wallace	Hamilton J
	25th	Marshall	Polland	Holt	Ferguson	Barry	Cumming	Rodger	Paton	Davidson	Wallace	Hamilton J
	29th	Marshall	Polland	Holt	Ferguson	Barry	Cumming	Rodger	Paton	Davidson	Wallace	Hamilton J
Sep	1st	Marshall	Polland	Holt	Cumming	Barry	Higgins	Wallace	Paton	Davidson	Hamilton W	Hamilton J
	8th	Marshall	Polland	Holt	Cumming	Barry	Higgins	Wallace	Paton	Davidson	Hamilton W	Hamilton J
	12th	Marshall	Polland	Holt	Cumming	Barry	Higgins	Wallace	Paton	Davidson	Hamilton W	Hamilton J
	15th	Marshall	Polland	Holt	Cumming	Barry	Higgins	Wallace	Paton	Davidson	Hamilton W	Hamilton J
	19th	Marshall	Polland	Holt	Cumming	Barry	Higgins	Wallace	Paton	Davidson	Hamilton W	Hamilton J
	22nd	Marshall	Polland	Holt	Cumming	Barry	Higgins	Wallace	Paton	Davidson	Hamilton W	Hamilton J
	29th	Marshall	Polland	Holt	Cumming	Barry	Higgins	Wallace	Paton	Davidson	Hamilton W	Hamilton J
Oct	6th	Marshall	Polland	Holt	Cumming	Barry	Higgins	Wallace	Paton	Davidson	Hamilton W	Hamilton J
	10th	Marshall	Polland	Holt	Cumming	Barry	Higgins	Wallace	Paton	Ross	Hamilton W	Hamilton J
	13th	Marshall	Polland	Holt	Cumming	Barry	Higgins	Wallace	Paton	Ross	Hamilton W	Hamilton J
	20th	Marshall	Polland	Holt	Ferguson	Barry	Higgins	Wallace	Docherty	Ross	Hamilton W	Hamilton J
	27th	Marshall	Polland	Holt	Cumming	Barry	Higgins	Wallace	Paton	Davidson	Hamilton W	Hamilton J
	30th	Marshall	Polland	Holt	Cumming	Barry	Higgins	Wallace	Ross	Davidson	Hamilton W	Hamilton J
Nov	3rd	Marshall	Polland	Holt	Ferguson	Barry	Higgins	Rodger	Paton	Wallace	Docherty	Hamilton J
	10th	Marshall	Polland	Holt	Ferguson	Barry	Docherty	Rodger	Paton	Wallace	Hamilton W	Hamilton J
	17th	Marshall	Polland	Holt	Ferguson	Barry	Cumming	Rodger	Paton	Wallace	Gordon	Hamilton J
	24th	Marshall	Polland	Holt	Cumming	Barry	Higgins	Rodger	Paton	Wallace	Gordon	Hamilton J
Dec	1st	Marshall	Polland	Holt	Ferguson	Cumming	Higgins	Rodger	Hamilton W	Wallace	Gordon	Hamilton J
	8th	Marshall	Polland	Holt	Ferguson	Cumming	Higgins	Rodger	Hamilton W	Davidson	Wallace	Hamilton J
	15th	Marshall	Polland	Holt	Ferguson	Cumming	Higgins	Rodger	Hamilton W	Davidson	Wallace	Hamilton J
Jan	12th	Marshall	Polland	Holt	Ferguson	Barry	Higgins	Hamilton J	Paton	Wallace	Hamilton W	Cumming
Mar	6th	Marshall	Polland	Holt	Ferguson	Barry	Higgins	Paton	Wallace	Davidson	Gordon	Cumming
	9th	Marshall	Polland	Holt	Ferguson	Cumming	Higgins	Paton	Wallace	Davidson	Gordon	Hamilton J
	13th	Marshall	Polland	Holt	Ferguson	Barry	Higgins	Ross	Hamilton W	Wallace	Gordon	Hamilton J
	16th	Marshall	Polland	Holt	Ferguson	Barry	Higgins	Ross	Hamilton W	Wallace	Gordon	Hamilton J
	18th	Marshall	Polland	Holt	Ferguson	Barry	Higgins	Ross	Hamilton W	Wallace	Gordon	Hamilton J
	23rd	Cruickshank	Polland	Holt	Ferguson	Barry	Higgins	Paton	Hamilton W	Wallace	Gordon	Hamilton J
	27th	Cruickshank	Polland	Holt	Ferguson	Barry	Higgins	Rodger	Hamilton W	Wallace	Gordon	Hamilton J
Apr	2nd	Marshall	Shevlane	Holt	Ferguson	Barry	Higgins	Hamilton J	Hamilton W	Wallace	Gordon	Cumming
	6th	Cruickshank	Holt	Cumming	Ferguson	Barry	Higgins	Ross	Hamilton W	Wallace	Gordon	Hamilton J
	10th	Cruickshank	Polland	Holt	Ferguson	Barry	Higgins	Rodger	Hamilton W	Wallace	Gordon	Hamilton J
	20th	Marshall	Holt	Shevlane	Ferguson	Cumming	Higgins	Ross	Hamilton W	Wallace	Gordon	Hamilton J
	24th	Marshall	Shevlane	Holt	Ferguson	Barry	Higgins	Hamilton J	Hamilton W	Wallace	Gordon	Cumming
	27th	Marshall	Shevlane	Holt	Ferguson	Barry	Higgins	Hamilton J	Wallace	Paton	Davidson	Traynor
	29th	Marshall	Shevlane	Holt	Ferguson	Barry	Higgins	Rodger	Wallace	Paton	Davidson	Hamilton
May	4th	Marshall	Shevlane	Holt	Ferguson	Barry	Higgins	Hamilton J	Hamilton W	Wallace	Gordon	Cumming
	6th	Marshall	Shevlane	Holt	Ferguson	Barry	Higgins	Rodger	Hamilton W	Paton	Wallace	Hamilton J
	11th	Marshall	Polland	Shevlane	Ferguson	Barry	Higgins	Rodger	Hamilton W	Paton	Wallace	Hamilton J
	13th	Cruickshank	Shevlane	Holt	Ferguson	Polland	Higgins	Rodger	Hamilton J	Paton	Wallace	Hamilton J
	18th	Cruickshank	Polland	Shevlane	Ferguson	Barry	Higgins	Wallace	Paton	Davidson	Hamilton W	Gordon

The Hearts squad in August 1963. (BACK) Jim Rodger, Danny Paton, Jim Thorburn, Jim Cruickshank, Derek Rutherford, Chris Shevlane, Robert Broome, Billy Higgins. MIDDLE - Donald McLeod (assistant-trainer), Johhny Hamilton, Davie Holt, Norrie Davidson, Brian Marjoribanks, John Cumming, Frank Sharp, Willie Polland, Colin Baillie, Johnny Harvey (trainer). FRONT - Maurice Elliott, Willie Wallace, Roy Barry, Danny Ferguson, Jim Kilgannon, Alan Gordon, John Binnie and Tommy Traynor.

Season 1963-64

Date		Opponents		Score	Crowd	Scorers
Aug 10th	LC	Falkirk	h	6-2	12,000	Davidson 3; Gordon; J. Hamilton; Traynor
14th	LC	Motherwell	a	0-3	18,000	-
17th	LC	Partick Thistle	a	2-2	10,000	Gordon; Wallace
21st	L	Airdrie	a	2-0	7,000	Traynor; J. Hamilton
24th	LC	Falkirk	a	3-0	6,000	Wallace; Traynor; J. Hamilton
28th	LC	Motherwell	h	0-0	20,000	-
31st	LC	Partick Thistle	h	2-2	8,500	Ferguson; Wallace
Sep 7th	L	Hibernian	h	4-2	24,000	Ferguson; Wallace 2; Davidson
14th	L	Dunfermline	a	2-2	15,000	Davidson; J. Hamilton (pen)
21st	L	Partick Thistle	h	4-1	11,000	Davidson; J. Hamilton 2; Harvey o.g.
25th	FC1	Lausanne Sports	a	2-2	6,000	Traynor; Ferguson
28th	L	Falkirk	a	2-1	8,000	Wallace; Davidson
Oct 5th	L	St Johnstone	h	3-3	12,000	Wallace 3
9th	FC1	Lausanne Sports	h	2-2 (4-4)	11,700	Cumming; J. Hamilton
12th	L	Queen of the South	h	0-1	10,000	-
15th	FC1	Lausanne Sports	Laus.*	2-3	7,000	Wallace; Ferguson
19th	L	Third Lanark	a	2-0	3,500	W. Hamilton; Wallace
26th	L	Kilmarnock	a	1-3	8,000	W. Hamilton
Nov 2nd	L	Aberdeen	h	0-0	8,000	-
9th	L	St Mirren	h	5-1	9,000	Paton; Wallace 3; J. Hamilton
16th	L	Dundee United	a	0-0	8,000	-
23rd	L	Dundee	h	1-3	10,000	Paton
30th	L	Rangers	a	3-0	24,000	White 2; Wallace
Dec 7th	L	Motherwell	h	1-1	12,000	J. Hamilton
14th	L	Celtic	h	1-1	25,000	White
21st	L	East Stirling	a	3-2	6,000	White 2; J. Hamilton
28th	L	Airdrie	h	4-0	12,000	White; Wallace 2; J. Hamilton
Jan 1st	L	Hibernian	a	1-1	35,000	Wallace
2nd	L	Dunfermline	h	2-1	20,000	J. Hamilton; White
4th	L	Partick Thistle	a	1-2	9,000	White
11th	L	East Stirling	h	4-0	11,000	Murphy 4
17th	L	Falkirk	h	4-1	8,000	J. Hamilton (pen); Murphy; White; Wallace
25th	SC2	Queen of the South	a	3-0	8,433	J. Hamilton (2 pens); White
Feb 1st	L	St Johnstone	a	4-1	9,400	Polland; White; Murphy 2
8th	L	Queen of the South	a	4-1	4,500	Wallace 3; White
15th	SC3	Motherwell	a	3-3	21,648	J. Hamilton (pen); White; Wallace
19th	SC3R	Motherwell	h	1-2	32,403	White
22nd	L	Kilmarnock	h	1-1	14,500	White
29th	L	Aberdeen	a	2-1	10,000	White 2
Mar 4th	L	Third Lanark	h	4-1	6,000	White 3; Gordon
7th	L	St Mirren	a	2-0	5,000	Wallace 2
14th	L	Dundee United	h	0-4	5,500	-
21st	L	Dundee	a	4-2	13,000	J. Hamilton 2; Ferguson; Wallace
Apr 1st	L	Rangers	h	1-2	29,000	Wallace
4th	L	Motherwell	a	1-0	5,000	Wallace
18th	L	Celtic	a	1-1	21,000	J. Hamilton
May 2nd	SuC	Hibernian	h	3-2	13,000	White 2; J. Hamilton (pen)
6th	SuC	Falkirk	a	4-1	3,000	White 3; Wallace
9th	SuC	Dunfermline	h	2-1	10,000	J. Hamilton; White
13th	SuC	Hibernian	a	0-1	11,000	-
16th	SuC	Falkirk	h	1-2	8,000	Wallace

*Play-off at Lausanne, Switzerland a.e.t, 2-2 after 90 mts.

Davie Holt - the hard-tackling Hearts left-back gained five caps for Scotland.

The Record		
League	-	**Fourth Place, Division One**
League Cup	-	**Qualifying stages only**
Scottish Cup	-	**Third round**
Fairs Cup	-	**First round**
Summer Cup	-	**Section winners****
Top Scorer	-	**Willie Wallace (30 goals)**
Av. Home Gate	-	**13,400**
Players used	-	**22**
Sent off	-	**None**

** Withdrew, already nominated for New York Tourney.

Cup Cash v. QOS £1,128; Motherwell (h) £4,374

Appearances

	League	L/Cup	S/Cup	F/Cup	Su/Cup	Total
Willie Wallace	34 (23)	6 (3)	3 (1)	3 (1)	6 (2)	52 (30)
Jim Cruickshank	34	6	3	3	5	51
Johnny Hamilton	34 (13)	6 (2)	2 (3)	3 (1)	6 (2)	51 (20)
Chris Shevlane	31	6	3	3	5	48
Tommy Traynor	29 (1)	5 (2)	3	3 (1)	5	45 (4)
Roy Barry	28	4	3	3	5	43
Willie Polland	26 (1)	6	3	2	6	43 (1)
Davie Holt	29	1	3	1	5	39
Billy Higgins	26	4	0	2	5	37
John Cumming	20	5	3	3 (1)	2	33 (1)
Danny Ferguson	16 (2)	6 (1)	0	3 (2)	5	30 (5)
Tommy White	19 (17)	0	3 (3)	0	6 (6)	28 (26)
Alan Gordon	10 (1)	4 (2)	0	1	2	17 (3)
Norrie Davidson	9 (4)	5 (3)	0	2	0	16 (7)
Alan Anderson	8	0	0	0	2	10
Jim Murphy	6 (7)	0	3	0	0	9 (7)
Danny Paton	6 (2)	0	1	0	0	7 (2)
Frank Sandeman	5	0	0	0	0	5
Willie Hamilton	3 (2)	0	0	1	0	4 (2)
David Anderson	0	0	0	0	1	1
Jim Rodger	1	1	0	0	0	1
Frank Sharp	0	1	0	0	0	1

Scottish League Division One

		Home			Away			Goals	
	P	W	D	L	W	D	L	F A	PTS
Rangers	34	13	1	3	12	4	1	85-21	55
Kilmarnock	34	14	2	1	8	3	6	77-40	49
Celtic	34	13	3	1	6	6	5	89-34	47
Hearts	**34**	**8**	**5**	**4**	**11**	**4**	**2**	**74-40**	**47**
Dunfermline	34	11	3	3	7	6	4	64-33	45
Dundee	34	11	3	3	9	2	6	94-50	45
Partick Thistle	34	11	3	3	4	2	11	55-54	35
Dundee United	34	10	2	5	3	6	8	65-49	34
Aberdeen	34	5	5	7	7	3	7	43-43	32
Hibernian	34	9	4	4	3	2	12	59-66	30
Motherwell	34	7	5	5	2	6	9	51-62	29
St Mirren	34	9	4	4	3	1	13	44-74	29
St Johnstone	34	6	2	8	5	3	9	54-70	28
Falkirk	34	7	4	6	4	2	11	54-84	28
Airdrie	34	7	3	7	4	1	12	52-97	26
Third Lanark	34	5	3	9	4	4	9	47-74	25
Queen of the South	34	3	3	11	2	3	12	40-92	16
East Stirling	34	4	2	11	1	0	16	37-91	12

Heart of Midlothian F.C. Line-Ups 1963-64

		1	2	3	4	5	6	7	8	9	10	11
Aug	10th	Cruickshank	Ferguson	Shevlane	Cumming	Polland	Higgins	Hamilton J	Wallace	Davidson	Gordon	Traynor
	14th	Cruickshank	Ferguson	Shevlane	Cumming	Polland	Higgins	Hamilton J	Wallace	Davidson	Gordon	Traynor
	17th	Cruickshank	Ferguson	Shevlane	Barry	Polland	Cumming	Rodger	Hamilton J	Davidson	Gordon	Wallace
	21st	Cruickshank	Ferguson	Shevlane	Barry	Polland	Cumming	Wallace	Hamilton J	Davidson	Higgins	Traynor
	24th	Cruickshank	Ferguson	Shevlane	Barry	Polland	Cumming	Wallace	Hamilton J	Davidson	Higgins	Traynor
	28th	Cruickshank	Ferguson	Shevlane	Barry	Polland	Cumming	Hamilton J	Davidson	Wallace	Higgins	Traynor
	31st	Cruickshank	Shevlane	Holt	Barry	Polland	Ferguson	Sharp	Hamilton J	Wallace	Gordon	Traynor
Sep	7th	Cruickshank	Shevlane	Holt	Barry	Polland	Higgins	Hamilton J	Ferguson	Davidson	Wallace	Traynor
	14th	Cruickshank	Shevlane	Cumming	Barry	Polland	Higgins	Hamilton J	Ferguson	Davidson	Wallace	Traynor
	21st	Cruickshank	Polland	Shevlane	Barry	Cumming	Higgins	Hamilton J	Ferguson	Davidson	Wallace	Traynor
	25th	Cruickshank	Polland	Shevlane	Barry	Cumming	Higgins	Hamilton J	Ferguson	Davidson	Wallace	Traynor
	28th	Cruickshank	Polland	Shevlane	Barry	Cumming	Higgins	Hamilton J	Ferguson	Davidson	Wallace	Traynor
Oct	5th	Cruickshank	Polland	Shevlane	Barry	Cumming	Higgins	Hamilton J	Ferguson	Davidson	Wallace	Traynor
	9th	Cruickshank	Polland	Shevlane	Cumming	Barry	Higgins	Hamilton J	Ferguson	Davidson	Wallace	Traynor
	12th	Cruickshank	Shevlane	Holt	Ferguson	Barry	Higgins	Hamilton J	Hamilton W	Davidson	Wallace	Traynor
	15th	Cruickshank	Shevlane	Holt	Ferguson	Barry	Cumming	Traynor	Hamilton W	Wallace	Gordon	Hamilton J
	19th	Cruickshank	Shevlane	Holt	Ferguson	Barry	Cumming	Hamilton J	Hamilton W	Davidson	Wallace	Traynor
	26th	Cruickshank	Shevlane	Holt	Ferguson	Barry	Cumming	Hamilton J	Hamilton W	Davidson	Wallace	Traynor
Nov	2nd	Cruickshank	Shevlane	Holt	Polland	Barry	Higgins	Hamilton J	Murphy	Ferguson	Wallace	Cumming
	9th	Cruickshank	Shevlane	Holt	Polland	Barry	Cumming	Rodger	Paton	Wallace	Ferguson	Hamilton J
	16th	Cruickshank	Shevlane	Holt	Polland	Barry	Cumming	Paton	Wallace	White	Ferguson	Hamilton J
	23rd	Cruickshank	Shevlane	Holt	Polland	Barry	Higgins	White	Paton	Wallace	Ferguson	Hamilton J
	30th	Cruickshank	Shevlane	Holt	Polland	Barry	Higgins	Hamilton J	Wallace	White	Gordon	Traynor
Dec	7th	Cruickshank	Shevlane	Holt	Polland	Barry	Higgins	Hamilton J	Wallace	White	Gordon	Traynor
	14th	Cruickshank	Shevlane	Holt	Polland	Barry	Cumming	Hamilton J	Wallace	White	Gordon	Traynor
	21st	Cruickshank	Shevlane	Holt	Cumming	Barry	Higgins	Hamilton J	Wallace	White	Gordon	Traynor
	28th	Cruickshank	Shevlane	Holt	Cumming	Barry	Higgins	Hamilton J	Wallace	White	Gordon	Traynor
Jan	1st	Cruickshank	Shevlane	Holt	Cumming	Barry	Higgins	Hamilton J	Wallace	White	Gordon	Traynor
	2nd	Cruickshank	Shevlane	Holt	Cumming	Anderson A	Higgins	Hamilton J	Paton	White	Wallace	Traynor
	4th	Cruickshank	Shevlane	Holt	Cumming	Anderson A	Higgins	Hamilton J	Paton	White	Wallace	Traynor
	11th	Cruickshank	Shevlane	Holt	Cumming	Polland	Higgins	Hamilton J	Murphy	White	Wallace	Traynor
	18th	Cruickshank	Shevlane	Holt	Polland	Anderson A	Cumming	Hamilton J	Murphy	White	Wallace	Traynor
	25th	Cruickshank	Shevlane	Holt	Polland	Barry	Cumming	Hamilton J	Murphy	White	Wallace	Traynor
Feb	1st	Cruickshank	Shevlane	Holt	Polland	Barry	Cumming	Hamilton J	Murphy	White	Wallace	Traynor
	8th	Cruickshank	Shevlane	Holt	Polland	Barry	Cumming	Hamilton J	Murphy	White	Wallace	Paton
	15th	Cruickshank	Shevlane	Holt	Polland	Barry	Cumming	Hamilton J	Murphy	White	Wallace	Traynor
	19th	Cruickshank	Shevlane	Holt	Polland	Barry	Cumming	Paton	Murphy	White	Wallace	Traynor
	22nd	Cruickshank	Shevlane	Holt	Polland	Barry	Higgins	Hamilton J	Gordon	White	Wallace	Traynor
	29th	Cruickshank	Shevlane	Holt	Polland	Barry	Higgins	Hamilton J	Wallace	White	Gordon	Traynor
Mar	4th	Cruickshank	Polland	Holt	Anderson A	Barry	Higgins	Hamilton J	Wallace	White	Gordon	Traynor
	7th	Cruickshank	Polland	Holt	Anderson A	Barry	Higgins	Hamilton J	Wallace	White	Murphy	Traynor
	14th	Cruickshank	Polland	Holt	Anderson A	Barry	Higgins	Hamilton J	Sandeman	Wallace	Gordon	Traynor
	21st	Cruickshank	Shevlane	Holt	Polland	Barry	Higgins	Hamilton J	Ferguson	Wallace	Sandeman	Traynor
Apr	1st	Cruickshank	Shevlane	Holt	Polland	Barry	Higgins	Hamilton J	Ferguson	Wallace	Sandeman	Traynor
	4th	Cruickshank	Shevlane	Holt	Polland	Anderson A	Higgins	Hamilton J	Ferguson	Wallace	Sandeman	Traynor
	18th	Cruickshank	Shevlane	Holt	Polland	Anderson A	Higgins	Hamilton J	Wallace	White	Sandeman	Traynor
May	2nd	Cruickshank	Shevlane	Holt	Polland	Barry	Higgins	Hamilton J	Ferguson	White	Wallace	Traynor
	6th	Cruickshank	Shevlane	Holt	Polland	Barry	Higgins	Hamilton J	Ferguson	White	Wallace	Traynor
	9th	Cruickshank	Shevlane	Holt	Polland	Barry	Higgins	Hamilton J	Ferguson	White	Wallace	Traynor
	13th	Anderson D	Polland	Ferguson	Barry	Anderson A	Higgins	Hamilton J	Cumming	White	Walace	Gordon
	16th	Cruickshank	Shevlane	Holt	Polland	Barry	Higgins	Hamilton J	Ferguson	White	Wallace	Traynor
	20th	Cruickshank	Shevlane	Holt	Polland	Anderson A	Cumming	Hamilton J	Wallace	White	Gordon	Traynor

League Cup Section

	P	W	D	L	F A	PTS
Motherwell	6	5	1	0	17-0	11
Hearts	**6**	**2**	**3**	**1**	**13-9**	**7**
Partick Thistle	6	1	3	2	9-12	5
Falkirk	6	0	1	5	6-24	1

Summer Cup Section

	P	W	D	L	F A	PTS
Hearts	**6**	**3**	**1**	**2**	**10-7**	**7**
Dunfermline	6	1	4	1	11-9	6
Hibs	6	1	2	2	11-9	6
Falkirk	6	2	1	3	12-19	5

Hearts then withdrew since they were due to participate in New York Tourney.
Hibs beat Dunfermline in a "play-off" and finished runners-up to Aberdeen.

New York Tourney

	P	W	D	L	F A	PTS
Werder Bremen	6	4	2	0	18-10	10
Hearts	**6**	**4**	**1**	**1**	**7-5**	**9**
LanerossiVicenza	6	2	2	2	12-11	6
Blackburn Rovers	6	1	1	4	7-11	3
Bahia Brazil	6	0	2	4	5-12	2

Hearts at training - Danny Ferguson and Johnny Hamilton are to the fore in this session under the watchful eye of trainer Johnny Harvey.

Season 1964-65

Date		Opponents		Score	Crowd	Scorers
Aug 8th	LC	Kilmarnock	a	1-1	6,000	Higgins
12th	LC	Celtic	h	0-3	20,000	-
15th	LC	Partick Thistle	a	1-2	7,500	White
19th	L	Airdrie	h	8-1	5,000	Gordon 2; Traynor; White; Ferguson 2; Wallace 2 (1 pen)
22nd	LC	Kilmarnock	h	0-1	15,000	-
26th	LC	Celtic	a	1-6	30,000	Wallace
29th	LC	Partick Thistle	h	4-3	7,000	Wallace 2; White (pen); Gordon
Sep 5th	L	Hibernian	a	5-3	18,000	Wallace; Traynor; Gordon 2; White;
12th	L	Dunfermline	h	1-1	24,000	Hamilton
19th	L	Third Lanark	a	5-1	10,000	Wallace; Traynor; Gordon 2; White
26th	L	Celtic	h	4-2	22,000	Hamilton; Wallace; Gordon 2
Oct 3rd	L	Partick Thistle	a	3-1	10,000	Wallace 2; Ford
10th	L	St Mirren	h	0-0	7,000	-
17th	L	Rangers	h	1-1	35,000	Wallace
24th	L	Dundee	a	2-1	16,000	Wallace; Hamilton
31st	L	Morton	h	4-1	22,000	Gordon; Barry; White 2
Nov 7th	L	Falkirk	a	2-2	8,000	Wallace; Barry
14th	L	Motherwell	a	3-1	6,000	Wallace; Hamilton (pen); White
21st	L	Clyde	h	3-0	14,000	White 2; Gordon
28th	L	St Johnstone	a	3-0	12,000	White 2; Hamilton
Dec 5th	L	Dundee United	h	3-1	11,000	White; Wallace; Barry
12th	L	Aberdeen	h	6-3	14,000	White; Hamilton 2 (1 pen); Gordon 3
19th	L	Kilmarnock	a	1-3	19,000	Gordon
26th	L	Airdrie	a	2-1	5,000	Wallace 2
Jan 1st	L	Hibernian	h	0-1	35,000	-
2nd	L	Dunfermline	a	2-3	20,000	Ford; Gordon
9th	L	Third Lanark	h	3-1	12,000	White; Gordon; Wallace (pen)
16th	L	Celtic	a	2-1	21,000	Hamilton 2
23rd	L	Partick Thistle	h	1-0	14,600	Jensen
30th	L	St Mirren	a	1-2	7,000	Gordon
Feb 6th	SC1	Falkirk	a	3-0	12,000	Hamilton 2 (1 pen); Traynor
13th	L	Rangers	a	1-1	50,000	Higgins
20th	SC2	Morton	a	3-3	16,560	Gordon; Hamilton; Wallace
24th	SC2R	Morton	h	2-0	31,796	Shevlane; Gordon
27th	L	Dundee	h	1-7	12,000	Cousin o.g.
Mar 6th	SC3	Motherwell	a	0-1	13,308	-
10th	L	Morton	a	3-2	12,000	Barry; Jensen; Ferguson
13th	L	Falkirk	h	5-2	10,000	Hamilton 3 (1 pen); Wallace; Jensen
20th	L	Motherwell	h	2-0	9,000	Hamilton; Barry
27th	L	Clyde	a	5-2	5,000	Hamilton 2 (1 pen); Barry; Wallace; McHugh o.g.
Apr 3rd	L	St Johnstone	h	4-1	12,000	Gordon 2; Wallace 2
10th	L	Dundee United	a	1-1	15,000	Wallace
17th	L	Aberdeen	a	3-0	15,000	Hamilton; Barry; Wallace
24th	L	Kilmarnock	h	0-2	37,275	-
May 1st	SU	Hibernian	a	0-3	13,600	-
5th	SU	Falkirk	h	2-0	3,000	Ford; Gordon
8th	SU	Dunfermline	a	2-1	3,000	Murphy; Hamilton (pen)
12th	SU	Hibernian	h	2-2	12,000	Wallace; Hamilton
15th	SU	Falkirk	a	2-1	2,000	Higgins; Barry
19th	SU	Dunfermline	h	2-2	5,000	Murphy; Higgins

Cup Cash Falkirk £1,840; Morton (a) £3,578, (h) £5,722; Motherwell £2,397

Alan Gordon - a clever forward who was particularly good in the air.

The Record		
League	-	Runners-up Division One
League Cup	-	Qualifying stages only
Scottish Cup	-	Quarter final
Summer Cup	-	Qualifying stages only
Top Scorer	-	Willie Wallace (26goals)
Av. Home Gate	-	18,200
Players used	-	21
Sent off	-	None

Appearances

	League	L/Cup	S/Cup	Su/Cup	Total
Jim Cruickshank	34	6	4	4	48
Billy Higgins	32 (1)	6 (1)	4	5 (2)	47 (4)
Davie Holt	32	6	4	2	44
Willie Wallace	34 (21)	4 (3)	4 (1)	3 (1)	45 (26)
Johnny Hamilton	32 (16)	5	4 (3)	6 (2)	47 (21)
Willie Polland	31	6	4	6	47
Alan Anderson	33	1	4	6	44
Alan Gordon	29 (19)	3 (1)	2 (2)	3 (1)	37 (23)
Chris Shevlane	25	4	1 (1)	4	34 (1)
Tommy Traynor	17 (3)	6	2 (1)	6	31 (4)
Roy Barry	16 (7)	5	3	6 (1)	30 (8)
Danny Ferguson	18 (3)	2	4	6	30 (3)
Tommy White	18 (13)	4 (2)	1	1	24 (15)
Roald Jensen	15 (3)	0	3	0	18 (3)
Donald Ford	7 (2)	0	0	2 (1)	9 (3)
Jim Murphy	1	2	0	3 (2)	6 (2)
Frank Sandeman	0	3	0	0	3
David Anderson	0	0	0	2	2
John Cumming	0	2	0	0	2
Derek Rutherford	0	1	0	0	1
Frank Sharp	0	0	0	1	1

Scottish League Division One

		Home			Away			Goals	
	P	W	D	L	W	D	L	F A	PTS
Kilmarnock	34	12	4	1	10	2	5	62-33	50
Hearts	**34**	**11**	**3**	**3**	**11**	**3**	**3**	**90-49**	**50**
Dunfermline	34	14	2	1	8	3	6	83-36	49
Hibernian	34	11	2	4	10	2	5	75-47	46
Rangers	34	9	5	3	9	3	5	78-35	44
Dundee	34	9	4	4	6	6	5	86-63	40
Clyde	34	10	3	4	7	3	7	64-58	40
Celtic	34	9	2	6	7	3	7	76-57	37
Dundee United	34	10	1	6	5	5	7	59-51	36
Morton	34	9	4	4	4	3	10	54-54	33
Partick Thistle	34	5	5	7	6	5	6	57-58	32
Aberdeen	34	8	5	4	4	3	10	59-75	32
St Johnstone	34	6	5	6	3	6	8	57-62	29
Motherwell	34	4	4	9	6	4	7	45-54	28
St Mirren	34	8	2	7	1	4	12	38-70	24
Falkirk	34	6	5	6	1	2	14	43-85	21
Airdrie	34	3	3	11	2	1	14	48-110	14
Third Lanark	34	2	0	15	1	1	15	26-99	7

League Cup Section

	P	W	D	L	F A	PTS
Celtic	6	4	1	1	18-5	9
Kilmarnock	6	3	2	1	9-5	8
Partick Thistle	6	1	2	3	6-14	4
Hearts	**6**	**1**	**1**	**4**	**7-16**	**3**

Heart of Midlothian F.C. Line-Ups 1964-65

		1	2	3	4	5	6	7	8	9	10	11
Aug	8th	Cruickshank	Shevlane	Holt	Polland	Barry	Higgins	Hamilton	Cumming	Murphy	Sandeman	Traynor
	12th	Cruickshank	Shevlane	Holt	Polland	Barry	Higgins	Hamilton	Cumming	Murphy	Sandeman	Traynor
	15th	Cruickshank	Shevlane	Holt	Polland	Barry	Higgins	Hamilton	Wallace	White	Sandeman	Traynor
	19th	Cruickshank	Shevlane	Holt	Polland	Barry	Higgins	Wallace	Ferguson	White	Gordon	Traynor
	22nd	Cruickshank	Shevlane	Holt	Polland	Barry	Higgins	Wallace	Ferguson	White	Gordon	Traynor
	26th	Cruickshank	Ferguson	Holt	Polland	Barry	Higgins	Hamilton	Wallace	White	Gordon	Traynor
	29th	Cruickshank	Rutherford	Holt	Polland	Anderson	Higgins	Hamilton	Wallace	White	Gordon	Traynor
Sep	5th	Cruickshank	Shevlane	Holt	Polland	Anderson	Higgins	Hamilton	Wallace	White	Gordon	Traynor
	12th	Cruickshank	Shevlane	Holt	Polland	Anderson	Higgins	Hamilton	Wallace	White	Gordon	Traynor
	19th	Cruickshank	Shevlane	Holt	Polland	Anderson	Higgins	Hamilton	Wallace	White	Gordon	Traynor
	26th	Cruickshank	Ferguson	Shevlane	Polland	Anderson	Higgins	Ford	Hamilton	Wallace	Gordon	Traynor
Oct	3rd	Cruickshank	Ferguson	Shevlane	Polland	Anderson	Higgins	Ford	Hamilton	Wallace	Gordon	Traynor
	10th	Cruickshank	Shevlane	Holt	Polland	Anderson	Higgins	Hamilton	Wallace	White	Gordon	Traynor
	17th	Cruickshank	Shevlane	Holt	Polland	Anderson	Higgins	Ford	Hamilton	Wallace	Gordon	Traynor
	24th	Cruickshank	Shevlane	Holt	Polland	Anderson	Higgins	White	Ferguson	Wallace	Gordon	Hamilton
	31st	Cruickshank	Shevlane	Holt	Polland	Anderson	Higgins	White	Barry	Wallace	Gordon	Hamilton
Nov	7th	Cruickshank	Shevlane	Holt	Polland	Anderson	Higgins	White	Barry	Wallace	Gordon	Hamilton
	14th	Cruickshank	Shevlane	Holt	Polland	Anderson	Higgins	Wallace	Barry	White	Gordon	Hamilton
	21st	Cruickshank	Shevlane	Holt	Polland	Anderson	Higgins	Wallace	Barry	White	Gordon	Hamilton
	28th	Cruickshank	Shevlane	Holt	Polland	Anderson	Higgins	Wallace	Barry	White	Gordon	Hamilton
Dec	5th	Cruickshank	Shevlane	Holt	Polland	Anderson	Higgins	Wallace	Barry	White	Gordon	Hamilton
	12th	Cruickshank	Shevlane	Holt	Polland	Anderson	Higgins	Wallace	Traynor	White	Gordon	Hamilton
	19th	Cruickshank	Shevlane	Holt	Polland	Anderson	Higgins	Wallace	Traynor	White	Gordon	Hamilton
	26th	Cruickshank	Shevlane	Holt	Polland	Anderson	Higgins	Traynor	Wallace	White	Gordon	Hamilton
Jan	1st	Cruickshank	Shevlane	Holt	Polland	Anderson	Higgins	Wallace	Ferguson	White	Gordon	Hamilton
	2nd	Cruickshank	Holt	Shevlane	Polland	Anderson	Higgins	Jensen	Wallace	Ford	Gordon	Hamilton
	9th	Cruickshank	Holt	Shevlane	Polland	Anderson	Higgins	Jensen	Wallace	White	Gordon	Traynor
	16th	Cruickshank	Shevlane	Holt	Ferguson	Anderson	Higgins	Hamilton	Jensen	Wallace	Gordon	Traynor
	23rd	Cruickshank	Shevlane	Holt	Ferguson	Anderson	Higgins	Hamilton	Jensen	Wallace	Gordon	Traynor
	30th	Cruickshank	Shevlane	Holt	Ferguson	Anderson	Higgins	Jensen	Wallace	White	Gordon	Hamilton
Feb	6th	Cruickshank	Ferguson	Holt	Polland	Anderson	Higgins	Jensen	Barry	Wallace	Hamilton	Hamilton
	13th	Cruickshank	Ferguson	Holt	Polland	Anderson	Higgins	Jensen	Barry	Wallace	Hamilton	Traynor
	20th	Cruickshank	Ferguson	Holt	Polland	Anderson	Higgins	Jensen	Barry	Wallace	Gordon	Hamilton
	24th	Cruickshank	Shevlane	Holt	Polland	Anderson	Higgins	Jensen	Ferguson	Wallace	Gordon	Hamilton
	27th	Cruickshank	Shevlane	Holt	Polland	Anderson	Higgins	Jensen	Ferguson	Wallace	Gordon	Hamilton
Mar	6th	Cruickshank	Ferguson	Holt	Polland	Anderson	Higgins	Hamilton	Barry	White	Wallace	Traynor
	10th	Cruickshank	Ferguson	Holt	Polland	Anderson	Higgins	Jensen	Barry	Ford	Hamilton	Wallace
	13th	Cruickshank	Ferguson	Holt	Barry	Anderson	Polland	Jensen	Hamilton	Ford	Wallace	Traynor
	20th	Cruickshank	Ferguson	Holt	Barry	Anderson	Polland	Jensen	Hamilton	Murphy	Wallace	Traynor
	27th	Cruickshank	Ferguson	Holt	Polland	Anderson	Higgins	Jensen	Barry	Ford	Wallace	Hamilton
Apr	3rd	Cruickshank	Ferguson	Holt	Polland	Anderson	Higgins	Jensen	Barry	Gordon	Wallace	Hamilton
	10th	Cruickshank	Ferguson	Holt	Polland	Anderson	Higgins	Jensen	Barry	Gordon	Wallace	Hamilton
	17th	Cruickshank	Ferguson	Holt	Polland	Anderson	Higgins	Jensen	Barry	Wallace	Gordon	Hamilton
	24th	Cruickshank	Ferguson	Holt	Polland	Anderson	Higgins	Jensen	Barry	Wallace	Gordon	Hamilton
May	1st	Cruickshank	Ferguson	Holt	Barry	Anderson	Polland	Ford	Hamilton	White	Wallace	Traynor
	5th	Cruickshank	Ferguson	Shevlane	Polland	Anderson	Higgins	Hamilton	Barry	Ford	Gordon	Traynor
	8th	Anderson D	Ferguson	Shevlane	Polland	Anderson	Higgins	Hamilton	Barry	Murphy	Gordon	Traynor
	12th	Cruickshank	Ferguson	Shevlane	Polland	Anderson	Higgins	Hamilton	Barry	Wallace	Gordon	Traynor
	15th	Cruickshank	Ferguson	Holt	Polland	Anderson	Higgins	Hamilton	Barry	Wallace	Murphy	Traynor
	19th	Anderson D	Ferguson	Shevlane	Polland	Anderson	Higgins	Hamilton	Barry	Murphy	Traynor	Sharp

Goals galore - Hearts finished the league's top scorers and here Willie Wallace shows how it's done as he sweeps the ball past George Niven in a match against Partick Thistle at Firhill. Harold Davis is on the left.

Season 1965-66

Date		Opponents		Score	Crowd	Scorers
Aug 14th	LC	Rangers	h	4-2	33,000	Wallace 2; Hamilton 2 (1 pen)
18th	LC	Aberdeen	a	1-1	18,000	Wallace
21st	LC	Clyde	h	1-2	15,000	Ford
25th	L	Hamilton	h	2-0	12,000	Wallace; Gordon
28th	LC	Rangers	a	0-1	40,000	-
Sep 1st	LC	Aberdeen	h	2-0	11,000	Hamilton (pen); Barry
4th	LC	Clyde	a	2-1	5,000	Ford; Wallace
11th	L	Dunfermline	a	1-1	15,000	Polland
18th	L	Hibernian	h	0-4	35,000	-
25th	L	St Johnstone	a	2-3	5,000	Gordon; Traynor
Oct 2nd	L	Dundee	h	0-0	10,000	-
9th	L	Celtic	a	2-5	30,000	Gordon 2
16th	L	Partick Thistle	a	3-3	3,500	Murphy 2; Hamilton
18th	FC2	Valerengen*	h	1-0	9,000	Wallace
23rd	L	Motherwell	h	5-2	10,000	Traynor 2; Wallace; Cumming; Kerrigan
27th	FC2	Valerengen	a	3-1 (4-1)	14,625	Kerrigan 2; Traynor
30th	L	Aberdeen	h	1-1	10,000	Ferguson
Nov 6th	L	Dundee United	a	2-2	10,000	Wallace; Kerrigan
13th	L	Rangers	h	0-2	28,000	-
20th	L	Morton	h	2-1	10,000	Wallace; Madsen o.g.
27th	L	Falkirk	a	1-0	4,500	Traynor
Dec 11th	L	Clyde	h	4-1	10,000	Traynor 2; Wallace; Hamilton (pen)
18th	L	Stirling Albion	a	2-2	4,000	Wallace; Sharp
25th	L	St Mirren	h	4-0	6,500	Higgins; Hamilton (pen); Wallace 2
Jan 1st	L	Hibernian	a	3-2	33,000	Wallace; Kerrigan 2
3rd	L	Dunfermline	h	0-0	25,000	-
8th	L	Hamilton	a	1-0	3,000	Wallace
12th	FC3	Zarragoza	h	3-3	25,000	Anderson; Wallace; Kerrigan
15th	L	St Johnstone	h	0-0	6,400	-
26th	FC3	Zarragoza	a	2-2 (5-5)	30,000	Anderson; Wallace
29th	L	Celtic	h	3-2	35,000	Kerrigan; Wallace 2
Feb 9th	SC1	Clyde	h	2-1	11,875	Kerrigan; Anderson
12th	L	Partick Thistle	h	3-1	8,000	Cunningham o.g.; Wallace; Fraser
21st	SC2	Hibernian	h	2-1	31,224	Traynor; Higgins
26th	L	Aberdeen	a	1-0	12,000	Shewan o.g.
Mar 2nd	FC3	Zarragoza	a*	0-1	30,000	-
5th	SCQ	Celtic	h	3-3	45,965	Wallace; Anderson; Hamilton
9th	SCQR	Celtic	a	1-3	72,000	Wallace
12th	L	Rangers	a	1-1	38,000	Anderson
16th	L	Dundee United	h	0-1	7,000	-
19th	L	Morton	a	3-0	7,000	Traynor; Wallace; Gordon
23rd	L	Motherwell	a	2-4	6,000	Traynor; Kerrigan
26th	L	Falkirk	h	1-2	6,000	Wallace
Apr 4th	L	Kilmarnock	a	2-2	5,000	Wallace 2
9th	L	Kilmarnock	h	2-3	8,000	Hamilton; Traynor
13th	L	Dundee	a	0-1	8,000	-
16th	L	Clyde	a	1-0	3,000	Wallace
23rd	L	Stirling Albion	h	1-1	4,000	Wallace
30th	L	St Mirren	a	1-1	4,000	Gordon

*From Norway; **Play-off in Zarragoza. Cup Cash v. Clyde £2,069; v. Hibs £5,869;

Willie Wallace - prolific scorer in his six years at Tynecastle.

The Record

League	-	Seventh Place, Division One
League Cup	-	Qualifying stages only
Scottish Cup	-	Quarter-final
Top Scorer	-	Willie Wallace (27 goals)
Av. Home Gate	-	13,600
Players used	-	23
Sent off	-	None

Cup Cash v. Celtic (h) £11,491; (a)£13,255

Appearances

	League	L/Cup	S/Cup	F/Cup	Total
Jim Cruickshank	34	6	4	5	49
Alan Anderson	34 (1)	5	4 (2)	5 (2)	48 (5)
Willie Wallace	33 (19)	5 (3)	4 (2)	5 (3)	47 (27)
Tommy Traynor	30 (9)	6	3 (1)	5 (1)	44 (11)
Johnny Hamilton	26 (4)	5 (3)	3 (1)	5	39 (8)
Chris Shevlane	23	3	4	1	31
Willie Polland	20 (1)	3	4	3	30 (1)
Roy Barry	17	6	2	0	25
Davie Holt	21	3	1	4	29
Danny Ferguson	17 (1)	6	0	4	27 (1)
Billy Higgins	18 (1)	2	3 (1)	3	26 (2)
Don Kerrigan	19 (6)	0	3 (1)	5 (3)	27 (10)
John Cumming	16 (1)	3	2	5	26 (1)
George Miller	17	0	4	3	24
Alan Gordon	15 (6)	4	0	0	19 (6)
Donald Ford	9	4	2	2	17
Raold Jensen	5	4	0	0	9
Jim Murphy	7 (2)	0	0	0	7 (2)
Frank Sharp	6 (1)	0	1	0	7 (1)
Frank O'Donnell	3	0	0	0	3
Bobby Aitchison	2	0	0	0	2
Billy Fraser	1 (1)	1	0	0	2
George Peden	1	0	0	0	1

Scottish League Division One

		Home			Away			Goals	
	P	W	D	L	W	D	L	F A	PTS
Celtic	34	16	1	0	11	2	4	106-30	57
Rangers	34	15	1	1	10	4	3	91-29	55
Kilmarnock	34	12	2	3	8	3	6	37-28	45
Dunfermline	34	11	2	4	8	6	5	94-55	44
Dundee United	34	10	3	4	9	2	6	79-51	43
Hibernian	34	8	6	3	8	0	9	81-55	38
Hearts	**34**	**7**	**5**	**5**	**6**	**7**	**4**	**56-48**	**38**
Aberdeen	34	8	3	6	7	3	7	61-54	36
Dundee	34	9	2	6	5	4	8	61-61	34
Falkirk	34	10	1	6	5	1	11	48-72	31
Clyde	34	7	2	8	6	2	9	62-64	30
Partick Thistle	34	9	5	4	1	5	10	55-64	30
Motherwell	34	9	0	8	3	4	10	52-69	28
St Johnstone	34	6	6	5	3	2	12	58-81	26
Stirling Albion	34	7	2	8	2	6	9	40-68	26
St Mirren	34	6	3	8	3	1	13	44-82	22
Morton	34	4	5	8	4	0	13	42-84	21
Hamilton	34	3	1	13	0	1	16	27-117	8

League Cup Section

	P	W	D	L	F A	PTS
Rangers	6	4	0	2	13-7	8
Aberdeen	6	3	1	2	10-7	7
Hearts	**6**	**3**	**1**	**2**	**7-8**	**7**
Clyde	6	1	0	5	5-13	2

Heart of Midlothian F.C. Line-Ups 1965-66

		1	2	3	4	5	6	7	8	9	10	11
Aug	14th	Cruickshank	Ferguson	Holt	Barry	Anderson	Higgins	Jensen	Gordon	Wallace	Traynor	Hamilton
	18th	Cruickshank	Ferguson	Holt	Barry	Anderson	Higgins	Jensen	Gordon	Wallace	Traynor	Hamilton
	21st	Cruickshank	Ferguson	Holt	Barry	Anderson	Gordon	Jensen	Wallace	Ford	Traynor	Fraser
	25th	Cruickshank	Ferguson	Shevlane	Barry	Anderson	Cumming	Jensen	Gordon	Wallace	Traynor	Hamilton
	28th	Cruickshank	Ferguson	Shevlane	Polland	Anderson	Cumming	Jensen	Barry	Ford	Traynor	Hamilton
Sep	1st	Cruickshank	Ferguson	Shevlane	Polland	Anderson	Cumming	Ford	Barry	Wallace	Traynor	Hamilton
	4th	Cruickshank	Ferguson	Shevlane	Polland	Barry	Cumming	Ford	Traynor	Wallace	Gordon	Hamilton
	11th	Cruickshank	Ferguson	Shevlane	Polland	Anderson	Cumming	Ford	Barry	Wallace	Traynor	Hamilton
	18th	Cruickshank	Ferguson	Shevlane	Barry	Anderson	Polland	Ford	Gordon	Wallace	Traynor	Hamilton
	25th	Cruickshank	Holt	Shevlane	Barry	Anderson	Polland	Wallace	Jensen	Ford	Gordon	Traynor
Oct	2nd	Cruickshank	Ferguson	Shevlane	Polland	Anderson	Cumming	Jensen	Barry	Wallace	Gordon	Traynor
	9th	Cruickshank	Ferguson	Shevlane	Polland	Anderson	Cumming	Jensen	Barry	Wallace	Gordon	Traynor
	16th	Cruickshank	Polland	Holt	Ferguson	Anderson	Cumming	Wallace	Ford	Murphy	Aitchison	Hamilton
	18th	Cruickshank	Ferguson	Holt	Polland	Anderson	Cumming	Ford	Traynor	Wallace	Kerrigan	Hamilton
	23rd	Cruickshank	Ferguson	Holt	Polland	Anderson	Cumming	Ford	Traynor	Wallace	Kerrigan	Hamilton
	27th	Cruickshank	Ferguson	Holt	Polland	Anderson	Cumming	Ford	Traynor	Wallace	Kerrigan	Hamilton
	30th	Cruickshank	Shevlane	Holt	Ferguson	Anderson	Polland	Ford	Kerrigan	Wallace	Traynor	Hamilton
Nov	6th	Cruickshank	Shevlane	Holt	Ferguson	Anderson	Polland	O'Donnell	Kerrigan	Wallace	Traynor	Hamilton
	13th	Cruickshank	Shevlane	Holt	Ferguson	Anderson	Polland	O'Donnell	Kerrigan	Wallace	Traynor	Hamilton
	20th	Cruickshank	Polland	Shevlane	Cumming	Anderson	Miller	Jensen	Murphy	Wallace	Kerrigan	Traynor
	27th	Cruickshank	Polland	Holt	Higgins	Anderson	Cumming	O'Donnell	Traynor	Wallace	Miller	Sharp
Dec	11th	Cruickshank	Ferguson	Holt	Cumming	Anderson	Miller	Hamilton	Higgins	Wallace	Traynor	Sharp
	18th	Cruickshank	Ferguson	Holt	Cumming	Anderson	Miller	Hamilton	Higgins	Wallace	Traynor	Sharp
	25th	Cruickshank	Ferguson	Holt	Cumming	Anderson	Miller	Hamilton	Higgins	Wallace	Traynor	Sharp
Jan	1st	Cruickshank	Ferguson	Holt	Cumming	Anderson	Miller	Hamilton	Higgins	Wallace	Kerrigan	Traynor
	3rd	Cruickshank	Ferguson	Holt	Cumming	Anderson	Miller	Hamilton	Higgins	Wallace	Kerrigan	Traynor
	8th	Cruickshank	Ferguson	Holt	Higgins	Anderson	Miller	Hamilton	Kerrigan	Wallace	Traynor	Sharp
	12th	Cruickshank	Ferguson	Holt	Cumming	Anderson	Miller	Hamilton	Higgins	Wallace	Kerrigan	Traynor
	15th	Cruickshank	Ferguson	Holt	Polland	Anderson	Higgins	Ford	Miller	Wallace	Kerrigan	Traynor
	26th	Cruickshank	Ferguson	Shevlane	Cumming	Anderson	Miller	Hamilton	Higgins	Wallace	Kerrigan	Traynor
	29th	Cruickshank	Polland	Shevlane	Higgins	Anderson	Miller	Hamilton	Cumming	Wallace	Kerrigan	Traynor
Feb	9th	Cruickshank	Holt	Shevlane	Polland	Anderson	Miller	Ford	Cumming	Wallace	Kerrigan	Sharp
	12th	Cruickshank	Polland	Shevlane	Aitchison	Anderson	Miller	Sharp	Kerrigan	Wallace	Cumming	Fraser
	21st	Cruickshank	Polland	Shevlane	Higgins	Anderson	Miller	Hamilton	Cumming	Wallace	Kerrigan	Traynor
	26th	Cruickshank	Polland	Holt	Higgins	Anderson	Miller	Hamilton	Cumming	Wallace	Kerrigan	Traynor
Mar	2nd	Cruickshank	Polland	Holt	Higgins	Anderson	Miller	Hamilton	Cumming	Wallace	Kerrigan	Traynor
	5th	Cruickshank	Polland	Shevlane	Higgins	Anderson	Miller	Hamilton	Barry	Wallace	Kerrigan	Traynor
	9th	Cruickshank	Polland	Shevlane	Higgins	Anderson	Miller	Hamilton	Barry	Wallace	Traynor	Ford
	12th	Cruickshank	Polland	Shevlane	Higgins	Anderson	Miller	Hamilton	Barry	Wallace	Kerrigan	Traynor
	16th	Cruickshank	Polland	Shevlane	Barry	Anderson	Miller	Hamilton	Gordon	Ford	Kerrigan	Traynor
	19th	Cruickshank	Polland	Shevlane	Barry	Anderson	Miller	Hamilton	Gordon	Wallace	Kerrigan	Traynor
	23rd	Cruickshank	Polland	Shevlane	Barry	Anderson	Miller	Hamilton	Gordon	Wallace	Kerrigan	Traynor
	26th	Cruickshank	Shevlane	Holt	Barry	Anderson	Miller	Kerrigan	Higgins	Wallace	Gordon	Hamilton
Apr	4th	Cruickshank	Shevlane	Holt	Anderson	Barry	Higgins	Hamilton	Murphy	Wallace	Gordon	Traynor
	9th	Cruickshank	Shevlane	Holt	Anderson	Barry	Higgins	Hamilton	Murphy	Wallace	Gordon	Traynor
	13th	Cruickshank	Shevlane	Holt	Anderson	Barry	Higgins	Ford	Murphy	Wallace	Gordon	Traynor
	16th	Cruickshank	Shevlane	Holt	Barry	Anderson	Higgins	Hamilton	Gordon	Wallace	Murphy	Traynor
	23rd	Cruickshank	Shevlane	Peden	Barry	Anderson	Higgins	Wallace	Gordon	Kerrigan	Murphy	Hamilton
	30th	Cruickshank	Shevlane	Holt	Barry	Anderson	Higgins	Hamilton	Gordon	Wallace	Kerrigan	Traynor

Heart of Midlothian F.C. 1965-66 (BACK, left to right) B. Higgins, A. Gordon, C. Shevlane, A. Thomson, J. Cruickshank, J Calder, J Brown, Sneddon, J. Lewry, J. Blyth. MIDDLE - D. McLeod (assistant-trainer), B. Elgin, J. Cumming, D. Holt, J. Murphy, W. Polland, G. Peden, R. Jensen, D. Kerrigan, B. Fraser, E. Thomson, R. Aichison, D. Clunie, J. Harvey (trainer). FRONT - W. Wallace, R. Barry, A. MacDonald, D. Ferguson, F. O'Donnell, A. Anderson, F. Sharp, J. Hamilton, D. Rutherford, T. Traynor, G. Fleming.

Season 1966-67

Date		Opponents		Score	Crowd	Scorers
Aug 13th	LC	Celtic	h	0-2	25,000	-
17th	LC	St Mirren	a	0-0	4,000	-
20th	LC	Clyde	h	4-3	6,000	Wallace 4
27th	LC	Celtic	a	0-3	46,000	-
31st	LC	St Mirren	h	3-1	4,000	Kerrigan 2; Traynor
Sep 3rd	LC	Clyde	a	3-1	3,000	Traynor; Jensen; Wallace
10th	L	Hibernian	a	1-3	21,300	Kerrigan
17th	L	Airdrie	h	1-1	7,000	Kerrigan
24th	L	Stirling Albion	a	3-0	5,000	Kerrigan; Wallace; Gordon
Oct 1st	L	Dundee	h	3-1	8,000	Wallace 2; Gordon
8th	L	Ayr United	a	1-0	8,000	Gordon
15th	L	Rangers	h	1-1	30,000	Anderson
22nd	L	St Johnstone	a	2-3	5,500	Wallace (pen); Shevlane
29th	L	Clyde	h	0-1	10,000	-
Nov 5th	L	Aberdeen	a	1-3	10,000	Murphy
12th	L	Dunfermline	h	1-1	10,000	Murphy
19th	L	St Mirren	h	4-0	6,000	Murphy 3; Gordon
26th	L	Celtic	a	0-3	40,000	-
Dec 3rd	L	Partick Thistle	a	1-1	3,000	Gordon
10th	L	Dundee United	h	2-1	12,000	Kemp; Anderson
17th	L	Falkirk	h	1-1	6,000	Anderson
24th	L	Kilmarnock	a	2-1	3,000	Murphy; McFadzean o.g.
31st	L	Motherwell	h	1-2	10,000	Kerrigan
Jan 2nd	L	Hibernian	h	0-0	31,000	-
14th	L	Dundee	a	1-1	8,500	Gordon
21st	L	Ayr United	h	1-0	5,000	Traynor
28th	SC1	Dundee United	h	0-3	17,139	-
Feb 4th	L	Rangers	a	1-5	33,000	Ferguson
11th	L	St Johnstone	h	1-0	6,700	G. Fleming
25th	L	Clyde	a	1-2	4,000	Miller
Mar 4th	L	Aberdeen	h	0-3	12,000	-
18th	L	St Mirren	a	0-3	4,000	-
22nd	L	Dunfermline	a	0-1	5,000	-
25th	L	Celtic	h	0-3	26,000	-
Apr 1st	L	Partick Thistle	h	0-0	5,500	-
8th	L	Dundee United	a	0-2	5,000	-
12th	L	Falkirk	a	1-2	5,000	Milne
19th	L	Stirling Albion	h	5-1	2,500	Murphy; Milne 3; Kemp
22nd	L	Kilmarnock	h	1-0	6,000	Kemp
26th	L	Airdrie	a	2-1	2,000	Kemp 2
29th	L	Motherwell	a	0-1	3,600	-

Cup Cash v. Dundee United £2,825

Billy Higgins - a stalwart midfielder at Tynecastle through the 1960's.

The Record		
League	-	11th Place, Division One.
League Cup	-	Qualifying stages only.
Scottish Cup	-	First round.
Top Scorer	-	Willie Wallace (9 goals)
Av. Home Gate	-	11,400
Players used	-	31
Sent off	-	One

Appearances

	League	L/Cup	S/Cup	Total
Jim Cruickshank	34	6	1	41
Alan Anderson	29 (3)	5	1	35 (3)
Tommy Traynor	24 (1)	6 (2)	1	31+1s (3)
Davie Holt	19	6	1	26
Alan Gordon	19 (6)	5	1	25+2s (6)
George Miller	20 (1)	5	0	25 (1)
Don Kerrigan	17 (4)	6 (2)	0	23 (6)
Jim Murphy	20 (7)	0	0	20+2s (7)
Danny Ferguson	16 (1)	0	1	17 (1)
George Fleming	16 (1)	0	1	17
Chris Shevlane	15 (1)	2	0	17 (1)
Johnny Hamilton	15	1	0	16+1s
Alan MacDonald	15	0	1	16
Willie Polland	12	4	0	16
Willie Wallace	10 (4)	6 (5)	0	16 (9)
Bobby Kemp	14 (5)	0	1	15 (5)
Billy Higgins	8	3	1	12
Roald Jensen	7	5 (1)	0	12 (1)
George Peden	12	0	0	12
Arthur Thomson	14	0	1	15
Jim Fleming	9	0	0	9
Eddie Thomson	9	0	0	9
Roy Barry	2	6	0	8
Andy Milne	5 (4)	0	0	5+1s (4)
Donald Ford	5	0	0	5
Tommy Davidson	2	0	0	2+1s
John Cumming	2	0	0	2
Derek Rutherford	2	0	0	2
Bobby Aitchison	1	0	0	1
Jim Townsend	1	0	0	1
Dave Clunie	0	0	0	0+3s

Scottish League Division One

		Home			Away			Goals	
	P	W	D	L	W	D	L	F A	PTS
Celtic	34	14	2	1	12	4	1	111-33	58
Rangers	34	13	3	1	11	4	2	92-31	55
Clyde	34	10	2	5	10	4	3	64-48	46
Aberdeen	34	11	3	3	6	5	6	72-38	42
Hibernian	34	10	3	4	9	1	7	72-49	42
Dundee	34	9	5	3	7	4	6	74-51	41
Kilmarnock	34	9	5	3	7	3	7	59-46	40
Dunfermline	34	9	4	4	5	6	6	72-52	38
Dundee United	34	7	5	5	7	4	6	68-62	37
Motherwell	34	7	6	4	3	5	9	59-60	31
Hearts	**34**	**7**	**6**	**4**	**4**	**2**	**11**	**39-48**	**30**
Partick Thistle	34	5	8	5	4	4	8	49-68	30
Airdrie	34	7	1	9	4	5	8	41-53	28
Falkirk	34	8	1	8	3	3	11	33-70	26
St Johnstone	34	8	3	6	2	2	13	53-73	25
Stirling Albion	34	3	6	8	2	3	12	31-85	19
St Mirren	34	4	1	12	0	6	11	25-81	15
Ayr United	34	1	4	12	0	3	14	20-86	9

League Cup Section

	P	W	D	L	F A	PTS
Celtic	6	6	0	0	23- 3	12
Hearts	**6**	**3**	**1**	**0**	**10-10**	**7**
Clyde	6	2	2	2	7-16	4
St Mirren	6	0	3	3	5- 9	3

Heart of Midlothian F.C. Line-Ups 1966-67

		1	2	3	4	5	6	7	8	9	10	11	12
Aug	13th	Cruickshank	Polland	Holt	Barry	Anderson	Higgins	Hamilton	Gordon	Wallace	Kerrigan	Traynor	Turnbull
	17th	Cruickshank	Polland	Holt	Barry	Anderson	Miller	Jensen	Gordon	Wallace	Kerrigan	Traynor	Hamilton
	20th	Cruickshank	Shevlane	Holt	Barry	Polland	Miller	Jensen	Gordon	Wallace	Kerrigan	Traynor	Hamilton (2)
	27th	Cruickshank	Shevlane	Holt	Barry	Anderson	Higgins	Jensen	Miller	Wallace	Kerrigan	Traynor	Gordon (2)
	31st	Cruickshank	Barry	Holt	Miller	Anderson	Higgins	Jensen	Gordon	Wallace	Kerrigan	Traynor	Murphy (6)
Sep	3rd	Cruickshank	Shevlane	Holt	Barry	Anderson	Miller	Jensen	Miller	Wallace	Kerrigan	Traynor	Murphy
	10th	Cruickshank	Shevlane	Holt	Polland	Anderson	Miller	Jensen	Barry	Wallace	Kerrigan	Traynor	Murphy
	17th	Cruickshank	Shevlane	Peden	Polland	Anderson*	Miller	Jensen	Murphy	Davidson	Kerrigan	Traynor	Gordon
	24th	Cruickshank	Shevlane	Peden	Anderson	Barry	Higgins	Hamilton	Kerrigan	Wallace	Gordon	Traynor	Miller
Oct	1st	Cruickshank	Shevlane	Peden	Anderson	Polland	Higgins	Hamilton	Kerrigan	Wallace	Gordon	Traynor	Clunie (8)
	8th	Cruickshank	Shevlane	Peden	Miller	Polland	Higgins	Hamilton	Murphy	Wallace	Gordon	Traynor	Clunie
	15th	Cruickshank	Shevlane	Peden	Anderson	Polland	Miller	Hamilton	Murphy	Wallace	Gordon	Traynor	Clunie (10)
	22nd	Cruickshank	Shevlane	Peden	Miller	Polland	Higgins	Jensen	Anderson	Wallace	Murphy	Hamilton	Clunie (2)
	29th	Cruickshank	Polland	Peden	McDonald	Miller	Higgins	Jensen	Anderson	Ford	Wallace	Hamilton	Davidson(6)
Nov	5th	Cruickshank	Polland	Peden	Cumming	Anderson	Gordon	Hamilton	Davidson	Wallace	Murphy	Traynor	Miller
	12th	Cruickshank	Ferguson	Peden	MacDonald	Anderson	Cumming	Jensen	Kerrigan	Murphy	Gordon	Hamilton	Sneddon
	19th	Cruickshank	Ferguson	Peden	MacDonald	Anderson	Miller	Hamilton	Kerrigan	Murphy	Gordon	Traynor	Polland
	26th	Cruickshank	Ferguson	Holt	MacDonald	Anderson	Miller	Wallace	Kerrigan	Murphy	Gordon	Traynor	Hamilton
Dec	3rd	Cruickshank	Ferguson	Holt	MacDonald	Thomson A	Anderson	Hamilton	Kerrigan	Wallace	Gordon	Traynor	Murphy
	10th	Cruickshank	Ferguson	Holt	MacDonald	Thomson A	Anderson	Traynor	Fleming G	Kerrigan	Gordon	Kemp	Hamilton
	17th	Cruickshank	Ferguson	Holt	MacDonald	Thomson A	Anderson	Traynor	Fleming G	Kerrigan	Gordon	Kemp	Hamilton
	24th	Cruickshank	Ferguson	Holt	MacDonald	Thomson A	Anderson	Fleming G	Kerrigan	Murphy	Gordon	Kemp	Sneddon
	31st	Cruickshank	Ferguson	Holt	MacDonald	Thomson A	Anderson	Fleming G	Kerrigan	Murphy	Gordon	Kemp	Traynor
Jan	2nd	Cruickshank	Shevlane	Holt	MacDonald	Thomson A	Anderson	Traynor	Kerrigan	Murphy	Gordon	Kemp	Hamilton
	14th	Cruickshank	Ferguson	Holt	MacDonald	Thomson A	Higgins	Fleming G	Anderson	Kemp	Gordon	Traynor	Hamilton
	21st	Cruickshank	Ferguson	Holt	Anderson	Thomson A	Higgins	Fleming G	MacDonald	Kemp	Gordon	Traynor	Aitchison
	28th	Cruickshank	Ferguson	Holt	Anderson	Thomson A	Higgins	Traynor	MacDonald	Gordon	Fleming G	Kemp	Aitchison
Feb	4th	Cruickshank	Polland	Holt	Anderson	Thomson A	Miller	Fleming G	Ferguson	Kerrigan	Gordon	Kemp	Traynor
	11th	Cruickshank	Polland	Holt	Anderson	Thomson A	Miller	Jensen	Fleming G	Ford	Kerrigan	Kemp	Murphy (11)
	25th	Cruickshank	Polland	Shevlane	MacDonald	Thomson A	Miller	Jensen	Fleming G	Ford	Kerrigan	Traynor	Ferguson
Mar	4th	Cruickshank	Polland	Shevlane	Ferguson	Thomson A	Aitchison	Kemp	Kerrigan	Milne	Gordon	Hamilton	Traynor (10)
	18th	Cruickshank	Ferguson	Shevlane	Anderson	Thomson A	Higgins	Hamilton	Fleming G	Fleming J	Gordon	Traynor	Murphy
	22nd	Cruickshank	Shevlane	Peden	Anderson	Thomson E	Miller	Ford	Ferguson	Fleming J	Murphy	Hamilton	Milne
	25th	Cruickshank	Shevlane	Peden	Thomson E	Anderson	Miller	Ford	Ferguson	Fleming J	Murphy	Hamilton	Milne (7)
Apr	1st	Cruickshank	Shevlane	Holt	Thomson E	Anderson	Miller	Fleming G	Ferguson	Fleming J	Murphy	Traynor	Gordon (7)
	8th	Cruickshank	Shevlane	Holt	Thomson E	Anderson	Miller	Hamilton	MacDonald	Fleming J	Murphy	Traynor	Milne
	12th	Cruickshank	Thomson E	Holt	MacDonald	Anderson	Miller	Fleming G	Milne	Thomson A	Murphy	Traynor	Sneddon
	19th	Cruickshank	Thomson E	Holt	Murphy	Anderson	Miller	Kemp	Fleming G	Fleming J	Milne	Traynor	Ferguson
	22nd	Cruickshank	Thomson E	Holt	Murphy	Anderson	Miller	Kemp	Fleming G	Fleming J	Milne	Traynor	Gordon
	26th	Cruickshank	Rutherford	Holt	Murphy	Thomson E	Miller	Kemp	Milne	Fleming J	Fleming G	Traynor	Gordon
	29th	Cruickshank	Rutherford	Holt	Townsend	Thomson E	Miller	Kemp	Fleming G	Fleming J	Murphy	Traynor	Gordon

Great save Jim - Jim Cruickshank gets down to push away a powerful shot from a Kilmarnock forward. Davie Holt and Tommy Traynor are the other Hearts players.

Season 1967-68

Date		Opponents		Score	Crowd	Scorers
Aug 12th	LC	St Johnstone	h	1-2	8,000	Jensen
16th	LC	Stirling Albion	a	1-0	4,000	G. Fleming
19th	LC	Falkirk	a	2-0	4,000	Miller; Ford
26th	LC	St Johnstone	a	2-3	5,000	Traynor; Miller o.g.
30th	LC	Stirling Albion	h	4-1	4,000	MacDonald; Irvine; Traynor; Ford;
Sep 2nd	LC	Falkirk	h	3-1	5,500	Traynor; Smith o.g.; G. Fleming
9th	L	Hibernian	h	1-4	22,000	Traynor
16th	L	Dunfermline	a	3-1	8,000	Irvine; J. Fleming; Ford
23rd	L	Dundee	h	1-0	10,000	Ford
30th	L	Rangers	a	1-1	30,000	G. Fleming
Oct 7th	L	Clyde	h	2-3	9,000	Miller 2 (1 pen)
14th	L	Raith Rovers	a	4-2	9,000	Traynor; Ford; Jensen 2
21st	L	Aberdeen	h	2-1	10,500	Jensen; Ford
28th	L	Motherwell	a	5-2	5,300	Townsend; Anderson; Jensen; J. Fleming; Ford
Nov 4th	L	Falkirk	h	1-0	9,000	Jensen
11th	L	Dundee United	h	1-0	8,500	G. Fleming
18th	L	Partick Thistle	a	3-3	9,000	J. Fleming; Ford; G. Fleming
25th	L	St Johnstone	h	1-1	9,000	Miller
Dec 2nd	L	Kilmarnock	a	2-3	6,000	Anderson 2
9th	L	Celtic	a	1-3	35,000	J. Fleming
16th	L	Airdrie	h	3-1	6,500	G. Fleming; J. Fleming; Kemp
23rd	L	Stirling Albion	a	4-1	4,000	Irvine 2; Kemp; Traynor
30th	L	Morton	h	3-0	10,000	Traynor 2; Anderson
Jan 1st	L	Hibernian	a	0-1		-
2nd	L	Dunfermline	h	1-2	16,000	Irvine
13th	L	Rangers	h	2-3	36,000	Irvine; Ford
20th	L	Clyde	a	3-6	5,000	Kemp 2; Irvine
27th	SC1	Brechin City	h	4-1	8,487	Jensen; Ford; G. Fleming; Anderson
Feb 10th	L	Aberdeen	a	0-2	12,000	-
17th	SC2	Dundee United	a	6-5	9,021	Ford; Moller 2; E. Thomson; Miller (pen); Irvine
28th	L	Motherwell	h	3-2	10,000	Irvine; E. Thomson; Moller
Mar 2nd	L	Falkirk	a	1-4	6,000	Moller
4th	L	Raith Rovers	h	0-2	6,200	-
9th	SCQ	Rangers	a	1-1	57,521	Irvine
13th	SCQR	Rangers	h	1-0	44,094	Ford
16th	L	Partick Thistle	h	0-1	7,000	-
20th	L	Dundee United	a	1-2	5,000	Moller
23rd	L	St Johnstone	a	2-3	4,000	Ford; G. Fleming
30th	SCS	Morton	Hamp	1-1	22,569	Jensen
Apr 3rd	SCSR	Morton	Hamp	2-1*	11,565	Miller; Jensen (pen)
6th	L	Celtic	h	0-2	27,000	-
10th	L	Kilmarnock	h	1-0	6,000	Miller (pen)
13th	L	Airdrie	a	2-2	4,000	Ford; Traynor
17th	L	Dundee	a	0-1	8,000	-
20th	L	Stirling Albion	h	2-1	6,000	Ford 2
27th	SCF	Dunfermline	Hamp	1-3	56,365	Lunn o.g.
29th	L	Morton	a	0-1	5,000	-

* a.e.t., 1-1 after 90 mts. Cup Cash v. Brechin £1,454, Rangers (h) £10, 042, Morton £5,588

George Fleming - an industrious and skilful midfielder.

The Record		
League	-	12th Place, Division One.
League Cup	-	Qualifying stages only
Scottish Cup	-	Runners-up
Top Scorer	-	Donald Ford (16 goals)
Av. Home Gate	-	12,300
Players used	-	22
Sent off	-	None

Appearances

	League	L/Cup	S/Cup	Total
George Miller	31 (4)	6 (1)	7 (2)	44 (7)
Donald Ford	29 (11)	6 (2)	6 (3)	41 (16)
Ian Sneddon	31	3	7	41
Arthur Thomson	30	0	6	36
Tommy Traynor	24 (6)	5 (3)	7	36+2s (9)
Alan Anderson	22 (4)	6	4 (1)	32+2s (5)
Jim Irvine	23 (7)	2 (1)	7 (2)	32+1s (10)
Jim Townsend	21 (1)	3	6	30 (1)
Jim Cruickshank	20	3	5	28
Arthur Mann	21	0	7	28
George Fleming	19 (5)	5 (2)	1 (1)	25+11s (8)
Davie Holt	18	6	0	24+1s
Jim Fleming	20 (5)	2	0	22+4s (5)
Raold Jensen	15 (5)	1 (1)	6 (3)	22 (9)
Kenny Garland	14	3	2	19
Eddie Thomson	9 (1)	3	4 (1)	16+1s (2)
Alan MacDonald	7	5 (1)	0	12 (1)
Rene Moller	8 (3)	0	2 (2)	10+2s (5)
Bobby Kemp	7 (4)	2	0	9+1s (4)
Willie Hamilton	3	5	0	8+1s
Andy Milne	1	0	0	1
Bobby Elgin	1	0	0	1

Scottish League Division One

		Home			Away			Goals	
	P	W	D	L	W	D	L	F A	PTS
Celtic	34	14	3	0	16	0	1	106-24	63
Rangers	34	14	2	1	14	3	0	93-34	61
Hibernian	34	12	2	3	8	3	6	67-49	45
Dunfermline	34	9	1	7	8	4	5	64-41	39
Aberdeen	34	11	1	5	5	4	8	65-48	37
Morton	36	10	4	3	5	2	10	57-53	36
Kilmarnock	34	9	4	4	4	4	9	59-57	34
Clyde	34	9	3	5	6	1	10	55-55	34
Dundee	34	8	2	7	5	5	7	62-59	33
Partick Thistle	34	6	5	6	6	2	9	51-67	31
Dundee United	34	7	7	3	3	4	10	53-72	31
Hearts	**34**	**9**	**1**	**7**	**4**	**3**	**10**	**56-61**	**30**
Airdrie	34	7	5	5	3	4	10	45-58	29
St Johnstone	34	6	2	9	4	5	8	43-52	27
Falkirk	34	3	6	8	4	6	7	36-45	26
Raith Rovers	34	5	4	8	4	3	10	58-86	25
Motherwell	34	4	3	10	2	4	11	40-66	19
Stirling Albion	34	4	3	10	0	1	16	29-105	12

League Cup Section

	P	W	D	L	F A	PTS
St Johnstone	6	4	1	1	10-5	9
Hearts	**6**	**4**	**0**	**2**	**13-7**	**8**
Stirling Albion	6	2	1	3	6-8	5
Falkirk	6	0	2	4	2-11	2

Heart of Midlothian F.C. Line-Ups 1967-68

	1	2	3	4	5	6	7	8	9	10	11	12
Aug 12th	Cruickshank	Thomson E	Holt	Townsend	Anderson	Miller	Jensen	Fleming G	Ford	Traynor	Kemp	Clunie
16th	Garland	Thomson E	MacDonald	Anderson	Holt	Townsend	Miller	Fleming G	Ford	Hamilton	Kemp	Milne
19th	Garland	Thomson E	Holt	MacDonald	Anderson	Miller	Fleming G	Townsend	Ford	Hamilton	Traynor	Fleming J (8)
26th	Garland	Sneddon	Holt	MacDonald	Anderson	Miller	Fleming G	Fleming J	Ford	Hamilton	Traynor	Irvine (8)
30th	Cruickshank	Sneddon	Holt	MacDonald	Anderson	Miller	Fleming J	Hamilton	Ford	Irvine	Traynor	Fleming G
Sep 2nd	Cruickshank	Sneddon	Holt	MacDonald	Anderson	Miller	Fleming G	Hamilton	Ford	Irvine	Traynor	Thomson E
9th	Cruickshank	Sneddon	Holt	MacDonald	Anderson	Miller	Fleming G	Hamilton	Ford	Irvine	Traynor	Fleming J
16th	Garland	Sneddon	Holt	MacDonald	Thomson A	Miller	Fleming J	Townsend	Ford	Irvine	Traynor	Fleming G (3)
23rd	Garland	Sneddon	Holt	MacDonald	Thomson A	Miller	Fleming J	Townsend	Ford	Irvine	Traynor	Fleming G
30th	Garland	Sneddon	Holt	MacDonald	Thomson A	Miller	Fleming J	Townsend	Ford	Irvine	Traynor	Fleming G (7)
Oct 7th	Garland	Sneddon	Holt	MacDonald	Thomson A	Miller	Fleming J	Townsend	Ford	Irvine	Traynor	Fleming G (11)
14th	Garland	Sneddon	Holt	MacDonald	Thomson A	Miller	Jensen	Townsend	Ford	Fleming J	Traynor	Fleming G (10)
21st	Garland	Sneddon	Holt	MacDonald	Thomson A	Miller	Jensen	Townsend	Ford	Irvine	Traynor	Fleming G (11)
28th	Garland	Sneddon	Holt	Anderson	Thomson A	Miller	Jensen	Townsend	Ford	Fleming J	Fleming G	Traynor (11)
Nov 4th	Garland	Sneddon	Holt	Anderson	Thomson A	Miller	Jensen	Townsend	Ford	Fleming J	Fleming G	Traynor
11th	Garland	Sneddon	Holt	Anderson	Thomson A	Miller	Jensen	Townsend	Ford	Fleming J	Fleming G	Traynor
18th	Cruickshank	Sneddon	Holt	Anderson	Thomson A	Miller	Jensen	Townsend	Ford	Fleming J	Fleming G	Traynor
25th	Cruickshank	Sneddon	Holt	Anderson	Thomson A	Miller	Jensen	Townsend	Ford	Fleming J	Fleming G	Traynor (8)
Dec 2nd	Cruickshank	Sneddon	Mann	Anderson	Thomson A	Miller	Jensen	Fleming G	Ford	Fleming J	Traynor	Kemp
9th	Cruickshank	Sneddon	Mann	Anderson	Thomson A	Miller	Jensen	Fleming G	Ford	Fleming J	Traynor	Kemp (7)
16th	Garland	Sneddon	Mann	Anderson	Thomson A	Miller	Kemp	Jensen	Ford	Fleming J	Traynor	Fleming G (9)
23rd	Garland	Sneddon	Mann	Anderson	Thomson A	Miller	Kemp	Fleming G	Fleming J	Irvine	Traynor	Hamilton
30th	Cruickshank	Sneddon	Mann	Anderson	Thomson A	Miller	Kemp	Fleming G	Fleming J	Irvine	Traynor	Hamilton (7)
Jan 1st	Cruickshank	Holt	Mann	Anderson	Thomson A	Miller	Hamilton	Fleming G	Fleming J	Irvine	Traynor	Kemp
2nd	Cruickshank	Holt	Mann	Anderson	Thomson A	Miller	Jensen	Fleming G	Fleming J	Irvine	Traynor	Hamilton
13th	Cruickshank	Sneddon	Mann	Anderson	Thomson A	Miller	Ford	Fleming G	Fleming J	Irvine	Kemp	McDonald
20th	Cruickshank	Sneddon	Mann	Thomson E	Thomson A	Anderson	Jensen	Hamilton	Ford	Irvine	Kemp	Fleming J (8)
27th	Garland	Sneddon	Mann	Anderson	Thomson A	Miller	Jensen	Fleming G	Ford	Irvine	Traynor	Thomson E (7)
Feb 10th	Garland	Sneddon	Mann	Thomson E	Thomson A	Miller	Ford	Townsend	Moller	Irvine	Traynor	Fleming G (9)
17th	Garland	Sneddon	Mann	Thomson E	Thomson A	Miller	Ford	Townsend	Moller	Irvine	Traynor	Fleming G (8)
28th	Garland	Sneddon	Mann	Thomson E	Thomson A	Miller	Ford	Townsend	Moller	Irvine	Traynor	Fleming J (11)
Mar 2nd	Garland	Sneddon	Mann	Thomson E	Thomson A	Miller	Ford	Townsend	Moller	Irvine	Kemp	Fleming G
4th	Cruickshank	Thomson E	Mann	Anderson	Thomson A	Miller	Fleming G	Townsend	Moller	Ford	Traynor	Fleming J
9th	Cruickshank	Sneddon	Mann	Thomson E	Thomson A	Miller	Jensen	Townsend	Moller	Irvine	Traynor	Ford
13th	Cruickshank	Sneddon	Mann	Thomson E	Anderson	Miller	Jensen	Townsend	Ford	Irvine	Traynor	Fleming G (4)
16th	Cruickshank	Sneddon	Mann	Thomson E	Anderson	Miller	Jensen	Townsend	Ford	Irvine	Traynor	Fleming G (7)
20th	Cruickshank	Sneddon	Holt	Miller	Anderson	Mann	Ford	Townsend	Moller	Irvine	Kemp	Fleming G
23rd	Cruickshank	Sneddon	Mann	Thomson E	Anderson	Miller	Ford	Townsend	Moller	Irvine	Fleming G	Holt (4)
30th	Cruickshank	Sneddon	Mann	Thomson E	Thomson A	Miller	Jensen	Townsend	Ford	Irvine	Traynor	Fleming G
Apr 3rd	Cruickshank	Sneddon	Mann	Anderson	Thomson A	Miller	Jensen	Townsend	Ford	Irvine	Traynor	Moller (11)
6th	Cruickshank	Sneddon	Mann	Anderson	Thomson A	Miller	Fleming J	Fleming G	Ford	Irvine	Traynor	Moller
10th	Cruickshank	Sneddon	Mann	Anderson	Thomson A	Miller	Traynor	Moller	Ford	Irvine	Fleming G	Fleming J (8)
13th	Cruickshank	Sneddon	Holt	Townsend	Thomson A	Miller	Traynor	Milne	Ford	Mann	Fleming G	Anderson (11)
17th	Cruickshank	Sneddon	Holt	Townsend	Thomson A	Miller	Jensen	Irvine	Ford	Mann	Traynor	Anderson (10)
20th	Cruickshank	Sneddon	Holt	Thomson E	Thomson A	Anderson	Jensen	Townsend	Ford	Irvine	Traynor	Fleming G (8)
27th	Cruickshank	Sneddon	Mann	Anderson	Thomson A	Miller	Jensen	Townsend	Ford	Irvine	Traynor	Moller (7)
29th	Cruickshank	Sneddon	Mann	Thomson E	Thomson A	Fleming G	Traynor	Fleming J	Moller	Irvine	Elgin	Anderson

Action stations - Ian Sneddon and George Miller watch Kenny Garland tip over a shot in the thrill-a-minute Scottish Cup tie against Dundee United at Tannadice. Hearts emerged 6-5 winners after a veritable feast of goals. DC Thomson

Season 1968-69

Date		Opponents		Score	Crowd	Scorers
Aug 10th	LC	Airdrie	a	3-2	5,500	Townsend; G. Fleming; Goodwin o.g.
14th	LC	Dundee	h	2-1	11,000	Ford 2
17th	LC	Kilmarnock	a	3-3	7,000	Ford 2; Moller
24th	LC	Airdrie	h	0-2	12,000	-
28th	LC	Dundee	a	0-4	8,300	-
31st	LC	Kilmarnock	h	0-0	8,000	-
Sep 7th	L	Hibernian	a	3-1	24,110	J. Fleming; G. Fleming; Moller
14th	L	Dunfermline	h	3-1	13,000	J. Fleming; Moller; Hamilton
21st	L	Airdrie	a	1-2	5,000	Hamilton
28th	L	Rangers	h	1-1	33,000	Ford
Oct 5th	L	Aberdeen	a	2-1	12,000	J. Fleming; Hamilton
12th	L	Celtic	h	0-1	30,000	-
19th	L	Falkirk	a	3-1	6,000	Ford; Hamilton 2
26th	L	Dundee	a	1-3	8,000	Traynor
Nov 2nd	L	Kilmarnock	h	0-1	8,500	-
9th	L	Partick Thistle	h	2-0	7,000	Jensen; Hamilton
16th	L	Dundee United	a	2-4	7,000	Veitch; Jensen
23rd	L	St Johnstone	h	2-2	7,000	G. Fleming 2
30th	L	Morton	a	2-0	5,000	Gordon; Traynor
Dec 7th	L	Clyde	h	2-3	8,000	Gordon 2
14th	L	Raith Rovers	h	1-0	7,000	Gordon
21st	L	Arbroath	a	3-2	3,000	G. Fleming; Traynor; Gordon
28th	L	St Mirren	a	1-1	8,000	J. Fleming
Jan 1st	L	Hibernian	h	0-0	30,000	-
2nd	L	Dunfermline	a	2-4	14,000	Ford; Gordon
4th	L	Airdrie	h	1-1	9,000	Jensen
11th	L	Rangers	a	0-2	40,000	-
18th	L	Aberdeen	h	3-2	8,000	Ford; Anderson; Hamilton
25th	SC1	Dundee	a	2-1	14,000	G. Fleming; Traynor
Feb 1st	L	Celtic	a	0-5	37,000	-
22nd	L	Kilmarnock	a	0-1	7,000	-
24th	SC2	Rangers	a	0-2	48,000	-
Mar 1st	L	Partick Thistle	a	1-5	3,300	Anderson
8th	L	Dundee United	h	1-0	7,000	Traynor
12th	L	Dundee	h	2-2	6,000	Traynor; Jensen
15th	L	St Johnstone	a	1-2	5,100	Jensen
24th	L	Morton	h	2-2	5,000	Jensen; Irvine
29th	L	Clyde	a	1-0	3,000	G. Fleming
Apr 2nd	L	Falkirk	h	2-1	6,000	Anderson; Veitch
5th	L	Raith Rovers	a	3-0	5,000	Irvine; Ford; Traynor
12th	L	Arbroath	h	2-2	6,500	Irvine; Ford
19th	L	St Mirren	h	2-1	8,000	MacDonald; Jensen

Alan Anderson - a pillar of strength in the Hearts defence.

The Record

League	-	Eighth Place, Division One.
League Cup	-	Qualifying stages only
Scottish Cup	-	Second round.
Top Scorer	-	Donald Ford (10 goals).
Av. Home Gate	-	11, 600
Players used	-	25
Sent Off	-	Four

Appearances

	League	L/Cup	S/Cup	Total
Eddie Thomson	34	6	2	42
Jim Cruickshank	31	5	2	38
George Fleming	30 (5)	5 (1)	2 (1)	37+1s (7)
Tommy Traynor	28 (6)	4	2 (1)	34+1s (7)
Donald Ford	23 (6)	6 (4)	2	31+3s (10)
Davie Holt	24	0	2	26
Raold Jensen	22 (7)	2	2	26 (7)
Alan MacDonald	20 (1)	2	0	22+4s (1)
Alan Anderson	19 (3)	0	2	21+2s (3)
Willie Hamilton	14 (7)	5	1	20+4s (7)
Arthur Thomson	14	4	2	20
Rene Moller	13 (2)	5 (1)	0	18
Arthur Mann	11	6	0	17
Jim Townsend	11	6 (1)	0	17 (1)
Dave Clunie	15	1	0	16 (3)
Alan Gordon	15 (6)	0	0	15 (6)
Billy McAlpine	12	0	2	14
Jim Fleming	13 (4)	0	1	14+2s (4)
Ian Sneddon	9	2	0	11
Tommy Veitch	6 (2)	0	0	6+4s (2)
Jim Irvine	5 (3)	0	0	5 (3)
George Miller	0	5	0	5+4s
Kenny Garland	3	1	0	4
Jim Brown	1	0	0	1+1s
Ernie Winchester	1	0	0	1
Roy Turnbull	0	0	0	0+1s
Bobby Elgin	0	1	0	1

Scottish League Division One

		Home			Away			Goals	
	P	W	D	L	W	D	L	F A	PTS
Celtic	34	12	3	2	11	5	1	89-32	54
Rangers	34	13	3	1	8	4	5	81-32	49
Dunfermline	34	12	4	1	7	3	7	63-45	45
Kilmarnock	34	10	6	1	5	8	4	50-32	44
Dundee United	34	12	3	2	5	6	6	61-49	43
St Johnstone	34	11	2	4	5	3	9	66-59	37
Airdrie	34	10	5	2	3	6	8	46-44	37
Hearts	**34**	**7**	**7**	**3**	**7**	**1**	**9**	**52-54**	**36**
Dundee	34	4	8	5	6	4	7	47-48	32
Morton	34	8	5	4	4	3	10	58-68	32
St Mirren	34	7	4	6	4	6	7	40-54	32
Hibernian	34	9	2	6	3	5	9	60-59	31
Clyde	34	6	7	4	3	6	8	35-50	31
Partick Thistle	34	7	3	7	2	7	8	39-53	28
Aberdeen	34	6	5	6	3	3	11	50-59	26
Raith Rovers	34	6	2	9	2	3	12	45-67	21
Falkirk	34	4	6	7	1	2	14	33-69	18
Arbroath	34	4	3	10	1	3	13	41-102	16

League Cup Section

	P	W	D	L	F A	PTS
Dundee	6	3	2	1	15- 5	8
Airdrie	6	3	1	2	10- 7	7
Hearts	**6**	**2**	**2**	**2**	**8-12**	**6**
Kilmarnock	6	0	3	3	5-14	3

Heart of Midlothian F.C. Line-Ups 1968-69

Date	1	2	3	4	5	6	7	8	9	10	11	12
Aug 10th	Cruickshank	Thomson E	Mann	Townsend	Thomson A	Miller	Fleming G	Hamilton	Ford	Moller	Traynor	MacDonald (8)
14th	Cruickshank	Thomson E	Mann	Townsend	Thomson A	Miller	Traynor	Hamilton	Ford	Moller	Fleming G	MacDonald
17th	Cruickshank	Thomson E	Mann	Townsend	Thomson A	Miller	Jensen	Hamilton	Ford	Moller	Fleming G	MacDonald (7)
24th	Garland	Thomson E	Mann	Townsend	Thomson A	Miller	Jensen	Hamilton	Ford	MacDonald	Moller	Fleming J
28th	Cruickshank	Sneddon	Mann	Townsend	Thomson E	Miller	Traynor	Hamilton	Ford	Moller	Fleming G	MacDonald
31st	Cruickshank	Sneddon	Mann	Townsend	Thomson E	Clunie	Traynor	MacDonald	Ford	Fleming G	Elgin	Fleming J
Sep 7th	Cruickshank	Sneddon	Mann	Townsend	Thomson E	MacDonald	Traynor	Hamilton	Fleming J	Moller	Fleming G	Jensen
14th	Cruickshank	Sneddon	Mann	Townsend	Thomson E	MacDonald	Traynor	Hamilton	Fleming J	Moller	Fleming G	Ford
21st	Cruickshank	Sneddon	Mann	Townsend	Thomson E	Veitch	Traynor	Hamilton	Fleming J	Moller	Fleming G	Ford (10)
28th	Cruickshank	Sneddon	Mann	Townsend	Thomson E	MacDonald	Traynor	Hamilton	Fleming J	Moller	Fleming G	Ford (7)
Oct 5th	Cruickshank	Holt	Mann	Townsend	Thomson E	MacDonald	Ford	Hamilton	Fleming J	Moller	Fleming G	Miller (9)
12th	Cruickshank	Sneddon	Mann	Townsend	Thomson E	MacDonald	Ford	Traynor	Moller	Hamilton	Fleming G	Miller (11)
19th	Cruickshank	Sneddon	Mann	Anderson	Thomson E	MacDonald	Jensen	Townsend	Ford	Hamilton	Traynor	Miller (8)
26th	Cruickshank	Holt	Mann	MacDonald	Thomson E	Gordon	Jensen	Fleming G	Ford	Hamilton	Traynor	Anderson (6)
Nov 2nd	Cruickshank	Holt	Mann	Veitch	Thomson E	MacDonald	Traynor	Hamilton	Ford	Moller	Fleming G	Anderson (10)
9th	Cruickshank	Holt	Mann	Veitch	Thomson E	Thomson A	Ford	Hamilton	Moller	Fleming G	Jensen	Turnbull (9)
16th	Cruickshank	Holt	Mann	Veitch	Thomson E	Thomson A	Fleming G	Hamilton	Gordon	Ford	Jensen*	Miller (8)
23rd	Cruickshank	Holt	McAlpine	Veitch	Thomson E	Thomson A	Moller	Ford	Gordon	Fleming G	Jensen	Traynor (4)
30th	Cruickshank	Holt	McAlpine	MacDonald	Thomson E	Anderson	Traynor	Ford	Gordon	Fleming G	Jensen	Hamilton
Dec 7th	Cruickshank	Clunie	Holt	MacDonald	Thomson E	Anderson	Traynor	Ford	Gordon	Fleming G	Jensen	Hamilton (6)
14th	Cruickshank	Clunie	Holt	MacDonald	Thomson E	Thomson A	Ford	Fleming J	Gordon	Fleming G	Traynor	Elgin
21st	Cruickshank	Clunie	Holt	MacDonald	Thomson E	Thomson A	Ford	Fleming J	Gordon	Fleming G	Traynor	Hamilton (4)
28th	Cruickshank	Clunie	Holt	MacDonald	Thomson E	Thomson A	Ford	Fleming J	Gordon	Fleming G	Traynor	Hamilton
Jan 1st	Cruickshank	Clunie	Holt	Anderson	Thomson E	Thomson A	Jensen	Fleming J	Gordon	Fleming G	Traynor	Ford (7)
2nd	Cruickshank	Clunie	Holt	Anderson	Thomson E	Thomson A	Ford	Fleming J	Gordon	Fleming G	Traynor	Hamilton (4)
4th	Cruickshank	Holt	McAlpine	Thomson E	Thomson A	Brown	Traynor	Ford	Fleming J	Gordon	Jensen	Fleming G
11th	Cruickshank	Holt	McAlpine	Anderson	Thomson E	Thomson A	Traynor	Ford	Gordon	Fleming G	Moller	Hamilton (9)
18th	Cruickshank	Holt	McAlpine	Thomson A	Thomson E	Anderson	Fleming J	Hamilton	Ford	Fleming G	Jensen	Brown (11)
25th	Cruickshank	Holt	McAlpine	Anderson	Thomson E	Thomson A	Traynor	Hamilton	Ford	Fleming G	Jensen	MacDonald (8)
Feb 1st	Cruickshank	Holt	McAlpine	Anderson	Thomson E	Thomson A	Traynor	Hamilton	Ford	Fleming G	Jensen	MacDonald(10)
22nd	Cruickshank	Holt	McAlpine	Anderson	Thomson E	Thomson A	Traynor	MacDonald	Ford	Hamilton	Jensen	Fleming J (10)
24th	Cruickshank	Holt	McAlpine	Anderson	Thomson E	Thomson A	Traynor	Fleming J	Ford	Fleming G	Jensen	Veitch (10)
Mar 1st	Cruickshank	Holt	McAlpine	Anderson	Thomson E	Thomson A	Traynor	Townsend	Fleming J	Fleming G	Jensen	Ford
8th	Cruickshank	Clunie	McAlpine	Thomson E	Anderson	Sneddon	Traynor	Townsend	Gordon	Fleming G	Jensen	Ford (9)
12th	Cruickshank	Clunie	McAlpine	Thomson E	Anderson	Sneddon	Traynor	Townsend	Gordon	Fleming G	Jensen	Ford
15th	Cruickshank	Clunie	McAlpine	Thomson E	Anderson	Sneddon	Traynor	Townsend	Gordon	Fleming G	Jensen	Ford
24th	Cruickshank	Clunie	Holt	MacDonald	Thomson E	Anderson	Traynor	Fleming G	Moller	Irvine	Jensen	Murray N
29th	Cruickshank	Clunie	Holt	MacDonald	Thomson E	Anderson	Traynor	Fleming G	Moller	Irvine	Jensen	Ford
Apr 2nd	Garland	Clunie	Holt	MacDonald	Anderson	Thomson E	Traynor	Moller	Ford	Fleming G	Jensen	Veitch (10)
5th	Garland	Clunie	Holt	MacDonald	Anderson	Thomson E	Traynor	Irvine	Ford	Fleming G	Jensen	Veitch (5)
12th	Garland	Clunie	Holt	MacDonald	Anderson	Thomson E	Traynor	Irvine	Ford	Fleming G	Jensen	Veitch (10)
19th	Cruickshank	Clunie	McAlpine	Thomson E	Anderson	MacDonald	Ford	Veitch	Winchester	Irvine	Jensen	Fleming G (8)

How did that get there - Hearts defenders Eddie Thomson and Jim Cruickshank wonder what went wrong after Celtic effort lands in the net at Tynecastle.

DC Thomson

Season 1969-70

Date		Opponents		Score	Crowd	Scorers
Aug 9th	LC	Dundee United	a	3-2	11,000	Winchester 2; Clunie
13th	LC	St Mirren	h	0-0	10,500	-
16th	LC	Morton	h	0-1	11,500	-
20th	LC	St Mirren	a	0-1	3,500	-
23rd	LC	Dundee United	h	1-0	7,000	Winchester
27th	LC	Morton	a	2-0	9,000	Winchester; MacDonald
30th	L	Morton	h	0-1	9,000	-
Sep 3rd	L	Airdrie	a	2-1	5,000	Moller; Winchester
6th	L	St Johnstone	a	3-3	9,000	Brown; Traynor; Moller
13th	L	Kilmarnock	h	4-1	9,000	Jensen 2; Ford 2
20th	L	Dunfermline	a	0-1	9,000	-
27th	L	Hibernian	h	0-2	26,000	-
Oct 4th	L	St Mirren	a	0-0	5,500	-
11th	L	Motherwell	h	2-2	10,000	Lynch; Brown
18th	L	Ayr United	a	0-0	11,000	-
25th	L	Partick Thistle	h	1-1	7,500	Traynor
Nov 1st	L	Raith Rovers	h	3-2	6,500	Moller; MacDonald 2
8th	L	Celtic	a	2-0	35,000	Jensen; Ford
15th	L	Aberdeen	h	2-2	11,500	Moller; Ford
22nd	L	Dundee	a	0-2	5,500	-
Dec 6th	L	Rangers	h	1-2	27,000	Brown
13th	L	Morton	a	3-2	3,000	Fleming; Ford; Townsend
16th	L	Clyde	a	1-2	2,000	Townsend
20th	L	Airdrie	h	5-0	6,000	Clunie; Townsend; Traynor; Ford 2
27th	L	Dundee United	h	2-2	11,500	J. Cameron o.g.; Townsend
Jan 1st	L	Hibernian	a	0-0	36,500	-
3rd	L	Dunfermline	h	2-0	14,000	Murray; Ford
10th	L	Dundee United	a	3-2	9,000	Fleming 2; Lynch
17th	L	Kilmarnock	a	0-0	5,000	-
24th	SC1	Montrose	a	1-1	4,500	Fleming
28th	SC1R	Montrose	h	1-0	13,000	Fleming
31st	L	St Johnstone	h	0-0	10,000	-
Feb 7th	SC2	Kilmarnock	a	0-2	13,934	-
21st	L	St Mirren	h	1-0	8,500	Anderson
28th	L	Motherwell	a	2-0	8,000	Townsend; Moller
Mar 7th	L	Ayr United	h	3-0	10,000	Clunie 2 (pens); Anderson
14th	L	Partick Thistle	a	0-1	3,000	-
21st	L	Raith Rovers	a	3-0	4,500	Townsend 2; Traynor
25th	L	Rangers	a	2-3	14,000	Winchester; Irvine
28th	L	Celtic	h	0-0	26,000	-
Apr 4th	L	Aberdeen	a	1-0	10,000	Moller
11th	L	Clyde	h	1-1	7,500	Winchester
18th	L	Dundee	h	1-3	7,500	Moller

Cup Cash v. Killie £3,138

Eddie Thomson - Hearts skipper and Scotland Under-23 international.

The Record		
League	-	**Fourth Place, Division One.**
League Cup	-	**Qualifying stages only.**
Scottish Cup	-	**Second round**
Top Scorer	-	**Donald Ford (8 goals)**
Av. Home Gate	-	**12,200**
Players used	-	**23**
Sent off	-	**1**

Appearances

	League		L/Cup		S/Cup		Total	
Alan Anderson	34	(2)	6		3		43	(2)
Dave Clunie	34	(3)	6	(1)	3		43	(4)
Jim Cruickshank	29		6		3		38	
Peter Oliver	33		0		3		36	
Rene Moller	32	(7)	0		2		34	(7)
Donald Ford	24	(8)	6		3		33+5s	(8)
Jim Townsend	20	(7)	4		3		27+3s	(7)
George Fleming	19	(3)	3		3	(2)	25+5s	(5)
Eddie Thomson	23		0		2		25	
Jim Brown	20	(3)	0		2		22+2s	(3)
Tommy Veitch	18		2		2		22+5s	
Tommy Traynor	16	(4)	3		1		20+1s	(4)
Alan MacDonald	16	(2)	3		0		19+2s	(2)
Ernie Winchester	13	(3)	6	(4)	0		19+4s	(7)
Neil Murray	8	(1)	6	(1)	2		16	(2)
Andy Lynch	13	(2)	0		1		14	(2)
Ian Sneddon	4		6		0		10+1s	
Billy McAlpine	1		6		0		7	
Kenny Garland	5		0		0		5	
Jim Irvine	5	(1)	0		0		5+1s	(1)
Raold Jensen	5	(3)	0		0		5	(3)
Arthur Thomson	0		3		0		3	
Eric Carruthers	2		0		0		2	

Scottish League Division One

		Home			Away			Goals	
	P	W	D	L	W	D	L	F A	PTS
Celtic	34	12	2	3	15	1	1	96-33	57
Rangers	34	13	1	3	6	6	5	67-40	45
Hibernian	34	12	3	2	7	3	7	65-40	44
Hearts	**34**	**6**	**7**	**4**	**7**	**5**	**5**	**50-36**	**38**
Dundee United	34	10	3	4	6	3	8	62-64	38
Dundee	34	11	2	4	4	4	9	49-44	36
Kilmarnock	34	10	5	2	3	5	9	62-57	36
Aberdeen	34	6	6	5	8	1	8	55-45	35
Dunfermline	34	12	2	3	1	7	9	52-52	35
Morton	34	9	5	3	6	0	11	45-45	35
Motherwell	34	8	4	5	3	6	8	49-51	32
Airdrie	34	8	3	6	4	5	8	59-64	32
St Johnstone	34	9	4	4	2	5	10	50-62	31
Ayr United	34	10	3	4	2	3	12	37-52	30
St Mirren	34	6	5	6	2	4	11	39-54	25
Clyde	34	8	4	5	1	3	13	34-56	25
Raith Rovers	34	4	6	7	1	5	11	32-69	21
Partick Thistle	34	4	4	9	1	3	13	41-82	17

League Cup Section

	P	W	D	L	F A	PTS
Morton	6	3	1	2	9-6	7
Hearts	**6**	**3**	**1**	**2**	**6-4**	**7**
St Mirren	6	2	2	2	5-5	6
Dundee United	6	2	0	4	6-11	4

Heart of Midlothian F.C. Line-Ups 1969-70

		1	2	3	4	5	6	7	8	9	10	11	12
Aug	9th	Cruickshank	Sneddon	Anderson	Thomson A	McAlpine	Fleming	Townsend	Clunie	Winchester	Ford	Murray	Veitch
	13th	Cruickshank	Sneddon	McAlpine	Anderson	Thomson A	Clunie	Ford	Townsend	Winchester	Fleming	Murray	Veitch
	16th	Cruickshank	Sneddon	Anderson	Thomson A	McAlpine	Fleming	Townsend	Clunie	Winchester	Ford	Murray	Traynor (6)
	20th	Cruickshank	Sneddon	McAlpine	MacDonald	Anderson	Clunie	Murray	Veitch	Winchester	Ford	Traynor	Townsend (8)
	23rd	Cruickshank	Sneddon	McAlpine	Clunie	Anderson	MacDonald	Murray	Veitch	Winchester	Ford	Traynor	Townsend
	27th	Cruickshank	Sneddon	McAlpine	Clunie	Anderson	MacDonald	Murray	Townsend	Winchester	Ford	Traynor	Veitch
	30th	Cruickshank	Sneddon	McAlpine	Clunie	Anderson	MacDonald	Murray	Townsend	Winchester	Ford	Moller	Veitch (10)
Sep	3rd	Cruickshank	Clunie	Oliver	Veitch	Anderson	MacDonald	Murray	Moller	Winchester	Brown	Traynor	Fleming
	6th	Cruickshank	Clunie	Oliver	Veitch	Anderson	MacDonald	Murray	Moller	Winchester	Brown	Traynor	Fleming (7)
	13th	Cruickshank	Clunie	Oliver	Veitch	Anderson	MacDonald	Ford	Moller	Winchester	Brown	Jensen	Fleming
	20th	Cruickshank	Clunie	Oliver	Veitch	Anderson	MacDonald	Fleming	Ford	Winchester	Brown	Moller	Townsend
	27th	Cruickshank	Clunie	Oliver	Veitch	Anderson	MacDonald	Ford	Moller	Winchester	Brown	Traynor	Fleming
Oct	4th	Cruickshank	Clunie	Oliver	Veitch	Anderson	MacDonald	Murray	Townsend	Ford	Brown	Moller	Fleming (4)
	11th	Cruickshank	Clunie	Oliver	Brown	Anderson	MacDonald	Murray	Moller	Ford	Fleming	Lynch	Townsend
	18th	Cruickshank	Clunie	Oliver	Brown	Anderson	MacDonald	Murray	Moller	Ford	Fleming	Lynch	Townsend (8)
	25th	Cruickshank	Clunie	Oliver	MacDonald	Anderson	Thomson E	Traynor	Moller	Ford	Brown	Lynch	Fleming
Nov	1st	Cruickshank	Clunie	Oliver	MacDonald	Anderson	Thomson E	Jensen	Moller	Ford	Brown	Lynch	Fleming
	8th	Cruickshank	Clunie	Oliver	McDonald	Anderson	Thomson E	Jensen	Moller	Ford	Brown	Lynch	Fleming (10)
	15th	Cruickshank	Clunie	Oliver	McDonald	Anderson	Thomson E	Jensen	Moller	Ford	Brown	Murray	Fleming (11)
	22nd	Cruickshank	Clunie	Oliver	McDonald	Anderson	Thomson E	Jensen	Moller	Ford	Fleming	Lynch	Veitch (7)
Dec	6th	Cruickshank	Clunie	Oliver	McDonald	Anderson	Thomson E	Ford	Fleming	Winchester	Brown	Moller	Townsend(9)
	13th	Garland	Clunie	Oliver	Brown	Anderson	Thomson E	Moller	Townsend	Ford	Fleming	Lynch	MacDonald(4)
	16th	Garland	Clunie	Oliver	Townsend	Anderson	Thomson E	Ford	MacDonald	Winchester	Fleming	Moller	Brown (8)
	20th	Garland	Clunie	Oliver	Brown	Anderson	Thomson E	Traynor	Townsend	Ford	Fleming	Moller	MacDonald(4)
	27th	Garland	Clunie	Oliver	Brown	Anderson	Thomson E	Moller	Townsend	Ford	Fleming	Lynch	Winchester (11)
Jan	1st	Cruickshank	Clunie	Oliver	Brown	Anderson	Thomson E	Moller	Townsend	Ford	Fleming	Lynch	Veitch
	3rd	Cruickshank	Clunie	Oliver	Brown	Anderson	Thomson E	Murray	Townsend	Ford	Fleming	Lynch	Veitch
	10th	Cruickshank	Clunie	Oliver	Brown	Anderson	Thomson E	Moller	Townsend	Ford	Fleming	Lynch	Veitch (8)
	17th	Cruickshank	Clunie	Oliver	Brown	Anderson	Veitch	Moller	Townsend	Ford	Fleming	Lynch	Sneddon (4)
	24th	Cruickshank	Clunie	Oliver	Brown	Anderson	Veitch	Moller	Townsend	Ford	Fleming	Murray	Winchester (11)
	28th	Cruickshank	Clunie	Oliver	Brown	Anderson	Thomson E	Moller	Townsend	Ford	Fleming	Murray	Veitch (6)
	31st	Cruickshank	Clunie	Oliver	Veitch	Anderson	Thomson E	Traynor	Townsend	Ford	Fleming	Lynch	Winchester
Feb	7th	Cruickshank	Clunie	Oliver	Veitch	Anderson	Thomson E	Traynor	Townsend	Ford	Fleming	Lynch	Brown (11)
	21st	Cruickshank	Clunie	Oliver	Veitch	Anderson	Thomson E	Traynor	Townsend	Carruthers	Fleming	Moller	Ford (10)
	28th	Cruickshank	Clunie	Oliver	Veitch	Anderson	Thomson E	Traynor	Townsend	Carruthers	Sneddon	Moller	Ford (9)
Mar	7th	Cruickshank	Clunie	Oliver	Veitch	Anderson	Thomson E	Traynor	Townsend	Ford	Sneddon	Moller	Brown
	14th	Cruickshank	Clunie	Oliver	Sneddon	Anderson	Veitch	Traynor	Townsend	Ford	Fleming	Moller	Winchester
	21st	Cruickshank	Clunie	Oliver	Veitch	Anderson	Thomson E	Traynor	Townsend	Winchester	Fleming	Moller	Irvine (9)
	25th	Cruickshank	Clunie	Oliver	Veitch	Anderson	Thomson E	Traynor	Townsend	Irvine	Fleming	Moller	Winchester (10)
	28th	Cruickshank	Clunie	Oliver	Veitch	Anderson	Thomson E	Traynor	Winchester	Irvine	Townsend*	Moller	Ford (11)
Apr	4th	Cruickshank	Clunie	Oliver	Veitch	Anderson	Thomson E	Traynor	Winchester	Irvine	Townsend	Moller	Ford (10)
	11th	Cruickshank	Clunie	Oliver	Veitch	Anderson	Thomson E	Traynor	Winchester	Irvine	Fleming	Moller	Ford (11)
	18th	Garland	Clunie	Oliver	Veitch	Anderson	Thomson E	Traynor	Townsend	Irvine	Winchester	Moller	Fleming (4)

Cracker - Donald Ford and Kilmarnock's Jim McLean watch as Raold Jensen blasts in an unstoppable shot for Hearts opening goal against Kilmarnock at Tynecastle.

Season 1970-71

Date			Opponents		Score	Crowd	Scorers
Aug	8th	LC	Celtic	h	1-2	34,000	Hegarty
	12th	LC	Dundee United	a	1-2	7,000	Wood
	15th	LC	Clyde	h	1-2	9,000	Ford
	19th	LC	Dundee United	h	0-0	8,000	-
	22nd	LC	Celtic	a	2-4	40,000	Hegarty 2
	26th	LC	Clyde	a	5-1	2,000	Lynch 2; Ford; Clunie; Jensen;
	29th	L	St Johnstone	h	1-3	11,000	Clunie
Sep	5th	L	Hibernian	a	0-0	24,000	-
	12th	L	Dunfermline	h	3-0	9,500	Hegarty 2; Jensen
	15th	TC1	Burnley	a	1-3	10,106	Fleming
	19th	L	Clyde	a	0-1	2,500	-
	26th	L	Airdrie	h	5-2	10,500	Lynch 2; Brown 2; Hegarty
	30th	TC1	Burnley	h	4-1 (5-4)	15,861	Brown; Hegarty; Lynch; Waldron o.g.
Oct	3rd	L	Kilmarnock	a	0-2	5,500	-
	10th	L	Rangers	h	0-1	32,500	-
	17th	L	Dundee	a	0-1	6,000	-
	19th	TCQ	Airdrie	a	5-0	11,000	Ford 4; Young
	28th	L	Celtic	a	2-3	18,000	Ford 2
Nov	4th	TCQ	Airdrie	h	2-3 (7-3)	7,203	Young; Ford
	7th	L	St Mirren	a	1-0	5,000	Fleming
	11th	L	Falkirk	h	1-1	8,000	Anderson
	14th	L	Dundee United	h	1-0	9,000	Anderson
	21st	L	Aberdeen	a	0-1	13,500	-
	28th	L	Ayr United	h	2-1	8,500	Ford; Brown
Dec	5th	L	Morton	h	2-2	10,000	Winchester; Anderson
	12th	L	Motherwell	a	2-1	6,000	Ford 2
	16th	TCS	Motherwell	h	1-1	21,301	Ford
	19th	L	Cowdenbeath	h	1-0	7,000	Ford
	26th	L	St Johnstone	a	1-2	3,000	Lynch
Jan	1st	L	Hibernian	h	0-0	28,000	-
	9th	L	Clyde	h	3-1	8,500	Brown; Ford; Lynch
	16th	L	Airdrie	a	0-0	5,000	-
	23rd	SC1	Stranraer	h	3-0	9,000	Ford 2; Lynch
	30th	L	Kilmarnock	h	2-0	9,500	Ford; Hegarty
Feb	6th	L	Rangers	a	0-1	29,500	-
	13th	SC2	Hibernian	h	1-2	30,000	Hegarty
	20th	L	Dundee	h	0-0	8,000	-
	27th	L	Celtic	h	1-1	24,000	Carruthers
Mar	3rd	TCS	Motherwell	a	2-1* (3-2)	25,259	Fleming; Ford
	6th	L	Falkirk	a	4-2	7,500	Miller o.g.; Fleming 3
	13th	L	St Mirren	h	1-0	8,500	Fleming
	20th	L	Dundee United	a	1-4	5,000	Ford
	24th	L	Dunfermline	a	2-1	7,000	Carruthers; Fleming
	27th	L	Aberdeen	h	1-3	13,500	Ford
Apr	3rd	L	Ayr United	a	0-1	6,000	-
	10th	L	Morton	a	0-3	4,500	-
	14th	TCF	Wolves	h	1-3	25,027	Ford
	17th	L	Motherwell	h	0-1	5,500	-
	24th	L	Cowdenbeath	a	4-0	1,500	Fleming; Laing; Townsend; Ford
May	3rd	TCF	Wolves	a	1-0 (2-3)	28,462	Fleming

* aet, 1-1 after 90 mts.

Ernie Winchester - a powerful figure in the Hearts front line.

The Record		
League	-	11th Place, Division One.
League Cup	-	Qualifying stages only
Scottish Cup	-	Second round
Texaco Cup	-	Runners up
Top Scorer	-	Donald Ford (23 goals)
Av. Home Gate	-	12,400
Players used	-	22
Sent off	-	One

Appearances

	League	L/Cup	S/Cup	T/Cup	Total
Jim Cruickshank	32	6	2	8	48
Donald Ford	32 (11)	6 (2)	2 (2)	8 (8)	48 (23)
Eddie Thomson	34	6	1	7	48
Alan Anderson	34 (3)	2	2	8	46 (3)
Jim Brown	33 (4)	3	2	7 (1)	45 (5)
Dave Clunie	29 (1)	6 (1)	2	6	43 (2)
Jim Townsend	29 (1)	0	2	8	39 (1)
George Fleming	26 (7)	3	2	5 (3)	36+6s (10)
Peter Oliver	20	6	0	5	31
Andy Lynch	20 (4)	4 (2)	1 (1)	3 (1)	28+1s (8)
Wilson Wood	15	3 (1)	0	6	24 (1)
Kevin Hegarty	13 (4)	5 (3)	2 (1)	2 (1)	22+4s (9)
Roy Kay	13	0	2	3	18
Eric Carruthers	10 (2)	1	0	3	14 (2)
Ian Sneddon	7	5	0	2	14
Drew Young	9	0	0	3 (2)	12+7s (2)
Tommy Veitch	3	5	1	1	10+1s
Raold Jensen	5 (1)	4 (1)	0	0	9 (2)
Ernie Winchester	5 (1)	1	1	1	8+7s (1)
Kenny Garland	2	0	0	0	2
Neil Murray	2	0	0	0	2+1s
Brian Laing	1 (1)	0	0	1	2 (1)
Billy McAlpine	0	0	0	1	1
Joe Morgan	0	0	0	0	0+1s

Scottish League Division One

	P	Home W	D	L	Away W	D	L	Goals F-A	PTS
Celtic	34	15	1	1	11	5	2	89-23	56
Aberdeen	34	11	6	0	13	0	4	68-18	54
St Johnstone	34	10	3	4	9	3	5	59-44	44
Rangers	34	10	5	2	6	4	7	58-34	41
Dundee	34	9	2	6	5	8	4	53-45	38
Dundee United	34	8	4	5	6	4	7	53-54	36
Falkirk	34	8	5	4	5	4	8	46-53	35
Morton	34	9	4	4	4	4	9	44-44	34
Airdrie	34	8	3	6	5	5	7	60-65	34
Motherwell	34	7	4	6	6	4	7	43-47	34
Hearts	**34**	**8**	**5**	**4**	**5**	**2**	**10**	**41-40**	**33**
Hibernian	34	8	4	5	2	6	9	47-53	30
Kilmarnock	34	5	6	6	5	2	10	43-67	28
Ayr United	34	7	5	5	2	3	12	37-54	26
Clyde	34	5	5	7	3	5	9	33-59	26
Dunfermline	34	6	5	6	0	6	11	44-56	23
St Mirren	34	4	3	10	3	6	8	38-56	23
Cowdenbeath	34	1	2	14	6	1	10	33-77	17

League Cup Section

	P	W	D	L	F A	PTS
Celtic	6	4	2	0	17-10	10
Dundee United	6	1	5	0	8- 7	7
Clyde	6	1	2	3	8-15	4
Hearts	**6**	**1**	**1**	**4**	**10-11**	**3**

Heart of Midlothian F.C. Line-Ups 1970-71

		1	2	3	4	5	6	7	8	9	10	11	12
Aug	8th	Cruickshank	Sneddon	Oliver	Veitch	Thomson	Wood	Ford	Clunie	Winchester	Fleming	Lynch	Hegarty (9)
	12th	Cruickshank	Sneddon	Oliver	Veitch	Thomson	Wood	Ford	Clunie	Hegarty	Fleming	Lynch	Winchester (11)
	15th	Cruickshank	Clunie	Oliver	Anderson	Thomson	Wood	Fleming	Veitch	Ford	Hegarty	Jensen	Murray (7)
	19th	Cruickshank	Sneddon	Oliver	Veitch	Thomson	Brown	Carruthers	Clunie	Ford	Hegarty	Jensen	Lynch
	22nd	Cruickshank	Sneddon	Oliver	Veitch	Thomson	Brown	Jensen	Clunie	Ford	Hegarty	Lynch	Winchester
	26th	Cruickshank	Sneddon	Oliver	Anderson	Thomson	Brown	Jensen	Clunie	Ford	Hegarty	Lynch	Carruthers
	29th	Cruickshank	Sneddon	Oliver*	Anderson	Thomson	Brown	Jensen	Clunie	Ford	Hegarty	Lynch	Fleming (9)
Sep	5th	Cruickshank	Clunie	Oliver	Anderson	Thomson	Brown	Jensen	Townsend	Winchester	Fleming	Lynch	Hegarty (11)
	12th	Cruickshank	Clunie	Oliver	Anderson	Thomson	Brown	Murray	Townsend	Hegarty	Fleming	Jensen	Winchester
	15th	Cruickshank	Clunie	Oliver	Anderson	Thomson	Brown	Ford	Townsend	Winchester	Hegarty	Fleming	Jensen
	19th	Cruickshank	Clunie	Oliver	Anderson	Thomson	Brown	Jensen	Townsend	Ford	Hegarty	Murray	Fleming (7)
	26th	Cruickshank	Clunie	Oliver	Anderson	Thomson	Brown	Fleming	Townsend	Ford	Hegarty	Lynch	Winchester (8)
	30th	Cruickshank	Clunie	Oliver	Anderson	Thomson	Brown	Fleming	Townsend	Ford	Hegarty	Lynch	Winchester
Oct	3rd	Cruickshank	Clunie	Sneddon	Anderson	Thomson	Brown	Fleming	Townsend	Ford	Hegarty	Lynch	Winchester (10)
	10th	Cruickshank	Clunie	Oliver	Anderson	Thomson	Brown	Fleming	Townsend	Ford	Hegarty	Lynch	Winchester (10)
	17th	Cruickshank	Clunie	Oliver	Anderson	Thomson	Brown	Fleming	Townsend	Ford	Hegarty	Lynch	Wood
	19th	Cruickshank	Clunie	Oliver	Anderson	Thomson	Brown	Young	Townsend	Ford	Wood	Lynch	Fleming
	28th	Garland	Clunie	Oliver	Anderson	Thomson	Brown	Young	Townsend	Ford	Wood	Lynch	Fleming
Nov	4th	Cruickshank	Clunie	Oliver	Anderson	McAlpine	Brown	Young	Townsend	Ford	Wood	Lynch	Fleming
	7th	Cruickshank	Clunie	Oliver	Thomson	Anderson	Brown	Young	Townsend	Ford	Wood	Lynch	Fleming (11)
	11th	Garland	Clunie	Oliver	Thomson	Anderson	Brown	Young	Townsend	Ford	Wood	Lynch	Fleming (11)
	14th	Cruickshank	Clunie	Oliver	Thomson	Anderson	Brown	Young	Townsend	Ford	Fleming	Lynch	Winchester
	21st	Cruickshank	Clunie	Oliver	Thomson	Anderson	Brown	Winchester	Townsend	Ford	Wood	Fleming	Young (10)
	28th	Cruickshank	Clunie	Oliver	Thomson	Anderson	Brown	Jensen	Townsend	Ford	Fleming	Lynch	Winchester (7)
Dec	5th	Cruickshank	Clunie	Oliver	Thomson	Anderson	Brown	Winchester	Townsend	Ford	Fleming	Lynch	Young (10)
	12th	Cruickshank	Clunie	Oliver	Thomson	Anderson	Brown	Carruthers	Townsend	Ford	Wood	Fleming	Young
	16th	Cruickshank	Clunie	Oliver	Thomson	Anderson	Brown	Carruthers	Townsend	Ford	Wood	Fleming	Lynch
	19th	Cruickshank	Clunie	Oliver	Thomson	Anderson	Brown	Carruthers	Townsend	Ford	Wood	Lynch	Fleming
	26th	Cruickshank	Clunie	Oliver	Thomson	Anderson	Brown	Carruthers	Townsend	Ford	Fleming	Lynch	Winchester
Jan	1st	Cruickshank	Clunie	Oliver	Thomson	Anderson	Brown	Fleming	Townsend	Ford	Hegarty	Lynch	Young
	9th	Cruickshank	Clunie	Oliver	Thomson	Anderson	Brown	Fleming	Townsend	Ford	Hegarty	Lynch	Young
	16th	Cruickshank	Clunie	Oliver	Thomson	Anderson	Brown	Fleming	Townsend	Ford	Hegarty	Lynch	Young (3)
	23rd	Cruickshank	Clunie	Kay	Thomson	Anderson	Wood	Fleming	Townsend	Ford	Hegarty	Lynch	Young (8)
	30th	Cruickshank	Clunie	Kay	Thomson	Anderson	Brown	Fleming	Townsend	Ford	Hegarty	Winchester	Young
Feb	6th	Cruickshank	Clunie	Kay	Thomson	Anderson	Brown	Fleming	Townsend	Ford	Hegarty	Winchester	Young
	13th	Cruickshank	Clunie	Kay	Veitch	Anderson	Wood	Fleming	Townsend	Ford	Hegarty	Winchester	Jensen (11)
	20th	Cruickshank	Clunie	Kay	Veitch	Anderson	Thomson	Young	Townsend	Ford	Brown	Hegarty	Fleming
	27th	Cruickshank	Clunie	Kay	Thomson	Anderson	Brown	Young	Townsend	Ford	Wood	Carruthers	Fleming
Mar	3rd	Cruickshank	Clunie	Kay	Thomson	Anderson	Brown	Young	Townsend	Ford	Wood	Carruthers	Fleming (7)
	6th	Cruickshank	Clunie	Kay	Thomson	Anderson	Brown	Fleming	Townsend	Ford	Wood	Carruthers	Young (11)
	13th	Cruickshank	Clunie	Kay	Thomson	Anderson	Brown	Young	Townsend	Ford	Wood	Fleming	Hegarty (8)
	20th	Cruickshank	Clunie	Kay	Thomson	Anderson	Brown	Fleming	Veith	Ford	Wood	Carruthers	Young
	24th	Cruickshank	Sneddon	Kay	Thomson	Anderson	Brown	Carruthers	Fleming	Ford	Wood	Lynch	Veitch
	27th	Cruickshank	Clunie	Kay	Thomson	Anderson	Brown	Carruthers	Fleming	Ford	Wood	Lynch	Veitch (7)
Apr	3rd	Cruickshank	Sneddon	Kay	Thomson	Anderson	Brown	Young	Fleming	Ford	Carruthers	Lynch	Veitch
	10th	Cruickshank	Sneddon	Kay	Thomson	Anderson	Brown	Fleming	Townsend	Ford	Wood	Carruthers	Young (11)
	14th	Cruickshank	Sneddon	Kay	Thomson	Anderson	Brown	Fleming	Townsend	Ford	Wood	Carruthers	Young (11)
	17th	Cruickshank	Sneddon	Kay	Thomson	Anderson	Brown	Young	Townsend	Ford	Wood	Fleming	Hegarty (7)
	24th	Cruickshank	Sneddon	Kay	Thomson	Anderson	Veitch	Townsend	Laing	Ford	Wood	Fleming	Morgan (11)
May	3rd	Cruickshank	Sneddon	Kay	Thomson	Anderson	Veitch	Townsend	Laing	Ford	Wood	Fleming	Carruthers

nb Garland was unused substitute goalkeeper in all the Texaco Cup ties

Heart of Midlothian F.C. 1970-71. BACK ROW (left to right) Wilson Wood, Alan Anderson, Dave Clunie, Kenny Garland, Jim Cruickshank, Tommy Veitch, Peter Oliver, Ernie Winchester, John Cumming (trainer). FRONT - Jim Brown, Raold Jensen, Eddie Thomson, Ian Sneddon, Andy Lynch, George Fleming, Jim Townsend. DC Thomson

Season 1971-72

Date			Opponents		Score	Crowd	Scorers
Aug	14th	LC	St Johnstone	h	4-1	11,500	Ford 2; Thomson; Lynch
	18th	LC	Airdrie	a	3-1	6,000	N. Murray 2; Lynch
	21st	LC	Dunfermline	a	0-1	7,500	-
	25th	LC	Airdrie	h	1-2	11,000	Fleming
	28th	LC	St Johnstone	a	0-1	8,000	-
Sep	1st	LC	Dunfermline	h	4-0	5,500	Carruthers; Ford; Brown; Lynch
	4th	L	Hibernian	h	0-2	28,000	-
	11th	L	Dunfermline	a	4-1	8,000	T. Murray 2; Ford; Thomson
	15th	TC1	Newcastle United	h	1-0	18,000	Lynch
	18th	L	St Johnstone	h	2-1	11,000	T. Murray; Lambie o.g.
	25th	L	Dundee	a	0-0	10,500	-
	28th	TC1	Newcastle United	a	1-2 (2-2)*	24,380	Anderson
Oct	2nd	L	Rangers	h	2-1	28,000	T. Murray; Brown
	9th	L	Clyde	a	1-0	3,500	Anderson
	16th	L	Airdrie	h	1-1	11,000	Ford
	23rd	L	Kilmarnock	a	2-2	5,000	Ford 2
	30th	L	East Fife	h	1-1	10,000	T. Murray
Nov	6th	L	Motherwell	a	3-5	5,500	T. Murray; Brown; Winchester
	13th	L	Morton	h	6-1	9,000	N. Murray; T. Murray; Townsend; Ford 3
	20th	L	Ayr United	h	1-0	9,500	Ford
	27th	L	Aberdeen	a	3-2	21,000	Ford 3
Dec	4th	L	Dundee United	h	3-2	10,000	Renton; Ford; Mollison o.g.
	11th	L	Falkirk	a	0-2	7,500	-
	18th	L	Partick Thistle	h	0-0	11,000	-
	25th	L	Celtic	a	2-3	34,000	Renton; Brown
Jan	1st	L	Hibernian	a	0-0	36,000	-
	3rd	L	Dunfermline	h	1-1	13,500	Townsend (pen)
	8th	L	St Johnstone	a	1-1	4,500	Ford
	15th	L	Dundee	h	2-5	9,000	Winchester; Steele o.g.
	22nd	L	Rangers	a	0-6	35,000	-
	29th	L	Clyde	h	2-0	7,000	Lynch; Ford
Feb	5th	SC1	St Johnstone	h	2-0	11,932	Anderson; Winchester
	12th	L	Airdrie	a	1-1	3,000	Kinnear
	19th	L	Kilmarnock	h	2-1	9,000	Thomson; Dickson o.g.
	26th	SC2	Clydebank	h	4-0	11,993	Hall o.g.; Ford; Kinnear 2
Mar	4th	L	East Fife	a	2-2	6,000	Kinnear; Anderson
	11th	L	Motherwell	h	0-0	9,000	-
	18th	SCQ	Celtic	a	1-1	47,000	Renton
	21st	L	Morton	a	1-1	4,000	Lynch
	25th	L	Ayr United	a	0-1	5,500	-
	27th	SCQR	Celtic	h	0-1	40,209	-
Apr	1st	L	Aberdeen	h	1-0	8,500	Renton
	8th	L	Dundee United	a	2-3	4,500	Carruthers 2
	15th	L	Falkirk	h	1-0	7,500	T. Murray
	22nd	L	Partick Thistle	a	2-2	7,000	T. Murray; Renton
	29th	L	Celtic	h	4-1	10,500	T. Murray; Ford; Renton; Brown

* aet 1-1 after 90 mts, Newcastle won 4-3 on pens.

Neil Murray - Hearts wing ace was rated a top prospect.

The Record

League	-	**Sixth Place, Division One**
League Cup	-	**Qualifying stages only**
Scottish Cup	-	**Quarter-final**
Top Scorer	-	**Donald Ford (19 goals)**
Av. Home gate	-	**11,900**
Players used	-	**23**
Sent off	-	**Two**

Cup Cash v. Celtic (a) £12,000, (h) £11,687

Appearances

	League	L/Cup	S/Cup	T/Cup	Total
Jim Brown	34 (4)	6 (1)	3	2	45+1s (5)
Ian Sneddon	31	6	4	2	43
Donald Ford	30 (15)	6 (3)	3 (1)	2	41 (19)
Eddie Thomson	29 (2)	6 (1)	4	2	41 (3)
Alan Anderson	28 (2)	6	4 (1)	2 (1)	40 (4)
Tommy Murray	29 (10)	0	4	2	35 (10)
Jim Townsend	23 (2)	6	1	2	32 (2)
Jim Cruickshank	20	6	0	2	28
Andy Lynch	16 (2)	6 (3)	4	2 (1)	28+1s (6)
Roy Kay	18	6	0	2	26
Ernie Winchester	21 (2)	0	1 (1)	0	22+1s (3)
Derek Renton	17 (5)	0	3 (1)	0	20 (6)
Kenny Garland	14	0	4	0	18
Neil Murray	8 (1)	5 (2)	0	2	15+4s (3)
Wilson Wood	10	2	3	0	15
Tommy Veitch	10	2	0	0	12+4s
Eric Carruthers	8 (2)	1 (1)	0	0	9+2s (3)
Jim Jefferies	7	0	2	0	9
Peter Oliver	7	0	2	0	9+1s
Harry Kinnear	4 (2)	0	2 (2)	0	6 (4)
Dave Clunie	5	0	0	0	5
George Fleming	2	2 (1)	0	0	4+2s (1)
John Gallacher	3	0	0	0	3

Scottish League Division One

	P	Home W	Home D	Home L	Away W	Away D	Away L	Goals F-A	PTS
Celtic	34	15	1	1	13	3	1	96-28	60
Aberdeen	34	13	3	1	8	5	4	80-26	50
Rangers	34	11	0	6	10	2	5	71-38	44
Hibernian	34	11	2	4	8	4	5	62-34	44
Dundee	34	8	6	3	6	7	4	59-38	41
Hearts	**34**	**10**	**5**	**2**	**3**	**8**	**6**	**53-49**	**39**
Partick Thistle	34	9	6	2	3	4	10	53-54	34
St Johnstone	34	7	5	5	5	3	9	52-58	32
Dundee United	34	7	5	5	5	2	10	55-70	31
Motherwell	34	9	3	5	2	4	11	49-69	28
Kilmarnock	34	7	3	7	4	3	10	49-64	28
Ayr United	34	5	6	6	4	4	9	40-58	28
Morton	34	5	7	5	5	0	12	46-52	27
Falkirk	34	7	4	6	3	3	11	44-60	27
Airdrie	34	4	6	7	3	6	8	44-76	26
East Fife	34	2	7	8	3	8	6	34-61	25
Clyde	34	5	4	8	2	6	9	33-66	24
Dunfermline	34	5	5	7	2	4	11	31-50	23

League Cup Section

	P	W	D	L	F A	PTS
St Johnstone	6	3	1	2	8-7	7
Hearts	**6**	**3**	**0**	**3**	**12-6**	**6**
Airdrie	6	3	0	3	7-9	6
Dunfermline	6	2	1	3	4-9	5

Heart of Midlothian F.C. Line-Ups 1971-72

	1	2	3	4	5	6	7	8	9	10	11	12
Aug 14th	Cruickshank	Sneddon	Kay	Brown	Anderson	Thomson	Murray N	Townsend	Ford	Wood	Lynch	Fleming
18th	Cruickshank	Sneddon	Kay	Brown	Anderson	Thomson	Murray N	Townsend	Ford	Wood	Lynch	Fleming
21st	Cruickshank	Sneddon	Kay	Brown	Anderson	Thomson	Murray N	Townsend	Ford	Fleming	Lynch	Veitch
25th	Cruickshank	Sneddon	Kay	Brown	Anderson	Thomson*	Murray N	Townsend	Ford	Fleming	Lynch	Veitch (7)
29th	Cruickshank	Sneddon	Kay	Veitch	Anderson	Thomson	Murray N	Townsend	Ford	Brown	Lynch	Fleming (10)
Sep 1st	Cruickshank	Sneddon	Kay	Veitch	Anderson	Thomson	Townsend	Carruthers	Ford	Brown	Lynch	Morgan
4th	Cruickshank	Sneddon	Kay	Veitch	Anderson	Thomson	Townsend	Carruthers	Ford	Brown	Lynch	Morgan
11th	Cruickshank	Sneddon	Kay	Brown	Anderson	Thomson	Townsend	Carruthers	Ford	Murray T	Lynch	Veitch (8)
15th	Cruickshank	Sneddon	Kay	Brown	Anderson	Thomson	Murray N	Townsend	Ford	Murray T	Lynch	Veitch (8)
18th	Cruickshank	Sneddon	Kay	Brown	Anderson	Thomson	Murray N	Townsend	Ford	Murray T	Lynch	Winchester (3)
25th	Cruickshank	Sneddon	Kay	Brown	Anderson	Veitch	Murray N	Townsend	Ford	Murray T	Lynch	Winchester
28th	Cruickshank	Sneddon	Kay	Brown	Anderson	Thomson	Murray N	Townsend	Ford	Murray T	Lynch	Winchester
Oct 2nd	Cruickshank	Sneddon	Kay	Brown	Anderson	Thomson	Townsend	Murray T	Ford	Winchester	Lynch	Renton
9th	Cruickshank	Sneddon	Kay	Brown	Anderson	Thomson	Townsend	Murray T	Ford	Winchester	Lynch	Veitch (8)
16th	Cruickshank	Sneddon	Kay	Brown	Anderson	Thomson	Townsend	Murray T	Ford	Winchester	Lynch	Carruthers 7)
23rd	Cruickshank	Sneddon	Kay	Brown	Anderson	Veitch	Townsend	Carruthers	Ford	Winchester	Murray T	Wood
30th	Cruickshank	Sneddon	Kay	Brown	Anderson	Veitch	Townsend	Carruthers	Ford	Winchester	Murray T	Murray N (8)
Nov 6th	Cruickshank	Sneddon	Kay	Brown	Anderson	Thomson	Townsend	Murray T	Ford	Winchester	Murray N	Lynch
13th	Cruickshank	Sneddon	Kay	Brown	Anderson	Thomson	Townsend	Murray T	Ford	Winchester	Murray N	Kinnear
20th	Cruickshank	Sneddon	Kay	Brown	Anderson	Thomson	Townsend	Murray T	Ford	Winchester	Murray N	Renton
27th	Cruickshank	Sneddon	Kay	Brown	Anderson	Thomson	Townsend*	Renton	Ford	Winchester	Murray T	Oliver
Dec 4th	Cruickshank	Sneddon	Kay	Brown	Anderson	Thomson	Townsend	Renton	Ford	Winchester	Murray T	Oliver (11)
11th	Garland	Sneddon	Kay	Brown	Anderson	Thomson	Townsend	Renton	Ford	Winchester	Murray T	Fleming (8)
18th	Cruickshank	Sneddon	Oliver	Brown	Anderson	Thomson	Townsend	Renton	Ford	Winchester	Fleming	Lynch
25th	Cruickshank	Sneddon	Oliver	Brown	Veitch	Thomson	Fleming	Renton	Ford	Winchester	Murray T	Wood
Jan 1st	Cruickshank	Sneddon	Oliver	Brown	Veitch	Thomson	Townsend	Renton	Ford	Winchester	Murray T	Murray N
3rd	Cruickshank	Sneddon	Oliver	Brown	Veitch	Thomson	Townsend	Renton	Ford	Winchester	Murray T	Murray N (3)
8th	Cruickshank	Sneddon	Kay	Brown	Anderson	Veitch	Townsend	Renton	Ford	Winchester	Murray T	Murray N
15th	Cruickshank	Sneddon	Kay	Brown	Veitch	Thomson	Townsend	Murray T	Ford	Winchester	Lynch	Oliver
22nd	Garland	Sneddon	Kay	Brown	Anderson	Thomson	Townsend	Renton	Ford	Winchester	Murray T	Lynch (11)
28th	Garland	Sneddon	Oliver	Brown	Anderson	Thomson	Murray N	Townsend	Ford	Winchester	Lynch	Wood
Feb 5th	Garland	Sneddon	Oliver	Brown	Anderson	Thomson	Murray T	Renton	Kinnear	Winchester	Lynch	Wood
12th	Garland	Sneddon	Oliver	Brown	Anderson	Thomson	Murray N	Renton	Kinnear	Winchester	Lynch	Menmuir
19th	Garland	Sneddon	Oliver	Thomson	Anderson	Wood	Murray T	Brown	Renton	Townsend	Lynch	Murray N
26th	Garland	Sneddon	Oliver	Thomson	Anderson	Wood	Murray T	Brown	Ford	Winchester	Lynch	Murray N (9)
Mar 4th	Garland	Sneddon	Jefferies	Thomson	Anderson	Wood	Murray T	Brown	Ford	Kinnear	Lynch	Carruthers (9)
11th	Garland	Sneddon	Jefferies	Thomson	Anderson	Wood	Murray T	Brown	Ford	Kinnear	Murray N	Lynch
18th	Garland	Sneddon	Jefferies	Thomson	Anderson	Wood	Murray T	Townsend	Ford	Renton	Lynch	Brown (8)
21st	Garland	Sneddon	Jefferies	Thomson	Anderson	Wood	Winchester	Brown	Ford	Renton	Lynch	Murray N
25th	Garland	Sneddon	Jefferies	Thomson	Anderson	Wood	Murray T	Brown	Kinnear	Veitch	Lynch	Clunie
27th	Garland	Sneddon	Jefferies	Thomson	Anderson	Wood	Murray T	Brown	Ford	Renton	Lynch	Murray N (2)
Apr 1st	Garland	Clunie	Jefferies	Thomson	Anderson	Wood	Murray T	Brown	Ford	Carruthers	Renton	Winchester
8th	Garland	Clunie	Jefferies	Thomson	Gallacher	Wood	Murray T	Brown	Ford	Carruthers	Renton	Lynch
15th	Garland	Clunie	Jefferies	Thomson	Gallacher	Wood	Murray T	Brown	Ford	Carruthers	Renton	Lynch
22nd	Garland	Sneddon	Clunie	Gallacher	Anderson	Wood	Murray T	Brown	Carruthers	Renton	Lynch	Ford
29th	Garland	Sneddon	Clunie	Thomson	Anderson	Wood	Murray T	Brown	Ford	Renton	Lynch	Carruthers

No chance - Hearts midfielder Derek Renton thunders the ball into the net at Tynecastle with Celtic right-back Jim Craig and keeper Dennis Connaghan too late to intervene. Hearts went on to beat the Parkhead side 4-1 in the final game of the season. DC Thomson

Season 1972-73

Date			Opponents		Score	Crowd	Scorers
Aug	12th	LC	Dumbarton	a	0-1	5,500	-
	16th	LC	Airdrie	h	0-0	7,500	-
	19th	LC	Berwick Rangers	a	1-1	5,000	Ford
	23rd	LC	Airdrie	a	1-2	3,500	Anderson
	26th	LC	Dumbarton	h	1-1	8,000	T. Murray
	30th	LC	Berwick Rangers	h	3-0	2,800	Ford; Lynch; Kay (pen)
Sep	2nd	L	St Johnstone	h	1-0	8,000	T. Murray
	9th	L	Hibernian	a	0-2	21,200	-
	13th	TC1	Crystal Palace	h	1-0	9,150	T. Murray
	16th	L	Dumbarton	h	1-0	7,000	Lynch
	23rd	L	Morton	a	4-2	3,500	Wood; Ford; Lynch 2
	26th	TC1	Crystal Palace	a	1-0 (2-0)	9,855	Lynch
	30th	L	East Fife	a	0-1	6,100	-
Oct	7th	L	Aberdeen	h	2-1	14,000	Ford; Carruthers
	14th	L	Dundee United	a	2-3	8,000	Ford; T. Murray
	16th	TC2	Motherwell	h	0-0	13,000	-
	21st	L	Motherwell	h	0-0	8,000	-
	28th	L	Arbroath	h	3-0	7,500	Carruthers; Clunie; Park
Nov	4th	L	Falkirk	a	3-1	7,500	Anderson; Park; Carruthers
	8th	TC2	Motherwell	a	2-4 (2-4)	10,929	T. Murray; Clunie (pen)
	11th	L	Ayr United	h	3-0	7,000	Park; Ford 2
	18th	L	Celtic	a	2-4	28,000	Ford 2
	25th	L	Partick Thistle	h	2-0	8,000	Anderson; Park
Dec	2nd	L	Rangers	a	1-0	22,000	Ford
	9th	L	Kilmarnock	h	0-0	7,000	-
	16th	L	Airdrie	a	2-0	3,500	T. Murray; Park
	23rd	L	Dundee	h	1-2	9,000	T. Murray
	30th	L	St Johnstone	a	2-3	5,700	Ford; Brown
Jan	1st	L	Hibernian	h	0-7	36,000	-
	6th	L	Dumbarton	a	2-0	2,500	Renton; Menmuir
	20th	L	East Fife	h	1-1	6,000	Thomson
	27th	L	Aberdeen	a	1-3	12,000	Renton
Feb	3rd	SC1	Airdrie	h	0-0	8,200	-
	7th	SC1R	Airdrie	a	1-3	10,000	Ford
	10th	L	Dundee United	h	0-2	7,000	-
	19th	L	Motherwell	a	2-2	4,800	T. Murray; Carruthers
Mar	3rd	L	Arbroath	a	0-3	3,400	-
	10th	L	Falkirk	h	1-0	6,500	Brown
	12th	L	Morton	h	0-0	5,500	-
	21st	L	Ayr United	a	0-2	6,000	-
	24th	L	Celtic	h	0-2	22,000	-
	31st	L	Partick Thistle	a	0-3	3,500	-
Apr	7th	L	Rangers	h	0-1	24,000	-
	14th	L	Kilmarnock	a	1-2	4,500	Carruthers
	21st	L	Airdrie	h	0-1	4,500	
	28th	L	Dundee	a	2-2	6,400	Sneddon; Park

Cup Cash v. Airdrie (h) £1,653

Donald Ford - the industrious striker was again top scorer.

The Record		
League	-	10th Place, Division One
League Cup	-	Qualifying stages only
Scottish Cup	-	First round
Texaco Cup	-	Second round
Top Scorer	-	Donald Ford (12 goals)
Av. Home Gate	-	11,000
Players used	-	23
Sent off (booked)	-	Four (9)

Appearances

	League	L/Cup	S/Cup	T/Cup	Total
Donald Ford	32 (9)	6 (2)	2 (1)	4	44 (12)
Jim Brown	31 (2)	6	2	4	43+1s (2)
Alan Anderson	30 (2)	6 (1)	2	4	42 (3)
Tommy Murray	27 (5)	6 (1)	2	4 (2)	39+1s (8)
Dave Clunie	25 (1)	6	1	4 (1)	36 (2)
Kenny Garland	23	6	2	4	35
Ian Sneddon	22 (1)	6	1	1	30 (1)
Eddie Thomson	23 (1)	0	2	3	28+1s (1)
Eric Carruthers	24 (5)	1	0	2	27+5s (5)
Roy Kay	15	6 (1)	2	3	26 (1)
Wilson Wood	17 (1)	5	0	4	26 (1)
Donald Park	16 (6)	0	2	1	19+2s (6)
Peter Oliver	15	0	0	3	18+2s
Andy Lynch	7 (3)	5 (1)	0	2 (1)	14+3s (5)
Derek Renton	9 (2)	4	1	0	14+3s (2)
Billy Menmuir	13 (1)	0	0	0	13 (1)
Jim Cruickshank	11	0	0	0	11
Kenny Aird	10	0	0	0	10
Jim Jefferies	8	0	2	0	10
John Gallacher	5	0	1	0	6
John Stevenson	5	0	0	0	5
Harry Kinnear	2	2	0	0	4
Neil Murray	3	1	0	0	4+3s
Jim Cant	1	0	0	0	1
Jim Townsend	0	0	0	1	1

Scottish League Division One

		Home			Away			Goals	
	P	W	D	L	W	D	L	F A	PTS
Celtic	34	14	3	0	12	2	3	93-28	57
Rangers	34	14	2	1	12	2	3	74-30	56
Hibernian	34	12	2	3	7	5	5	74-33	45
Aberdeen	34	10	6	1	6	5	6	61-34	43
Dundee	**34**	**13**	**4**	**0**	**4**	**5**	**8**	**68-43**	**43**
Ayr United	34	11	4	2	5	4	8	50-51	40
Dundee United	34	11	3	3	6	2	9	56-51	39
Motherwell	34	5	6	6	6	3	8	38-48	31
East Fife	34	8	3	6	3	5	9	46-54	30
Hearts	**34**	**7**	**4**	**6**	**5**	**2**	**10**	**39-50**	**30**
St Johnstone	34	8	3	6	2	6	9	52-67	29
Morton	34	8	4	5	2	4	11	47-53	28
Partick Thistle	34	4	5	8	6	3	8	40-43	28
Falkirk	34	6	4	7	1	8	8	38-56	26
Arbroath	34	8	3	6	1	5	11	39-63	26
Dumbarton	34	3	9	5	3	2	12	43-72	23
Kilmarnock	34	6	3	8	1	5	11	40-71	22
Airdrie	34	2	4	11	2	4	11	34-75	16

League Cup Section

	P	W	D	L	F A	PTS
Airdrie	6	3	2	1	9-7	8
Dumbarton	6	2	2	2	9-7	6
Hearts	**6**	**1**	**3**	**2**	**6-5**	**5**
Berwick Rangers	6	1	3	2	5-10	5

Heart of Midlothian F.C. Line-Ups 1972-73

		1	2	3	4	5	6	7	8	9	10	11	12
Aug	12th	Garland	Sneddon	Clunie	Kay	Anderson	Wood	Murray T	Brown	Ford	Carruthers	Renton	Murray N (11)
	16th	Garland	Sneddon	Clunie	Kay	Anderson	Wood	Murray T	Brown	Ford	Renton	Lynch	Murray N (11)
	19th	Garland	Sneddon	Clunie	Kay	Anderson	Wood	Murray T	Brown	Ford	Renton	Lynch	Murray N (10)
	23rd	Garland	Sneddon	Clunie	Kay	Anderson	Wood	Murray T	Brown	Ford	Kinnear	Lynch	Murray N
	26th	Garland	Sneddon	Clunie	Kay	Anderson	Wood	Murray T	Brown	Ford	Kinnear	Lynch	Renton (10)
	30th	Garland	Sneddon	Clunie	Kay	Anderson	Brown	Murray N	Renton	Ford	Murray T	Lynch	Wood
Sep	2nd	Garland	Clunie	Oliver	Kay	Anderson	Brown	Murray N	Renton*	Ford	Murray T	Lynch	Wood
	9th	Garland	Clunie	Oliver	Kay	Anderson	Brown	Murray N	Renton	Ford	Murray T	Lynch	Wood
	13th	Garland	Clunie	Oliver	Kay	Anderson	Wood	Murray T	Brown	Ford	Townsend	Lynch	Renton (10)
	16th	Garland	Clunie	Oliver	Kay	Anderson	Wood	Murray T	Ford	Thomson	Brown	Lynch	Renton
	23rd	Garland	Clunie	Oliver	Kay	Anderson	Wood	Murray T	Ford	Thomson	Brown	Lynch	Renton
	26th	Garland	Clunie	Oliver	Kay	Anderson	Wood	Murray T	Ford	Thomson	Brown	Lynch	Renton
	30th	Garland	Clunie	Oliver	Kay	Anderson	Wood	Murray T	Ford	Thomson	Brown	Lynch	Carruthers (9)
Oct	7th	Garland	Clunie	Oliver	Kay	Anderson	Wood	Murray T	Brown	Ford	Carruthers	Lynch	Renton
	14th	Garland	Clunie	Oliver	Kay	Anderson	Wood	Murray T	Brown	Ford	Carruthers	Lynch	Thomson (11)
	16th	Garland	Clunie	Oliver	Kay	Anderson	Wood	Murray T	Brown	Thomson	Carruthers	Ford	Renton
	21st	Garland	Clunie	Oliver	Thomson	Anderson	Wood	Murray T	Renton	Ford	Carruthers	Murray N	Brown (8)
	28th	Garland	Sneddon	Clunie	Thomson	Anderson	Wood	Park	Brown	Ford	Carruthers	Murray T	Kay
Nov	4th	Garland	Sneddon	Clunie	Thomson	Anderson	Wood	Park	Brown	Ford	Carruthers	Murray T	Lynch
	8th	Garland	Sneddon*	Clunie	Thomson	Anderson	Wood	Park	Brown	Ford	Carruthers	Murray T	Lynch (7)
	11th	Garland	Sneddon	Clunie	Thomson	Anderson	Wood	Park	Brown	Ford	Carruthers	Murray T	Lynch
	18th	Garland	Sneddon	Clunie	Thomson	Anderson	Brown	Park	Menmuir	Ford	Carruthers	Murray T	Lynch (10)
	25th	Garland	Sneddon	Clunie	Thomson	Anderson	Brown	Park	Menmuir	Ford	Carruthers	Murray T	Renton
Dec	2nd	Garland	Sneddon	Clunie	Thomson	Anderson	Brown	Park	Menmuir	Ford	Carruthers	Murray T	Renton
	9th	Garland	Sneddon	Clunie	Thomson	Anderson	Brown	Park	Menmuir	Ford	Carruthers	Murray T	Renton
	16th	Garland	Sneddon	Jefferies	Thomson	Anderson	Brown	Park	Menmuir	Ford	Carruthers	Murray T	Wood
	23rd	Garland	Sneddon	Clunie	Thomson	Anderson	Brown	Park	Menmuir	Ford	Carruthers	Murray T	Stevenson
	30th	Garland	Sneddon	Clunie	Thomson	Anderson	Brown	Park	Menmuir	Ford	Carruthers	Murray T	Lynch (10)
Jan	1st	Garland	Clunie	Jefferies	Thomson	Anderson	Wood	Park	Brown	Ford	Carruthers	Murray T	Lynch (10)
	6th	Garland	Clunie	Jefferies	Thomson	Anderson	Brown	Park	Menmuir	Ford	Renton	Murray T	Carruthers
	20th	Garland	Clunie	Jefferies	Thomson	Anderson	Kay	Park	Renton	Ford	Brown	Murray T	Carruthers
	27th	Garland	Clunie	Jefferies	Thomson	Anderson	Kay	Park	Renton	Ford	Brown	Murray T	Carruthers (7)
Feb	3rd	Garland	Clunie	Jefferies	Thomson	Anderson	Kay	Park	Renton	Ford	Brown	Murray T	Carruthers (8)
	7th	Garland	Sneddon	Jefferies	Gallacher	Anderson	Kay	Park	Ford	Thomson	Brown	Murray T	Carruthers (7)
	10th	Garland	Sneddon	Jefferies*	Kay	Gallacher	Oliver	Park	Ford	Thomson	Brown	Murray T	Carruthers (11)
	19th	Cruickshank	Sneddon	Jefferies	Thomson	Gallacher	Brown	Carruthers	Menmuir	Ford	Renton	Murray T	Oliver (6)
Mar	3rd	Cruickshank	Sneddon	Jefferies	Thomson	Gallacher	Wood	Aird	Menmuir	Kinnear	Ford	Murray T	Oliver (9)
	10th	Cruickshank	Sneddon	Clunie	Wood	Anderson	Thomson	Aird	Carruthers	Ford	Brown	Murray T	Renton
	12th	Cruickshank	Sneddon	Clunie	Thomson	Anderson	Wood	Aird	Carruthers	Ford	Renton	Brown	Menmuir
	21st	Cruickshank	Sneddon	Oliver	Gallacher	Anderson	Kay	Aird	Wood	Carruthers	Renton	Brown	Menmuir
	24th	Cruickshank	Sneddon	Oliver	Kay	Anderson	Brown	Aird	Menmuir	Ford	Carruthers	Murray T	Renton (11)
	31st	Cruickshank	Sneddon	Oliver	Kay	Gallacher	Brown	Aird	Menmuir	Ford	Stevenson	Carruthers	Murray T (8)
Apr	7th	Cruickshank	Sneddon	Oliver	Kay	Anderson	Wood	Aird	Stevenson	Ford	Brown	Carruthers	Park (8)
	14th	Cruickshank	Sneddon	Oliver	Kay	Anderson	Wood	Aird	Stevenson	Ford	Brown	Carruthers	Murray
	21st	Cruickshank	Sneddon	Oliver	Clunie	Anderson	Wood	Aird	Stevenson	Ford	Brown	Carruthers	Park (6)
	28th	Cruickshank	Sneddon	Clunie	Menmuir	Anderson	Cant	Park	Stevenson	Kinnear	Carruthers	Aird	Ford

nb Cruickshank was the unused substitute keeper for all Texaco Cup games

Heads down - Eric Carruthers dives full length to head a spectacular goal against Dundee United at Tannadice. Donald Ford, Derek Renton and Eddie Thomson look suitably impressed. McAlpine, Copland, Gray and Fleming are the United players. DC Thomson

Season 1973-74

Date			Opponents		Score	Crowd	Scorers
Aug	11th	LC	Partick Thistle	h	2-0	10,000	Ford 2 (1 pen)
	15th	LC	St Johnstone	a	1-2	5,000	Ford
	18th	LC	Dundee	a	1-2	8,000	Busby
	22nd	LC	St Johnstone	h	4-1	6,000	Busby; Aird; Ford 2
	25th	LC	Dundee	h	0-0	13,500	-
	29th	LC	Partick Thistle	a	0-0	4,000	-
Sep	1st	L	Morton	a	3-2	5,000	Ford (3 pens)
	8th	L	Hibernian	h	4-1	29,000	Schaedler o.g.; Aird; Ford; Busby;
	15th	L	Motherwell	a	2-2	10,000	Stevenson; Ford
	18th	TC1	Everton	a	1-0	12,500	Busby
	22nd	L	Dundee	h	2-2	14,000	Ford 2 (1 pen)
	29th	L	Rangers	a	3-0	30,000	Prentice; Busby 2
Oct	3rd	TC1	Everton	h	0-0 (1-0)	24,903	-
	6th	L	Dunfermline	h	3-0	15,500	Prentice; Aird; Busby
	13th	L	St Johnstone	a	2-0	7,000	Ford; Brown
	20th	L	Dumbarton	h	0-0	10,500	-
	24th	TC2	Burnley	h	0-3	21,824	-
	27th	L	Celtic	h	1-3	33,000	Ford
Nov	3rd	L	Arbroath	a	3-2	4,000	Ford 2 (1 pen); Park
	6th	TC2	Burnley	a	0-5 (0-8)	9,500	-
	10th	L	Dundee United	h	1-1	11,000	Kay
	17th	L	Aberdeen	a	1-3	10,800	Ford
	24th	L	Falkirk	h	2-1	7,500	Ford; Stevenson
Dec	8th	L	East Fife	a	0-0	3,800	-
	15th	L	Ayr United	h	0-1	5,500	-
	22nd	L	Partick Thistle	a	3-1	4,000	Busby; Ford; Stevenson
	29th	L	Morton	h	0-2	8,000	-
Jan	1st	L	Hibernian	a	1-3	35,400	Ford
	5th	L	Motherwell	h	2-0	10,000	Park; Ford (pen)
	19th	L	Rangers	h	2-4	20,000	Busby; Brown
	26th	SC3	Clyde	h	3-1	9,100	Busby; Gibson; Prentice
Feb	9th	L	St Johnstone	h	0-2	10,500	-
	16th	SC4	Partick Thistle	h	1-1	12,000	Gibson
	19th	SC4R	Partick Thistle	a	4-1	10,000	Ford 3; Gibson
	23rd	L	Dumbarton	a	1-0	5,000	Gibson
Mar	2nd	L	Celtic	a	0-1	32,000	-
	9th	SCQ	Ayr United	h	1-1	18,500	Anderson
	13th	SCQR	Ayr United	a	2-1*	15,200	Ford 2
	16th	L	Dundee United	a	3-3	7,000	Busby 2; Park
	23rd	L	Aberdeen	h	0-0	13,500	-
	30th	L	Falkirk	a	2-0	6,000	Prentice; Busby
Apr	2nd	L	Arbroath	h	4-0	7,500	Gibson 2; Park; Stevenson
	6th	SCS	Dundee United	Hamp	1-1	22,700	Anderson
	9th	SCSR	Dundee United	Hamp	2-4*	12,800	Ford; Gibson
	13th	L	East Fife	h	2-2	6,500	Ford (pen); Gibson
	17th	L	Dunfermline	a	3-2	5,500	Ford; Gibson 2
	20th	L	Ayr United	a	1-2	2,500	Wells o.g.
	24th	L	Clyde	a	0-2	3,000	-
	27th	L	Partick Thistle	h	3-1	5,500	Busby 3
May	4th	L	Clyde	h	0-0	6,000	-
	6th	L	Dundee	a	0-0	5,100	-

* a.e.t. 0-0 after 90 minutes

Kenny Aird - right wing buzz-bomb for the Maroons.

The Record		
League	-	Sixth Place, Division One
League Cup	-	Qualifying stages only
Scottish Cup	-	Semi-final
Texaco Cup	-	Second round
Top Scorer	-	Donald Ford (29 goals)
Av. Home Gate	-	12,600
Players used	-	23
Sent off (booked)	-	One (10)

Appearances

	League	L/Cup	S/Cup	T/Cup	Total
John Stevenson	30 (4)	6	7	4	47 (4)
Donald Ford	29 (18)	6 (5)	7 (6)	4	46+1s (29)
Dave Clunie	31	6	5	4	46
Alan Anderson	27	6	7 (2)	4	44 (2)
Drew Busby	27 (12)	6 (2)	4 (1)	4 (1)	41+2s (16)
Jim Jefferies	23	6	7	2	38+1s
Rab Prentice	26 (3)	3	5 (1)	3	37+4s (4)
Jim Cant	26	6	0	4	36
Jim Brown	25 (2)	1	7	2	35+3s (2)
Ian Sneddon	18	6	6	3	33
Kenny Aird	17 (2)	6 (1)	6	3	32 (3)
Kenny Garland	20	6	0	4	30
Tommy Murray	15	2	2	1	20+12s
Jim Cruickshank	11	0	7	0	18
Roy Kay	14 (1)	0	3	1	18 (1)
Donald Park	13 (4)	0	1	1	15+7s (4)
Willie Gibson	10 (6)	0	3 (4)	0	13+3s (10)
John Gallacher	5	0	0	0	5
David Graham	3	0	0	0	3
Ralph Callachan	1	0	0	0	1
Eric Carruthers	1	0	0	0	1
Harry Kinnear	1	0	0	0	1
Peter Oliver	1	0	0	0	1

Scottish League Division One

		Home			Away			Goals	
	P	W	D	L	W	D	L	F A	PTS
Celtic	34	12	4	1	11	3	3	82-27	53
Hibernian	34	14	2	1	6	7	4	75-42	49
Rangers	34	9	3	5	12	3	2	67-34	48
Aberdeen	34	7	9	1	6	7	4	46-26	42
Dundee	34	7	3	7	9	4	4	67-48	39
Hearts	**34**	**6**	**6**	**5**	**8**	**4**	**5**	**54-43**	**38**
Ayr United	34	9	4	4	6	4	7	44-40	38
Dundee United	34	7	3	7	8	4	5	55-41	37
Motherwell	34	8	5	4	6	2	9	45-40	35
Dumbarton	34	7	3	7	4	4	9	43-58	29
Partick Thistle	34	7	4	6	2	6	9	33-46	28
St Johnstone	34	3	6	8	6	4	7	41-60	28
Arbroath	34	5	2	10	5	5	7	52-69	27
Morton	34	4	5	8	4	5	8	37-49	26
Clyde	34	5	2	10	3	7	7	29-65	25
Dunfermline	34	3	5	9	5	3	9	43-65	24
East Fife	34	3	2	12	6	4	7	26-51	24
Falkirk	34	1	11	5	3	3	11	33-58	22

League Cup Section

	P	W	D	L	F A	PTS
Dundee	6	4	2	0	11- 2	10
St Johnstone	6	3	1	2	12- 9	7
Hearts	**6**	**2**	**2**	**2**	**8- 5**	**6**
Partick Thistle	6	0	1	5	2-17	1

Heart of Midlothian F.C. Line-Ups 1973-74

Date	1	2	3	4	5	6	7	8	9	10	11	12	14
Aug 11th	Garland	Sneddon	Clunie	Cant	Anderson	Jefferies	Ford	Murray	Busby	Stevenson	Aird	Brown	Park
15th	Garland	Sneddon	Clunie	Cant	Anderson	Jefferies	Ford	Murray	Busby	Stevenson	Aird	Brown	Park (8)
18th	Garland	Sneddon	Clunie	Cant	Anderson	Jefferies	Ford	Brown	Busby	Stevenson	Aird	Prentice (8)	Murray
22nd	Garland	Sneddon	Clunie	Cant	Anderson	Jefferies	Aird	Ford	Busby	Stevenson	Prentice	Murray	Brown
25th	Garland	Sneddon	Clunie	Cant	Anderson	Jefferies	Aird	Ford	Busby	Stevenson	Prentice	Murray (6)	Brown
29th	Garland	Sneddon	Clunie	Cant	Anderson	Jefferies	Aird	Ford	Busby	Stevenson	Prentice	Murray (9)	Brown
Sep 1st	Garland	Sneddon	Clunie	Cant	Anderson	Jefferies	Aird	Ford	Carruthers	Stevenson	Prentice	Murray (11)	Brown
8th	Garland	Sneddon	Clunie	Cant	Anderson	Jefferies	Aird	Ford	Busby	Stevenson	Prentice	Murray	Brown
15th	Garland	Sneddon	Clunie	Cant	Anderson	Jefferies	Aird	Ford	Busby	Stevenson	Prentice	Murray (6)	Park (11)
18th	Garland	Sneddon	Clunie	Cant	Anderson	Jefferies	Aird	Ford	Busby	Stevenson	Prentice	Murray	Cruickshank
22nd	Garland	Sneddon	Clunie	Cant	Anderson	Brown	Aird	Ford	Busby	Stevenson	Prentice	Murray (6)	Park
29th	Garland	Sneddon	Clunie	Cant	Anderson	Brown	Aird	Ford	Busby	Stevenson	Prentice	Murray	Park
Oct 3rd	Garland	Sneddon	Clunie	Cant	Anderson	Brown	Aird	Ford	Busby	Stevenson	Prentice	Murray	Cruickshank
6th	Garland	Sneddon	Clunie	Cant	Anderson	Brown	Aird	Ford	Busby	Stevenson	Prentice	Murray	Park
13th	Garland	Sneddon	Clunie	Cant	Anderson	Brown	Aird	Ford	Busby	Stevenson	Prentice	Murray	Park
20th	Garland	Sneddon	Clunie	Cant	Anderson	Brown	Aird	Ford	Busby	Murray	Prentice	Park	Menmuir
24th	Garland	Sneddon	Clunie	Cant	Anderson	Brown	Aird	Ford	Busby	Stevenson	Prentice	Murray (11)	Cruickshank
27th	Garland	Sneddon	Clunie	Cant	Anderson	Jefferies	Aird	Ford	Busby	Stevenson	Prentice	Park	Brown
Nov 3rd	Garland	Kay	Clunie	Cant	Anderson	Jefferies	Park	Ford	Busby	Stevenson	Aird	Murray (11)	Brown
6th	Garland	Kay	Clunie	Cant	Anderson	Jefferies	Park	Ford	Busby	Stevenson	Murray	Brown	Cruickshank
10th	Garland	Kay	Clunie	Cant	Anderson	Jefferies	Park	Ford	Kinnear	Stevenson	Prentice	Murray	Brown
17th	Garland	Kay	Clunie	Cant	Anderson	Jefferies	Park	Ford	Busby	Stevenson	Prentice	Brown (10)	Murray (11)
24th	Garland	Kay	Clunie	Cant	Anderson	Jefferies	Murray	Ford	Busby	Stevenson	Prentice	Brown (6)	Gibson
Dec 8th	Garland	Kay	Clunie	Cant	Anderson	Jefferies	Murray	Ford	Busby	Stevenson	Prentice	Brown (6)	Gibson
15th	Garland	Kay	Clunie	Cant	Anderson	Brown	Murray	Ford	Busby	Stevenson	Prentice	Jefferies	Gibson
22nd	Garland	Kay	Clunie	Cant	Anderson	Brown	Ford	Stevenson	Busby	Murray	Prentice	Jefferies	Gibson
29th	Garland	Kay	Clunie	Cant	Anderson	Brown	Stevenson	Ford	Busby	Murray	Prentice	Park (7)	Gibson (8)
Jan 1st	Garland	Kay	Clunie	Cant	Anderson	Brown	Stevenson	Ford	Busby	Murray	Prentice	Park (6)	Jefferies
5th	Cruickshank	Kay	Clunie	Cant	Anderson	Brown	Park	Ford	Busby	Stevenson	Prentice	Jefferies (6)	Murray
19th	Cruickshank	Kay	Clunie	Cant	Anderson	Brown	Park	Ford	Busby	Stevenson	Prentice	Murray	Jefferies
26th	Cruickshank	Kay	Clunie	Jefferies	Anderson	Brown	Park	Busby	Ford	Stevenson	Prentice	Murray	Gibson (1)
Feb 9th	Cruickshank	Sneddon	Kay	Jefferies	Gallacher	Brown	Aird	Ford	Busby	Stevenson	Prentice	Park (7)	Murray (11)
16th	Cruickshank	Sneddon	Kay	Jefferies	Anderson	Brown	Aird	Gibson	Ford	Stevenson	Prentice	Park (11)	Murray (6)
19th	Cruickshank	Sneddon	Kay	Jefferies	Anderson	Brown	Aird	Gibson	Ford	Stevenson	Murray	Park	Prentice
23rd	Cruickshank	Sneddon	Kay	Jefferies	Anderson	Brown	Aird	Gibson	Ford	Stevenson	Murray	Park	Prentice (7)
Mar 2nd	Cruickshank	Sneddon	Kay	Jefferies	Anderson	Brown	Aird	Gibson	Ford	Stevenson	Murray	Prentice (10)	Busby
9th	Cruickshank	Sneddon	Clunie	Jefferies	Anderson	Brown	Aird	Gibson	Ford	Stevenson	Murray	Prentice (11)	Busby (7)
13th	Cruickshank	Sneddon	Clunie	Jefferies	Anderson	Brown	Aird	Ford	Busby	Stevenson	Prentice	Murray	Gibson
16th	Cruickshank	Sneddon	Clunie	Jefferies	Anderson	Brown	Park	Gibson	Busby	Stevenson	Prentice	Murray (10)	Aird
23rd	Cruickshank	Sneddon	Clunie	Jefferies	Anderson	Brown	Aird	Ford	Busby	Stevenson	Prentice	Murray	Park
30th	Cruickshank	Sneddon	Clunie	Jefferies	Anderson	Brown	Aird	Busby	Ford	Stevenson	Prentice	Murray	Park (11)
Apr 2nd	Cruickshank	Sneddon	Clunie	Jefferies	Anderson	Brown	Park	Gibson	Busby	Stevenson	Murray	Ford	Kay
6th	Cruickshank	Sneddon	Clunie	Jefferies	Anderson	Brown	Aird	Busby	Ford	Stevenson	Prentice	Murray (10)	Gibson
9th	Cruickshank	Sneddon	Clunie	Jefferies	Anderson	Brown	Aird	Busby	Ford	Stevenson	Prentice	Gibson (7)	Murray
13th	Cruickshank	Sneddon	Clunie	Jefferies	Anderson	Brown	Park	Gibson	Ford	Murray	Prentice	Aird	Callachan
17th	Cruickshank	Sneddon	Clunie	Cant	Jefferies	Brown	Park	Gibson	Ford	Callachan	Murray	Aird	Stevenson
20th	Garland	Clunie	Oliver	Cant	Jefferies	Brown	Aird	Gibson	Ford	Park	Murray	Busby (11)	Stevenson
24th	Garland	Clunie	Jefferies	Cant	Gallacher	Brown	Park*	Gibson	Busby	Stevenson	Aird	Ford (11)	Murray
27th	Graham	Clunie	Jefferies	Cant	Gallacher	Brown	Park	Gibson	Busby	Stevenson	Prentice	Ford	Murray
May 4th	Graham	Clunie	Jefferies	Cant	Gallacher	Brown	Murray	Ford	Busby	Stevenson	Prentice	Gibson (7)	Park
6th	Graham	Clunie	Jefferies	Cant	Gallacher	Brown	Park	Gibson	Busby	Stevenson	Murray	Aird	Callachan

Nice one - Hearts striker Donald Ford jumps for joy after cracking home the first of a double in a 2-2 draw with Dundee at Tynecastle. Thomson Allan can only watch as the ball heads for the back of the net. DC Thomson

Season 1974-75

Date			Opponents		Score	Crowd	Scorers
Aug	10th	LC	Aberdeen	a	1-0	11,000	Ford
	14th	LC	Dunfermline	h	2-3	9,000	Cant; Ford (pen)
	17th	LC	Morton	a	5-0	6,000	Ford 2; Aird; Stevenson; Busby
	21st	LC	Dunfermline	a	1-2	8,500	Ford (pen)
	24th	LC	Morton	h	2-0	10,000	Cant 2
	28th	LC	Aberdeen	h	2-1	14,000	Aird 2
	31st	L	St Johnstone	h	1-2	10,000	Ford
Sep	7th	L	Hibernian	a	1-2	26,600	Ford (pen)
	11th	LCQ	Falkirk	h	0-0	11,000	-
	14th	L	Kilmarnock	h	1-1	8,000	Busby
	17th	TC1	Oldham Athletic	a	0-1	11,465	-
	21st	L	Dunfermline	a	2-2	6,000	Busby; Ford
	25th	LCQ2	Falkirk	a	0-1	9,500	-
	28th	L	Partick Thistle	a	1-4	6,500	Busby
	30th	TC1	Oldham Athletic	h	1-1 (1-2)	10,000	Ford (pen)
Oct	5th	L	Aberdeen	h	1-4	8,500	Park
	12th	L	Dundee United	a	0-5	5,500	-
	19th	L	Airdrie	h	2-1	8,000	Gibson; Stevenson
	21st	L	Rangers	h	1-1	28,000	Gibson
Nov	2nd	L	Ayr United	a	3-3	5,000	Ford 3 (1 pen)
	9th	L	Dumbarton	h	2-1	10,000	T. Murray; Callachan
	16th	L	Arbroath	a	1-3	3,500	T. Murray
	23rd	L	Celtic	h	1-1	23,000	Busby
	30th	L	Clyde	a	2-2	2,800	McVie o.g.; Ford (pen)
Dec	7th	L	Morton	h	3-1	8,000	Ford; Donaldson; Gibson
	14th	L	Motherwell	a	3-1	5,100	Ford 2 (1 pen); Callachan
	21st	L	Dundee	h	0-0	11,000	-
	28th	L	St Johnstone	a	3-2	5,000	Busby; Ford (pen); Gibson
Jan	1st	L	Hibernian	h	0-0	36,500	-
	4th	L	Kilmarnock	a	1-1	7,000	Ford
	11th	L	Dunfermline	h	1-0	13,000	Gibson
	18th	L	Partick Thistle	h	3-1	11,500	Callachan (pen); Busby; Prentice
	29th	SC3	Kilmarnock	h	2-0	21,054	Busby 2
Feb	1st	L	Aberdeen	a	2-2	11,000	Gibson; Callachan
	8th	L	Dundee United	h	3-1	12,500	Gibson; Busby 2 (1 pen)
	15th	SC4	Queen of the South	a	2-0	14,000	Callachan; Gibson
	22nd	L	Airdrie	a	1-1	8,500	Gibson
Mar	1st	L	Rangers	a	1-2	38,000	Callachan
	8th	SCQ	Dundee	h	1-1	27,300	T. Murray
	12th	SCQR	Dundee	a	2-3	22,200	Callachan (pen); Busby
	15th	L	Dumbarton	a	1-0	4,000	Gibson
	19th	L	Ayr United	h	1-0	8,000	Prentice
	22nd	L	Arbroath	h	0-0	9,000	-
	29th	L	Celtic	a	1-4	21,100	Busby
Apr	5th	L	Clyde	h	0-1	5,000	-
	12th	L	Morton	a	0-0	2,500	-
	19th	L	Motherwell	h	4-1	8,000	Busby 2; Ford; MacLaren o.g.
	23rd	L	Dundee	a	0-2	4,900	-

Cup Cash v. Killie £7,072; QOS £5,500;Dundee (h) £9,498

Drew Busby - formed a lethal partnership up front with Donald Ford. DC Thomson

The Record		
League	-	Eighth Place, Division One
League Cup	-	Quarter final
Scottish Cup	-	Semi-final
Top Scorer	-	Donald Ford (18 goals)
Av. Home Gate	-	12,800
Players used	-	26
Sent off (booked)	-	One (16)

Appearances

	League	L/Cup	S/Cup	T/Cup	Total
Drew Busby	30 (11)	7 (1)	4 (3)	2	43 (15)
Ralph Callachan	27 (5)	4	4 (2)	1	36+2s (7)
Jim Jefferies	27	6	4	1	34+1s
Alan Anderson	28	0	4	1	33
Roy Kay	28	1	3	2	34
Willie Gibson	27 (9)	1	4 (1)	1	33+3s (10)
Dave Clunie	27	1	4	0	32
Donald Ford	21 (13)	8 (5)	2	1 (1)	32+2s (19)
Jim Cruickshank	27	0	4	0	31
Jim Brown	18	8	2	2	30+3s
Tommy Murray	18 (2)	1	4 (1)	1	24+5s (3)
Kenny Aird	12	8 (3)	0	2	22+5s (3)
Don Murray	16	0	3	0	19
John Stevenson	10 (1)	7 (1)	1	0	18+7s (2)
Kenny Garland	7	8	0	2	17
Jim Cant	8	8 (3)	0	2	16 (3)
Ian Sneddon	6	8	0	1	15
John Gallacher	4	8	0	1	13
Bobby Prentice	5 (2)	4	1	1	11+12s (2)
George Donaldson	10 (1)	0	0	0	10+5s (1)
Donald Park	7 (1)	0	0	0	7+8s (1)
Eric Carruthers	5	0	0	0	5+2s
Sandy Burrell	2	0	0	1	3
Cammy Fraser	3	0	0	0	3
Billy Bennett	1	0	0	0	1

Scottish League Division One

		Home			Away			Goals		
	P	W	D	L	W	D	L	F	A	PTS
Rangers	34	14	1	2	11	5	1	86	33	56
Hibernian	34	12	2	3	8	7	2	69	37	49
Celtic	34	11	2	4	9	3	5	81	41	45
Dundee United	34	10	5	2	9	2	6	72	43	45
Aberdeen	34	9	6	2	7	3	7	66	43	41
Dundee	34	11	1	5	5	5	7	48	42	38
Ayr United	34	9	5	3	5	3	9	50	61	36
Hearts	**34**	**8**	**6**	**3**	**3**	**7**	**7**	**47**	**52**	**35**
St Johnstone	34	8	4	5	3	8	6	41	44	34
Motherwell	34	8	2	7	6	3	8	52	57	33
Airdrie	34	7	7	3	4	2	11	43	55	31
Kilmarnock	34	5	7	5	3	8	6	52	68	31
Partick Thistle	34	7	5	5	3	5	9	48	62	30
Dumbarton	34	3	5	9	4	5	8	44	55	24
Dunfermline	34	3	6	8	4	3	10	46	66	23
Clyde	34	4	6	7	2	4	11	40	63	22
Morton	34	4	5	8	2	5	10	31	62	22
Arbroath	34	4	5	8	1	2	14	34	66	17

League Cup Section

	P	W	D	L	F	A	PTS
Hearts	**6**	**4**	**0**	**2**	**13**	**6**	**8**
Dunfermline	6	2	3	1	8	9	7
Aberdeen	6	2	1	3	10	7	5

Heart of Midlothian F.C. Line-Ups 1974-75

	1	2	3	4	5	6	7	8	9	10	11	12	14
Aug 10th	Garland	Sneddon	Jefferies	Cant	Gallacher	Brown	Aird	Ford	Busby	Stevenson	Prentice	Clunie	Gibson
14th	Garland	Sneddon	Jefferies	Brown	Gallacher	Cant	Aird	Ford	Busby	Stevenson	Prentice	Gibson	Callachan (11)
17th	Garland	Sneddon	Jefferies	Cant	Gallacher	Brown	Aird	Ford	Busby	Stevenson	Callachan	Murray N	Park
21st	Garland	Sneddon	Jefferies	Cant	Gallacher	Brown	Aird	Ford	Busby	Stevenson	Callachan	Park (11)	Murray
24th	Garland	Sneddon	Jefferies	Cant	Gallacher	Brown	Aird	Ford	Busby	Stevenson	Callachan	Donaldson (11)	Gibson
28th	Garland	Sneddon	Jefferies	Cant	Gallacher	Brown	Aird	Ford	Busby	Stevenson	Callachan	Donaldson	Gibson
31st	Garland	Sneddon	Jefferies	Cant	Gallacher	Brown	Aird	Ford	Busby	Donaldson	Stevenson	Callachan (2)	Gibson (9)
Sep 7th	Garland	Sneddon	Clunie	Cant	Gallacher	Brown	Aird	Ford	Busby	Donaldson	Stevenson	Gibson (9)	Prentice (10)
11th	Garland	Sneddon	Clunie	Cant	Gallacher	Brown	Aird	Ford	Gibson	Stevenson	Prentice	Park	Callachan
14th	Garland	Sneddon	Kay	Cant	Gallacher	Brown	Aird	Gibson	Busby	Callachan	Prentice	Park	Stevenson (6)
17th	Garland	Sneddon	Kay	Cant	Gallacher	Brown	Aird	Gibson	Busby	Callachan	Prentice	Ford (10)	Graham
21st	Garland	Sneddon	Kay	Cant	Gallacher	Brown	Aird	Ford	Busby	Stevenson	Murray T	Prentice (10)	Gibson
25th	Garland	Sneddon	Kay	Cant	Gallacher	Brown	Aird	Ford	Busby	Murray T	Prentice	Park (5)	Gibson
28th	Garland	Sneddon	Kay	Cant	Jefferies	Brown	Aird	Ford	Busby	Murray T	Prentice	Callachan	Gibson (11)
30th	Garland	Kay	Burrell	Cant	Anderson	Jefferies	Aird	Ford	Busby	Brown	Murray T	Park (4)	Callachan
Oct 5th	Garland	Kay	Burrell	Jefferies	Anderson	Brown	Aird	Ford	Busby	Park	Murray T	Cant	Callachan
12th	Garland	Kay	Clunie	Cant	Anderson	Brown	Gibson	Ford	Busby	Murray T	Callachan	Aird (9)	Carruthers
19th	Cruickshank	Kay	Clunie	Brown	Anderson	Jefferies	Park	Gibson	Ford	Carruthers	Callachan	Stevenson (9)	Prentice(4)
21st	Cruickshank	Sneddon	Clunie	Kay	Anderson	Jefferies	Gibson	Busby	Carruthers	Murray T	Callachan	Stevenson (9)	Prentice (11)
Nov 2nd	Cruickshank	Kay	Clunie	Jefferies	Anderson	Murray T	Gibson	Busby	Ford	Carruthers	Callachan	Stevenson (11)	Prentice (8)
9th	Cruickshank	Kay	Clunie	Cant	Anderson	Jefferies	Aird	Gibson	Ford	Murray T	Callachan	Park (7)	Prentice
16th	Cruickshank	Kay	Clunie	Brown	Jefferies	Bennett	Aird	Gibson	Ford	Murray T	Callachan	Park	Prentice (4)
23rd	Cruickshank	Kay	Park	Jefferies	Anderson	Murray T	Gibson	Busby	Ford	Carruthers	Callachan	Aird	Donaldson (8)
30th	Cruickshank	Kay	Burrell	Brown	Anderson	Jefferies	Gibson	Carruthers	Ford	Murray T	Callachan	Stevenson (10)	Donaldson (4)
Dec 7th	Cruickshank	Kay	Clunie	Jefferies	Anderson	Donaldson	Gibson	Busby	Ford	Murray T	Callachan	Burrell	Stevenson
14th	Cruickshank	Kay	Clunie	Jefferies	Anderson	Murray D	Gibson	Busby	Ford	Stevenson	Callachan	Prentice	Burrell
21st	Cruickshank	Kay	Clunie	Jefferies	Anderson	Murray D	Gibson	Busby	Ford	Stevenson	Callachan	Carruthers (7)	Donaldson
28th	Cruickshank	Kay	Clunie	Jefferies	Anderson	Murray D	Gibson	Busby	Ford	Stevenson	Callachan	Murray T	Carruthers
Jan 1st	Cruickshank	Kay	Clunie	Jefferies	Anderson	Murray D	Gibson	Busby	Ford	Stevenson	Callachan	Murray T (11)	Carruthers
4th	Cruickshank	Kay	Clunie	Jefferies	Anderson	Murray D	Gibson	Busby	Ford	Stevenson	Callachan	Carruthers (11)	Prentice (2)
11th	Cruickshank	Kay	Clunie	Jefferies	Anderson	Murray D	Gibson	Busby	Ford	Stevenson	Callachan	Prentice (9)	Murray T
18th	Cruickshank	Kay	Clunie	Jefferies	Anderson	Murray T	Park	Busby	Gibson	Stevenson	Callachan	Prentice (7)	Brown (10)
29th	Cruickshank	Kay	Clunie	Jefferies	Anderson	Brown	Callachan	Busby	Gibson	Murray T	Prentice	Stevenson (11)	Park
Feb 1st	Cruickshank	Kay	Clunie	Jefferies	Anderson	Brown	Park	Busby	Gibson	Murray T	Callachan	Aird (7)	Stevenson
8th	Cruickshank	Kay	Clunie	Jefferies	Anderson	Brown	Park	Busby	Gibson	Murray T	Callachan	Stevenson (10)	Aird (11)
15th	Cruickshank	Kay	Clunie	Jefferies	Anderson	Murray D	Stevenson	Busby	Gibson	Murray T	Callachan	Brown (7)	Aird
22nd	Cruickshank	Kay	Clunie	Jefferies	Anderson	Murray D	Brown	Busby	Gibson	Murray T	Callachan	Donaldson (10)	Aird (11)
Mar 1st	Cruickshank	Kay	Clunie	Murray D	Anderson	Murray T	Aird	Busby	Ford	Gibson	Callachan	Brown (2)	Jefferies (9)
8th	Cruickshank	Kay	Clunie	Jefferies	Anderson	Murray D	Gibson	Busby	Ford	Murray T	Callachan	Brown	Park
12th	Cruickshank	Brown	Clunie	Jefferies	Anderson	Murray D	Gibson	Busby	Ford	Murray T	Callachan	Park (9)	Prentice (10)
15th	Cruickshank	Brown	Clunie	Jefferies	Anderson	Murray D	Gibson	Donaldson	Busby	Park	Callachan	Prentice (11)	Murray T (10)
19th	Cruickshank	Kay	Clunie	Jefferies	Anderson	Murray D	Gibson	Brown	Busby	Donaldson	Prentice	Murray T	Callachan
22nd	Cruickshank	Kay	Clunie	Callachan	Anderson	Murray D	Gibson	Brown	Busby	Donaldson	Prentice	Murray T (4)	Park (7)
29th	Cruickshank	Kay	Clunie	Jefferies	Anderson	Murray D	Gibson	Brown	Busby	Donaldson	Callachan	Murray T (5)	Prentice (7)
Apr 5th	Cruickshank	Kay	Clunie	Jefferies	Anderson	Murray D	Gibson	Brown	Busby	Murray T	Prentice	Donaldson (4)	Aird (8)
12th	Cruickshank	Clunie	Jefferies	Donaldson	Anderson	Murray D	Aird	Busby	Fraser	Murray T	Callachan	Park (11)	Ford (9)
19th	Cruickshank	Jefferies	Clunie	Donaldson	Anderson	Murray D	Aird	Busby	Fraser	Ford	Callachan	Murray T	Park
23rd	Cruickshank	Cant	Clunie	Donaldson	Anderson	Murray D	Aird	Busby	Fraser	Gibson	Callachan	Park (10)	Murray T (9)

Razor sharp - Dundee defenders converge but Hearts striker Tommy Murray wastes no time in finding the net in this Scottish Cup tie at Tynecastle. Drew Busby is the other Heart with Bobby Robinson, Iain Anderson and Tommy Gemmell the Dundee men. DC Thomson

Season 1975-76

Date		Comp	Opponents		Score	Crowd	Scorers
Aug	2nd	ASC1	Queen of South	a	3-2	4,500	Callachan; Fraser; Ford;
	9th	LC	Dumbarton	a	1-2	4,000	Callachan
	13th	LC	Celtic	h	2-0	19,000	Hancock; Ford (pen)
	16th	LC	Aberdeen	a	2-1	7,750	Ford; Hancock
	20th	LC	Celtic	a	1-3	28,000	Busby
	23rd	LC	Aberdeen	h	1-0	8,000	Prentice
	27th	LC	Dumbarton	h	6-0	5,000	Hancock; Busby 2; Callachan; Prentice; Park
	30th	L	Hibernian	a	0-1	23,646	-
Sep	3rd	ASC1	QOS	h	3-1 (6-3)	3,000	Busby; Gibson; Park
	6th	L	Rangers	h	0-2	25,000	-
	13th	L	Dundee	a	3-2	6,700	Busby (pen); Park 2
	17th	ASC2	Fulham	a	2-3	6,000	Gibson 2
	20th	L	Aberdeen	h	2-2	7,750	Gibson; Prentice
	27th	L	Motherwell	a	1-1	6,100	Busby
Oct	1st	ASC2	Fulham	h	2-2 (4-5)	14,000	Jefferies; Gibson
	4th	L	Celtic	a	1-3	20,000	Busby
	11th	L	Dundee United	h	1-0	9,000	Prentice
	18th	L	Ayr United	h	2-1	9,000	Brown; Busby
	25th	L	St Johnstone	a	1-0	4,700	Aird
Nov	1st	L	Hibernian	h	1-1	25,000	Callachan
	8th	L	Rangers	a	2-1	24,000	Gibson 2
	15th	L	Dundee	h	1-1	10,000	Gibson
	22nd	L	Aberdeen	a	0-0	11,400	-
	29th	L	Motherwell	h	3-3	15,500	Aird; Brown; Busby (pen)
Dec	6th	L	Celtic	h	0-1	21,000	-
	13th	L	Dundee United	a	1-0	4,550	Callachan
	20th	L	Ayr United	a	1-1	5,500	Aird
	27th	L	St Johnstone	h	2-0	9,000	Aird; Busby (pen)
Jan	1st	L	Hibernian	a	0-3	33,000	-
	3rd	L	Rangers	h	1-2	23,000	Forsyth o.g.
	10th	L	Dundee	a	1-4	6,550	Shaw
	17th	L	Aberdeen	h	3-3	10,300	Gibson; Anderson; Prentice
	24th	SC3	Clyde	h	2-2	10,165	Gibson; Park
	28th	SC3R	Clyde	a	1-0	5,378	Gibson
	31st	L	Motherwell	a	0-2	10,050	-
Feb	7th	L	Celtic	a	0-2	22,000	-
	14th	SC4	Stirling Albion	h	3-0	10,390	Callachan; Busby 2 (1 pen)
	21st	L	Dundee United	h	0-1	9,500	-
	28th	L	Ayr United	h	1-0	8,000	Gibson
Mar	6th	SCQ	Montrose	a	2-2	8,200	McNicoll o.g.; Shaw
	9th	SCQR	Montrose	h	2-2*	16,228	Shaw; Gibson
	13th	L	Hibernian	h	0-1	19,000	-
	16th	SCQR	Montrose	Muirton	2-1**	10,050	Shaw; Callachan
	20th	L	Rangers	a	1-3	30,000	Aird
	27th	L	Dundee	h	3-0	8,500	Busby (pen); Aird; Shaw
Apr	3rd	SCS	Dumbarton	Hamp.	0-0	16,087	-
	7th	L	Aberdeen	a	3-0	6,500	Gibson 2; Aird
	10th	L	Motherwell	h	1-2	11,500	Busby
	14th	SCSR	Dumbarton	Hamp.	3-0	11,273	W. Smith o.g.; Prentice; Busby
	17th	L	Dundee United	a	0-2	6,600	-
	21st	L	Ayr United	a	1-0	5,200	Park
	24th	L	St Johnstone	h	1-0	8,500	Prentice
	26th	L	St Johnstone	a	0-0	3,500	-
May	1st	SCF	Rangers	Hamp.	1-3	85,250	Shaw
	3rd	L	Celtic	h	1-0	9,000	Brown

* aet 2-2 at 90 mts,:** aet 1-1 after 90 mts. Cup Cash v. Clyde (h) £4,177. v. Stirling £4,645, v. Montrose (a) £4,099, (h) £7,880, Dumbarton replay £3,200

Appearances

	League		L/Cup		S/Cup		AS/Cup		Total	
Jim Cruickshank	35		5		9		3		52	
Jim Brown	33	(3)	5		9		3		50+2s	
Ralph Callachan	34	(2)	3	(2)	8	(2)	4	(1)	49+2s	(7)
Drew Busby	32	(8)	6	(3)	7	(3)	4	(1)	49	(15)
Bobby Prentice	30	(4)	5	(2)	6	(1)	1		42+4s	(7)
Dave Clunie	26		6		6		4		42	
Jim Jefferies	26		4		8		3	(1)	41+3s	(1)
Don Murray	22		6		5		3		36	
Kenny Aird	26	(7)	0		8		1		35+3s	(7)
Willie Gibson	24	(8)	0		7	(3)	3	(4)	34+5s	(15)
Roy Kay	23		5		4		1		33+1s	
Alan Anderson	22	(1)	6		2		3		33	(1)
Donald Park	18	(3)	0	(1)	3	(1)	2	(1)	23+14s	(6)
John Gallacher	14		0		7		1		22	
Graham Shaw	13	(2)	0		6	(4)	0		19	
Sandy Burrell	6		0		2		2		10+1s	
Donald Ford	2		6	(2)	1		1	(1)	10	(3)
Cammy Fraser	5		1		1		1	(1)	8+13s	(1)

Jim Cruickshank - a tremendous servant to Hearts in his 17 years at Tynecastle.

The Record		
League	-	**Fifth Place, Premier Division**
League Cup	-	**Qualifying stages only**
Scottish Cup	-	**Runners up**
Anglo Scottish Cup	-	**Second round**
Top Scorer	-	**Drew Busby, Willie Gibson (both 15 goals)**
Av. Home Gate	-	**13,300**
Players used	-	**25**
Sent Off (booked)	-	**One (22)**

Scottish League Premier Division

		Home			Away			Goals	
	P	W	D	L	W	D	L	F A	PTS
Rangers	36	14	2	2	8	6	4	58-26	52
Celtic	36	10	5	3	11	1	6	71-42	48
Hibernian	36	13	2	3	5	5	8	55-43	43
Motherwell	36	11	4	3	5	4	9	57-48	40
Hearts	**36**	**7**	**5**	**6**	**6**	**5**	**8**	**39-45**	**35**
Ayr United	36	10	3	5	5	2	11	48-57	35
Aberdeen	36	8	5	5	3	5	10	49-50	32
Dundee United	36	9	3	6	3	5	10	46-48	32
Dundee	36	8	5	5	3	5	10	49-72	32
St Johnstone	36	3	4	11	0	1	17	28-79	11

League Cup Section

	P	W	D	L	F A	PTS
Celtic	6	5	0	1	17-4	10
Hearts	**6**	**4**	**0**	**2**	**13-8**	**8**
Aberdeen	6	2	0	4	4-6	4
Dumbarton	6	1	0	5	5-21	2

Appearances

	League	L/Cup	S/Cup	AS/Cup	Total
Stevie Hancock	2	5 (3)	0	1	8+2s (3)
Jim Cant	0	1	0	1	2
George Donaldson	2	0	0	0	2
Kenny Garland	0	1	0	1	2
John Stevenson	0	1	0	1	2
David Graham	1	0	0	0	1

Heart of Midlothian F.C. Line-Ups 1975-76

		1	2	3	4	5	6	7	8	9	10	11	12	13
Aug	2nd	Garland	Clunie	Jefferies	Cant	Anderson	Murray D	Stevenson	Busby	Ford	Fraser	Callachan	Prentice	Brown
	9th	Garland	Clunie	Jefferies	Cant	Anderson	Murray D	Stevenson	Busby	Ford	Fraser	Callachan	Prentice (9)	Brown (7)
	13th	Cruickshank	Clunie	Jefferies	Cant	Anderson	Murray D	Brown	Busby	Ford	Hancock	Prentice	Park	Fraser
	16th	Cruickshank	Kay	Clunie	Callachan	Anderson	Murray D	Brown	Busby	Hancock	Ford	Prentice	Park (2)	Fraser
	20th	Cruickshank	Kay	Clunie	Jefferies	Anderson	Murray D	Brown	Busby	Hancock	Ford	Prentice	Park (9)	Callachan
	23rd	Cruickshank	Kay	Clunie	Jefferies	Anderson	Murray D	Brown	Busby	Hancock	Ford	Prentice	Callachan (11)	Park
	27th	Cruickshank	Kay	Clunie	Callachan	Anderson	Murray D	Brown	Busby	Hancock	Ford	Prentice	Park (9)	Gibson (10)
	30th	Cruickshank	Kay	Clunie	Jefferies	Anderson	Murray D	Brown	Busby	Hancock	Callachan	Prentice	Park (11)	Gibson
Sep	3rd	Cruickshank	Clunie	Burrell	Brown	Gallacher	Murray D	Park	Busby	Hancock	Gibson	Callachan	Aird (8)	Jefferies
	6th	Cruickshank	Clunie	Burrell	Brown	Anderson	Murray D	Park	Busby	Hancock	Gibson	Prentice	Callachan (9)	Aird
	13th	Cruickshank	Clunie	Burrell	Brown	Anderson	Murray D	Park	Busby	Gibson	Callachan	Prentice	Jefferies	Hancock
	17th	Cruickshank	Clunie	Burrell	Jefferies	Anderson	Murray D	Park	Busby	Gibson	Brown	Callachan	Kay (3)	Hancock
	20th	Cruickshank	Clunie	Kay	Brown	Anderson	Murray D	Park	Busby	Gibson	Callachan	Prentice	Aird (4)	Jefferies
	27th	Cruickshank	Clunie	Kay	Brown	Anderson	Murray D	Park	Busby	Gibson	Callachan	Prentice	Jefferies (6)	Aird
Oct	1st	Cruickshank	Clunie	Kay	Brown	Anderson	Jefferies	Aird	Busby	Gibson	Callachan	Prentice	Aird	Jefferies
	4th	Cruickshank	Clunie	Kay	Jefferies	Anderson	Murray D	Aird	Brown	Busby	Callachan	Prentice	Gibson (11)	Park (8)
	11th	Cruickshank	Clunie	Kay	Brown	Anderson	Murray D	Aird	Busby	Gibson	Callachan	Prentice	Hancock (7)	Jefferies (2)
	18th	Cruickshank	Clunie	Kay	Brown	Anderson	Murray D	Aird	Busby	Gibson	Callachan	Prentice	Hancock	Jefferies
	25th	Cruickshank	Clunie	Kay	Brown	Anderson	Murray D	Aird	Busby	Gibson	Callachan	Prentice	Hancock (9)	Jefferies
Nov	1st	Cruickshank	Kay	Jefferies	Brown	Anderson	Murray D	Aird	Busby	Gibson	Callachan	Prentice	Park	Hancock
	8th	Cruickshank	Clunie	Jefferies	Brown	Anderson	Murray D	Aird	Busby	Gibson	Callachan	Prentice	Kay (6)	Park (10)
	15th	Cruickshank	Clunie	Kay	Brown	Anderson	Jefferies	Aird	Busby	Gibson	Callachan	Prentice	Park (10)	Donaldson
	22nd	Cruickshank	Clunie	Jefferies	Brown	Gallacher	Murray D	Park	Busby	Gibson	Callachan	Prentice	Kay	Fraser (11)
	29th	Cruickshank	Clunie	Jefferies	Brown	Anderson	Murray D	Aird	Busby	Gibson	Callachan	Prentice	Park	Fraser
Dec	6th	Cruickshank	Clunie	Jefferies	Brown	Anderson	Murray D	Aird	Busby	Gibson	Park	Callachan	Prentice (11)	Fraser
	13th	Cruickshank	Clunie	Jefferies	Brown	Anderson	Murray D	Park	Busby	Fraser	Callachan	Prentice	Kay	Gibson
	20th	Cruickshank	Clunie	Jefferies	Brown	Anderson	Murray D	Park	Busby	Fraser	Callachan	Prentice	Gibson (9)	Aird (3)
	27th	Cruickshank	Clunie	Brown	Callachan	Anderson	Murray D	Aird	Busby	Gibson	Park	Prentice	Jefferies	Fraser (7)
Jan	1st	Cruickshank	Clunie	Brown	Callachan	Anderson	Murray D	Fraser	Busby	Gibson	Park	Prentice	Jefferies (7)	Kay
	3rd	Cruickshank	Clunie	Jefferies	Brown	Anderson	Murray D	Park	Busby	Gibson	Donaldson	Callachan	Prentice (10)	Kay
	10th	Cruickshank	Kay	Clunie	Donaldson	Gallacher	Murray D	Aird	Busby	Shaw	Park	Callachan	Gibson	Fraser
	17th	Graham	Clunie	Jefferies	Callachan	Anderson	Kay	Aird	Park	Gibson	Shaw	Prentice	Fraser (8)	Brown (10)
	24th	Cruickshank	Clunie	Jefferies	Brown	Anderson	Murray D	Aird	Park	Gibson	Callachan	Prentice	Kay	Fraser (4)
	28th	Cruickshank	Clunie	Jefferies	Brown	Anderson	Murray D	Aird	Park	Gibson	Busby	Shaw	Fraser (11)	Kay
	31st	Cruickshank	Clunie	Jefferies	Brown	Anderson	Kay	Aird	Park	Gibson	Busby	Callachan	Fraser (8)	Prentice(9)
Feb	7th	Cruickshank	Clunie	Jefferies	Brown	Gallacher	Murray D	Aird	Busby	Ford	Callachan	Shaw	Park (7)	Prentice
	14th	Cruickshank	Clunie	Jefferies	Brown	Gallacher	Murray D	Aird	Busby	Ford	Callachan	Prentice	Gibson	Park
	21st	Cruickshank	Clunie	Jefferies	Brown	Gallacher	Kay	Aird	Busby	Ford	Park	Prentice	Fraser (11)	Gibson (7)
	28th	Cruickshank	Clunie	Jefferies	Brown	Gallacher	Murray D	Aird	Busby	Gibson	Callachan	Shaw	Fraser	Kay
Mar	6th	Cruickshank	Clunie	Jefferies	Brown	Gallacher	Murray D	Aird	Busby	Gibson	Callachan	Shaw	Fraser	Park
	9th	Cruickshank	Clunie	Jefferies	Brown	Gallacher	Murray D	Aird	Busby	Gibson	Callachan*	Shaw	Park (8)	Fraser (3)
	13th	Cruickshank	Clunie	Jefferies	Callachan	Gallacher	Kay	Aird	Park	Shaw	Fraser	Prentice	Gibson (9)	Burrell
	16th	Cruickshank	Brown	Clunie	Callachan	Gallacher	Kay	Aird	Park	Gibson	Fraser	Prentice	Shaw (9)	Burrell (3)
	20th	Cruickshank	Brown	Burrell	Callachan	Gallacher	Kay	Aird	Callachan	Shaw	Fraser	Prentice	Park (9)	Hay
	27th	Cruickshank	Brown	Burrell	Jefferies	Gallacher	Kay	Aird	Busby	Shaw	Callachan	Prentice	Park	Fraser
Apr	3rd	Cruickshank	Brown	Burrell	Jefferies	Gallacher	Kay	Aird	Busby	Shaw	Callachan	Prentice	Park	Gibson
	7th	Cruickshank	Brown	Jefferies	Callachan	Gallacher	Kay	Aird	Busby	Shaw	Gibson	Prentice	Fraser (6)	Park
	10th	Cruickshank	Brown	Jefferies	Callachan	Gallacher	Kay	Aird	Busby	Gibson	Park	Prentice	Fraser (10)	Burrell
	14th	Cruickshank	Brown	Jefferies	Callachan	Gallacher	Kay	Aird	Busby	Shaw	Gibson	Prentice	Park	Fraser
	17th	Cruickshank	Brown	Jefferies	Callachan	Gallacher	Kay	Aird	Busby	Shaw	Gibson	Prentice	Fraser (11)	Park (7)
	21st	Cruickshank	Brown	Jefferies	Callachan	Gallacher	Kay	Aird	Busby	Shaw	Gibson	Prentice	Park (7)	Burrell
	24th	Cruickshank	Brown	Jefferies	Callachan	Gallacher	Kay	Aird	Busby	Shaw	Gibson	Prentice	Park (9)	Fraser (8)
	26th	Cruickshank	Brown	Burrell	Jefferies	Anderson	Kay	Aird	Park	Shaw	Callachan	Prentice	Fraser (9)	Gibson
May	1st	Cruickshank	Brown	Burrell	Jefferies	Gallacher	Kay	Gibson	Busby	Shaw	Callachan	Prentice	Aird (3)	Park (7)
	3rd	Cruickshank	Brown	Burrell	Jefferies	Gallacher	Kay	Aird	Busby	Shaw	Callachan	Prentice	Park	Fraser

No penalty - said referee Bob Valentine as Aberdeen's Davie Robb hits the deck in theatrical fashion after this clash with Dave Clunie at Pittodrie. Rab Prentice and Jim Brown of Hearts and Aberdeen's Doug Rougvie are the spectators. DC Thomson

Season 1976-77

Date			Opponents		Score	Crowd	Scorers
Aug	14th	LC	Dundee	h	2-0	10,000	Busby; Gibson
	18th	LC	Partick Thistle	a	2-0	4,000	Gallacher; Aird
	21st	LC	Motherwell	h	2-1	13,000	Gibson 2
	25th	LC	Partick Thistle	h	3-3	12,000	Park; Busby 2 (1 pen)
	28th	LC	Motherwell	a	4-1	7,800	Busby 2 (1 pen); Callachan; Park
Sep	1st	LC	Dundee	a	2-3	4,733	Park; Shaw
	4th	L	Aberdeen	a	2-2	11,077	Busby; Park
	11th	L	Partick Thistle	h	0-0	10,000	-
	15th	CWC1	Locomotiv Leipzig	a	0-2	25,000	-
	18th	L	Celtic	a	2-2	27,000	Busby (pen); Shaw
	22nd	LCQ	Falkirk	h	4-1	12,000	Prentice; Gallacher; Callachan; Gibson
	25th	L	Rangers	a	2-4	20,000	Gibson; Miller o.g.
	29th	CWC1	Locomotiv Leipzig	h	5-1 (5-2)	18,000	Kay; Gibson 2; Brown; Busby
Oct	2nd	L	Kilmarnock	h	2-2	10,000	Gallacher 2
	6th	LCQ2	Falkirk	a	3-4	5,000	Busby; Shaw; Prentice
	9th	L	Ayr United	h	2-2	11,000	Park; Shaw
	16th	L	Motherwell	a	1-1	7,932	Gibson
	20th	CWC2	SV Hamburg	a	2-4	20,000	Busby; Park
	23rd	L	Dundee United	h	1-2	12,000	Gibson
	25th	LCS	Celtic	Hamp.	1-2	21,700	Brown
	30th	L	Hibernian	a	1-1	23,723	Prentice
Nov	3rd	CWC2	SV Hamburg	h	1-4 (3-8)	25,000	Gibson
	10th	L	Aberdeen	h	2-1	12,000	Jefferies 2
	20th	L	Celtic	h	3-4	20,500	Gibson 3
	27th	L	Rangers	h	0-1	19,000	-
	30th	L	Partick Thistle	a	1-2	4,000	Shaw
Dec	11th	L	Ayr United	a	1-0	5,100	Gibson
	18th	L	Motherwell	h	2-1	10,000	Shaw; Stevens o.g.
	27th	L	Dundee United	a	1-1	10,000	Callachan
Jan	3rd	L	Aberdeen	a	1-4	18,761	Callachan (pen)
	8th	L	Partick Thistle	h	1-0	9,000	Whittaker o.g.
	22nd	L	Rangers	a	2-3	22,000	Gallacher; Shaw
	26th	L	Hibernian	h	0-1	24,100	-
	29th	SC1	Dumbarton	h	1-1	7,969	Callachan
Feb	2nd	SC1R	Dumbarton	a	1-0*	3,000	Gibson
	5th	L	Kilmarnock	h	4-0	8,000	Jefferies; Gibson 3
	7th	L	Celtic	a	1-5	21,000	Gibson
	15th	L	Kilmarnock	a	1-2	3,000	Shaw
	19th	L	Motherwell	a	1-2	6,900	Gibson
	26th	SC2	Clydebank	h	1-0	13,618	Busby
Mar	5th	L	Dundee United	h	1-1	8,000	Brown
	12th	SCQ	East Fife	h	0-0	10,300	-
	15th	SCQR	East Fife	a	3-2	8,550	Gibson; Prentice; Gallacher
	19th	L	Aberdeen	h	1-1	8,500	Park
	23rd	L	Hibernian	a	1-3	13,625	Gibson
	26th	L	Partick Thistle	a	0-2	5,500	-
	30th	SCS	Rangers	Hamp	0-2	23,222	
Apr	2nd	L	Celtic	h	0-3	17,000	-
	6th	L	Ayr United	h	1-2	11,500	Brown
	9th	L	Rangers	h	1-3	12,500	Busby
	13th	L	Hibernian	h	2-2	11,100	Gibson; Brown
	16th	L	Kilmarnock	a	2-2	3,000	Smith; Prentice
	20th	L	Dundee United	a	2-1	3,266	Robertson; Shaw
	23rd	L	Ayr United	a	1-1	3,781	Gallacher
	30th	L	Motherwell	h	3-2	6,500	Gibson; Smith; Bannon

* aet, 0-0 after 90 mts.Cup Cash Dumbarton (h) £4,737; Clydebank £7,112; East Fife £6,991

Ralph Callachan - talented perfomer in midfield for Hearts.

The Record		
League	-	**Ninth Place, Premier Division**
League Cup	-	**Semi-final**
Scottish Cup	-	**Semi-final**
European Cup -Winners Cup	-	**Second round**
Top Scorer	-	**Willie Gibson (24 goals)**
Av. Home Gate	-	**12,300**
Players used	-	**22**
Sent off (bookings)	-	**Three (14)**

Scottish League Premier Division

		Home			Away			Goals	
	P	W	D	L	W	D	L	F A	PTS
Celtic	36	13	5	0	10	4	4	79-39	55
Rangers	36	12	4	2	6	6	6	62-37	46
Aberdeen	36	12	4	2	4	7	7	56-42	43
Dundee United	36	8	5	5	8	4	6	54-45	41
Partick Thistle	36	9	5	4	2	8	8	40-44	35
Hibernian	36	4	10	4	4	8	6	34-35	34
Motherwell	36	8	7	3	2	5	11	57-60	32
Ayr United	36	5	5	8	6	3	9	44-68	30
Hearts	**36**	**5**	**6**	**7**	**2**	**7**	**9**	**49-66**	**27**
Kilmarnock	36	4	3	6	1	3	9	32-71	17

League Cup Section

	P	W	D	L	F A	PTS
Hearts	**6**	**4**	**1**	**1**	**15- 8**	**9**
Dundee	6	3	1	2	9-10	7
Partick Thistle	6	2	2	2	8- 7	6
Motherwell	6	0	2	4	7-14	2

Heart of Midlothian F.C. Line-Ups 1976-77

		1	2	3	4	5	6	7	8	9	10	11	12	13
Aug	14th	Wilson	Kay	Burrell	Jefferies	Gallacher	Murray D	Aird	Busby	Gibson	Park	Prentice	Callachan (11)	Brown
	18th	Wilson	Kay	Burrell	Jefferies	Gallacher	Clunie	Aird	Busby	Gibson	Park	Prentice	Brown (10)	Callachan
	21st	Wilson	Kay	Burrell	Jefferies	Gallacher	Clunie	Aird	Busby	Gibson	Park	Prentice	Callachan (4)	Brown
	25th	Wilson	Kay	Burrell	Jefferies	Gallacher	Clunie	Callachan	Busby	Gibson	Park	Prentice	Shaw (9)	Brown (3)
	28th	Wilson	Brown	Kay	Jefferies	Gallacher	Clunie	Park	Busby	Gibson	Callachan	Prentice	Shaw (9)	Fraser (8)
Sep	1st	Cruickshank	Brown	Kay	Jefferies	Gallacher	Cant	Park	Busby	Shaw	Callachan	Prentice	Burrell	Fraser
	4th	Cruickshank	Brown	Kay	Jefferies	Gallacher	Clunie	Park	Busby	Gibson	Callachan	Prentice	Burrell	Shaw (4)
	11th	Wilson	Brown	Kay	Jefferies	Gallacher	Clunie	Park	Busby	Gibson	Callachan	Prentice	Shaw (10)	Aird (9)
	15th	Cruickshank	Brown	Kay	Callachan	Gallacher	Clunie	Aird	Shaw	Busby	Park	Prentice	Fraser (8)	Jefferies
	18th	Cruickshank	Brown	Kay	Callaghan	Gallacher	Clunie	Aird	Busby	Gibson	Park	Shaw	Fraser (7)	Burrell (12)
	22nd	Cruickshank	Brown	Kay	Callachan	Gallacher	Clunie	Shaw	Busby	Gibson	Park	Prentice	Burrell	Aird
	25th	Cruickshank	Brown	Kay	Callachan	Gallacher	Clunie	Shaw	Busby	Gibson	Park	Prentice	Jefferies	Cant (4)
	29th	Cruickshank	Brown	Kay	Callachan	Gallacher	Clunie	Aird	Busby	Gibson	Park	Prentice	Shaw (7)	Jefferies (5)
Oct	2nd	Cruickshank	Brown	Kay	Callachan	Gallacher	Clunie	Aird	Busby	Gibson	Park	Prentice	Shaw (9)	Jefferies (10)
	6th	Cruickshank	Brown	Kay	Callachan	Gallacher	Clunie	Aird	Busby	Shaw	Park	Prentice	Jefferies (4)	Fraser
	9th	Cruickshank	Brown	Kay	Jefferies	Gallacher	Clunie	Shaw	Busby	Gibson	Park	Prentice	Fraser	Bannon
	16th	Wilson	Brown	Kay	Jefferies	Gallacher	Clunie	Shaw	Busby	Gibson	Park	Prentice	Fraser	Cruickshank
	20th	Wilson	Brown	Kay	Jefferies	Gallacher	Clunie	Aird	Park	Shaw	Busby	Prentice	Fraser (7)	Gibson (11)
	23rd	Wilson	Brown	Kay	Fraser	Gallacher	Cant	Shaw	Busby	Gibson	Park	Prentice	Burrell	Bannon
	25th	Wilson	Brown	Kay	Fraser	Gallacher	Clunie	Shaw	Busby	Gibson	Park	Prentice*	Jefferies	Cant
	30th	Wilson	Brown	Kay	Fraser	Gallacher	Clunie	Shaw	Busby	Gibson	Park	Prentice	Jefferies (10)	Cant
Nov	3rd	Wilson	Brown	Kay	Jefferies	Gallacher	Clunie	Shaw	Busby	Gibson	Park	Prentice	Fraser (4)	Bannon
	10th	Wilson	Brown	Kay	Jefferies	Gallacher	Clunie	Shaw	Busby	Gibson	Park	Prentice	Fraser	Burrell
	20th	Wilson	Brown	Kay	Jefferies	Gallacher	Clunie	Shaw	Busby	Gibson	Park	Prentice	Fraser	Burrell
	27th	Wilson	Brown	Kay	Jefferies	Gallacher	Clunie	Aird	Busby	Gibson	Shaw	Prentice	Park (7)	Burrell
	30th	Wilson	Brown	Kay	Jefferies	Gallacher	Clunie	Aird	Busby	Gibson	Shaw	Prentice	Park (11)	Burrell
Dec	11th	Cruickshank	Clunie	Kay	Jefferies	Gallacher	Fraser	Shaw	Brown	Gibson	Park	Callachan	Burrell	Prentice (8)
	18th	Cruickshank	Clunie	Kay	Jefferies	Gallacher	Fraser	Shaw	Callachan	Gibson	Park	Prentice	Aird	Burrell
	27th	Cruickshank	Kay	Clunie	Jefferies	Gallacher	Fraser	Aird	Brown	Gibson	Callachan	Shaw	Bannon	Smith G
Jan	3rd	Cruickshank	Clunie	Kay	Jefferies	Gallacher	Fraser	Shaw	Brown	Gibson	Callachan	Prentice	Park (2)	Aird (6)
	8th	Cruickshank	Brown	Kay	Jefferies	Gallacher	Fraser	Aird	Shaw	Gibson	Callachan	Prentice	Clunie	Park (10)
	22nd	Cruickshank	Brown	Clunie	Jefferies	Gallacher	Fraser	Aird	Busby	Shaw	Callachan	Prentice	Park (11)	Kay
	26th	Cruickshank	Brown	Kay	Jefferies	Gallacher	Fraser	Aird	Busby	Shaw	Callachan	Prentice	Clunie (9)	Park (5)
	29th	Cruickshank	Brown	Kay	Callachan	Jefferies	Fraser	Aird	Busby	Shaw	Park	Prentice	Bannon (7)	Clunie
Feb	2nd	Cruickshank	Brown	Burrell	Clunie	Jefferies	Fraser	Gibson	Shaw	Busby	Callachan	Park	Prentice (5)	Kay (9)
	5th	Cruickshank	Brown	Burrell	Jefferies	Clunie	Fraser	Bannon	Park	Gibson	Callachan	Shaw	Prentice (11)	Kay (9)
	7th	Cruickshank	Clunie	Burrell	Jefferies	Gallacher	Fraser	Bannon	Park	Gibson	Brown	Shaw	Prentice (2)	Kay
	15th	Cruickshank	Brown	Burrell	Jefferies	Gallacher	Fraser	Bannon	Busby	Gibson	Park	Shaw	Prentice (10)	Kay (11)
	19th	Cruickshank	Kay	Burrell	Brown	Gallacher	Fraser	Bannon	Busby	Gibson	Park	Prentice	Aird	Clunie
	26th	Cruickshank	Kay	Burrell	Brown	Gallacher	Fraser	Bannon	Busby	Gibson	Park	Prentice	Clunie	Aird
Mar	5th	Cruickshank	Kay	Burrell	Brown	Gallacher	Fraser	Bannon	Busby	Gibson	Park	Prentice	Clunie	Shaw (8)
	12th	Cruickshank	Kay	Burrell	Brown	Gallacher	Fraser	Bannon	Busby	Gibson	Park	Prentice	Clunie	Shaw (7)
	15th	Cruickshank	Clunie	Burrell	Kay	Gallacher	Fraser	Bannon	Busby	Gibson	Brown	Park	Shaw (3)	Prentice (7)
	19th	Cruickshank	Brown	Kay	Bannon	Gallacher	Clunie	Robertson	Busby	Gibson	Park	Prentice	Shaw (4)	Fraser
	23rd	Cruickshank	Kay	Clunie	Brown	Gallacher	Fraser	Robertson	Busby	Gibson	Park	Shaw	Prentice (8)	Bannon
	26th	Cruickshank	Brown	Kay	Bannon	Gallacher	Clunie	Robertson	Busby	Gibson	Park	Shaw	Prentice (7)	Fraser
	30th	Cruickshank	Brown	Kay	Clunie	Gallacher	Fraser	Bannon	Busby	Gibson	Park	Shaw	Prentice (10)	Aird
Apr	2nd	Cruickshank	Kay	Burrell	Clunie	Gallacher	Fraser	Bannon	Busby	Shaw	Park*	Robertson	Prentice (11)	Aird (7)
	6th	Cruickshank	Brown	Kay	Clunie	Gallacher	Fraser	Robertson*	Park	Gibson	Shaw	Prentice	Burrell (10)	Busby (7)
	9th	Cruickshank	Brown	Kay	Shaw	Gallacher	Clunie	Aird	Busby	Gibson	Park	Prentice	Bannon (10)	Fraser
	13th	Cruickshank	Brown	Kay	Shaw	Gallacher	Clunie	Aird	Busby	Gibson	Park	Prentice	Fraser	Bannon
	16th	Cruickshank	Brown	Kay	Bannon	Gallacher	Clunie	Aird	Busby	Gibson	Shaw	Prentice	Fraser (3)	Smith (9)
	20th	Cruickshank	Brown	Rodger	Fraser	Gallacher	Clunie	Aird	Smith	Shaw	Bannon	Robertson	Park (3)	Prentice
	23rd	Cruickshank	Brown	Rodger	Fraser	Gallacher	Clunie	Aird	Smith	Shaw	Bannon	Prentice	Robertson	Park
	30th	Wilson	Brown	Rodger	Park	Gallacher	Fraser	Gibson	Smith	Shaw	Bannon	Robertson	Prentice (4)	Busby

Appearances

	League	L/Cup	S/Cup	CWC	Total
John Gallacher	35 (4)	9 (2)	4 (1)	4	52 (7)
Jim Brown	34 (3)	5 (1)	6	4 (1)	49+2s (5)
Roy Kay	29	9	5	4 (1)	47+3s (1)
Willie Gibson	31 (15)	7 (4)	5 (2)	2 (3)	45+1s (24)
Donald Park	26 (3)	9 (3)	6	4 (1)	45+7s (7)
Drew Busby	25 (3)	9 (6)	6 (1)	4 (2)	44+1s (12)
Dave Clunie	29	7	3	4	43+1s
Bobby Prentice	25 (2)	9 (2)	3 (1)	4	41+11s (5)
Graham Shaw	30 (7)	4 (2)	3	3	40+10s (9)
Jim Cruickshank	27	3	6	2	38
Jim Jefferies	18 (3)	6	2	2	28+4s (3)
Cammy Fraser	20	1	6	0	27+5s
Ralph Callachan	13 (2)	5 (2)	2 (1)	2	22+2s (5)
Kenny Aird	13	4 (1)	1	3	21+3s (1)
Brian Wilson	9	6	0	2	17
Eammon Bannon	12 (1)	0	4	0	16+2s (1)
Sandy Burrell	6	4	4	0	14+2s
Malcolm Robertson	7 (1)	0	0	0	7 (1)
Paul Rodger	3	0	0	0	3
Gordon Smith	3 (2)	0	0	0	3+1s (2)
Jim Cant	1	1	0	0	2+1s
Don Murray	0	1	0	0	1

In defence - John Gallacher, Jim Jefferies and Dave Clunie feel the power of this shot from Aberdeen's Joe Harper at Pittodrie.

Season 1977-78

Date			Opponents		Score	Crowd	Scorers
Aug	13th	L	Dumbarton	a	2-2	4,100	I. Smith; Gibson
	20th	L	Dundee	h	2-1	12,000	Shaw; Busby
	27th	L	Kilmarnock	a	1-1	6,500	Gibson
	29th	LC1	Stenhousemuir	h	1-0	6,500	Park
Sep	3rd	LC1	Stenhousemuir	a	5-0 (6-0)	3,350	Shaw; Gibson 2; Bannon 2; Park
	10th	L	East Fife	h	4-1	8,500	Gibson; Busby; Prentice; Shaw
	14th	L	QOS	a	3-3	2,800	Bannon 2; O'Hara o.g.
	17th	L	St Johnstone	h	3-0	9,200	Bannon; Busby; I. Smith
	24th	L	Stirling Albion	a	4-2	6,800	Shaw; Gibson 3
	28th	L	Alloa Athletic	h	1-0	8,000	Park
Oct	1st	L	Hamilton Accies	h	0-2	9,000	-
	5th	LC2	Morton	h	3-0	12,000	Bannon 2; Busby (pen)
	8th	L	Morton	a	3-5	9,000	Park 2; Fraser
	15th	L	Airdrie	h	3-2	9,000	Jefferies; Gibson; Bannon
	19th	L	Montrose	a	1-3	2,100	Busby
	22nd	L	Dumbarton	h	2-1	9,200	Gibson; Tierney
	26th	LC2	Morton	a	0-2 (3-2)	7,500	
	29th	L	Dundee	a	1-1	9,074	Prentice
Nov	5th	L	Kilmarnock	h	1-2	8,000	Busby
	9th	LCQ	Dundee United	a	1-3	7,514	Busby
	12th	L	East Fife	a	0-2	3,898	-
	16th	LCQ	Dundee United	h	2-0* (3-3)	7,514	Kidd; Busby
	19th	L	St Johnstone	a	1-0	3,897	Robertson
	26th	L	Stirling Albion	h	2-0	8,500	Gibson; Park
Dec	10th	L	Morton	h	1-1	12,500	Anderson o.g.
	17th	L	Airdrie	a	4-2	6,500	Gibson 2; Park; Black o.g.
	24th	L	Arbroath	a	7-0	3,165	Gibson 3 (1 pen); Busby 3; Robertson
	31st	L	Kilmarnock	h	3-0	13,000	Bannon 3 (1 pen)
Jan	2nd	L	East Fife	a	2-1	7,774	Busby 2
	7th	L	Dundee	h	2-2	19,700	Gibson; Caldwell o.g.
	14th	L	QOS	h	1-0	12,300	Tierney
Feb	4th	L	Hamilton Accies	h	1-0	7,400	Gibson
	6th	SC1	Airdrie	a	3-2	6,800	Park; Busby; Gibson
	18th	SC2	Dumbarton	a	1-1	6,700	Bannon (pen)
	25th	L	Airdrie	h	3-0	9,600	Busby; Bannon (pen); Robertson
	27th	SC2R	Dumbarton	h	0-1	12,906	-
Mar	1st	LCS	Celtic	Hamp	0-2	18,800	-
	4th	L	Dumbarton	h	1-1	6,900	Fraser
	8th	L	Morton	a	1-0	10,000	Gibson
	11th	L	Alloa Athletic	a	2-0	4,500	Busby; McNicoll
	15th	L	Stirling Albion	a	2-1	4,700	Robertson; Gibson
	18th	L	Montrose	h	2-2	8,600	Bannon; Gibson
	25th	L	Montrose	a	0-0	2,500	-
Apr	2nd	L	Hamilton Accies	a	2-0	6,000	Busby; Bannon
	8th	L	Arbroath	h	3-2	9,644	Bannon; Busby; Gibson
	12th	L	St Johnstone	a	2-0	4,224	Bannon; Robertson
	15th	L	QOS	a	1-1	4,000	Park
	22nd	L	Alloa Athletic	h	2-1	11,222	Robertson; Busby
	29th	L	Arbroath	a	1-0	8,389	Bannon

* aet 3-3 after 90 mts. Hearts won 4-3 on pens. Cup Cash v. Dumbarton (h) £6,958

Jim Brown - an inspirational skipper for Hearts down the years.

The Record		
League	-	Runners-up, Division One
League Cup	-	Semi-final
Scottish Cup	-	Second round
Top Scorer	-	Willie Gibson (23 goals)
Av. Home Gate	-	10,100
Players used	-	22
Sent off (booked)	-	n/a

Appearances

	League	L/Cup	S/Cup	Total
Eamonn Bannon	39 (13)	7 (3)	3 (1)	49 (17)
Cammy Fraser	39 (2)	7	3	49 (2)
Jim Jefferies	38 (1)	7	2	47 (1)
Willie Gibson	36 (20)	7 (2)	3 (1)	46+3s (23)
Drew Busby	36 (15)	6 (3)	3 (1)	45 (19)
Ray Dunlop	34	7	3	44
Donald Park	32 (6)	6 (2)	3 (1)	41+2s (9)
Malcolm Robertson	26 (6)	4	3	33+4s (6)
Lawrie Tierney	23 (2)	5	3	31+6s (2)
Dave McNicoll	27 (1)	0	3	30 (1)
Walter Kidd	21	4 (1)	3	28+2s (1)
Graham Shaw	23 (3)	4 (1)	0	27+6s (4)
Bobby Prentice	17 (2)	4	0	21+12s (2)
Jim Brown	15	4	0	19
John Gallacher	7	2	0	9
Paul Rodger	5	3	1	9
John Brough	5	0	0	5
Ian Smith	3 (2)	0	0	3+5s (2)
Gordon Smith	2	0	0	2+2s
David Johnston	1	0	0	1
Gordon Brown	0	0	0	0+4s

Scottish League Division One

		Home			Away			Goals	
	P	W	D	L	W	D	L	F A	PTS
Morton	39	12	3	5	13	5	1	85-42	58
Hearts	**39**	**13**	**4**	**2**	**11**	**6**	**3**	**77-41**	**58**
Dundee	39	14	2	3	11	5	4	91-44	57
Dumbarton	39	11	8	1	5	9	5	65-48	49
Stirling Albion	39	7	6	7	8	6	5	59-52	42
Kilmarnock	39	8	7	4	6	5	9	52-46	40
Hamilton	39	10	5	5	2	7	10	54-55	36
St Johnstone	39	7	2	10	8	4	8	52-64	36
Arbroath	39	7	7	6	4	6	9	41-56	35
Airdrie	39	8	5	7	4	5	10	50-64	34
Montrose	39	7	5	7	3	4	13	55-71	29
Queen of the South	39	6	7	6	2	6	12	44-68	29
Alloa Athletic	39	4	6	9	4	2	14	71-84	24

Heart of Midlothian F.C. Line-Ups 1977-78

		1	2	3	4	5	6	7	8	9	10	11	12	14
Aug	13th	Dunlop	Brown J	Jefferies	Fraser	Gallacher	Shaw	Gibson	Bannon	Smith I	Busby	Smith G	Tierney (11)	Rodger
	20th	Dunlop	Brown J	Jefferies	Fraser	Gallacher	Shaw	Gibson	Bannon	Smith I	Busby	Johnston D	Tierney	Rodger
	27th	Dunlop	Brown J	Jefferies	Fraser	Gallacher	Shaw	Robertson	Bannon	Gibson	Busby	Prentice	Tierney (6)	Smith I (7)
	29th	Dunlop	Brown J	Jefferies	Fraser	Gallacher	Shaw	Robertson	Bannon	Gibson	Busby	Prentice	Park (11)	Tierney
Sep	3rd	Dunlop	Brown J	Jefferies	Fraser	Gallacher	Shaw	Park	Bannon	Gibson	Busby	Robertson	Prentice (11)	Tierney (6)
	10th	Dunlop	Brown J	Jefferies	Fraser	Gallacher	Shaw	Park	Bannon	Gibson	Busby	Prentice	Tierney (8)	Robertson
	14th	Dunlop	Brown J	Jefferies	Fraser	Gallacher	Shaw	Park	Bannon	Gibson	Busby	Prentice	Tierney	Smith I
	17th	Dunlop	Brown J	Jefferies	Fraser	Gallacher	Tierney	Park	Bannon	Gibson	Busby	Prentice	Smith I (9)	Rodger
	24th	Dunlop	Brown J	Jefferies	Fraser	Gallacher	Shaw	Park	Bannon	Gibson	Busby	Prentice	Tierney (5)	Smith I
	28th	Dunlop	Brown J	Jefferies	Fraser	Tierney	Shaw	Park	Bannon	Gibson	Busby	Prentice	Smith I (9)	Rodger
Oct	1st	Dunlop	Brown J	Jefferies	Fraser	Tierney	Shaw	Park	Bannon	Gibson	Busby	Prentice	Smith I (11)	Rodger
	5th	Dunlop	Brown J	Jefferies	Fraser	Tierney	Shaw	Park	Bannon	Gibson	Busby	Prentice	Robertson (11)	Rodger
	8th	Dunlop	Brown J	Jefferies	Fraser	Tierney	Shaw	Robertson	Bannon	Smith I	Park	Prentice	Gibson (9)	Brown G
	15th	Dunlop	Brown J	Jefferies	Fraser	Rodger	Shaw	Park	Bannon	Gibson	Tierney	Robertson	Prentice (5)	Smith I (11)
	19th	Dunlop	Brown J	Jefferies	Fraser	Tierney	Shaw	Park	Bannon	Gibson	Busby	Prentice	Kidd (5)	Smith G
	22nd	Dunlop	Brown J	Jefferies	Fraser	McNicoll	Shaw	Park	Bannon	Gibson	Tierney	Prentice	Kidd (6)	Smith I
	26th	Dunlop	Brown J	Jefferies	Fraser	Tierney	Shaw	Park	Bannon	Gibson	Kidd	Prentice	Robertson (11)	Rodger
	29th	Dunlop	Brown J	Jefferies	Fraser	McNicoll	Shaw	Park	Bannon	Gibson	Busby	Prentice	Robertson (11)	Tierney
Nov	5th	Dunlop	Brown J	Jefferies	Fraser	McNicoll	Shaw	Park	Bannon	Gibson	Busby	Prentice	Smith G (11)	Tierney (2)
	9th	Dunlop	Kidd	Rodger	Fraser*	Jefferies	Tierney	Park	Bannon	Gibson	Busby	Prentice	Robertson (7)	Brown G
	12th	Dunlop	Kidd	Rodger	McNicoll	Jefferies	Fraser	Park	Bannon	Gibson	Busby	Robertson	Smith I	Brown G
	16th	Dunlop	Kidd	Rodger	Fraser	Jefferies	Tierney	Park	Bannon	Gibson	Busby	Robertson	Prentice (9)	Brown G (6)
	19th	Dunlop	Fraser	Rodger	McNicoll	Jefferies	Tierney	Robertson	Bannon	Park	Busby	Prentice	Gibson (3)	Brown G
	26th	Dunlop	Kidd	Fraser	McNicoll	Jefferies	Tierney	Park	Bannon	Gibson	Busby	Robertson	Prentice	Rodger
Dec	10th	Dunlop	Kidd	Fraser	McNicoll	Jefferies	Tierney	Park	Bannon	Gibson	Busby	Robertson	Prentice (11)	Rodger
	17th	Dunlop	Kidd	Fraser	McNicoll	Jefferies	Tierney	Park	Bannon	Gibson	Busby	Robertson	Prentice	Brown G
	24th	Dunlop	Kidd	Fraser	McNicoll	Jefferies	Tierney	Park	Bannon	Gibson	Busby	Robertson	Prentice	Rodger
	31st	Dunlop	Kidd	Fraser	McNicoll	Jefferies	Tierney	Park	Bannon	Gibson	Busby	Robertson	Prentice (7)	Brown G
Jan	2nd	Dunlop	Kidd	Fraser	McNicoll	Jefferies	Tierney	Prentice	Bannon	Gibson	Busby	Robertson	MacLaren	Rodger
	7th	Dunlop	Kidd	Fraser	McNicoll	Jefferies	Tierney	Shaw	Bannon	Gibson	Busby	Prentice	Brown G (7)	Rodger
	14th	Dunlop	Kidd	Fraser	McNicoll	Jefferies	Tierney	Prentice	Bannon	Gibson	Busby	Robertson	Shaw (11)	Brown G
Feb	4th	Dunlop	Kidd	Fraser	McNicoll	Jefferies	Tierney	Prentice	Bannon	Gibson	Busby	Robertson	Shaw (7)	Park (11)
	6th	Dunlop	Kidd	Fraser	McNicoll	Jefferies	Tierney	Park	Bannon	Gibson	Busby	Robertson	Shaw (6)	Prentice (7)
	18th	Dunlop	Kidd	Fraser	McNicoll	Jefferies	Tierney	Park	Bannon	Gibson	Busby	Robertson	Prentice	Shaw
	25th	Dunlop	Kidd	Fraser	McNicoll	Rodger	Tierney	Park	Bannon	Gibson	Busby	Robertson	Shaw (6)	Prentice (11)
	27th	Dunlop	Kidd	Fraser	McNicoll	Rodger	Tierney	Park	Bannon	Gibson	Busby	Robertson	Shaw (9)	Prentice (7)
Mar	1st	Dunlop	Kidd	Fraser	Jefferies	Rodger	Tierney	Park	Bannon	Gibson	Busby	Robertson	Shaw (5)	Prentice (7)
	4th	Dunlop	Kidd	Fraser	McNicoll	Jefferies	Tierney	Park	Bannon	Shaw	Busby	Robertson	Gibson (6)	Rodger
	8th	Dunlop	Kidd	Fraser	McNicoll	Jefferies	Shaw	Park	Bannon	Gibson	Busby	Robertson	Brown G	Tierney
	11th	Dunlop	Kidd	Fraser	McNicoll	Jefferies	Shaw	Park	Bannon	Gibson	Busby	Robertson	Brown G (6)	Tierney
	15th	Dunlop	Kidd	Fraser	McNicoll	Jefferies	Tierney	Park	Bannon	Gibson	Busby	Robertson	Brown G	Prentice
	18th	Dunlop	Kidd	Fraser	McNicoll	Jefferies	Tierney	Park	Bannon	Gibson	Busby	Robertson	Prentice (6)	Brown G
	25th	Dunlop	Fraser	Rodger	McNicoll	Jefferies	Smith G	Park	Bannon	Gibson	Busby	Robertson	Prentice (11)	Black
Apr	2nd	Dunlop	Kidd	Fraser	McNicoll	Jefferies	Tierney	Park	Bannon	Gibson	Busby	Robertson	Smith G (4)	Prentice
	8th	Brough	Tierney	Fraser	McNicoll	Jefferies	Shaw	Park	Bannon	Gibson	Busby	Robertson	Smith G (11)	Paterson (2)
	12th	Brough	Kidd	Fraser	McNicoll	Jefferies	Shaw	Park	Bannon	Gibson	Busby	Robertson	Smith G	Rodger
	15th	Brough	Kidd	Fraser	McNicoll	Jefferies	Shaw	Park	Bannon	Gibson	Busby	Robertson	Smith G	Rodger
	22nd	Brough	Kidd	Fraser	McNicoll	Jefferies	Shaw	Park	Bannon	Gibson	Busby	Robertson	Prentice (9)	Rodger
	29th	Brough	Kidd	Fraser	McNicoll	Jefferies	Shaw	Park	Bannon	Gibson	Busby	Robertson	Paterson (9)	Smith G

Celebrations - a happy Hearts squad celebrate in the dressing room after their promotion-clinching win at Arbroath.

Season 1978-79

Date			Opponents		Score	Crowd	Scorers
Aug	12th	L	Aberdeen	h	1-4	11,500	Bannon
	16th	ASC1	Partick Thistle	a	1-2	4,000	Gibson
	19th	L	Celtic	a	0-4	24,000	-
	23rd	ASC1	Partick Thistle	h	1-1 (2-3)	7,500	Bannon
	26th	L	Hibernian	h	1-1	20,000	Park
	30th	LC1	Morton	h	1-3	7,000	Shaw
Sep	2nd	LC1	Morton	a	1-4 (2-7)	5,000	Bannon (pen)
	9th	L	Partick Thistle	a	2-3	5,000	Bannon (pen); Busby
	16th	L	Morton	h	1-1	7,200	McQuade
	23rd	L	Motherwell	a	1-0	5,200	Robertson
	30th	L	Dundee United	a	1-3	6,300	Bannon
Oct	7th	L	St Mirren	h	1-1	9,500	Gibson
	14th	L	Rangers	h	0-0	18,200	-
	21st	L	Aberdeen	a	2-1	12,750	O'Connor; McQuade
	28th	L	Celtic	h	2-0	18,500	Busby 2
Nov	4th	L	Hibernian	a	2-1	20,100	McQuade; O'Connor
	11th	L	Partick Thistle	h	0-1	11,000	-
	18th	L	Morton	a	2-3	7,500	Bannon (pen); O'Connor
	25th	L	Motherwell	h	3-2	9,000	O'Connor; Robertson; Fraser
Dec	9th	L	St Mirren	a	0-4	6,050	-
	16th	L	Rangers	a	3-5	18,000	Busby 2; Bannon
	23rd	L	Aberdeen	h	0-0	9,500	-
Jan	20th	L	Motherwell	a	2-3	3,900	Robertson; O'Connor
	27th	SC1	Raith Rovers	a	2-0	10,000	Robertson 2
Feb	10th	L	St Mirren	h	1-2	8,000	Gibson
	24th	L	Rangers	h	3-2	16,500	O'Connor 2; Robertson
Mar	3rd	SC2	Morton	h	1-1	9,000	Gibson (pen)
	5th	SC2R	Morton	a	1-0	8,000	Busby
	10th	SCQ	Hibernian	a	1-2	22,616	O'Connor
	17th	L	Hibernian	a	1-1	13,300	Gibson (pen)
	28th	L	Hibernian	h	1-2	16,000	Gibson
	31st	L	Morton	a	2-2	6,000	Busby; Gibson (pen)
Apr	4th	L	Dundee United	h	2-0	6,700	Shaw; O'Connor
	7th	L	Motherwell	h	3-0	7,000	Dempsey o.g; Fraser 2 (1 pen)
	11th	L	Partick Thistle	h	0-2	10,000	-
	14th	L	Dundee United	h	0-3	7,800	-
	18th	L	Celtic	h	0-3	12,000	-
	21st	L	St Mirren	a	1-2	5,800	McQuade
	25th	L	Dundee United	a	1-2	6,000	Gibson (pen)
	28th	L	Rangers	a	0-4	21,000	-
May	2nd	L	Aberdeen	a	0-5	6,000	-
	5th	L	Partick Thistle	a	0-2	4,000	-
	7th	L	Morton	h	0-1	2,700	-
	14th	L	Celtic	a	0-1	18,000	-

Cup Cash v. Raith £12,000; Morton (h) 6,309 exc. stand; Hibs £24,842

Frank Liddell - hard-tackling and strong in the air

The Record		
League	-	Ninth Place, Premier Division
League Cup	-	First round
Scottish Cup	-	Quarter-final
Anglo-Scottish Cup	-	First round
Top Scorer	-	Derek O'Connor (9 goals)
Av. Home Gate	-	11,200
Players used	-	29
Sent off (bookings)	-	Six (30)

Appearances

	League	L/Cup	S/Cup	AS/Cup	Total
Cammy Fraser	36 (3)	0	3	2	41 (3)
Willie Gibson	33 (6)	1	4 (1)	2 (1)	40+1s (8)
Frank Liddell	31	2	3	2	38
Malcolm Robertson	27 (4)	2	4 (2)	1	34+2s (6)
Walter Kidd	29	0	4	2	35+1s
Jim Jefferies	26	2	4	2	34+2s
Drew Busby	25 (6)	1	3 (1)	0	29+2s (7)
Jim Brown	22	2	4	0	28+4s
Derek O'Connor	18 (8)	0	4 (1)	0	22 (9)
Eamonn Bannon	19 (5)	2 (1)	0	2 (1)	23 (7)
Ray Dunlop	18	0	2	2	22
Dave McNicoll	16	2	1	2	21+1s
John Craig	14	0	3	0	17+4s
Thomson Allan	16	0	0	0	16
Dennis McQuade	13 (4)	0	0	0	13+11s (4)
Ian Black	10	0	2	0	12+4s
Graham Shaw	8 (1)	1 (1)	1	2	12+2s (2)
Lawrie Tierney	8	1	0	0	9+7s
Bobby Prentice	6	1	0	1	8+6s
John Brough	2	2	2	0	6
Donald Park	2 (1)	1	0	2	5+1s (1)
Colin More	4	0	0	0	4

Scottish League Premier Division

	P	Home W	Home D	Home L	Away W	Away D	Away L	Goals F-A	PTS
Celtic	36	12	4	2	9	2	7	61-37	48
Rangers	36	12	5	1	6	4	8	52-35	45
Dundee United	36	12	4	2	6	4	8	56-37	44
Aberdeen	36	9	4	5	4	10	4	59-36	40
Hibernian	36	7	9	2	5	4	9	44-48	37
St Mirren	36	8	3	7	7	3	8	45-41	36
Morton	36	9	4	5	3	8	7	52-53	36
Partick Thistle	36	10	2	6	3	6	9	42-39	34
Hearts	**36**	**5**	**5**	**8**	**3**	**2**	**13**	**39-71**	**23**
Motherwell	36	2	5	11	3	2	13	33-86	17

Appearances

	League	L/Cup	S/Cup	AS/Cup	Total
Paul Rodger	2	1	0	0	3
David Scott	3	0	0	0	3+2s
Kenny McLeod	2	0	0	0	2+1s
Des O'Sullivan	2	0	0	0	2
Gordon Smith	0	1	0	0	1+2s
Ian Paterson	0	0	0	0	0+2s

Heart of Midlothian F.C. Line-Ups 1978-79

	1	2	3	4	5	6	7	8	9	10	11	12	13
Aug 12th	Dunlop	Kidd	Fraser	McNicoll	Jefferies	Liddell	Park	Bannon	Gibson	Shaw	Robertson	Prentice (9)	Tierney (11)
16th	Dunlop	Kidd	Fraser	McNicoll	Jefferies	Liddell	Park	Bannon	Gibson	Shaw	Robertson	Prentice ?	Tierney ?
19th	Dunlop	Kidd	Fraser	McNicoll	Jefferies	Liddell	Robertson	Bannon	Gibson	Shaw	Prentice	Tierney (10)	Park (7)
23rd	Dunlop	Kidd	Fraser	McNicoll	Jefferies	Liddell	Park	Bannon	Gibson	Shaw	Prentice	Tierney (2)	Paterson
26th	Brough	Fraser	Jefferies*	McNicoll	Liddell	Shaw	Park*	Bannon	Gibson	Tierney	Prentice	Robertson (9)	Smith (10)
30th	Brough	Brown	Jefferies	McNicoll	Liddell	Shaw	Robertson	Bannon	Gibson	Tierney*	Prentice	Smith G (11)	Busby (8)
Sep 2nd	Brough	Brown	Rodger	McNicoll	Jefferies	Liddell	Park	Bannon	Busby	Smith G	Robertson	Prentice	Shaw
9th	Brough	Brown	Fraser	McNicoll	Liddell	Jefferies	McQuade	Bannon	Busby	Craig	Robertson	Gibson (6)	Tierney (11)
16th	Dunlop	Kidd	Fraser	Jefferies	Liddell	Shaw	McQuade	Bannon	Gibson	Busby	Robertson	Tierney (6)	Brown
23rd	Dunlop	Kidd	Fraser	Jefferies	Liddell	Tierney	Robertson	Bannon	Gibson	Busby	McQuade	McNicoll (10)	Prentice
30th	Dunlop	Kidd	Fraser	Jefferies	Liddell	Craig	Robertson	Bannon	Gibson	Busby	McQuade	Tierney (4)	Brown (10)
Oct 7th	Dunlop	Kidd	Fraser	McNicoll	Liddell	Tierney	Robertson	Bannon	Gibson	Busby	Prentice	Brown (6)	McQuade (7)
14th	Dunlop	Kidd	Jefferies	McNicoll	Liddell	Fraser	Robertson	Bannon	Gibson	Busby	Prentice	Brown	McQuade (9)
21st	Dunlop	Kidd	Jefferies	McNicoll	Liddell	Fraser	Gibson	Bannon	O'Connor	Busby	Robertson	Brown (2)	McQuade (11)
28th	Dunlop	Brown	Jefferies	McNicoll	Liddell	Fraser	Gibson	Bannon	O'Connor	Busby	Robertson*	Tierney (6)	McQuade
Nov 4th	Dunlop	Brown	Jefferies	McNicoll	Liddell	Fraser	Gibson	Bannon	O'Connor	Busby	McQuade	Craig	Prentice
11th	Dunlop	Brown	Jefferies	McNicoll	Liddell	Fraser	Gibson	Bannon	O'Connor	Busby	McQuade	Craig (8)	Robertson (11)
18th	Dunlop	Brown	Jefferies	McNicoll	Liddell	Fraser	Gibson	Bannon	O'Connor	Craig	Robertson	Prentice (7)	Kidd (2)
25th	Dunlop	Kidd	Jefferies	McNicoll	Liddell	Fraser	Robertson	Bannon	O'Connor	Busby	Prentice	McQuade (11)	Craig
Dec 9th	Dunlop	Kidd	Brown	McNicoll	Liddell	Fraser	McQuade	Bannon	O'Connor	Busby	Robertson	Prentice (7)	Craig (4)
16th	Dunlop	Kidd	Brown	Jefferies	Liddell	Fraser	Gibson	Bannon	O'Connor	Busby	Robertson	McQuade (7)	Craig (5)
23rd	Dunlop	Kidd	Fraser	McNicoll	Jefferies	Craig	Gibson	Bannon	O'Connor	Busby	Robertson	McQuade (7)	Brown
Jan 20th	Dunlop	Kidd	Fraser	McNicoll	Jefferies	Craig	Gibson	Bannon	O'Connor	Busby	Robertson	Brown (6)	McQuade (7)
27th	Dunlop	Kidd	Brown	McNicoll	Jefferies	Black	Gibson	Busby	O'Connor	Fraser	Robertson	McQuade	Tierney
Feb 10th	Dunlop	Kidd	Brown	McNicoll	Jefferies	Craig	Gibson	Fraser	O'Connor	Busby	Robertson	McQuade	Black
24th	Allan	Kidd	Brown	Liddell	Jefferies	Craig	Gibson	Fraser	O'Connor	Busby	Robertson	McQuade (11)	Black
Mar 3rd	Dunlop*	Kidd	Brown	Liddell	Jefferies	Craig	Gibson	Fraser	O'Connor	Shaw	Robertson	Black	McQuade
5th	Brough	Kidd	Brown	Liddell	Jefferies	Craig	Gibson	Fraser	O'Connor	Busby	Robertson	McQuade	Black
10th	Brough	Brown	Black	Liddell	Jefferies	Craig	Gibson	Kidd	O'Connor	Busby	Robertson	Shaw (10)	McQuade (7)
17th	Allan	Kidd	Black	Liddell	Jefferies	Craig	Gibson	Fraser	O'Connor	Busby	Robertson	Prentice (11)	Shaw
28th	Allan	Kidd	Black	Jefferies	Liddell	Craig	Gibson	Fraser	O'Connor	Busby	Robertson	Brown J	McQuade
31st	Allan	Kidd	Brown	Jefferies	Liddell	Shaw	Gibson	Fraser	O'Connor	Busby	Robertson	Black (11)	McQuade
Apr 4th	Allan	Kidd	Brown	Jefferies	Liddell	Shaw	Gibson	Fraser	O'Connor	Busby	Robertson	Black (10)	McQuade
7th	Allan	Kidd	Brown	Jefferies	Liddell	Shaw	Gibson	Fraser	O'Connor	Busby	Robertson	Black (11)	McQuade (7)
11th	Allan	Kidd	Brown	Jefferies	Shaw	Gibson	Fraser	O'Connor	Black	Rodger	Robertson	Craig	McQuade (6)
14th	Allan	Kidd	Black	Liddell	Jefferies	Brown	Robertson	Fraser	Gibson	Busby	McQuade	Craig (3)	Prentice (11)
18th	Allan	Kidd	Brown	Tierney	Liddell	Craig	Robertson	Fraser	Gibson	Busby	Prentice	Paterson (9)	Black
21st	Allan	Kidd	Brown	Fraser	Rodger	Craig	McQuade	Tierney	Gibson	Busby	Robertson	Paterson (11)	Black (8)
25th	Allan	Kidd	Black	Fraser	Liddell	Craig	Gibson	Brown	Scott	Tierney	McQuade	Prentice(8)	Busby (10)
28th	Allan	Kidd	Black	Fraser	Liddell	Tierney	Gibson	Brown	Scott	Craig	McQuade	Stewart (7)	Prentice
May 2nd	Allan	Brown	Black	Fraser	Liddell	More	Gibson	Tierney	Stewart	Craig	McQuade	Scott (10)	Jefferies (8)
5th	Allan	Kidd	Black	More	Liddell	Brown	Gibson	Fraser	Scott	Stewart	McQuade	McLeod (9)	More
7th	Allan	Kidd	Black	Liddell	Fraser	O'Sullivan	Gibson	More	Brown	Stewart	McLeod	McQuade	McLeod (9)
14th	Allan	Kidd	Black	More	Liddell	Brown	O'Sullivan	Fraser	Gibson	Stewart	McLeod	Scott (11)	Jefferies (7)

On the wing - Malcolm Robertson shows Dundee United's Scottish international defender Paul Hegarty the ball before beating him down the line. Former Hearts midfielder George Fleming and Dennis McQuade are the others on view. DC Thomson

Season 1979-80

Date			Opponents		Score	Crowd	Scorers
Aug	11th	L	Arbroath	a	2-1	2,600	Fraser; Robertson
	18th	L	Ayr United	h	4-2	5,700	Gibson; O'Connor; Fraser; Robertson
	25th	L	Berwick Rangers	a	3-1	4,500	O'Connor 3
Sep	1st	LC1	Ayr United	a	2-2	2,100	Gibson (pen); Robertson
	3rd	LC1	Ayr United	h	0-1	6,800	-
	5th	L	St Johnstone	h	2-1	5,000	Gibson 2
	8th	L	Clydebank	h	2-1	6,000	Kidd 2
	11th	L	Raith Rovers	a	2-3	4,000	O'Connor 2
	15th	L	Stirling Albion	h	2-1	5,500	J. Kennedy o.g.; Gibson (pen)
	18th	L	Motherwell	a	2-4	6,000	Gibson (2 pens)
	22nd	L	Airdrie	h	2-2	5,000	O'Connor; Fraser
	29th	L	Clyde	h	4-1	5,700	Fraser 2; Gibson 2 (1 pen)
Oct	6th	L	Dumbarton	a	1-1	3,500	Sinclair o.g.
	13th	L	Hamilton Accies	a	1-3	6,000	Fraser
	20th	L	Dunfermline	h	2-1	6,000	Fraser 2
	27th	L	Ayr United	a	0-2	4,500	-
Nov	3rd	L	Berwick Rangers	a*	0-0	2,650	-
	10th	L	Clydebank	a	1-1	2,000	Fraser
	17th	L	Stirling Albion	h	1-0	4,500	O'Connor
	24th	L	Motherwell	h	2-1	4,800	Shaw; Gibson
Dec	1st	L	Clyde	a	2-2	1,500	Fraser; O'Connor
	8th	L	Dumbarton	h	1-0	5,600	O'Sullivan
	15th	L	Hamilton Accies	h	0-0	4,750	-
Jan	5th	L	Clydebank	h	3-3	5,000	O'Connor 3
	12th	L	Stirling Albion	a	1-0	2,800	Stewart
	19th	L	Motherwell	a	0-0	5,000	-
	30th	SC3	Alloa Athletic	a	1-0	3,400	Fraser
Feb	9th	L	Dumbarton	a	1-1	4,500	Robinson
	16th	SC4	Stirling Albion	h	2-0	6,000	Shaw 2
	23rd	L	Hamilton Accies	h	1-0	5,400	O'Connor
Mar	1st	L	Arbroath	h	2-1	4,650	Gibson 2 (1 pen)
	8th	SCQ	Rangers	a	1-6	31,000	T. Forsyth o.g.
	15th	L	Raith Rovers	a	0-0	4,000	-
	25th	L	Dunfermline	a	3-0	4,700	Gibson; Fraser; Shaw
	29th	L	Arbroath	h	1-0	4,200	Robertson
Apr	1st	L	Ayr United	h	0-1	5,200	-
	5th	L	Airdrie	a	1-0	1,000	Gibson
	9th	L	Raith Rovers	h	2-2	6,150	Gibson; Fraser
	13th	L	Clyde	a	1-2	4,000	Fillipi o.g.
	16th	L	St Johnstone	a	1-0	3,100	Gibson
	19th	L	Dunfermline	h	0-0	6,550	-
	23rd	L	Berwick Rangers	h	1-1	4,800	Liddell
	26th	L	St Johnstone	a	3-0	3,500	Gibson 2 (1 pen); Jefferies
	30th	L	Airdrie	h	1-0	13,229	Liddell

* Played at Tynecastle. ** Earlier tie on 26/1 abandoned after 51 mts due to fog. Alloa led 1-0

Graham Shaw - power play in the Hearts midfield.

The Record		
League	-	Division One Champions
League Cup	-	First round
Scottish Cup	-	Quarter-final
Top Scorer	-	Willie Gibson (18 goals)
Av. Home Gate	-	5,700
Players Used	-	24
Sent off (booked)	-	n/a

Appearances

	League	L/Cup	S/Cup	Total
Willie Gibson	39 (17)	2 (1)	3	44 (18)
Frank Liddell	37 (2)	2	3	42 (2)
Cammy Fraser	36 (12)	2	3 (1)	41 (13)
Jim Denny	34	0	3	37
Bobby Robinson	31 (1)	2	3	36+4s (1)
Jim Jefferies	32 (1)	1	3	36 (1)
John Brough	31	0	3	34
Malcolm Robertson	28 (3)	2 (1)	2	32+2s (4)
Crawford Boyd	28	0	3	31
Walter Kidd	27 (2)	2	1	30+7s (2)
Derek O'Connor	25 (13)	1	2	28+2s (13)
Graham Shaw	15 (2)	2	2 (2)	19+6s (4)
Ian Black	17	2	0	19+1s
Bobby Masterton	9	1	2	12+7s
Thomson Allan	8	2	0	10
Archie White	9	0	0	9
Colin More	6	1	0	7
Lawrie Tierney	6	0	0	6+1s
Steve Hamilton	5	0	0	5+1s
Rab Stewart	3 (1)	0	0	3+2s
Des O'Sullivan	2 (1)	0	0	2+6s (1)
Jim Docherty	1	0	0	1+5s
David Scott	0	0	0	0+4s
Pat McShane	0	0	0	0+2s

Scottish League Division One

		Home			Away			Goals	
	P	W	D	L	W	D	L	F A	PTS
Hearts	**39**	**13**	**7**	**0**	**7**	**6**	**6**	**58-39**	**53**
Airdrie	39	14	2	4	7	7	5	78-47	51
Ayr United	39	11	5	4	5	7	7	64-51	44
Dumbarton	39	10	4	5	9	2	9	59-51	44
Raith Rovers	39	8	7	5	7	5	8	59-64	43
Motherwell	39	9	7	3	7	4	9	59-48	43
Hamilton Accies	39	11	5	3	4	5	11	60-59	40
Stirling Albion	39	7	6	7	6	7	6	40-40	39
Clydebank	39	9	6	5	5	2	12	58-57	36
Dunfermline	39	7	7	5	4	6	10	39-57	35
St Johnstone	39	5	5	9	7	5	8	57-74	34
Berwick Rangers	39	5	7	7	3	8	9	57-64	31
Arbroath	39	7	5	7	2	5	13	50-79	28
Clyde	39	3	6	10	3	7	10	45-69	25

Heart of Midlothian F.C. Line-Ups 1979-80

	1	2	3	4	5	6	7	8	9	10	11	12	13
Aug 11th	Allan	Jefferies	Black	More	Liddell	Robinson	Gibson	Fraser	O'Connor	Tierney	Robertson	Kidd	McShane
18th	Allan	Jefferies	Black	More	Liddell	Robinson	Gibson	Fraser	O'Connor	Tierney	Robertson	Kidd (8)	McShane
25th	Allan	Jefferies	Black	More	Liddell	Robinson	Gibson	Fraser	O'Connor	Tierney	Robertson	Kidd (7)	McShane (10)
Sep 1st	Allan	Jefferies	Black	More	Liddell	Robinson	Gibson	Fraser	Shaw	Kidd	Robertson	Scott (11)	Masterton (2)
3rd	Allan	Kidd	Black	Fraser	Liddell	Robinson	Gibson	Masterton	Shaw	O'Connor	Robertson	Scott (10)	Hamilton (8)
5th	Allan	Hamilton	Black	Denny	Liddell	Robinson	Gibson	Fraser	Shaw	Kidd	Robertson	Masterton (9)	Scott
8th	Allan	Hamilton	Black	Denny	Liddell	Robinson	Gibson	Fraser	Shaw	Kidd	Robertson	Masterton (2)	O'Connor (9)
11th	Allan	Jefferies	Black	Denny	Liddell	Robinson	Gibson	Fraser	O'Connor	Kidd	Robertson	Shaw (10)	Masterton
15th	Allan	Hamilton	Jefferies	Denny	Liddell	Robinson	Gibson	Fraser	O'Connor	Kidd	Robertson	Black (2)	Scott (3)
18th	Allan	Denny	Black	Boyd	Liddell	Robinson	Gibson	Fraser	O'Connor	Kidd	Robertson	More	Masterton
22nd	Brough	Kidd	Denny	Boyd	Liddell	Robinson	Gibson	Fraser	O'Connor	Tierney	Robertson	Masterton (6)	Scott (7)
29th	Brough	Kidd	Black	Boyd	Liddell	Robinson	Gibson	Fraser	Denny	Tierney	Robertson	Shaw (9)	Scott
Oct 6th	Brough	Kidd	Black	Boyd	Liddell	Robinson	Gibson	Fraser	Denny	Tierney	Robertson	Masterton (10)	McShane
13th	Brough	Kidd	Black	Boyd	Liddell	Shaw	Gibson	Fraser	Denny	Masterton	Robinson	Tierney (11)	McShane (6)
20th	Brough	Kidd	Black	Boyd	Liddell	Jefferies	Gibson	Fraser	Stewart	Robinson	Masterton	O'Sullivan (8)	Shaw (10)
27th	Brough	Kidd	Black	Boyd	Liddell	Jefferies	Gibson	Fraser	Stewart	Shaw	Masterton	O'Sullivan (11)	Robinson (4)
Nov 3rd	Brough	Kidd	Black	Boyd	Liddell	Jefferies	Gibson	Fraser	O'Connor	Denny	Robertson	O'Sullivan	Robinson (2)
10th	Brough	Denny	Black	Boyd	Jefferies	Kidd	Gibson	Fraser	O'Connor	Robinson	Robertson	O'Sullivan (11)	Masterton (3)
17th	Brough	Kidd	Jefferies	Denny	Boyd	Robinson	Gibson	Fraser	O'Connor	Masterton	Robertson	O'Sullivan (11)	Shaw (10)
24th	Brough	Kidd	Denny	Boyd	Liddell	Jefferies	Gibson	Fraser	O'Connor	Shaw	Robertson	O'Sullivan	Robinson (4)
Dec 1st	Brough	Kidd	Denny	Boyd	Liddell	Jefferies	Gibson	Fraser	O'Connor	Shaw	Robertson	McShane	Black
8th	Brough	Kidd	Black	Boyd	Liddell	Jefferies	Gibson	Fraser	O'Connor	Denny	Robertson	Masterton	O'Sullivan (9)
15th	Brough	Kidd	Black	Boyd	Liddell	Jefferies	Gibson	Fraser	O'Connor	Denny	O'Sullivan	Stewart (7)	Masterton (11)
Jan 5th	Brough	Kidd	Black	Boyd	Liddell	Jefferies	Gibson	Denny	O'Connor	Masterton	Stewart	Robinson (2)	O'Sullivan (7)
12th	Brough	Kidd	Denny	Boyd	Liddell	Jefferies	O'Sulllivan	Robinson	O'Connor	Masterton	Gibson	Black	Stewart (7)
19th	Brough	Kidd	Denny	Boyd	Liddell	Jefferies	Gibson	Fraser	O'Connor	Robinson	Robertson	Masterton	Stewart
30th	Brough	Kidd	Denny	Boyd	Liddell	Jefferies	Masterton	Fraser	Gibson	Robinson	Robertson	O'Sullivan	Stewart
Feb 9th	Brough	Kidd	Denny	Boyd	Liddell	Jefferies	Gibson	Robinson	O'Connor	Masterton	Robertson	Stewart	Docherty (11)
16th	Brough	Robinson	Denny	Boyd	Liddell	Jefferies	Gibson	Fraser	O'Connor	Masterton	Shaw	Stewart	Black
23rd	Brough	Robinson	Denny	Boyd	Liddell	Jefferies	Gibson	Fraser	O'Connor	Shaw	Robertson	Docherty	Stewart
Mar 1st	Brough	Robinson	Denny	Boyd	Liddell	Jefferies	Gibson	Fraser	O'Connor	Shaw	Robertson	Docherty (11)	Kidd
8th	Brough	Robinson	Denny	Boyd	Liddell	Jefferies	Gibson	Fraser	O'Connor	Shaw	Robertson	Docherty (9)	Kidd
15th	Brough	Robinson	Denny	Masterton	Liddell	Jefferies	Gibson	Fraser	White	Shaw	Robertson	Docherty	Kidd (10)
25th	Brough	Robinson	Denny	More	Liddell	Jefferies	Gibson	Fraser	White	Shaw	Masterton	Docherty	Kidd (11)
29th	Brough	Robinson	Denny	More	Liddell	Jefferies	Gibson	Fraser	White	Shaw	Kidd	Robertson (11)	Docherty
Apr 1st	Brough	Robinson	Denny	More	Liddell	Jefferies	Gibson	Fraser	White	Shaw	Robertson	Kidd	Docherty
5th	Brough	Hamilton	Denny	Boyd	Liddell	Jefferies	Gibson	Fraser	White	Kidd	Robertson	Docherty	O'Connor
9th	Brough	Hamilton	Denny	Boyd	Liddell	Jefferies	Gibson	Fraser	White	Robinson	Robertson	Docherty (11)	Kidd (2)
13th	Brough	Robinson	Denny	Boyd	Liddell	Jefferies	Gibson	Fraser	Docherty	Shaw	White	Kidd (9)	O'Connor (11)
16th	Brough	Robinson	Denny	Boyd	Liddell	Jefferies	Gibson	Fraser	O'Connor	Shaw	White	Robertson	Kidd
19th	Brough	Robinson	Denny	Boyd	Liddell	Jefferies	Gibson	Fraser	O'Connor	Shaw	White	Kidd (11)	Robertson (10)
23rd	Brough	Robinson	Denny	Boyd	Liddell	Jefferies	Gibson	Fraser	O'Connor	Kidd	Robertson	White	Shaw
26th	Brough	Robinson	Denny	Boyd	Liddell	Jefferies	Gibson	Fraser	O'Connor	Kidd	Robertson	Shaw (3)	White
30th	Brough	Robinson	Denny	Boyd	Liddell	Jefferies	Gibson	Fraser	O'Connor	Kidd	Robertson	Shaw (3)	White

Heart of Midlothian F.C. 1979-80. (BACK, left to right) - Walter Kidd, Cammy Fraser, John Brough, Thomson Allan, Ronnie McLafferty, Grant Tierney, David Scott. MIDDLE - Andy Stevenson (trainer), Bobby Masterton, Rab Stewart, Graham Shaw, Pat McShane, Colin More, Frank Liddell, Des O'Sullivan, Derek O'Connor, Alex. Rennie. FRONT - Peter Johnstone, Gordon Marr, Ian Black, Kenny McLeod, Jim Jefferies, Willie Gibson, Malcolm Robertson, Francis Farmer, Lawrie Tierney.

Season 1980-81

Date			Opponents		Score	Crowd	Scorers
Jul	30th	AS1	Airdrie	a	0-3	2,000	-
Aug	6th	AS1	Airdrie	h	3-3 (3-6)	3,334	C. Robertson; O'Connor 2
	9th	L	Partick Thistle	a	2-3	4,000	F. Liddell; Fraser (pen)
	16th	L	Airdrie	h	0-2	6,711	-
	23rd	L	St Mirren	a	3-1	7,553	Conn; O'Connor 2
	27th	LC1	Montrose	h	2-1	3,500	C. Robertson; MacDonald
	30th	LC1	Montrose	a	3-1 (5-2)	1,600	C. Robertson 3
Sep	3rd	LC2	Ayr United	h	2-3	5,400	C. Robertson; Bowman
	6th	L	Kilmarnock	a	1-0	4,000	Gibson
	13th	L	Celtic	h	0-2	17,169	-
	20th	L	Morton	h	0-1	5,996	-
	24th	LC2	Ayr United	a	0-4 (2-7)	4,800	-
	27th	L	Dundee United	a	1-1	6,263	O'Connor
Oct	4th	L	Aberdeen	h	0-1	10,873	
	11th	L	Rangers	a	1-3	23,700	MacDonald
	18th	L	Partick Thistle	h	0-1	5,905	-
	25th	L	Airdrie	a	0-3	3,500	-
Nov	1st	L	St Mirren	h	1-1	5,707	Conn
	8th	L	Dundee United	h	0-3	5,800	-
	15th	L	Morton	a	2-2	3,500	Conn; O'Connor
	22nd	L	Rangers	h	0-0	16,300	-
Dec	6th	L	Kilmarnock	h	2-0	5,183	MacDonald; O'Brien
	13th	L	Celtic	a	2-3	13,800	MacDonald; Gibson
	20th	L	Morton	h	0-0	5,900	-
	27th	L	Dundee United	a	1-4	6,928	Gibson
Jan	1st	L	Airdrie	h	2-3	8,086	Gibson; O'Brien
	3rd	L	Partick Thistle	a	0-1	3,500	-
	10th	L	Aberdeen	h	0-2	7,999	-
	24th	SC1	Morton	a	0-0	4,700	
	28th	SC1	Morton	h	1-3	8,000	MacDonald
	31st	L	Celtic	h	0-3	14,596	-
Feb	21st	L	St Mirren	a	1-2	3,412	McShane
	28th	L	Partick Thistle	h	1-1	3,491	Kidd
Mar	7th	L	Aberdeen	a	1-4	11,000	Hamill
	14th	L	Rangers	h	2-1	11,500	Redford o.g.; F. Liddell
	21st	L	Morton	a	0-3	3,500	-
	24th	L	Kilmarnock	a	0-2	1,445	-
	28th	L	Dundee United	h	0-4	3,776	-
Apr	1st	L	Celtic	a	0-6	13,300	-
	4th	L	Kilmarnock	h	1-0	1,866	Bowman
	11th	L	Aberdeen	a	0-1	6,000	-
	18th	L	St Mirren	h	1-2	2,500	Maxwell
	25th	L	Airdrie	a	2-1	2,000	G. Liddell 2
May	2nd	L	Rangers	a	0-4	7,000	-

Malcolm Robertson - dangerman on the left for Hearts

The Record

League	-	10th Place, Premier Division
League Cup	-	Second round
Scottish Cup	-	First round
Anglo Scottish Cup	-	First round
Top Scorer	-	Derek O'Connor Chris Robertson (both 6 goals)
Av. Home Gate	-	7,700
Players used	-	27
Sent off (booked)	-	One (29)

Appearances

	League	L/Cup	S/Cup	ASC	Total
John Brough	34	4	2	2	42
Willie Gibson	30 (4)	2	2	1	35+4s (4)
Alex. MacDonald	28 (3)	4 (1)	2 (1)	0	34 (5)
Peter Shields	30	1	2	0	33
Walter Kidd	25 (1)	3	2	2	32 (1)
Frank Liddell	24 (2)	4	2	2	32 (2)
Colin More	21	0	2	0	23+4s
Alex. Hamill	20 (1)	0	2	0	22+1s (1)
Dave Bowman	16 (1)	4 (1)	0	0	20+2s (2)
Jim Denny	19	1	0	1	21
Bobby Robinson	13	4	0	2	19+6s
Derek O'Connor	13 (4)	4	0	1 (2)	18+4s (6)
Chris Robertson	12	4 (5)	0	2 (1)	18+1s (6)
Alfie Conn	13 (3)	2	0	2	17+4s (3)
Jim Jefferies	12	4	0	1	17+1s
Paul O'Brien	13 (2)	0	2	0	15+2s (2)
Steve Hamilton	12	0	2	0	14
Gary Mackay	11	0	2	0	13+2s
Gary Liddell	13 (2)	0	0	0	13 (2)
Willie McVie	12	0	0	1	13
Crawford Boyd	5	3	0	1	9
Bobby Masterton	8	0	0	0	8+3s
Malcolm Robertson	6	0	0	2	8+3s
Pat McShane	3 (1)	0	0	0	3+2s (1)
Cammy Fraser	0 (1)	0	0	2	2+1s (1)

Scottish League Premier Division

		Home			Away			Goals	
	P	W	D	L	W	D	L	F A	PTS
Celtic	36	12	3	3	14	1	3	84-37	58
Aberdeen	36	11	4	3	8	7	3	61-26	49
Rangers	36	12	3	3	4	9	5	60-37	44
St Mirren	36	9	6	3	9	2	7	56-47	44
Dundee United	36	8	5	5	9	4	5	66-42	43
Partick Thistle	36	6	6	6	4	4	10	32-48	30
Airdrie	36	6	5	7	4	4	10	36-55	29
Morton	36	7	2	9	3	6	9	36-58	28
Kilmarnock	36	3	5	10	2	4	12	23-65	19
Hearts	**36**	**3**	**4**	**11**	**3**	**2**	**13**	**27-71**	**18**

Appearances (Ctd)

	League	L/Cup	S/Cup	ASC	Total
Ian Westwater	2	0	0		2
Scott Maxwell	1 (1)	0	0	0	1 (1)
Archie White	0	0	0	0	0+4s
Jim Docherty	0	0	0	0	0+1s

Heart of Midlothian F.C. Line-Ups 1980-81

	1	2	3	4	5	6	7	8	9	10	11	12	14
Jul 30th	Brough	Robinson	Denny	McVie	Liddell F	Fraser	Gibson	Conn	Robertson C	Kidd	Robertson M	Bowman (7)	O'Connor (9)
Aug 6th	Brough	Robinson	Jefferies	Boyd	Liddell F	Kidd	Conn	Fraser	O'Connor	Robertson C	Robertson M	More (4)	Denny
9th	Brough	Robinson	Denny	More	Liddell F	Kidd	Conn	MacDonald	O'Connor	Robertson C	Robertson M	Gibson	Fraser (7)
16th	Brough	Robinson	Jefferies	Boyd	Liddell F	MacDonald	Conn	Bowman	O'Connor	Robertson C	Robertson M	Kidd	Docherty (11)
23rd	Brough	Robinson	Jefferies	Boyd	Liddell F	Kidd	Bowman	Conn	O'Connor	Robertson C	MacDonald	Gibson (8)	More (9)
27th	Brough	Robinson	Jefferies	Boyd	Liddell F	Kidd	Bowman	Conn	O'Connor	Robertson C	MacDonald	White (10)	Gibson (8)
30th	Brough	Robinson	Jefferies	Boyd	Liddell F	Kidd	Bowman	Gibson	O'Connor	Robertson C	MacDonald	Robertson M (10)	More
Sep 3rd	Brough	Robinson	Jefferies	Boyd	Liddell F	Kidd	Bowman	Gibson	O'Connor	Robertson C	MacDonald	Robertson M (6)	More
6th	Brough	Robinson	Jefferies	Boyd	Liddell F	Kidd	Bowman	Gibson	O'Connor	Robertson C	MacDonald	More (7)	Robertson M
13th	Brough	Robinson	Jefferies	Boyd	Liddell F	Kidd	Bowman	Gibson	O'Connor	Robertson C	MacDonald	Conn (7)	More
20th	Brough	Jefferies	Shields	Boyd	Liddell F	Robinson	Bowman	Gibson	O'Connor	Robertson C	MacDonald	Robertson M (10)	Conn (8)
24th	Brough	Robinson	Shields	Denny	Liddell F*	Jefferies	Bowman	Conn	O'Connor	Robertson C	MacDonald	Gibson (8)	Mackay (2)
27th	Brough	Jefferies	Shields	Denny	McVie	Kidd	Bowman	Gibson	O'Connor	Robertson C	MacDonald	Robinson (10)	More
Oct 4th	Brough	Jefferies	Shields	Denny	McVie	Kidd	Bowman	Gibson	O'Connor	Robertson M	MacDonald	Robinson (4)	More
11th	Brough	Jefferies	Shields	Denny	McVie	Kidd	Bowman	Gibson	O'Connor	Robertson M	MacDonald	Robinson (8)	Conn (7)
18th	Brough	Jefferies	Shields	Denny	McVie	Kidd	Bowman	Gibson	Robertson C	Robertson M	MacDonald	Robinson	Mackay
25th	Brough	Jefferies	Shields	Denny	McVie	Kidd	Bowman	Gibson	O'Connor	Robertson M	MacDonald	Robinson (7)	Conn (8)
Nov 1st	Westwater	Jefferies	Shields	Denny	Liddell F	Kidd	Bowman	Robinson	Conn	Gibson	MacDonald	Masterton (7)	White
8th	Westwater	Jefferies	Shields	Denny	Liddell F	Kidd	Bowman	Masterton	Conn	Gibson	MacDonald	White (7)	Mackay (6)
15th	Brough	Hamilton	Shields	Liddell F	McVie	Robinson	Masterton	Gibson	Conn	O'Connor	MacDonald	More	White
22nd	Brough	Hamilton	Shields	McVie	Liddell F	Robinson	Masterton	Gibson	Conn	O'Connor	MacDonald	More (2)	White
Dec 6th	Brough	More	Shields	Denny	McVie	Robinson	Masterton	Gibson	Conn	O'Brien	MacDonald	Hamill (7)	O'Connor
13th	Brough	More	Shields	Denny	McVie	Robinson	Hamill	Gibson	Conn	O'Brien	MacDonald	Masterton (9)	O'Connor (10)
20th	Brough	More	Shields	Denny	McVie	Robinson	Hamill	Gibson	Conn	O'Brien	MacDonald	Masterton (11)	O'Connor(8)
27th	Brough	More	Shields	Denny	McVie	Robinson	Hamill	Gibson	O'Connor	O'Brien	Masterton	Mackay	Kidd
Jan 1st	Brough	More	Shields	Denny	McVie	Masterton	Hamill	Gibson	Conn	O'Brien	MacDonald	Robinson	Hamilton
3rd	Brough	Hamilton	Shields	More	Liddell F	Masterton	Hamill	Gibson	Conn	O'Brien	MacDonald	Robinson (2)	O'Connor
10th	Brough	Hamilton	Shields	More	Liddell F	Masterton	Hamill	Gibson	Conn	O'Brien	MacDonald	Robinson (6)	O'Connor(9)
24th	Brough	Hamilton	Shields	More	Liddell F	Mackay	Kidd	Gibson	Hamill	O'Brien	MacDonald	McShane	O'Connor
28th	Brough	Hamilton	Shields	More	Liddell F	Mackay	Kidd	Gibson	Hamill	O'Brien	MacDonald	McShane (6)	White (10)
31st	Brough	Hamilton	Shields	More	Liddell F	Mackay	Kidd	MacDonald	Gibson	Hamill	O'Brien	McShane (8)	White (6)
Feb 21st	Brough	Hamilton	Hamill	More	Liddell F	Bowman	Mackay	Gibson	McShane	Liddell G	Kidd	Masterton	O'Brien
28th	Brough	Hamilton	Shields	More	Liddell F	Hamill	Mackay	Gibson	McShane	Liddell G	Kidd	Bowman	O'Brien
Mar 7th	Brough	Hamilton	Shields	More	Liddell F	Hamill	Mackay	Gibson	McShane	Liddell G	Kidd	Bowman (7)	O'Brien (9)
14th	Brough	Hamilton	Shields	More	Liddell F	Hamill	Mackay	Gibson	Liddell G	MacDonald	Kidd	O'Brien	McShane
21st	Brough	Hamilton	Shields	More	Liddell F	Hamill	Mackay	Gibson	Liddell G	MacDonald	Kidd	O'Brien (9)	Bowman
24th	Brough	Hamilton	Shields	More	Liddell F	Hamill	O'Brien	Gibson	Liddell G	MacDonald	Kidd	Bowman	McShane
28th	Brough	Hamilton	Shields	More	Liddell F	Hamill	O'Brien	Gibson	Liddell G	MacDonald	Kidd	McShane	Bowman
Apr 1st	Brough	Denny	Shields	Kidd	More	Hamill	Mackay	Gibson	Liddell G	Bowman	MacDonald	O'Brien	Robertson C
4th	Brough	Denny	Shields	Bowman	More	Hamill	Mackay	Gibson	Liddell G	MacDonald	Kidd	Robertson C (8)	Gauld
11th	Brough	Denny	Shields	Bowman	Liddell F	Hamill	Mackay	Gibson	Liddell G	Robertson C	Kidd	Gauld	O'Brien
18th	Brough	Denny	Shields	More	Liddell F	Hamill	Maxwell	Robertson C	Liddell G	O'Brien	Kidd	Hamilton	Masterton
25th	Brough	Denny	Shields	More	Liddell F	Hamill	Mackay	Robertson C	Liddell G	O'Brien	Kidd	Gauld	Jefferies
May 2nd	Brough	Denny	Shields	More	Liddell F	Hamill	Mackay	Robertson C	Liddell G	O'Brien	Kidd	Jefferies (7)	Gibson (10)

Just a touch - Hearts Scotland Under-21 international goalkeeper John Brough gets down to push away this shot in the match against Dundee United at Tannadice.

Season 1981-82

Date			Opponents		Score	Crowd	Scorers
Aug	8th	LC	Airdrie	a	1-0	3,000	C. Robertson
	12th	LC	Aberdeen	h	1-0	10,400	C. Robertson
	15th	LC	Kilmarnock	h	1-1	7,750	G. Liddell
	19th	LC	Aberdeen	a	0-3	11,000	-
	22nd	LC	Airdrie	h	2-3	4,900	G. Liddell; McCoy
	26th	LC	Kilmarnock	a	0-2	2,500	-
	29th	L	Dunfermline	a	1-1	4,300	G. Liddell
Sep	5th	L	Kilmarnock	h	0-1	4,796	-
	12th	L	Falkirk	a	0-0	6,500	-
	16th	L	Hamilton Accies	h	2-1	3,500	Mackay; Hamill
	19th	L	Clydebank	h	1-0	6,000	O'Connor
	23rd	L	Ayr United	a	0-0	3,500	-
	26th	L	Dumbarton	h	2-1	3,627	R. MacDonald; O'Connor
Oct	3rd	L	Queens Park	a	0-1	2,450	-
	7th	L	St Johnstone	h	3-1	4,077	Pettigrew; O'Connor 2
	10th	L	QOS	a	2-1	2,400	Shields; Addison
	17th	L	Raith Rovers	h	2-1	5,001	R. MacDonald; G. Liddell
	24th	L	Motherwell	a	2-2	7,662	Pettigrew 2
	31st	L	East Stirling	h	0-1	5,093	-
Nov	7th	L	Kilmarnock	a	0-0	3,400	-
	14th	L	Dunfermline	h	1-1	5,570	C. Robertson
	21st	L	Hamilton Accies	a	2-0	2,200	Mackay; Addison
	28th	L	Dumbarton	a	1-3	1,200	Marinello
Dec	5th	L	Queens Park	h	1-1	3,516	Pettigrew
Jan	28th	SC1	East Stirling	a	4-1	4,000	R. MacDonald; C. Robertson; Marinello; Byrne
	30th	L	Motherwell	h	0-3	11,054	-
Feb	6th	L	East Stirling	a	1-0	1,100	Byrne
	9th	L	Falkirk	h	3-0	2,700	McCoy; Marinello; Pettigrew
	13th	SC2	Forfar Athletic	h	0-1	5,600	-
	17th	L	QOS	h	4-1	2,397	C. Robertson; R. MacDonald; McCoy; Pettigrew
	20th	L	Ayr United	a	3-0	2,902	McCoy; Pettigrew; Byrne
	23rd	L	St Johnstone	a	1-2	3,700	McCoy
	27th	L	Raith Rovers	h	4-0	4,000	C. Robertson; McCoy 2; Bowman
Mar	6th	L	Falkirk	a	1-3	2,500	C. Robertson
	13th	L	QOS	a	5-1	2,620	Pettigrew 3; Addison; Byrne (pen)
	20th	L	Queens Park	h	1-0	3,777	Byrne
	27th	L	Clydebank	a	1-2	1,731	Byrne
	31st	L	Raith Rovers	a	3-0	3,050	McCoy 2 (1 pen); R. MacDonald
Apr	3rd	L	St Johnstone	h	3-0	4,577	R. MacDonald; C. Robertson 2
	10th	L	Hamilton Accies	a	2-0	3,432	A. MacDonald; Pettigrew
	14th	L	Clydebank	a	5-1	960	Pettigrew 4; Byrne
	21st	L	Ayr United	h	2-1	4,675	Hamill; Addison
	24th	L	Dunfermline	a	2-1	1,620	C. Robertson; R. MacDonald
	27th	L	East Stirling	h	2-0	4,300	Byrne (pen); McCoy
May	1st	L	Dumbarton	h	2-5	4,861	Byrne; Pettigrew
	8th	L	Kilmarnock	a	0-0	10,000	-
	15th	L	Motherwell	h	0-1	14,709	-

Alex. MacDonald - the gritty midfielder proved good value for money.

The Record		
League	-	**Third Place, Division One**
League Cup	-	**Qualifying stages only**
Scottish Cup	-	**Second round**
Top Scorer	-	**Willie Pettigrew (16 goals)**
Av. Home Gate	-	**5,200**
Players used	-	**25**
Sent off (booked)	-	**Five (40)**

Appearances

	League	L/Cup	S/Cup	Total
Pat Byrne	37 (8)	4	2 (1)	43 (9)
Peter Shields	37 (1)	4	2	43 (1)
Stewart MacLaren	34	6	2	42
Roddy MacDonald	35 (6)	4	2 (1)	41 (7)
Henry Smith	33	6	2	41
Willie Pettigrew	35 (16)	0	2	37 (16)
Derek Addison	32 (4)	0	2	34 (4)
Walter Kidd	29	2	2	33+2s
Chris Robertson	24 (7)	5 (2)	1 (1)	30+7s (10)
Gerry McCoy	19 (9)	3 (1)	1	23+2s (10)
Dave Bowman	16 (1)	5	2	23 (1)
Alex. Hamill	16 (2)	6	0	22+4s (2)
Alex. MacDonald	15 (1)	4	0	19+1s (1)
Brian McNeill	15	2	0	17+2s
Gary Liddell	9 (2)	5 (2)	0	14+2s (4)
Gary Mackay	10 (2)	2	0	12+8s (2)
Peter Marinello	10 (2)	0	2 (1)	12+8s (3)
Derek O'Connor	12 (4)	0	0	12+3s (4)
Colin More	3	6	0	9
John Brough	6	0	0	6
Stuart Gauld	2	0	0	2
Frank Liddell	0	1	0	1+1s
Paul O'Brien	0	1	0	1+1s
John Robertson	0	0	0	0+1s
Derek Strickland	0	0	0	0+1s

Scottish League Division One

		Home			Away			Goals	
	P	W	D	L	W	D	L	F A	PTS
Motherwell	39	12	7	0	14	2	4	92-36	61
Kilmarnock	39	6	12	2	11	5	3	60-29	51
Hearts	**39**	**12**	**2**	**5**	**9**	**6**	**5**	**65-37**	**50**
Clydebank	39	12	3	5	7	5	7	61-53	46
St Johnstone	39	12	3	4	5	5	10	68-59	42
Ayr United	39	12	6	1	3	6	11	56-50	42
Hamilton Accies	39	10	3	6	6	5	9	52-49	40
Queens Park	39	11	5	4	2	5	12	43-44	36
Falkirk	39	8	8	4	3	6	10	49-52	36
Dunfermline	39	3	9	7	8	5	7	47-58	36
Dumbarton	39	10	1	9	3	8	8	49-61	35
Raith Rovers	39	5	2	13	6	5	8	31-59	29
East Stirling	39	4	6	9	3	4	13	38-77	24
Queen of the South	39	2	5	13	2	5	12	42-89	18

League Cup Section

	P	W	D	L	F A	PTS
Aberdeen	6	4	1	1	12-1	9
Kilmarnock	6	2	2	2	5-8	6
Hearts	**6**	**2**	**1**	**3**	**5-9**	**5**
Airdrie	6	1	2	3	4-8	4

Heart of Midlothian F.C. Line-Ups 1981-82

	1	2	3	4	5	6	7	8	9	10	11	12	13
Aug 8th	Smith	More	Shields	Byrne	MacDonald R	MacLaren	Mackay	Robertson C	Liddell G	Bowman	Hamill	Liddell F (3)	O'Connor
12th	Smith	More	Shields	Byrne	MacDonald R	MacLaren	Bowman	Robertson C	Liddell G	MacDonald A	Hamill	Liddell F	O'Connor
15th	Smith	More	Shields	Byrne	MacDonald R	MacLaren	Bowman	Robertson C	Liddell G*	MacDonald A	Hamill	Liddell F	McCoy
19th	Smith	More	Shields	Byrne	MacDonald R	MacLaren	Bowman	Robertson C	McCoy	MacDonald A	Hamill	Kidd (4)	O'Connor (7)
22nd	Smith	Kidd	McNeill	Bowman	More	MacLaren	O'Brien	McCoy	Liddell G	Hamill	MacDonald A	Robertson C(11)	Mackay
26th	Smith	More	McNeill	Kidd	Liddell F	MacLaren	McCoy	Robertson C	Liddell G	Mackay	Hamill	O'Brien	Strickland
29th	Smith	McNeill	Shields	Byrne	MacDonald R	MacLaren	Bowman	McCoy	Liddell G	Hamill	Kidd	Robertson C	Liddell F
Sep 5th	Smith	McNeill	Shields	Byrne	MacDonald R	MacLaren	Bowman	McCoy	Liddell G	Hamill	Kidd	O'Connor(10)	O'Brien (7)
12th	Smith	McNeill	Shields	Byrne	MacDonald R	MacLaren	McCoy	Robertson C	Liddell G	Hamill	Mackay	O'Connor (8)	Kidd
16th	Smith	McNeill	Shields	Byrne	MacDonald R	MacLaren	McCoy	Robertson C	O'Connor	Hamill	Mackay	Strickland	Kidd (8)
19th	Smith	McNeill	Shields	Byrne	MacDonald R	MacLaren	McCoy	Pettigrew	O'Connor	Addison	Mackay	Robertson C	Hamill (10)
23rd	Smith	McNeill	Shields	Byrne	MacDonald R	MacLaren	Bowman	Pettigrew	O'Connor	Addison	Hamill	Robertson C	Mackay
26th	Smith	McNeill	Shields	Byrne	MacDonald R	MacLaren	Mackay	Pettigrew	O'Connor	Addison	Hamill	Robertson C	Strickland (2)
Oct 3rd	Smith	Kidd	Shields	Byrne	MacDonald R	MacLaren	MacDonald A	Pettigrew	O'Connor	Addison	Hamill G	Robertson C	Mackay (7)
7th	Smith	Kidd	Shields	Byrne	MacDonald R	MacLaren	Mackay	Pettigrew	O'Connor	Addison	Liddell G	Robertson C(11)	Hamill
10th	Smith	Kidd	Shields	Byrne	MacDonald R	MacLaren	Mackay	Pettigrew	O'Connor	Addison	Liddell G	Robertson C(11)	Hamill (7)
17th	Smith	Kidd	Shields	Byrne	MacDonald R	MacLaren	Mackay	Pettigrew	O'Connor	Addison	Liddell G	Robertson C (7)	Strickland
24th	Smith	Kidd	Shields	Byrne	MacDonald R	MacLaren	Liddell G	Pettigrew	O'Connor	Addison	MacDonald A	Robertson C	Hamill (2)
31st	Smith	Kidd	Shields	Byrne	MacDonald R	MacLaren	Liddell G	Pettigrew	O'Connor	Addison	Hamill	Marinello (11)	McNeill (2)
Nov 7th	Brough	Kidd	Shields	Byrne	MacDonald R	McNeill	Liddell G	Pettigrew	O'Connor	Bowman	Hamill	C Robertson (7)	Mackay
14th	Brough	Kidd	Shields	Byrne*	MacDonald R	McNeill	Robertson C	Pettigrew	O'Connor	Addison	Hamill	Mackay (7)	Strickland
21st	Brough	Kidd	Shields	Bowman	MacDonald R	McNeill	Robertson C	Pettigrew	Mackay	Addison	MacDonald A	Hamill (11)	O'Connor
28th	Smith	Kidd	Shields	Byrne	More	McNeill	Robertson C	Pettigrew	Mackay	Addison	MacDonald A	Marinello (10)	Hamill
Dec 5th	Smith	Kidd	Shields	Byrne	MacDonald R	McNeill	Marinello	Pettigrew	Robertson C	Addison	MacDonald A	Liddell G (9)	Strickland
Jan 28th	Smith	Kidd	Shields	Byrne	MacDonald R	MacLaren	Bowman	Pettigrew	Robertson C	Addison	Marinello	McNeill	McCoy
30th	Smith	Kidd	Shields	Byrne	MacDonald R	MacLaren	Bowman	Pettigrew	Robertson C	Addison	Marinello	McNeill (10)	McCoy (2)
Feb 6th	Smith	McNeill	Shields	Byrne	MacDonald R	MacLaren	Bowman	Pettigrew	McCoy	Addison	Marinello	Liddell G (11)	Mackay (7)
9th	Smith	McNeill	Shields	Byrne	MacDonald R	MacLaren	Bowman	Pettigrew	McCoy	Addison	Marinello	Robertson C (9)	Mackay
13th	Smith	Kidd	Shields	Byrne	MacDonald R	MacLaren	Bowman	Pettigrew	McCoy	Addison	Marinello	Robertson C (7)	Mackay (11)
17th	Smith	Kidd	Shields	Byrne	MacDonald R	MacLaren	Bowman	Pettigrew	McCoy	Addison	Robertson C	Robertson J (9)	Marinello
20th	Smith	Kidd	Shields	Byrne	MacDonald R	MacLaren	Bowman	Pettigrew	McCoy	Addison	Robertson C	Robertson J	Hamill
23rd	Smith	Kidd	Shields	Byrne	MacDonald R	MacLaren	Bowman	Pettigrew	McCoy	Addison	Robertson C	Hamill	Mackay
27th	Smith	Kidd	Shields	Byrne	MacDonald R	MacLaren	Bowman	Pettigrew	McCoy	Addison	Robertson C	Marinello (11)	Mackay (9)
Mar 6th	Smith	Kidd	Shields	Byrne	MacDonald R	MacLaren	Bowman	Pettigrew	McCoy	Addison	Robertson C	Marinello (11)	Mackay (7)
13th	Brough	Kidd	Shields	Byrne	MacDonald R	MacLaren	Bowman	Pettigrew	McCoy*	Addison	Robertson C	MacDonald A (7)	Mackay
20th	Brough	Kidd	Shields	Byrne	MacDonald R	MacLaren	Addison	Pettigrew	Mackay	MacDonald A	Robertson C	Marinello (9)	Bowman
27th	Brough	Kidd	Shields	Byrne	MacDonald R	MacLaren	Addison	Pettigrew	McCoy	MacDonald A	Robertson C	Marinello (6)	Bowman
31st	Smith	Kidd	Shields	Byrne	MacDonald R	MacLaren	Addison	Pettigrew	Robertson C	McCoy	MacDonald A	Marinello	Bowman
Apr 3rd	Smith	Kidd	Shields	Byrne	MacDonald R	MacLaren	Addison	Pettigrew	Robertson C	McCoy	MacDonald A	Marinello (10)	McNeill
10th	Smith	Kidd	Shields*	Byrne	McDonald R	MacLaren	Addison	Pettigrew	Robertson C	MacDonald A	Marinello	Robertson J	Bowman
14th	Smith	Kidd	Hamill	Byrne	McDonald R	MacLaren	Addison	Pettigrew	Robertson C	MacDonald A	Marinello	Bowman	Mackay
21st	Smith	Kidd	Shields	Hamill	MacDonald R	MacLaren	Addison	Pettigrew	Robertson C	MacDonald A	Marinello	Robertson J	Bowman
24th	Smith	Kidd	Hamill	Byrne	MacDonald R	MacLaren	Addison	Pettigrew	Robertson C	MacDonald A	Marinello	McCoy (11)	Bowman
27th	Smith	Kidd	Shields	Byrne	MacDonald R	MacLaren	Addison	Pettigrew	Robertson C	McCoy	MacDonald A	Hamill	Marinello
May 1st	Smith	Hamill	Shields	Byrne	McNeill	MacLaren	Addison	Pettigrew	Robertson C	McCoy	MacDonald A	Marinello (9)	Bowman
8th	Smith	Gauld	Shields	Byrne	More	MacLaren	Marinello	Pettigrew	McCoy*	Hamill	Bowman	McNeill	Mackay (7)
15th	Smith	Gauld	Shields	Byrne	More	MacLaren	Marinello	Pettigrew	Robertson C	Hamill	Bowman	Mackay (10)	Robertson J

Heart of Midlothian F.C. 1981-82 (BACK, left to right), Tony Ford (manager), Walter Kidd, Stewart MacLaren, Derek O'Connor, Roddy MacDonald, John Brough, Colin More, Frank Liddell, Jim Jefferies and Gary Liddell. FRONT - Peter Shields, Alex. Hamill, Gerry McCoy, Alex. MacDonald, Chris Robertson, Gerry Byrne, Derek Strickland and Willie Gibson. DC Thomson

Season 1982-83

Date			Opponents		Score	Crowd	Scorers
Aug	14th	LC	Motherwell	a	1-2	5,100	O'Connor
	18th	LC	Forfar Athletic	h	2-1	1,900	O'Connor 2
	21st	LC	Clyde	a	7-1		Pettigrew 4; Brogan o.g.; Bowman; Shields
	25th	LC	Forfar Athletic	a	2-0	2,000	A. MacDonald; Marinello
	28th	LC	Motherwell	h	1-0	9,000	A. MacDonald
Sep	1st	LC	Clyde	h	3-0	5,000	Shields; Pettigrew; Bowman
	4th	L	Queens Park	a	2-1	1,817	Bowman; Marinello
	8th	LCQ	St Mirren	a	1-1	5,523	Pettigrew
	11th	L	Ayr United	h	1-1	5,601	O'Connor
	15th	L	St Johnstone	a	1-1	3,900	Pettigrew
	18th	L	Falkirk	a	1-1	3,500	O'Connor
	22nd	LCQ	St Mirren	h	2-1 (3-2)	12,000	A. MacDonald; Pettigrew
	25th	L	Clyde	h	1-0	4,734	Bowman
	29th	L	Clydebank	h	4-1	5,500	Pettigrew; O'Connor; Byrne; Jardine (pen)
Oct	2nd	L	Raith Rovers	a	0-1	3,000	-
	6th	L	Dumbarton	h	1-1	5,000	O'Connor
	9th	L	Alloa Athletic	h	3-0	4,382	R. MacDonald; Holt o.g.; J. Robertson
	16th	L	Hamilton Accies	a	3-1	2,204	A. MacDonald; Byrne; O'Connor
	23rd	L	Dunfermline	h	4-1	5,997	O'Connor; Bowman; A. MacDonald; Johnston
	27th	LCS	Rangers	a	0-2	22,500	-
	30th	L	Partick Thistle	a	1-1	3,045	J. Robertson
Nov	6th	L	Airdrie	h	2-4	5,656	O'Connor; Jardine (pen)
	10th	LCS	Rangers	h	1-2 (1-4)	18,983	O'Connor
	13th	L	Clydebank	a	3-0	2,116	Mackay; O'Connor; J. Robertson
	20th	L	Falkirk	h	3-1	4,847	Johnston; J. Robertson 2
	27th	L	Dumbarton	a	1-1	3,000	O'Connor
Dec	4th	L	Raith Rovers	h	2-0	4,190	Mackay; Johnston (pen)
	11th	L	Clyde	a	3-2	2,300	A. MacDonald; Pettigrew 2
	27th	L	Ayr United	a	3-0	2,500	O'Connor; Pettigrew; A. MacDonald
Jan	1st	L	St Johnstone	h	1-0	14,554	Pettigrew
	3rd	L	Airdrie	a	1-0	4,500	Pettigrew
	8th	L	Hamilton Accies	h	2-1	5,081	Pettigrew; O'Connor
	15th	L	Alloa Athletic	a	0-0	2,591	-
	22nd	L	Partick Thistle	h	0-1	7,061	-
	29th	SC3	QOS	a	1-1	6,034	Shields
Feb	2nd	SC3R	QOS	h	1-0	5,500	O'Connor
	9th	L	Dunfermline	a	1-2	3,500	R. MacDonald
	12th	L	Ayr United	h	5-1	4,294	O'Connor; Pettigrew; Mackay; Bowman; Byrne
	20th	SC4	East Fife	h	2-1	9,300	R. McDonald; O'Connor
	26th	L	Queens Park	a	3-0	1,468	J. Robertson 3
Mar	5th	L	Falkirk	h	1-2	5,500	O'Connor
	12th	SCQ	Celtic	a	1-4	25,400	A. MacDonald
	19th	L	Partick Thistle	h	4-0	7,000	J. Robertson 3; Pettigrew
	26th	L	Clyde	h	3-1	4,647	J. Robertson; Mackay; R. MacDonald
	29th	L	Raith Rovers	a	2-4	2,100	Johnston 2 (1 pen)
Apr	2nd	L	Airdrie	a	2-0	3,000	Mackay (pen); J. Robertson
	6th	L	Queens Park	h	2-0	5,050	J. Robertson; O'Connor
	9th	L	St Johnstone	a	1-2	7,501	Bowman
	16th	L	Clydebank	h	2-2	6,432	J. Robertson 2
	23rd	L	Alloa Athletic	a	1-1	2,395	A. MacDonald
	30th	L	Dunfermline	h	3-3	6,427	J. Robertson 3
May	7th	L	Dumbarton	a	4-0	4,000	J. Robertson 2; O'Connor; Mackay
	14th	L	Hamilton Accies	h	2-0	9,136	Johnston; O'Connor

Dave Bowman - midfield powerhouse for Hearts

The Record		
League	-	Runners up, Division One
League Cup	-	Semi-final
Scottish Cup	-	Quarter final
Top Scorer	-	Derek O'Connor (22goals)
Av. Home Gate	-	6,054
Players used	-	17
Sent off (booked)	-	Five

Appearances

	League		L/Cup		S/Cup		Total	
Sandy Jardine	39	(2)	10		4		53	(2)
Roddy MacDonald	39	(3)	10		4	(1)	53	(4)
Henry Smith	39		10		4		53	
Dave Bowman	39	(5)	9	(2)	4		52	(7)
Walter Kidd	37		10		3		50	
Derek O'Connor	37	(16)	9	(4)	3	(2)	49+3s	(22)
Alex MacDonald	29	(5)	9	(3)	3	(1)	41+2s	(9)
Peter Shields	25		10	(2)	4	(1)	39	(3)
Willie Pettigrew	26	(10)	9	(7)	3		38+8s	(17)
Pat Byrne	25	(3)	10		1		36+5s	(3)
Gary Mackay	26	(6)	2		4		32+9s	(6)
Willie Johnston	24	(6)	1		3		28+4s	(6)
John Robertson	19	(21)	1		3		23+5s	(21)
Stuart Gauld	14		0		1		15	
Stewart MacLaren	8		4		0		12+9s	
Peter Marinello	2	(1)	4	(1)	0		6+2s	(2)
Gerry McCoy	1		2		0		3+8s	

Scottish League Division One

		Home			Away			Goals	
	P	W	D	L	W	D	L	F A	PTS
St Johnstone	39	17	1	2	8	4	7	59-39	55
Hearts	**39**	**13**	**4**	**3**	**9**	**6**	**4**	**79-39**	**54**
Clydebank	39	8	5	6	12	5	3	72-49	50
Partick Thistle	39	9	6	4	11	3	6	66-45	49
Airdrie	39	7	3	9	9	4	7	62-47	39
Alloa Athletic	39	8	7	5	6	4	9	52-52	39
Falkirk	39	8	2	9	7	4	9	45-55	36
Dumbarton	39	6	7	6	7	3	10	50-62	36
Hamilton Accies	39	7	6	7	4	6	9	54-66	34
Raith Rovers	39	8	3	8	5	5	10	64-63	34
Clyde	39	8	2	10	6	4	9	55-65	34
Ayr United	39	9	4	7	3	4	12	45-59	32
Dunfermline	39	5	9	6	2	8	9	39-69	31
Queens Park	39	3	6	10	3	5	12	44-80	23

League Cup Section

	P	W	D	L	F A	PTS
Hearts	**6**	**5**	**0**	**1**	**16-4**	**10**
Motherwell	6	3	2	1	10-7	8
Forfar Athletic	6	2	1	3	5-6	5
Clyde	6	0	1	5	5-19	1

Heart of Midlothian F.C. Line-Ups 1982-83

		1	2	3	4	5	6	7	8	9	10	11	12	13
Aug	14th	Smith	Kidd	Shields	Byrne	MacDonald R	Jardine	MacLaren	Pettigrew	Mackay	MacDonald A	Marinello	O'Connor (9)	McCoy (11)
	18th	Smith	Kidd	Shields	Byrne	MacDonald R	Jardine	Bowman	Pettigrew	O'Connor	MacDonald A	Marinello	O'Connor	Mackay
	21st	Smith	Kidd	Shields	Byrne	MacDonald R	Jardine	Bowman	Pettigrew	O'Connor	MacDonald A	Marinello	Mackay (10)	MacLaren
	25th	Smith	Kidd	Shields	Byrne	MacDonald R	Jardine	Bowman	Pettigrew	O'Connor	MacDonald A	Marinello	MacLaren (11)	Mackay
	28th	Smith	Kidd	Shields	Byrne	MacDonald R	Jardine	Bowman	Pettigrew	O'Connor	MacDonald A	McCoy	MacLaren	Mackay
Sep	1st	Smith	Kidd	Shields	Byrne	MacDonald R	Jardine	Bowman	Pettigrew	O'Connor	MacDonald A	McCoy	Robertson J (8)	MacLaren (10)
	4th	Smith	Kidd	Shields	Byrne	MacDonald R	Jardine	Bowman	Pettigrew	O'Connor	MacDonald A	McCoy	MacLaren (10)	Marinello (11)
	8th	Smith	Kidd	Shields	Byrne	MacDonald R	Jardine	Bowman	Pettigrew	O'Connor	MacLaren	MacDonald A	McCoy	Mackay
	11th	Smith	Kidd	Shields	Byrne	MacDonald R	Jardine	Bowman	Pettigrew	O'Connor	MacDonald A	Marinello	McCoy (11)	MacLaren
	15th	Smith	Kidd	Shields	Byrne	MacDonald R	Jardine	Bowman	Pettigrew	O'Connor	MacLaren	MacDonald A	Marinello	Mackay
	18th	Smith	Kidd	Shields	Byrne	MacDonald R	Jardine	Bowman	Pettigrew	O'Connor	MacDonald A	Marinello	MacLaren (4)	Mackay (8)
	22nd	Smith	Kidd	Shields	Byrne	MacDonald R	Jardine	Bowman	Pettigrew	O'Connor	MacLaren	MacDonald A	Johnston (10)	Mackay
	25th	Smith	Kidd	Shields	Byrne	MacDonald R	Jardine	Bowman	Pettigrew	O'Connor	Mackay	Johnston	MacLaren	Marinello
	29th	Smith	Kidd	Shields	Byrne	MacDonald R	Jardine	Bowman	Pettigrew	O'Connor	MacDonald A	Johnston	MacLaren	Mackay
Oct	2nd	Smith	Kidd	Shields	Byrne	MacDonald R	Jardine	Bowman	Pettigrew	O'Connor	Mackay	Johnston	McCoy (9)	MacLaren (3)
	6th	Smith	Kidd	Shields	Byrne	MacDonald R	Jardine	Bowman	Pettigrew	O'Connor	Mackay	Johnston	MacLaren	Marinello
	9th	Smith	Kidd	Shields	Byrne	MacDonald R	Jardine	Bowman	Pettigrew	O'Connor	Mackay	Johnston	MacDonaldA(11)	Robertson J 8
	16th	Smith	Kidd	Shields	Byrne	MacDonald R	Jardine	Bowman	Pettigrew	O'Connor	MacDonald A	Johnston	Robertson J (8)	Mackay
	23rd	Smith	Kidd	Shields	Byrne	MacDonald R	Jardine	Bowman	Pettigrew	O'Connor	MacDonald A	Johnston	Robertson J (9)	MacLaren (11)
	27th	Smith	Kidd	Shields	Byrne	MacDonald R	Jardine	Bowman	Pettigrew	O'Connor	MacLaren	MacDonald A	Johnston (10)	Mackay
	30th	Smith	Kidd	Shields	Byrne	MacDonald R	Jardine	Bowman	Pettigrew	O'Connor	MacDonald A	Johnston	Robertson J (8)	Mackay (4)
Nov	6th	Smith	Kidd	Shields	Byrne	MacDonald R	Jardine	Bowman	Robertson J	O'Connor	MacLaren	Johnston	McCoy (11)	Mackay (4)
	10th	Smith	Kidd	Shields	Byrne	MacDonald R	Jardine	Bowman	Robertson J	O'Connor	Mackay	Johnston	MacLaren	Pettigrew (8)
	13th	Smith	Kidd	Shields	Mackay	MacDonald R	Jardine	Bowman	Robertson J	O'Connor	MacDonald A	Johnston	Byrne	Pettigrew
	20th	Smith	Kidd	Shields	Mackay	MacDonald R	Jardine	Bowman	Robertson J	O'Connor	MacDonald A	Johnston	Byrne (10)	Pettigrew (11)
	27th	Smith	Kidd	Gauld	Mackay	MacDonald R	Jardine	Bowman	Robertson J	O'Connor	MacDonald A	Johnston	Pettigrew (10)	Byrne (11)
Dec	4th	Smith	Kidd	Gauld	Mackay	MacDonald R	Jardine	Bowman	Robertson J	O'Connor	MacDonald A	Johnston	Pettigrew (8)	Byrne
	11th	Smith	Kidd	Gauld	Byrne	MacDonald R	Jardine	Bowman	Pettigrew	O'Connor	Mackay	MacDonald A	Johnston	Robertson J
	27th	Smith	Kidd	Shields	Byrne	MacDonald R	Jardine	Bowman	Pettigrew	O'Connor	Mackay	MacDonald A*	MacLaren	Johnston
Jan	1st	Smith	Kidd	Shields	Byrne	MacDonald R	Jardine	Bowman	Pettigrew	O'Connor	Mackay	MacLaren	Johnston	Robertson J
	3rd	Smith	Kidd	Shields	Byrne	MacDonald R	Jardine	Bowman	Pettigrew	O'Connor	MacLaren	MacDonald A	Mackay (4)	Johnston
	8th	Smith	Kidd	Shields	Byrne	MacDonald R	Jardine	Bowman	Pettigrew	O'Connor	Mackay	MacDonald A	Johnston (10)	MacLaren
	15th	Smith	Kidd	Shields	Byrne	MacDonald R	Jardine	Bowman	Pettigrew	O'Connor	MacDonald A	Johnston	Mackay (11)	MacLaren
	22nd	Smith	Kidd	Shields	Byrne	MacDonald R	Jardine	Bowman	Pettigrew	O'Connor	MacLaren	MacDonald A	Mackay (4)	Johnston (8)
	29th	Smith	Kidd	Shields	Bowman	MacDonald R	Jardine	Mackay	Pettigrew	Robertson J*	MacDonald A	Johnston	Byrne (2)	MacLaren
Feb	2nd	Smith	Kidd	Shields	Bowman	MacDonald R	Jardine	Mackay	Pettigrew	O'Connor	MacDonald A	Johnston*	McCoy (8)	Byrne (4)
	9th	Smith	Kidd	Shields	Bowman	MacDonald R	Jardine	Byrne	Pettigrew	O'Connor	Mackay	Robertson J	McCoy	MacLaren
	12th	Smith	Kidd	Shields	Bowman	MacDonald R	Jardine	Byrne	Pettigrew	O'Connor	Mackay	Johnston	Robertson J	MacLaren
	20th	Smith	Gauld	Shields	Bowman	MacDonald R	Jardine	Byrne	Pettigrew	O'Connor	Mackay	Robertson J	McCoy (9)	MacLaren
	26th	Smith	Gauld	Shields	Bowman	MacDonald R	Jardine	Byrne	Pettigrew	O'Connor	Mackay	Robertson J	MacDonald A(9)	MacLaren
Mar	5th	Smith	Gauld	Shields	Bowman	MacDonald R	Jardine	Byrne	Pettigrew	O'Connor	MacDonald A	Robertson J	Mackay (7)	McCoy (8)
	12th	Smith	Kidd	Shields	Bowman	MacDonald R	Jardine	Mackay	Robertson J	O'Connor	MacDonald A	Johnston*	Pettigrew (9)	MacLaren (3)
	19th	Smith	Kidd	Gauld	Bowman	MacDonald R	Jardine	Mackay	Pettigrew	O'Connor	MacDonald A	Robertson J	MacLaren	Marinello
	26th	Smith	Kidd	Gauld	Bowman	MacDonald R	Jardine	Mackay	Robertson J	O'Connor	MacDonald A	Johnston	Pettigrew(9)	MacLaren
	29th	Smith	Kidd	Gauld	Bowman	MacDonald R	Jardine	Mackay	Robertson J	Pettigrew	MacDonald A*	Johnston	O'Connor (9)	MacLaren (6)
Apr	2nd	Smith	Kidd	Gauld	Bowman	MacDonald R	Jardine	Mackay	Robertson J	O'Connor	MacLaren	Johnston	Byrne	McCoy
	6th	Smith	Kidd	Gauld	Bowman	MacDonald R	Jardine	Mackay	Robertson J	O'Connor	MacDonald A	Johnston	MacLaren	McCoy
	9th	Smith	Kidd	Gauld	Bowman	MacDonald R	Jardine	Mackay	Robertson J	O'Connor	MacDonald A	Johnston	Pettigrew (11)	MacLaren
	16th	Smith	Kidd	MacLaren	Bowman	MacDonald R	Jardine	Mackay	Robertson J	O'Connor	MacDonald A	Johnston	Pettigrew (9)	Gauld
	23rd	Smith	Kidd	MacLaren	Bowman	MacDonald R	Jardine	Byrne	Robertson J	Pettigrew	MacDonald A	Mackay	O'Connor (9)	Johnston (7)
	30th	Smith	Kidd	Gauld	Bowman	MacDonald R	Jardine	Mackay	Robertson J	O'Connor	MacDonald A	Johnston	McCoy (9)	Byrne
May	7th	Smith	Kidd	Gauld	Bowman	MacDonald R	Jardine	Mackay	Robertson J	O'Connor	MacDonald A	Johnston	McCoy	Byrne
	14th	Smith	Kidd	Gauld	Bowman	MacDonald R	Jardine	Mackay	Robertson J	O'Connor	MacDonald A	Johnston	Pettigrew (9)	Byrne (2)

Five of Hearts - (left to right) Alex. MacDonald, Roddy MacDonald, Willie Pettigrew, Sandy Jardine and Willie Johnston.

Season 1983-84

Date			Opponents		Score	Crowd	Scorers
Aug	20th	L	St Johnstone	a	1-0	6,600	Bone
	24th	LC2	Cowdenbeath	a	0-0	2,600	-
	27th	LC2	Cowdenbeath	h	1-1* (1-1)	5,000	Mackay
	31st	LC3	St Mirren	a	2-2	4,226	Bone; Robertson (pen)
Sep	3rd	L	Hibernian	h	3-2	20,002	Robertson 2; Bone
	7th	LC3	Rangers	h	0-3	11,287	-
	10th	L	Rangers	h	3-1	16,173	A. MacDonald; Robertson; Bone
	17th	L	Dundee	a	2-1	6,765	Bone; Robertson
	24th	L	St Mirren	a	1-0	6,000	R. MacDonald
Oct	1st	L	Aberdeen	h	0-2	18,200	-
	5th	LC3	Clydebank	h	1-1	2,527	Park
	8th	L	Motherwell	h	0-0	7,900	-
	15th	L	Celtic	a	1-1	12,207	Bone
	22nd	L	Dundee United	a	0-1	13,200	-
	25th	LC3	Rangers	a	0-2	12,000	-
	29th	L	St Johnstone	h	2-0	8,207	Robertson 2 (1 pen)
Nov	5th	L	Hibernian	a	1-1	22,000	Robertson
	9th	LC3	St Mirren	h	3-1	2,000	O'Connor; Mackay (pen); Robertson
	13th	L	Dundee	h	1-3	12,300	Mackay (pen)
	19th	L	Aberdeen	a	0-2	20,000	-
	26th	L	St Mirren	h	2-2	9,500	Mackay 2 (1 pen)
	30th	LC3	Clydebank	a	3-0	587	Robertson 2; Johnston
Dec	3rd	L	Rangers	a	0-3	22,500	-
	10th	L	Dundee United	h	0-0	9,288	-
	17th	L	Celtic	h	1-3	15,298	Robertson
	26th	L	Motherwell	a	1-1	7,589	Bone
	31st	L	St Johnstone	a	2-1	9,670	Park; Cowie
Jan	2nd	L	Hibernian	h	1-1	23,499	Park
	7th	L	Dundee	a	1-4	5,960	Robertson
Feb	6th	SC3	Partick Thistle	h	2-0	7,000	Cowie; Bone
	11th	L	Rangers	h	2-2	18,083	O'Connor; Robertson
	18th	SC4	Dundee United	a	1-2	14,371	Robertson (pen)
	25th	L	Celtic	a	1-4	17,950	Park
Mar	3rd	L	Motherwell	h	2-1	6,098	Robertson 2
	11th	L	Dundee United	a	1-3	10,058	Kidd
	17th	L	St Mirren	a	1-1	4,215	Johnston
	24th	L	St Mirren	h	2-1	6,500	Robertson; Bone
	31st	L	Dundee United	h	0-0	7,852	-
Apr	2nd	L	Aberdeen	a	1-1	16,240	Robertson
	7th	L	Rangers	a	0-0	22,000	-
	21st	L	Hibernian	a	0-0	19,000	-
	28th	L	St Johnstone	h	2-2	6,799	R. MacDonald; Park
May	2nd	L	Aberdeen	h	0-1	12,600	-
	5th	L	Celtic	h	1-1	12,281	Johnston
	9th	L	Dundee	h	1-1	6,571	Mackay
	12th	L	Motherwell	a	1-0	3,781	Robertson (pen)

* aet 1-1 after 90 mts.Hearts won 4-2 on pens

Jimmy Bone - the veteran striker brought out the best in the youngsters.

The Record		
League	-	Fifth Place, Premier Division
League Cup	-	Third round
Scottish Cup	-	Fourth round
Top Scorer	-	John Robertson (20 goals)
Av. Home Gate	-	12,000
Players used	-	24
Sent off (booked)	-	One (55)

Appearances

	League	L/Cup	S/Cup	Total	
George Cowie	35 (1)	7	2 (1)	44	(2)
Henry Smith	36	6	2	44	
Sandy Jardine	33	7	2	42	
John Robertson	34 (15)	5 (4)	2 (1)	41+2s	(20)
Jimmy Bone	34 (7)	5 (1)	2 (1)	41	(9)
Roddy MacDonald	34 (2)	7	0	41	(2)
Walter Kidd	31 (1)	7	2	40	(1)
Davie Bowman	32	7	0	39+2s	
Gary Mackay	29 (4)	7 (2)	2	38+3s	(6)
Donald Park	26 (4)	7 (1)	1	34+4s	(5)
Stewart MacLaren	18	5	2	25+1s	
Alex. MacDonald	19 (1)	4	0	23+5s	(1)
Craig Levein	20	0	2	22+2s	
Derek O'Connor	5 (1)	4 (1)	1	10+6s	(2)
Willie Johnston	2 (2)	4 (1)	0	6+19s	(3)
Gregor Stevens	3	0	2	5	
Stuart Gauld	2	2	0	4+1s	
Peter Shields	2	2	0	4+1s	
Ian Westwater	0	2	0	2	
Malcolm Murray	1	0	0	1	
Alan Redpath	0	0	0	0+2s	
Gerry McCoy	0	0	0	0+1s	
Willie Pettigrew	0	0	0	0+1s	

Scottish League Premier Division

		Home			Away			Goals	
	P	W	D	L	W	D	L	F A	PTS
Aberdeen	36	14	3	1	11	4	3	78-21	57
Celtic	36	13	5	0	8	3	7	80-41	50
Dundee United	36	11	3	4	7	8	3	67-39	47
Rangers	36	7	8	3	8	4	6	43-41	42
Hearts	**36**	**5**	**9**	**4**	**5**	**7**	**6**	**38-47**	**36**
St Mirren	36	8	6	4	1	8	9	55-59	32
Hibernian	36	7	4	7	5	3	10	45-55	31
Dundee	36	6	1	11	5	4	9	50-74	27
St Johnstone	36	6	1	11	4	2	12	36-81	23
Motherwell	36	2	5	11	2	2	14	31-75	15

League Cup Section

	P	W	D	L	F A	PTS
Rangers	6	6	0	0	18-0	12
Hearts	**6**	**2**	**2**	**2**	**9- 9**	**6**
Clydebank	6	1	2	3	6-14	4
St Mirren	6	1	2	3	6-16	2

Heart of Midlothian F.C. Line-Ups 1983-84

	1	2	3	4	5	6	7	8	9	10	11	12	13
Aug 20th	Smith	Kidd	Cowie	Jardine	MacDonald R	Bowman	MacLaren	Robertson	Park	Bone	MacDonald A	Johnston	Murray
24th	Smith	Kidd	Cowie	Jardine	MacDonald R	Bowman	MacLaren	Robertson	Park	Bone	Johnston	Mackay (11)	Gauld
27th	Smith	Kidd	Cowie	Jardine	MacDonald R	Bowman	Park	Robertson	Bone	MacLaren	Mackay	Johnston (9)	Gauld
31st	Smith	Kidd	Cowie	Jardine	MacDonald R	MacLaren	Bowman	Robertson	Bone	Park	Mackay	Johnston	Gauld
Sep 3rd	Smith	Gauld	Cowie	Jardine	MacDonald R	MacLaren	Bowman	Robertson	Bone	Park	Mackay	MacDonald A(11)	Johnston(9)
7th	Smith	Gauld	Cowie	Jardine	MacDonald R	MacDonaldA	Bowman	Mackay	O'Connor	Park	Johnston	MacLaren	Pettigrew(9)
10th	Smith	Kidd	Cowie	Jardine	MacDonald R	MacLaren	Bowman	Robertson	Bone	MacDonald A	Park	Gauld	Mackay
17th	Smith	Kidd	Cowie	Jardine	MacDonald R	MacLaren	Bowman	Robertson	Bone	MacDonald A	Park	Mackay (11)	Johnston
24th	Smith	Kidd	Cowie	Jardine	MacDonald R	MacLaren	Bowman	Robertson	Bone	Mackay	Park	MacDonald A (7)	Gauld
Oct 1st	Smith	Kidd	Cowie	Jardine	MacDonald R	MacLaren	Bowman	Robertson	Bone	MacDonald A	Park	Johnston (6)	Park
5th	Westwater	Kidd	Shields	Gauld	MacDonald R	Cowie	Bowman	Robertson	Park	Mackay	Johnston	McCoy (8)	MacLaren
8th	Smith	Kidd	Cowie	Jardine	MacDonald R	MacLaren	Bowman	Robertson	Bone	MacDonald A	Park	Johnston (11)	Gauld
15th	Smith	Kidd	Cowie	Jardine	MacDonald R	MacLaren	Bowman	Robertson	Bone	MacDonald A	Park	Mackay (6)	Gauld
22nd	Smith	Kidd	Cowie	Jardine	MacDonald R	Mackay	Bowman	Park	Bone	Robertson	MacDonald A	Johnston (8)	Gauld
25th	Smith	Kidd	Shields	Jardine	MacDonald R	Mackay	Bowman	Connor	Bone	MacDonald A	Park	Johnston (2)	Robertson (9)
29th	Smith	Kidd	Shields	Jardine	MacDonald R	Park	Bowman	Mackay	Bone	MacDonald A	Robertson	Gauld (10)	O'Connor
Nov 5th	Smith	Kidd	Cowie	Jardine	MacDonald R	Park	Bowman	Mackay	Bone	MacDonald A	Robertson	MacLaren (7)	O'Connor(12)
9th	Smith	Kidd	Cowie	Jardine	MacDonald R	MacLaren	Mackay	Bone	O'Connor	MacDonald A	Park	Robertson (9)	Redpath (6)
13th	Smith	Kidd	Cowie	Jardine	MacDonald R	MacLaren	Park	Mackay	Bone	MacDonald A	Robertson	O'Connor (7)	Gauld
19th	Smith	Kidd	Cowie	Jardine	MacDonald R	MacLaren	Park	Mackay	Bone	MacDonald A	Robertson	O'Connor (10)	Johnston (6)
26th	Smith	Kidd	Cowie	Jardine	MacDonald R	MacLaren	Park	Mackay	Bone	Johnston	Robertson	O'Connor (3)	Bowman (6)
30th	Westwater	Kidd	Cowie	Jardine	MacLaren	MacDonald A	Bowman	Mackay	O'Connor	Robertson	Johnston	Redpath (4)	Scott (6)
Dec 3rd	Smith	Kidd	Cowie	Jardine	MacDonald R	Levein	Bowman	Mackay	Bone	Robertson	Park	O'Connor (9)	Johnston (11)
10th	Smith	Kidd	Cowie	Jardine	MacDonald R	Levein	Bowman	Mackay	Bone	Robertson	Park	O'Connor	Johnston
17th	Smith	Kidd	Cowie	Jardine	MacDonald R	Levein	Bowman	Mackay	Bone	Robertson	Park	Johnston (11)	MacLaren
26th	Smith	Kidd	Cowie	Jardine	MacDonald R	Levein	Bowman	Mackay	Bone	Robertson	Park	MacDonald A (6)	Johnston (10)
31st	Smith	Kidd	Cowie	Levein	MacDonald R	MacLaren	Bowman	Mackay	Bone	Park	O'Connor	Robertson	Johnston
Jan 2nd	Smith	MacLaren	Cowie	Levein	MacDonald R	Mackay	Bowman	Park	Bone	Robertson	O'Connor	Shields	Johnston
7th	Smith	MacLaren	Cowie	Levein	McDonald R	Park	Bowman	Mackay	Bone	Robertson	O'Connor	Shields (2)	Johnston(11)
Feb 6th	Smith	Kidd	Cowie	Jardine	Stevens	MacLaren	Mackay	Levein	O'Connor	Bone	Robertson	Johnston	Shields
11th	Smith	Kidd	Cowie	Jardine	Stevens	MacLaren	Levein	Robertson	Bone	Shields	Mackay	Johnston (7)	O'Connor (9)
18th	Smith	Kidd	Cowie	Jardine	Stevens	MacLaren	Mackay	Robertson	Bone*	Levein	Park	Johnston (10)	Bowman (6)
25th	Smith	Kidd	Cowie	Jardine	Stevens	Levein	MacLaren	Bowman	Mackay	Park	Robertson	Johnston (6)	Macdonald R
Mar 3rd	Smith	Kidd	Cowie	Jardine	MacDonald R	Stevens	Bowman	Robertson	O'Connor	Levein	Park	MacDonald A(6)	MacLaren
11th	Smith	Kidd	Cowie	Jardine	MacDonald R	Levein	Bowman	Robertson	Bone	MacDonald A	Mackay	Park (6)	O'Connor
17th	Smith	Kidd	Cowie	Jardine	MacDonald R	Levein	Bowman	Mackay	Bone	MacDonald A	Robertson	Johnston (6)	MacLaren
24th	Smith	Kidd	Cowie	Jardine	MacDonald R	MacLaren	Bowman	Mackay	Bone	MacDonald A	Robertson	Johnston (9)	Levein (6)
31st	Smith	Kidd	Cowie	Jardine	MacDonald R	MacLaren	Bowman	Mackay	Bone	MacDonald A	Robertson	Levein (6)	Johnston
Apr 2nd	Smith	Kidd	Cowie	Jardine	MacDonald R	Levein	Bowman	Mackay	Bone	MacDonald A	Robertson	Johnston (10)	Park (6)
7th	Smith	Kidd	Cowie	Jardine	MacDonald R	Levein	Bowman	Mackay	Bone	Park	Robertson	Johnston	MacLaren
21st	Smith	Kidd	Cowie	Jardine	MacDonald R	Levein	Bowman	Mackay	Bone	O'Connor	Park	MacDonald A (8)	Johnston (10)
28th	Smith	Kidd	Cowie	Jardine	MacDonald R	Levein	Bowman	Mackay	Bone	Robertson	Johnston	Park (6)	O'Connor
May 2nd	Smith	Kidd	Cowie	Jardine	MacDonald R	Levein	Bowman	Mackay	Bone	Robertson	Park	Johnston (11)	MacDonald A
5th	Smith	Kidd	Cowie	Jardine	MacDonald R	Levein	Bowman	Mackay	Bone	Robertson	MacDonald A	Johnston (11)	Park
9th	Smith	Gauld	Cowie	Jardine	MacDonald R	Levein	Bowman	Mackay	Bone	Robertson	MacDonald A	Johnston (5)	Park
13th	Smith	Murray	Cowie	Jardine	MacDonald R	Levein	Bowman	Mackay	Bone	Robertson	MacDonald A	Park (8)	Johnston

Just wide - Hearts defender George Cowie looks on anxiously but keeper Henry Smith has the ball covered in this game against Dundee United at Tannadice.

DC Thomson

Season 1984-85

Date			Opponents		Score	Crowd	Scorers
Aug	11th	L	Dundee United	a	0-2	10,027	-
	18th	L	Morton	h	1-2	7,377	Whittaker
	22nd	LC2	East Stirling	h	4-0	3,755	Bone; Levein; Johnston; Whittaker
	25th	L	Hibernian	a	2-1	18,000	Levein; O'Connor
	29th	LC3	Ayr United	h	1-0	5,377	O'Connor
Sep	1st	L	Dumbarton	h	1-0	6,914	Park
	4th	LCQ	Dundee	a	1-0	8,818	R. MacDonald
	8th	L	St Mirren	h	1-2	7,669	Robertson (pen)
	15th	L	Celtic	a	0-1	18,411	-
	19th	UEF1	Paris St Germain	a	0-4	21,639	-
	22nd	L	Dundee	h	0-2	7,511	-
	26th	LCS	Dundee United	h	1-2	10,541	Robertson
	29th	L	Aberdeen	a	0-4	16,300	-
Oct	3rd	UEF1	Paris St Germain	h	2-2	10,023	Robertson 2
	6th	L	Rangers	h	1-0	18,097	Robertson
	10th	LCS	Dundee United	a	1-3 (2-5)	13,468	Park
	13th	L	Dundee United	h	2-0	7,066	Park; Robertson
	20th	L	Morton	a	3-2	2,500	Black (pen); Robertson; Clark
	27th	L	Hibernian	h	0-0	20,156	-
Nov	3rd	L	Dumbarton	a	1-0	2,500	Bone
	10th	L	St Mirren	a	3-2	5,514	Clark 2; Bone
	17th	L	Celtic	h	1-5	20,117	Johnston
	24th	L	Dundee	a	1-2	6,414	Bowman
Dec	1st	L	Aberdeen	h	1-2	10,037	A. MacDonald
	8th	L	Rangers	a	1-1	16,700	Park
	15th	L	Dundee United	a	2-5	7,359	Black (pen); Bone
	29th	L	Morton	h	1-0	7,226	Black (pen)
Jan	1st	L	Hibernian	a	2-1	22,500	Mackay; Clark
	5th	L	Dumbarton	h	5-1	7,713	Black 3 (1 pen); Clark; Bone
	12th	L	St Mirren	h	0-1	11,103	-
	30th	SC3	Inverness Caley	h	6-0	7,075	R. MacDonald; Mackay 4; Robertson
Feb	3rd	L	Dundee	h	3-3	10,063	Robertson; Mackay; McNaughton
	9th	L	Aberdeen	a	2-2	14,700	Watson; Robertson
	16th	SC4	Brechin City	a	1-1	6,250	Robertson
	20th	SC4R	Brechin City	h	1-0	8,942	McNaughton
	23rd	L	Rangers	h	2-0	14,004	Watson; R. MacDonald
Mar	2nd	L	Morton	a	1-0	3,000	A. MacDonald
	9th	SCQ	Aberdeen	h	1-1	23,896	Clark
	13th	SCQR	Aberdeen	a	0-1	23,000	
	16th	L	Dundee United	h	0-1	7,663	-
	20th	L	Celtic	a	2-3	11,522	Robertson; Watson
	23rd	L	Dumbarton	a	3-1	3,000	Kidd; Clark 2
Apr	2nd	L	Hibernian	h	2-2	17,814	Robertson; Clark
	6th	L	Celtic	h	0-2	14,883	-
	20th	L	Dundee	a	0-3	7,421	-
	27th	L	Rangers	a	1-3	12,193	McNaughton
May	4th	L	Aberdeen	h	0-3	8,251	-
	11th	L	St Mirren	a	2-5	4,817	Black (pen); Clarke o.g.

Cup Cash v. Inverness Caley £10,527

Roddy MacDonald - a key defender in the Hearts revival.

Appearances

	League	L/Cup	S/Cup	UEF	Total
Henry Smith	36	5	5	2	48
Sandy Jardine	34	5	5	1	45
Craig Levein	35 (1)	5 (1)	4	2	46+1s (2)
John Robertson	33 (8)	5 (1)	5 (2)	2 (2)	45 (13)
Walter Kidd	33 (1)	5	4	2	44 (1)
Kenny Black	32 (7)	2	5	2	41 (7)
Roddy MacDonald	28 (1)	5 (1)	5 (1)	0	38 (3)
Brian Whittaker	25 (1)	0 (1)	5	2	32+6s (2)
Sandy Clark	25 (8)	0	5 (1)	0	30 (9)
Donald Park	16 (3)	4 (1)	0	1	21+7s (4)
Jimmy Bone	16 (4)	5 (1)	0	2	23+6s (5)
Gary Mackay	16 (2)	0	5 (4)	1	22+1s (6)
George Cowie	14	5	0	1	20+1s
Alex. MacDonald	14 (2)	3	0	1	18+11s (2)
Andy Watson	14 (3)	0	3	0	17+4s (3)
Davie Bowman	9 (1)	4	0	2	15+2s (1)
Willie Johnston	4 (1)	1 (1)	1	1	7+11s (2)
Neil Berry	2	0	3	0	5+1s
Malcolm Murray	4	0	0	0	4
Brian McNaughton	3 (2)	0	0 (1)	0	3+8s (3)
Derek O'Connor	0 (1)	1 (1)	0	0	1+5s (2)
Jimmy Sandison	2	0	0	0	2+1s
Stewart MacLaren	1	0	0	0	1
Paul Cherry	0	0	0	0	0+3s
Jim Cowell	0	0	0	0	0+1s

The Record

League	-	**Seventh Place, Premier Division**
League Cup	-	**Semi final**
Scottish Cup	-	**Quarter final**
Top Scorer	-	**John Robertson (13 goals)**
Av. Home Gate	-	**11,300**
Players used	-	**25**
Sent off (booked)	-	**Three (49)**

Scottish League Premier Division

		Home			Away			Goals		
	P	W	D	L	W	D	L	F	A	PTS
Aberdeen	36	13	4	1	14	1	3	89-26		59
Celtic	36	12	3	3	10	5	3	77-30		52
Dundee United	36	13	2	3	7	5	6	67-33		47
Rangers	36	7	6	5	6	6	6	47-38		38
St Mirren	36	10	2	6	7	2	9	51-56		38
Dundee	36	9	3	6	6	4	8	48-50		37
Hearts	**36**	**6**	**3**	**9**	**7**	**2**	**9**	**47-64**		**31**
Hibernian	36	5	4	9	5	3	10	38-61		27
Dumbarton	36	4	4	10	2	3	13	29-64		19
Morton	36	3	1	14	2	1	15	29-100		12

Heart of Midlothian F.C. Line-Ups 1984-85

	1	2	3	4	5	6	7	8	9	10	11	12	13
Aug 11th	Smith	Kidd	Whittaker	Jardine	MacDonald R	MacLaren	Park	Robertson	Bone	MacDonald A	Black	Johnston (6)	Levein (7)
18th	Smith	Kidd	Whittaker	Jardine	MacDonald R	Levein	Bowman	Robertson	Bone	Black	Johnston	Park (3)	MacDonald A (10)
22nd	Smith	Kidd	Cowie	Jardine	MacDonald R	Levein	Bowman	Robertson	Bone	MacDonald	Johnston	Whittaker (11)	Park (9)
25th	Smith	Kidd	Cowie	Jardine	MacDonald R	Levein	Bowman	Park	Bone	Robertson	MacDonald A	O'Connor (11)	Whittaker
29th	Smith	Kidd	Cowie	Jardine	MacDonald R	Levein	Bowman	Robertson	O'Connor	Bone	Park	Johnston (9)	MacDonald A (6)
Sep 1st	Smith	Kidd	Cowie	Jardine	MacDonald R	Levein	Bowman	Park	Bone	Robertson	Johnston	O'Connor (9)	MacDonald A (7)
4th	Smith	Kidd	Cowie	Jardine	MacDonald R	Levein	Bowman	Bone	Robertson	MacDonald A	Park	Johnston (2)	Whittaker (10)
8th	Smith	Kidd	Cowie	Jardine	MacDonald R	Levein	Bowman	Robertson	Bone	MacDonald A	Park	Johnston (11)	Whittaker (10)
15th	Smith	Kidd	Cowie	Jardine	MacDonald R	Levein	Bowman	Mackay	Bone	MacDonald A	Robertson	Park (10)	Whittaker* (2)
19th	Smith	Kidd	Whittaker	Jardine	Levein	Mackay	Bowman	Black	Bone	MacDonald A	Robertson	Johnston (10)	Park, O'Connor
22nd	Smith	Kidd	Cowie	Jardine	MacDonald R	Levein	Bowman	Mackay	Bone	Black	Park	Johnston (8)	Cherry (9)
26th	Smith	Kidd	Cowie	Jardine	MacDonald R	Levein	Bowman*	Robertson	Bone	Park	Black	O'Connor (8)	Johnston (10)
29th	Smith	Kidd	Cowie	Jardine	MacDonald R	Levein	Park	Robertson	Bone	MacDonald A	Black	Whittaker (7)	O'Connor (4)
Oct 3rd	Smith	Cowie	Whittaker	Levein	Kidd	Black	Bowman	Bone	Park	Robertson	Johnston	O'Connor (8)	MacDonald A (9)
6th	Smith	Kidd	Cowie	Jardine	MacDonald R	Levein	Park	Robertson	Bone	MacDonald A	Black	Whittaker (7)	O'Connor (4)
10th	Smith	Kidd	Cowie	Jardine	MacDonald R	Levein	Park	Robertson	Bone	MacDonald A	Black	Whittaker (4)	Johnston (10)
13th	Smith	Kidd	Whittaker	Levein	MacDonald R	Black	Park	Cowie	Bone	Robertson	Johnston	Cherry (11)	Sandison
20th	Smith	Kidd	Whittaker	Jardine	MacDonald R	Levein	Park	Robertson	Clark	Bone	Black	Johnston (7)	MacDonaldA(10)
27th	Smith	Kidd	Whittaker	Jardine	MacDonald R	Levein	Black	Robertson	Clark	Bone	MacDonald A	Johnston	Park
Nov 3rd	Smith	Kidd	Black	Jardine	Whittaker	Levein	Park	Robertson	Clark	Bone	MacDonald A	Johnston	Sandison
10th	Smith	Kidd	Whittaker	Jardine	MacDonald R	Levein	Black	Park	Clark	Bone	MacDonald A	Bowman (6)	Johnston
17th	Smith	Kidd	Whittaker	Jardine	MacDonald R	Levein	Park	Bone	Clark	MacDonald A	Black	Bowman (10)	Johnston (7)
24th	Smith	Kidd	Whittaker	Jardine	MacDonald R	Levein	Bowman	Robertson	Clark	Bone	Black	Park (5)	MacDonald A (10)
Dec 1st	Smith	Kidd	Whittaker	Jardine	Levein	Black	Bowman	Robertson	Clark	MacDonald A	Park	Johnston (10)	Bone
8th	Smith	Kidd	Whittaker	Jardine	Black	Levein	Bowman	Robertson	Clark	Park	MacDonald A	Mackay (11)	Bone (8)
15th	Smith	Cowie	Whittaker	Jardine	Black	Levein	Mackay	Robertson	Clark	MacDonald A	Park	Berry (2)	Bone (11)
29th	Smith	Cowie	Whittaker	Jardine	Black	Levein	Mackay	Watson	Clark	Robertson	MacDonald A	Bone (11)	Park
Jan 1st	Smith	Kidd	Cowie	Jardine	MacDonald R	Levein	Mackay	Watson	Clark	Robertson	Black	Bone	MacDonald A
5th	Smith	Kidd	Whittaker	Jardine	MacDonald R	Levein	Watson	Mackay	Clark	Robertson	Black	Bone (5)	Johnston
12th	Smith	Kidd	Whittaker	Jardine	MacDonald R	Levein	Watson	Mackay	Clark	Robertson	Black	Bone (5)	MacDonald A
30th	Smith	Kidd	Whittaker	Jardine	MacDonald R	Levein	Mackay	Watson	Clark	Robertson	Black	Johnston (8)	Bone
Feb 3rd	Smith	Kidd	Whittaker	Jardine	MacDonald R	Levein	Mackay	Robertson	Clark	Black	Johnston	Watson (2)	McNaughton (11)
9th	Smith	Kidd	Whittaker	Jardine	MacDonald R	Levein	Watson	Mackay	Clark	Robertson	Black	McNaughton	Berry
16th	Smith	Kidd	Whittaker	Jardine	MacDonald R	Levein	Mackay	Watson	Clark	Robertson	Black	Berry	McNaughton (11)
20th	Smith	Berry	Whittaker	Jardine	MacDonald R	Levein	Mackay	Robertson	Clark	Black	Johnston	Watson (10)	McNaughton(11)
23rd	Smith	Kidd	Whittaker	Levein	MacDonald R	Berry	Watson	Mackay	Clark	Robertson	Black	McNaughton	MacDonald A
Mar 2nd	Smith	Kidd	Whittaker	Jardine	MacDonald R	Levein	Berry	Mackay	Clark	Robertson	Black	McNaughton (2)	MacDonaldA(9)
9th	Smith	Kidd	Whittaker	Jardine	MacDonald R	Berry	Mackay	Watson	Clark	Robertson	Black	MacDonaldA(8)	McNaughton
13th	Smith	Kidd	Whittaker	Jardine	MacDonald R*	Levein	Mackay	Berry	Clark	Robertson	Black	Watson (8)	McNaughton (10)
16th	Smith	Kidd	Whittaker	Jardine	Murray	Levein	McNaughton	Watson	Clark	Robertson	Black	MacDonaldA(7)	Cowie (3)
20th	Smith	Kidd	Cowie	Jardine	MacDonald R	Levein	Watson	Clark	Whittaker	Robertson	Black	MacDonaldA(9)	McNaughton (10)
23rd	Smith	Kidd	Whittaker	Jardine	MacDonald R	Levein	Mackay	Watson	Clark	Robertson	Black	McNaughton (7)	MacDonald A
Apr 2nd	Smith	Kidd	Whittaker	Jardine	MacDonald R	Levein	Mackay	Watson	Clark	Robertson	Black	Park (7)	Cowie
6th	Smith	Kidd	Whittaker	Jardine	MacDonald R	Levein	Mackay	Watson	Clark	Robertson	Black	Park (10)	MacDonald A
20th	Smith	Kidd	Whittaker	Jardine	MacDonald R	Levein	Watson	Mackay	Clark	Robertson	Black	Park (4)	MacDonaldA(7)
27th	Smith	Kidd	Murray	Jardine	MacDonald R	Levein	Watson	Robertson	Clark	McNaughton	Black	Sandison (7)	MacDonaldA
May 4th	Smith	Kidd	Murray	Jardine	Cowie	Levein	Sandison	Robertson	Clark	Mackay	Black	Watson (5)	McNaughton(10)
11th	Smith	Murray	Cowie	Jardine	Sandison	Levein	Watson	McNaughton	Robertson	Park	Black	Cowell (1)	Cherry (10)

So close - Henry Smith dives but he is beaten by this effort by Celtic's Frank McGarvey. Roddy MacDonald, Sandy Jardine and George Cowie are powerless to intervene.

DC Thomson

Season 1985-86

Date			Opponents		Score	Crowd	Scorers
Aug	10th	L	Celtic	h	1-1	21,786	Colquhoun
	17th	L	St Mirren	a	2-6	6,327	Colquhoun; Robertson
	20th	LC2	Montrose	a	3-1	1,992	Kidd; Robertson; Colquhoun
	24th	L	Rangers	a	1-3	35,483	Robertson
	27th	LC3	Stirling Albion	h	2-1*	4,479	Cherry; McNaughton
	31st	L	Hibernian	h	2-1	17,457	Colquhoun; Clark
Sep	4th	LCQ	Aberdeen	a	0-1	13,066	-
	7th	L	Aberdeen	a	0-3	12,000	-
	14th	L	Dundee United	h	2-0	7,617	R. MacDonald; Robertson
	21st	L	Motherwell	a	1-2	4,806	I. Jardine
	28th	L	Clydebank	a	0-1	3,641	-
Oct	5th	L	Dundee	h	1-1	8,512	I. Jardine
	12th	L	Celtic	a	1-0	26,683	Robertson
	19th	L	St Mirren	h	3-0	8,638	Robertson 2; Mackay
	30th	L	Aberdeen	h	1-0	12,886	Levein
Nov	2nd	L	Dundee United	a	1-1	10,142	I. Jardine
	9th	L	Hibernian	a	0-0	19,700	-
	16th	L	Rangers	h	3-0	23,083	Clark 2; Robertson
	23rd	L	Motherwell	h	3-0	10,119	Clark 2; I. Jardine
	30th	L	Clydebank	h	4-1	10,267	Berry; Clark; Black (pen): Robertson
Dec	7th	L	Dundee	a	1-1	10,780	I. Jardine
	14th	L	Celtic	h	1-1	22,163	Robertson
	21st	L	St Mirren	a	1-0	6,498	Black (pen)
	28th	L	Rangers	a	2-0	33,410	Colquhoun 2
Jan	1st	L	Hibernian	h	3-1	25,605	I. Jardine; Robertson; Clark
	4th	L	Motherwell	a	3-1	9,850	Jardine; Berry; Robertson
	11th	L	Dundee United	h	1-1	19,043	Mackay
	18th	L	Aberdeen	a	1-0	21,500	Colquhoun
	25th	SC3	Rangers	h	3-2	27,442	McAdam; Mackay; Robertson
Feb	1st	L	Clydebank	a	1-1	6,095	Clark
	8th	L	Dundee	h	3-1	15,065	Colquhoun; Robertson; Mackay
	22nd	L	Celtic	a	1-1	45,346	Robertson
Mar	3rd	SC4	Hamilton Accies	a	2-1	10,000	Robertson; Mackay
	9th	SCQ	St Mirren	h	4-1	20,655	Colquhoun; Robertson 2 (1 pen); Black
	15th	L	Motherwell	h	2-0	12,071	R. MacDonald; Robertson (pen)
	22nd	L	Hibernian	a	2-1	20,000	Clark; Robertson (pen)
	25th	L	St Mirren	h	3-0	13,287	Levein; Robertson; Clark
	29th	L	Rangers	h	3-1	24,740	Robertson 2 (1 pen); Clark
Apr	5th	SCS	Dundee United	Hamp	1-0	30,872	Colquhoun
	12th	L	Dundee United	a	3-0	22,515	Robertson 2; Clark
	20th	L	Aberdeen	h	1-1	19,047	Colquhoun
	26th	L	Clydebank	h	1-0	20,100	Mackay
May	3rd	L	Dundee	a	0-2	19,567	-
	10th	SCF	Aberdeen	Hamp	0-3	62,800	-

* aet 1-1 after 90 mts.

Craig Levein - classy defender went on to play for Scotland

Appearances

	League	L/Cup	S/Cup	Total	
Henry Smith	36	3	5	44	
John Colquhoun	36 (8)	2 (1)	5 (2)	43+1s	(11)
Sandy Jardine	35	3	5	43	
John Robertson	34 (20)	3 (1)	5 (4)	42+1s	(25)
Craig Levein	33 (2)	3	5	41	(2)
Sandy Clark	33 (12)	2	5	40	(12)
Neil Berry	32 (2)	0	5	37	(2)
Gary Mackay	30 (4)	2	5 (2)	37+2s	(6)
Walter Kidd	28	2 (1)	5	35	(1)
Brian Whittaker	24	3	4	31+1s	
Kenny Black	23 (2)	2	5 (1)	30+6s	(3)
Ian Jardine	19 (7)	0	1	20+5s	(7)
Roddy MacDonald	10 (2)	3	0	13+1s	(2)
Andy Watson	8	3	0	11+5s	
George Cowie	8	1	0	9	
Brian McNaughton	2	1 (1)	0	3+2s	(1)
Paul Cherry	3	0 (1)	0	3+4s	(1)
Jimmy Sandison	2	0	0	2+3s	
Colin McAdam	0	0	0 (1)	0+6s	(1)
Billy Mackay	0	0	0	0+4s	
Alex. MacDonald	0	0	0	0+1s	

The Record		
League	-	Runners-up, Premier Division
League Cup	-	Quarter-final
Scottish Cup	-	Runners-up
Top Scorer	-	John Robertson (25 goals)
Av. Home Gate	-	16,200
Players used	-	21
Sent off (booked)	-	Two (39)

Scottish League Premier Division

	P	Home W	Home D	Home L	Away W	Away D	Away L	Goals F-A	PTS
Celtic	36	10	6	2	10	4	4	67-38	50
Hearts	**36**	**13**	**5**	**0**	**7**	**5**	**6**	**59-33**	**50**
Dundee United	36	10	6	2	8	5	5	59-31	47
Aberdeen	36	11	4	3	5	8	5	62-31	44
Rangers	36	10	4	4	3	5	10	53-45	35
Dundee	36	11	2	5	3	5	10	45-51	35
St Mirren	36	9	2	7	4	3	11	42-63	31
Hibernian	36	6	4	8	5	2	11	49-63	28
Motherwell	36	7	3	8	0	3	15	33-66	20
Clydebank	36	4	6	8	2	2	14	29-77	20

Heart of Midlothian F.C. Line-Ups 1985-86

	1	2	3	4	5	6	7	8	9	10	11	12	13
Aug 10th	Smith	Sandison	Whittaker	Jardine S	Levein	Berry	Colquhoun	Watson	Clark	Robertson	Mackay G	McNaughton	Cherry (6)
17th	Smith	Sandison	Whittaker	Jardine S	MacDonald	Levein	Colquhoun	Watson	Clark	Robertson	Mackay G	McNaughton	Cherry
20th	Smith	Kidd	Whittaker	Jardine S	MacDonald	Levein	Colquhoun	Watson	Clark	Mackay G	Robertson	McNaughton	Sandison (6)
24th	Smith	Kidd*	Whittaker	Jardine S	MacDonald	Levein	Colquhoun	Watson	Clark*	Cowie	Robertson	McNaughton (3)	Cherry (7)
27th	Smith	Cowie	Whittaker	Jardine S	MacDonald	Levein	Colquhoun	Watson	McNaughton	Robertson	Black	Sandison (9)	Cherry (4)
31st	Smith	Kidd	Cowie	Jardine S	MacDonald	Levein	Colquhoun	Watson	Clark	Robertson	Black	Mackay G (8)	Whittaker
Sep 4th	Smith	Kidd	Whittaker	Jardine S	MacDonald	Levein	Watson	Mackay G	Clark	Robertson	Black	Cherry (8)	Colquhoun (10)
7th	Smith	Cowie	Whittaker	Jardine S	MacDonald	Levein	Colquhoun	Watson	McNaughton	Cherry	Black	Mackay G (7)	Sandison (11)
14th	Smith	Cowie	Whittaker	Jardine S	MacDonald	Levein	Colquhoun	Watson	McNaughton	Berry	Cherry	Robertson (9)	Jardine I
21st	Smith	Cowie	Whittaker	Jardine S	MacDonald	Levein	Watson	Robertson	Colquhoun	Berry	Cherry	Jardine I (5)	McNaughton (7)
28th	Smith	Kidd	Whittaker	Jardine S	Berry	Levein	Colquhoun	Watson	Clark	Robertson	Black	Mackay G	MacDonaldA(11)
Oct 5th	Smith	Kidd	Whittaker	Jardine S	Berry	Levein	Colquhoun	Jardine I	Clark	Mackay G	Robertson	Black (7)	Watson
12th	Smith	Kidd	Whittaker	Jardine S	Berry	Levein	Colquhoun	Jardine I	Clark	Mackay G	Robertson	Black (7)	Watson (11)
19th	Smith	Kidd	Whittaker	Jardine S	Berry	Levein	Colquhoun	Jardine I	Clark	Mackay G	Robertson	Watson	Black
30th	Smith	Kidd	Whittaker	Jardine S	Berry	Levein	Colquhoun	Jardine I	Clark	Robertson	Mackay G	Black (8)	Watson
Nov 2nd	Smith	Kidd	Whittaker	Jardine S	Berry	Levein	Colquhoun	Jardine I	Clark	Mackay G	Robertson	Black (11)	Watson
9th	Smith	Kidd	Whittaker	Jardine S	Berry	Levein	Colquhoun	Jardine I	Clark	Mackay G	Robertson	Black (7)	MacDonald R
16th	Smith	Kidd	Whittaker	Jardine S	Berry	Levein	Colquhoun	Jardine I	Clark	Mackay G	Robertson	Black	Watson
23rd	Smith	Kidd	Black	Jardine S	Berry	Levein	Colquhoun	Jardine I	Clark	Mackay G	Robertson	Watson	Cherry
30th	Smith	Kidd	Black	Jardine S	Berry	Levein	Colquhoun	Jardine I	Clark	Mackay G	Robertson	Watson	Cherry
Dec 7th	Smith	Kidd	Black	Jardine S	Levein	Berry	Colquhoun	Jardine I	Clark	Mackay G	Robertson	Watson (10)	Whittaker (4)
14th	Smith	Kidd	Black	Jardine S	Levein	Berry	Colquhoun	Jardine I	Clark	Mackay G	Robertson	Whittaker	Watson (10)
21st	Smith	Kidd	Black	Jardine S	Berry	Levein	Colquhoun	Jardine I	Clark	Mackay G	Robertson	Watson (7)	McAdam
28th	Smith	Kidd	Black	Jardine S	Berry	Levein	Colquhoun	Jardine I	Clark	Mackay G	Robertson	Watson	McAdam
Jan 1st	Smith	Kidd	Black	Jardine S	Berry	Levein	Colquhoun	Jardine I	Clark	Mackay G	Robertson	Watson	McAdam
4th	Smith	Kidd	Black	Jardine S	Berry	Levein	Colquhoun	Jardine I	Clark	Mackay G	Robertson	Watson	McAdam (7)
11th	Smith	Kidd	Whittaker	Jardine S	Berry	Levein	Colquhoun	Black	Clark	Mackay G	Robertson	Watson	McAdam
18th	Smith	Kidd	Black	Jardine S	Berry	Levein	Colquhoun	Jardine I	Clark	Mackay G	Robertson	Watson	McAdam (11)
25th	Smith	Kidd	Black	Jardine S	Berry	Levein	Colquhoun	Jardine I	Clark	Mackay G	Robertson	Watson	McAdam (9)
Feb 1st	Smith	Kidd	Black	Jardine S	Berry	MacDonald	Colquhoun	Jardine I	Clark	Mackay G	Robertson	Watson	McAdam (8)
8th	Smith	Kidd	Black	Jardine S	Berry	MacDonald	Colquhoun	Whittaker	Clark	Mackay G	Robertson	Watson	McAdam
22nd	Smith	Kidd	Black	Jardine S	Berry	Levein	Colquhoun	Jardine I	Clark	Mackay G	Robertson	Whittaker	Mackay B (11)
Mar 3rd	Smith	Kidd	Black	Jardine S	Berry	Levein	Colquhoun	Whittaker	Clark	Mackay G	Robertson	Watson (11)	Cowie
9th	Smith	Kidd	Whittaker	Jardine S	Berry	Levein	Colquhoun	Black	Clark	Mackay G	Robertson	MacDonald R(4)	Mackay B (7)
15th	Smith	Kidd	Whittaker	Levein	Berry	MacDonald	Colquhoun	Black	Clark	Mackay G	Robertson	Mackay B (11)	Cowie
22nd	Smith	Kidd	Whittaker	Jardine S	Berry	Levein	Colquhoun	Black	Clark	Mackay G	Robertson	Jardine I	McAdam
25th	Smith	Kidd	Whittaker	Jardine S	Berry	Levein	Colquhoun	Black	Clark	Mackay G	Robertson	Jardine I	Mackay B
29th	Smith	Kidd	Whittaker	Jardine S	Berry	Levein	Colquhoun	Black	Clark	Mackay G	Robertson	McAdam (7)	Jardine I (10)
Apr 5th	Smith	Kidd	Whittaker	Jardine S	Berry	Levein	Colquhoun	Black	Clark	Mackay G	Robertson	Jardine I (10)	Mackay B
12th	Smith	Cowie	Whittaker	Jardine S	Berry	Levein	Colquhoun	Black	Clark	Mackay G	Robertson	Jardine I	McAdam (10)
20th	Smith	Cowie	Whittaker	Jardine S	Berry	Levein	Colquhoun	Black	Clark	Mackay G	Robertson	McAdam	Jardine I (10)
26th	Smith	Cowie	Whittaker	Jardine S	Berry	Levein	Colquhoun	Black	Clark	Mackay G	Robertson	Jardine I (8)	Mackay B
May 3rd	Smith	Kidd	Whittaker	Jardine S	Berry	MacDonald	Colquhoun	Jardine I	Clark	Mackay G	Robertson	Mackay B (8)	Black (3)
10th	Smith	Kidd*	Whittaker	Jardine S	Berry	Levein	Colquhoun	Black	Clark	Mackay G	Robertson	Mackay B	Cowie

So near - Sandy Clark just fails to connect in the crucial league game against Dundee at Dens. Sadly, that was the Hearts story in both league and Scottish Cup in an otherwise memorable 1985-86 season. DC Thomson

Season 1986-87

Date			Opponents		Score	Crowd	Scorers
Aug	9th	L	St Mirren	a	0-0	8,869	-
	13th	L	Hamilton Accies	h	1-0	10,103	Robertson
	16th	L	Falkirk	h	1-0	11,918	Watson
	19th	LC2	Montrose	h	0-2	7,028	-
	23rd	L	Dundee United	a	0-1	11,068	-
	30th	L	Hibernian	a	3-1	21,500	Robertson; I. Jardine; Clark
Sep	6th	L	Clydebank	h	2-1	10,158	G. Mackay; Foster
	13th	L	Aberdeen	a	1-0	15,000	Clark
	17th	UEF1	Dukla Prague	h	3-2	18,869	Clark; Foster; Robertson
	20th	L	Motherwell	h	4-0	11,113	Clark; Colquhoun; Watson; Robertson
	27th	L	Dundee	a	0-0	9,947	-
Oct	1st	UEF1	Dukla Prague	a	0-1 (3-3)*	3,500	-
	4th	L	Rangers	h	1-1	28,637	Berry
	8th	L	Celtic	a	0-2	35,382	-
	11th	L	St Mirren	h	0-0	11,420	-
	18th	L	Hamilton Accies	a	3-1	5,405	Colquhoun; G. Mackay (pen); Foster
	25th	L	Dundee United	h	2-2	14,320	Colquhoun; G. Mackay (pen)
	29th	L	Falkirk	a	0-2	8,200	-
Nov	1st	L	Hibernian	h	1-1	22,178	G. Mackay (pen)
	8th	L	Clydebank	a	3-0	3,910	Colquhoun 2; MacDonald
	15th	L	Aberdeen	h	2-1	17,108	Colquhoun; Robertson
	19th	L	Motherwell	a	3-2	6,341	Berry; MacDonald 2
	22nd	L	Dundee	h	3-1	12,094	Colquhoun; Black; Robertson
	29th	L	Rangers	a	0-3	38,733	-
Dec	3rd	L	Celtic	h	1-0	25,886	Berry
	6th	L	St Mirren	a	0-0	6,177	-
	13th	L	Hamilton Accies	h	7-0	9,324	Clark; G. Mackay (pen); Robertson 2; S. Jardine; MacDonald; Colquhoun
	20th	L	Dundee United	a	1-3	11,749	Robertson
	27th	L	Falkirk	h	4-0	13,214	Clark; Robertson 2; Manley o.g.
Jan	3rd	L	Clydebank	h	3-0	12,022	Clark; G. Mackay; Robertson
	6th	L	Hibernian	a	2-2	24,000	Colquhoun 2
	21st	L	Aberdeen	a	1-2	14,942	Watson
	24th	L	Dundee	a	1-0	8,397	G. Mackay
	31st	SC3	Kilmarnock	h	0-0	15,227	-
Feb	4th	SC3	Kilmarnock	a	1-1**	15,000	Foster
	7th	L	Rangers	h	2-5	29,000	Robertson (2 pens)
	9th	SC3	Kilmarnock	a	3-1	14,150	G. Mackay; Black; Foster
	14th	L	Celtic	a	1-1	38,198	Foster
	21st	SC4	Celtic	h	1-0	28,891	Robertson
	25th	L	Motherwell	h	1-1	9,639	Robertson
	28th	L	St Mirren	h	1-0	12,002	Colquhoun
Mar	7th	L	Hamilton Accies	a	1-0	4,778	Colquhoun
	14th	SCQ	Motherwell	h	1-1	22,045	Robertson
	17th	SCQ	Motherwell	a	1-0	15,275	Colquhoun
	21st	L	Falkirk	a	0-0	8,000	-
	28th	L	Clydebank	a	1-1	3,357	Colquhoun
Apr	4th	L	Hibernian	h	2-1	19,731	MacDonald; Clark
	11th	SCS	St Mirren	Hamp	1-2	32,390	G. Mackay
	15th	L	Motherwell	a	1-0	3,907	Clark
	18th	L	Aberdeen	h	1-1	12,539	Foster
	25th	L	Rangers	a	0-3	43,205	-
May	2nd	L	Dundee	h	1-3	7,818	Cowie
	9th	L	Celtic	h	1-0	12,596	Robertson (pen)
	11th	L	Dundee United	h	1-1	6,779	Robertson (pen)

* Hearts lose on away goals rule. ** After extra-time, 1-1 at 90 mts.

Gary Mackay - inspirational midfielder for the Maroons.

Sandy Clark - key man in the Hearts front line.

The Record		
League	-	**Fifth Place, Premier Division**
League Cup	-	**Second round**
Scottish Cup	-	**Semi final**
UEFA Cup	-	**First round**
Top Scorer	-	**John Robertson (19 goals)**
Av. Home Gate	-	**14,500**
Players used	-	**22**
Sent off (booked)	-	**Six (50)**

Scottish League Premier Division

		Home			Away			Goals	
	P	W	D	L	W	D	L	F A	PTS
Rangers	44	18	2	2	13	5	4	85-23	69
Celtic	44	16	5	1	11	4	7	90-41	63
Dundee United	44	15	5	2	9	7	6	66-36	60
Aberdeen	44	13	6	3	8	10	4	63-28	58
Hearts	**44**	**13**	**6**	**2**	**8**	**7**	**7**	**64-43**	**55**
Dundee	44	11	6	5	7	6	9	74-57	48
St Mirren	44	9	5	8	3	7	12	36-51	36
Motherwell	44	7	5	10	4	7	11	43-64	34
Hibernian	44	6	8	8	4	5	13	44-70	33
Falkirk	44	4	9	9	4	1	17	31-70	26
Clydebank	44	3	7	12	3	5	14	35-93	24
Hamilton	44	2	4	16	4	5	13	39-93	21

Heart of Midlothian F.C. Line-Ups 1986-87

	1	2	3	4	5	6	7	8	9	10	11	12	14
Aug 9th	Smith	Cowie	Whittaker	Sandison	Berry	Levein	Colquhoun	Jardine I	Clark	Black	Robertson	Mackay B (11)	Watson (8)
13th	Smith	Kidd	Whittaker	Jardine S	Berry	Levein	Colquhoun	Jardine I	Clark	Black	Robertson	Watson	Mackay B
16th	Smith	Kidd	Black	Jardine S	Berry	Levein	Colquhoun	Jardine I	Clark	Mackay G	Robertson	Watson (8)	Mackay B (7)
19th	Smith	Kidd	Black	Jardine S	Berry	Levein	Colquhoun	Jardine I	Clark	Mackay G	Robertson	Watson (8)	Mackay B (11)
23rd	Smith	Murray	Whittaker	Jardine S	Berry	Levein	Colquhoun	Jardine I	Clark	Mackay G	Foster	Black (5)	Robertson (11)
30th	Smith	Kidd	Whittaker	Jardine S	Black	Levein	Colquhoun	Jardine I	Clark	Mackay G	Robertson	Watson (10)	Foster (11)
Sep 6th	Smith	Kidd	Whittaker	Jardine S	Black	Levein	Colquhoun	Jardine I	Clark	Mackay G	Robertson	Watson (3)	Foster (11)
13th	Smith	Kidd	Whittaker	Jardine S	Black	Levein	Colquhoun	Jardine I	Clark	Mackay G	Foster	Watson (8)	Robertson (10)
17th	Smith	Kidd	Whittaker	Jardine S	Black	Levein	Colquhoun	Jardine I	Clark	Mackay G	Foster	Watson (8)	Robertson (7)
20th	Smith	Kidd	Whittaker	Jardine S	Black	Levein	Colquhoun	Jardine I	Clark	Mackay G	Foster	Watson (5)	Robertson (7)
27th	Smith	Kidd	Whittaker	Jardine S	Berry	Levein	Robertson	Black	Clark	Watson	Foster	Colquhoun (7)	Cowie
Oct 1st	Smith	Kidd	Whittaker	Jardine S	Berry	Levein	Colquhoun	Black	Clark	Mackay G	Foster	Robertson (11)	Watson (2)
4th	Smith	Kidd	Whittaker	Jardine S	Berry	Levein	Colquhoun	Black	Clark	Mackay G	Robertson	Watson (5)	Foster (11)
8th	Smith	Kidd	Whittaker	Jardine S	Berry	Levein	Colquhoun	Black	Clark	Mackay G	Robertson	Watson (10)	Foster (11)
11th	Smith	Kidd	Whittaker	Jardine S	Berry	Levein	Colquhoun	Mackay G	Clark	Foster	Black	Robertson (8)	Watson (11)
18th	Smith	Kidd	Whittaker	Jardine S	Berry	MacDonald	Black	Mackay G	Clark	Colquhoun	Foster	Watson	Robertson (2)
25th	Smith	Kidd	Whittaker	Jardine S	Berry	MacDonald	Colquhoun	Mackay G	Clark	Black	Foster	Mackay B	Watson
29th	Smith	Kidd	Whittaker	Jardine S	Berry	MacDonald	Colquhoun	Mackay G	Clark	Black	Foster	Watson (8)	Mackay B
Nov 1st	Smith	Kidd	Whittaker	Jardine S	Berry	MacDonald	Colquhoun	Mackay G	Clark	Black	Foster	Mackay B	Watson
8th	Smith	Kidd	Whittaker	Jardine S	Berry	MacDonald	Colquhoun	Mackay G	Clark	Black	Foster	Mackay B	Watson
15th	Smith	Kidd	Whittaker	Jardine S	Berry	MacDonald	Colquhoun	Mackay G	Clark	Black	Foster	Robertson (11)	Watson
19th	Smith	Kidd	Whittaker	Jardine S	Berry	MacDonald	Colquhoun	Mackay G	Clark	Black	Robertson	Foster	Watson (11)
22nd	Smith	Kidd	Whittaker	Jardine S	Berry	MacDonald	Colquhoun	Jardine I	Clark	Black	Robertson	Foster (8)	Watson
29th	Smith	Kidd	Whittaker	Jardine S	Berry	MacDonald	Colquhoun	Mackay G	Clark	Black	Robertson	Foster (7)	Jardine I (2)
Dec 3rd	Smith	Kidd	Whittaker	Jardine S	Berry	MacDonald	Colquhoun	Black	Clark	Mackay G	Robertson	Jardine I	Foster
6th	Smith	Kidd	Whittaker	Jardine S	Berry	MacDonald	Colquhoun	Black	Clark	Mackay G	Robertson	Sandison (4)	Foster
13th	Smith	Kidd	Whittaker	Jardine S	Berry	MacDonald	Colquhoun	Black	Clark	Mackay G	Robertson	Moore (7)	Jardine I (5)
20th	Smith	Kidd	Whittaker	Jardine S	Berry	MacDonald	Colquhoun	Black	Clark	Mackay G	Robertson	Foster	Jardine I
27th	Smith	Kidd	Black	Jardine S	Berry	MacDonald	Colquhoun	Jardine I	Clark	Mackay G	Robertson	Moore (7)	Watson (4)
Jan 3rd	Smith	Kidd	Black	Sandison	Berry	MacDonald	Colquhoun	Jardine I	Clark	Mackay G	Robertson	Foster	Crabbe (7)
6th	Smith	Kidd	Black	Sandison	Berry	MacDonald	Colquhoun	Jardine I	Clark	Mackay G	Robertson	Foster	Watson (10)
21st	Smith	Kidd	Black	Sandison	Whittaker	MacDonald*	Colquhoun	Watson	Clark	Mackay G	Robertson	Foster (9)	Jardine I (10)
24th	Smith	Watson	Whittaker	Sandison	Kidd	Foster	Cowie	Black	Colquhoun	Mackay G	Robertson	Murray	Moore
31st	Smith	Cowie	Black	Sandison	Berry	MacDonald	Colquhoun	Watson	Clark	Mackay G	Robertson	Foster (7)	Kidd
Feb 4th	Smith	Cowie	Whittaker*	Sandison	Berry	MacDonald	Colquhoun	Mackay G	Clark	Black	Robertson	Foster (8)	Watson (7)
7th	Smith	Kidd	Cowie	Sandison	Berry	MacDonald	Colquhoun	Watson	Clark	Black	Robertson	Murray	Moore (8)
9th	Smith	Kidd	Whittaker	Sandison	Cowie	MacDonald	Colquhoun	Mackay G	Clark	Black	Robertson	Foster (9)	Watson (5)
14th	Smith	Kidd	Whittaker	Sandison	Black	MacDonald	Colquhoun	Foster	Clark	Watson	Robertson	Taylor	Moore (9)
21st	Smith	Kidd	Whittaker	Jardine S	Berry	MacDonald	Colquhoun	Black	Clark	Foster	Robertson	Mackay G (10)	Watson (7)
25th	Smith	Kidd	Whittaker	Sandison	Berry	MacDonald	Colquhoun	Black	Clark	Foster	Robertson	Mackay G (10)	Watson (5)
28th	Smith	Kidd	Whittaker	Jardine S	Berry	MacDonald	Colquhoun	Black	Clark	Foster	Robertson	Mackay G (5)	Watson (2)
Mar 7th	Smith	Kidd	Whittaker	Sandison	Berry	MacDonald	Colquhoun	Black	Clark	Foster	Robertson	Mackay G (10)	Watson
14th	Smith	Kidd	Whittaker	Sandison	Berry	MacDonald	Colquhoun	Black	Clark	Foster	Robertson	Mackay G (9)	Watson
17th	Smith	Kidd	Whittaker	Jardine S	Berry	MacDonald	Mackay G	Black	Clark	Foster	Robertson	Colquhoun (5)	Watson (2)
21st	Smith	Cowie	Whittaker	Jardine S	Watson	MacDonald	Mackay G	Black	Colquhoun	Foster	Robertson*	Sandison	Crabbe (7)
28th	Smith	Jardine S	Whittaker	Sandison	Murray	MacDonald	Colquhoun	Moore	Clark	Watson	Crabbe	Mackay B	Mackay G (11)
Apr 4th	Smith	Murray	Black	Jardine S	MacDonald	Cowie	Colquhoun	Watson	Clark	Foster	Mackay G	Crabbe	Sandison
11th	Smith	Murray	Cowie	Jardine S	Watson	MacDonald	Colquhoun	Mackay G	Clark	Black	Foster	Crabbe (5)	Sandison
15th	Smith	Bruce	Cowie	Whittaker	Jardine S	Black	Sandison	Colquhoun	Watson	Clark	Crabbe	Foster	Moore (10)	MacDonald A
18th	Smith	Murray	Cowie	Jardine S	Whittaker	Black	Colquhoun	Watson	Clark	Robertson	Foster	Crabbe	Moore (10)
25th	Smith	Murray	Whittaker	Jardine S	MacDonald	Watson	Colquhoun	Black	Clark	Robertson	Foster	Mackay G (5)	Moore (10)
May 2nd	Smith	Murray	Black	Jardine S	Whittaker	Watson	Colquhoun	Foster	Clark	Mackay G	Robertson	Cowie (6)	Moore (8)
9th	Smith	Murray	Black	Jardine S	Whittaker	Berry	Colquhoun	Cowie	Clark	Mackay G	Robertson	Foster (9)	Kidd (10)
11th	Smith	Murray	Cowie	Sandison	MacDonald	Berry	Moore	Crabbe*	Foster	Mackay G	Robertson	Watson (12)	Kidd (2)

Appearances

	League	L/Cup	S/Cup	ECWC	Total
Henry Smith	43	1	7	2	53
Kenny Black	41 (1)	1	7 (1)	2	51+1s (2)
John Colquhoun	42 (13)	1	6 (1)	2	51+2s (14)
Sandy Clark	41 (8)	1	7	2 (1)	51+1s (9)
Brian Whittaker	37	0	5	2	44
Sandy Jardine	34 (1)	1	3	2	40 (1)
Walter Kidd	33	1	4	2	40+2s
Gary Mackay	31 (7)	1	5 (2)	2	39+7s (9)
John Robertson	31 (16)	1	6 (2)	0 (1)	38+8s (19)
Neil Berry	30 (3)	1	5	1	37 (3)
Roddy MacDonald	27 (5)	0	7	0	34 (5)
Wayne Foster	23 (4)	0	4 (2)	2 (1)	29+11s (7)
Jimmy Sandison	12	0	4	0	16+1s
Craig Levein	12	1	0	2	15
Andy Watson	12 (3)	0	2	0	14+23s (3)
Ian Jardine	12 (1)	1	0	1	14+3s (1)
George Cowie	9 (1)	0	4	0	13 (1)
Malcolm Murray	8	0	1	0	9
Scott Crabbe	3	0	0	0	3+3s
Allan Moore	2	0	0	0	2+8s
Andy Bruce	1	0	0	0	1
Billy Mackay	0	0	0	0	0+3s

John Robertson dives full-length to head home against Dundee

Season 1987-88

Date			Opponents		Score	Crowd	Scorers
Aug	8th	L	Falkirk	h	4-2	12,163	Colquhoun; Clark; Robertson 2
	12th	L	Celtic	a	0-1	29,815	-
	15th	L	St Mirren	a	1-1	7,408	Robertson (pen)
	19th	LC1	Kilmarnock	h	6-1	9,188	Clark 2; McPherson; Mackay; Berry; Foster
	22nd	L	Dundee United	h	4-1	14,548	Clark 2; Robertson (pen); I. Jardine;
	25th	LC2	Clyde	h	2-0	11,711	Robertson 2 (1 pen)
	29th	L	Hibernian	h	1-0	24,496	Robertson
Sep	2nd	LCQ	Rangers	a	1-4	39,303	Robertson
	5th	L	Morton	a	2-1	5,000	Colquhoun; Robertson (pen)
	12th	L	Motherwell	h	1-0	11,488	Moore
	19th	L	Dundee	a	3-1	9,199	Colquhoun 2; Robertson (pen)
	26th	L	Dunfermline	a	1-0	13,873	Colquhoun
Oct	3rd	L	Rangers	h	0-0	28,906	
	7th	L	Aberdeen	h	2-1	17,843	Robertson; McPherson
	10th	L	Falkirk	a	5-1	9,300	Colquhoun 2; I. Jardine; Robertson (pen); Foster
	17th	L	Hibernian	a	1-2	23,396	Robertson
	24th	L	Morton	h	3-0	11,516	Black 2; Mackay
	27th	L	Motherwell	a	3-0	6,699	Foster; Robertson (pen); Caughey o.g.
	31st	L	Dundee	h	4-2	13,806	Robertson 2; Colquhoun; Black
Nov	7th	L	Celtic	h	1-1	28,992	Colquhoun
	14th	L	Aberdeen	a	0-0	20,000	-
	18th	L	Dundee United	a	3-0	14,258	Robertson 2; Foster
	21st	L	St Mirren	h	0-0	14,879	-
	24th	L	Dunfermline	h	3-2	14,157	Robertson; McPherson; Clark
	28th	L	Rangers	a	2-3	43,557	Robertson; Galloway
Dec	5th	L	Falkirk	h	1-0	12,729	Robertson (pen)
	12th	L	Celtic	a	2-2	43,968	Robertson; Galloway
	16th	L	Motherwell	h	1-1	9,407	Mackay
	19th	L	Dundee	a	0-0	10,806	-
	26th	L	Morton	a	0-0	8,000	-
Jan	2nd	L	Hibernian	h	0-0	28,992	-
	9th	L	Dunfermline	a	4-0	11,963	Robertson 2; Colquhoun; Galloway
	16th	L	Rangers	h	1-1	28,967	Clark
	30th	SC3	Falkirk	a	3-1	16,000	Robertson 2; Foster
Feb	3rd	L	Dundee United	h	1-1	13,710	Mackay
	6th	L	St Mirren	a	6-0	6,659	Colquhoun 3; Robertson 2 (1 pen); Foster
	13th	L	Aberdeen	h	2-2	18,817	Clark; Robertson (pen)
	20th	SC4	Morton	h	2-0	13,646	Clark; Mackay
	27th	L	Falkirk	a	0-2	9,009	-
Mar	8th	L	Motherwell	a	2-0	5,831	Robertson; Colquhoun
	12th	SCQ	Dunfermline	h	3-0	21,969	Colquhoun; Foster; Mackay
	19th	L	Hibernian	a	0-0	20,847	-
	26th	L	Morton	h	2-0	8,787	Galloway 2
	30th	L	Dundee	h	2-0	9,649	Black; Colquhoun
Apr	2nd	L	Rangers	a	2-1	41,125	McPherson; Robertson (pen)
	9th	SCS	Celtic	Hamp	1-2	65,886	Whittaker
	13th	L	Dunfermline	h	2-1	7,307	McPherson; Mackay
	16th	L	Celtic	h	2-1	26,200	Galloway; Mackay
	23rd	L	Aberdeen	a	0-0	11,000	-
	30th	L	St Mirren	h	0-1	8,570	-
May	7th	L	Dundee United	a	0-0	9,820	-

Dave McPherson - developed into an international class defender.

John Robertson - the deadly striker grabbed his best-ever haul of 31 goals.

The Record		
League	-	Runners-up, Premier Division
League Cup	-	Quarter- final
Scottish Cup	-	Semi-final
Top Scorer	-	John Robertson (31 goals)
Av. Home Gate	-	16,600
Players used	-	22
Sent off (booked)	-	None (54)

Scottish League Premier Division

		Home			Away			Goals		
	P	W	D	L	W	D	L	F	A	PTS
Celtic	44	16	5	1	15	5	2	79-23		72
Hearts	**44**	**13**	**8**	**1**	**10**	**8**	**4**	**74-32**		**62**
Rangers	44	14	4	4	12	4	6	85-34		60
Aberdeen	44	11	7	4	10	10	2	56-25		59
Dundee United	44	8	7	7	8	8	6	54-47		47
Hibernian	44	8	8	6	4	11	7	41-42		43
Dundee	44	9	5	8	8	2	12	70-64		41
Motherwell	44	10	2	10	3	8	11	37-56		36
St Mirren	44	5	11	6	5	4	13	41-64		35
Falkirk	44	8	4	10	2	7	13	41-75		31
Dunfermline	44	6	6	10	2	4	16	41-84		26
Morton	44	3	7	12	0	3	19	27-100		16

Heart of Midlothian F.C. Line-Ups 1987-88

		1	2	3	4	5	6	7	8	9	10	11	12	13
Aug	8th	Smith	Kidd	Whittaker	Jardine S	Berry	McPherson	Colquhoun	Black	Clark	Mackay	Robertson	Jardine I	Foster (9)
	12th	Smith	Kidd	Whittaker	Jardine S	Berry	McPherson	Colquhoun	Black	Clark	Mackay	Robertson	Jardine I	Foster (11)
	15th	Smith	Kidd	Whittaker	Jardine S	Berry	McPherson	Colquhoun	Black	Clark	Mackay	Robertson	Jardine I (10)	Foster (7)
	19th	Smith	Kidd	Whittaker	Jardine S	Berry	McPherson	Colquhoun	Black	Clark	Mackay	Robertson	Foster (9)	Jardine I (6)
	22nd	Smith	Kidd	Whittaker	Jardine S	Berry	McPherson	Colquhoun	Jardine I	Clark	Mackay	Robertson	Sandison	Foster (9)
	25th	Smith	Kidd	Whittaker	Jardine S	Berry	McPherson	Colquhoun	Jardine I	Clark	Mackay	Robertson	Foster	Burns (8)
	29th	Smith	Kidd	Whittaker	Jardine S	Berry	McPherson	Colquhoun	Jardine I	Clark	Mackay	Robertson	Black (2)	Foster (11)
Sep	2nd	Smith	Kidd	Whittaker	Jardine S	Berry	McPherson	Colquhoun	Jardine I	Clark	Mackay	Robertson	Foster (9)	Black (8)
	5th	Smith	Kidd	Whittaker	Jardine S	Berry	McPherson	Moore	Black	Colquhoun	Mackay	Robertson	Crabbe (11)	Jardine I
	12th	Smith	Kidd	Whittaker	Jardine S	Berry	McPherson	Moore	Black	Colquhoun	Mackay	Robertson	Jardine I (7)	Foster (9)
	19th	Smith	Kidd	Whittaker	Jardine S	Berry	McPherson	Foster	Black	Colquhoun	Mackay	Robertson	Jardine I (9)	Moore (7)
	26th	Smith	Kidd	Whittaker	Jardine S	Berry	McPherson	Foster	Black	Colquhoun	Mackay	Robertson	Jardine I (3)	Clark (11)
Oct	3rd	Smith	Burns	Whittaker	Levein	Berry	McPherson	Foster	Black	Colquhoun	Mackay	Robertson	Jardine S	Clark
	7th	Smith	Burns	Whittaker	Levein	Berry	McPherson	Foster	Black	Colquhoun	Mackay	Robertson	Jardine I	Clark (9)
	10th	Smith	Burns	Whittaker	Levein	Berry	McPherson	Foster	Black	Colquhoun	Mackay	Robertson	Clark (9)	Jardine I (5)
	17th	Smith	Kidd	Whittaker	Levein	Berry	McPherson	Foster	Black	Colquhoun	Mackay	Robertson	Jardine I (8)	Clark (7)
	24th	Smith	Burns	Whittaker	Levein	Berry	McPherson	Foster	Black	Colquhoun	Mackay	Robertson	Jardine I(10)	Clark (7)
	27th	Smith	Burns	Whittaker	Levein	Berry	McPherson	Foster	Black	Colquhoun	Mackay	Robertson	Kidd	Clark (9)
	31st	Smith	Burns	Whittaker	Levein	Berry	McPherson	Foster	Black	Colquhoun	Mackay	Robertson	Kidd	Clark (11)
Nov	7th	Smith	Burns	Whittaker	Levein	Berry	McPherson	Foster	Black	Colquhoun	Mackay	Robertson	Kidd	Clark (9)
	14th	Smith	Burns	Whittaker	Levein	Berry	McPherson	Foster	Black	Colquhoun	Mackay	Robertson	Kidd (5)	Clark (11)
	18th	Smith	Burns	Whittaker	Levein	Kidd	McPherson	Foster	Black	Colquhoun	Mackay	Robertson	Galloway(5)	Clark (7)
	21st	Smith	Burns	Whittaker	Levein	Kidd	McPherson	Foster	Black	Colquhoun	Mackay	Robertson	Clark (7)	Galloway(10)
	24th	Smith	Burns	Whittaker	Levein	Kidd	McPherson	Foster	Black	Colquhoun	Mackay	Robertson	Clark (9)	Galloway (5)
	28th	Smith	Burns	Whittaker	Levein	Galloway	McPherson	Foster	Black	Colquhoun	Mackay	Robertson	Clark (4)	Kidd (8)
Dec	5th	Smith	Burns	Whittaker	Levein	Galloway	McPherson	Foster	Black	Colquhoun	Mackay	Robertson	Clark (9)	Kidd
	12th	Smith	Kidd	Whittaker	Levein	Galloway	McPherson	Colquhoun	Black	Foster	Mackay	Robertson	Clark	Berry (11)
	16th	Smith	Kidd	Whittaker	Levein	Galloway	McPherson	Colquhoun	Black	Foster	Mackay	Robertson	Clark (11)	Berry
	19th	Smith	Kidd	Whittaker	Levein	Galloway	McPherson	Colquhoun	Black	Foster	Mackay	Robertson	Moore (11)	Berry (2)
	26th	Smith	Burns	Whittaker	Levein	Galloway	McPherson	Colquhoun	Black	Foster	Mackay	Robertson	Berry (2)	Moore (9)
Jan	2nd	Smith	Burns	Whittaker	Levein	Galloway	McPherson	Colquhoun	Black	Foster	Mackay	Robertson	Berry (8)	Clark (11)
	9th	Smith	Burns	Whittaker	Levein	Galloway	McPherson	Mackay	Foster	Robertson	Colquhoun	Black	Berry	Moore (8)
	16th	Smith	Burns	Whittaker	Levein	Galloway	McPherson	Mackay	Clark	Robertson	Colquhoun	Berry	Moore	Jardine I (4)
	30th	Smith	Kidd	Whittaker	Berry	Galloway	McPherson	Mackay	Black	Robertson	Colquhoun	Foster	Clark	Jardine I (2)
Feb	3rd	Smith	Burns	Whittaker	Berry	Galloway	McPherson	Mackay	Black	Robertson	Colquhoun	Foster	Clark (11)	Jardine I (2)
	6th	Smith	Berry	Whittaker	Black	Galloway	McPherson	Mackay	Jardine I	Robertson	Colquhoun	Foster	Clark (10)	Burns
	13th	Smith	Berry	Whittaker	Black	Galloway	McPherson	Mackay	Jardine I	Robertson	Colquhoun	Clark	Burns	Moore
	20th	Smith	Berry	Whittaker	Black	Galloway	McPherson	Mackay	Jardine I	Robertson	Colquhoun	Clark	Burns (8)	Moore (10)
	27th	Smith	Berry	Whittaker	Black	Galloway	McPherson	Mackay	Burns	Robertson	Colquhoun	Foster	Sandison	Clark (9)
Mar	8th	Smith	Burns	Whittaker	Black	Galloway	McPherson	Mackay	Berry	Robertson	Colquhoun	Foster	Clark (10)	Jardine I (4)
	12th	Smith	Burns	Whittaker	Black	Berry	McPherson	Mackay	Jardine I	Robertson	Colquhoun	Foster	Clark	Sandison (8)
	19th	Smith	Burns	Whittaker	Black	Galloway	McPherson	Mackay	Berry	Robertson	Colquhoun	Foster	Clark (9)	Jardine I (4)
	26th	Smith	Murray	Whittaker	Black	Galloway	McPherson	Mackay	Jardine I	Robertson	Colquhoun	Foster	Crabbe (8)	Gavin (10)
	30th	Smith	Burns	Whittaker	Black	Galloway	McPherson	Mackay	Berry	Robertson	Colquhoun	Foster	Clark (11)	Jardine I (7)
Apr	2nd	Smith	Murray	Whittaker	Black	Galloway	McPherson	Mackay	Berry	Clark	Colquhoun	Robertson	Jardine I	Gavin (10)
	9th	Smith	Murray	Whittaker	Black	Galloway	McPherson	Mackay	Berry	Foster	Colquhoun	Robertson	Clark (9)	Jardine I (7)
	13th	Smith	Murray	Black	McPherson	Berry	Galloway	Gavin	Jardine I	Clark	Crabbe	Foster	Colquhoun(11)	Mackay (8)
	16th	Smith	Murray	Whittaker	Black	Berry	McPherson	Mackay	Gavin	Foster	Galloway	Colquhoun	Burns	Clark (11)
	23rd	Smith	Murray	Whittaker	Black	Galloway	McPherson	Colquhoun	Sandison	Foster	Berry	Gavin	Clark (11)	Burns (9)
	30th	Smith	Murray	Whittaker	Black	Galloway	McPherson	Colquhoun	Clark	Foster	Berry	Gavin	Crabbe (9)	Sandison
May	7th	Smith	Burns	McLaren	Sandison	Murray	McPherson	Colquhoun	Clark	Black	Crabbe	Gavin	Moore (8)	Stewart

Appearances

	League	L/Cup	S/Cup	Total	
Dave McPherson	44 (4)	3 (1)	4	51	(5)
Henry Smith	44	3	4	51	
John Colquhoun	43 (15)	3	4 (1)	50+1s	(16)
Brian Whittaker	42	3	4 (1)	49	(1)
Gary Mackay	40 (5)	3 (1)	4 (2)	47+1s	(8)
Kenny Black	41 (4)	1	4	46+2s	(4)
John Robertson	39 (26)	3 (3)	4 (2)	46	(31)
Neil Berry	31	3 (1)	4	38+4s	(1)
Wayne Foster	33 (4)	0 (1)	3 (2)	36+8s	(7)
Mike Galloway	22 (6)	0	3	25+3s	(6)
Hugh Burns	23	0	1	24+3s	
Craig Levein	21	0	0	21	
Walter Kidd	16	3	1	20+2s	
Sandy Clark	11 (6)	3 (2)	1 (1)	15+25s	(9)
Sandy Jardine	9	3	0	12	
Ian Jardine	6 (2)	2	2	10+15s	(2)
Malcolm Murray	7	0	1	8	
Mark Gavin	5	0	0	5+2s	
Scott Crabbe	2	0	0	2+3s	
Alan Moore	2 (1)	0	0	2+6s	(1)
Jimmy Sandison	2	0	0	2+1s	
Alan McLaren	1	0	0	1	

John Colquhoun lashes the ball past Dunfermline keeper Hans Segars.

Season 1988-89

Date			Opponents		Score	Crowd	Scorers
Aug	13th	L	Celtic	a	0-1	46,845	-
	17th	LC1	St Johnstone	h	5-0	10,474	Ferguson 3; Mackay; Jardine
	20th	L	Hamilton Accies	h	3-2	12,032	Ferguson; Clark; Colquhoun
	23rd	LC2	Meadowbank	a*	2-0	6,800	Black; Murray
	27th	L	Hibernian	a	0-0	25,000	-
	31st	LCQ	Dunfermline	a	4-1	16,494	Mackay; Colquhoun; Ferguson 2
Sep	3rd	L	St Mirren	h	1-2	11,386	Foster (pen)
	7th	UEF1	St Patrick's Athl'c.	a	2-0	9,000	Foster (pen); Galloway
	17th	L	Rangers	h	1-2	25,401	Butcher o.g.
	21st	LCS	Rangers	Hamp	0-3	53,623	-
	24th	L	Aberdeen	a	0-1	15,500	-
	28th	L	Dundee	h	1-1	8,392	Ferguson
Oct	1st	L	Dundee United	a	0-0	10,838	-
	5th	UEF1	St Patrick's Athl'c	h	2-0 (4-0)	11,142	Galloway; Black
	8th	L	Motherwell	h	2-2	8,809	Moore 2
	11th	L	Hamilton Accies	a	4-0	4,764	Ferguson 2; Black; Colquhoun
	22nd	L	Celtic	h	0-2	24,017	-
	26th	UEF2	Austria Vienna	h	0-0	14,021	-
	30th	L	Aberdeen	h	1-1	12,644	Jardine
Nov	1st	L	Rangers	a	0-3	36,505	-
	5th	L	St Mirren	a	1-1	7,653	Godfrey o.g.
	9th	UEF2	Austria Vienna	a	1-0 (1-0)	15,000	Galloway
	12th	L	Hibernian	h	1-2	23,062	McPherson
	19th	L	Dundee United	h	0-0	10,124	-
	23rd	UEF3	Velez Mostar	h	3-0	17,417	Colquhoun; Bannon; Galloway;
	26th	L	Motherwell	a	0-2	6,230	-
Dec	3rd	L	Dundee	a	1-1	6,902	Colquhoun
	7th	UEF3	Velez Mostar	a	1-2 (4-2)	17,000	Galloway
	10th	L	Rangers	h	2-0	26,424	Galloway; Ferguson
	17th	L	Hamilton Accies	h	2-0	11,490	McLaren; McPherson
	31st	L	Celtic	a	2-4	44,646	Robertson 2 (1 pen)
Jan	4th	L	Hibernian	a	0-1	27,022	-
	7th	L	St Mirren	h	2-0	11,961	Colquhoun; McKinlay
	14th	L	Motherwell	h	0-0	13,283	-
	21st	L	Dundee United	a	0-0	13,674	-
	28th	SC3	Ayr United	h	4-1	15,916	McIntyre o.g.; Colquhoun; Galloway; McPherson
Feb	11th	L	Dundee	h	3-1	10,432	Colquhoun; Bannon; Mackay
	20th	SC4	Partick Thistle	h	2-0	18,350	Bannon; Colquhoun
	25th	L	Aberdeen	a	0-3	15,000	-
	28th	UEFQ	Bayern Munich	h	1-0	26,294	Ferguson
Mar	11th	L	Celtic	h	0-1	23,087	-
	14th	UEFQ	Bayern Munich	a	0-2 (1-2)	25,000	-
	18th	SCQ	Celtic	a	1-2	46,348	Bannon
	25th	L	Hamilton Accies	a	2-0	3,854	Mackay; McPherson
Apr	1st	L	Hibernian	h	2-1	22,090	Bannon; Robertson
	8th	L	St Mirren	a	1-1	6,970	Robertson
	15th	L	Dundee	a	1-2	6,993	McPherson
	22nd	L	Aberdeen	h	1-0	13,367	Galloway
	29th	L	Rangers	a	0-4	42,856	-
May	6th	L	Dundee United	h	0-0	8,613	-
	13th	L	Motherwell	a	1-1	6,020	Berry

*played at Brockville for safety reasons

Eamonn Bannon - back on his old beat after a nine year absence.

The Record		
League	-	Sixth Place, Premier Division
League Cup	-	Semi-final
Scottish Cup	-	Quarter-final
UEFA Cup	-	Quarter-final
Top Scorer	-	Iain Ferguson (11 goals)
UEFA Cup	-	Quarter-final
Av. Home Gate	-	15,400
Players used	-	24
Sent off (booked)	-	Five (59)

Appearances

	League	L/Cup	S/Cup	UEFA	Total	
Henry Smith	36	4	3	8	51	
John Colquhoun	34 (5)	4 (1)	3 (2)	7 (1)	48+3s	(9)
Neil Berry	32 (1)	4	3	8	47	(1)
Dave McPherson	32 (4)	4	3 (1)	8	47	(5)
Mike Galloway	30 (2)	4	3 (1)	8 (5)	45+1s	(8)
Gary Mackay	29 (2)	4 (2)	3	6	42+2s	(4)
Kenny Black	33 (1)	3 (1)	0	8 (1)	44+1s	(3)
Eamonn Bannon	23 (2)	3	3 (2)	7 (1)	36+9s	(5)
Iain Ferguson	23 (5)	3 (5)	1	4 (1)	31+10s	(11)
Brian Whittaker	24	4	0	6	34	
Walter Kidd	20	1	1	6	28+1s	
Tosh McKinlay	17 (1)	0	3	2	22	(1)
Alan McLaren	11 (1)	0	3	2	14+1s	(1)
Wayne Foster	8 (1)	2	0	3 (1)	13+4s	(3)
Craig Levein	8	0	2	2	12+1s	
Jimmy Sandison	11	0	0	1	12+5s	
John Robertson	8 (4)	0	2	0	10+9s	(4)
Malcolm Murray	8	2 (1)	0	0	10+1s	(1)
Alan Moore	5 (2)	0	0	1	6+8s	(2)
Ian Jardine	2 (1)	0 (1)	0	1	3+17s	(2)
Sandy Clark	1 (1)	2	0	0	3+1s	(1)
Scott Crabbe	1	0	0	0	1	
Mark Gavin	0	0	0	0	0+2s	
Murray McDermott	0	0	0	0	0+1s	

Scottish League Premier Division

		Home			Away			Goals		
	P	W	D	L	W	D	L	F	A	PTS
Rangers	36	15	1	2	11	3	4	62	26	56
Aberdeen	36	10	7	1	8	7	3	51	25	50
Celtic	36	13	1	4	8	3	7	66	44	46
Dundee United	36	6	8	4	10	4	4	44	26	44
Hibernian	36	8	4	6	5	5	8	37	36	35
Hearts	**36**	**7**	**6**	**5**	**2**	**7**	**9**	**35**	**42**	**31**
St Mirren	36	5	6	7	6	1	11	39	55	29
Dundee	36	8	4	6	1	6	11	34	48	28
Motherwell	36	5	7	6	2	6	10	35	44	27
Hamilton	36	5	0	13	1	2	15	19	76	14

Heart of Midlothian F.C. Line-Ups 1988-89

	1	2	3	4	5	6	7	8	9	10	11	12	13
Aug 13th	Smith	Murray	Black	Whittaker	Galloway	McPherson	Colquhoun	Berry	Ferguson	Mackay	Bannon	Jardine I	Clark (10)
17th	Smith	Galloway	Murray	Whittaker	Berry	McPherson	Colquhoun	Mackay	Clark	Ferguson	Bannon	Jardine I (9)	Gavin
20th	Smith	Galloway	Murray	Whittaker	Berry	McPherson	Colquhoun	Mackay	Clark	Ferguson	Black	Bannon (11)	Gavin (7)
23rd	Smith	Galloway	Murray	Whittaker	Berry	McPherson	Colquhoun	Black	Clark	Mackay	Ferguson	Bannon (10)	Foster (9)
27th	Smith	Murray	Berry	Whittaker	Galloway	McPherson	Mackay	Ferguson	Colquhoun	Black	Foster	Bannon (7)	Jardine I
31st	Smith	Berry	Black	Whittaker	Galloway	McPherson	Colquhoun	Mackay	Ferguson	Foster	Bannon	Jardine I (7)	Gavin
Sep 3rd	Smith	Berry	Murray	Whittaker	Black	McPherson	Colquhoun	Mackay	Ferguson	Foster	Bannon	Kidd	Gavin (3)
7th	Smith	Kidd	Berry	Whittaker	Black	McPherson	Colquhoun	Mackay	Ferguson	Galloway	Foster	Bannon (11)	McDermott (1)
17th	Smith	Berry	Kidd	Whittaker	Galloway	McPherson	Colquhoun	Mackay	Ferguson	Black	Foster	Bannon (9)	Moore (7)
21st	Smith	Kidd	Berry	Whittaker	Galloway	McPherson	Colquhoun	Mackay	Foster	Black	Bannon	Ferguson (9)	Murray (6)
24th	Smith	Kidd	Berry	Whittaker	Galloway	Murray	Colquhoun	Mackay	Foster	Black	Bannon	Ferguson (7)	Jardine I (10)
28th	Smith	Kidd	Berry	Whittaker	Galloway	McPherson	Colquhoun	Mackay	Ferguson	Black	Bannon	Jardine I (10)	Moore (2)
Oct 1st	Smith	Kidd	Berry	Whittaker	Galloway	McPherson	Colquhoun	Mackay	Ferguson	Black	Bannon	Jardine I	Moore (9)
5th	Smith	Kidd	Berry	Whittaker	Galloway	McPherson	Colquhoun	Mackay	Ferguson	Black	Bannon	Jardine I	Foster (11)
8th	Smith	Kidd	Berry	Whittaker	Galloway	McPherson	Colquhoun	Mackay	Foster	Black	Moore	Ferguson (9)	Jardine I (8)
11th	Smith	Kidd	Murray	Whittaker	Berry	McPherson	Colquhoun	Mackay	Ferguson	Black	Moore	Crabbe	Jardine I
22nd	Smith	Kidd	Murray	Whittaker	Berry	McPherson	Colquhoun	Mackay	Ferguson	Black	Moore	Bannon (5)	Galloway (8)
26th	Smith	Kidd	Berry	Whittaker	Galloway	McPherson	Colquhoun	Moore	Foster	Black	Bannon	Mackay (9)	Ferguson (11)
30th	Smith	Kidd	Whittaker	Berry	Galloway	McPherson	Moore	Mackay	Ferguson	Black	Bannon	Jardine I (4)	Colquhoun (9)
Nov 1st	Smith	Kidd	Murray	Whittaker	Galloway	McPherson	Colquhoun	Mackay	Foster	Black	Bannon	Jardine I (2)	Moore (7)
5th	Smith	Kidd	Sandison	Jardine I	Whittaker	McPherson	Mackay	Galloway	Foster	Black	Bannon	Colquhoun (6)	Ferguson
9th	Smith	Kidd	Berry	McPherson	Whittaker	Sandison	Galloway	Mackay	Foster	Black	Bannon	Colquhoun (9)	Jardine I (8)
12th	Smith	Kidd	Berry	McPherson	Whittaker	Jardine I	Galloway	Mackay	Colquhoun	Black	Bannon	Sandison (6)	Moore (2)
19th	Smith	Kidd	Sandison	McPherson	Whittaker	Berry	Colquhoun	Mackay	Ferguson	Black	Bannon	Jardine I (2)	Crabbe
23rd	Smith	Kidd	Berry	McPherson	Whittaker	Black	Colquhoun	Mackay	Ferguson	Galloway	Bannon	Jardine I (2)	Sandison (11)
26th	Smith	Kidd	Sandison	McPherson*	Whittaker	Berry	Colquhoun	Crabbe	Ferguson	Black	Mackay	Moore (8)	Jardine I (11)
Dec 3rd	Smith	Kidd	Sandison	Berry	Whittaker	Bannon	Galloway	Mackay	Colquhoun	Black	Ferguson	Jardine I (11)	McLaren (6)
7th	Smith	Kidd	Jardine I	McPherson	Whittaker	Berry	Galloway	Mackay	Colquhoun	Black	Bannon	Ferguson	Moore (7)
10th	Smith	Kidd	McKinlay	McPherson	Whittaker	Berry	Galloway*	Mackay	Colquhoun	Black	Robertson	Bannon (9)	Ferguson (11)
17th	Smith	Kidd	McKinlay	McPherson	Whittaker	McLaren	Ferguson	Mackay	Colquhoun	Black	Robertson	Bannon (6)	Jardine I (9)
31st	Smith	Kidd	McKinlay	Sandison	Whittaker	McPherson	Galloway	Mackay	Colquhoun	Black	Robertson	Jardine I (2)	Ferguson
Jan 4th	Smith	Kidd	McKinlay	Berry	Whittaker	McPherson	Galloway	Mackay	Colquhoun	Black	Robertson	Foster (3)	Sandison
7th	Smith	McLaren	McKinlay	McPherson	Whittaker	Berry	Galloway	Mackay	Colquhoun	Black	Robertson	Bannon	Ferguson (11)
14th	Smith	McLaren	McKinlay	McPherson	Whittaker	Berry	Galloway	Mackay	Colquhoun	Black	Ferguson	Foster	Bannon (9)
21st	Smith	McLaren	McKinlay	McPherson	Berry	Levein	Galloway	Mackay	Colquhoun	Robertson	Bannon	Ferguson (7)	Sandison
28th	Smith	McLaren	McKinlay	McPherson	Berry	Levein	Galloway	Mackay	Colquhoun	Robertson	Bannon	Ferguson	Sandison (6)
Feb 11th	Smith	McLaren	McKinlay	McPherson	Berry	Sandison	Galloway	Mackay	Colquhoun	Robertson	Bannon	Kidd	Ferguson
20th	Smith	McLaren	McKinlay	McPherson	Kidd	Berry	Galloway	Mackay	Colquhoun	Robertson	Bannon	Black (8)	Ferguson (10)
25th	Smith	McLaren	McKinlay	McPherson	Berry	Levein	Galloway	Robertson	Colquhoun	Black	Bannon	Sandison (9)	Ferguson (8)
28th	Smith	McLaren	McKinlay	McPherson	Berry	Levein	Galloway	Ferguson	Colquhoun	Black	Bannon	Mackay (8)	Foster (9)
Mar 11th	Smith	McLaren	McKinlay	Levein	Berry	McPherson	Galloway	Mackay	Colquhoun	Ferguson	Bannon	Robertson (11)	Sandison
14th	Smith	McLaren	McKinlay	Levein	Berry	McPherson	Galloway	Mackay	Colquhoun	Black	Bannon	Ferguson (11)	Robertson (3)
18th	Smith	McLaren*	McKinlay*	Levein	Berry	McPherson	Colquhoun	Mackay	Galloway	Ferguson	Bannon	Robertson (10)	Kidd (4)
25th	Smith	Kidd	Black	Levein	Berry	McPherson	Colquhoun	Mackay	Galloway	Ferguson	Bannon	Robertson (11)	Sandison (6)
Apr 1st	Smith	Sandison	McKinlay	Levein	Berry	Black	Colquhoun	Mackay	Galloway	Ferguson	Bannon	Robertson (9)	Jardine I (8)
8th	Smith	Sandison	McKinlay	Levein*	Berry	Black	Foster	Ferguson	Galloway	Bannon	Colquhoun	Robertson (7)	Wright
15th	Smith	Kidd	McKinlay	McPherson	Berry	Sandison	Galloway	Bannon	Ferguson	Black	Colquhoun	Robertson (2)	Jardine I
22nd	Smith	McLaren	McKinlay	McPherson	Berry	Sandison	Galloway	Ferguson	Colquhoun	Black	Bannon	Robertson (8)	Jardine I (11)
29th	Smith	McLaren	McKinlay	McPherson	Berry	Sandison	Colquhoun	Galloway	Ferguson	Black	Bannon	Robertson (8)	Levein (2)
May 6th	Smith	McLaren	McKinlay	McPherson	Berry	Levein	Galloway	Bannon	Ferguson	Black	Colquhoun	Moore (7)	Sandison
13th	Smith	McLaren	McKinlay	Levein	McPherson	Berry	Moore	Galloway	Colquhoun	Black	Bannon	Crabbe	Jardine I (11)

What a stramash - Tosh McKinlay of Hearts and Celtic's Mick McCarthy are pulled away by referee David Syme as mayhem breaks out in the Scottish Cup tie at Parkhead. Both players were ordered off.

DC Thomson

Season 1989-90

Date			Opponents		Score	Crowd	Scorers
Aug	12th	L	Celtic	h	1-3	25,932	McPherson
	16th	LC2	Montrose	h	3-0	7,024	Crabbe 2; Musemic
	19th	L	St Mirren	a	2-1	7,122	Musemic; Berry
	23rd	LC3	Falkirk	a	4-1	9,700	Crabbe; Bannon; Kidd; Kirkwood
	26th	L	Hibernian	h	1-0	22,731	Musemic
	30th	LCQ	Celtic	h	2-2*	25,221	Crabbe; Robertson
Sep	9th	L	Dundee	a	2-2	8,440	McPherson; Crabbe (pen)
	16th	L	Motherwell	a	3-1	8,948	Robertson; Crabbe 2
	23rd	L	Dundee United	h	1-1	14,008	McPherson
	30th	L	Rangers	a	0-1	39,544	-
Oct	4th	L	Dunfermline	h	1-2	14,165	Musemic
	14th	L	Aberdeen	a	3-1	15,000	McKinlay; Crabbe 2
	21st	L	Celtic	a	1-2	40,500	Crabbe
	28th	L	St Mirren	h	4-0	9,911	Robertson 2; Colquhoun; Crabbe
Nov	4th	L	Hibernian	a	1-1	19,700	Bannon
	11th	L	Dundee	h	6-3	11,869	Colquhoun 3; Foster; Robertson; Crabbe
	18th	L	Motherwell	h	3-0	12,035	Crabbe; Colquhoun; Sandison
	25th	L	Dundee United	a	1-2	12,201	Crabbe (pen)
Dec	2nd	L	Rangers	h	1-2	24,771	Bannon
	9th	L	Dunfermline	a	2-0	11,295	Robertson 2
	20th	L	Aberdeen	h	1-1	11,370	Robertson
	26th	L	Celtic	h	0-0	23,259	-
	30th	L	St Mirren	a	0-2	7,287	-
Jan	1st	L	Hibernian	h	2-0	25,224	Robertson 2 (1 pen)
	6th	L	Dundee	a	1-0	8,300	Craib o.g.
	13th	L	Motherwell	a	3-0	8,822	Colquhoun; Robertson 2 (1 pen)
	20th	SC3	Falkirk	h	2-0	14,520	Robertson 2
	27th	L	Dundee United	h	3-2	13,083	Kidd; Crabbe; Robertson
Feb	3rd	L	Aberdeen	a	2-2	17,000	Sandison; Ferguson
	10th	L	Dunfermline	h	0-2	14,204	-
	17th	L	Rangers	a	0-0	41,884	-
	24th	SC4	Motherwell	h	4-0	19,161	Robertson 2; Crabbe: Colquhoun;
Mar	3rd	L	Motherwell	h	2-0	9,205	Crabbe; Robertson
	10th	L	Celtic	a	1-1	34,792	Robertson
	17th	SCQ	Aberdeen	a	1-4	22,500	Colquhoun
	24th	L	St Mirren	h	0-0	8,066	-
	31st	L	Hibernian	a	2-1	18,000	Robertson 2
Apr	4th	L	Dundee	h	0-0	10,761	-
	14th	L	Dunfermline	a	1-0	10,829	McPherson
	21st	L	Aberdeen	h	1-0	11,616	Mackay
	28th	L	Dundee United	a	1-1	7,679	McLaren
May	5th	L	Rangers	h	1-1	20,283	Robertson (pen)

* aet 1-1 after 90 mts. Celtic won 3-1 on pens

Alan McLaren - outstanding young defender for the Maroons.

Appearances

	League	L/Cup	S/Cup	Total
John Colquhoun	36 (6)	3	3 (2)	42 (8)
Henry Smith	36	3	3	42
Craig Levein	35	3	3	41
Dave McPherson	35 (4)	3	3	41 (4)
Eamonn Bannon	31 (2)	3 (1)	3	37+2s (3)
Gary Mackay	31 (1)	2	1	34+3s (1)
Scott Crabbe	27 (12)	3 (4)	3 (1)	33+8s (17)
Tosh McKinlay	29 (1)	0	2	31 (1)
John Robertson	25 (17)	0 (1)	3 (4)	28+8s (22)
Alan McLaren	26 (1)	2	0	28+2s (1)
Dave McCreery	20	0	3	23+2s
Walter Kidd	12 (1)	1 (1)	3	16+6s (2)
Wayne Foster	14 (1)	0	0	14+5s (1)
Dave Kirkwood	10	3 (1)	1	14+9s (1)
Neil Berry	10 (1)	2	1	13+1s (1)
Brian Whittaker	6	2	1	9+1s
Jimmy Sandison	8 (2)	0	0	8+4s (2)
Husref Musemic	4 (3)	3 (1)	0	7+2s (4)
Iain Ferguson	1 (1)	0	0	1+12s (1)
George Wright	0	0	0	0+1s

The Record

League	-	**Third Place, Premier Division**
League Cup	-	**Quarter-final**
Scottish Cup	-	**Quarter-final**
Top Scorer	-	**John Robertson (22 goals)**
Av. Home Gate	-	**15,700**
Players used	-	**20**
Sent off (bookings)	-	**Six (44)**

Scottish League Premier Division

		Home			Away			Goals	
	P	W	D	L	W	D	L	F A	PTS
Rangers	36	14	2	2	6	9	3	48-19	51
Aberdeen	36	12	4	2	5	6	7	56-33	44
Hearts	**36**	**8**	**6**	**4**	**8**	**6**	**4**	**54-35**	**44**
Dundee United	36	8	8	2	3	5	10	36-39	35
Celtic	36	6	6	6	4	8	6	37-37	34
Motherwell	36	7	6	5	4	6	8	43-47	34
Hibernian	36	8	5	5	4	5	9	34-41	34
Dunfermline	36	5	6	7	6	2	10	37-50	30
St Mirren	36	6	6	6	4	4	10	28-48	30
Dundee	36	4	8	6	1	6	11	41-65	24

Heart of Midlothian F.C. Line-Ups 1989-90

		1	2	3	4	5	6	7	8	9	10	11	12	13
Aug	12th	Smith	McLaren	Kirkwood	Levein	Berry	McPherson	Colquhoun	Mackay	Musemic	Ferguson	Bannon	Crabbe (11)	Kidd
	16th	Smith	McLaren	Kirkwood	Levein	Berry	McPherson	Colquhoun	Mackay	Musemic	Crabbe	Bannon	Ferguson	Whittaker (4)
	19th	Smith	Kidd	McLaren	Whittaker	Berry	McPherson	Colquhoun	Mackay	Musemic	Kirkwood	Crabbe	Bannon (8)	Ferguson (9)
	23rd	Smith	Levein	Kidd	Whittaker	Berry	McPherson	Colquhoun	Kirkwood	Musemic	Crabbe	Bannon	Ferguson (10)	McLaren (5)
	26th	Smith	McLaren	Whittaker	Kirkwood	Levein	McPherson	Colquhoun	Mackay	Musemic	Crabbe	Bannon	Ferguson (10)	Kidd (9)
	30th	Smith	McLaren	Whittaker	Kirkwood	Levein	McPherson	Colquhoun	Mackay	Musemic	Crabbe	Bannon	Robertson (10)	Kidd (3)
Sep	9th	Smith	McLaren	McKinlay	Kirkwood	Levein	McPherson	Colquhoun	Mackay	Musemic	Crabbe	Bannon*	Robertson (10)	McCreery (9)
	16th	Smith	Kidd*	McKinlay	Levein	Kirkwood	McPherson	Colquhoun	Mackay	Robertson	Crabbe	McCreery	Musemic	McLaren (10)
	23rd	Smith	McLaren	McKinlay	Levein	Kirkwood	McPherson	Colquhoun	Mackay	Robertson	Crabbe	McCreery	Musemic (10)	Bannon
	30th	Smith	McLaren	McKinlay	Levein	Kirkwood	McPherson	Colquhoun	Mackay	Robertson	Crabbe	McCreery	Foster	Bannon (10)
Oct	4th	Smith	McLaren	McKinlay	Levein	McCreery	McPherson	Bannon	Mackay	Colquhoun	Crabbe	Robertson	Kirkwood (8)	Musemic (11)
	14th	Smith	McLaren	McKinlay	Levein	McCreery	McPherson	Colquhoun	Mackay	Foster	Crabbe	Bannon	Robertson (9)	Kirkwood
	21st	Smith	McLaren	McKinlay	Levein	McCreery	McPherson	Colquhoun	Mackay	Foster	Crabbe	Bannon	Robertson (9)	Kirkwood (10)
	28th	Smith	McLaren	McKinlay	Levein	McCreery	McPherson	Colquhoun	Mackay	Foster	Crabbe	Bannon	Robertson (2)	Kirkwood (9)
Nov	4th	Smith	McLaren	McKinlay	Levein	McCreery	McPherson	Colquhoun	Mackay	Foster	Crabbe	Bannon	Robertson (10)	Kirkwood (11)
	11th	Smith	McLaren	McKinlay	Levein	Kirkwood	McPherson	Colquhoun	Mackay	Foster	Robertson	Bannon	Crabbe (8)	Kidd (4)
	18th	Smith	McLaren	McKinlay	Levein	Kirkwood	Sandison	Colquhoun	Mackay	Foster*	Crabbe	Bannon	Ferguson (10)	Wright
	25th	Smith	McLaren	McKinlay	Levein	Kirkwood	McPherson	Colquhoun	Mackay	Robertson	Crabbe	Bannon	Ferguson (9)	Sandison
Dec	2nd	Smith	McLaren	McKinlay	Levein	McCreery	McPherson	Colquhoun	Mackay	Foster	Crabbe	Bannon	Robertson (10)	Kidd (5)
	9th	Smith	McLaren	McKinlay	Levein	McCreery	McPherson	Colquhoun	Kidd	Foster*	Robertson	Bannon	Crabbe (10)	Kirkwood (8)
	20th	Smith	McLaren	McKinlay	Levein	McCreery	McPherson	Colquhoun	Mackay	Robertson	Crabbe	Bannon	Kidd (10)	Sandison (5)
	26th	Smith	McLaren	McKinlay	Levein	McCreery	McPherson	Colquhoun	Mackay	Robertson	Crabbe	Bannon	Sandison (2)	Kidd (5)
	30th	Smith	Kidd	McKinlay	Levein	Sandison	McPherson	Colquhoun	Mackay	Robertson	Crabbe	Bannon	Ferguson (2)	Kirkwood
Jan	1st	Smith	Kidd	Whittaker	Levein	Sandison	McPherson	Colquhoun	Mackay	Foster	Robertson	Bannon	Crabbe (9)	Kirkwood (7)
	6th	Smith	Kidd	Whittaker	Levein	Sandison	McPherson	Colquhoun	Mackay	Crabbe	Robertson	Bannon	Ferguson (9)	Kirkwood
	13th	Smith	Kidd	Whittaker	Levein	Sandison	McPherson	Colquhoun	Mackay*	Robertson	Crabbe	Bannon	Ferguson (9)	McCreery (10)
	20th	Smith	Kidd	Whittaker	Levein	McCreery	McPherson	Colquhoun	Kirkwood	Robertson	Crabbe	Bannon	Ferguson (10)	McKinlay
	27th	Smith	Kidd	McKinlay	Levein	McCreery	McPherson	Colquhoun	Sandison	Robertson	Crabbe	Bannon	Ferguson (7)	Mackay (5)
Feb	3rd	Smith	Kidd*	McKinlay	Levein	McCreery	McPherson	Colquhoun	Sandison	Robertson	Crabbe	Bannon	Mackay (5)	Ferguson (3)
	10th	Smith	McLaren	Whittaker	Levein	Sandison	McPherson	Colquhoun	Mackay	Robertson	Crabbe	Bannon	Ferguson	McCreery
	17th	Smith	Kidd	McKinlay	Levein	McCreery	McPherson	Colquhoun	Mackay	Robertson	Crabbe	Bannon	Sandison (8)	Wright
	24th	Smith	Kidd	McKinlay	Levein	McCreery	McPherson	Colquhoun	Mackay	Robertson	Crabbe	Bannon	Foster (9)	Berry (5)
Mar	3rd	Smith	Kidd	McKinlay	Levein	McCreery	McPherson	Colquhoun	Berry	Robertson	Crabbe	Bannon	Foster (10)	Sandison (2)
	10th	Smith	Kidd	McKinlay	Levein	McCreery	McPherson	Colquhoun	Berry	Robertson	Crabbe	Bannon	Mackay	Foster (7)
	17th	Smith	Kidd	McKinlay	Levein	McCreery	McPherson	Colquhoun	Berry	Robertson	Crabbe	Bannon	Foster (10)	Mackay (11)
	24th	Smith	McLaren	McKinlay	Levein	McCreery	McPherson	Colquhoun	Mackay	Robertson	Crabbe	Bannon	Foster (11)	Berry
	31st	Smith	McLaren	McKinlay	Levein	Berry	McPherson	Colquhoun	Mackay	Robertson	Foster	Bannon	Crabbe (9)	Kirkwood (10)
Apr	4th	Smith	McLaren	McKinlay	Levein	Berry	McPherson	Colquhoun	Mackay	Robertson	Foster	Bannon	Crabbe	McCreery
	14th	Smith	McLaren	McKinlay	Levein	Berry	McPherson	Colquhoun	Mackay	Robertson	Foster	Bannon	Crabbe (9)	Kirkwood (7)
	21st	Smith	McLaren	McKinlay	Levein	Berry	McPherson	Colquhoun	Mackay	Robertson	Foster	Bannon	Crabbe (11)	Kirkwood (7)
	28th	Smith	McLaren	McKinlay	Levein	Berry	McPherson	Colquhoun	Mackay	Crabbe	McCreery	Bannon	Robertson (9)	Wright
May	5th	Smith	McLaren	McKinlay	Levein	Berry	McPherson	Colquhoun	Mackay	Robertson	McCreery	Foster	Crabbe (7)	Wright (8)

Ace of Hearts - a John Robertson header flashes towards the net for the first of a double in this 2-1 derby win for Hearts at Easter Road. Wayne Foster and Dave McPherson and Pat McGinlay of Hibs watch the action. DC Thomson

Season 1990-91

Date			Opponents		Score	Crowd	Scorers
Aug	21st	LC2	Cowdenbeath	a*	2-0	5,133	Robertson; Bannon
	25th	L	St Mirren	h	1-1	12,215	Robertson
	29th	LC3	St Mirren	a	1-0**	6,916	Crabbe
Sep	1st	L	Dunfermline	a	0-2	10,602	-
	5th	LCQ	Aberdeen	a	0-3	14,853	-
	8th	L	Rangers	h	1-3	22,001	Wright
	15th	L	Hibernian	a	3-0	16,913	Robertson 2; Levein
	19th	UEF1	Dniepr Dneprop.^	a	1-1	15,500	Robertson
	22nd	L	Celtic	a	0-3	38,409	-
	29th	L	Dundee United	h	1-0	12,052	Bannon
Oct	3rd	UEF1	Dniepr Dneprop.^	h	3-1 (4-2)	18,760	Robertson 2 (1 pen); McPherson
	6th	L	Motherwell	a	1-1	6,780	I. Ferguson
	13th	L	St Johnstone	h	2-3	12,856	I. Ferguson; Kirkwood
	20th	L	Aberdeen	a	0-3	14,800	-
	24th	UEF2	Bologna	h	3-1	11,155	Foster 2; I. Ferguson
	27th	L	St Mirren	a	1-2	5,441	Colquhoun
Nov	3rd	L	Dunfermline	h	1-1	11,897	Colquhoun
	7th	UEF2	Bologna	a	0-3 (3-4)	12,224	-
	10th	L	Celtic	h	1-0	19,189	Colquhoun
	17th	L	Dundee United	a	1-1	10,821	Levein
	24th	L	Hibernian	h	1-1	19,004	Berry
Dec	1st	L	Rangers	a	0-4	37,623	-
	8th	L	Aberdeen	h	1-0	9,839	Colquhoun
	15th	L	St Johnstone	a	1-2	8,500	Crabbe
	22nd	L	Motherwell	h	3-2	8,635	McPherson; Mackay; Robertson (pen)
	29th	L	Celtic	a	1-1	28,118	Colquhoun
Jan	2nd	L	Hibernian	a	4-1	13,601	McKinlay; McPherson; Mackay; Levein
	5th	L	Rangers	h	0-1	20,956	-
	12th	L	St Mirren	h	2-0	10,914	Robertson 2 (1 pen)
	26th	SC3	Airdrie	a	1-2	9,500	Mackay
Feb	2nd	L	Aberdeen	a	0-5	13,000	-
	16th	L	Dundee United	h	2-1	7,216	Robertson; McLaren
	23rd	L	Dunfermline	a	1-3	7,273	Wilson o.g.
Mar	2nd	L	Motherwell	a	3-1	5,212	Robertson; Sandison; Foster
	6th	L	St Johnstone	h	2-1	8,135	D. Ferguson; Colquhoun
	9th	L	Rangers	a	1-2	36,128	D. Ferguson
	23rd	L	Hibernian	h	3-1	14,211	Levein; Wright; Robertson
	30th	L	St Mirren	a	0-0	4,823	-
Apr	6th	L	Dunfermline	h	4-1	8,102	Robertson 2; Crabbe; McKinlay
	13th	L	Aberdeen	h	1-4	16,877	McKimmie o.g.
	20th	L	St Johnstone	a	2-0	6,822	Colquhoun; Mackay
	27th	L	Celtic	h	0-1	17,085	-
May	4th	L	Dundee United	a	1-2	6,820	Crabbe
	11th	L	Motherwell	h	2-1	7,055	Robertson; Bannon

* Played at East End Park, Dunfermline for safety reasons; ** After extra-time. ^ Dnepropetrovsk = Russia.

Iain Ferguson - netted some spectacular goals in his time at Hearts

Appearances

	League	L/Cup	S/Cup	UEFA	Total
John Colquhoun	36 (7)	2	1	4	43 (7)
Dave McPherson	34 (2)	3	1	3 (1)	41 (3)
Craig Levein	33 (4)	3	0	4	40 (4)
Tosh McKinlay	31 (2)	3	1	4	39+2s (2)
John Robertson	31 (12)	3 (1)	1	3 (3)	38 (16)
Gary Mackay	27 (3)	3	1 (1)	1	32+4s (4)
Henry Smith	23	3	1	4	31
Derek Ferguson	25 (2)	2	1	0	28+5s (2)
Jimmy Sandison	24 (1)	0	1	1	26+1s (1)
Wayne Foster	21 (1)	2	0	2 (2)	25+8s (3)
Neil Berry	18 (1)	2	1	3	24+1s (1)
Alan McLaren	18 (1)	1	1	3	23+6s (1)
Eamonn Bannon	15 (2)	1 (1)	0	3	19+6s (3)
George Wright	14 (2)	0	0	2	16+3s (2)
Scott Crabbe	13 (3)	1 (1)	1	0	15+10s (4)
Nicky Walker	13	0	0	0	13
Davie Kirkwood	8 (1)	0	0	3	11+2s (1)
Iain Ferguson	7 (2)	0	0	3 (1)	10+5s (3)
Dave McCreery	4	3	0	1	8+3s
Walter Kidd	1	1	0	0	2+5s
Tommy Harrison	0	0	0	0	0+3s

The Record		
League	-	Fifth Place, Premier Division
League Cup	-	Quarter final
Scottish Cup	-	Third round
Top Scorer	-	John Robertson (16 goals)
Av. Home Gate	-	13,236
Players used	-	21
Sent off (booked)	-	Four (48)

Scottish League Premier Division

		Home			Away			Goals		
	P	W	D	L	W	D	L	F	A	PTS
Rangers	36	14	3	1	10	4	4	62-23		55
Aberdeen	36	12	5	1	10	4	4	62-27		53
Celtic	36	10	4	4	7	3	8	52-38		41
Dundee United	36	11	3	4	6	4	8	41-29		41
Hearts	**36**	**10**	**3**	**5**	**4**	**4**	**10**	**48-55**		**35**
Motherwell	36	9	5	4	3	4	11	51-50		33
St Johnstone	36	6	4	8	5	5	8	41-54		31
Dunfermline	36	5	7	6	3	4	11	38-61		27
Hibernian	36	6	5	7	0	8	10	24-51		25
St Mirren	36	4	5	9	1	4	13	28-59		19

Heart of Midlothian F.C. Line-Ups 1990-91

	1	2	3	4	5	6	7	8	9	10	11	12	14
Aug 21st	Smith	Kidd	McKinlay	Levein	McCreery	McPherson	Ferguson D	Mackay	Robertson	Crabbe	Foster	Bannon (11)	Berry
25th	Smith	Wright	McKinlay	Levein	McCreery	McPherson	Colquhoun	Ferguson D	Robertson	Mackay	Crabbe	Bannon (5)	Berry (7)
29th	Smith	McLaren	McKinlay	Levein	McCreery	McPherson	Colquhoun	Ferguson D	Robertson	Mackay	Berry	Crabbe (7)	Bannon (5)
Sep 1st	Smith	McLaren	McKinlay	Levein	McCreery	McPherson	Colquhoun	Ferguson D	Robertson	Mackay	Berry	Crabbe (8)	Bannon (3)
5th	Smith	Berry	McKinlay	Levein	McCreery	McPherson	Colquhoun	Mackay	Robertson	Foster	Bannon	Ferguson D	Kidd (5)
8th	Smith	Kidd	McKinlay	McCreery	Berry	McPherson	Colquhoun	Ferguson D	Robertson	Mackay	Foster	Kirkwood (10)	Wright (7)
15th	Smith	McLaren	McKinlay	Levein	Berry	Wright	Robertson	Mackay	Foster	Sandison	Colquhoun	Ferguson I (9)	Kidd (6)
19th	Smith	McLaren	McKinlay	Levein	Berry	Wright	Robertson	McCreery	Foster	Sandison	Colquhoun	Kidd (8)	Kirkwood (5)
22nd	Smith	McLaren	McKinlay	Levein	McPherson	Wright	Robertson	Kirkwood	Foster	Sandison	Colquhoun	Ferguson I (7)	Kidd
29th	Smith	McLaren	McKinlay	Levein	Kirkwood	McPherson	Colquhoun	Wright	Foster	Ferguson I	Bannon	Sandison (9)	Ferguson D (11)
Oct 3rd	Smith	McLaren	McKinlay	Levein	Kirkwood	McPherson	Colquhoun	Wright	Robertson	Ferguson I	Bannon	Mackay (8)	Ferguson D (7)
6th	Smith	McLaren	McKinlay	Levein	Kirkwood	McPherson	Colquhoun	Mackay	Robertson	Ferguson I	Bannon	Foster (9)	Ferguson D (4)
13th	Smith	McLaren	McKinlay	Levein	Kirkwood	McPherson	Colquhoun	Mackay	Robertson	Ferguson I	Bannon	Foster	Ferguson D (8)
20th	Smith	McLaren	McKinlay	Levein	Kirkwood	McPherson	Colquhoun	Berry	Robertson	Ferguson I	Bannon	Foster (9)	Mackay
24th	Smith	McLaren	McKinlay	Levein	Kirkwood	McPherson	Colquhoun	Berry	Foster	Ferguson I	Bannon	Crabbe	Ferguson D (5)
27th	Smith	McLaren	McKinlay	Levein	Kirkwood	McPherson	Colquhoun	Berry	Foster	Ferguson I	Bannon	Mackay (11)	Crabbe (9)
Nov 3rd	Smith	Mackay	McKinlay	Levein	Kirkwood	McPherson	Colquhoun	Berry	Foster	Ferguson I	Bannon	Crabbe (10)	Kidd
7th	Smith	Mackay	McKinlay	Levein	Kirkwood	McPherson	Colquhoun	Berry	Robertson	Ferguson I	Bannon	McLaren (11)	Crabbe (9)
10th	Smith	Sandison	McKinlay	Levein	Mackay	McPherson	Colquhoun	Berry	Foster	Ferguson D*	Robertson	Ferguson I (9)	Kidd (11)
17th	Smith	Sandison	McKinlay	Levein	Mackay	McPherson	Colquhoun	Berry	Foster	Kirkwood	Robertson	Ferguson I (11)	Kidd
24th	Smith	Sandison	McKinlay	Levein	Mackay	McPhersson	Colquhoun	Berry	Foster	Ferguson D	Robertson	Ferguson I (9)	McLaren
Dec 1st	Smith	Sandison	Wright	Levein	Mackay	McPherson	Colquhoun	Berry	Foster	Ferguson D	Ferguson I	Crabbe (9)	McLaren
8th	Smith	Sandison	McKinlay	Levein	Mackay	McPherson	Colquhoun	Berry	Foster	Ferguson D	Robertson	Crabbe (9)	McLaren
15th	Smith	Sandison	McKinlay	Levein	Mackay	McPherson	Colquhoun	Berry	Foster	Ferguson D	Robertson	Crabbe (9)	McLaren
22nd	Smith	Sandison	McKinlay	Levein	Mackay	McPherson	Colquhoun	Berry	Crabbe	Ferguson D	Robertson	Foster (9)	McLaren (4)
29th	Smith	Sandison	McKinlay	McLaren	Mackay	McPherson	Colquhoun	Berry	Crabbe	Ferguson D	Robertson	Foster (11)	Kidd
Jan 2nd	Smith	Sandison	McKinlay	Levein	Mackay	McPherson	Colquhoun	Berry	Crabbe	Ferguson D	Robertson	Foster (9)	McLaren (4)
5th	Smith	Sandison	McKinlay	Levein*	Mackay	McPherson	Colquhoun	Berry	Crabbe	Ferguson D	Robertson	Bannon (9)	McLaren (11)
12th	Smith	Sandison	McKinlay	McLaren	Mackay	McPherson	Colquhoun	Berry	Crabbe	McCreery	Robertson	Foster (9)	Wright
26th	Smith	Sandison	McKinlay	McLaren	Mackay	McPherson	Colquhoun	Berry	Crabbe	Ferguson D	Robertson	Foster (9)	McCreery
Feb 2nd	Smith	Sandison	McKinlay	Levein	Mackay	McPherson	Colquhoun	Berry	Foster	Ferguson D	Robertson	McCreery (11)	McLaren
16th	Walker	Sandison	McLaren	Levein	Mackay	McPherson	Colquhoun	Bannon	Foster	Ferguson D	Robertson	Harrison (8)	Kidd (4)
23rd	Walker	Sandison	McKinlay	Levein	Mackay	McPherson	Colquhoun	McLaren	Foster	Ferguson D	Robertson	Harrison	Wright (6)
Mar 2nd	Walker	Sandison	McKinlay	Levein	Mackay	McPherson	Colquhoun	McLaren	Foster	Ferguson D	Robertson	Harrison	Wright
6th	Walker	Sandison	McKinlay	Levein	Mackay	McPherson	Colquhoun	McLaren	Foster	Ferguson D	Robertson	Crabbe	Wright (8)
9th	Walker	Sandison	Wright	Levein	Mackay	McPherson	Colquhoun	Crabbe	Foster	Ferguson D	Robertson	Harrison (8)	Bannon (9)
23rd	Walker	Sandison	McKinlay	Levein	Wright	McPherson	Colquhoun	Bannon	Crabbe	Ferguson D	Robertson	Harrison (11)	McLaren (8)
30th	Walker	Sandison	McKinlay	Levein	Wright	McPherson	Colquhoun	Bannon	Crabbe	Ferguson D	Robertson	Harrison	McLaren
Apr 6th	Walker	Sandison	McKinlay	Levein	Wright	McPherson	Colquhoun	Bannon	Crabbe	Ferguson D	Robertson	Mackay (8)	McLaren
13th	Walker	Sandison	McKinlay	Levein	Wright	McPherson	Colquhoun	Bannon	Crabbe	Ferguson D	Robertson*	Mackay (3)	McLaren (2)
20th	Walker	McLaren	Mackay*	Levein	Wright	McPherson	Colquhoun	Bannon	Crabbe	Ferguson D	Foster	McCreery (11)	McKinlay (7)
27th	Walker	McLaren	McKinlay	Levein	Wright	McPherson	Colquhoun	Bannon	Crabbe	Ferguson D	Robertson	McCreery	Foster (7)
May 4th	Walker	McLaren	McKinlay	Levein	Wright	Sandison	Colquhoun	Bannon	Robertson	Mackay	Foster	Crabbe (7)	McCreery (5)
11th	Walker	McLaren	Mackay	Levein	Wright	McPherson	Colquhoun	Bannon	Robertson	Ferguson D	Foster	Crabbe (7)	McKinlay (11)

In the net - Wayne Foster celebrates as Craig Levein finds the net against Dundee United at Tannadice. Jim McInally fails to prevent the ball going in while Billy McKinlay and Alan Main are the other United defenders. **DC Thomson**

Season 1991-92

Date			Opponents		Score	Crowd	Scorers
Aug	10th	L	Dunfermline	a	2-1	10,520	Crabbe; Robertson
	13th	L	Airdrie	a	3-2	5,650	Robertson 2 (1 pen)
	17th	L	Rangers	h	1-0	22,534	Crabbe
	20th	LC2	Clydebank	h	3-0	7,867	Crabbe; Baird; Robertson
	24th	L	St Johnstone	a	1-0	7,516	Levein
	28th	LC3	Hamilton Accies	a	2-0	4,006	Robertson (pen); Baird
	31st	L	Hibernian	h	0-0	22,208	-
Sep	3rd	LCQ	Rangers	h	0-1	22,878	-
	7th	L	Motherwell	h	2-0	9,003	Crabbe; Baird
	14th	L	St Mirren	a	3-2	5,836	Millar; McPherson; Crabbe
	21st	L	Dundee United	h	1-1	11,746	McKinlay
	28th	L	Falkirk	a	2-1	8,339	Crabbe; Millar
Oct	5th	L	Celtic	a	1-3	33,106	Robertson
	9th	L	Aberdeen	h	1-0	15,569	Crabbe
	12th	L	Dunfermline	h	1-0	9,002	McLaren
	19th	L	Rangers	a	0-2	36,481	-
	26th	L	Motherwell	a	1-0	5,417	I. Ferguson
	30th	L	St Mirren	h	0-0	8,683	-
Nov	2nd	L	Hibernian	a	1-1	19,831	Robertson
	9th	L	St Johnstone	h	2-1	10,222	Baird; Hogg
	16th	L	Celtic	h	3-1	22,666	Wright; Levein; Crabbe
	20th	L	Aberdeen	a	2-0	15,338	Robertson; Baird
	23rd	L	Dundee United	a	1-0	12,796	Robertson
	30th	L	Airdrie	h	1-0	12,073	Crabbe (pen)
Dec	4th	l	Falkirk	h	1-1	11,742	Crabbe
	7th	L	Dunfermline	a	2-0	8,774	Millar; Crabbe (pen)
	14th	L	Motherwell	h	3-1	10,006	Millar; Crabbe (pen); Baird
	21st	L	St Mirren	a	1-0	5,216	Millar
	28th	L	St Johnstone	a	5-0	10,064	Baird; Robertson 2; Crabbe 2
Jan	1st	L	Hibernian	h	1-1	20,358	I. Ferguson
	4th	L	Celtic	a	2-1	30,415	Crabbe; Millar
	11th	L	Aberdeen	h	0-4	16,291	-
	18th	L	Airdrie	a	1-2	8,000	Robertson
	25th	SC3	St Mirren	a	0-0	8,952	-
Feb	1st	L	Rangers	h	0-1	24,356	-
	5th	SC3R	St Mirren	h	3-0	12,130	Robertson 3
	8th	L	Dundee United	h	1-0	10,516	Bannon
	15th	SC4	Dunfermline	a	2-1	12,882	Hogg; Crabbe
	29th	L	Celtic	h	1-2	20,683	Robertson (pen)
Mar	4th	L	Falkirk	a	2-1	6,225	Mackay; D. Ferguson
	8th	SCQ	Falkirk	h	3-1	11,227	I. Ferguson; Robertson; Mackay
	14th	L	St Johnstone	h	2-0	8,799	McKinlay; Millar
	18th	L	Aberdeen	a	0-2	10,581	-
	21st	L	Hibernian	a	2-1	13,766	Baird; I. Ferguson
	28th	L	Dunfermline	h	1-0	7,488	Robertson
Apr	4th	SCS	Airdrie	Hamp.	0-0	27,310	-
	7th	L	Motherwell	a	1-0	4,502	Robertson
	11th	L	St Mirren	h	0-0	6,200	-
	14th	SCSR	Airdrie	Hamp.	1-1*	11,163	McLaren
	18th	L	Dundee United	a	0-2	6,711	-
	25th	L	Airdrie	h	2-2	5,310	Crabbe; McPherson
	29th	L	Rangers	a	1-1	36,129	Robertson (pen)
May	2nd	L	Falkirk	h	2-0	7,348	Bannon; I. Ferguson

aet 1-1 after 90 minutes, Airdrie won 4-2 on pens.

Scott Crabbe - the speedy striker bounced back with 17 goals.

The Record		
League	-	Runners up, PremierDivision
League Cup	-	Quarter-final
Scottish Cup	-	Semi-final
Top Scorer	-	John Robertson (20 goals)
Av. Home Gate	-	13,300
Players used	-	19
Sent off (booked)	-	Nine (73)

Appearances

	League		L/Cup		S/Cup		Total	
Dave McPherson	44	(2)	3		6		53	(2)
Henry Smith	44		3		6		53	
John Robertson	42	(14)	3	(2)	6	(4)	51	(20)
John Millar	40	(7)	3		5		48+1s	(7)
Gary Mackay	41	(1)	3		3	(1)	47+2s	(2)
Derek Ferguson	37	(1)	3		6		46+1s	(1)
Tosh McKinlay	37	(2)	3		5		45+2s	(2)
Alan McLaren	38	(2)	1		6	(1)	45	(3)
Scott Crabbe	37	(15)	3	(1)	2	(1)	42+7s	(17)
Craig Levein	36	(2)	3		4		43	(2)
Ian Baird	30	(6)	3	(2)	3		36	(8)
George Wright	15	(1)	0		4		19+12s	(1)
Ian Ferguson	12	(4)	0		4	(1)	16+20s	(5)
Graeme Hogg	13	(1)	2		1	(1)	16+5s	(2)
Eamonn Bannon	10	(2)	0		4		14 +4s	(2)
Glynn Snodin	4		0		1		5+3s	
Steve Penney	3		0		0		3+8s	
Wayne Foster	1		0		0		1+9s	
Tommy Harrison	0		0		0		0+2s	

Scottish League Premier Division

		Home			Away			Goals	
	P	W	D	L	W	D	L	F A	PTS
Rangers	44	14	5	3	19	1	2	101-31	72
Hearts	**44**	**12**	**7**	**3**	**15**	**2**	**5**	**60-37**	**63**
Celtic	44	15	3	4	11	7	4	88-42	62
Dundee United	44	10	7	5	9	6	7	66-50	51
Hibernian	44	7	8	7	9	9	4	53-45	49
Aberdeen	44	9	6	7	8	8	6	55-42	48
Airdrie	44	7	5	10	6	5	11	50-70	36
St Johnstone	44	5	7	10	8	3	11	52-73	35
Falkirk	44	7	2	13	5	9	8	54-73	35
Motherwell	44	5	6	11	5	8	9	43-61	34
St Mirren	44	2	5	15	4	7	11	33-73	24
Dunfermline	44	2	7	13	2	3	17	22-80	18

Heart of Midlothian F.C. Line-Ups 1991-92

	1	2	3	4	5	6	7	8	9	10	11	12	13
Aug 10th	Smith	McLaren	McKinlay*	Levein	Mackay	McPherson	Crabbe	Ferguson D	Baird	Millar	Robertson	Bannon (7)	Foster (9)
13th	Smith	McLaren	Bannon	Levein*	Mackay	McPherson	Crabbe	Ferguson D	Baird	Millar	Robertson	Foster (9)	Wright
17th	Smith	McLaren	Bannon	McKinlay	Mackay	McPherson	Crabbe	Ferguson D	Baird	Millar	Robertson	Foster (7)	Wright
20th	Smith	McLaren	McKinlay	Levein	Mackay	McPherson	Crabbe	Ferguson D	Baird	Millar	Robertson	Foster (2)	Wright (8)
24th	Smith	Hogg	McKinlay	Levein	Mackay	McPherson	Crabbe	Ferguson D	Baird	Millar	Robertson	Harrison	Penney (7)
28th	Smith	Hogg*	McKinlay	Levein	Mackay	McPherson	Crabbe	Ferguson D	Baird	Millar	Robertson	Harrison (10)	Foster (11)
31st	Smith	McLaren	McKinlay	Levein	Mackay	McPherson	Crabbe	Ferguson D	Baird	Millar	Robertson	Foster (7)	Wright
Sep 3rd	Smith	Hogg	McKinlay	Levein	Mackay	McPherson	Crabbe	Ferguson D	Baird	Millar	Robertson	Penney (11)	Wright
7th	Smith	Hogg	McKinlay	Levein	Mackay	McPherson	Crabbe	Ferguson D	Baird	Millar	Robertson	Penney (5)	Wright (8)
14th	Smith	Hogg	McKinlay	Levein	Mackay	McPherson	Crabbe	Ferguson D	Baird*	Millar	Robertson	Penney (7)	Wright
21st	Smith	Hogg	McKinlay	Levein	Mackay	McPherson	Crabbe	Ferguson D	Penney	Millar	Robertson	Harrison	Wright
28th	Smith	Hogg	McKinlay	Levein	Mackay	McPherson	Crabbe	Ferguson D	Penney	Millar	Robertson	Harrison (9)	Wright
Oct 5th	Smith	McLaren	McKinlay	Levein	Mackay	McPherson	Crabbe	Ferguson D	Baird	Millar	Robertson	Penney (9)	Wright (6)
9th	Smith	McLaren	McKinlay	Levein	Mackay	McPherson	Crabbe	Ferguson D	Baird	Millar	Robertson	Ferguson I (9)	Wright
12th	Smith	McLaren	McKinlay	Levein	Mackay	McPherson	Crabbe	Ferguson D	Baird	Millar	Robertson	Ferguson I (11)	Wright
19th	Smith	McLaren	McKinlay	Levein	Mackay	McPherson	Crabbe	Ferguson D	Baird	Millar	Robertson	Penney (7)	Wright
26th	Smith	McLaren	McKinlay	Levein	Mackay	McPherson	Crabbe	Ferguson D	Ferguson I	Millar	Robertson	Penney	Wright (11)
30th	Smith	McLaren	McKinlay	Levein	Mackay	McPherson	Crabbe	Ferguson D	Ferguson I	Millar	Robertson	Penney (7)	Wright (4)
Nov 2nd	Smith	McLaren	Hogg	Wright	Mackay	McPherson	Crabbe	Ferguson D	Baird	Millar	Robertson	Penney	Ferguson I (7)
9th	Smith	McLaren	Hogg	Wright	Mackay	McPherson	Crabbe	Ferguson D	Baird	Penney	Robertson	Williams	Ferguson I
16th	Smith	McLaren	McKinlay	Levein	Mackay	McPherson	Crabbe	Ferguson D	Baird	Millar	Robertson	Ferguson I (9)	Wright (8)
20th	Smith	McLaren	McKinlay	Levein	Mackay	McPherson	Crabbe	Wright	Baird	Millar	Robertson	Ferguson I (9)	Hogg (11)
23rd	Smith	McLaren	McKinlay	Levein	Mackay*	McPherson	Crabbe	Wright	Baird	Millar	Robertson	Ferguson I (11)	Hogg (7)
30th	Smith	McLaren	McKinlay	Levein	Bannon	McPherson	Crabbe	Wright	Baird	Millar	Robertson	Ferguson I (9)	Hogg
Dec 4th	Smith	McLaren	McKinlay	Levein	Mackay	McPherson	Crabbe	Wright	Baird	Millar	Robertson	Ferguson I (3)	Hogg (8)
7th	Smith	McLaren	McKinlay	Levein	Mackay	McPherson	Crabbe	Wright	Baird	Millar	Robertson	Ferguson I (11)	Bannon
14th	Smith	McLaren	McKinlay	Levein	Mackay	McPherson	Crabbe	Wright	Baird	Millar	Robertson	Ferguson I (7)	Hogg (4)
21st	Smith	McLaren	McKinlay	Hogg	Mackay	McPherson	Crabbe	Wright	Baird	Millar	Robertson	Ferguson I (11)	Ferguson D (8)
28th	Smith	McLaren	McKinlay	Levein	Mackay	McPherson	Crabbe	Ferguson D	Baird	Millar	Robertson	Ferguson I (9)	Hogg
Jan 1st	Smith	McLaren	McKinlay	Levein	Mackay	McPherson	Crabbe	Ferguson D	Baird	Millar	Robertson	Ferguson I (7)	Hogg (4)
4th	Smith	McLaren	McKinlay	Levein	Mackay	McPherson	Crabbe	Ferguson D	Baird	Millar	Robertson	Ferguson I (7)	Wright (5)
11th	Smith	McLaren	McKinlay	Levein	Mackay	McPherson	Crabbe	Ferguson D	Baird	Millar	Robertson	Ferguson I	Wright
18th	Smith	McLaren	McKinlay	Levein	Mackay	McPherson	Crabbe	Ferguson D	Baird	Millar	Robertson	Ferguson I (7)	Wright (4)
25th	Smith	McLaren	McKinlay	Levein	Wright	McPherson	Crabbe	Ferguson D	Baird*	Millar	Robertson	Ferguson I (11)	Hogg
Feb 1st	Smith	McLaren	McKinlay	Levein	Wright	McPherson	Crabbe	Ferguson D	Ferguson I	Millar	Robertson	Mackay (5)	Hogg
5th	Smith	McLaren	McKinlay	Levein	Wright	McPherson	Ferguson I	Ferguson D	Baird	Millar	Robertson	Crabbe (8)	Bannon (9)
8th	Smith	McLaren	McKinlay	Levein*	Wright	McPherson	Ferguson I	Ferguson D	Bannon	Millar	Robertson	Crabbe (7)	Mackay (9)
15th	Smith	McLaren	McKinlay	Hogg	Mackay	McPherson	Ferguson I	Ferguson D	Bannon	Millar	Robertson	Crabbe (9)	Wright (5)
29th	Smith	McLaren	McKinlay	Hogg	Mackay	McPherson	Crabbe	Ferguson D	Baird	Millar	Robertson	Ferguson I (7)	Wright
Mar 4th	Smith	McLaren	McKinlay	Mackay	Hogg*	McPherson	Ferguson I	Ferguson D	Baird	Millar	Robertson	Foster (7)	Wright (11)
8th	Smith	McLaren	McKinlay	Wright	Mackay	McPherson	Ferguson I	Ferguson D	Bannon	Millar	Robertson	Foster (9)	Penney (3)
14th	Smith	McLaren	McKinlay	Hogg	Mackay	McPherson	Ferguson I	Ferguson D	Bannon	Millar	Robertson	Foster (9)	Snodin (2)
18th	Smith	McLaren	McKinlay	Levein	Mackay	McPherson	Crabbe	Ferguson D	Ferguson I	Millar	Robertson	Snodin (7)	Wright (11)
21st	Smith	McLaren	McKinlay	Levein	Mackay	McPherson	Bannon	Ferguson D	Ferguson I	Wright	Robertson	Crabbe (5)	Snodin
28th	Smith	McLaren	McKinlay	Levein	Mackay	McPherson	Bannon	Ferguson D	Ferguson I	Wright	Robertson	Crabbe (7)	Millar (10)
Apr 4th	Smith	McLaren	McKinlay	Levein	Mackay	McPherson	Bannon	Ferguson D	Ferguson I	Wright	Robertson	Crabbe (7)	Snodin
7th	Smith	Hogg	Snodin	Levein	Mackay	McPherson	Ferguson I	Ferguson D	Crabbe	Wright	Robertson	Foster	McKinlay (10)
11th	Smith	McLaren	McKinlay	Hogg	Mackay	McPherson	Crabbe	Ferguson D	Ferguson I	Millar	Robertson	Bannon (5)	Snodin (3)
14th	Smith	McLaren	Snodin	Levein	Bannon	McPherson	Crabbe	Ferguson D	Baird	Millar	Robertson	Ferguson I (9)	Wright (5)
18th	Smith	McLaren	Snodin	Levein	Mackay	McPherson	Crabbe	Ferguson D	Foster	Millar	Wright	Bannon (11)	Hogg
25th	Smith	McLaren	Snodin	Levein	Mackay	McPherson	Crabbe	Ferguson D	Baird	Millar	Bannon	Ferguson I (9)	McKinlay
29th	Smith	McLaren	Snodin	Levein	Mackay	McPherson	Bannon	Ferguson D	Baird	Millar	Robertson	Ferguson I (9)	McKinlay (3)
May 2nd	Smith	McLaren	McKinlay	Levein	Mackay	McPherson	Bannon	Ferguson D	Ferguson I	Millar	Robertson	Crabbe (11)	Snodin

In where it hurts - Ian Baird collides with St Johnstone keeper Alan Main as he heads the ball into the net at McDiarmid Park. DC Thomson

Season 1992-93

Date			Opponents		Score	Crowd	Scorers
Aug	1st	L	Celtic	h	0-1	18,510	-
	5th	L	Falkirk	h	3-0	8,198	Robertson 2 (1 pen); Crabbe
	8th	L	Dundee United	a	1-1	9,112	Levein
	12th	LC2	Clydebank	h	1-0	5,758	McLaren
	15th	L	Partick Thistle	h	2-1	7,911	Mackay; Baird
	19th	LC3	Brechin City	a	2-1*	1,903	McKinlay; Robertson
	22nd	L	Hibernian	a	0-0	15,889	-
	26th	LCQ	Celtic	h	1-2	21,502	Mackay
	29th	L	Motherwell	h	1-0	7,285	Berry
Sep	1st	L	Dundee	a	3-1	5,878	Robertson; D. Ferguson; Levein
	12th	L	Aberdeen	h	1-0	10,630	Robertson
	16th	UEF1	Slavia Prague	a	0-1	4,549	-
	19th	L	Rangers	a	0-2	41,888	-
	26th	L	Airdrie	a	0-1	4,372	-
	30th	UEF1	Slavia Prague	h	4-2 (4-3)	16,139	Baird; Mackay; Levein; Snodin
Oct	3rd	L	St Johnstone	h	1-1	7,738	Robertson
	7th	L	Celtic	a	1-1	26,059	Preston
	17th	L	Dundee United	h	1-0	8,209	Hogg
	21st	UEF2	Standard Liege	h	0-1	16,897	-
	24th	L	Motherwell	a	3-1	5,171	Robertson; Martin o.g; I.Ferguson
	31st	L	Dundee	h	1-0	7,452	Baird
Nov	4th	UEF2	Standard Liege	a	0-1 (0-2)	17,000	-
	7th	L	Hibernian	h	1-0	17,342	Baird
	10th	L	Partick Thistle	a	1-1	6,137	McLaren
	21st	L	Rangers	h	1-1	20,831	Baird
	28th	L	Aberdeen	a	2-6	13,555	Baird; Hogg
Dec	2nd	L	Falkirk	a	1-2	5,675	Robertson (pen)
	5th	L	Airdrie	h	1-3	6,665	Baird
	12th	L	St Johnstone	a	1-1	4,362	I. Ferguson
	19th	L	Celtic	h	1-0	13,554	I. Ferguson
	26th	L	Partick Thistle	h	1-1	9,922	Mackay
Jan	2nd	L	Hibernian	a	0-0	21,649	-
	9th	SC3	Huntly	h	6-0	9,520	Baird; D. Ferguson; Snodin; Robertson; Boothroyd 2
	20th	L	St Johnstone	h	2-0	5,060	Robertson; Baird
	23rd	L	Motherwell	h	0-0	6,610	-
	30th	L	Dundee United	a	1-0	7,732	Robertson
Feb	3rd	L	Dundee	a	0-1	4,335	-
	6th	SC4	Dundee	h	2-0	12,021	I. Ferguson; Robertson
	13th	L	Falkirk	h	3-1	7,700	McKinlay; Thomas; Taylor o.g.
	20th	L	Airdrie	a	0-0	3,347	-
	27th	L	Rangers	a	1-2	42,128	Millar
Mar	6th	SCQ	Falkirk	h	2-0	12,700	Preston; Robertson (pen)
	10th	L	Celtic	a	0-1	16,984	-
	13th	L	Dundee United	h	1-0	7,087	Baird
	20th	L	Hibernian	h	1-0	13,740	Robertson
	27th	L	Partick Thistle	a	1-1	5,150	Preston
Apr	3rd	SCS	Rangers	Parkhd.	1-2	41,700	Preston
	10th	L	Dundee	h	0-0	6,033	-
	14th	L	Rangers	h	2-3	14,622	Robertson; Bannon
	17th	L	Aberdeen	a	2-3	9,700	Levein; I. Ferguson
	20th	L	Motherwell	a	1-2	4,355	Baird
May	1st	L	Falkirk	a	0-6	4,124	-
	5th	L	Aberdeen	h	1-2	6,038	Thomas
	8th	L	Airdrie	h	1-1	5,104	Johnston
	15th	L	St Johnstone	a	1-3	3,900	Harrison

* After extra-time, 1-1 after 90 mts.

Graeme Hogg - a powerful central defender who was particularly strong in the air.

The Record		
League	-	Fifth Place, Premier Division
League Cup	-	Quarter-final
Scottish Cup	-	Semi-final
Top Scorer	-	John Robertson (15 goals)
Av. Home Gate	-	9,800
Players used	-	27
Sent off (booked)	-	Six (67)

Scottish League Premier Division

		Home			Away			Goals		
	P	W	D	L	W	D	L	F	A	PTS
Rangers	44	20	2	0	13	5	4	97-35		73
Aberdeen	44	13	7	2	14	3	5	87-36		64
Celtic	44	13	5	4	11	7	4	68-41		60
Dundee United	44	8	7	7	11	2	9	56-49		47
Hearts	**44**	**12**	**6**	**4**	**3**	**8**	**11**	**46-51**		**44**
St Johnstone	44	8	10	4	2	10	10	52-66		40
Hibernian	44	8	8	6	4	5	13	54-64		37
Partick Thistle	44	5	6	11	7	6	9	50-71		36
Motherwell	44	7	4	11	4	9	9	46-62		35
Dundee	44	7	4	11	4	8	10	48-68		34
Falkirk	44	7	5	10	4	2	16	60-86		29
Airdrie	44	4	9	9	2	8	12	35-70		29

Appearances

	League	L/Cup	S/Cup	UEFA	Total
John Robertson	41 (11)	3 (1)	4 (3)	4	52+1s (15)
Gary Mackay	36 (2)	3 (1)	4	4 (1)	47+1s (4)
Derek Ferguson	37 (1)	3	4 (1)	3	47 (2)
Craig Levein	37 (3)	3	3	3 (1)	46 (4)
Peter Van De Ven	37	1	3	4	45
Ian Baird	34 (9)	2	4 (1)	3 (1)	43 (11)
Tosh McKinlay	32 (1)	3 (1)	3	4	42+2s (2)
Alan McLaren	34 (1)	2 (1)	4	2	42+1s (2)
Henry Smith	25	3	0	4	32
Graeme Hogg	20 (2)	3	0	3	26+2s (2)
John Millar	23 (1)	0	1	1	25+1s (1)
Ally Mauchlen	16	2	3	2	23+2s
Nicky Walker	18	0	4	0	22
Alan Preston	19 (2)	0	3 (2)	0	22+2s (4)
Glynn Snodin	16	0	1 (1)	2 (1)	19+15s (2)
Neil Berry	16 (1)	0	1	1	18+2s (1)
Ian Ferguson	9 (4)	0	1 (1)	1	11+17s (5)
George Wright	8	1	1	0	10+5s
Wayne Foster	7	2	0	1	10+7s
Eamonn Bannon	8 (1)	0	0	2	10+14s (1)

Appearances (Ctd.)

	League	L/Cup	S/Cup	UEFA	Total
Scott Crabbe	4 (1)	2	0	0	6+6s (1)
Tommy Harrison	3 (1)	0	0	0	3+1s (1)
Alan Johnston	2 (1)	0	0	0	2 (1)
Kevin Thomas	2 (2)	0	0	0	2+3s (2)
Adrian Boothroyd	0	0	0 (2)	0	0+6s (2)
Gary Locke	0	0	0	0	0+1s
Tommy Wilson	0	0	0	0	0+1s

Heart of Midlothian F.C. Line-Ups 1992-93

	1	2	3	4	5	6	7	8	9	10	11	12	13
Aug 1st	Smith	McLaren	McKinlay	Levein	Mackay	Van de Ven	Crabbe	Mauchlen	Baird	Wright	Bannon	Robertson (7)	Hogg (5)
5th	Smith	McLaren	McKinlay	Levein	Hogg	Van de Ven	Robertson	Mauchlen	Baird	Wright	Bannon	Snodin (11)	Crabbe (9)
8th	Smith	McLaren	McKinlay	Levein	Hogg	Van de Ven	Robertson	Ferguson D	Baird	Mauchlen	Bannon	Crabbe (11)	Wright (7)
12th	Smith	McLaren	McKinlay	Levein	Hogg	Mackay	Robertson	Ferguson D	Baird	Wright	Crabbe	Foster (6)	Snodin
15th	Smith	McLaren	McKinlay	Levein	Hogg	Mackay	Robertson	Ferguson D	Baird	Mauchlen	Crabbe	Foster (6)	Wright
19th	Smith	McLaren	McKinlay	Levein	Hogg	Mackay	Robertson	Ferguson D	Baird	Mauchlen	Foster	Snodin (8)	Crabbe (9)
22nd	Smith	McLaren	McKinlay	Levein	Mackay	Van de Ven	Robertson	Ferguson D	Baird	Mauchlen	Foster	Crabbe (2)	Hogg (5)
26th	Smith	Hogg	McKinlay	Levein	Mackay	Van de Ven	Robertson	Ferguson D	Crabbe	Mauchlen	Foster	Snodin (3)	Berry (10)
29th	Smith	Hogg	McKinlay	Levein	Mackay	Van de Ven	Robertson	Ferguson D	Crabbe	Berry	Foster	Snodin (5)	Bannon (9)
Sep 1st	Smith	Hogg	McKinlay	Levein	Mackay	Van de Ven	Robertson	Ferguson D	Wright	Berry	Foster	Snodin	Johnston
12th	Smith	Hogg	McKinlay	Levein	Mackay	Van de Ven	Robertson	Ferguson D	Baird	Mauchlen	Foster	Crabbe (9)	Snodin (8)
16th	Smith	Hogg	McKinlay	Berry	Mackay	Van de Ven	Robertson	Ferguson D	Baird	Mauchlen	Foster	Crabbe (7)	Bannon (11)
19th	Smith	Hogg	McKinlay	Levein	Mackay	Van de Ven	Crabbe	Ferguson D	Baird	Mauchlen	Berry	Bannon (5)	Snodin (10)
26th	Smith	Hogg	McKinlay	Levein	Wright	Van de Ven	Snodin	Ferguson D	Baird	Berry	Foster	Bannon (9)	Millar (10)
30th	Smith	Hogg	McKinlay	Levein	Mackay	Van de Ven	Robertson	McLaren	Baird	Snodin	Bannon	Wright (8)	Wilson (10)
Oct 3rd	Smith	Hogg	McKinlay	Levein	Wright	Van de Ven	Robertson	McLaren	Baird	Snodin	Preston	Bannon (11)	Mauchlen (10)
7th	Smith	Hogg	McKinlay	Levein	Mackay	Van de Ven	Robertson	Mauchlen	Baird	Snodin	Preston	Bannon (11)	Millar
17th	Smith	Hogg	McKinlay	Levein	Mackay	Van de Ven	Robertson	Ferguson D	Baird	Millar	Preston	Bannon (11)	Snodin (3)
21st	Smith	Hogg	McKinlay	Levein	Mackay	Van de Ven	Robertson	Ferguson D	Baird	Snodin	Bannon	Ferguson I (8)	McLaren (4)
24th	Smith	McLaren	McKinlay	Wright	Mackay	Van de Ven	Robertson	Ferguson D	Baird	Millar	Preston	Ferguson I (11)	Snodin (5)
31st	Smith	McLaren	McKinlay	Levein	Mackay	Van de Ven	Robertson	Snodin	Baird	Millar	Preston	Ferguson I (8)	Harrison
Nov 4th	Smith	McLaren	McKinlay	Levein	Mackay	Van de Ven	Robertson	Ferguson D	Ferguson I	Millar	Mauchlen	Foster (5)	Snodin (10)
7th	Smith	McLaren	McKinlay	Levein	Mackay	Van de Ven	Robertson	Ferguson D	Baird	Millar	Mauchlen	Ferguson I (7)	Snodin (5)
10th	Smith	McLaren	McKinlay	Levein	Mauchlen	Van de Ven	Robertson	Ferguson D	Baird	Millar	Preston	Ferguson I (11)	Snodin (4)
21st	Smith	McLaren	McKinlay	Levein	Berry	Van de Ven	Robertson	Ferguson D	Baird	Millar	Bannon	Ferguson I (11)	Snodin (6)
28th	Smith	McLaren	McKinlay*	Levein	Mackay	Hogg	Robertson	Ferguson D	Baird	Millar	Berry	Ferguson I (11)	Snodin (7)
Dec 2nd	Smith	McLaren	Snodin	Levein	Mackay	Van de Ven	Robertson	Ferguson D	Baird	Millar	Berry	Ferguson I	Foster (5)
5th	Walker	McLaren	McKinlay	Levein	Mackay	Van de Ven	Robertson	Ferguson D	Baird	Millar	Ferguson I	Preston (11)	Snodin
12th	Walker	McLaren	McKinlay	Levein	Mackay	Van de Ven	Robertson	Ferguson D	Ferguson I	Millar	Preston	Foster	Boothroyd (8)
19th	Walker	McLaren	McKinlay	Levein	Mackay	Van de Ven	Robertson	Ferguson D	Ferguson I	Millar	Preston	Foster (9)	Boothroyd (11)
26th	Walker	McLaren	Snodin	Levein	Mackay	Van de Ven	Robertson	Ferguson D	Foster	Millar	Preston	Bannon (11)	Boothroyd (9)
Jan 2nd	Walker	McLaren	Snodin	Levein	Mackay	Van de Ven	Robertson	Ferguson D	Baird	Millar	Mauchlen	Preston (5)	Berry
9th	Walker	McLaren	Snodin	Levein	Mackay	Van de Ven	Robertson	Ferguson D	Baird	Mauchlen	Preston	Foster (11)	Boothroyd (8)
20th	Walker	McLaren	Snodin	Levein	Mackay	Van de Ven	Robertson	Ferguson D	Baird	Mauchlen	Preston	Ferguson (11)	McKinlay
23rd	Walker	McLaren	Snodin	Levein	Mackay	Van de Ven	Robertson	Ferguson D	Baird	Mauchlen	Preston	Foster (5)	McKinlay
30th	Walker	McLaren	Snodin	Levein	Mackay	Van de Ven	Robertson	Ferguson D	Baird	Mauchlen	Preston	Boothroyd(11)	McKinlay (7)
Feb 3rd	Walker	McLaren	Snodin	Hogg	Mackay	Van De Ven	Robertson	Ferguson D	Baird	Millar	Preston	Ferguson I (11)	Berry
6th	Walker	McLaren	McKinlay	Levein	Mackay	Van de Ven	Robertson	Ferguson D	Baird	Mauchlen	Ferguson I	Bannon (9)	Boothroyd (11)
13th	Walker	McLaren	McKinlay	Berry	Mackay	Van de Ven	Robertson	Ferguson D	Ferguson I	Mauchlen	Preston	Thomas (11)	Bannon (9)
20th	Walker	McLaren	McKinlay	Berry	Mackay	Van de Ven	Robertson	Millar	Ferguson I	Mauchlen	Preston	Wright (10)	Thomas
27th	Walker	McLaren	McKinlay	Berry	Mackay	Van de Ven	Robertson	Ferguson D	Ferguson I	Millar	Preston	Wright (8)	Bannon (9)
Mar 6th	Walker	McLaren	McKinlay	Berry	Mackay	Wright	Robertson	Ferguson D	Baird	Mauchlen	Preston	Bannon (10)	Thomas (7)
10th	Walker	McLaren	McKinlay	Berry	Mackay	Levein	Robertson	Ferguson D	Baird	Millar	Preston	Wright (3)	Ferguson I (11)
13th	Walker	McLaren	Snodin	Levein	Hogg	Wright	Robertson	Ferguson D	Baird	Millar	Ferguson I	Mauchlen (6)	Bannon (11)
20th	Walker	McLaren	Snodin	Levein	Hogg	Van de Ven	Robertson	Ferguson D	Baird	Millar	Ferguson I	Mackay (5)	Bannon (11)
27th	Walker	McLaren	Snodin	Levein	Mackay	Berry	Robertson	Wright	Baird	Millar	Preston	Ferguson I (9)	McKinlay (3)
Apr 3rd	Walker	McLaren	McKinlay	Levein	Mackay	Van de Ven	Robertson	Ferguson D	Baird	Millar	Preston	Ferguson I (11)	Snodin (8)
10th	Walker	McLaren	McKinlay	Levein	Mackay	Van de Ven	Robertson	Ferguson D	Baird	Millar	Preston	Ferguson I (11)	Berry (2)
14th	Walker	Berry	McKinlay	Levein	Mackay	Van de Ven	Robertson	Ferguson D	Baird	Millar	Bannon	Snodin	Harrison
17th	Baird	Hogg	McKinlay	Levein	Mackay	Van de Ven	Robertson	Ferguson D	Ferguson I	Berry	Bannon	Harrison (6)	Snodin (3)
20th	Smith	McLaren	Snodin	Levein	Mackay	Hogg	Robertson	Ferguson D	Baird	Millar	Bannon	Ferguson I (6)	Ferguson I
May 1st	Smith	McLaren	Snodin	Levein	Mackay	Van de Ven	Robertson	Ferguson D	Baird	Berry	Bannon	Ferguson I (11)	Hogg
5th	Smith	Hogg	McKinlay	Harrison	McLaren	Van de Ven	Foster	Ferguson D	Baird*	Mackay	Robertson	Thomas (7)	Thomas
8th	Smith	Hogg	McKinlay	Levein	McLaren	Harrison	Johnston	Ferguson D	Thomas	Mackay	Robertson	Ferguson I (4)	Locke
15th	Smith	Hogg	McKinlay	Harrison	Berry	Van de Ven	Johnston	Ferguson D	Thomas	Mackay	Robertson	Ferguson I (11)	Locke (8)

Power run - Glyn Snodin leaves a defender trailing in the Scottish Cup tie against Highland League Huntly at Tynecastle. DC Thomson

Season 1993-94

Date			Opponents		Score	Crowd	Scorers
Aug	7th	L	Rangers	a	1-2	43,261	Ferguson
	11th	LC2	Stranraer	h	2-0	5,332	Robertson 2
	14th	L	Raith Rovers	h	1-0	8,587	Robertson
	21st	L	Hibernian	h	1-0	17,283	A. Johnston
	25th	LC3	Falkirk	h	0-1	9,583	-
	28th	L	Dundee United	a	0-0	8,502	-
Sep	4th	L	Partick Thistle	h	2-1	7,273	Levein; Fashanu
	11th	L	Motherwell	a	0-2	7,662	-
	14th	UEF1	Atletico Madrid	h	2-1	15,596	Colquhoun; Robertson
	18th	L	Kilmarnock	h	0-1	8,309	-
	25th	L	Celtic	h	1-0	14,761	Robertson
	29th	UEF1	Atletico Madrid	a	0-3 (2-4)	35,000	-
Oct	2nd	L	Dundee	a	0-2	5,021	-
	5th	L	Aberdeen	a	0-0	13,798	-
	9th	L	St Johnstone	h	1-1	6,028	Robertson
	16th	L	Raith Rovers	a	0-1	5,375	-
	23rd	L	Partick Thistle	a	0-0	7,895	-
	30th	L	Hibernian	a	2-0	18,952	Colquhoun 2
Nov	3rd	L	Rangers	h	2-2	18,370	Mackay; Colquhoun
	6th	L	Dundee United	h	1-1	8,362	M. Johnston
	13th	L	Dundee	h	1-2	7,681	Pittman o.g.
	20th	L	Celtic	a	0-0	25,981	-
	30th	L	Kilmarnock	a	0-0	6,948	-
Dec	4th	L	Aberdeen	h	1-1	9,402	Colquhoun
	11th	L	St Johnstone	a	0-2	4,612	-
	15th	L	Motherwell	h	2-3	5,531	M. Johnston; Leitch
	18th	L	Raith Rovers	h	0-1	6,227	-
	27th	L	Rangers	a	2-2	45,116	Millar; Robertson (pen)
Jan	8th	L	Dundee United	a	0-3	8,583	-
	12th	L	Hibernian	h	1-1	24,139	Millar
	15th	L	Partick Thistle	h	1-0	7,619	Millar
	22nd	L	Kilmarnock	h	1-1	9,204	Robertson
	29th	SC3	Partick Thistle	a	1-0	9,619	M. Johnston
Feb	5th	L	Motherwell	a	1-1	7,009	Robertson
	12th	L	Celtic	h	0-2	14,049	-
	20th	SC4	Hibernian	a	2-1	20,700	Robertson; Foster
Mar	1st	L	Dundee	a	2-0	3,965	M. Johnston 2
	5th	L	Aberdeen	a	1-0	13,059	Leitch
	12th	SCQ	Rangers	a	0-2	41,666	-
	19th	L	Raith Rovers	a	2-2	5,697	Colquhoun; Levein
	26th	L	Rangers	h	1-2	18,108	Foster
	30th	L	Motherwell	h	0-0	7,979	-
Apr	2nd	L	Kilmarnock	a	1-0	8,022	Millar
	6th	L	St Johnstone	h	2-2	8,938	McGowne o.g.; Robertson
	9th	L	Celtic	a	2-2	18,761	Colquhoun; Frail
	16th	L	Dundee	h	0-2	7,028	-
	23rd	L	St Johnstone	a	0-0	6,763	-
	26th	L	Aberdeen	h	1-1	13,811	Robertson (pen)
	30th	L	Hibernian	a	0-0	14,344	-
May	7th	L	Dundee United	h	2-0	13,827	Frail; Levein
	14th	L	Partick Thistle	a	1-0	10,012	McLaren

George Wright - on verge of big breakthrough in the Hearts midfield.

The Record		
League	-	Seventh Place, Premier Division
League Cup	-	Third round
Scottish Cup	-	Quarter final
UEFA Cup	-	First Round
Top Scorer	-	John Robertson (12 goals)
Av. Home gate	-	11,000
Players used	-	25
Sent off (booked)	-	Four (53)

Appearances

	League	L/Cup	S/Cup	UEFA	Total
Tosh McKinlay	43	2	3	2	50
John Colquhoun	38 (6)	2	3	2 (1)	45+3s (7)
Alan McLaren	37 (1)	0	3	2	42 (1)
Gary Mackay	34 (1)	2	2	2	40+2s (1)
John Robertson	32 (8)	2 (2)	2 (1)	2 (1)	38+5s (12)
Craig Levein	30 (3)	2	3	2	37 (3)
Gary Locke	29	2	1	2	34+5s
Neil Berry	30	1	3	0	34
Maurice Johnston	31 (4)	0	3 (1)	0	34 (5)
Henry Smith	27	2	3	2	34
Scott Leitch	24 (2)	0	3	2	29+4s (2)
Jim Weir	25	0	1	1	27+2s
John Millar	16 (4)	0	2	0	18+4s (4)
Graeme Hogg	16	1	0	1	18+1s
Nicky Walker	17	0	0	0	17
Justin Fashanu	10 (1)	2	0	2	14+1s (1)
George Wright	10	2	0	0	12+3s
Wayne Foster	8 (1)	0	1 (1)	0	9+12s (2)
Stevie Frail	9 (2)	0	0	0	9 (2)
Kevin Thomas	7	0	0	0	7+9s
Allan Johnston	5 (1)	0	0	0	5+25s (1)

Scottish League Premier Division

		Home			Away			Goals		
	P	W	D	L	W	D	L	F	A	PTS
Rangers	44	12	6	4	10	8	4	74	41	58
Aberdeen	44	11	9	2	6	12	4	58	36	55
Motherwell	44	11	7	4	9	7	6	58	43	54
Celtic	44	8	11	3	7	9	6	51	38	50
Hibernian	44	11	7	4	5	8	9	53	48	47
Dundee United	44	5	11	6	6	9	7	47	48	42
Hearts	**44**	**6**	**9**	**7**	**5**	**11**	**6**	**37**	**43**	**42**
Kilmarnock	44	6	10	6	6	6	10	36	45	40
Partick Thistle	44	9	8	5	3	8	11	46	57	40
St Johnstone	44	7	7	8	3	13	6	35	47	40
Raith Rovers	44	3	12	7	3	7	12	46	80	31
Dundee	44	6	7	9	2	6	14	42	57	29

Appearances (Ctd.)

	League	L/Cup	S/Cup	UEFA	Total
Ian Ferguson	3 (1)	0	0	0	3+4s (1)
Peter Van De Ven	2	1	0	0	3
Tommy Harrison	1	0	0	0	1
Ally Mauchlen	0	1	0	0	1

Heart of Midlothian F.C. Line-Ups 1993-94

	1	2	3	4	5	6	7	8	9	10	11	12	14
Aug 7th	Smith	Locke	McKinlay	Levein	Berry	Van de Ven	Colquhoun	Mackay	Fashanu	Wright	Robertson	Ferguson (9)	Johnston A(11)
11th	Smith	Locke	McKinlay	Levein	Berry	Van de Ven	Colquhoun	Mackay	Fashanu	Wright	Robertson	Johnston A (7)	Thomas (9)
14th	Smith	Locke	McKinlay	Levein	Berry	Van de Ven	Colquhoun	Mackay	Fashanu	Wright	Robertson	Johnston A(11)	Thomas (9)
21st	Smith	Locke	McKinlay	Levein	Berry	Weir	Colquhoun	Mackay	Fashanu	Wright	Robertson	Johnston A(5)	Thomas (11)
25th	Smith	Locke	McKinlay	Levein	Hogg	Mauchlan	Colquhoun	Mackay	Fashanu	Wright	Robertson	Johnston A(6)	Thomas (9)
28th	Smith	Locke	McKinlay	Levein	Hogg	Weir	Colquhoun	Mackay	Fashanu	Wright	Thomas	Johnston A(9)	Leitch (2)
Sep 4th	Smith	Locke	McKinlay	Levein	Hogg	Berry	Colquhoun	Mackay	Fashanu*	Wright	Thomas	Johnston A(11)	Leitch (7)
11th	Smith	Locke	McKinlay	Levein	Berry	McLaren	Colquhoun	Mackay	Thomas	Wright	Robertson	Johnston A(11)	Leitch (7)
14th	Smith	Locke	McKinlay	Levein	Weir	McLaren	Colquhoun	Mackay	Fashanu	Leitch	Robertson	Johnston A	Thomas (11)
18th	Smith	Locke	McKinlay	Levein	Weir	McLaren	Colquhoun	Mackay	Johnston A	Leitch	Robertson	Hogg (5)	Thomas (6)
25th	Smith	Locke	McKinlay	Levein	Hogg	McLaren	Colquhoun	Mackay	Fashanu	Leitch	Robertson	Ferguson (9)	Weir (10)
29th	Smith	Locke	McKinlay	Levein	Hogg	McLaren	Colquhoun	Mackay	Fashanu	Leitch	Robertson	Ferguson (9)	Thomas (11)
Oct 2nd	Walker	Locke	McKinlay	Berry	Hogg	McLaren	Colquhoun	Weir	Fashanu	Leitch	Robertson	Ferguson (8)	Johnston A (7)
5th	Walker	Locke	McKinlay	McLaren	Hogg	Berry	Weir	Mackay	Fashanu	Leitch	Ferguson	Colquhoun (11)	Robertson
9th	Walker	Locke	McKinlay	McLaren	Hogg	Berry	Ferguson	Mackay	Fashanu	Leitch	Robertson	Weir	Johnston A(6)
16th	Walker	Locke	McKinlay	McLaren	Hogg	Weir	Ferguson	Mackay	Fashanu	Harrison	Robertson	Johnston A(11)	Colquhoun (9)
23rd	Walker	McLaren	McKinlay	Levein	Hogg	Weir	Mackay	Leitch	Colquhoun	Johnston A	Johnston M	Berry	Thomas
30th	Walker	Weir	McKinlay	Levein	Hogg	McLaren	Leitch	Locke	Colquhoun	Johnston M	Robertson	Mackay	Johnston A (9)
Nov 3rd	Walker	Weir	Wright	Levein	Hogg	McLaren	Locke	Leitch	Colquhoun	Johnston M	Robertson	Johnston A (2)	Mackay (4)
6th	Walker	Locke	McKinlay	Wright	Hogg	McLaren	Leitch	Mackay	Colquhoun	Johnston M	Robertson	Johnston A (8)	Berry
13th	Walker	Locke	McKinlay	Wright	Hogg	McLaren	Leitch	Mackay	Colquhoun	Johnston M	Robertson	Johnston A (8)	Thomas (11)
20th	Walker	Weir	McKinlay	McLaren	Hogg	Berry	Leitch	Locke	Colquhoun	Johnston M	Johnston A	Robertson	Millar (7)
30th	Walker	Weir	McKinlay	McLaren	Hogg	Leitch	Colquhoun	Locke	Robertson	Johnston M	Mackay	Johnston A (5)	Thomas (10)
Dec 4th	Walker	Weir	McKinlay	McLaren	Berry	Leitch	Colquhoun	Mackay	Thomas	Robertson	Johnston M	Locke	Johnston A (7)
11th	Walker	Weir	McKinlay	McLaren	Berry	Leitch	Colquhoun	Mackay	Thomas	Robertson	Johnston M	Fashanu (11)	Locke (3)
15th	Walker	Weir	McKinlay	McLaren	Berry	Leitch	Colquhoun	Johnston M	Thomas	Locke	Mackay	Foster (7)	Millar (10)
18th	Walker	Weir	McKinlay	McLaren	Berry	Leitch	Colquhoun	Mackay	Thomas	Johnston M	Locke	Johnston A (2)	Foster (9)
27th	Walker	Berry	McKinlay	McLaren	Weir	Locke	Johnston A	Johnston M	Colquhoun	Millar	Foster	Robertson (9)	Wright (7)
Jan 8th	Walker	Berry	McKinlay	McLaren	Weir	Locke	Johnston A	Leitch	Colquhoun	Millar	Foster	Mackay (2)	Robertson (7)
12th	Smith	Locke	McKinlay	Levein	Berry	McLaren	Leitch	Mackay	Foster	Johnston M	Robertson	Colquhoun (9)	Millar (2)
15th	Smith	McLaren	McKinlay	Levein	Berry	Millar	Colquhoun	Mackay	Leitch	Johnston M	Robertson	Foster	Locke (9)
22nd	Smith	Locke	McKinlay	Levein	Berry	McLaren	Colquhoun	Mackay	Leitch	Johnston M	Robertson	Foster (10)	Johnston A
29th	Smith	McLaren	McKinlay	Levein	Berry	Locke	Colquhoun*	Mackay	Leitch	Johnston M	Robertson	Foster (10)	Wright (9)
Feb 5th*	Smith	Locke	McKinlay	Levein	Berry	McLaren	Leitch	Mackay	Foster	Johnston M	Robertson	Wright (11)	Johnston A
12th	Smith	Locke	McKinlay	Levein	Weir	McLaren	Leitch	Mackay	Foster	Johnston M	Robertson	Wright	Johnston A (2)
20th	Smith	McLaren	McKinlay	Levein	Berry	Millar	Colquhoun	Mackay	Robertson	Johnston M	Leitch	Foster (9)	Weir (11)
Mar 1st	Smith	Weir	McKinlay	Levein	Berry	McLaren	Colquhoun	Mackay	Foster	Johnston M	Millar	Robertson	Leitch (8)
5th	Smith	Weir	McKinlay	Levein	Berry	McLaren	Colquhoun	Leitch	Foster	Johnston M	Millar	Robertson (7)	Locke (9)
12th	Smith	Weir	McKinlay	Levein	Berry	McLaren	Colquhoun	Leitch	Foster	Johnston M	Millar	Robertson (7)	Locke (5)
19th	Smith	Weir	McKinlay	Levein	Hogg	McLaren	Colquhoun	Leitch	Foster	Johnston M	Millar	Robertson (9)	Locke (3)
26th	Smith	Weir	McKinlay	Levein	Hogg	McLaren	Colquhoun	Locke	Robertson	Johnston M	Millar	Johnston A (3)	Foster (2)
29th	Smith	Wright	McKinlay	Levein	Berry	McLaren	Colquhoun	Mackay	Robertson	Johnston M	Millar	Foster (9)	Johnston A (2)
Apr 2nd	Smith	Frail	McKinlay	Levein	Berry	McLaren	Colquhoun	Mackay	Robertson	Johnston M	Millar	Foster (9)	Johnston A
6th	Smith	Frail	McKinlay	Levein	Berry	McLaren	Colquhoun	Mackay	Robertson	Johnston M	Millar	Foster	Johnston A (6)
9th	Smith	Frail	McKinlay	Levein	Berry	McLaren	Colquhoun	Mackay	Robertson	Johnston M	Millar	Foster (7)	Johnston A (8)
16th	Smith	Frail	McKinlay	Levein	Berry	Weir	Colquhoun	Mackay	Robertson	Johnston M	Millar	Johnston A (7)	Foster (11)
23rd	Smith	Frail	McKinlay	Levein	Berry	Weir	Colquhoun	Mackay	Robertson	Johnston M	Millar	Foster	Johnston A
27th	Smith	Frail	McKinlay	Levein	Berry	McLaren	Colquhoun	Mackay	Robertson	Johnston M	Millar	Foster	Johnston A
30th	Smith	Frail	McKinlay	Levein	Berry	McLaren	Colquhoun	Mackay	Robertson	Johnston M	Millar	Johnston A	Foster (10)
May 7th	Smith	Frail	McKinlay	Levein	Berry	McLaren	Colquhoun	Locke	Robertson	Johnston M	Millar	Johnston A	Foster (10)
14th	Smith	Frail	McKinlay	Levein	Weir	McLaren	Colquhoun	Mackay	Robertson	Johnston M	Locke	Foster	Millar (5)

Heart of Midlothian F.C. 1993-94. (BACK, left to right) - Scott Leitch, Adrian Boothroyd, Neil Berry, Graeme Hogg, Ian Ferguson, Tosh McKinlay. MIDDLE - Alan Rae (physio), John Millar, George Wright, Wayne Foster, Justin Fashanu, Peter Van De Ven, Gary Mackay, John Colquhoun, Hugh McCann (assistant-manager). FRONT - Nicky Walker, John Robertson, Craig Levein, Sandy Clark (manager), Alan McLaren, Ally Mauchlen, Henry Smith.

DC Thomson

Season 1994-95

Date			Opponents		Score	Crowd	Scorers
Aug	13th	L	Aberdeen	a	1-3	14,238	Colquhoun
	16th	LC2	Dumbarton	a	4-0	2,700	J. Millar; Robertson; A. Johnston 2
	20th	L	Motherwell	a	1-1	8,249	M. Johnston
	27th	L	Hibernian	h	0-1	12,371	-
	31st	LC3	St Johnstone	h	2-4	8,467	Locke; Colquhoun
Sep	11th	L	Rangers	a	0-3	41,041	-
	17th	L	Dundee United	h	2-1	7,392	Thomas; Frail
	24th	L	Kilmarnock	h	3-0	9,302	J. Millar; McLaren; Mackay
Oct	1st	L	Falkirk	a	1-2	7,581	Robertson
	8th	L	Partick Thistle	a	1-0	5,384	Robertson
	15th	L	Celtic	h	1-0	12,086	Robertson
	22nd	L	Aberdeen	h	2-0	10,655	Frail; Robertson
	29th	L	Hibernian	a	1-2	13,606	Robertson (pen)
Nov	5th	L	Motherwell	h	1-2	8,889	Robertson
	9th	L	Rangers	h	1-1	12,347	Colquhoun
	19th	L	Dundee United	a	2-5	7,717	Thomas 2
	26th	L	Kilmarnock	a	1-3	8,029	Robertson
Dec	3rd	L	Falkirk	h	1-1	8,960	Thomas
	26th	L	Partick Thistle	h	3-0	8,920	Hagen; Robertson; Bett
	31st	L	Aberdeen	a	1-3	11,392	Thomas
Jan	8th	L	Motherwell	a	2-1	5,117	Hamilton; C. Miller
	11th	L	Celtic	a	1-1	26,491	Bett (pen)
	14th	L	Dundee United	h	2-0	8,656	J. Millar; Jamieson
	18th	L	Hibernian	h	2-0	12,630	McPherson; J. Millar
	21st	L	Rangers	a	0-1	44,231	-
Feb	1st	SC3	Clydebank	a	1-1	3,606	Robertson (pen)
	4th	L	Falkirk	a	0-2	6,028	-
	7th	SC3R	Clydebank	h	2-1	8,503	Robertson; Thomas
	11th	L	Kilmarnock	h	2-2	8,374	J. Millar; Mackay
	20th	SC4	Rangers	h	4-2	12,375	C. Miller; McPherson; Robertson; Thomas
	25th	L	Celtic	h	1-1	11,185	Jamieson
Mar	12th	SCQ	Dundee United	h	2-0	12,515	J. Millar 2
	18th	L	Rangers	h	2-1	9,806	Robertson; J. Millar
	21st	L	Dundee United	a	1-1	6,862	A. Johnston
Apr	1st	L	Falkirk	h	0-1	9,003	-
	4th	L	Partick Thistle	a*	1-3	5,500	J. Millar
	8th	SCS	Airdrie	Hamp	0-1	22,538	-
	12th	L	Kilmarnock	a	2-3	7,239	Cramb; Jamieson
	15th	L	Partick Thistle	h	0-1	9,007	-
	19th	L	Celtic	a	1-0	18,638	Hagen
	29th	L	Aberdeen	h	1-2	11,466	McPherson
May	6th	L	Hibernian	a	1-3	7,146	Hagen
	13th	L	Motherwell	h	2-0	11,172	Hamilton; Robertson (pen)

* Replay of earlier game played on April 4th but abandoned at half-time with score 0-0 due to snowbound pitch

Mo Johnston - former Scotland striker was an ambitious signing

Appearances

	League	L/Cup	S/Cup	Total
John Robertson	27 (10)	2 (1)	5 (3)	34+4s (14)
Neil Berry	29	1	2	32
Stevie Frail	25 (2)	2	4	31 (2)
Jim Bett	26 (2)	0	4	30 (2)
Craig Levein	24	2	4	30
John Millar	25 (6)	2 (1)	3 (2)	30+3s (9)
Dave McPherson	23 (2)	0	5 (1)	28 (3)
Gary Mackay	21 (2)	1	4	26+14s (2)
John Colquhoun	23 (2)	2 (1)	2	27+11s (3)
Craig Nelson	20	0	5	25
David Hagen	16 (3)	0	5	21+4s (3)
Colin Miller	16 (1)	0	3 (1)	19+1s (2)
Scott Leitch	18	0	0	18+5s
Brian Hamilton	13 (2)	0	5	18 (2)
Willie Jamieson	13 (2)	0	2	15+3s (2)
Henry Smith	14	0	0	14
Kevin Thomas	11 (5)	0	2 (2)	13+10s (7)
Tosh McKinlay	11	1	0	12
Alan McLaren	10 (1)	2	0	12 (1)
Allan Johnston	9 (1)	2 (2)	0	11+12s (3)
Fraser Wishart	8	0	0	8
Gary Locke	3	1 (1)	0	4+6s (1)
Nicky Walker	2	2	0	4
Maurice Johnston	3 (1)	1	0	4+1s (1)
Jim Weir	2	1	0	3+1s
Colin Cramb	3 (1)	0	0	3+3s (1)
Walter Kidd	1	0	0	1

The Record

League	-	**Sixth Place, Premier Division**
League Cup	-	**Second round**
Scottish Cup	-	**Semi-final**
Top Scorer	-	**John Robertson (14 goals)**
Av. Home gate	-	**10,100**
Players used	-	**31**
Sent off (booked)	-	**Three (58)**

Scottish League Premier Division

		Home			Away			Goals		
	P	W	D	L	W	D	L	F	A	PTS
Rangers	36	11	5	2	9	4	5	60-	35	69
Motherwell	36	8	6	4	6	6	6	50-	50	54
Hibernian	36	9	7	2	3	10	5	49-	37	53
Celtic	36	6	8	4	5	10	3	39-	33	51
Falkirk	36	8	3	7	4	9	5	48-	47	48
Hearts	**36**	**9**	**4**	**5**	**3**	**3**	**12**	**44-**	**51**	**43**
Kilmarnock	36	8	4	6	3	6	9	40-	48	43
Partick Thistle	36	4	9	5	6	4	8	40-	50	43
Aberdeen**	36	7	7	4	3	4	11	43-	46	41
Dundee United*	36	6	6	6	3	3	12	40-	56	36

* Relegated; ** Won play-off 6-1 on aggregate against Division One Runners-up, Dunfermline.

Appearances (Ctd.)

	League	L/Cup	S/Cup	Total
George Wright	0	0	0	0+2s
Wayne Foster	0	0	0	0+1s
Tommy Harrison	0	0	0	0+1s
Graeme Hogg	0	0	0	0+1s

Heart of Midlothian F.C. Line-Ups 1994-95

	1	2	3	4	5	6	7	8	9	10	11	12	14	15
Aug 13th	Smith	Frail	McKinlay	Locke	Weir	McLaren	Colquhoun	Mackay	Robertson	Leitch	Millar J	Johnston A (4)	Thomas (3)	O'Connor (6)
16th	Walker	Frail	McKinlay	Levein	Mackay	McLaren	Colquhoun	Johnston A	Robertson	Johnston M	Millar J	Leitch (3)	Weir (5)	Smith
20th	Walker	Frai!	McKinlay	Levein	Weir	McLaren	Colquhoun	Mackay	Robertson	Johnston M	Millar J	Johnston A (8)	Leitch (9)	Smith
27th	Walker	Frail	McKinlay	Levein	Berry	McLaren	Colquhoun	Mackay	Robertson	Johnston M	Leitch	Johnston A (11)	Millar J (3)	Smith
31st	Walker	Frail*	Weir	Levein	Berry	McLaren	Colquhoun	Locke	Robertson	Johnston A	Millar J	Foster (14)	Harrison (10)	Smith
Sep 11th	Smith	Locke	McKinlay	Levein	Berry	McLaren	Colquhoun	Leitch	Johnston M	Millar J	Robertson	Johnston A (11)	Hogg (2)	O'Connor
17th	Smith	Frail	McKinlay	Levein	Berry	McLaren	Colquhoun	Leitch	Robertson	Millar J	Thomas	Johnston M(11)	Johnston A (7)	Hogarth
24th	Smith	Frail	McKinlay	Levein	Berry	McLaren	Colquhoun	Leitch	Robertson	Millar J	Thomas	Johnston A (11)	Mackay (7)	Hogarth
Oct 1st	Smith	Frail	McKinlay	Levein	Berry	McLaren	Colquhoun	Leitch	Robertson	Millar J	Thomas	Johnston A (8)	Mackay (7)	O'Connor
8th	Smith	Frail	McKinlay	Levein	Berry	McLaren	Colquhoun	Bett	Robertson	Millar J	Thomas	Johnston A (11)	Mackay (7)	O' Connor
15th	Smith	Frail	McKinlay	Levein	Berry	McLaren	Mackay	Bett	Robertson	Leitch	Thomas	Colquhoun (11)	Millar (10)	O'Connor
22nd	Smith	Frail	McKinlay	Levein	Berry	McLaren	Mackay	Bett	Robertson	Millar J	Johnston A	Colquhoun (10)	Leitch (7)	O'Connor
29th	Smith	Frail	McKinlay	Levein	Berry	McPherson	Mackay	Bett	Robertson	Leitch	Johnston A	Colquhoun (7)	Millar J (10)	O'Connor
Nov 6th	Smith	Frail	Millar J	Bett	Berry	McPherson	Colquhoun	Mackay	Robertson	Leitch	Johnston A	Thomas (11)	Locke	O'Connor
9th	Smith	Frail	Millar J	Mackay	Berry	McPherson	Colquhoun	Bett	Robertson	Leitch	Johnston A	Thomas (11)	Wright (7)	O'Connor
19th	Smith	Miller C	Millar J	Mackay	Berry	McPherson	Colquhoun	Bett	Robertson	Leitch	Thomas	Johnston A	Locke (4)	O'Connor
26th	Smith	Locke	Miller C	Mackay	Kidd	McPherson	Colquhoun	Bett	Robertson	Millar J	Thomas	Leitch (11)	Johnston A (2)	O'Connor
Dec 3rd	Nelson	Frail	Miller C	Jamieson	Berry	McPherson	Colquhoun	Bett	Robertson	Millar J	Thomas	Mackay (8)	Hagen (11)	Smith
26th	Nelson	Frail	Miller C	Jamieson	Berry	McPherson	Colquhoun	Bett	Robertson	Millar J	Hagen	Thomas (11)	Mackay (3)	Smith
31st	Nelson	Frail	Miller C	Jamieson	Berry	McPherson	Colquhoun	Bett	Robertson	Mackay	Hagen	Thomas (9)	Wright (4)	Smith
Jan 8th	Nelson	Frail	Miller C	Jamieson	Berry	McPherson	Hamilton	Bett	Thomas	Leitch	Hagen	Robertson (10)	Mackay (9)	Smith
11th	Nelson	Frail	Miller C	Jamieson	Berry	McPherson	Hamilton	Bett	Thomas	Leitch	Hagen	Robertson (9)	Mackay (10)	Smith
14th	Nelson	Frail	Miller C	Jamieson	Berry	McPherson	Hamilton	Bett	Robertson	Millar J	Hagen	Mackay (9)	Colquhoun (8)	Smith
18th	Nelson	Frail	Miller C	Levein	Jamieson	McPherson	Hamilton	Bett	Robertson	Millar J	Hagen	Mackay (9)	Colquhoun (8)	Smith
21st	Nelson	Frail	Miller C	Levein	Jamieson	McPherson	Hamilton	Bett	Colquhoun	Millar J	Hagen	Mackay (9)	Robertson (4)	Smith
Feb 1st	Nelson	Frail	Miller C	Levein	Mackay	McPherson	Hamilton	Bett	Thomas	Robertson	Hagen	Colquhoun (8)	Jamieson (9)	Smith
4th	Nelson	Frail	Miller C	Levein	Berry	McPherson	Hamilton	Bett	Robertson	Mackay	Hagen	Colquhoun (3)	Johnston A (10)	Smith
7th	Nelson	Frail	Berry	Levein	Bett	McPherson	Colquhoun	Hamilton	Thomas	Robertson	Hagen	Mackay (7)	Miller C (9)	Smith
11th	Nelson	Frail	Berry	Levein	Bett	McPherson	Colquhoun	Hamilton	Robertson	Millar J	Thomas	Mackay (6)	Hagen (3)	Smith
20th	Nelson	Frail	Miller C	Levein	Bett	McPherson	Hamilton	Mackay	Robertson	Millar J	Hagen	Colquhoun (3)	Thomas (11)	Smith
25th	Nelson	Frail	Leitch	Levein	Jamieson	McPherson	Hamilton	Mackay	Johnston A	Millar J	Hagen	Colquhoun (9)	Thomas (3)	Smith
Mar 12th	Nelson	Frail	Miller C	Berry	Jamieson	McPherson	Colquhoun	Hamilton	Robertson	Mackay	Hagen	Thomas (7)	Leitch (11)	Smith
18th	Nelson	Frail	Leitch	Berry	Jamieson	McPherson	Mackay	Bett	Robertson	Millar J	Hagen	Johnston A (11)	Colquhoun (9)	Smith
21st	Nelson	Frail	Leitch	Levein	Jamieson	Berry	Mackay	Bett	Johnston A	Millar J	Hagen	Cramb (11)	Locke (2)	Smith
Apr 1st	Nelson	Wishart	Miller C	Levein	Berry	McPherson	Mackay	Bett	Robertson	Leitch	Johnston A	Hagen (5)	Cramb (10)	Smith (1)
4th	Smith	Wishart	Miller C	Levein	Bett	McPherson	Colquhoun	Hamilton	Robertson	Millar J	Hagen	Thomas (9)	Mackay (3)	O'Connor
8th	Nelson	Mackay	Miller C	Levein	Jamieson	McPherson	Hamilton	Bett	Robertson	Millar J	Hagen	Colquhoun (7)	Thomas (5)	Smith
12th	Nelson	Wishart	Miller C	Levein	Berry	McPherson	Colquhoun	Mackay	Cramb	Millar J	Johnston A	Jamieson (6)	Locke (3)	Smith
15th	Nelson	Wishart	Leitch	Levein	Jamieson	Berry	Colquhoun	Mackay	Cramb	Millar J	Johnston A	Hagen (5)	Locke (3)	Smith
19th	Nelson	Wishart	Miller C	Levein	Jamieson	Berry	Hamilton	Bett	Cramb	Mackay	Hagen	Colquhoun (9)	Locke (2)	Smith
29th	Nelson	Wishart	Miller C	Levein	Berry	McPherson	Hamilton	Bett	Colquhoun	Mackay	Hagen	Robertson (9)	Jamieson (2)	Smith
May 6th	Nelson	Wishart	Miller C	Levein	Berry	McPherson	Colquhoun	Bett	Robertson	Hamilton	Hagen	Mackay (6)	Johnston A (3)	Smith
13th	Nelson	Mackay	Wishart	Levein	Berry	McPherson	Colquhoun	Bett	Robertson	Hamilton	Hagen	Cramb (7)	Locke (8)	Smith

It's there - John Millar and John Robertson jump with joy as the Hearts midfielder's header beats Dundee United keeper Guido Van De Kamp for Hearts second goal in the Scottish Cup quarter-final at Tynecastle.

DC Thomson

Season 1995-96

Date		Opponents		Score	Crowd	Scorers
Aug 19th	LC2	Alloa Athletic	h	3-0	7,732	McPherson; Hamilton; Leitch
26th	L	Motherwell	h	1-1	10,971	Hagen
30th	LC3	Dunfermline	h	2-1	12,498	Hagen; McPherson
Sep 9th	L	Falkirk	h	4-1	11,531	Lawrence; Colquhoun 2; Robertson (pen)
16th	L	Partick Thistle	a	0-2	5,534	-
20th	LCQ	Dundee	a	4-4*	9,528	Colquhoun; McPherson; Robertson (pen); Lawrence;
23rd	L	Celtic	h	0-4	13,696	-
Oct 1st	L	Hibernian	a	2-2	13,500	McPherson; Robertson^
4th	L	Aberdeen	h	1-2	10,927	Robertson
7th	L	Kilmarnock	a	1-3	6,721	Lawrence
14th	L	Raith Rovers	h	4-2	10,133	Millar; Lawrence 2; Robertson
21st	L	Rangers	a	1-4	45,155	Millar
28th	L	Falkirk	a	0-2	6,775	-
Nov 4th	L	Partick Thistle	h	3-0	10,094	McWilliams o.g; Millar; Eskilsson
7th	L	Motherwell	a	0-0	5,595	-
11th	L	Kilmarnock	h	2-1	10,442	Locke; Robertson
19th	L	Hibernian	h	2-1	12,074	Millar; Robertson (pen)
25th	L	Celtic	a	1-3	33,936	Bruno
Dec 2nd	L	Rangers	h	0-2	15,105	-
9th	L	Raith Rovers	a	1-1	6,348	Robertson
16th	L	Aberdeen	a	2-1	12,200	Johnston; Colquhoun
Jan 1st	L	Hibernian	a	1-2	15,500	Pointon
6th	L	Partick Thistle	a	1-0	4,900	McManus
10th	L	Motherwell	h	4-0	9,288	Fulton; Colquhoun; Johnston 2
13th	L	Falkirk	h	2-1	11,560	Robertson; Fulton
17th	L	Celtic	h	1-2	15,871	Robertson
20th	L	Rangers	a	3-0	45,096	Johnston 3
31st	SC3	Partick Thistle	h	1-0	13,770	Ritchie
Feb 3rd	L	Raith Rovers	h	2-0	10,183	Robertson; Locke
10th	L	Aberdeen	h	1-3	14,314	Robertson
17th	SC4	Kilmarnock	a	2-1	15,173	Berry; Ritchie
24th	L	Kilmarnock	a	2-0	8,022	Colquhoun; Robertson
Mar 2nd	L	Celtic	a	0-4	37,193	-
7th	SCQ	St Johnstone	a	2-1	9,951	Lawrence; McPherson
16th	L	Hibernian	h	1-1	14,923	Mackay
23rd	L	Partick Thistle	h	2-5	9,610	Johnston; Eskilsson
30th	L	Falkirk	a	2-0	5,164	Ritchie; Locke
Apr 6th	SCS	Aberdeen	Hampden	2-1	27,785	Robertson; Johnston
10th	L	Rangers	h	2-0	15,350	Pointon; Johnston
13th	L	Raith Rovers	a	3-1	4,765	Cameron; Pointon: Mackay
20th	L	Aberdeen	a	1-1	11,303	Locke
27th	L	Kilmarnock	h	1-0	11,329	McManus
May 4th	L	Motherwell	a	1-1	8,301	Cameron
18th	SCF	Rangers	Hampden	1-5	37,730	Colquhoun

* After extra-time, 3-3 after 90 minutesDundee win 5-4 on pens.

Gilles Rousset - the big Frenchman is a commanding figure in goal.

The Record		
League	-	Fourth Place, Premier Division
League Cup	-	Quarter-final
Scottish Cup	-	Runners-up
Top Scorer	-	John Robertson (14 goals)
Av. Home gate	-	12,100
Players used	-	34
Sent off (booked)	-	Five (47)

Appearances

	League	L/Cup	S/Cup	Total
Gary Locke	29 (4)	3	4	36 (4)
Allan Johnston	30 (8)	2	4 (1)	36+4s (9)
Paul Ritchie	28 (1)	0	5 (2)	33 (3)
John Robertson	27 (12)	2 (1)	2 (1)	31+8s (14)
Steve Fulton	26 (2)	0	4	30 (2)
Gilles Rousset	25	0	5	30
Dave McPherson	22 (1)	3 (3)	4 (1)	29+5s (5)
Gary Mackay	21 (2)	3	5	29+5s (2)
John Colquhoun	20 (5)	3 (1)	5 (1)	28+11s (7)
Pasquale Bruno	22 (1)	0	4	26 (1)
Neil Pointon	21 (3)	0	5	26+1s (3)
Alan Lawrence	17 (4)	1 (1)	3 (1)	21+10s (6)
Alan McManus	16 (2)	0	3	19+3s (2)
Neil Berry	16	1	1 (1)	18+4s (1)
John Millar	16 (4)	0	1	17+5s (4)
Brian Hamilton	8	3 (1)	0	11+4s (1)
Hans Eskilsson	9 (2)	0	0	9+2s (2)
David Hagen	5 (1)	3 (1)	0	8+2s (2)
David Winnie	6	2	0	8
Henry Smith	3	3	0	6
Craig Levein	1	2	0	3
Colin Cameron	4 (2)	0	0	4 (2)
Craig Nelson	4	0	0	4
Scott Leitch	4	1 (1)	0	5+3s
Paul Smith	4	0	0	4+5s (1)

Scottish League Premier Division

	P	Home W	Home D	Home L	Away W	Away D	Away L	Goals F-A	PTS
Rangers	36	13	3	2	14	3	1	85-25	87
Celtic	36	12	5	1	12	6	0	74-25	83
Aberdeen	36	11	1	6	5	6	7	52-45	55
Hearts	**36**	**10**	**2**	**6**	**6**	**5**	**7**	**55-53**	**55**
Hibernian	36	7	5	6	4	5	9	43-57	43
Raith Rovers	36	7	5	6	5	2	11	41-57	43
Kilmarnock	36	8	4	6	3	4	11	39-54	41
Motherwell	36.	6	6	6	3	6	9	28-39	39
Partick Thistle	36	3	5	10	5	1	12	29-62	30
Falkirk	36	4	4	10	2	2	14	31-60	24

* Relegated after losing 3-2 on aggregate to First Division Runners-up, Dundee United

Appearances (Ctd.)

	League	L/Cup	S/Cup	Total
Gary O'Connor	3	0	0	3
Willie Jamieson	2	0	0	2+4s
Colin Miller	2	0	0	2+1s
Fraser Wishart	1	1	0	2
George Wright	2	0	0	2
Myles Hogarth	1	0	0	1
Kevin Thomas	0	0	0	0+3s
Gary Naysmith	0	0	0	0+1s
Stuart Callaghan	0	0	0	0+2s

Heart of Midlothian F.C. Line-Ups 1995-96

	1	2	3	4	5	6	7	8	9	10	11	12	14	15
Aug 19th	Smith	Locke	Wishart	Levein	McPherson	Hamilton	Colquhoun	Mackay	Hagen	Johnston	Leitch	Jamieson	Callaghan (11)	Nelson
26th	Smith	Locke	Wishart	Levein	McPherson	Hamilton	Colquhoun	Mackay	Hagen	Johnston	Lawrence	Leitch (11)	Berry (3)	Nelson
30th	Smith	Locke	Winnie	Levein	McPherson	Hamilton	Colquhoun	Mackay	Hagen	Johnston	Robertson	Lawrence (7)	Berry (4)	Nelson
Sep 9th	Smith	Locke	Winnie	Berry	McPherson	Hamilton	Colquhoun	Lawrence	Robertson	Johnston	Hagen	Jamieson (2)	Leitch (11)	Nelson
16th	Smith	Locke	Winnie	Berry	McPherson	Hamilton	Colquhoun	Lawrence	Robertson	Johnston	Leitch	Mackay (11)	Hagen (7)	Nelson
20th	Smith	Locke	Winnie	Berry	McPherson	Hamilton	Colquhoun	Mackay	Robertson	Hagen	Lawrence	Jamieson (3)	Leitch (8)	Nelson
23rd	Nelson	Locke	Ritchie	Jamieson	McPherson	Hamilton	Colquhoun	Leitch*	Robertson	Johnston	Hagen	Lawrence (6)	McManus	Smith
Oct 1st	Nelson	Locke	Winnie	Miller C	McPherson	Hamilton	Mackay*	Lawrence	Robertson	Wright	Hagen	Colquhoun (4)	Millar J (2)	Smith
4th	Nelson	Wright	Winnie	Miller C	McPherson	Hamilton	Leitch	Lawrence	Robertson	Millar J	Hagen	Colquhoun (8)	Ritchie	Smith
7th	O'Connor	Berry	Ritchie	Mackay	McPherson	Winnie	Colquhoun	Lawrence	Robertson	Millar J	Leitch	Hamilton (4)	Hagen (11)	Smith
14th	O'Connor	Locke	Pointon	Berry	McPherson	Hamilton	Colquhoun	Lawrence	Robertson	Fulton	Millar J	Johnston (7)	Jamieson (8)	Smith
21st	O'Connor	Locke	Pointon	Berry	McPherson	Hamilton	Johnston	Lawrence	Robertson	Fulton	Millar J	Colqhoun	Miller C (6)	Smith
28th	Rousset	Locke	Pointon	Jamieson	McPherson	Winnie	Colquhoun	Lawrence	Robertson	Fulton	Millar J	Johnston (3)	Berry (5)	O'Connor
Nov 4th	Rousset	Locke	Ritchie	Smith P	Berry	Bruno	Johnston	Lawrence	Robertson	Fulton	Millar J	Eskillson (8)	Jamieson (10)	O'Connor
7th	Rousset	Locke	Ritchie	Smith P	Berry	Bruno	Johnston	Eskilsson	Robertson	Fulton	Millar J	Lawrence	Jamieson	O'Connor
11th	Rousset	Locke	Ritchie	Smith P	Berry^	Bruno	Johnston	Eskilsson	Robertson	Fulton	Millar J	Lawrence (9)	Jamieson	Colquhoun
19th	Rousset	Locke	Ritchie	Mackay	Berry	Bruno	Johnston	Eskilsson	Robertson	Fulton	Millar J	Lawrence	Colquhoun (9)	Hamilton
25th	Rousset	Locke	Ritchie	Mackay	Berry	Bruno	Johnston	Eskilsson	Lawrence	Fulton	Millar J	Colquhoun (9)	Smith (4)	Nelson
Dec 2nd	Rousset	Locke	Ritchie	Mackay	Berry	Bruno	Johnston	Eskilsson	Robertson	Fulton	Millar J	Colquhoun (4)	Smith	Hamilton (10)
9th	Rousset	Locke*	Ritchie	Mackay	Berry*	Bruno	Johnston	Eskilsson	Robertson	Fulton	Millar J	Pointon (9)	Colquhoun (15)	Hamilton (10)
16th	Rousset	McManus	Ritchie	Mackay	Pointon	Bruno	Johnston	Eskilsson	Robertson	Fulton	Millar J	Colquhoun (8)	Smith	Hamilton (10)
Jan 1st	Rousset	McManus	Ritchie	Mackay	Pointon	Bruno	Johnston	Eskilsson	Robertson	Fulton	Millar J	Colquhoun (8)	Smith (4)	Lawrence (5)
6th	Rousset	Locke	Ritchie	Mackay	McManus	Bruno	Johnston	Lawrence	Colquhoun	Millar	Pointon	Robertson (8)	Smith	Fulton
10th	Rousset	Locke	Ritchie	Mackay	McManus	Bruno	Johnston	Colquhoun	Robertson	Fulton	Pointon	Lawrence (8)	Smith (4)	McPherson (6)
13th	Rousset	Locke	Ritchie	Mackay	McManus	Bruno	Johnston	Colquhoun	Robertson	Fulton	Pointon	Lawrence (8)	Smith	McPherson (11)
17th	Rousset	Locke	Ritchie	Mackay	McManus	Bruno	Johnston	Colquhoun	Robertson	Fulton	Pointon	Lawrence (9)	Smith	McPherson (5)
20th	Rousset	Locke	Ritchie	McPherson	McManus	Bruno	Johnston	Colquhoun	Lawrence	Fulton	Pointon	Robertson (8)	Mackay (6)	Nelson
31st	Rousset	Locke	Ritchie	McPherson	McManus	Bruno	Johnston	Colquhoun	Robertson	Mackay	Pointon	Lawrence	Smith	Millar J
Feb 3rd	Rousset	Locke	Ritchie	Eskillson	McManus	Bruno	Johnston	Colquhoun	Robertson	Mackay	Pointon	Lawrence (9)	Smith (6)	Millar J
10th	Rousset	Locke	Ritchie	McPherson	McManus	Bruno*	Johnston	Colquhoun	Robertson	Mackay	Pointon	Lawrence	Smith	Millar J (5)
17th	Rousset	Berry	Ritchie	McPherson	Mackay	Millar J	Johnston	Colquhoun	Lawrence	Fulton	Pointon	Robertson (7)	McManus (6)	Nelson
24th	Rousset	Locke	Ritchie	McPherson	McManus	Mackay	Colquhoun	Lawrence	Robertson	Fulton	Pointon	Johnston (9)	Smith (6)	Callaghan (8)
Mar 2nd	Nelson	Locke	Ritchie	McPherson	Bruno	Mackay	Johnston	Lawrence	Colquhoun	Fulton	Pointon	Robertson (5)	McManus	Millar J (8)
7th	Rousset	Locke	Ritchie	McPherson	Mackay	Bruno	Lawrence	Colquhoun	Robertson	Fulton	Pointon	Johnston (9)	Millar J (5)	McManus (10)
16th	Rousset	Locke	Ritchie	McPherson	McManus	Bruno	Johnston	Colquhoun	Robertson	Fulton	Pointon	Lawrence (5)	Mackay (11)	Millar J (6)
23rd	Rousset	Smith	Ritchie	McPherson	Mackay	Bruno	Johnston	Colquhoun	Lawrence	Fulton	Millar J	Eskilsson (9)	Robertson (11)	McManus(2)
30th	Rousset	Locke	Ritchie	Berry	McManus	Bruno	Johnston	Mackay	Colquhoun	Fulton	Pointon	McPherson (8)	Lawrence (9)	Thomas (9)
Apr 6th	Rousset	Locke	Ritchie	Mackay	McManus	Bruno	Johnston	Colquhoun	Lawrence	Fulton	Pointon	McPherson (10)	Thomas	Robertson (9)
10th	Rousset	McManus	Ritchie	Mackay	McPherson	Bruno	Johnston	Cameron	Robertson	Fulton	Pointon	Berry (4)	Thomas (9)	Colquhoun (11)
13th	Rousset	McManus	Ritchie	Mackay	McPherson	Bruno	Johnston	Cameron	Robertson	Fulton	Pointon	Colquhoun	Lawrence	Berry
20th	Rousset	Locke	Ritchie	McManus	McPherson	Berry	Johnston	Cameron	Robertson	Fulton	Pointon	Colquhoun (3)	Mackay (8)	Thomas
27th	Rousset	Locke	Ritchie	McManus	McPherson	Berry	Johnston	Colquhoun	Robertson	Fulton	Pointon	Mackay (9)	Thomas (7)	Lawrence (8)
May 4th	Hogarth	Locke	Ritchie	McManus	McPherson	Berry	Johnston	Cameron	Lawrence	Fulton	Pointon	Naysmith (11)	Colquhoun (9)	Robertson (7)
18th	Rousset	Locke	Ritchie^	McManus	McPherson	Bruno	Johnston	Mackay	Colquhoun	Fulton	Pointon	Lawrence (2)	Robertson (6)	Hogarth

Man's game - Neil Pointon wins the ball after this he-man clash with the Raith Rovers left-back at Stark's Park. DC Thomson

Season 1996-97

Date		Opponents		Score	Crowd	Scorers
Aug 8th	CWPP	Red Star Belgrade	a	0-0	24,500	-
13th	LC2	Stenhousemuir	h	1-1*	9,303	McCann
17th	L	Kilmarnock	h	3-2	10,854	Ritchie 2; Weir
22nd	CWPP	Red Star Belgrade	h	1-1^	15,062	McPherson
25th	L	Aberdeen	a	0-4	13,600	-
Sep 3rd	LC3	St Johnstone	a	3-1**	6,806	Cameron; Beckford; Robertson
7th	L	Dundee United	h	1-0	11,848	Robertson (pen)
10th	L	Dunfermline	a	1-2	7,787	Weir
14th	L	Rangers	a	0-3	47,240	-
17th	LCQ	Celtic	h	1-0*	14,442	Robertson
21st	L	Motherwell	h	1-1	10,932	Weir
28th	L	Hibernian	a	3-1	14,746	Cameron 2; Robertson
Oct 12th	L	Raith Rovers	a	1-1	6,240	Robertson
20th	L	Celtic	h	2-2	13,352	Cameron; McPherson
23rd	LCS	Dundee	Easter Rd	3-1	15,653	Beckford; Cameron (pen); Paille
26th	L	Dundee United	a	0-1	9,353	-
Nov 2nd	L	Dunfermline	h	2-0	12,517	Weir; Cameron
11th	L	Motherwell	a	2-0	5,441	Paille; Robertson
16th	L	Hibernian	h	0-0	15,129	-
24th	LCF	Rangers	Hampden	3-4	48,559	Fulton; Robertson; Weir
30th	L	Celtic	a	2-2	50,034	Cameron; McCann
Dec 7th	L	Raith Rovers	h	0-0	10,719	-
11th	L	Aberdeen	h	1-2	11,477	Cameron
14th	L	Kilmarnock	a	0-2	5,832	-
21st	L	Rangers	h	1-4	15,139	Robertson
26th	L	Dunfermline	a	3-2	9,736	Mackay; Fulton; Robertson (pen)
28th	L	Motherwell	h	4-1	11,164	Weir; Robertson 2 (1 pen); Hamilton
Jan 1st	L	Hibernian	a	4-0	15,826	Robertson; Cameron; Hamilton 2
4th	L	Raith Rovers	a	2-1	6,460	Robertson; Hamilton
11th	L	Celtic	h	1-2	15,424	Hamilton
18th	L	Dundee United	h	1-2	12,777	Robertson
25th	SC3	Cowdenbeath	h	5-0	11,485	Robertson 2 (1 pen); Cameron; Weir; Pointon
Feb 1st	L	Rangers	a	0-0	50,024	-
8th	L	Kilmarnock	h	2-0	11,020	McCann; Ritchie
10th	L	Aberdeen	a	0-0	8,672	-
16th	SC4	Dundee United	h	1-1	14,833	Hamilton
22nd	L	Raith Rovers	h	3-2	10,341	McCann 2; Weir
25th	SC4	Dundee United	a	0-1	12,283	-
Mar 1st	L	Celtic	a	0-2	49,729	-
15th	L	Hibernian	h	1-0	15,136	McCann
22nd	L	Motherwell	a	1-0	6,245	Paille
Apr 5th	L	Kilmarnock	a	0-1	7,787	-
12th	L	Aberdeen	h	0-0	11,186	-
19th	L	Dunfermline	h	1-1	10,174	Robertson
May 3rd	L	Dundee United	a	0-1	7,405	-
10th	L	Rangers	h	3-1	13,097	Cameron; Robertson 2 (1 pen)

* aet 1-1 after 90 mts.5-4 on penalties. Scorers - McCann, Beckford, Mackay, Cameron, Pointon. ** aet 1-1 after 90 mts
^ Red Star go through on away goals rule.

Paul Ritchie - has gone from strength to strength in the Hearts defence.

The Record		
League	-	Fourth Place, Premier Division
League Cup	-	Runners-up
Scottish Cup	-	Fourth Round
European Cup Winners Cup	-	Preliminary Stage
Top Scorer	-	John Robertson (19 goals)
Av. Home Gate	-	12,300
Players used	-	30
Sent off	-	Seven (69)

Appearances

	League	L/Cup	S/Cup	ECW	Total
Colin Cameron	36 (8)	5 (2)	3 (1)	2	45 (11)
Davie Weir	34 (6)	4 (1)	3 (1)	2	43+7s (8)
Gilles Rousset	33	5	3	2	43
Dave McPherson	26 (1)	3	3	2 (1)	34 (2)
Paul Ritchie	27 (3)	3	1	2	33+2s (3)
Neil Pointon	24	4	2 (1)	2	32+1s (1)
Steve Fulton	25 (1)	2 (1)	3	1	31+6s (2)
Neil McCann	25 (5)	3 (1)	2	1	31+6s (6)
John Robertson	25 (14)	4 (3)	1 (2)	0	30+6s (19)
Gary Mackay	20 (1)	5	1	2	28+9s (1)
Pasquale Bruno	11	4	0	2	17+2s
Jim Hamilton	12 (5)	0	3 (1)	0	15+6s (6)
Stefan Salvatori	12	1	2	0	15+2s
Stefan Paille	12 (2)	2 (1)	0	0	14+8s (3)
Gary Locke	11	0	3	0	14
Alan McManus	10	2	1	0	13+6s
Gary Naysmith	10	1	1	0	12
John Colquhoun	4	2	0	2	8+7s
Jeremy Goss	7	0	0	1	8+6s
Darren Beckford	6	1 (2)	0	0	7+4s (2)
Steve Frail	4	1	0	1	6
David Murie	6	0	0	0	6+1s
Kevin Thomas	4	1	0	0	5+11s
Stuart Callaghan	4	1	0	0	5
Roddy McKenzie	3	0	0	0	3
Grant Murray	2	0	0	0	2+3s
Andy Thorn	1	1	0	0	2
Derek Holmes	1	0	0	0	1
Robbie Horn	1	0	0	0	1
John-Paul Burns	0	0	0	0	0+2s

Scottish League Premier Division

		Home			Away			Goals	
	P	W	D	L	W	D	L	F A	PTS
Rangers	36	13	2	3	12	3	3	85-33	80
Celtic	36	14	2	2	9	9	4	78-32	75
Dundee United	36	10	4	4	10	7	5	46-33	60
Hearts	**36**	**8**	**6**	**4**	**6**	**4**	**8**	**46-43**	**52**
Dunfermline	36	8	4	6	4	5	9	52-65	45
Aberdeen	36	6	8	4	4	6	8	45-44	44
Kilmarnock	36	8	4	6	3	2	13	41-61	39
Motherwell	36	5	5	8	4	6	8	44-55	38
Hibernian*	36	6	4	8	3	7	8	38-55	38
Raith Rovers	36	3	5	10	3	2	13	29-73	25

* Won Premier League play-off with First Division Runners-up Airdrie 5-3 on aggregate.

Heart of Midlothian F.C. Line-Ups 1996-97

	1	2	3	4	5	6	7	8	9	10	11	12	14	15
Aug 8th	Rousset	Frail	Ritchie	Weir	McPherson	Bruno	Mackay	Cameron	Colquhoun	Goss	Pointon	Fulton	McManus (2)	Robertson
14th	Rousset	Frail	Ritchie	Weir	Mackay	Bruno	Colquhoun	Cameron	Robertson	Fulton	Pointon	Thomas (9)	Beckford (7)	McCann (3)
17th	Rousset	Frail	Ritchie	Weir	Mackay	Bruno	McCann	Cameron	Beckford*	Fulton	Pointon	McManus (11)	Colquhoun (7)	Thomas (6)
22nd	Rousset	Weir	Ritchie	Mackay	McPherson	Bruno	McCann	Cameron	Colquhoun	Fulton	Pointon	Frail	McManus	Robertson (4)
25th	Rousset	McManus	Ritchie	Weir	McPherson	Mackay	Goss	Cameron	Thomas	Fulton	Pointon	McCann (6)	Colqhuoun (9)	Frail (2)
Sep 3rd	Rousset	Mackay	Ritchie	Weir	McPherson	Bruno	McCann	Colquhoun	Beckford	Cameron	Pointon	Frail (9)	Fulton (6)	Robertson (8)
7th	Rousset	Weir	Ritchie	Fulton	McPherson	Bruno	McCann	Beckford	Robertson	Cameron	Pointon	Mackay (4)	Frail	Colquhoun
10th	Rousset	Weir	Ritchie	Mackay	McPherson	Bruno	Colquhoun	Beckford	Robertson	Cameron	Pointon	Fulton (8)	Salvatori (4)	Thomas (7)
14th	Rousset	Weir*	Ritchie*	Mackay	McPherson	Bruno*	McCann	Salvatori	Robertson	Cameron	Pointon*	Frail (8)	Fulton (9)	Thomas (4)
17th	Rousset	McManus	Naysmith	Salvatori*	McPherson	Thorn	Thomas	Mackay	Robertson	Cameron	McCann	Goss (7)	Fulton (8)	Colquhoun
21st	Rousset	Weir	Naysmith	McManus	McPherson	Thorn	Colquhoun	Bruno	Thomas	Cameron	McCann	Mackay (6)	Robertson (9)	Ritchie
28th	Rousset	McManus	Pointon	Weir	McPherson	Mackay	Beckford	Salvatori	Robertson	Cameron	McCann	Colquhoun	Ritchie (3)	Goss
Oct 12th	Rousset	McManus	Pointon	Weir	McPherson	Mackay	Paille	Salvatori	Robertson	Cameron	Colquhoun	Ritchie	Goss (11)	Thomas (7)
20th	Rousset	McManus	Pointon	Weir	McPherson	Mackay	Paille	Salvatori	Robertson	Cameron	Callaghan	Ritchie	Bruno (8)	Beckford (6)
23rd	Rousset	McManus	Pointon	Weir	McPherson	Mackay	Paille	Bruno	Robertson	Cameron	Callaghan	Ritchie (5)	Goss (7)	Beckford (9)
26th	Rousset	McManus	Pointon	Weir	Ritchie	Mackay	Paille	Bruno	Beckford	Cameron	Callaghan	Goss (11)	Colquhoun (9)	Fulton (10)
Nov2nd	Rousset	Weir	Pointon	Mackay	McPherson	Ritchie	Paille	Goss	Colquhoun	Cameron	Callaghan	Fulton (4)	Bruno	Beckford (9)
11th	Rousset	Weir	Pointon	Mackay	McPherson	Ritchie	Paille	Goss	Robertson	Cameron	Fulton	Callaghan	Colquhoun (7)	Bruno
16th	Rousset	Weir	Naysmith	Mackay	McPherson	Ritchie	Paille	Fulton	Robertson	Cameron	McCann	Goss (8)	Bruno (5)	Thomas (11)
24th	Rousset	Weir	Pointon	Mackay	Ritchie	Bruno	Paille	Fulton	Robertson	Cameron	McCann	Goss	Beckford (7)	McManus
30th	Rousset	McManus	Pointon	Goss	Ritchie	Bruno	Paille	Fulton	Robertson	Cameron	McCann	Frail	Beckford	Callaghan
Dec 7th	Rousset	McManus	Pointon	Goss	Ritchie	Bruno	Paille	Fulton	Robertson	Cameron	McCann	Mackay (4)	Frail (7)	Thomas (9)
11th	Rousset	Weir	Pointon	Mackay	McManus	Bruno	Paille	Fulton	Robertson	Cameron	McCann	Frail (4)	Goss	Colquhoun (7)
14th	Rousset	Frail	Pointon	Goss	Weir	Bruno	Beckford	Fulton	Hamilton	Cameron	McCann	McManus (2)	Colquhoun (7)	Burns (4)
21st	Rousset	Weir	Pointon*	Mackay	McManus	Ritchie	Paille	Fulton	Robertson	Cameron	McCann	Colquhoun (2)	Hamilton (11)	Murray (8)
26th	Rousset	Murie	Naysmith	Weir	Ritchie	Mackay	McCann	Fulton	Robertson	Cameron	Hamilton	Goss	Murray	Thomas
28th	Rousset	Murie	Naysmith	Weir	Ritchie	Mackay	Goss	Fulton	Robertson	Cameron	Hamilton	McCann (6)	Murray (7)	Thomas (9)
Jan 1st	Rousset	Murie	Naysmith	Weir	McPherson	Ritchie	Mackay	Fulton	Robertson	Cameron	Hamilton	Goss	McCann (9)	Pointon
4th	Rousset	Murie	Naysmith	Weir	McPherson	Ritchie	Mackay	Fulton	Robertson	Cameron	Hamilton	Goss	McCann (3)	Murray
11th	Rousset	Murie	Ritchie	Weir	McPherson	Mackay	McCann	Fulton	Robertson	Cameron	Hamilton	Goss	Naysmith	Paille (6)
18th	Rousset	Murie	Ritchie	Weir	McPherson	Mackay	McCann	Fulton	Robertson	Cameron	Hamilton	Goss	Paille	Pointon (2)
25th	Rousset	Locke	Pointon	Weir	McPherson	Mackay	McCann	Fulton	Robertson	Cameron	Hamilton	Goss (7)	Paille (11)	Frail (6)
Feb 1st	Rousset	Locke	Pointon	Weir	McPherson	Ritchie	Salvatori	Fulton	Robertson	Cameron	McCann	Mackay (7)	Hamilton	Paille
8th	Rousset	Locke	Pointon	Weir	McPherson	Ritchie	Salvatori	Fulton	Hamilton	Cameron	McCann	Mackay (7)	Paille (9)	McManus
10th	McKenzie	Locke	Pointon	Weir	Bruno	Ritchie	Salvatori	Fulton	Hamilton	Cameron	McCann	Mackay (3)	Paille (9)	McManus (5)
16th	Rousset	Locke	Pointon	Weir	McPherson	McManus	Salvatori	Fulton	Hamilton	Cameron	McCann	Mackay (7)	Robertson (3)	Murray (2)
22nd	Rousset	Locke	Naysmith	Weir	McPherson	Salvatori	McCann	Fulton	Robertson	Cameron	Hamilton	Mackay (10)	Paille (9)	McManus (11)
25th	Rousset	Locke	Naysmith	Weir	McPherson	Ritchie	Salvatori	Fulton	Hamilton	Cameron	McCann	Robertson (2)	Mackay (7)	Murray
Mar 1st	Rousset	Locke	Naysmith	Weir	McPherson	Ritchie	Mackay	Salvatori	Robertson	Cameron	McCann	Fulton	Paille (9)	Burns(11)
15th	Rousset	Locke	Pointon	Weir	McPherson	Ritchie	McCann	Fulton	Robertson	Cameron	Hamilton	Paille (11)	Callaghan	Murray
22nd	Rousset	Locke	Pointon	Weir	McPherson	Ritchie	Salvatori	Fulton	Paille	Cameron	McCann	Hamilton (9)	McManus	Thomas (10)
Apr 5th	Rousset	Locke	Pointon	Weir	McPherson	Ritchie	Salvatori	Fulton	Paille	Cameron	McCann	Hamilton (9)	McManus	Thomas (7)
12th	Rousset	Locke	Pointon	Weir	McPherson	Ritchie	Salvatori	Fulton	Hamilton	Cameron	McCann	Paille (8)	McManus(12)	Robertson (9)
19th	Rousset	Locke	Naysmith	Weir	McPherson	Ritchie	Thomas	Fulton	Robertson	Cameron	McCann	Hamilton (8)	Salvatori (2)	Frail (6)
May 8th	McKenzie	Murray	Naysmith	Weir	McPherson	Horn	Thomas	Frail	Robertson	Cameron	Callaghan	Hamilton (9)	McCann (7)	McManus
10th	McKenzie	Locke	Pointon	Weir	McPherson	Murray	Holmes	Frail	Robertson	Cameron	McCann	Hamilton (7)	Murie (6)	McManus

Gilles to the rescue - Hearts keeper Gilles Rousset comes off his line to thwart a Dundee attack in the Coca Cola Cup semi-final against Dundee. David Weir is on the left with Neil Pointon on the right.

Hearts Challenge Matches, Benefit Games and other Matches

John Cumming - two goals against Chelsea at Stamford Bridge in 1952

Date	Opponents		Score	Crowd	Scorers
Apr 21st, 1947	Chelsea	h	1-4	11,086	Urquhart
Sep 24th, 1947	Charlton Athletic	h	1-3	18,431	Sloan
Apr 26th, 1948	Chelsea	a	1-4	16,000	Flavell
Mar 26th, 1949	Middlesbrough	a	0-4	18,000	-
Apr 27th, 1949	Chelsea	h	1-1	15,728	Flavell
May 7th, 1949	Scottish Command	h	7-0	4,000	Bauld 2; Conn 3; Wardhaugh; Cox
Apr 26th, 1950	Chelsea	a	2-3	17,000	Armstrong o.g.; Conn
Apr 28th, 1950	Brighton & H. Albion	a	1-1	8,000	Sloan
Mar 10th, 1951	Manchester City	h	1-0	20,995	Conn
May 12th, 1951	Chelsea	h	0-2	16,520	- -
May 18th, 1951	Belfast Distillery	h	4-0	5,521	Bauld; Sloan; Cumming; Urquhart
Tour of West Germany					
May 26th, 1951	Fortuna Dusseldorf		2-0	10,000	Conn; Wardhaugh
May 27th, 1951	Offenbach Kickers		0-3		-
May 30th, 1951	FC Augsburg		1-5		Wardhaugh
Jun 2nd, 1951	VFB Stuttgart		3-3	10,000	Bauld 2; Conn
Jul 14th, 1951	Celtic*	a	1-2	51,000	Bauld
Apr 23rd, 1952	Chelsea	a	2-3	7,471	Cumming 2
May 15th, 1953	Tottenham Hotspur	h	2-0	14,294	Urquhart; Wardhaugh

* 1st round of the St Mungo's Cup - Scotland's contribution to the Festival of Great Britain

Date	Opponents		Score	Crowd	Scorers
Tour of Sweden					
May 19th, 1953	AIK Stockholm	a	4-1	6,000	Wardhaugh 2; Blackwood; Parker
May 21st, 1953	Djurgardens IF	a	1-5	10,000	Conn
Sep 28th, 1953	Portsmouth	a	2-2	15,500	Urquhart 2
Oct 7th, 1953	Newcastle United	a	2-2	38,000	Wardhaugh; Conn
Oct 14th, 1953	Manchester City	a	3-6	23,979	Parker (pen); Wardhaugh; Cumming
Oct 19th, 1953	West Ham United	a	0-7	19,000	-
Nov 9th, 1953	Doncaster Rovers	a	3-1	15,000	Urquhart; Wardhaugh 2
Mar 31st, 1954	Chelsea*	h	1-3	8,000	Urquhart
Apr 12th, 1954	Admira Vienna	h	0-2	10,000	-

* Stamford Bridge Trophy, commenced 1951

Date	Opponents		Score	Crowd	Scorers
South African Tour					
May 22nd, 1954	Southern Transvaal (Jo'burg)		2-0	17,000	Wardhaugh; Conn
May 26th, 1954	Northern Transvaal (Pretoria)		4-0	10,000	Conn 2; Urquhart; Blackwood
May 29th, 1954	Natal (Durban)		11-2	17,000	Bauld 4; Wardhaugh 4; Conn 2; Cumming (pen)
May 31st, 1954	Western Province (Cape Town)		5-2		Wardhaugh 3; Bauld; Conn
Jun 5th, 1954	Eastern Transvaal (Benoni)		3-0	13,000	Bauld; Conn; Urquhart
Jun 9th, 1954	Orange Free State (Bloemfontein)		4-0		Conn 2; McKenzie 2
Jun 12th, 1954	South Africa (Jo'burg)		2-0	25,000	Wardhaugh 2
Jun 16th, 1954	Natal (Pietermarizburg)		1-0		Conn
Jun 19th, 1954	South Africa (Durban)		1-2	20,000	Bauld
Jun 22nd, 1954	Southern Transvaal (Jo'burg*)		3-2	16,000	Conn;Wardhaugh; Bauld

* Played under floodlights

Date	Opponents		Score	Crowd	Scorers
Oct 13th, 1954	Newcastle United	a	3-2	22,590	Parker; Bauld; Conn
Oct 18th, 1954	Hibernian	a^	2-0		Urquhart; Whittle
Nov 3rd, 1954	Leeds United	a	4-2	10,000	Wardhaugh 4
Nov 10th, 1954	Sunderland	a	3-3	10,000	McDonald o.g.; Conn; Urquhart
Oct 10th, 1955	Newcastle United	a	2-2	22,000	Young; Murray
Nov 7th, 1955	Newcastle United*	h	4-6	12,700	Wardhaugh; Cumming; Parker; Urquhart
Feb 6th, 1956	Sheffield United	a	2-4	12,000	Conn; Wardhaugh
Sep 19th, 1956	Newcastle United	a	2-1	23,000	Young; McFadzean
Oct 15th, 1956	Tottenham Hotspur*	h	3-2	16,000	Young; Mackay; Hamilton
Nov 5th, 1956	Newcastle United*	h	0-0	18,000	-
Nov 12th, 1956	Tottenham Hotspur	a	2-4	17,504	Crawford; Hamilton
Nov 19th, 1956	Manchester City*	h	3-4	20,000	Murray; Young; Hamilton
Nov 26th, 1956	Linfield	a	9-1	12,500	Wardhaugh 3; Bauld 2; Young; Bowman; Hamilton; P. Smith
Feb 16th, 1957	Bolton Wanderers	h	3-6	11,000	Young; Murray; Hamilton
Apr 17th, 1957	Combined Services X1	h	3-2	2,500	Conn 2; Bauld
Oct 7th, 1957	Hibernian**	h	2-4		Bauld; Wardhaugh
Oct 14th, 1957	Bolton Wanderers	a	1-1	21,058	Wardhaugh
Oct 30th, 1957	Norwich City	a	4-3	17,090	Wardhaugh 2; Murray; Young
Nov 4th, 1957	Manchester City	h	3-5	18,000	Murray 2; Bauld
Nov 20th, 1957	Newcastle United	h	2-2	15,000	Cumming; Wardhaugh
Nov 27th, 1957	Newcastle United	a	0-2	10,260	-
Dec 2nd, 1957	British Army	h	3-5	6,000	Conn; Mackay; Wardhaugh
Mar 3rd, 1958	Scotland X1	h	3-2	29,000	Young; Hamilton; Mackay
Apr 23rd, 1958	British Army	h	3-1	17,000	Crawford (pen); Murray; Young

^ Opening of Easter Road Floodlights * Played at Easter Road ** Opening of Tynecastle Floodlights

Head man - Willie Bauld flashes a header past Manchester City keeper Bert Trautman.

Tour of Canada and USA (Empire State Cup celebrating 25 years of American Soccer League)

Date	Opponent		Score	Att.	Scorers
May 23rd, 1958	Ontario All Stars (Toronto)		6-0	10,000	Bauld 2; Wardhaugh 2; Hamilton; Young
May 25th, 1958	Manchester City (New York)		6-5	20,600	Wardhaugh 3; Young; Hamilton; Bauld
May 28th, 1958	Manitoba All Stars (Winnipeg)		13-2		Conn 4; Hamilton 2; Wardhaugh 2; Cumming; Bowman; Paton; Bauld; Young
May 31st, 1958	Manchester City (Vancouver)		5-2	20,975	Bauld 2; Crawford; Young; Wardhaugh
Jun 2nd, 1958	British Columbia All Stars*		4-1	15,554	Hamilton; Wardhaugh 2; Young
Jun 4th, 1958	Alberta All Stars (Edmonton)		13-2	5,000	Hamilton 3; Blackwood 2; Conn 2; Paton 2; Crawford 2; Wardhaugh; Bowman
Jun 7th, 1958	Manchester City (Toronto)		1-7	24,000	Crawford
Jun 9th, 1958	Northern All Stars (Sudbury)		10-0	3,000	Conn 4; Young 3; Blackwood 2;
Jun 11th, 1958	Manchester City (Montreal)		6-0	10,200	Wardhaugh 4; Conn 2

* Vancouver

Date	Opponent		Score	Att.	Scorers
Oct 13th, 1958	Blackpool	a	1-2	15,437	Bauld
Oct 30th, 1958	South Africa X1	h	3-3	10,000	Young; Paton (pen); P. Smith
Nov 3rd, 1958	Djurgardens IF	h	0-2		
Nov 19th, 1958	Aston Villa	a	3-3	22,000	Young; Blackwood; Wardhaugh
Feb 28th, 1959	Ipswich Town	a	0-1	9,378	-
Apr 4th, 1959	Inverness Select	a	7-2	3,000	Young 2; Wardhaugh 2; Crawford; Hamilton; Murray;

Dave Mackay - missed Canadian tour due to 1958 World Cup duties.

Tour of Australia

Date	Opponent		Score	Att.	Scorers
May 9th, 1959	Australia (Sydney)		7-1	16,000	Crawford 2; Murray; Cumming; Hamilton; Bauld; Young
May 10th, 1959	New South Wales (Newcastle)		6-1	11,000	Bauld 3; Wardhaugh; Blackwood; Crawford
May 12th, 1959	Queensland (Brisbane)		3-3	8,000	Rankin; Bauld 2
May 16th, 1959	Australia (Brisbane)		7-1		Young 2; Hamilton; Bauld; Thomson; Murray; Pagani o.g.;
May 20th, 1959	Northern Districts (Wallsend)		8-2		Bauld 3; Blackwood; Young; Murray; Hamilton; Thomson
May 23rd, 1959	Australia (Sydney)		7-1	8,000	Wardhaugh 3; Murray 2; Young 2
May 24th, 1959	South Coast (Wellongong)		7-0		Bauld 2; Young 2;Wardhaugh; Thomson; Hamilton
May 30th, 1959	Australia (Melbourne)		9-1	20,000	Hamilton 3; Wardhaugh; Crawford 2; Young 2; Murray
May 31st, 1959	Victoria (Melbourne)		5-0	16,000	Bauld 2; Blackwood; Wardhaugh; Crawford
Jun 3rd, 1959	Tasmania (Hobart)		10-0	3,000	Rankin 3; Blackwood 3; Young 2; Crawford; Hamilton
Jun 6th, 1959	Australia (Adelaide)		6-0	11,000	Wardhaugh 2; Thomson (pen); Crawford 2; Young
Jun 7th, 1959	Victoria (Melbourne)		7-1		Young 4; Crawford; Wardhaugh; Bauld
Jun 10th, 1959	South Australia (Adelaide)		8-0	15,000	Wardhaugh 3; Bauld 2; Young 2; Cumming
Jun 13th, 1959	Australia (Perth)		9-0	9,317	Bauld 4; Crawford 2; Young; Blackwood; Cumming
Jun 15th, 1959	West Australia (Perth)		10-1	3,000	Bauld 4; Crawford 4; Young; Hamilton

Date	Opponent		Score	Att.	Scorers
Aug 31st, 1959	British Army	h	8-1	7,000	Murray 2; Blackwood 2; Thomson 2 (pens); Hamilton; Smith
Oct 12th, 1959	Norwich City	h	0-0	10,000	
Apr 25th, 1960	Aston Villa	h	2-2	20,000	Murray; Bauld

Tour of Canada and USA

Date	Opponent		Score	Att.	Scorers
May 14th, 1960	Manchester United (Toronto)		2-2	17,849	Thomson (pen); Blackwood
May 16th, 1960	Montreal Cantalia (Ottawa)		3-0	3,000	Hamilton; Thomson (pen); Bauld
May 18th, 1960	Montreal Concordia (Montreal)		2-0	5,000	Blackwood; Crawford
May 22nd, 1960	Manchester United (New York)		0-3	10,411	-
May 28th, 1960	Manchester United (Vancouver)		2-3	18,644	Blackwood; Crawford
Jun 1st, 1960	Manchester United (Los Angeles)		4-0	10,500	Thomson (pen); Bauld 2; Crawford
Jun 4th, 1960	British Columbia All Stars		2-2	17,500	Blackwood; Bauld
Jun 6th, 1960	Victoria All Stars (Victoria)		3-0	2,500	Thomson (pen); Crawford; Blackwood
Jun 8th, 1960	Alberta All Stars (Edmonton)		6-2	7,000	Bauld 3; Smith; Crawford; Murray
Jun 9th, 1960	Burnley (Toronto)		1-2	15,020	Bauld

Date	Opponent		Score	Att.	Scorers
Oct 31st, 1960	Raith Rovers	h	2-2	6,000	Hamilton;Crawford (George Dobbie Testimonial)
Nov 7th, 1960	British Army	h	3-2	7,000	Johnston 2; Finlay
Nov 13th, 1961	British Army	h	0-3	6,000	-
Sep 25th, 1962	Sportsklub Brann	a	4-0	10,500	Wallace; Davidson 2; J. Hamilton
Nov 5th, 1962	Sheffield United*	h	2-2	18,000	Rodger; Wallace
Nov 12th 1962	Sportsklub Brann	h	8-2	10,000	Rodger 4; Gordon 2; Ross; Wallace

* Willie Bauld Testimonial

Star attraction - four games with Manchester United in Canada.

Hearts Challenge Matches, Benefit Games and other Matches

Date	Opponents		Score	Crowd	Scorers
Dec 6th, 1962	Moscow Torpedo	h	6-0	20,000	Davidson 2; W. Hamilton 2; Wallace; Ostrovsky o.g.
Apr 24th, 1964	Chelsea	h	2-0	8,500	J. Hamilton; Wallace

New York Tourney 1964

Date	Opponents		Score	Crowd	Scorers
May 31st, 1964	Blackburn Rovers		1-0		White
Jun 5th, 1964	East Canada Pro All Stars* (Toronto)		2-0		Barry; Gordon
Jun 7th, 1964	Lanerossi Vicenza		1-1		White
Jun 14th, 1964	Bahia Brazil		1-0	14,069	Wallace
Jun 19th, 1964	Werder Bremen (Chicago)		0-3		-
Jun 21st, 1964	Lanerossi Vicenza		2-1	14,000	J. Hamilton 2
Jun 24th, 1964	Blackburn Rovers		2-0		Traynor; White

* Friendly. See P165 for placings

Date	Opponents		Score	Crowd	Scorers
Oct 19th, 1964	Stoke City	h	1-2	10,000	Wallace

Tour of Norway

Date	Opponents		Score	Crowd	Scorers
Jun 8th, 1965	Sportsklub Brann		2-0	15,700	Ford 2
Jun 10th, 1965	Valerengens IF		4-1	14,300	Kerrigan; Ford; Jensen; Polland
Jun 14th, 1965	Larvik Turn		5-0	10,000	Traynor 2; Ford; Barry; Sharp
Jun 17th, 1965	Nidelv Trondheim		3-0	6,100	J. Hamilton 2; Ford

Date	Opponents		Score	Crowd	Scorers
Sept 27th 1965	Coleraine	h	1-2	3,900	Anderson
Oct 11th, 1965	Newcastle United	h	2-1	5,683	J. Hamilton 2
Aug 1st, 1966	Maccabi Tel Aviv	h	4-2	5,000	Wallace 3; Miller
Sep 26th, 1966	Newcastle United	a	7-2	5,160	Anderson; J. Hamilton 2 (1 pen);
Feb 14th, 1967	Slovan Bratislava	h	3-1	8,000	Gordon 2; Ford
Feb 17th, 1967	Preston North End	a	3-0	7,737	Ford 2; Gordon
Mar 10th, 1967	Carlisle United	a	1-1	7,489	Traynor
Apr 3rd, 1967	Hartlepool United	a	1-1	3,443	Gordon
May 8th, 1967	Derby County	a	1-1	5,000	Townsend
May 9th, 1967	Lincoln City	a	0-3	3,336	-

Tour of Iceland

Date	Opponents		Score	Crowd	Scorers
May 19th, 1967	KBR Reykjavik		6-0		Kemp 3; Milne; Ford; Traynor
May 22nd, 1967	Valur		4-0		J. Fleming 3; Murphy
May 25th, 1967	Rekyavik Select		3-3		Ford; Traynor; Milne

Date	Opponents		Score	Crowd	Scorers
Aug 5th, 1967	Preston North End	h	2-0	9,000	Irvine; Ford
Aug 8th, 1967	Hull City	a	0-4	11,665	-
May 21st, 1968	Linfield	a	5-1	5,000	J. Fleming; Ford 2; Traynor; Miller (pen)
May 24th, 1968	Coleraine	a	0-0	3,000	-
May 26th, 1968	Dundalk^	a	2-0	5,000	Irvine J., Fleming
Aug 3rd 1968	Middlesbrough	a	3-4	7,510	Moller 2; Anderson
Sep 23rd 1968	Sunderland	a	1-2	2,568	J. Fleming
Oct 21st, 1968	Middlesbrough	h	2-4	6,319	Ford; Gordon
Apr 14th, 1969	Eintracht Frankfurt	h	1-1	10,500	Winchester
Jul 26th, 1969	Carlisle United	a	0-5	5,000	-
Jul 30th, 1969	Newcastle United	a	0-1	21,000	-
Aug 2nd, 1969	Tottenham Hotspur	h	1-1	14,000	Beal o.g.
Oct 6th, 1969	Dallas Tornado	h	4-1	5,500	Moller; Murray 2; Brown
Apr 24th, 1970	Coventry City	h	0-0	5,554	-
Aug 1st, 1970	Dunfermline	h	4-2	6,000	Ford; Clunie; Lynch; Hegarty
Aug 3rd, 1970	West Brom	a	0-2	11,000	-
Dec 2nd, 1970	Gornik Zabrze*	h	0-0	3,000	-

* abandoned after 33 mts due to flooding ^ Harp Lager Cup

Tour of USA and Canada 1971

Date	Opponents		Score	Crowd	Scorers
May 6th, 1971	Dallas Tornado		0-0		-
May 10th, 1971	St Louis All Stars		2-1		Ford 2
May 12th, 1971	Atlanta Chiefs		0-1		-
May 16th, 1971	Washington Darts		3-0	4,063	Lynch 2; Ford
May 18th, 1971	Philadelphia Spartans		4-0		Hegarty 3; Lynch
May 21st, 1971	New York Cosmos		4-2		Ford 3; Fleming
May 24th, 1971	Toronto Metros		3-0		Ford; Carruthers; Wood
May 26th, 1971	Rochester Lancers		0-0		-
May 27th, 1971	Newton (Boston)		1-1		Lynch
May 30th, 1971	Montreal Olympic		7-0		Carruthers 5; Ford; Thomson Anderson; T. Murray
Jul 31st, 1971	QOS	a	2-0	1,200	Lynch 2

Tourist class - Hearts undertook a North American Tour in 1971.

Andy Lynch - two goals against the Washington Darts in 1971.

Date	Opponents		Score	Crowd	Scorers
Aug 7th, 1971	Tottenham Hotspur	h	2-1	15,020	N. Murray; Kay
Nov 2nd, 1971	Carlisle United	a	2-3	3,500	Brown 2
Nov 24th, 1971	Gornik Zabrze	h	2-1	7,000	Winchester; Renton
Tour of Holland					
Jul 29th, 1972	Den Haag		1-0		Anderson
Aug 2nd, 1972	Alkmaar		1-0		Lynch
Aug 6th, 1972	Sparta Rotterdam		0-1		-
Aug 7th, 1972	Den Haag	h	2-1	9,000	Clunie; Anderson
Mar 17th, 1973	Brechin City	a	3-0	500	Carruthers 3
May 4th, 1973	Orkney Select	a	2-0	400	Carruthers; Kinnear
May 5th, 1973	Orkney Select	a	8-2	300	Carruthers 2; Ford 2; Gibson 2;
Aug 4th, 1973	Sparta Rotterdam	h	1-0	9,000	Ford
Aug 3rd, 1974	Tottenham Hotspur	h	1-1	13,326	Ford (pen)
May10th, 1975	Newcastle United	h	2-2	8,500	Ford 2
Jul 26th, 1975	Roda JC	h	0-0	9,500	-
Jul 30th, 1975	Arsenal	h	0-2	11,000	-
May 8th, 1976	Southampton	a	3-2	7,526	Park; Callachan; Aird
World Tour					
May19th, 1976	SK Brann Bergen		2-0	2,700	Park; Prentice
May 26th, 1976	Christchurch United (New Zealand)		0-1		-
May 29th, 1976	Wellington		2-0		Busby (pen); Gibson
May 30th, 1976	Auckland X1		3-0		Fraser; Callachan; Gibson
Jun 2nd, 1976	New South Wales X1 (Sydney)		2-0		Busby; Prentice
Jun 3rd, 1976	Northern NSW (Newcastle)		2-0		Busby; Prentice
Jun 4th, 1976	Wollongong City		1-1		Brown
Jun 6th, 1976	Mauritius X1		1-1		Busby
Aug 5th, 1976	Southampton	h	3-0	10,000	Gibson 2; Prentice
Nov 13th, 1976	Middlesbrough	a	0-3	8,000	-
Aug 5th, 1977	OFK Kikinda	h	2-1	8,000	Gallacher; I. Smith
Aug 9th, 1977	Middlesbrough	h	1-0	7,620	I. Smith
Aug 5th, 1978	Rangers (Ten. Caled)	Ibrox	1-3	25,000	Park
Aug 6th, 1978	West Brom ..	Ibrox	2-0	10,000	Gibson; Bannon
Aug 9th, 1978	Middlesbrough	h	3-0	7,500	Park; Gibson; Prentice (pen)
Aug 2nd, 1979	Aston Villa	h	1-3	8,000	Fraser
Aug 4th, 1979	Hibernian^	a	1-2	13,000	Gibson
Aug 6th, 1979	Coventry City^	h	1-3	6,000	O'Connor
Aug 8th, 1979	Manchester City^	Easter Rd.	1-1	4,000	Fraser
Jul 26th, 1980	Chelsea	h	0-1	6,128	-
Aug 2nd, 1980	Glenavon	a	3-3	800	O'Connor; C. Robertson 2
Aug 4th, 1980	Newcastle United	h	1-1	3,334	C. Robertson
Jul 25th, 1981	North Shields	a	4-2	600	McCoy 2; G. Liddell; Shields (pen)
Jul 27th, 1981	Whitley Bay	a	1-1	400	C. Robertson
Jul 28th, 1981	Blyth Spartans	a	3-1	500	G. Liddell; O'Brien; McCoy
Aug 1st, 1981	Sunderland	h	0-1	4,937	-
Jul 27th, 1982	North Shields	a	1-1	600	own-goal
Jul 29th, 1982	Blyth Spartans	a	3-0	500	Pettigrew; J. Robertson 2
Jul 31st, 1982	Whitley Bay	a	3-1	510	Byrne (pen); McCoy; Pettigrew
Aug 4th, 1982	Sheffield United	h	4-2	3,600	Mackay 2; Kidd; Bowman
Aug 7th, 1982	Leeds United	h	1-0	5,800	Hart o.g.
Nov 24th, 1982	Dynamo Kiev	h	0-2	4,600	-
Apr 18th, 1983	Ross County	a	5-1	600	Mackay 2 (1p); Robertson; Byrne 2
Aug 1st, 1983	Nairn County ^ Skol Festival Trophy	a	8-0	300	Bowman 2; Mackay; A. MacDonald; Park 2; MacDonald R. 2
Aug 3rd, 1983	Inverness Caley	a	0-2	1,100	-
Aug 6th, 1983	Elgin City	a	1-0	400	Cowie
Aug 9th, 1983	Leeds United	h	0-0	5,235	-
Aug 13th, 1983	Leicester City	h	2-3	4,003	J. Robertson 2
Feb 28th, 1984	Arsenal	h	3-2	10,500	Kidd; Bone; Mackay
May 15th, 1984	Rangers* *Alex. MacDonald Testimonial	h	2-3	17,853	Mackay; J. Robertson
Tour of Scottish Highlands					
Jul 28th, 1984	Ross County	a	2-2	1,300	Mackay 2
Jul 30th, 1984	Wick Academy	a	7-1	2,200	O'Connor 3; Park; Black (pen); Whittaker;A. MacDonald
Aug 1st, 1984	Clachnacuddin	a	5-2	1,100	Bone; Robertson; Mackay; Black (pen); R. MacDonald

Jim Cruickshan - Hearts veteran of several foreign tours.

Down South - a memento of a visit to Ayresome Park

Hearts Challenge Matches, Benefit Games and other Matches

Date		Opponents		Score	Crowd	Scorers
Aug 4th,	1984	Elgin City	a	2-0	1,000	Levein; Black (pen)
Aug 7th,	1984	Queens Park Rangers	h	3-2	5,068	R. MacDonald; Robertson; Allen o.g.
Apr 24th,	1985	Eintracht Frankfurt	h	3-1	5,009	Clark; McNaughton; Robertson
		* Abandoned due to hailstorm.				
Tour of West Germany						
Jul 25th,	1985	FSV Saarwellingen*		2-0	600	Watson; McNaughton
Jul 26th,	1985	SV Wiesbaden		0-0	500	-
Jul 29th,	1985	SPVGG Ingleheim		5-1	375	Watson; Robertson; McNaughton; Black; MacDonald R.
Aug 3rd,	1985	SG Eintracht Bad Kreuznach		4-1	400	Robertson 2; Kidd; Mackay
Aug 4th,	1985	SC Birkenfeld		2-1	750	Mackay 2
Oct 23rd,	1985	Arbroath	a	4-1	300	Clark; Mackay 2; Robertson
Tour of Trinidad and Tobago						
May 19th,	1986	Barbados		3-1		Clark 3
May 21st,	1986	Trinidad and Tobago		3-0		Kidd 2; Watson
May 23rd,	1986	Tintoc (Trinidad)		2-0		Watson; Robertson
Isle of Man Festival Trophy						
Jul 28th,	1986	Stoke City		0-1	600	-
Jul 30th,	1986	Wigan Athletic		1-1	375	Colquhoun
Jul 31st,	1986	Bohemians Dublin		3-0	300	Colquhoun; Watson; W. Irvine
Aug 5th,	1986	Watford	h	2-1	8,500	Colquhoun; Clark
Sep 2nd,	1986	Manchester United	h	2-2	11,741	I. Jardine; Watson
May 12th,	1987	Watford*	a	3-4	4,402	Robertson (pen); Clark; Mackay
		*S. Sherwood Testimonial				
Tour of the USA						
May 24th,	1987	San Diego Nomads		4-4		Foster; Clark 2; Black
May 26th,	1987	San Jose Earthquakes		4-1		Watson 2; Colquhoun; Robertson
May 29th,	1987	California Kickers		2-1		Berry; Colquhoun
May 31st,	1987	Seattle Storm		1-1		Moore
Tour of West Germany						
Jul 18th,	1987	Homburg		1-2	1,800	Watson
Jul 21st,	1987	Preussen Munster		2-0	300	G. Mackay; Watson
Jul 24th,	1987	Eintracht Bad Kreuznach		3-1	250	Moore; Watson; Clark
Jul 25th,	1987	SC Birkenfeld		1-1	450	G. Mackay
Jul 27th,	1987	Remscheid		1-2	300	Robertson (pen)
Aug 1st,	1987	Berwick Rangers	a	2-1	1,200	McPherson; Robertson
Aug 3rd,	1987	Newcastle United	h	0-1	10,113	-
Sep 29th,	1987	Inverness Caley	a	4-3	2,500	Burns; Clark; Robertson; Colquhoun
Oct 18th,	1987	Everton	h	*1-1	8,171	Moore
Apr 24th,	1988	Falkirk Select	a	**2-4	6,000	Black (pen); A. MacDonald

* Walter Kidd Testimonial ** Andy Nicol (Falkirk) Testimonial ^John Docherty Testimonial

Sandy Clark - a welcome tour of Trinidad after disappointment of 1986.

Nice'n easy - John Colquhoun races through to roll the ball past the helpless Falkirk keeper in a match at Tynecastle. DC Thomson

Kenny Black - on the mark in 1988 West German tour.

Date	Opponents		Score	Crowd	Scorers
Tour of West Germany					
Jul 13th, 1988	TSV Battenberg		3-3	800	Galloway; Mackay (pen); Crabbe
Jul 15th, 1988	Rot-Weiss Essen		1-1	2,500	Galloway
Jul 16th, 1988	Fortuna Dusseldorf		0-1	1,500	-
Jul 20th, 1988	Reimscheid		2-0	200	I. Jardine; Clark
Jul 23rd, 1988	ASC Schoeppingen		2-2	500	Black; Gavin
Jul 24th, 1988	TUS Zielpich		4-2	600	Clark 2; Galloway; Colquhoun
Jul 30th, 1988	Forres Mechanics	a	5-1	1,50	Galloway 2; Ferguson; Mackay; Foster
Aug 1st, 1988	Lossiemouth	a	4-0	900	Colquhoun; Ferguson; Clark; own-goal
Aug 6th, 1988	Airdrie	a	5-0	3,500	Colquhoun; Clark; Galloway; Ferguson; I. Jardine
Aug 9th, 1988	Cruzeiro	h	2-1	12,403	Black (pen); Ferguson
Sep 12th, 1988	Nottingham Forest	h	0-3	8,876	-
Dec 18th, 1988	Dunfermline	a	5-3	3,400	Ferguson 2; Galloway 2; Foster
	* George Cowie Testimonial				
Rothes Tourney					
Jul 29th, 1989	Nairn County	a	5-1	1,034	Crabbe 2; McPherson; Colquhoun; Ferguson
Jul 31st 1989	Inverness Caley	a	3-2	2,000	Mackay; Ferguson (pen); Kirkwood
Aug 2nd, 1989	Peterhead	a	4-0	1,300	Ferguson 2; Musemic; Berry
Aug 5th, 1989	Sunderland	h	1-0	6,650	Musemic
Aug 8th, 1989	Dynamo Tbilisi	h	0-2	6,005	-
Sep 26th, 1989	Manchester United^	h	2-4	9,001	Crabbe; Bannon (pen)
Jul 30th, 1990	Raith Rovers	a	3-2	2,500	Robertson 2 (1 pen); McPherson
Aug 2nd, 1990	RFC Liege*		1-1	9,500	Kirkwood
Aug 3rd, 1990	Brighton and H.A..*		2-2	9,700	Robertson 2 (3/4th place game, Hts lost 4-2 on pens)
Aug 7th, 1990	Valencia**		1-3	14,900	Colquhoun
Aug 8th, 1990	Levante UD**		0-0	8,000	- ..
	*Bucharest Tournament **Valencia Tournament ^Eamonn Bannon Testimonial)				
Aug 13th, 1990	Tottenham Hotspur	h	1-1	18,068	Foster
Aug 17th, 1990	Airdrie	h	2-1	3,124	Foster 2
Mar 15th, 1991	IFK Gothenburg	h	2-1	4,530	Robertson; Colquhoun
May 13th, 1991	Everton^	h	2-0	5,575	Jordan 2
Aug 3rd, 1991	Real Sociedad	h	3-1	7,677	Crabbe; Baird (pen); Robertson (pen)
Jul 18th, 1992	Raith Rovers	a	2-1	1,519	Crabbe; Foster
Jul 22nd, 1992	Hamilton Accies.	a	2-0	1,299	Mackay; D. Ferguson
Jul 25th, 1992	Tottenham Hotspur	h	1-2	7,018	Levein
Jul 27th, 1992	Newcastle United*	h	1-0	11,105	Baird
	^ Gary Mackay Testimonial *John Robertson Testimonial				
Jul 22nd, 1993	Kickers Emden		2-1	1,500	A. Johnson; Locke
Jul 24th, 1993	F.C. Melle		8-0	700	Ferguson 3; Robertson; Locke; Mackay; Thomas; Wright
Jul 28th, 1993	F.C. Colppenburg		1-0	600	Boothroyd
Jul 30th, 1993	Borrussia Munchengladbach*		1-3	3,500	Robertson
Jul 31st, 1993	Twente Enschede*		1-3	3,500	Thomas
Aug 2nd, 1993	Everton^	h	0-2	9,213	-
Jul 30th, 1994	Clachnacuddin	a	5-0	550	A. Johnston 2; Colquhoun; Robertson (pen); Hogg
	* Four team tourney ^ Henry Smith Testimonial				
Jul 31st, 1994	Forres Mechanics	a	9-1	1,000	A. Johnston 2; Colquhoun 2; M. Johnston; Robertson; Millar; Frail
Aug 4th, 1994	Morton	a	3-1	500	Robertson; Frail; Leitch
Aug 6th, 1994	Middlesbrough	a	1-3	11,591	Robertson (pen)
Aug 9th, 1994	Raith Rovers	a	0-2	2,172	-
Dec 14th, 1994	West Ham United*	a	0-1	1,200	-
	* Benfit for West Ham fan with motor neurone abandoned due to floodlight failure				
Jul 28th, 1995	Peterhead	a	6-0	400	Hamilton; Cramb; Leitch; Murie; Colquhoun; Robertson (pen)
Jul 29th, 1995	Elgin City	a	4-0	900	Wright; Robertson 2 (1 pen); Locke
Jul 30th, 1995	Montrose	a	3-3	800	Mackay; Levein; Hamilton
Aug 5th, 1995	Derby County	a	3-3	5,079	Robertson (pen); Hagen; own goal
Aug 9th, 1995	Newcastle United	h	0-1	13,337	-
Aug 12th, 1995	Manchester City	h	5-1	6,879	Colquhoun 2; Hamilton; Hagen; Johnston
Oct 8th, 1995	Coventry*	h	1-5	3,500	Hagen
Mar 18th, 1996	Olympique Lyonnais^	h	1-3	6,500	A. Johnston
	* Craig Levein Testimonial Neil Berry Testimonial				
Jul 19th, 1996	Dundalk	a	3-1	200	Colquhoun; Robertson; Cameron
Jul 21st, 1996	Shamrock Rovers	a	1-1	2,000	Thomas
Jul 27th, 1996	Berwick Rangers	a	5-0	1,159	McPherson; Fulton; Pointon; Robertson; Lawrence
Jul 31st, 1996	FC Porto	h	1-3	9,986	Thomas
Aug 3rd, 1996	Southampton	h	1-0	8,542	Thomas
Mar27th, 1997	Ross County	a	4-4	1,308	McCann 3; Weir
Jul 16th, 1997	Blyth Spartans	a	0-0	800	-
Jul 18th 1997	Hull City	a	3-2	3,471	Salvatori; Flogel; Hamilton
Jul 20th 1997	Berwick Rangers	a	3-0	1,754	Robertson; Hamilton 2
Jul 26th, 1997	Rangers^	h	3-2	9,284	Hamilton 3
Jul 29th, 1997	Grimsby Town	a	0-2	6,348	-
Oct 10th, 1997	Hibernian*	h	0-1	8,800	-
	^ Dave McPherson Testimonial * Craig Levein Second Testimonail				

Match programme from the John Robertson Testimonial game